"*The Owner's Manual for the Personality from 12 to 22* represents cutting edge personality data and is filled with imaginative and poignant examples. The straightforward writing style will appeal to young people as well as those who try to understand and guide them."

Bob Augelli, Ph.D., Director, Multicultural Business Scholars Program, and Lecturer, Management
School of Business, University of Kansas

"I was captivated and frequently astonished by your combined genius, creativity, writing ability, and fortitude in writing this. I am usually not easily impressed but this is an exception. I think this is a brilliant piece of work and so many people could benefit by reading it—and, of course, taking the profile."

Judy Nelson, Attorney and Executive Coach
Los Angeles, California

"As a science journalist and as a father, I highly recommend this thoughtfully researched book, a must-read for professionals, parents and students. It shows us why the adolescent years are a great opportunity and how you can effectively help teenagers getting the best start for adult life."

Bart van Eldert, Health & Science Reporter
Algemeen Dagblad (Dutch daily newspaper with 1.2+ million readership)

"I like the book very much—quite respectful toward teens, relevant, well-researched, witty, enjoyable to read."

Jennifer Parker, Education Consultant
Charlotte, North Carolina

"Your style of writing is very personal, engaging, and easy to follow. I can almost hear your voice as I read through the pages. It feels as if you were having a conversation with the reader! Your tone and the examples from your personal experience make the material feel accessible and immediate. Moreover, I was amazed by your thorough analysis and careful treatment of every subject. Are you sure you were never a principal?? Maybe in another life?? Psychologists, organizational consultants, parents, counselors, educators, and students owe you and Jane a big thanks for providing us with such a comprehensive and user-friendly resource."

Monica Vergara, Education Consultant
The Woodlands, Texas

"At Invisionit, we continue to be amazed at how the SchoolPlace Big Five Profile has 'cracked the code' for teens. There is now NO reason for young people to be lost, confused or frustrated about how their life could unfold--for their benefit and the benefit of all those around them. Thank you, Pierce & Jane, for an astounding tool. Our goal is to show millions of youth a path that is uniquely 'them' using SchoolPlace Big Five. And now, we have this book to support our work!"

Judi Spear, Founder, Invisionit, LLC
Buffalo, New York

"As a psychologist who specializes in psychological assessment, I very much believe in a holistic approach to evaluation. I think the strategies/recommendations that you provide are practical, not just abstract theory about what to do. The various learning models you present allow a teacher or school to choose what best suits them. I only wish schools could get to the point where they use the 'In Class' chapter."

Roslyn Walker, Clinical Psychologist
Charlotte, North Carolina

"I loved the latest installment of your book—especially the myth section and 'Distractors from School Success'—it was a pleasure to read!"

Lauren Thomas, Graduate Student in Psychology
University of Louisville

"As a psychotherapist and career counselor who has used the Big Five extensively with clients around their life choices and relationship issues, I cannot recommend this book highly enough. The Big Five is the most useful way for us to understand the needs and motivations of our personalities that I know of. How do we apply that understanding? Whether you are a teacher, a parent, a therapist, a partner, or simply a seeker, it's here in this gem of a book."

Tammie Lesesne, MA, MAT; NC Licensed Professional Counselor
Charlotte, North Carolina

The Owner's Manual for Personality from 12 to 22

How the Big Five Personality Traits Affect
Adolescents at School and at Home,
in Their Careers and in Their Relationships

Pierce J. Howard, Ph.D.
Jane Mitchell Howard, M.B.A.

CENTER FOR
APPLIED COGNITIVE STUDIES
CentACS--Charlotte

The Owner's Manual for Personality from 12 to 22

The Owner's Manual for Personality from 12 to 22
How the Big Five Personality Traits Affect Adolescents at School and at Home, in their Careers and in their Relationships

Printed in the United States of America

CentACS Press
4701 Hedgemore Drive, Suite 210
Charlotte NC 28209-2200
Phone +1.704.331.0926 Fax +1.704.331.9408
www.centacs.com

Library of Congress Preassigned Control Number

Howard, Pierce J. & Howard, Jane Mitchell
The owner's manual for personality from 12 to 22: how the big five personality traits affect adolescents at school and at home, in their careers and in their relationships / Pierce J. Howard, Jane Mitchell Howard
Library of Congress Control Number: 2010912960

ISBN 978-0-578-05337-0 (pbk)

The authors may be contacted through
CentACS—Center for Applied Cognitive Studies
4701 Hedgemore Plaza, Suite 210
Charlotte NC 28209-2200
704-331-0926 phone
704-331-9408 fax
info@centacs.com or www.centacs.com

A CentACS Book
Design and Indexing: The Authors
Editing: Steve Carrell
Cover: Wendy Accetta of W. Accetta Design
Printing: Lightning Source
Font: Calibri

First Printed: March 2011

Preface

When we developed the *WorkPlace Big Five Profile* for use with working adults, we realized that we needed to provide a book to help test users. The result was *The Owner's Manual for the Workplace.* Then, when our users asked us for a parallel instrument to use with high school and college students, we developed the SchoolPlace Big Five Profile. So, in like manner, we herewith provide a book to help those who use personality information in working with adolescents.

Some comments on style...

1. We have resolved the thorny issue of referring to singular males and females by eschewing the awkward s/he and his/her constructions. We prefer the "singular their" as recommended by the Manhattan Institute's John McWhorter in his 2008 book, *Our Magnificent Bastard Tongue.* Hence, "One should mind *their* p's and q's."
2. Where one of us is telling a story, we parenthetically identify the narrator, as in: "I (Jane) went to Canada." With the next use of "I" by the other of us, we again identify ourselves.
3. Some material is taken from our earlier books, either word for word (very little, however) or modified. No apologies. Example: Speed Reading paragraph in Chapter 15.
4. For ease of reading, we have chosen to use the simple "scientific" footnote style, whereby, when citing a source, we list the author's last name and the year their work was published, as in Wright (1998). To fully identify the source, refer to the bibliography.
5. This book's punctuation comes mainly from the *Chicago Manual of Style*. However, readers of this book will range from academics who mainly use APA style to a general audience that commonly reads AP style. Therefore, this book uses a mixed collection of punctuation rules, chosen for their ability to communicate and not distract readers from the narrative.

Thanks to Dr. Pam Ey and her teenagers Taylor and Jason, to Hilary and Jy Murphy, to Laura and Paul Solitario and two teenagers Christine and Elizabeth, and to our 2009 summer research intern Emily Crowder (an undergraduate at the University of North Carolina at Chapel Hill) for contributing examples of trait behavior from popular culture. Further thanks to readers who have offered encouragement and suggestions: Judy Nelson, Amy Ramsey, Bob Augelli, Brandy Stamper, Derrick Flakkoll, Lisa Struckmeyer, Caryn Lee, Emily Crowder, Jennifer Parker, Judi Spear, Kim Buch, Lauren Thomas, Monica Vergara, Pam Ey, Robin McClure, Roslyn Walker, Tammy Lesesne, Bart van Eldert, and Susan Close.

We dedicate this book to all of the youth in schools where we have taught, studied, consulted, and frolicked over the years for giving us real material: West Charlotte High School (NC); Chapel Hill High School (NC); Grainger High School (NC); Opelika High School (AL); Tuscaloosa Junior High School (AL); Covenant Presbyterian Church (NC); East Carolina University (NC); the North Carolina Advancement School (NC); N.C. State University; Davidson College (NC); University of North Carolina, both at Chapel Hill and Charlotte; University of Montevallo (AL); Wake Forest University (NC); University of South Carolina at Columbia; Central Piedmont Community College (NC); Myers Park High School(NC); Queens University of Charlotte (NC); and Providence Day School (NC).

About the Authors

Pierce J. Howard grew up in Kinston, North Carolina, the youngest of seven, attending public schools until college at Davidson College (B.A.), East Carolina University (M.A.), and the University of North Carolina at Chapel Hill (Ph.D.). While studying at Chapel Hill, he taught English at Chapel Hill High School and later at North Carolina State University in Raleigh. Following his studies at Chapel Hill, he took a position as head of School Services at the North Carolina Advancement School in Winston-Salem—a special program for research and dissemination regarding underachievement among teenagers. He moved to Charlotte, NC, to teach and administer in a school-within-a school at West Charlotte High School. Since that time, Pierce has worked as an organization development consultant in a variety of settings around the world, while continuing to teach undergraduate and graduate students at Queens University (Charlotte), University of North Carolina at Charlotte, and Pfeiffer University at Charlotte. He has worked with over four dozen high school, undergraduate, and graduate interns, many of whose theses he advised. Meanwhile, he raised two teenage girls and looks forward to four grandchildren going through adolescence. Author of *The Owner's Manual for the Brain* (3rd edition) and (with Jane) *The Owner's Manual for Personality at Work* (2nd edition), he devotes most of his time now at the Center for Applied Cognitive Studies as the Managing Director of Research and Development involved in research, writing, and product development, mostly focused on the Five-Factor Model of personality.

Jane Mitchell Howard grew up in Opelika, Alabama, the youngest of three, attending public schools until obtaining a B.M.E. in music education from the University of Montevallo. After teaching high school and middle school choral music, she assumed the position of education director for Spirit Square Arts Center, in Charlotte, where she planned and managed arts programs for children, adolescents, and adults. As Jane completed her M.B.A at Wake Forest University, she and Pierce began their own firm, Howard Management Consulting, in 1986. Subsequently, the company evolved into the Center for Applied Cognitive Studies (CentACS) where Jane is Managing Director of Programs. Over the years, she has served as a choir mother, chaperoned a youth venture to Canada, worked with undergraduate interns, and raised two teenagers. She, along with Pierce, hopes to apply the principles of this book to their four grandchildren, just as she has coached many students in examining career options. Since the late 1980s, Jane has presented, led training courses, and consulted with business clients on five continents, co-authored (with Pierce) the WorkPlace Big Five Profile™, the SchoolPlace Big Five Profile™, *The Owner's Manual for Personality at Work* (1st and 2nd editions), professional manuals for both profiles, numerous trade-journal articles, and various scripts/products/exercises to teach the Big Five to learners of all ages. She also teaches in the Organization Development Certificate Program for the University of North Carolina at Charlotte.

About the Center for Applied Cognitive Studies (CentACS)

The vision of CentACS, the Center for Applied Cognitive Studies, is to optimize people through a global professional network. The company is the primary location of Pierce and Jane Howard's work and research with the Big Five. It is an information-based e-commerce company, developing and publishing materials, training and certifying consultants to use the Big Five, and conducting research to support the Five-Factor Model of personality and other brain-related research designed to help people learn, work, and grow more effectively.

Established in Charlotte, North Carolina, in July 1986 by Jane Mitchell Howard, M.B.A., managing director, and Pierce J. Howard, Ph.D., director of research, the company is currently located near downtown Charlotte. At this writing, CentACS has eight full-time employees, five part-time employees, and a growing network of over three thousand certified and qualified Big Five consultants around the world, trained by the Howards and other CentACS Master Trainers.

The mission of CentACS is to establish personality assessment and brain research standards for the twenty-first century by building a global network of internal and external consultants and international affiliate companies who use the Five-Factor Model of personality, the Human Resource Optimization Model, and related brain research in their work. Through in-class and online certification and advanced training programs, learning conferences, valid and respected test instruments, on-line e-services, a scoring services bureau, consulting and selection projects for clients, and other resources, CentACS provides cutting-edge information, high-quality products, and support services.

CENTER FOR
APPLIED COGNITIVE STUDIES

Primarily, the company operates within the United States with certified consultants located from California to Massachusetts, from Florida to Wisconsin. Many Fortune 500 companies, medium-to-small companies, university MBA and undergraduate programs, public and private high schools, and large and small consulting companies are customers of CentACS. Outside the United States, CentACS is currently affiliated with four companies that work with the Big Five in their respective geographic areas.

For further information about how you may use the Big Five in your school, organization, or in your work, or to contact CentACS or its affiliate companies, or inquire how your organization may become an affiliate, please refer to the following information:

United States and all other countries not listed below:
The Center for Applied Cognitive Studies
4701 Hedgemore Drive, Suite 210, Charlotte, NC 28209-2200, USA

Contact: Lisa Struckmeyer, Sales & Marketing Director
Contact: Caryn Lee, Managing Director--Operations

Telephone: +1.704.331.0926
Toll Free in the US: +1.800.BIG.55Fax: +1.704.331.9408

E-mail: info@centacs.com
Website: www.centacs.com

SchoolPlace Big Five Profile and WorkPlace Big Five Profile project set-up form and related products and materials on-line: www.centacs.com

Additional copies of this book available through Amazon.com or through CentACS.

Mexico: People Value
Contact: Celina del Castillo
E-mail: cdelcastillo@peoplevalue.com.mx
Website: www.peoplevalue.com.mx

Singapore and Hong Kong: DisTinctions Asia
Contact: George Quek
E-mail: enquiry@distinctions-asia.com
Website: www.distinctions-asia.com

India: Chatur Knowledge Networking
Contact: Sheetal Gore
Email: sheetal.gore@chatur.com
Website: www.chatur.com

Table of Contents

The Owner's Manual for Personality from 12 to 22

by Pierce J. Howard, Ph.D., & Jane Mitchell Howard, M.B.A.

Introduction

An Overview of What We Know About Youth from 12 to 22, and How This Book Will Contribute to That Knowledge

> "There is no such thing as a *typical* teenager."
>
> –Phillip Graham in *The Death of Adolescence*

Teenagers put up with bad rap. Not bad rap music, not bad rap sheets, not bad rapping on the front door. Bad reputation. Aristotle philosophized in the 4th century BCE that "the young...in regard to sexual desire...exercise no self-restraint" (Graham, 2004, p. 26). Almost 2,000 years later, William Shakespeare laments through the Old Shepherd in *The Winter's Tale* that, "I would there were no age between ten and three and twenty... for there is nothing in the between but getting wenches with child, wronging the ancientry, stealing, fighting..." (III,iii). And more recently, we hear that, "Mother Nature is providential. She gives us twelve years to develop a love for our children before turning them into teenagers" (attributed to William Galvin). And stirring the pot with the academic trappings of authority, G. Stanley Hall (1904) writes in the first textbook on adolescence of the "sturm und drang" (storm and stress/urge) of the teen years.

But wait. Current research tells us that all behavior is "normally distributed." Yes, teens have tempers, but so do toddlers and grandparents. For any given age group, one in three persons will be atypically calm, 1 in 3 will be atypically distressed, and the rest of us will alternate between calm and distress. So why the bad rap? This invites our first definition of terms: what is adolescence?

The word derives from the Latin infinitive *adolescere,* meaning "to grow up," while the Latin past participle *adultus* gives us "adult," or "having grown up." The word "adolescence," and its softer synonym "youth," tend to be used more by scholars and professionals, while "teenagers" and "teens" tend to be used more by the young people themselves and by marketing professionals appealing to a thriving market segment. In fact, the very word "teenager" seems to have first appeared in 1941 in *Popular Mechanics* magazine as part of an effort to create a marketing niche (Graham, 2004). Those who study adolescence typically mark its beginning with puberty (from the Latin word *pubertas*, meaning "ripe age"), when one's body undergoes changes that result in procreative ability (Note: Puberty can start as early as age 8). The end of adolescence is typically marked by readiness for work and a family, or more simply, readiness to be fully independent. The phases within this period are most typically described (cf. Lerner and Steinberg, 2004) as early adolescence, middle adolescence, and late adolescence. Because of the different biological timelines in the sexes, different age brackets are associated with each (see Table 0.1).

Table 0.1 Stages of Adolescence by Sex

	Male	Female
Early Adolescence	12-14	10-12
Late Adolescence	14-18	12-18
Emerging Adulthood	18-27	18-25

It is this in-between time of being neither child nor adult that is associated with the bad rap. As we hope to show in this book, the rap is undeserved. Pleasant and unpleasant behaviors accompany every stage of life. Certainly, conformity decreases throughout these years as a result of the identity formation process (Cobb, 2007). However, as we will see in later chapters, this increasing nonconformity is essential for maturity. And, it is a process that parents can facilitate, so long as they interpret the nonconformity as growthful and not rejecting. Sure, a slight rise in negative emotions comes with the middle school years, but only to rebound to earlier levels of positive emotions by the end of high school (Cobb, 2007). This blip in negativity comes with learning how to handle major changes in body chemistry, neurological structures, and physical characteristics, just as parents show blips in negativity when undergoing changes at work, in relationships, and elsewhere in their lives. For the most part, the stress of living around teens is self-inflicted, inasmuch as parents tend to take their teens' outbursts seriously and personally when they are no more serious and personally directed than a cat's hiss, both soon followed by purring and hugging.

Furthermore, the characteristics we associate with the teen years—sexuality, stress, emotional volatility, experimentation with a variety of mind-altering substances, search for identity, and family/relational conflicts—are as typical of adults as of teens. The evolution of society, particularly in the latter half of the 20th century, not only created a youth culture different from the past, it created an adult culture different from the past. The Women's Movement, contraception technology, ever larger homes and multiple homes (with more opportunities for risky behavior), the availability of a personal car (a bedroom/bar/forum on wheels), the development of media, widespread mores that condone sexual freedom and cohabitation, improvements in transportation and material distribution (making alcohol, drugs, etc. cheaper and more accessible), cell phones and Internet communication, racial integration and cultural diversity, the Vietnam/Iraq wars with ensuing distrust of government and institutions—all have a cumulative effect on creating a youth culture—AND an adult culture—like none before. For example, one social practice associated with the new youth culture—two-worker families—affects adults as much as kids.

10 Myths about the Teen Years

Phillip Graham (2004, pp. 12-22) writes convincingly of 10 "myths" of teens and systematically tears each down. Graham's myths and explanations follow, along with additional research that has emerged since his book was published.

Myth #1: "Normal adolescent development is tumultuous."

Reality: This is true only for about 1 in 9 youth, and can be attributed to normal differences in the two personality traits of extraversion and the need for stability, as we will see in Part One. Tantrums peak around age 2 and all but disappear by 14. Otherwise, about 1/9 of the population, from the teen years through old age, experience tumultuous emotional volatility (the third of the population who score highest on need for stability [e.g., negative emotions, such as anxiety, anger, and sadness], AND the emotionally volatile also score in the highest third of the population on extraversion [e.g., positive emotions, such as ecstasy, joy, and excitement]—these terms are further defined in Chapter 1). For a relatively low percentage of the population, levels of suicide, depression, irritability, and distress do, in fact, increase somewhat around the time of puberty. That statistic remains stable into the late 20s, then decreases somewhat. This is consistent with Costa and McCrae's (2003) observation of behavioral changes occurring around age 30 (explained in more detail in Chapter 1).

The distress of youth, to the extent that it does exist, comes from two sources: temperament (which is inherited) and environment (primarily poverty and lack of advantage). The latter can be addressed through opportunities for young people to make their own money, receive better nutrition/vitamins/minerals/variety of foods (fruits and vegetables), move into more adequate housing/safer neighborhoods, have access to educational resources/experiences/computers, receive positive feedback from a caring parent or guardian, and gain access to youth organizations with a positive mission (sport, arts, environment, politics, caregiving, and so forth), rather than gangs.

Myth #2: "The teen years are marked by an upsurge of aggression."

Reality: The incidence of aggression is similar to the incidence of emotional volatility described in Myth #1. In fact, aggression is more common for persons over 21 than under. That said, approximately 1 in 20 youth exhibit anti-social behavior (aggression/violence with the intent to harm), with boys 20 times more likely to be the culprit than girls. This anti-social behavior comes in two forms: Life-Course Persistent (LCP) and Adolescence Limited (AL). The former is more likely to be primarily birth given (either genetic or traumatic—e.g., neurological damage in utero). Adolescent Limited aggression has less of an origin in genetics (some of it is caused by maturity gaps, which are primarily genetic) and more origin in personal situations (Graham, 2004, p. 98 ff). Graham provides remedies for both kinds of aggression in *The End of Adolescence* (2004), beginning on page 111.

Myth #3: "Adolescents are obsessed with sex, because they are suddenly flooded with hormones that drive them into sexual promiscuity."

Reality: Chaim Potok starts his novel about growing up, *In the Beginning*, with the sentence, "All beginnings are hard." Yes, hormone levels increase. However, the changes are gradual, beginning as early as the age of five, with a surge around nine or ten, then reaching adult levels around age 14 on average. Moreover, the hormone levels achieved at the height of youth do not decrease—these adult levels remain stable for quite some time—until middle age ushers in decreases. The only sense in which teens are any different is in the sense of Potok's observation that "Beginnings are hard." What do I do with these hormones? Actually 20-somethings have more sex, more sex partners, and more abortions than teens. And, the sexual fantasies that characterize youth typically continue well into advanced age.

An aspect of this myth has to do with the notion that menarche (a girl's first menstrual period) happens earlier than ever before. And, the earlier menarche occurs, the less mature the girl. The less mature the girl, the less time to accumulate experience that is helpful in managing hormone-associated emotions. Some explanation is in order. In the early Victorian era (early 19th century), the average age of menarche was 15. Dramatic improvements in diet saw this average age fall to 12.5 by 1950. In addition, this change in timing of menarche was accompanied by an average increase in height. Both of these changes are associated with improvements in nutrition and diet. These group statistics are different from individual statistics, whereby some girls experience menarche earlier than others, mostly as a result of their genetic inheritance (with one exception: father-absent girls have menarche earlier, a relationship unexplained satisfactorily to date).

One factor that appears to be contributing to earlier onset of menarche in some metropolitan areas has to do with chemical crossovers from waste disposal systems to their parallel fresh water supply systems. The CBS program *60 Minutes* aired a segment in 2008 that showed hormones and other drugs being flushed down toilets after their expiration dates. Because of this action, *60 Minutes* reported that hormones and drugs were infiltrating some cities' water supplies, thereby potentially accelerating maturity ages among children.

Myth #4: "The teen years are inevitably a time of violent disagreement between parents and their children."

Reality: Family conflict is the exception, not the rule. Most teens have healthy attachment with parents. Conflicts occur but do not cripple the relationship, and are rather a part of identity formation and learning to be independent (on both sides—parents and teens). Most conflict comes from emerging differences (and disappointing similarities) between traits/abilities/physical characteristics of youth in comparison with their parents/other family members. We will discuss this phenomenon in more detail in this chapter in the upcoming section headed "Living with Differences."

In a 2002 survey of 500 teens (Graham, 2004, p. 47), 85% said they were happy with their family life, 10% said they did not get along with their parents (probably attributed to low levels of two traits—Accommodation and Consolidation—that will be explained in upcoming chapters), and 33% said they had not had an argument with their parents in the past year. In another survey in 1999 with 2,500 teens, only 3% emerged as "often unhappy, down-hearted, or tearful," while the vast majority said this phrase was definitely not true of them (80% of boys, 75% of girls).

Myth #5: "Those in their teen years, although they may appear superficially clever, are immature in their thinking process when compared to adults."

Reality: Thinking processes such as syllogisms, searching for assumptions, inductive pattern finding, creating analogies and metaphors, determining meaning from context, searching for evidence, and separating fact from fiction are to experience as roadmaps are to terrain. The more kinds of terrain one has experienced (through travel, camping, and so forth), the more maps come alive upon inspection. Similarly, the more life has been lived (through reading, relationships, work, travel, exposure to diversity, and so forth), the more one's thinking processes will have to work with.

Yes, teens are lacking in years of experience, but they demonstrate adult-like mastery of basic thinking skills. If you remove experience differences, as in matching youth and adults who have had no experience with, say, computer programming, then the thinking abilities of both groups are equal. It is not the ability to think that teens lack. Rather, they lack years of experience. Evidence shows that teens who have travelled more, read more, and interacted with others more, show comparable reasoning ability with the typical adult.

Myth #6: "The teen years form a separate phase of life."

Reality: There is no evidence that this statement is true. As Graham (2004) writes, "It is society that creates our teenagers, not their brains" (p. 16). Physical and neurological changes occur throughout life, with teen-relevant changes beginning as early as 5 years of age and continuing through the late 20s. There is no clear span of time bracketed by the stop and start of teendom. Only the conventional bookends of puberty and marriage/career normally define adolescence. The emphasis on teendom as a clear segment of society is primarily a marketing strategy.

Myth #7: "Adolescents have constant doubts about their identity."

Reality: The raw material of identity (traits, abilities, and physical characteristics, each described in detail in Part One) is present from birth. Kids know when they are more sociable or more solitary than others, more reactive or more able to chill, more imaginative or more literal, more verbal or more kinesthetic, and so forth. By age 8, trait and talent strengths are clear—assuming that they enjoy a reasonably supportive environment. It is how they express themselves that can change, as in, "What will I do with my sociability? Politics, sales, management, cheerleading, social work, trial law?"

Myth #8: "Those in their teen years are emotionally immature."

Reality: Emotional maturity, more popularly called emotional intelligence ("EQ"), is a function of 1) temperament and 2) memory. Some people are less volatile temperamentally than others, and history/experience (i.e., memory) gives us points of reference to inform new choices ("last time I did that, I threw up"). Less volatile people naturally learn more quickly from experience than the more volatile. It takes time for the latter to get beyond their sense of invulnerability, with some, sadly, taking their impulsivity (and its consequences) to their graves.

Much of what passes as immaturity is what David Elkind describes as the "personal fable" (Cobb, 2007), according to which young people often feel "unique, invulnerable, and omnipotent" (121). However, this outlook is a function of experience (e.g., broken legs, hurt feelings, etc.) as well as inherited temperament (spontaneity, distractibility, nerves of steel), which lasts a lifetime. The more one experiences—the more one bumps up against one's limitations—the better one's memory of these experiences is able to serve as a reminder of undesirable consequences. According to Elkind, risky behavior of (some) teens is not so much self-destructive as it is springing from a sense of indestructibility (i.e., that one is not subject to the rules/natural laws operating in the universe). For many teens, this sense of indestructibility is corrected by the school of hard knocks. However, this sense of indestructibility is not characteristic of all teens. Clearly, many young people have a certain temperament that is coupled with an environment (parents, school, friends, and so forth) that provides good information that, in fact, one is not indestructible (e.g., family councils, drug education).

Myth #9: "Those in their teens are characteristically full of naïve idealism."

Reality: No evidence supports this. Naïve idealism is primarily an inherited temperament, just like naïve pragmatism, and it continues throughout one's lifetime. Naïve idealism is associated with several inherited traits—trust, enthusiasm, comfort with change, and assertiveness, to name a few. However, one does not inherit the specific content of one's naïve idealism. What we are naively idealistic about ("eat no meat" or "abstain from sex" or "women are made for homemaking" or "the right to bear arms") is influenced by family, peers, needs of the moment, and other contextual factors.

Myth #10: "The teens have the greater abundance of creativity and new ideas."

Reality: No, it just isn't true. There are just too many counterexamples. Creativity is more a function of inherited temperament that lasts for a lifetime (one small exception is that creative mathematics appears to peak in one's 20s). We will discuss this in more depth in the chapter relating to "O," which stands for "Originality."

Living with Differences

The task of living with adolescents is no different than the task of living with adults. Let us explain. As we will show in Parts One and Two of this book, personality (from the Latin *persona*, referring to the masks worn by stage actors) comprises three sets of "raw materials" that we inherit: behavioral traits (such as sociability and methodicalness), mental abilities (such as memory and language), and physical characteristics (such as height and a taste for spicy foods). Each of these kinds of raw materials is distributed among us, such that about 1/3 of us tend to be towards one extreme (e.g., more solitary, poorer memory, and shorter), another 1/3 of us tend to be towards the opposite extreme (e.g., more sociable, stronger memory, and taller), while the remaining 1/3 of us tend to be in between (e.g., sometimes solitary and sometimes sociable, modest memory, and medium height).

It is the differences among us that make it possible to build civilizations, that make us interesting to one another, and, yes, that make it hard to live with each other. When a solitary person lives with a sociable person, the solitary one can feel pressured to change and be more sociable (as a friend in graduate school said to her scholarly, and solitary, husband: "What do you have against people?"). On the other hand, the sociable one can feel misunderstood by the solitary one (as the same friend's husband said back to her, "Why can't you learn to be comfortable with yourself?"). When a person with one extreme behavior lives or interacts with someone at the opposite extreme, there is a tendency to take the differences *personally.* The solitary person feels that the sociable person is being sociable *just to get away from the solitary person.* In other words, the solitary person can go crazy thinking they are being judged by the sociable person's desire to be around other people ("What's wrong with me? Why do you need these other people? Why can't you be happy just being with me?"). And the sociable person can go crazy thinking they are being judged by the solitary person's choice not to go out ("What's wrong with me? Why won't you go out with me? Are you embarrassed to be in public with me?").

The coexistence of extremes, when taken so personally, can make you crazy, depressed, insecure, angry, or bored; UNLESS you learn to see such differences as God-given, inherited, natural, and NOT something the other person is doing to get back at you, as a way to judge you, or as a way to make you uncomfortable. The teen/spouse/partner/coworker is not a slob in order to get under your skin—they would be that way with anyone. So, we must learn not to take differences personally.

With marriage and career, we can make choices to be around persons who are similar to us, and whose extremes don't bother us. However, parents can't choose the qualities of their offspring, and children can't choose the qualities of their parents. We are best served by the attitude of, "Hmmm, it's interesting and amusing how different we are." Or, as we read years ago in a book on individual differences, "I can regard my difference from you as superior, and feel smug. Or I can view my difference from you as inferior, and feel depressed. Or I can see our differences as merely differences, neither being better than the other, and be amused and appreciative of our mutual uniqueness." In other words, it makes no more sense to regard personality differences with pride, envy, or despair, than it does to regard differences in fingerprints in a like manner. This book is devoted to helping us understand what these basic differences are and how to live with them.

The Tree of Life

Every task in life has two components: the *skill* with which we perform the task and the personal *resources* we bring to the task. For example, take "doing math homework." Performance on this task involves completing the assignment in a timely and accurate manner, which requires that we master the knowledge and skills associated with the task:

- knowing and understanding the relevant mathematical concepts and procedures
- organizing the homework itself
- timely completion of the task

- accurate completion of the task

To the degree that we complete the task on time and accurately, we are said to be "competent" at that task and its associated skills/knowledge. In the world of work, that task is called a competency, something that we are, or are not, competent at doing (the word comes from the Latin *competere*, meaning "to compete").

However, being competent at a task does not mean that we necessarily have the optimal personal resources for doing that task. For example, the optimal personal resources for the competency "math homework" would include:

- concentration
- preference for, and comfort with, solitude
- preference for methodicalness
- perfectionist streak
- patience and stick-with-it-ness
- ambition, wanting to do well/make good grades/salvage earlier bad grades
- mathematics ability
- legible handwriting
- problem-solving spirit

A student with all of these personal resources, coupled with a supportive home atmosphere, will find it natural to excel at the competency of "math homework." However, as you begin to remove these resources one by one, students who lack one or more of these optimal resources for "math homework" will find it increasingly unnatural to perform that competency or task. *That does not mean that the student cannot do it well, just that it will not be natural for them.* The student will have to find ways to compensate for missing resources. For example, a student who is more gregarious and who is uncomfortable with solitude, could compensate by setting up circumstances so the temptation to join in social activities with others is minimized (e.g., have a study area away from any windows, door closed, no telephone in the same room, announce to parents/siblings not to be interrupted, keep the family pet away from the study area, and so forth).

These two sets of competency-related attributes—the **performance skills** and the **personal resources**—relate to each other much like a tree (i.e., performance) and its root system (i.e. resources). Consider five different trees, each showing a different condition with respect to its leafiness (or performance) and roots (or resources). A unique strategy is associated with each condition:

1) The typical tree will most likely flourish (i.e., high performance) with a wide root system (i.e., abundant personal resources).

   Strategy: **Capitalize**, or build on it.

2) A tree will languish (i.e., poor performance) if it has shallow roots (i.e., sparse personal resources).

   Strategy: **Compensate**, or find a work-around.

3) A tree might flourish initially yet have a small root system (e.g., where bound by rocks), but the flourishing is doomed ultimately to turn into languishing.

Strategy: **Caution**, or plan to prevent burnout.

4) Another tree might languish (because, e.g., shade and/or drought is stunting its growth), while nonetheless having a strong, wide root system. In time, it could flourish if freed of its constraints.

    Strategy: **Develop**, or provide training and practice.

5) A tree with some good roots and some bad ones will languish without special attention.

    Strategy: **Develop with Support**, or provide special attention and resources.

These five conditions are illustrated in Figure A. Each condition can be visualized as falling somewhere on a two-dimensional graph, as shown in Figure B. If you compare Figure A and Figure B, you will see that the five tree-and-root systems of Figure A can actually be superimposed on Figure B, as illustrated in Figure C.

We call this series of relationships between performance skills and personal resources "Human Resource Optimization" (HRO). HRO will be explained more in Chapter 4. The tree-root relationship is critical to understanding teens (and adults) in their various contexts: 1) what is expected of them (=performance skills in many areas, e.g., relational, academic, familial, and athletic); 2) what they bring to the task (=personal resources including traits, abilities, and physical characteristics). You will see the tree-and-root-system icon throughout this book as a reminder of these critical relationships.

Figure A HRO Trees

Figure B HRO Performance versus Resources Model

Figure C Trees and Model Superimposed

You will soon discover that the focus in this book is on the behavioral personality traits that constitute a large portion of the "personal resources" that we bring to a task, with less emphasis on the mental abilities and physical characteristics—they are the subject of a future book.

The Owner's Manual for Personality from 12 to 22

What Teens Must Accomplish

Nancy Cobb, in her book *Adolescence: Continuity, Change, and Diversity* (2007, p. 15), says research shows there are eight developmental tasks of adolescence. She states these should be the large challenges that each young person must successfully address during the school years:

Early Adolescence:

- achieving new and more mature relations with age-mates
- achieving a masculine or feminine [somewhere along the continuum] social role
- accepting one's physique and using the body effectively
- achieving emotional independence from parents and other adults

Late Adolescence:

- preparing for marriage and family [or partner] life
- preparing for an economic career
- acquiring a set of values/ethical system as a guide to behavior
- desiring and achieving socially responsible behavior

We will see in the following chapters how one's personal resources affect each of these developmental tasks. Enjoy the journey!

Part One

All About Personality

1

Traits

How the Stable Part of Personality Develops

> "When my student does well, I favor environmental explanations. When poorly, genetic. "
>
> --Unknown teacher
>
> "When my child does well, I favor environmental explanations. When poorly, genetic."
>
> –Unknown parent
>
> "When I do well, I attribute it to my effort. When poorly, to my genes."
>
> --Unknown student

Guide to this chapter:

- What is Personality?
- How to Measure the "Givens"—and How to Understand the Measurements!
- The "Big Five" Personality Traits: a Brief Introduction
- So, Where Does Personality Come From?
- How Do Nature and Nurture Work Together Over Time?
- What about Birth Order?
- Do Traits Work the Same Way Around the World?
- Are Traits the Same for Males and Females?
- Can Levels of a Trait Be Increased or Decreased?
- What Happens to Traits Over Time?

Personality is a set of predictable behaviors that make us recognizable. When I (Pierce) got home after a long high school day in eastern North Carolina, I knew whether my mother had been in my room by whether my dirty clothes were off the floor and in the hamper. Her neatness made her recognizable. Similarly, she could tell when I had been in the kitchen, as something was likely to be left out on the counter—a loaf of bread, a spreading knife, perhaps a jar of peanut butter. While nature abhors a vacuum, I abhor unrelenting order. I did not share my mother's neatness genes. Nor do I today! Unmade beds, piles here and there, clippings and notes stuck all over.... And I married a woman with the same set of predictable behaviors: Jane's desktop is typically stacked and chaotic until she has a periodic "clean up" day, and then she delights in imagining her mother (no longer with us) smiling approvingly at the freshly neatened desktop. A. A. Milne described it as the wonderful chaos called home.

Similar to the form of a geometric proof, this initial chapter starts with the "givens"—the raw materials of personality that we bring into the world with us. You will see that each piece of raw material, such as a mother's neatness gene, forms a set of characteristics that makes each of us unique as a person. These raw materials can be described as belonging to one of three categories:

- Behavioral Traits
- Mental Abilities
- Physical Characteristics

Traits are correlated sets of *behaviors*, behaviors that tend to occur together. As we have said earlier, behavioral traits are the main subject of this book. Neatness is an example of such a behavioral trait (or just "trait," for short). Neatness is composed of a variety of correlated behaviors such as:

- putting tools back after using them
- putting dirty clothes in the hamper
- taking out the trash regularly
- arranging items on a shelf in an orderly fashion
- returning papers to their proper file folders/drawers
- saving computer documents to the proper folders
- sweeping after living in an area
- "policing" the campground after an outing for any non-natural scraps
- keeping one's study area organized
- wiping the crumbs off a counter after making a snack
- ...plus, hundreds of similar behaviors

These behaviors are correlated in the sense that a person who tends to do one of them will also tend to do the others. But they are only "correlated"—they are not absolutely related to one another. Some people are neat in some ways but not in other ways. We might put up tools, but otherwise be a slob. We might police a campground (as a well–trained scout or soldier), but allow a room and study area to go wild. At a house of worship, we might present ourselves dressed up in designer clothes, yet go to school or work in ripped jeans and a stained t-shirt. On the other hand, some people are neat and orderly just about ALL the time! And, at the other end, some are almost never inclined to bother about organization and neatness.

Mental abilities are correlated sets of *skills*—that is, skills that tend to occur together. "Memory" is an example of a mental ability (or just "ability," for short). Memory is comprised of a correlated set of skills:

- short-term memory

- long-term memory
- memory for faces
- memory for names
- memory for dates
- memory for procedures
- memory for words and their meanings
- memory for formulas and how they work

These skills, like the behaviors listed earlier, are correlated in the sense that a person who tends to do one of them well is likely to do many of them well. But they are only "correlated"—they are not absolutely related to one another. People who do most of them well are said to have good memories, while those who do only one are said to have a specific kind of memory, such as having a "good memory for faces."

Physical characteristics are neither behaviors nor skills, but rather are attributes of our bodies that make us more similar or more different than others. These characteristics don't really cluster in groups the way that behaviors and skills cluster into different traits and abilities. Rather, these physical characteristics are like a geographical map of how our bodies are laid out:

- height
- weight
- eye color
- hair color
- hair texture
- skin color
- skin texture
- tendency to motion sickness
- sleep requirements
- tolerance for heat/cold
- visual acuity
- auditory acuity
- allergies
- taste preferences
- tolerance for hot/spicy foods
- predispositions for specific diseases
- deformities
- and so forth

How to Measure the "Givens"—and How to Interpret the Measurements!

Most people reading this book will have test results in hand from the SchoolPlace Big Five Profile, the WorkPlace Big Five Profile, or maybe even some other Big Five assessment. So you may read your report responsibly and knowledgeably, here are some of the basic principles of personality measurement and interpretation.

In order to describe each other's behavioral traits, mental abilities, and physical characteristics, we need to agree on several principles of description. So let us take a few moments to review the tools of the trade that are used in measuring these attributes. In order, these tools are:

- The "normal bell curve" describes how traits occur throughout the population.
- Some types of scores are univalent; others are bivalent.
- Scores are not absolutes.
- Small point differences (at least 5 points) can represent significant differences between individuals.

All About Personality

- Most trait scores are arrived at by administering a "self-report" survey to an individual.
- Test scores are only meaningful when they are based on a good set of "norms."

These are the tools that permit us to see how we are all similar and different.

1. The "Normal Bell Curve." Behavioral traits, mental abilities, and physical characteristics have one thing in common. Namely, they are all "normally distributed" throughout the world. This means that, for each trait, ability, and physical characteristic, some people are more towards one extreme, some are more towards the opposite extreme, and most are in between. This pattern is described as the normal curve. Figure 1.1 uses the example of "height" to illustrate the normal curve. You will notice

Figure 1.1 The Normal Curve

a. The normal curve, with U.S. adult height (in feet) as an illustration:

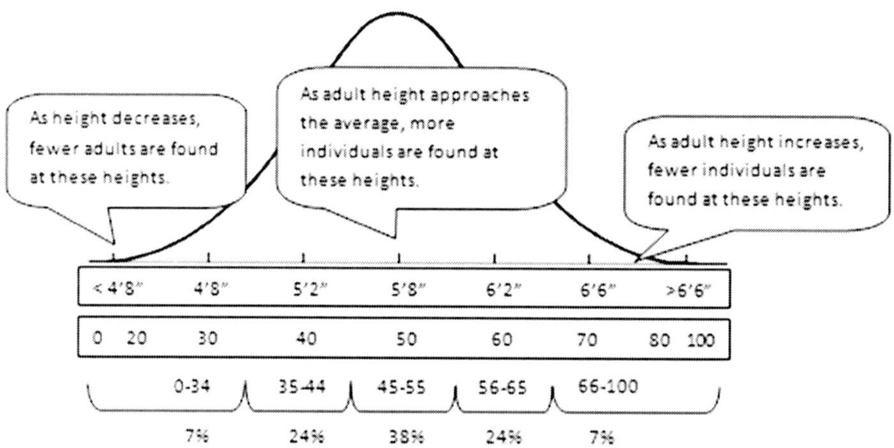

b. The normal curve, using "Sociability" as an illustration:

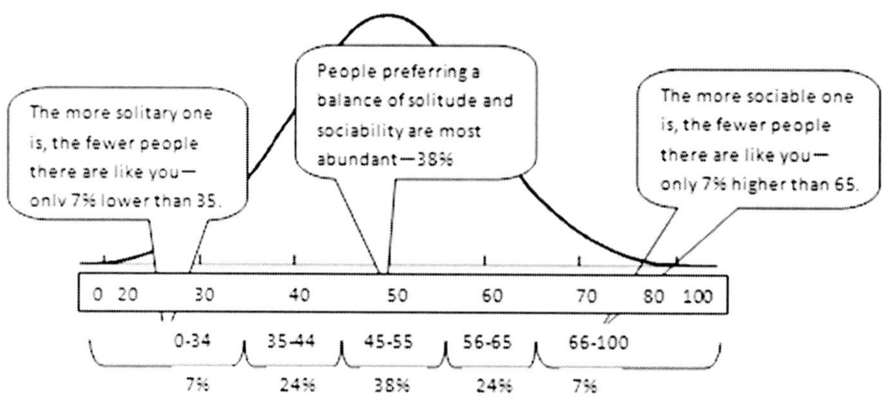

two curves: Figure 1.1a uses "height" as an illustration, and Figure 1.1b uses the trait of "Sociability" as an illustration. The curve that forms the upper border of Figure 1.1a is the "normal curve." At any given point on the curve, the higher the curve, the more people are associated with the "score" on the horizontal line just below it. The lower the curve, or the closer it gets to that horizontal line, the fewer people are associated with the "score" on the horizontal line. In the very center of the horizontal line, you will see 5'8", which represents the average height of adults in the U.S.A. Notice that the curve is at its tallest just above this "score." As the heights get taller to the right, ending at 7 feet, notice the curve drops, meaning that fewer and fewer people are found at these increasing heights. The same is true as scores go to the left side towards 4'6".

Instead of measurement based on feet and inches, we use something called a "standard score" with the three groups of personality attributes. The reason it is called "standard" is that it takes a bunch of different kinds of scores, such as height, weight, neatness, and IQ, and translates them into a common "language" or "score type." The nature of standard scores is such that a 50 always represents the average score of a specific attribute. Standard scores range from 0 to 100, with very few people ever scoring below 20 or above 80. For the sake of convenience, we group the scores into five levels:

- Very Low, or below 35, where about 7% of the people score on a given attribute
- Low, from 35 to 45, where about 24% score
- Mid-range, from 45 to 55, where about 38% score
- High, from 55 to 65, where about 24% score
- Very High, above 65, where about 7% score

> "All things come into being by conflict of opposites."
> --Heraclitus

An easy way to remember this is that roughly 1/3 of the population score in the mid-range (from 45 to 55), with about 1/3 scoring lower and 1/3 scoring higher. A score of 50, the average, will have the most scores that are similar to it. As a score moves further away from 50, the number of similar scores decreases. Extreme scorers on personality traits and abilities are rare. Not bad or weird, just rare.

2. Univalent and Bivalent. There are two ways to interpret standard scores:

a. Scores in one direction are better than scores in the opposite direction. We call these "univalent" scales, or scales for which there is only one right direction to score. Examples of univalent scores are golf scores (the lower the better), word knowledge (the more the better), and mathematical ability (the higher the better). Of the three sets of personality characteristics, only the mental abilities group has univalent scores for all characteristics in the group. With respect to physical characteristics, some are univalent (such as visual acuity—there's nothing of value in not being able to focus visually) and others are *bivalent.*

b. Scores in either direction are fine. We call these "bivalent," meaning that any score in the range—from very low to mid-range to very high—has value. Examples of bivalent attributes are height and sociability. It is fine to be short (e.g., to be a jockey) or tall (e.g., to be a basketball center), and it is fine to be solitary (e.g., to be a scholar) or to be sociable (e.g., to be a salesperson). There is nothing intrinsically good or bad about high or low scores on a bivalent scale. It depends on the context.

> "Without Contraries is no progression. Attraction and Repulsion, Reason and Energy, Love and Hate, are necessary to Human existence."
> --William Blake

Traits are, by their very nature, bivalent. As Ralph Waldo Emerson put it (in *Society and Solitude,* 1870), "Every individual nature has its own beauty." Or, there is no one right way to be. Each personality trait is comprised of opposites, such as solitude and sociability. In most of us, we are aware of some struggle between these opposites: "I need to stop texting with my friends and do my homework, " or "I need to get out of the library, breathe some fresh air, and hang with my friends for a while." One's score on a trait represents the balance that we tend to exhibit between each pair of opposites. So,

- A score of 30 on sociability would be someone who finds it more natural to spend time alone, yet who will from time to time feel the need for, and enjoyment of, other people. This kind of person will be happier in a job or relationship in which the majority of their time is spent in relative solitude or working alone on a project.

- A score of 80 on sociability, on the other hand, would be someone who finds it more natural to be around other people, yet who will from time to time (hopefully!) feel the need for closing the door and doing some reading or computer work. This kind of person will be happier in a job or relationship in which the majority of their time is spent around other people and interacting with them.

- A score of 50 on sociability would be someone who would prefer a balance of social and solitary activities, as in a musician who is comfortable spending half the time practicing alone and the other half playing/singing with groups. Or it could be someone who dislikes both solitude AND large groups, and prefers spending most of the time with a few friends, coworkers, or family. In other words, mid-range scores can represent either a) persons who behave half the time like one extreme, and half the time like the other, or b) persons who behave all the time in-between the two extremes. The first kind of person would be like someone who likes very sweet drinks some of the time, and plain water at other times. The second kind of person would be like someone who likes a moderately sweet drink all the time.

Think of a trait as being comprised of two "fuel cans" with each can representing the amount of energy one has for each opposing trait. Someone with an 80 for Sociability has a relatively large fuel can for being sociable and a rather small can of fuel for being solitary. Literally, after 30 minutes of intense solitary study, this person is likely to feel something like, "I've used up my energy for being still, quiet, and alone. I need to switch fuel tanks and allow my tank for solitude to fill back up. Then I'll continue studying later." Our grandsons recently spent the night at our house, then we attended a children's symphony concert on Saturday morning (a "Lollipop" concert), and then visited a botanical garden to experience a special butterfly exhibit. We wore each other out and returned home late in the afternoon, after depositing the boys with their parents, and slept for almost two hours! Later, we asked how the kids enjoyed their stay with us, and their dad said, "At supper, Liam (the 6-year-old), clearly worn out, said to us, 'I'm all out of puff.'" Which, in Thomas the Tank Engine's Land of Sodor, means out of fuel—just can't get up a head of steam/puff. Liam was saying that he had used up his tank for being around other people and was ready for some quiet, alone time, perhaps even to sleep! He needed to refill his tank for being around the sensory bombardment that others often generate. Figure 1.2 illustrates the fuel-can analogy using Liam's lower score on Sociability as an example. As you can observe, Liam's small fuel can for sociability had been used up at the end of the day—all that was left was fumes. It was then time to switch to his other, and much larger, fuel can for solitude and quiet.

3. Scores are not absolutes. The trait score is broad-brush. While a 55 on sociability suggests that person is more sociable than about 2/3 of the population, one can still exhibit different levels of sociability in different aspects of one's life. On average, across all areas of one's life, one may be more sociable than 2/3 of the population, but that sociability score could be comprised of 99th percentile on sports, 75th on religious activities, 60th on family, 50th on music, 30th on hobbies, and so forth. On the other hand, one could be more consistent than that, and, for example, enjoy being around active groups of people in nearly every aspect of life.

Figure 1.2 The Fuel Can Metaphor for Understanding the Bivalent Nature of Traits

In the typical individual, these varying levels of behavior all average out to one's "score" on a behavioral trait range. The score is a best estimate of one's total natural energy for that kind of trait-related behavior. And while the score/level doesn't change, one can redistribute the way the energy is used. For example, each of us has a finite amount of energy for being around crowds. You may like sports events and rock concerts, but if at one period of your life you happen to experience a spate of sports events, you may lose your taste for rock concerts. If one declines to redistribute, and instead tries to raise or lower one's score/level by unnaturally behaving more in one direction or the other, then one risks health complications. It is like borrowing without either collateral or hope of future income to pay back the energy "debt."

4. *Small point differences* (at least five points) *can represent significant differences between individuals.* The cumulative effect of a single daily behavior can be dramatic. You might be only five points lower than me on a measure of "methodicalness," and that difference in scores might mean that you engage in only one more spontaneous behavior (i.e., a nonmethodical behavior) than I do. While being more spontaneous only once a day doesn't sound like much, over a year this will result in 365 more instances of spontaneity. This can make a big difference, for example, in being able to stay within your budget. If you make one more small impulse purchase daily than I do, it could mean upwards of a thousand dollars over a year.

5. *Most trait scores are arrived at by administering a "self-report" survey to an individual.* In other words, the individual answers questions about him/herself. For example, one might be asked to agree or disagree with a statement like this: "I am a neat and tidy person." Some critics say that answers to such questions are unreliable because people can't be trusted to be truthful about themselves. McCrae and Costa (2003) defend this practice, however, and point to a study in which researchers observed college students and timed their walking speed. The study found that:

> The fastest walkers were the ones who reported the highest activity level and who were rated by their peers as most energetic—not a particularly exciting result for the average reader, but a revelation for those psychologists who thought that self-reports were totally untrustworthy. (p. 40)

6. *Test scores are only meaningful when they are based on a good set of "norms."* Norms come from studying individuals. The norm group is the group of individuals to whom one is being compared. To say that a score of 50 is the "average" means that half of the norm group scores higher than this person, and the other half scores lower. This makes the composition of the norm group extremely important. In one infamous instance, a personality test was "normed" by testing and comparing 300 patients in an insane asylum. The test was intended for use with a sane population. Therefore, using this norm group would make the scores meaningless. It is imperative that the norm group that scores are based on is representative for how you will use the test. The two tests that we refer to in this book, the SchoolPlace Big Five Profile and the WorkPlace Big Five Profile, are parallel assessments with two well-designed, robust, norm groups:

- The SchoolPlace assessment is intended for students ages 12 to 22. The norm group, appropriately, had about 150 students at each of these eleven age levels, evenly distributed between public schools and private schools in the U.S., and evenly balanced with respect to sex and race according to U.S. census data in 2000.

- The WorkPlace Big Five Profile is intended for adults who hold full time jobs. The norm group contained only adults who in fact work full time, with balanced representation from different industries, job types, sex, age, and race.

Having such a balanced norm group makes it more appropriate to compare an individual such as you or me to others in the group, so long as you and I reflect the makeup of the norm group.

The "Big Five" Personality Traits: a brief introduction

[*Note to reader:* In Part Two of this book, we present relatively detailed descriptions of the personality traits that we will refer to throughout the remainder of the book. Here, we provide a brief overview. The remainder of this chapter's material would not make much sense without such a brief overview. But we will wait until Chapter 5 before giving detailed definitions of the behavioral traits. So, let's begin. But first, if you do not have a SchoolPlace Big Five Profile report to help make this discussion personally meaningful, we suggest that you go now to Appendix A and complete the "Table for Estimating Scores on the SchoolPlace Big Five Profile." This will make reading this book more personally meaningful for you.]

In 1936, Gordon Allport and Henry Odbert threw out a challenge to the psychological research community. Allport pointed to the 4,500 words in the unabridged dictionary that described everyday differences in behavior. Then, he challenged researchers to find the smallest number of synonym clusters to account for the differences in meaning among those 4,500 words and phrases. Over the next 50 years, many researchers attempted to answer Allport's challenge, but it was not until the advent of the microcomputer in the late 1970s and early 1980s that researchers were able to agree on the answer: five. Five synonym clusters account for most of the meaning in those 4,500 words. The history of this discovery is told in many places (Howard and Howard, 2001, 2010; McCrae and Costa, 2003; Nettle, 2007, to name a few). Here, we will omit the detailed history and present the results. Today, these five clusters are most typically referred to with five letters: N, E, O, A, and C. Here is a summary definition for each of the Big Five supertraits:

- N: **Need for Stability**. This measures how much **stress** (the fight/flight response) we experience, with high scorers experiencing more stress, low scorers less stress.
- E: **Extraversion**. This dimension is about how we react to **sensory bombardment** (like being in a crowd), with high scorers typically enjoying being in the thick of the action, lower scorers liking it quieter, with less action.
- O: **Originality**. This is about our comfort with **novelty** and complexity, with higher scorers enjoying more creative pursuits, lower scorers more practical ones.
- A: **Accommodation**. This is about **power** and hierarchy, with higher scorers tending to defer to power, lower scorers tending to challenge it.
- C: **Consolidation**. This deals with the degree to which we **focus** our energy on our goals, with higher scorers naturally focusing on one or a few goals, low scorers' energy more naturally diffused and spontaneous.

These five supertraits—N, E, O, A, and C—are the core elements of the Big Five. As we begin to talk about them, we will frequently refer to different levels of these traits. For the sake of brevity and convenience, we will use the following scheme:

- Very high levels are indicated with "++", as in E++ *(i.e., very high score on Extraversion)*[1].
- High levels are indicated with "+" as in N+ *(i.e., high score on Need for Stability).*
- Mid-range levels are indicated with "=", as in O= *(i.e., mid-range score on Originality).*
- Low levels are indicated with "-", as in C- *(i.e., low score on Consolidation).*
- Very low levels are indicated with "- -", as in A- - *(i.e., very low score on Accommodation).*

So we would describe a person high in E (say a 61), very low in O (maybe a 32), and mid-range in C (say a 49), as being E+O--C=. Okay, so much for the abbreviations. Now, here are slightly longer definitions of the five supertraits, with labels to help remember and understand the high, medium, and low levels of each.

N: Need for Stability

"N" has to do with how we respond to various kinds of stressful situations. Higher scorers ("Reactives") are people who tend to react more strongly to stress, whether through fear, anger, pessimism, or paralysis. Lower scorers ("Resilients") tend not to react to stress, and are typically more calm, at ease, optimistic, and resilient. Mid-range scorers ("Responsives") are more situational (reactive) in some stressful situations and not in others, or perhaps just moderately reactive in all stressful situations, but seldom highly reactive or calm during stress. Remember our recent discussion of the two kinds of mid-range scorers?

E: Extraversion

"E" has to do with how we respond and feel about sensory bombardment and being in the center of the action. Higher scorers ("Extraverts") are people who are enthusiastic, gregarious, energetic, eager to take charge, prone to trust, and tactful around others. Remember that these behaviors are correlated, no absolutes, so an E+ or E++ person might not exhibit all of these extraverted behaviors to the same degree. Lower scorers ("Introverts") are people who are more sedate, solitary, sedentary, independent (i.e., resist leading others), skeptical, and tending towards bluntness. Mid-range scorers ("Ambiverts") tend to be more extraverted in some situations and introverted in others (like enjoying both teaching and studying), or neither solitary nor comfortable with larger groups, instead preferring smaller, more intimate gatherings of friends, associates, study team, or family.

O: Originality

"O" has to do with how we respond to new ideas, situations, people, and so forth. Higher scorers ("Explorers") tend to welcome, seek out, and even create novelty. They tend to be imaginative, comfortable with complexity, comfortable with change, and to have a preference for the "big picture." Lower scorers ("Preservers") tend to prefer the familiar. They are prone to dealing with the here-and-now, the simpler, the traditional, and the details. Mid-range scorers ("Moderates") tend to welcome

---

[1] From time to time you will see a notation that has three, not two, symbols, as in "E+++" or "A- - -". This is meant to suggest that a trait has an extraordinarily strong association with a specific behavior. i.e., the number of pluses or minuses following a trait name is suggestive of the strength of the relationship between the trait and the associated behavior.

change or novelty in some areas of their lives and not in other areas, or, they tend to prefer small, incremental change rather than either the status quo or major, rapid change.

A: Accommodation

"A" has to do with issues involving power, status, and authority. Higher scorers ("Adapters") tend to defer to those in authority, through preferring to focus on others' needs and agendas, through minimizing conflict, showing humility, and through keeping their opinions largely to themselves and staying more in the background. Lower scorers ("Challengers") tend to establish themselves as dominant in relationships through focusing on their own needs and agenda, welcoming conflict, showing pride, and in freely expressing their opinions and relishing the opportunity to be in the foreground. Mid-range scorers ("Negotiators") tend to be dominant in some situations and more submissive in others, or, they tend to be neither strongly dominant nor deferential, preferring to work for the compromise or win-win solution.

"It is not human nature to be selfish, but it might be one particular person's nature to be selfish!"
--Authors

C: Consolidation

"C" has to do with how we focus on our goals. Higher scorers ("Focused") tend to be more perfectionistic, more organized, more ambitious, naturally concentrating, and more methodical. Lower scorers ("Flexible") tend to be more casual about standards, more comfortable with less order, more satisfied with current levels of achievement, more distractible, and more spontaneous. Mid-range scorers ("Balanced") tend to be more focused in some aspects of their lives and more flexible in other aspects, or their actions and attitudes mostly are midway between extremely focused and extremely flexible.

At the beginning of the next chapter, and for all succeeding chapters, we will insert this table as a reminder of the names of the traits:

N	E	O	A	C
Need for Stability	**Extraversion**	**Originality**	**Accommodation**	**Consolidation**
N+ Reactive	E+ Extravert	O+ Explorer	A+ Adapter	C+ Focused
N= Responsive	E= Ambivert	O= Moderate	A= Negotiator	C= Balanced
N- Resilient	E- Introvert	O- Preserver	A- Challenger	C- Flexible

By placing this reminder at the beginning of each chapter, we hope to make it easier for you the reader to keep in mind the names of all of the suptertraits, the names for the three levels of each supertrait, and, after they have been introduced in Chapters 5 through 9, the names of the subtraits. All behavior is attributable to some combination of these five "supertraits." N-E+ tends to explain "happy people." N-E+A-C+ explains most sales and entrepreneurial behavior. N+E+O+C- explains much risk-taking behavior. E+C- explains speedy decision making, while N-C+ explains sound decision making. Clearly, mental abilities (math, spatial, verbal, kinesthetic, etc.) and physical characteristics (eye-hand coordination, fear of heights, etc.) also explain certain aspects of behavior. However, the physical aspects of behavior are more obvious than the behavioral traits, and are not the focus of this book. They will be explained in moderate detail in Chapter 3. For now, and in the majority of this book, we will focus on how these five supertraits (and their subtraits, or subcategories) help to explain everyday behavior.

A word of caution is necessary. People often talk about "human nature," as in, "it is human nature to want to get ahead." What we have already hinted at, and will learn repeatedly throughout this book adventure together, is that human nature in this sense does not exist. What does exist are behavioral tendencies based on opposing kinds of needs. Yes, some people want to get ahead, but others are content with their current achievement, and still others want to get ahead in some areas of their lives and not in other areas. So, when we talk about "human nature," we must not be absolutist. Yes, it is human nature to be neat (for some people), but is also human nature to be comfortable with clutter (for some people). There just are no traits found in equal amounts in all people and in all cultures. Hence, "human nature" is a moving target.

The trait approach to personality resists the absolutist approach that ends up saying things like: "People have a [*enter the quality here*] nature." Some would say: "It is human nature to be suspicious." The truth: Suspiciousness is a continuum, with some people extremely suspicious, and others completely trusting. It is human nature to be BOTH trusting AND suspicious, with people preferring these two opposing behaviors to different degrees in different situations. And it is managing the tension between these opposing sets of behaviors that makes us all different and interesting. It is living closely with someone who possesses one extreme of a trait when we possess the other extreme (e.g., you are more trusting, and I am more suspicious, or you are neater, and I am more comfortable with clutter, or I am more gregarious, and you are more solitary) that makes life more stressful (but hopefully more interesting!). But, as we shall see, these differences among us are necessary for humanity's survival. It is the differences that permit the building of civilizations: leaders and followers, thinkers and doers, worriers and cool cucumbers, liberals and conservatives.

In short, there is no one right way to be. There is no one ideal profile. Yes, there are ideal profiles for specific tasks or situations, but there is not one ideal profile that is the perfect fit for every task or situation. As the Bible suggests, people have "differing gifts." Or, as Ralph Waldo Emerson writes, "Every individual nature has its own beauty." (We love this quotation, and you'll see it a couple more times before you're through!) Lee Cronbach writes: "If for each environment there is a best organism, for each organism there is a best environment" (Nettle, 2007, p. 54). Put more simply: For each task or situation in life, there is a best personality, and for each personality, there is a best task or situation. Our task in growing up is then to find our best match in our vocation and in a life partner.

So, Where Does Personality Come From?

The three quotes at the beginning of this chapter point to an age-old debate on the origins of personality. Did I inherit my personality, or did I acquire it over time from the environment in which I was raised, educated, married, and worked? Or, more simply, does personality come from our genes or from our environment? Nature or nurture? Shakespeare reveals his own struggle with this issue through the voice of Prospero near the end of *The Tempest*. Prospero, shipwrecked and alone on a deserted island save for his daughter Miranda and the local primitive man, Caliban, has throughout the play been trying to civilize Caliban by putting him through Prospero's own personal charm school. At this point in the play, Prospero is giving up by saying that Caliban is:

> "Professors are inclined to attribute the intelligence of their children to nature, and the intelligence of their students to nurture."
> --Roger Masters

> "A devil, a born devil, on whose nature
> Nurture can never stick, on whom my pains,
> Humanely taken, all, all lost, quite lost..."
> (IV,i, 188-190)

One might guess that this was the first published use in literature of "nature versus nurture" as a term, but that is not the case. Shakespeare is said to have taken this phrase from the schoolmaster Richard Mulcaster, who in 1581 wrote "...by Nature emplanted, for nurture to enlarge...." (in *Positions Concerning the Training Up of Children).* Mulcaster makes a point that he restated the following year in his work *Elementaries*: "...Nature makes him toward, but...nurture sets him forward." Mulcaster makes the point in the 16th century that only recently has been answered once and for all: Neither nature nor nurture alone accounts for our personality similarities and differences, but rather both together. Nature determines the underlying temperament (e.g., how sociable versus how solitary), and nurture determines how that temperament expresses itself (e.g., as salesperson, cheerleader, chemist, and so forth). Many recent books provide detailed, well-reasoned treatments of this debate, and its current resolution (e.g., Wright, 1998; Pinker, 2003; Freeman, 1999).

Derek Freeman (1999) in his *The Fateful Hoaxing of Margaret Mead: A Historical Analysis of Her Samoan Research,* sums up the nature/nurture issue by quoting from R. J. Rose:

> We inherit dispositions, not destinies. Life outcomes are consequences of lifetimes of behavior choices. The choices are guided by our dispositional tendencies, and the tendencies find expression within environmental opportunities that we actively create. (p. 216)

And again from biochemist Daniel Koshland Jr.:

> "The debate on nature and nurture in regard to behavior is basically over. Both are involved, and we are going to have to live with that complexity." This is unquestionably the case, and at the end of the twentieth century, it is crystal clear that anthropology, of necessity, must operate within an interactionist paradigm. And this, ineluctably, involves the abandonment of Boasian culturalism, which is now a completely super-

> seded belief system. In adolescent behavior, as in *all* human behavior, *both* 'physiological conditions' *and* 'cultural conditions (to use Boas's terms) are *always involved,* in varying degree: It is *never* 'nature *or* nurture' but always 'nature *and* nurture.' (p. 217)

With such emphatic statements, why has there even been a debate? If we knew in the 16th century that nature AND nurture influenced personality, why did we not heed this knowledge? The answer is relatively simple: sheer, unadulterated prejudice, primarily in the form of one Adolf Hitler. He maintained that a superior race existed that was genetically determined, that its superiority was intrinsic, and that nurture/the environment was not able to destroy its superiority. Neither was nurture/the environment able to overcome the alleged inferiority of other races. With Hitler, the pendulum had swung to one extreme. After World War II and the demise of Nazism, the pendulum swung in the other direction, saying we are born a "blank slate," a *tabula rasa,* such that everyone, every person born to this earth, was born with equal potential. They called this the notion of equipotentiality. In psychology, its adherents were called learning theorists, in the sense that they strongly believed, in contrast to Hitler, that anything could be learned. Reduced to the absurd, they were saying that we are all dogs being taught to fetch.

This extreme position on Nurture as dictator of personality is best summed up by this statement from John Watson (1925):

> Give me a dozen healthy infants, well-formed, and my own specified world to bring them up in and I'll guarantee to take any one at random and train him [or her!] to become any type of specialist I might select—doctor, lawyer, artist, merchant-chief, and yes, even beggar-man and thief, regardless of his [or her] talents, penchants, tendencies, and abilities, vocations, and race of his [or her] ancestors.

Watson was writing well before Hitler set out to destroy his "inferiors," which highlights dramatically what it was that Hitler was trying to refute. If you believe Watson completely, then there can be no such thing as an intrinsically superior group of people, for the only thing keeping one person from being a perfect copy of another is proper training, in his opinion.

And that is clearly not the case. Training is for knowledge and skills, not for temperament. We are born with set levels for each of the Big Five traits. These set levels, or set points, can change in the presence of trauma, abuse, drugs, surgery, and major prolonged illness. This is especially true of brain diseases—dementia is accompanied by increases in N, along with decreases in E and C. Diseases of the heart and other organs do not typically entail changes in traits levels (McCrae & Costa, 2003, p. 132). We may be born with a strong preference for solitude, but our genes do not dictate what we choose to do with that preference for solitude. When our grandson Liam was three, we all attended a birthday party in the park across from our home. I (Pierce) needed to return the ice cream cake to our freezer, and asked Liam if he wanted to walk back to the house with me. He cheerily said, "OK, Opa." After leaving the frosty dessert in the freezer, I started for the door to return to the party. Liam had crawled up on

> "Nature is often hidden, sometimes overcome, seldom extinguished."
> --Sir Francis Bacon

our sofa with his favorite Richard Scarry wordbook. Me: "Liam, hop up and let's go back to the party." He to me: "NO MORE PARTY!!!" My best effort at negotiation failed. He had used up all his allotment of sociability for the time being and needed some time to restore some "sociability energy." I sat on the sofa with him and (to my delight) enjoyed the cool and quiet of reading together. Liam will likely (and hopefully) end up in a career that incorporates his preference for solitude and quiet: architecture, information technology, research, or some such. His preference for solitude originates in nature. What he chooses to do with it originates in nurture.

Judith Rich Harris (1998, 2006) identifies the largest single environmental influence on the formation of personality between the ages of 8 and 25 is the "salient peer group," that peer group at any one time in a youth's life that the youth tries most to be like. We will discuss this in more detail in Chapter 2.

Based on these conclusions, we can sum up the thesis of this book with one passage from English trait psychologist Daniel Nettle (2007):

> If your personality is causing you trouble and worry, you need to find alternative, and less destructive, outlets for the same characteristics. You don't have to change yourself. You just have to change your self's outlet. (p. 239)

How do Nature and Nurture Work Together Over Time?

The University of Jyvaskyla (Finland) psychologist Jari-Erik Nurmi describes (in Lerner and Steinberg, 2004, p. 87) the interplay of nature and nurture in creating personality during the teen years as a four–phase process:

1. Channeling—one's environment (parents, neighborhood, school, arts groups, athletic teams, volunteer programs, religion) determines what a young person will be exposed to.
2. Selection—one's nature (or temperament or genes) chooses from environmental options those features that resonate or tend to be compatible with one's nature.
3. Adjustment—feedback from one's environment rewards the selections that make sense (e.g., "you're a genius at designing things" punishes those that do not make sense, e.g., "you're no leader", leading to modifications and adjustments, e.g., "guess I'll focus on my drawing and stop worrying about getting elected class president").
4. Reflection—one's nature sorts things out and makes new selections as environment evolves ("I sort of like leadership responsibility, but maybe not leadership of a cross-section of kids—perhaps my solitary temperament would find leadership more natural among people more like me—more solitary people, like art club, computer club, and so forth").

The exposure during channeling includes roles, tasks, institutions, events, travel, peer groups, and so forth. The selection involves establishing goals, solving problems, making commitments, exploring paths (a path could be a school subject, extra-curricular or community interests, or a value such as thrift or patriotism). The adjustment includes coping skills, goal reformulations, and belief systems (e.g., what causes certain phenomena such as luck, hard work, money, social status). Reflection over time builds the sense of self, including one's identity, self-concept, and life narrative.

What About Birth Order?

No discussion of the origins of personality could be complete without some mention of birth order. Suffice it to be said that the order in which one was born in one's family (e.g., first child, middle child, youngest of two, youngest of ten, and so forth) has no effect on the permanent formation of personality. In a solid refutation of the birth order hypothesis (i.e., that firstborns are different temperamentally from later borns, for example, more responsible, with later borns more playful), Judith Rich Harris (2006, ch. 4) presents the evidence supporting the view that birth order does not produce systematic lifelong differences in personality. She shows that while there are birth order effects *within* the family, they don't generalize *outside* the family. For example, an older child dominating a younger sibling does not necessarily show the same tendency to dominate with peers at school. Submissive children at home can rise to the occasion outside the home. A boisterous second child fighting for attention and toys at home can turn around and be meek at school around peers. The home behavior is temporary and limited: temporary in that, unless it is genetically based, the child will grow out of it when the older sibling is out of the nest, and limited in that, unless it is genetically based, the child will abandon the behavior when in neutral territory, a level playing field away from the older sibling, as in school, a birthday party, and so forth. Behavioral differences are often attributed to birth order when in fact they are nothing but behaviors associated with age differences, with older ones more responsible (at least at home) and younger ones grabbing attention (at least at home), a pattern that is not permanent (again, unless it is, in fact, genetically based). We already see this with our second grandson, Rowan, who is seldom quiet around family members. He is so boisterous, in fact, that our first-born grandson, Liam, often tells his younger brother to "be quiet!" when Rowan—not unlike a circus master—bounds down the circular staircase disturbing Liam, who is reading or playing quietly by himself. Yet, Rowan's teachers report that he is typically quiet at day care.

Do Traits Work the Same Way Around the World?

Yes. Traits, again, have two components: the genetic part and the environmental, or cultural, part. The genetic part is essentially universal. The average levels of dopamine are essentially the same throughout the human species, and the deviations around the average are the same throughout the world. In other words, dopamine is normally distributed everywhere. And as dopamine levels influence the "O" trait, O(riginality) is normally distributed around the world. However, for whatever reason, within a particular culture, imagination and creativity may be more emphasized or more deemphasized. Singapore may emphasize creativity and innovation as part of a social engineering program, and Iran may deemphasize creativity and innovation as part of an anti-Western politicization program. However, in both cases, the distribution of the "O" temperament is the same in both cultures. It is just that in one culture, O behavior is encouraged, and in the other, discouraged. Such cultural variations are brilliantly summarized in Dutch researcher Geert Hofstede's classic work *Culture's Consequences* (2nd Ed., 2001).

Climate, geography, politics, religion, financial conditions—all can influence the way that a particular trait is expressed. One of the most commonly acknowledged variations in behavior is the notion that parts of East Asia are more polite (i.e., higher in "A[ccommodation]") than most areas of the west (i.e., the west would be lower in "A"). In fact, we know that "A" behavior is strongly influenced by the ratio of estrogen to androgen (as explained in Chapter 8). As such, the biology of A is the same in China as in France. However, because of centuries of the *I Ching*'s influence, the Chinese, as a people, have learned ways of expressing their low A in more benign, socially acceptable ways: "Your honorable servant wishes to honorably suggest that honorable master may have made a statement that would benefit from some honorable modification." In other words, "You're wrong!" as might be said in France by the people marching with signs in the streets with the same genetic, biological disposition as the Chinese speaker. In traveling, working, and socializing, we all need to be sensitive to how persons from different cultures express our common traits differently. One interesting treatment of this is the entertaining and useful book *Kiss, Bow, or Shake Hands* (Morrison and Conaway, 2006), although some of our international colleagues have dismissed some of the findings as no longer current in the global economy.

Are Traits the Same for Males and Females?

Yes, with a couple of minor exceptions. All of our research suggests that the average scores, as well as the distribution from high to low scores around the means, are the same for males and females. Males average slightly higher on openness to new ideas (an aspect of O), slightly lower on N, and slightly lower on A (McCrae and Costa, 2003). However, these differences are small, and they do not suggest that you can assume anything about the trait differences between two individuals solely based on a difference in gender. In all of the studies done by our Center for Applied Cognitive Studies, there were no statistically significant differences between males and females or between the major racial groups on any of the Big Five traits, regardless of age (in the U.S. sample that provided our original norms).

Can Levels of a Trait be Changed? Can They be Increased or Decreased?

The biological basis of a trait is permanent, unchangeable, except of course by such methods as surgery, use of pharmaceuticals, or the experience of trauma or abuse. (See Chapter 2 for a discussion of *temporary* changes in trait levels.) In other words, temperament, what we inherit (our "genotype") comes with us into this world and stays with us for a lifetime. If we are high in sociability as a kid, we'll be highly sociable as a senior. The same goes for all of the traits. In this sense, people do not, cannot, truly change. The tiger cannot change his stripes, the human cannot change his/her extraversion into introversion.

However, the way we *express* a trait can change. Let me illustrate. Once I (Pierce) was coaching a young sales executive who was concerned about his temper. He had been told that, if he wanted a promotion, he needed to learn to "control" his temper. I got the job of trying to help him accomplish this goal. My approach with him was to start with the assumption that his quick trigger, his tendency to get angry at the slightest provocation, would not change. What he could do was to change the way he expressed his anger in everyday behavior. After considering several alternatives, he/we decided on this: whenever he felt the urge to blow up during a meeting, he should bite down on an "imaginary" corncob pipe. He loved the idea, and it worked for him. Some six months later he called me and asked, "Hey Doc, I've bitten through most of the pipe stems. Could you order me some more?!" This bit of play-acting had become a regular part of his behavior. The anger was still felt, but the way he expressed it to others had changed. In the next chapter, we will discuss this in more detail.

McCrae and Costa (2003), globally acknowledged leaders in study of the Five-Factor Model (the Big Five), write, "There is no contradiction at all in saying that personality remains stable whereas behavior changes" (p. 208). Lottery winners experience a temporary increase in euphoria only to return to their "set point" weeks or months later. Julie Andrews temporarily quietened upon entering a convent in the role of Maria in *The Sound of Music,* only to recover her irrepressible extraversion to the degree that her fellow nuns sing in puzzlement, "How do you solve a problem like Maria?... How do you hold a moonbeam in your hand?" Roberto Benigni in the role of Guido in *La Vita é bella* does not vary from his set point of happiness even when in a concentration camp with son—his happiness stays, but its expression morphs into pranks played with his son at the expense of their guards. Little Orphan Annie, in the Broadway musical *Annie*, in spite of bullying, threats, deprivation, and the loss of her parents, nonetheless clings to her optimism, when Aileen Quinn, who is playing the part of Annie, sings "The sun'll come out tomorrow, bet your bottom dollar that tomorrow there'll be sun!"

What Happens to Traits Over Time?

Not much. Basically there are two kinds of change, neither being particularly dramatic. The first change occurs during the teenage years. In the early teens, more experimentation typically occurs, as described above by Jari-Erik Nurmi's four-phase process of identity formation comprising channeling, selection, adjustment, and reflection. As teens in the early years explore various talents, behaviors, values, and physical capabilities, they tend over time to settle on those that provide the greatest satisfaction. By and large, peer approval appears to influence this process more than other sources of approval and reinforcement, although all reinforcement is important. Here are two personal examples:

- I (Pierce) played drums, piano, trumpet, and French horn all within the middle school years. There were plenty of drummers, trumpeters, and pianists, but I was the only one in my group who played the treacherous, monstrous French horn, with its 20 feet of brass tubing and unsettling unpredictability. I liked being the only one playing my instrument. Plus, in the eighth grade, I won the "second chair" in the high school horn section, sitting between two lovely senior high girls! My choice of playing French horn over the other instruments was fixed.
- From an early age, I (Jane) created plays, songs, and dances, complete with a curtained stage on Tobi Miller's front porch, where she and I would entertain family and other neighborhood kids for polite applause and 10¢ each (two positive reinforcements). Comfort being in front of people led to my acting in legitimate plays and singing vocal solos in my teenage years, followed by a career as an educator, train-

> er, and business coach/consultant, where I teach, train, coach, and advise others. And, I even still sing solos in public on occasion.

So, to complete the thought, teens experiment more in the early years, then settle over the next several years on the options that have the most positive influence on getting along with one's peers. Our behavior moves from more unpredictable to more conforming, as a result of our personal identity beginning to jell (Cobb, 2007, p. 266). This can be tracked by looking at how the standard deviation of teens' trait scores decreases throughout adolescence. The standard deviation is a measure of consistency, and teens become more consistent in how they describe themselves as they progress in years.

The second kind of change involves a shift sometime between late adolescence and early adulthood. During this phase, N, E, and O tend to decrease slightly, while A and C tend to increase slightly. This pattern is global. With few exceptions, people as a group in emerging from school to family and career tend to become a little calmer (somewhat lower in N), a little less of a social animal (a little lower in E), somewhat less curious and desirous of change (lower in O), somewhat more of a team player (higher in A), and somewhat more ambitious and disciplined (higher in C). This pattern is evident in many cartoon/comic characters who derive their humor from, in essence never growing up, never lessening N, E, and O, and increasing A and C. For those who have enjoyed years of "Calvin and Hobbes" cartoons, Calvin is the perfect example. Reactive to everything, so outgoing he has to have an imaginary playmate to avoid being alone, imaginative to the point of absurdity (Spaceman Spiff), never deferring to authority (especially teachers), and totally unfocused on goals.

McCrae and Costa (2003) explain the likely reasons for the changes, based on evolutionary psychology and human development needs:

> Openness to Experience [what we call Originality] and Extraversion both make individuals more adventurous and help them explore the natural and interpersonal worlds; they may thus be helpful in solving the tasks of adolescents. Once settled in, however, with a home, a mate, and a family to raise, these traits become less valuable—in fact, they may be distractions. Instead, love and work should now become priorities, and these are related to Agreeableness [the Big Five's Accommodation] and Conscientiousness [the Big Five's Consolidation]. It is less clear why adolescents should be high in N[eed for Stability] compared to adults, but it is hard to complain about its decline! (p. 96)

Conventional wisdom says that major personality changes occur during adolescence, but as we explained in the Introduction, that is a myth. In fact, in the norms for our SchoolPlace Big Five Profile, the average scores on all traits remain unchanged for all age groups from age 12 well into the college years. Some individuals may experience significant changes in personality, for a variety of reasons, but, as a group, most teens do not change. As Haan, Millsap, and Hartka (1986) put it: "More marked shifts occur, not during adolescence, but at its end when most people make the profound role shifts entailed by entry into full-time work and marriage" (quoted in McCrae and Costa [2003], p.10).

What happens after this transition into adulthood trait levels? McCrae and Costa (2003, p. 11) follow through with this:

> The data suggest to us that personality change is the exception rather than the rule after age 30; somewhere in the decade between 20 and 30, individuals attain a configuration of traits that will characterize them for years to come. From the perspective of the trait psychologist, adulthood begins at that point.

Other than this shift during transition to adulthood, personality doesn't change. College students who work full time while taking a full load of courses tend to undergo this shift earlier than college students who do not have to work full time. (Howard & Howard, 2007) But, once the shift has occurred, personality is set. Incidentally, the changes during this shift are not dramatic. Typically they are in the range of 5 to 10 standard score points. We're not speaking here of going from one extreme to another, but rather of toning things a little up or down. McCrae and Costa (2003) conclude emphatically: "For the most part, it appears that perceptions of change in personality are misperceptions. Most people think they are stable, and those who think they have changed are probably wrong." (p. 128)

2

States

What Influences Trait Levels to Vary

> Later that night, I [Amir] was passing by my father's study when I overheard him speaking to Rahim Khan [friend of the family]. I pressed my ear to the closed door.
>
> "—grateful that he's healthy," Rahim Khan was saying.
>
> "I know, I know. But he's always buried in those books or shuffling around the house like he's lost in some dream."
>
> "And?"
>
> "I wasn't like that." Baba sounded frustrated, almost angry.
>
> Rahim Khan laughed. "Children aren't coloring books. You don't get to fill them with your favorite colors."
>
> --Khaled Hosseini, *The Kite Runner,* Riverhead Books/Penguin, 2003. p. 21

Guide to this chapter:

- the difference between traits and states
- learned habits that can affect trait expression
- social relationships that can affect trait expression (peers, gender roles, hierarchies)
- physical influences on trait expression (food, drink, drugs, sleep, the environment)

Now that we have established that traits are stable over one's lifetime, with the "set points" shifting somewhat as one leaves school and enters into work and family responsibilities, we need to add a wrinkle. Traits can in fact vary from time to time, although they typically, but not always, return to the set point. When a trait increases or decreases from its established set point, we call this new level a "state." Traits and states. Traits refer to the permanent set points. States refer to temporary deviations from a set point. If my normal trait level for sociability is moderately high, and I were to suddenly acquire triplets, it is highly likely that my level of sociability would decrease. I would be in a temporary "state" of lessened sociability. The constant care and attention given to the triplets would

N	E	O	A	C
Need for Stability	Extraversion	Originality	Accommodation	Consolidation
N+ Reactive	E+ Extravert	O+ Explorer	A+ Adapter	C+ Focused
N= Responsive	E= Ambivert	O= Moderate	A= Negotiator	C= Balanced
N- Resilient	E- Introvert	O- Preserver	A- Challenger	C- Flexible

likely deplete my fuel for sociability on a daily basis, and I would begin craving quiet, alone time for myself. Or, for a more short-term example, if my normal trait level for enthusiasm is medium, and I learn that I have won an award, I would immediately go in a "state" of heightened enthusiasm, whooping it up in an unaccustomed manner. "What got into him?" someone observing me might say, "He's in a *state*!" But soon, back to normal.

This deviation from normal trait levels, or "states," is the topic of this chapter. Simply put, it is this: What are the factors that cause trait levels to vary from normal, and how can we use knowledge of these factors to manage our lives effectively? Our discussion is organized around three kinds of factors:

- habits that we learn, and that we can unlearn or modify
- social relationships in which we engage, and from which we can disengage
- physical influences that we can manage, or can allow to manage us

First, some general thoughts about "states"

The set point is rather resilient. McCrae and Costa (2003) report on a study in which researchers recorded the frequency of 30 highly stressful events in peoples' lives over six years. These events included divorce, death of a loved one, serious illness, loss of a job, and that sort of thing. The results of the study were that, while some individuals showed changes in trait levels after certain events, there were no lasting changes at the end of the six years, *regardless of how many of these 30 events had occurred in an individual's life.* Some of the temporary trait level changes included many women showing increases in E and O after a divorce, and people in general showing increases in N and decreases in C after losing a job. In other words, losing a job may make you temporarily more anxious and/or angry and less disciplined and ambitious. In effect, you are in a "state." But you return to normal. The same is true following divorce—many women tend to become more outgoing and creative, but then return to normal.

Another interesting point about variations in trait levels is summed up by Roberts, Wood, and Smith (2005) in what they call "social investment theory." According to this school of thought, when an individual commits to an institution (religious, school, employer) or to an organization (club, gang, team, music group), they often will take up the behaviors that they perceive to be the norms of the institution or organization. I (Pierce) remember that, in my 20s, I accepted a teaching position at a local university. After a couple of weeks, in which I had been my usual self—I love to tell jokes, make puns, share stories, and so forth, a fellow professor offered me some advice: "Pierce, I appreciate your jokes.

However, you should be aware that most professors around here look down on jokes and joke tellers. For your own sake, you might want to limit your joke telling to me and one or two others who appreciate them." Here I was faced with the decision of whether to adapt my behavior to the apparent norm of the institution—seriousness. Well, I'm a serious guy, but I love to lighten up from time to time—I love a good joke. I decided to adapt, and to limit my joke telling. In the process, my respect for the institution decreased, and I left after one year. Free, at last! Back to my set point.

Here's another example: The summer that I (Jane) was 20, I was earning money for college by working as a rotating secretary in a large law firm, where I would substitute for secretaries while they went on vacation. The second week I was there, I found myself working for an attorney who really had nothing for me to do. After catching up on filing papers and finding myself very bored without a book to read (this was before the days of texting, the Internet, or iPods), my altruistic nature surfaced, and I decided to organize the desk drawer of the secretary I was replacing for the week. The clutter of paper clips, pens, pencils, metal brads, punched-out holes of paper, gum, and loose change quickly yielded to my control. I thought I had performed a great service for the vacationing secretary. When she returned the following week, however, I quickly noticed that subsequently vacationing secretaries specifically asked that I not reorganize their desks while they were gone. I only organized one drawer, but from that point for the rest of the summer, I held my altruism in check and brought a book with me to manage my boredom. Although they invited me to return the next summer, I sought work where altruism would be appreciated.

In the very last section of this chapter, we will talk about disorders of personality. Looking ahead to that section, it is of interest to note that, when a person prolongs a "state" that is not natural for a very long period, the body reacts. In other words, when one changes the level of a trait in order to blend in with an institution or organization, one's body reacts negatively.

A couple of examples: A pediatrician entered practice. His personality was E-O+C+: solitary, quiet, creative, curious, and disciplined. However, the pediatric practice demanded the opposite: an active day around lots of people with many sick children, mostly with boring "same old, same old," (as in one rhinovirus after another) and jumping from one thing to another. Within ten years of this and in spite of being a healthy distance runner, he had developed high blood pressure. Behaving in a manner opposite to his nature had stressed his body, and his body had rebelled in its own way. He left the practice and took a job with a diagnostic medical program away from the big city, where he could study one problem child exclusively at a time for days with a few other specialists. He loved it. It was a perfect match for his set points. The high blood pressure disappeared.

Or, consider the case of an 18-year-old boy who took an entry job as an assembly worker at a plant in eastern Kentucky. He rose through the ranks, attaining the position of plant manager some 20 years later. Being the plant manager required him to be calm, outgoing, visionary, tough, and disciplined (N-E+O+A-C+), yet his natural temperament was nervous, solitary, down-to-earth, kind, and disciplined (N+E-O-A+C+). He had the disciplined part (C+), but the rest of the job was unnatural for him. He adapted his behavior to fit the demands of being a manager, and within five years he had developed ulcers and a heart condition. He was able to take a new position in the company—he moved north to the company's headquarters and took a job as Vice-President for Research and Development. Here, he was able to lead a relatively quiet day (E-) around a handful of engineers and related scientists. He could also express his down-to-earth (O-) outlook to his innovative team by doing reality testing with his colleagues' wild ideas. Essentially, he found a job that matched the set points for all his traits. The heart and ulcer problems went away.

In terms of the "HRO" model we presented in the Introduction, the man in the previous case study had, as a plant manager, been a flourishing tree with a poor root system—he had been performing his job well, in spite of his unfit temperament. By moving to a job that better fit his personality, he became a flourishing tree with a well-developed root system.

Here's one more general comment about traits and states, and then we'll look at the specific factors that influence states. Daniel Nettle (2007, p. 46) writes about two ways that situations influence behavior: **Situation Selection**, whereby one chooses situations that represent opportunities to express a trait, as in an O- choosing to take a course in bookkeeping or an E+ selecting parties, dance clubs, sporting events, or other situations that involve crowds, noise, and activity. D. C. Rowe (1994) calls this "niche picking" (p. 21). "Situation selection" is at work whenever we make a choice that permits us to use a trait for which we have a large fuel can (i.e., lots of natural energy). Two contrasting examples would be a more extraverted student choosing to study with a group of friends, or a more introverted student choosing to spend the time in the library. On the other hand, Nettle writes about **Situation Evocation**, whereby one starts a chain reaction. By engaging in a behavior that elicits a fairly predictable response, one sets things up so as to come back with a customary behavior associated with a particular trait. In other words, we choose a situation that initially is not natural for us, but we know can set the stage for behavior that is natural. For example, a "take charge" type person might say to someone: "Have you figured out how to X?" The other says, "No, not yet." Then the "take charge" predictably comes back with something like, "Well, let me show you how to do it" and then launches in a step-by-step plan, in charge.

Both situation selection and situation evocation end up with an individual making healthy choices that permit him or her to "be oneself." It is when an individual makes choices that do not permit them to be themselves that temporary (or longer) changes in trait level occur. When a sedentary boy chooses to date an energetic girl, he is likely, initially, to join in on the girl's many activities—running, dancing, and such. The boy is thus in an unnatural "state." Over time, his body will rebel, as his sedentary nature is highly unlikely to change to match that of the girl. Some possible outcomes of this state behavior would be resentment, physical accidents (to allow some restful recuperation time), aggression (verbal or otherwise), strong suggestions—even coercion—to engage in more sedentary activity, domineering so as to discourage further activity, and so forth.

Now, on to the three primary ways that we see trait levels change: habits, social relations, and physical factors.

Habits We Learn, that We Can Unlearn

The genetic part of traits we cannot change. How we express our genes, we can change. As we have said earlier, we cannot change our degree of preference for solitude, but we can switch from being a religious renunciate to being a forest ranger spending our days alone on a trail. In Table 2.1, which we have entitled "Genes and Jeans", we present the 23 subtraits of the Big Five supertraits (they will be defined in more detail in Chapters 5 through 9). In the left hand column, we say what it is about the traits that *cannot* be changed, e.g., the level of solitude/sociability, and in the right hand column, we say how we can express the trait in a different way. Genes cannot be changed, but jeans can. We can't exchange our genes for a different set, but we can exchange our jeans for cords, khakis, chinos, shorter skirts, longer skirts, rayon, woolies, seersucker, plaids, and so forth. The importance of this table is that it can stimulate our thinking about ways that we can change so as to lead a more satisfying life. For example, we once knew a Suzuki violin student whose parents made him practice several hours daily. There was only one problem—the child was tone deaf. He loved music, but he couldn't match pitches. With the violin, if you can't hear when your finger is properly placed on the fingerboard so as to render the precise pitch, then you'll never make a satisfactory violinist. In this situation, the thing you cannot change is the tone deafness. What you can change is how you express your musical interest. For example, the child could have changed to piano, which does not require a good sense of pitch. Study this table for opportunities to make adjustments in your life or in the lives of others you care about.

Table 2.1 Genes & Jeans—Behaviors that You Cannot Change (e.g., Genes), and Those that You Can (e.g., Jeans, Khakis, Shorts, and So Forth)

Note: In the "cannot change" column, the first phrase in each pair represents the left/lower end of the trait continuum, and the second word/phrase represents the right/upper end; these are the two "buckets" of fuel/energy we talked about earlier.

Trait:	What You *Cannot Change*	What You *Can Change* (plus some illustrative examples)
N1 Worry	Capacities for Calm & Worry/ Anxiety	How you deal with anxious feelings: e.g., eating, exercising, having a milkshake with a friend, grooming the family pet, reading, playing with your siblings, watching TV, and so forth
N2 Temper	Capacities for Being at Ease & Being Angry	How you deal with angry feelings: counting to ten before responding, hitting a pillow, chomping down on gum, arguing, jumping up and down, isometric exercises, deep breathing, hyperventilating
N3 Outlook	Capacities for Optimism & Pessimism	How you explain outcomes: your fault, others' fault, temporary, permanent, limited to one aspect of your life, affecting all areas of your life

Table 2.1 (continued)

N4 Coping Level	Capacities for Recovery & Distress	How you get back on track after a crisis: planning, emotional release, sleeping/resting, aerobic exercise, hard physical labor (raking leaves, gardening), devoting yourself to your homework, starting a new project, working with a therapist, being with family/friends
E1 Approach Level	Capacities for Aloofness & Warmth	How you express your feelings: writing notes, smiling, laughing, touching, sending gifts/flowers/food, going out for a chat, taking a stroll with someone, going dancing, playing games together, reading together (silently or spoken), making something for someone, sending a card, texting, practicing your handshake and smile before an interview
E2 Group Orientation	Capacities for Solitude & Being around Others	How you realize your capacity: for solitude (study, long walks, meditation, hobbies, reading, practice, working out, sleeping, cooking, cleaning your room, video games) and for being with others (parties, family gatherings, club meetings, public events (sports, concerts, dances), speaking, group projects, political campaigns, tutoring little kids, team sports, music/theatrical groups, scouts, volunteering)
E3 Pace	Capacities for Being Still & Being Active	What you do: while sedentary (reading, writing, painting, smaller scale construction such as models or repairs], practice, computer and videogames, texting, watch television, drive) and while active (physical exercise, athletics, gardening, dog training, coaching kids, marching band, baking, dancing, skate-boarding, cycling, canoeing, hiking, swimming, rollerblading, painting your room or fence, horse riding, gymnastics, ice skating)
E4 Leadership	Capacities for Independence & Being the Boss	What you do alone (just doing a job or role for the team, but not taking charge of directing others' activities) and taking charge (starting and coordinating a group [music, intramural sports team, community service, chess group], club president, student-government officer, organizing a dance/fund-raising/homecoming event, study team leader, organizing a group dinner, organizing a group project)
E5 Trust	Capacities for Skepticism & Trust	How you express your skepticism: casual questions, withholding information, specifying how information is to be managed, expressing lack of confidence in someone/something, planning ahead, dry runs, simulations, telling others how to do something, practice, over-practice, perfectionism, rehearsal, orienting others, careful delegation, training others, offering support or assistance
E6 Tact	Capacities for Direct Talk & Smooth Talk	How direct or indirect talk is accompanied (smiles, nods, neutral expression, anger, fear, trembling, eye contact, standing face-to-face, blunt versus elaborate, standing closer or farther, hand written, email, telephone, with a sneer, with sympathy, or with disdain) or how the tact is formulated (simple paraphrase, deception, lying, using others' vocabulary/values/interests, keeping the audience in mind, avoiding guilt, making things look rosy, leaving out information that makes your position less favorable)
O1 Imagination	Capacities for Literalness & Creativity	What you apply your imagination to: daydreaming, scheming, plotting revenge, asking "what if?" questions, inventing, thinking up new uses, dreaming up variations, finding a new way to express something, playing out various scenarios in your mind, brainstorming, making connections, identifying assumptions, forming/asking probing questions
O2 Range of Interests	Capacities for Simplicity & Complexity	How you exercise your comfort with complexity: interdisciplinary studies, keeping up with more than one field of specialization, having dialogue with colleagues from other areas of knowledge/skill to identify commonalities/linkages, helping others solve problems, creating order out of chaos, making things more complex than they need to be, reducing the more complex to the simpler, documenting your experiences/observations for others to learn from
O3 Innovation	Capacities for Routine & Novelty	How you satisfy your preference for predictability (the same route to work every day, the same kind of outfit daily, same daily diet/menu, approaching a task the same way repeatedly, spending time with the same set of friends/family/associates, doing only what you already know, becoming expert in your area of specialty, following the same basic daily pattern) and how you satisfy your need for variety (changing plans in midstream, meeting new people, learning something new [skills, knowledge, languages, exercises] experimenting with different approaches to work/tasks, varied diet, exploring different services/products, embracing the latest technology or Internet innovations, rearranging, reorganizing, redesigning)

Table 2.1 (continued)

Trait:	What You *Cannot Change*	What You *Can Change*
O4 **Zoom Scale**	Capacities for Details & Big Picture	Where you choose to spend time on the details: comparing online prices, doing exhaustive research, spending time practicing, proofreading, editing, paperwork, getting organized, hobbies, cleaning, maintenance, yard work, filing, documenting, journal writing, exercising, weeding out, shopping, cooking, scrapbooking, indexing, illustrating, memorizing
A1 **Service**	Capacities for Addressing Self vs. Others' Needs	How you choose to be of service to others: regularly asking what others (peers, family, friends) need, offering to help by doing something you are good at, offering to help by learning to do something new or by doing something you don't particularly care for, regularly observing others' birthdays/anniversaries and how you prioritize your own needs (always get your own way, negotiate with family/friends/associates for a balanced meeting of needs, find ways for meeting your own needs that allows others to also meet their needs [i.e., a win-win], creating a wish list for self and others and mutually setting priorities)
A2 **Compliance**	Capacities for Arguing & Conceding	How you conduct yourself in an argument or conflict: using a communications model for managing conflict, using a model for negotiating, telling people what is important to you and asking what is important to them, identifying key issues in advance that you will not back away from, using a third party to facilitate, putting your thoughts/opinions in writing, consciously keeping emotions out of a disagreement, revisiting a decision/action later after the heat of the moment has worn off, agreeing with significant others on how you prefer to conduct yourselves when disagreeing, practicing standing your ground
A3 **Humility**	Capacities for Pride & Humility	How you ask for recognition (asking "How'd I do?, How do you think it went?, What did you see as my strong/weak points? How should I do it differently?") and how you accept it (saying thank you, identifying others who helped and who should share the recognition)
A4 **Speak Out Level**	Capacities for Being Out Front & in the Background	How you time your speaking (finishing others' sentences, interrupting others, waiting for a lull before talking, using an imaginary "talking stick," speaking in twenty-five-word sound bites or tweets, speaking in the format of a "Quaker sermon," timing your participation so that it does not exceed your "share" of air time), how you let your thoughts be known other than writing (emails, memos, letters, blogs, position papers, white papers, wish lists, instant messaging, nonverbal expressions (head nods, smiles, eye contact, touch, jittery/still), and how you preface/ finish your remarks ("to build on what X just said," "Let me see if I understand what you are saying," "Is this consistent with your meaning")
C1 **Thoroughness**	Capacities for Approximation & Exactitude	How you prioritize your tasks with respect to their need for perfection/adherence to the highest standards (except certain tasks which must always be perfect, e.g., college applications, job resumes, important letters/emails): assign levels of approval, review five times, delegate review to another, reserve one final review for yourself, delegate the task completely with no review by you, no review necessary, confer with friends about which items on your "to-do" list should get which level of approval/review/perfection
C2 **Structure**	Capacities for Clutter & Order	How you go about your preferred level and manner of organization: piles vs. files, color-coded folders, paperless office, Urgent/Important priority system, ABC system, Outlook task reminders, "never handle an email or a piece of paper more than once," "never do a "B" priority when you still have an "A" remaining to do; never do a "C" when you still have a "B," vertical file stands, slotted book shelves, wall calendars/boards/etc. cardboard boxes, bulletin boards, weekly/monthly/end-of-semester/etc. review and clear out all files, get a friend to get and keep you organized, use Outlook or other planners' "Tasks" with reminder alarms
C3 **Ambition**	Capacities for Content with Achievement & Wanting More	How you go formulate and monitor your goals: stickers on the mirror, asking others what your goals need to be, having goals in different areas (spiritual, family, friends, siblings, parents, hobbies, special interests, political, degrees, licenses, bodies of knowledge, skills, physical condition, maintenance of your living space, getting hired for your first job), having a weekly/monthly/quarterly meeting with parents/teachers/counselors/friends to determine progress towards goals, asking a friend to periodically check with you on progress towards goals, using the salami technique [breaking larger goals up into smaller ones], having competitions with friends as to who will achieve goals first/best, e.g., get accepted at your university of choice)

Table 2.1 (continued)

Trait:	What You *Cannot Change*	What You *Can Change*
C4 Concentration	Capacities for Multi-tasking & Single-tasking	How you organize your work in such a way as to enhance concentration (eliminating all distractions [auditory, visual, people, odors, food/drink, textural (as in scratchy clothing)], closing windows/shades, turning off television/radio [or getting away from it], announcing a study hour with the door shut—no interruptions/calls", establishing a signal for others around you to know when you're trying to concentrate and wish not to be disturbed [e.g., wearing a hat, turning off your cell phone, moving to a different room or space], establishing a home policy regarding interruptions)
C5 Methodicalness	Capacities for Spontaneity & Going Stepwise	How you go about planning your work: no planning at all—just jump into it, using PERT charts, Gantt charts, Microsoft Plan, Action Planning (what/who/by-when), prototype project/program planning chart on the wall, flow charting, wall calendar, reading a manual, following directions, reading the plan for critical steps and dependencies but then jumping in without the plan, using potential problem analysis/threat analysis, mind mapping technique to get organized for term papers and other projects)

Internationally acclaimed University of Pennsylvania psychologist Martin E. P. Seligman in his classic book *Learned Optimism* writes about a habit we learn in our youth that can have a tremendous impact on our satisfaction with life. He calls it "explanatory style," or how we explain why good or bad things happen to us. When good things happen (make a good grade, get a good job or promotion, score a touchdown), the optimist essentially takes credit—I did it, I earned it, I ran hard. However, the pessimist discounts the good fortune by calling it luck, a one-time piece of good fortune with little promise for more of the same in the future. On the other hand, when bad things happen (fail a test, lose an election, rejected for a date), optimists do what pessimists do after something good: Optimists say the bad outcome was luck, a one-time piece of bad fortune, and tomorrow could be a brighter day. The pessimist does what the optimist did for good outcomes: The pessimist says the bad outcome was due to personal inadequacy, undesirability, and is part of a pattern that is likely to continue.

In short, according to Seligman, explanatory style comprises three elements: personalness, pervasiveness, and permanence. Personalness deals with whether one sees oneself as the primary cause of an outcome (internal), or one sees others or "fate" as the primary cause(s) of an outcome (external). Pervasiveness deals with whether one sees an outcome as confined only to this one part of life (limited), or whether the outcome is typical of outcomes in many or all other areas of life (pervasive). Permanence deals with whether one sees an outcome as occurring at this one, current point in time (temporary), or whether one will experience similar outcomes for a lifetime (permanent). Some examples of these three elements of explanatory style are presented in Table 2.2.

The relation of the three ingredients to optimism and pessimism is illustrated in Figure 2.2. Here we can see that optimistic explanations of good outcomes are identical to pessimistic explanations of bad outcomes—internal, pervasive, and permanent, while pessimistic explanations of good outcomes are identical to optimistic explanations of bad outcomes—external, limited, and temporary. Seligman has demonstrated that these explanatory styles are learned, and that they can be unlearned.

Table 2.2 Seligman's Explanatory Styles

Explanation of Adversity	
Optimist:	**Pessimist:**
It's someone else's fault *(external personalization)* It's only temporary *(not permanent)* It won't affect other areas of my life *(limited pervasiveness)*	It's my fault *(internal personalization)* It's will last forever *(permanent)* It'll affect every area of my life *(universal pervasiveness)*
Explanation of Success	
Optimist:	**Pessimist:**
I made it happen *(internal personalization)* This is one in a line of many successes *(permanent)* This outcome will affect every part of my life *(universal pervasiveness)*	Someone else made it happen *(external personalization)* It'll never happen again *(not permanent)* It won't help me in other areas of my life *(limited pervasiveness)*

His research shows that pessimistic styles are associated with depression and other undesirable mental states. And his research further shows that people can learn to avoid pessimistic styles with an accompanying increase in positive mood. In one interesting strain of his research, he found that teenage girls tend to use pessimistic explanations more than boys do. This can explain the higher incidence of depression among teen girls. And the good news is that this condition can, potentially, be fixed.

Figure 2.1 Martin Seligman's Model of Explanatory Style

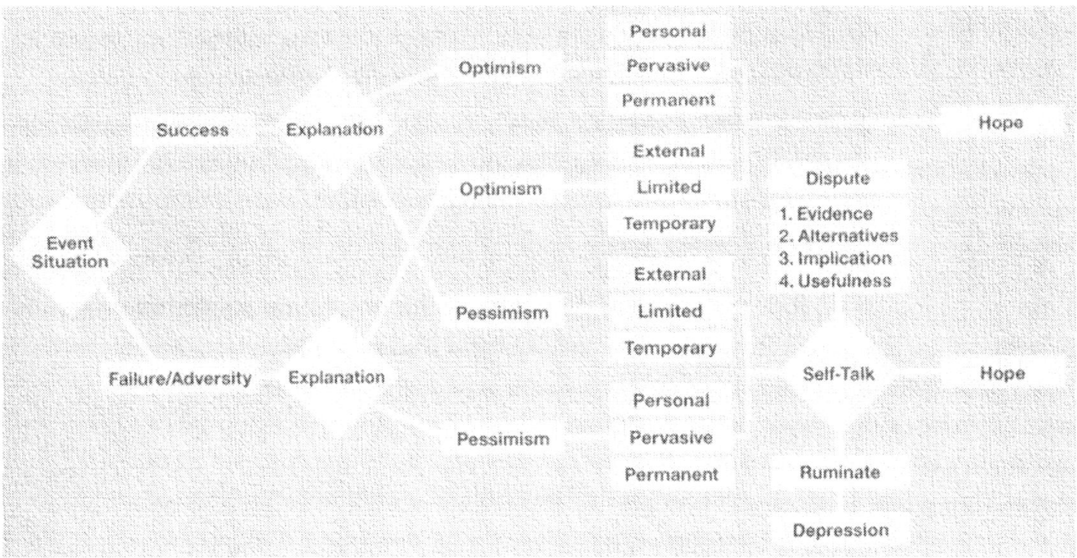

The goal in training someone in explanatory style is not to turn them into Pollyannaish optimists, but rather to help them become more realistic in their explanations of life's outcomes. The simplest way to encourage someone to shake loose a pessimistic style is to invite them to suggest alternative explanations whenever you hear them languishing over a pessimistic response. Here is one such scenario:

Mother: How was school today?

Daughter: Awful.

M: What happened?

D: I learned that Deedee is throwing a party this weekend, and I'm not invited.

M: I wonder how that happened?

D: She doesn't like me because I'm so tall (*internal, permanent*). Everyone thinks tall girls are weird (*pervasive*).

M: I wonder if there might be some other explanation?

D: Like what? Like she totally overlooked me (*external, limited, temporary*) or something?

M: Why not? I remember the time Fran wouldn't talk to me when she thought I had intentionally ignored her at the airport. She didn't know that I was preoccupied with rebooking my cancelled flight and didn't even see her.

D: I suppose it is possible.

M: Any other possible explanation?

D: Well, her next-door neighbor is dating my ex-boyfriend, and Deedee *has* to invite her. Maybe she's trying to be sensitive to my feelings (*external, limited, temporary*), or she would be embarrassed for both of us to be there.

Perhaps you catch the drift. By inviting someone who has uttered a pessimistic explanation to consider other possible explanations, you begin to break a pattern of putting oneself down. Always consider more than one explanation of outcomes, and select the explanation that makes the most sense. It won't always be a completely optimistic explanation, and it won't always be pessimistic either.

Social relationships in which we engage, and from which we can disengage

Judith Rich Harris has written two major books on the topic of youth development: *The Nurture Assumption* (1998) and *No Two Alike* (2006). In her first book, she announced a discovery that shook the foundations of development theory: that peers, not parents, are the primary environmental influence on the formation of personality between the ages of 8 and 25. Finding that parents are primarily responsible for teaching values and skills, peer groups on the other hand tend to have a stronger effect on modifying and reinforcing basic personality traits. During the period from ages 8 to 25, at any one time a youth might have anywhere from a few to several dozen "peer groups." A peer group consists of a group of peers that regularly convenes. With this definition, every class at school is a peer group. A study group for a class is another peer group. If you play in the band, sing in a chorus, or play a team sport, then those three groups become peer groups. If you play trumpet, the trumpet section is another peer group. If you play solo trumpet (i.e., "first chair"), then the other kids who play first in their sections become a peer group. If you play on the defensive line of a football team, then the defensive line is a peer group.

Harris finds that, at any one time during this 17-year period, one peer group stands out as "salient." For some reason, one peer group has stronger meaning for a youth than any of the other peer groups. It could be that the youth is a "leader," and all the other peer groups already have strong leaders, while one particular group, the "salient" one, has no leader, or a weak one, and that peer group eagerly embraces this youth's leadership initiatives. I (Pierce) remember when I was 16. Miss McClees, my high school science teacher (she taught biology, chemistry, and physics), talked the local DuPont plant into putting on a once-a-week science seminar for some of her more enthusiastic science students. For the next two years, we drove out to the DuPont plant one day a week, after school, for a two-hour seminar in which DuPont scientists introduced us to the mysterious world of experiments, analysis, and so forth, with all of their expensive equipment and bright researchers. For two years, those select science students became my salient peer group.

Harris talks about "peer pressure" not as something that your peers do to you, but as something that you do to yourself. Peer pressure is what happens when you try your darnedest to be like your peers, to minimize the differences between you and them. If your salient peer group wears nose rings, you wear nose rings. If they use a particular set of words, like "cool," "awesome," "rad," and so forth, then you use those words also. Minimize differences, blend in, be like Mike. That is peer pressure. The peer group doesn't need you, you need it. That is what she found.

Now for the clincher: The salient peer group can be positive or negative, healthy or toxic. If the peer group is positive, in both the parents' and youth's eyes, so much the better. No problem. However, if the salient peer group is toxic (leading to undesirable behavior—drugs, alcohol, sex, tobacco, etc.), then the only solution is to eliminate the peer group. No, not by pulling out your AK-47 and offing them, but by figuring out a way to make it impossible for the youth to continue associating with that group. This could be accomplished by moving to another city, moving to another school district, or, as in the case of one of our friends, cutting off the teen's allowance—no money, no new clothes, etc.—if the association with that toxic group continued. The youth refused to speak to the parents for over a month, but eventually sat down with them and said, "Thanks, I needed that. Things were out of control, and I felt too helpless to do anything about it. I knew I should have backed out, but I couldn't." Today, one of the kids in that peer group is, as an adult, in prison for selling drugs. In support of Harris' observations on toxic peer groups, Rowe (1994) found that siblings (not twins) who hung out with the same friends showed similar levels of alcohol/drug/tobacco use (p. 72).

In Harris' second book, she goes into much more detail about how the peer group process works. We believe her insights are so important that we devote considerable space here to summarizing her thinking.

Her process involves three phases: our database of acquaintances, our various groupings of people in that database, and our evaluation of how we stack up within these groups. The three phases are very much like a high school or college yearbook: the database is like the pictures of everyone in the class, the groups are like clubs and teams, and the evaluations are like the officers of the clubs/teams.

> For social development, the learning tasks that have to be accomplished in childhood fall into three categories. The first involves managing relationships; the second, becoming socialized; and the third has to do with besting one's rivals—or at least not being bested by them—in Darwinian-style competition. (p. 160)

She calls these "departments of the mind," or "systems" (p. 162).

> The three systems are products of evolution; they are organs of the mind. Like other essential organs, they are present in all physically normal humans, and (though the organs themselves will vary somewhat from one individual to another) their function is the same in everyone.

How do these three systems relate to the Big Five? The first system, "relationships," or the database, would appear to be primarily a function of one's E and A scores, with higher E and A having more database entries, and lower E and A having fewer. The second system, "socialization", or the groups/teams/clubs, would seem to be primarily a function of O, in the sense that O determines the breadth of our interests, with O+ people having more interests, hence more likely to have membership or involvement in more groups, and O- people having fewer interests, hence more likely to be involved with fewer groups. The third system entails how we evaluate ourselves relative to others in our groups (i.e., how we fare competitively within a group). This system would appear to be primarily a function of N and C, with N-C+ showing greater confidence and ambition and N+C- showing greater concern and spontaneity. These three systems work together to form the other half of personality that complements genetics. Let us now take a more in-depth look at each of the three systems.

Relationships: The Database of Everyone We Know

This system stores information about individuals in our life, like a database of family, friends, colleagues, customers, teachers, employers, enemies, resources, and so forth. Harris calls it a "lexicon for people, with a separate entry for each individual we know anything about." (p. 167) She describes this as a "self-organizing system" (p. 175), similar to a school of fish or a flying flock of birds that intuitively knows how to move with respect to others. This system's catalog includes not only faces, names and qualities, but our attitudes toward them, as in whom we want to attract, to avoid, to approach, to hang with, to party with, to work with, to learn from, to borrow money from, and so forth. In other words, it is a living database with "rules of engagement." Hierarchies (sometimes called "pecking order") are associated with this system, and they determine those at whom we look. Meanwhile, it also has a detection device that provides us with a sense of who is looking at us—people higher in the hierarchy are looked at more frequently (p. 178). Our database determines what we do with these gazes, whether we become aggressive, submissive, engaged, seductive, amused, and so forth. It is this system that causes me to try to think of a joke or something funny every time I see Alan Hickock, a friend in my church choir who suffers from chronic fatigue syndrome and who benefits from the effects of belly laughs. Harris calls this system "a discriminator, not a generalizer—a splitter, not a lumper. Its purpose is to make fine distinctions among individuals, even between identical twins." (p. 181) This system also determines our sense of status in every group we associate with, in that we store our judgments of who is superior/inferior to us in a multitude of domains: musical talent, verbal ability, street smarts, negotiation skills, and so forth.

Socialization: The Various Groupings of the Database Entries

The relationships and socialization systems both store data on people. The former is limited to individuals, the latter to groups or categories. It is like the difference between Clinton and Democrats or Martin Luther King, Jr., and African Americans. This socialization system is the storehouse of stereotypes. It is especially akin to what Harris described in *The Nurture Assumption*, in that socialization is what makes people similar, growing like each other, minimizing the differences between one and the salient peer group. It doesn't explain what makes people different, but it does explain how it makes them similar, apart from genetic influences, to their peers.

This includes the phenomenon of moving from one culture to another. Harris cites research of Yasuko Minoura, who found that Japanese immigrants arriving in California under age nine, and who stayed a minimum of four years, became completely acculturated, or assimilated (p. 185). Moreover, these kids experienced difficulties if and when they moved back to Japan, in that they found it hard to re-assimilate into their original Japanese culture. The upper limit for being able to re-assimilate appeared to be around 14 - 15, by which time re-assimilation appeared to be well-nigh impossible.

The system that supports socialization is an evolutionary build on the "self-organizing" system of relationships. This system employs implicit memory, which is the memory for rules and procedures, rather than explicit memory, which is the memory for facts, faces, figures, and so forth, that is employed in the relationships system. Harris observes that these first two systems can be in strong conflict: "I love Juliet, but Juliet is a Capulet." Or: "I hate Democrats, but some of my best friends are Democrats" (p. 193).

The socialization system attempts to find the "average" pattern of behavior for a group, and socialization then comes from striving to mimic that concept of the average, rather than mimicking any single individual in that group: be like an NBA player, not "be like Mike." Harris explains: "Children become socialized, I propose, not by imitating specific people in their lives, but by tailoring their behavior to that of the appropriate prototype" (p. 194). She points out that this average is skewed towards the higher status members of the group. Socialization is, in essence, "self-categorization," in which the young individual selects the group, or category, and its prototype to emulate. Peer pressure is self-initiated, not imposed (p. 195).

All About Personality

To varying degrees, individuals tend to change the prototypes to which they aspire depending on the category/group they currently find themselves with. McCrae and Costa (2003) report that differentiated personalities are less healthy. A differentiated personality means one that is different in different contexts, as opposed to someone who is essentially the same across all contexts—"What you see is what you get." Using Harris' model, this would suggest that kids are healthier when they tend to stick with a single, or at least a narrow range, of prototypes. In other words, all other things being equal, it is healthier to stick with the behaviors associated with your salient peer group, even when around other peer groups. "I'm a mathematician/musician/jock/geek/etc. wherever I am, take it or leave it." Interestingly, the category that one chooses to emulate does not have to be real—it can be virtual (p. 198), as in an imagined conceptual prototype of the kind of people who read my favorite author or watch my favorite TV show.

Successes at socialization and relationships are independent. One can have high group acceptance and few or no friends, while others can have satisfying friendships with no or low group acceptance.

Status: How We Stack Up in Each of Our Groups

Neither of Harris' first two systems explains how we become different (above and beyond genetic causes) from one another as we grow up—the second system explains how we become similar, and the first explains nothing. But the three systems together account for the other half of determining how we grow to be different, the half other than genes. Harris calls this the "status" system—the drive to excel in relation to others in one's group or category (p. 209). Just as relationships and socialization are independent of each other, so is status independent of, yet simultaneously related to, relationships and socialization. For example, one can achieve high status in a group (e.g., soloist in a performing group) at the expense of acceptance within that group (e.g., jealousy, resentment, fear, mistrust, on the part of other performers). Inasmuch as the first two systems gather information about others (individuals and groups), this third system gathers information about oneself—i.e., how I rank among or am perceived by other individuals in the group.

This sense of status is developed, particularly during the teen years, with the sense of status around age 16 continuing as a powerful, life-long sense of self. The sense is acquired by intuitively averaging all of the judgments of significant others in one's group(s), what Harris calls the "generalized other." (p. 221) Our sense of status is determined by the way we read this generalized other. One of the specific sets of data that we compute into this average is the frequency that others gaze at us, as opposed to gazing at others in our group (p. 224). In essence, our sense of status is developed by trying to figure out how others around us have filed us in their database, their relationship files.

In the small town where I (Jane) grew up, there had long been an established pattern in my church that teenagers would sit in the back of the balcony to sleep, talk, laugh, write/pass notes, and engage in nonworshipful activities. My mother was the organist of this church, so from age 4 onward, I was instructed to sit on the third row of the congregation where she could keep an eye on me. As a teenager, and especially my final two years of high school, I evolved into one of the informal leaders of the youth in my church. As a result of my leadership of this peer group, other teenagers my age and younger started joining me on the third row. Before I left for college, almost all the high school students would sit together most Sundays on three or four full pews at the front of the church. My leadership exerted enough "peer" pressure that the youth moved from the back balcony to the front rows. My sense of status that emerged provided a solid launch pad for confidently entering and taking on the demands of adulthood.

Harris found an intriguing relationship between acceptance and status. Persons who feel accepted by others tend to be less aggressive, while those who have high status tend to be the targets of others' jealousy and upward ambitions, and hence tend to be more aggressive in defense of that higher status. While some high-status individuals also feel accepted, they are more often lonely and the objects of attack. One major life task is for such leaders to find appropriate ways to maintain their status without resorting to aggression (p. 212):

> Evolution is all about competition, and one of the purposes of childhood is to prepare children to compete successfully in adulthood. But humans have many ways of competing, and what works for one could be a disaster for another. Behaving aggressively, for example, can be a successful strategy for some people but not for others. Big, strong individuals versus puny ones, physically attractive individuals versus unattractive ones—they're going to have different sets of options. In order to succeed in adult life, children have to work out a long-term strategy of behavior that is tailored to their own particular assets and liabilities. (p. 161)

Eric Erikson (1950) writes that a paramount requirement for a young person making it through the teen years is to have a skill in which they are better than others. Such skill mastery elicits acceptance and recognition in a way that contributes to forming one's identity. Erikson's observation is exactly what Harris is talking about here with the "status" system.

Harris says that even identical twins can become differentiated because of the complex relationship between these three systems: The relationship system causes other individuals to file the twins separately, with different data for each. The socialization system causes the twins to develop each other's "generalized other" independently, and the competition system causes each twin to assess his or her status within their various categories.

> ...within a group of boys, only one can be the toughest. Within a group of girls, only one can be the prettiest.... Even if they're both very tough or very pretty, one will inevitably be the second best, and the other will rank higher in the attention structure. The twin who receives more gazes will tend to speak out more in the group and will consequently receive yet more gazes, so that what might have started out as a tiny difference will widen. (p. 230)

Even random events can have profound effects in creating differences. For example, in 1997, I (Pierce) had the fortune to be asked by Oprah Winfrey's producers to appear on her talk show. They happened to find my name via an Internet search, while looking for a brain expert. My practical orientation must have appealed to them. I had not appeared on a major television program prior to that.

That appearance, then, was "random." Not part of a pattern. However, people who see that I have been on "Oprah" tend to make certain assumptions about my fame, credibility, wealth, and so forth. In truth, my appearance on Oprah's show should not be any more valid an indicator of my permanent character than the fact that I once slipped on a banana peel. Only when the pattern becomes repeated should it be regarded as an indicator. If I appear on Oprah regularly, or slip on a banana peel weekly, then go right ahead and make inferences about me therefrom!

However, as Harris continues explaining:

> The incidents may be random but their consequences are not. The status system is designed not to be hijacked by random events and to look for consistencies and trends, but a random event can cause everyone in your group to think you're wise or clumsy or funny or brave, and to go on thinking that for years.... Some random events are isolated occurrences—they happen once and then they are over—but others have repercussions that echo through the years. It is this second kind of random event—the kind that has long-term effects on a person's experiences---that can produce long-term changes in personality. What shapes personality is not the event itself but the persisting experiences that follow from the event. (p. 231)

Harris summarizes as follows:

> Parents do have some power to produce long-term effects on their children's behavior, but their power is indirect: it comes by way of the socialization system. It resides in their ability to determine where and by whom their children will be socialized. The parents decide which society to live in, which culture their children will grow up in, where they will go to school. To some extent, they can even determine which group or groups within the society their children will become members of.
>
> Parents do not, however, have the power to influence the personality development of their children via the status system. This system either discounts information obtained from close relatives or averages it together with so much other information that it doesn't have much impact. The way you are regarded by the 'generalized other' is unlikely to be the same as the way you are regarded by your mother. Mother doesn't always know best. (p. 233)
>
> The status system doesn't give a damn about the group's welfare; it asks, 'How can *I* best compete?' To find the best answer requires self-knowledge, so the status system searches for self-knowledge in the social cues provided by others. It then uses this information to plot a long-term strategy that will involve direct competition only in those arenas of endeavor in which the individual has a hope of succeeding and, if possible, avoid competition in other areas. The result is that individuals seek unoccupied niches; they specialize in different things. (p. 239)

The point: Change the peer group and you change the child. Sometimes, the child may consciously, or unconsciously, create a new peer group as an alternative to one that has become toxic. My senior year of high school, I (Jane) had become very active in both theater and choral music at school. I was president of the Drama Club and vice president of the Women's Chorus. Because of all the plays I had been in, I was awarded membership in the National Thespian Society. For this, I received a great deal of teasing from a few class members (such as Crawford Melton) who equated "thespian" with "lesbian," even though I clearly had a preference for boys. I regarded the class members' behavior as childish and immature and saw myself as more of an artist and began writing poetry as a way to separate myself from those I perceived as culturally ignorant. I dearly loved my English teacher, Miss

Trammel (who called me Carolyn since she had taught my older sister, Carolyn, 16 years before me). Trusting Miss Trammel's knowledge and wisdom, I asked her to read and evaluate the poetry that I was writing outside of my regular school assignments. Imagine my surprise and pleasure when Miss Trammel proposed that I write the class poem and read it (dramatically) at graduation. I had found an unoccupied "niche."

While boys and girls must both navigate these forces of socialization, the playing field is not always equal for the two. In some cultures, in fact, girls, and later as women, are not only denied education but also denied normal social relations in the community, particularly with men outside their family. In the U.S., Mary Belenky (1997) and her colleagues found a pattern that hampers the way that females deal with Harris' three developmental forces. It has to do with the different way that our culture encourages boys and girls in the management of their internal "voice." Traditional families rear their girls differently than their boys. Males are typically encouraged to fend for themselves, to tough it out, to take responsibility.

In short, from an early age boys are encouraged to find their own "voice" and to exercise it, grow confident in it, to learn to speak for themselves. In the traditional U.S. family, girls, on the other hand, are encouraged to take on the voice of significant elders in their lives, be it mother, father, grandparent, priest, rabbi, imam, or teacher. As a result, the pattern that emerges is that the traditional boy is encouraged to think for himself, while the typical girl is encouraged to divine the way others would think. Belenky observes that, in school, this manifests itself as the girl who is helpless in answering a test question unless she knows how the teacher wishes it to be answered. In an essay question, such as "What are the underlying causes of economic disparity in the U.S.?", the typical "traditional" girl attempts to answer the question based on what the teacher or other significant figures in her life have said, while the typical boy will more likely answer based without reference to the views of specific authority figures in his life.

Belenky calls for teachers in U.S. high schools, colleges, and universities to emphasize, for all students, but especially for girls, critical thinking in all aspects of the curriculum. The opposite of critical thinking is rote learning—spitting back what one has heard. Critical thinking forces the student to figure out an answer without reference to any memorized material. For example, a critical thinking approach to interpreting a poem would be for the teacher to ask the student a series of questions such as:

- Who is the speaker in this poem?
- What does the poem tell you about the speaker?
- What is the speaker's attitude towards the subject of the poem?
- What well-known contemporary person could be the speaker in this poem?
- Support your answers to these questions with details from the text of the poem.
- If you were the speaker, how might you express these thoughts?

This critical thinking approach assumes that the student has not previously seen the poem and has not heard the teacher or anyone else express opinions on these questions.

In short, Belenky calls for parents and teachers and counselors—anyone who works with youth—to encourage young people to think for themselves in every area of their lives, taking their book knowledge and applying it to real life. I (Pierce) remember Dr. Thomas Clark's question on the first semester examination in his New Testament class at Davidson College: "Compare and contrast St. Paul's journeys to the experiences of the freedom riders in the deep south of the 1960s." There was no right answer. Students were on their own to think for themselves. Fostering critical thinking in this way increases the chances that a young person will form an identity free of coercion and will thus experience the gentlest possible entry into adulthood. The cost of coerced identity and inexperience in thinking for oneself is many false starts and unsatisfying choices in young adulthood and beyond.

Gender: How Our Notions of What Boys and Girls are Supposed to Be Like Affects Trait Levels

Much has been written about the differences in male and female behavior. The Mars/Venus dichotomy, the doer/talker notion—all try to establish differences among the sexes. However, the basic question that underlies all of these treatments is this: Are sex differences in behavior inevitable or cultural, inherited or learned, genetic or environmentally influenced, nature-driven or nurture-driven? The answer to date is: We don't really know. The data appear to support the notion that sex differences (boys better at math, girls at language, etc.) are cultural in origin. It is beyond the scope of this book to deal completely with this subject. However, we can make one clear statement: *no goal (legal goal, that is) is off limits for either sex.* The only limitations that should affect a youth's individual goal setting are the limitations that we accept as unavoidable at the time, such as geographical, financial, religious, cultural, or physical constraints.

To the degree that we accept gender-differences in behavior—boys are supposed to be this way, and girls are supposed to be that way—this can affect the level of a trait, regardless of our "set point." We may have a low set point for A (Accommodation, in the Five-Factor Model), such that, under normal circumstances, we would be competitive, argumentative, aggressive. However, low A girls living in a culture that expects girls to be submissive (i.e., they are to be silent partners to the men in their lives) will live in a "state" of mid to high A. One example that comes to mind is the character of Nora in Norwegian-born Henrik Ibsen's play, *A Doll's House.* Throughout the play, Nora patiently defers to her husband Torvald with submissive phrases such as "Whatever you say, dear." Or "You are quite right, dear." And then, at the end of the play, she walks out, slamming the door on Torvald and, some say, opening the door of the feminist revolution. If one were to guess at Nora's level of A during the first half of the play, one would definitely describe her as A+. But we learn towards the end that this A+ behavior is a "state," a deviation from her natural temperament, which is considerably lower in A. Such assumed gender roles, then, are states, unless by chance they happen to match one's nature. In Nora's case, that was not true.

Physical influences that we can manage, or can allow to manage us

In this last section, we want to run through several physical factors that can influence trait levels. We begin with food; continue with beverages, sleep, exercise, media, and the environment; and end with some thoughts about mental illness.

Food: Proteins, Complex Carbohydrates, Simple Carbs, and Fats

Proteins: Proteins are the chemical basis of all cell structure. Eating proteins (e.g., skimmed dairy products, meat trimmed of fat, seafood, eggs, grains, legumes, nuts) maximizes the availability of L-tyrosine, an amino acid associated with mental alertness. The effect of proteins on behavior is increased idea generation, which means an increase in O (Originality, in the Five-Factor Model), and also an increase in concentration and task focus, which means an increase in C (Consolidation, in the Five-Factor Model). **General Recommendation:** When you need to eat before a period of optimal mental functioning, prefer proteins (and also complex carbohydrates, as you shall see below).

Complex Carbohydrates: The effect of eating complex carbohydrates (e.g., whole grain breads, pastas, cereals, beans, most vegetables, berries, and so forth) is to provide sustaining energy over time. Unlike protein, which does not provide energy, complex carbohydrates, simple carbs, and fats are all fuels that provide energy. In short, they provide calories. Complex carbohydrates are superior to simple ones in that their form of energy is steady and long-lasting, whereas simple carbs provide spurts of energy. This behavioral effect of increased energy means primarily an increase in E (Extraversion) and C (Consolidation). **General Recommendation:** Eat complex carbohydrates when you need physical energy over time in order to stay focused in the thick of the action. That is why people talk about carbohydrate "loading" before a sporting event requiring endurance, such as a marathon.

Simple Carbohydrates: Simple carbohydrates are, for example, products with significant sugar content and little if any fiber, such as watermelon; they're foods that are high on the glycemic index—for the glycemic values of various foods, check websites such as http://www.mendosa.com/gilists.htm. These foods quickly raise blood sugar for a quick boost in energy. However, a trough-like low in blood sugar follows that causes drowsiness, irritability, and a "blah" feeling. The behavioral effect is a brief increase in E and C (this is why some people eat candy for a quick burst of energy), followed by an increase in N (Need for Stability), and decreases in E, O, A, and C. **Recommendation:** Study the glycemic index charts in order to find snacks that are both satisfying and with a low glycemic index, i.e., more complex carbohydrates, in order to avoid the "troughs" or lows that don't feel very good. For example, instead of cookies or chips, try nuts or fruits. We keep a bag of unsalted nuts and a bag of dried fruit in our desk drawer at all times for a convenient snack.

Fats: The general effect of eating fats (e.g., products with cream, butter, oils, and so forth) is to increase levels of serotonin in one's body. This rise of serotonin has the behavioral effect of making one more relaxed and agreeable. With respect to the Big Five, eating fats can temporarily reduce N and increase A, making one calmer and less aggressive. Excessive consumption of fats could also reduce E,

O, and C, inasmuch as being too relaxed, even sleepy, will reduce energy level, idea generation, and concentration. **General Recommendation:** Avoid fats in the middle of the school or workday in order to maximize alertness. Prefer to eat fats when 1) you need to calm down, or 2) at the evening meal, to facilitate ultimate sleepiness. It also happens that evening is the time when one's body craves fats the most. Our bodies have evolved so as to crave fats when we need to calm down for our evening's rest.

Summary of Effects of Foods on Trait Levels:

	N	E	O	A	C
Proteins			↑		↑
Complex Carbs		↑			↑
Simple Carbs	↑	↕	↓	↓	↓
Fats	↓	↓	↓	↑	↓

One example of the effect of food consumption on behavior is a case study of one of my students. When I (Pierce) taught at West Charlotte (NC) High School back in the 1970s, I had a student who came into my home room around 7:15 a.m. every morning, straight from the bus drop-off. He came into my room literally "off the wall." He was so hyped up that he would jump high into the air and kick himself off of the concrete classroom wall, then try to land upright. He would bump other students, talk loudly/shout, brag, accuse, laugh—in short, his behavior was out of control. Otherwise, he was a nice kid with plenty of ability. For the sake of the students and other teachers, we needed to figure out how to obtain a softer early morning landing from him. I called for a parent/teacher/student/counselor conference. The four of us met one day after school: mother, 16-year-old boy, counselor, and me. Wanting to look at the context of this young person's life, I asked mother and son to narrate a typical day, minute by minute, from midnight to midnight.

To shorten the story, suffice it to say that we found that the father was a truck driver and seldom at home, that the student woke up to his alarm at 5:30 a.m., quickly dressed, and hurried (his mother still asleep, meanwhile) to a nearby convenience store, where he grabbed a grape soda and a pack of powdered doughnuts, then headed for the bus. I felt that I knew the problem then: He was coming to school on a "sugar high" (E+). He wasn't a problem in later classes—the sugar wore off, and he was irritable, lethargic, and inattentive, but not a particular problem. After lunch, his behavior evened out. He was coming to school without having consumed any protein or complex carbs, and without having had any loving maternal contact. I asked his mother if she would cook breakfast for him. She said she had tried, but he wouldn't eat it. When I asked him why, he said he didn't like eggs. I said, "How about a hamburger and a glass of milk." He said, "Sounds great." I said, "Mom, will you cook him a hamburger every morning for breakfast?" Taken aback, she agreed. After a couple of days, the "off the wall" behavior disappeared. Before, the student was coming to school in a "state," not having received either proper physical or emotional nourishment before leaving home. With proper nourishment—protein and Mom time, this "state" abated.

Beverages: Caffeine, Alcohol, Sugar, Sugar Substitutes

Caffeine: Caffeine does not actually have a direct effect on our body—it is not in and of itself an "accelerant." Instead, it works its magic in this way: When the body is at work—mental, physical, or otherwise—our neurons release adenosine into the immediately surrounding area. As adenosine accumulates, it makes its way back into the cell, like a thermostat, having the effect of making us drowsy, signaling us that it is time for a break, to slow down and rest. The caffeine molecule is similar to the adenosine molecule and fits very nicely into these adenosine receptors, with the effect that the adenosine remains in the immediate area outside the neurons while the caffeine enters the neurons, thus keeping us alert. The result is that we don't get drowsy—we stay charged up, continuing to do our work. So, while alcohol (as we will see in the next paragraph) is like putting a rock under your accelerator—it slows down all systems, caffeine is like putting a rock under your brake—it keeps you from slowing down (Braun, 1996, p. 130).

Caffeine—through blocking adenosine—has been shown to disrupt the balance of female hormones, so it's a likely cause of, or at least a contributor to, PMS (pre-menstrual syndrome). As a way to minimize chances of PMS, Braun (p. 154) recommends staying off caffeine from four days before menses, through menstruation, and until the next ovulation. Unfortunately, many females think caffeine will counteract the unpleasant symptoms accompanying menstruation, but, in fact, it is more likely that the caffeine aggravates the problems. Experiments show that that the body tends to adapt quickly (i.e., to tolerate) caffeine levels, such that people who average 900 mg of caffeine per day showed no physical, emotional, or mental performance edge over abstainers. In other words, much of our perception about caffeine's effects is an illusion (Braun, p. 170). In effect, then, caffeine tends to increase N through elevating arousal, increase E through maintaining energy level, decrease A through hormone imbalance and heightened arousal, and decrease C through nervous edge and accompanying easy distractibility (especially in higher doses). Note: The recommended dose of caffeine is approximately 1 milligram of caffeine per pound of body weight, and it takes about 7 hours to metabolize. One 5 oz. cup of drip coffee contains about 150 mg. of caffeine. An 8 oz. can of Red Bull has 80 mg. Thus, two 8-ounce Red Bulls (160 mg of caffeine) within 7 hours is the limit for a 160-pound person. **General Recommendation:** Limit caffeine consumption to one dose every seven hours, and avoid it if possible. Rest when fatigued; don't drink more caffeine.

Alcohol: (We know alcohol sales are illegal to teens, but we also know that they often find ways to obtain it; so we feel a need to discuss it.) Alcohol is the rock under the accelerator, as mentioned earlier. It has the effect, then, of slowing down all systems, a temporary form of old age, as it were. Alcohol decreases executive ability in the brain (planning, organizing, memory storage, and so forth). Enzymes that metabolize alcohol (i.e., render it impotent) are much less efficient in females than in males, such that normally females require only half the amount of alcohol to experience the same effect as males. From an evolutionary perspective, this is likely associated with the survival advantage of infants whose mothers drink less alcohol during gestation—such consumption has a disastrous effect on the embryo (e.g., fetal alcohol syndrome, wherein an embryo's brain cells literally get drunk from the mother's alcohol and then lose their way when migrating from one location to the next). Safe drinking rules have established "one drink per hour" as the standard, because it takes about one hour for the stomach/intestines/liver to process 0.5 oz. of ethanol. More alcohol than that invites intoxication.

With respect to the interaction of alcohol and caffeine (traditional wisdom is that taking caffeine after alcohol "sobers you up"), research indicates no appreciable effect (except with very low levels of alcohol). Coffee after alcohol only produces a wide-awake drunk. Alcohol anesthetizes by depressing various central nervous system processes. This occurs by binding with glutamate receptors (excitatory), thus generally slowing things down (downing two drinks in one hour has been measured as decreasing glutamate functioning by around 80% [Braun, p. 49])—speech begins to slur, reaction time becomes protracted, stepping becomes foot-dragging, and so forth. Alcohol binds with receptors for NMDA (N-methyl-D-aspartic acid, a specific type of glutamate), thereby preventing the formation of new memories (one drink reduces memory efficiency by around 3%, two drinks by around 80%. Quantity obviously relates to the "alcoholic blackout" phenomenon—perception with no recording).

Alcohol triggers the same dopamine receptors as cocaine and amphetamines, thus activating the reward/pleasure pathway. Alcohol and Valium bind with receptors for the inhibitory neurotransmitter GABA (gamma-aminobutyric acid); so the substances have similar calming effects. Alcohol increases serotonin production, and, in some studies, alcoholics show reduced serotonin levels, with the suggestion that some alcoholics are self-medicating with alcohol as an alternative to Prozac. In fact, studies have shown that being on Prozac can reduce alcohol consumption. Braun (1996, pp. 53, 59) describes this process as disabling the accelerator (glutamate) and sensitizing the brakes (GABA).

In summary, alcohol tends to lower N (calming, also reducing arousal), lower E (slowing down), lowering A (by reducing inhibitions), and lowering C (through decreased executive function). Alcohol raises O by reducing inhibitions and efficiency and lowers O by interfering with neural connectivity. **General Recommendation:** Don't consume alcohol if you are under-age. If you can legally drink, limit alcohol use. Especially limit it to times when you don't need to shine mentally. While alcohol is regarded as a social lubricant (by reducing inhibitions), it is also a social irritant (also from reducing inhibitions!).

Sugared drinks (e.g., soft drinks/sodas, sugared fruit drinks) have the same effect as simple carbohydrate foods (see previous discussion). Sugar substitutes have an effect similar but lesser than caffeine because both heighten arousal. The most benign sugar substitute at this time appears to be sucralose (e.g., Splenda).

Summary of Effects of Beverages on Trait Levels:

	N	E	O	A	C
Caffeine	↑	↑		↓	↓
Alcohol	↓	↓	↕	↓	↓
Sugared	↑	↕	↓	↓	↓
Sugar Substitues	↑	↑		↓	↓

Here is an example of the effects of caffeine. I (Pierce) was teaching a college class. One day after class, a bright, 20-something student approached me for help. She complained that she was a nervous wreck, couldn't concentrate, had trouble remembering material she had studied, and so forth. I noticed that she was rather thin. After some conversation, I learned that she was a diet fanatic, and that she ate so few calories daily that she consumed large quantities of caffeine (coffee, sugar-free cola drinks) to get through the day. I explained what the caffeine was doing to her. Then I suggested drinking only one dose of caffeine every seven hours and consuming one or two tablespoons of peanut butter on whole-grain toast for breakfast as a source of energy for the day. She was horrified, thinking that she'd get fat. I convinced her that she would feel better and that she could make up her mind to limit the peanut butter to that one serving. Several months later, she returned to share with me that she was successful in maintaining the new diet, and that her mood and mental performance had improved considerably without her having gained additional weight.

Drugs: Marijuana, Ecstasy, and So Forth

Illegal drugs, while they do have a variety of temporary effects on trait levels, are not an option due to their dangerous side effects. Even though we could identify the specific effects of various illegal drugs on specific trait levels, we will not do that here, for fear that we might encourage drug use in order to achieve a desired state of mind or level of behavior. As is plainly visible throughout this section, plenty of legal options are available for achieving the same effects.

Rest and Exertion: the Effects of Sleep Cycles, Naps, Aerobic Exercise, Nonaerobic Exercise, and Athletic Competition

Sleep: A good night's sleep is widely misunderstood by many, who consider it a matter of how many hours of sleep one gets. That is not quite the case: A good night's sleep is a matter of how many uninterrupted cycles of sleep one gets. The average sleep cycle covers about 90 minutes, with the average teen requiring about five cycles, which take at least a total of about 7½ hours. When a sleep cycle is interrupted (e.g., by an alarm clock or someone waking you up), one loses the restorative effect of that particular cycle. Teens, in addition to needing five complete cycles, tend to have a body clock that differs from younger and older family members. Teens they tend to fall asleep later, and wake later, than others. Studies of school start times in places like Edina, Minnesota have found that delaying the start time of junior and senior high school by one or more hours can have a significant impact on students' mood, alertness, performance, health, and attendance. **General Recommendation:** Allow a teen to wake up naturally after about 7½ hours sleep, or if an alarm must be set, make it go off within the first 30 minutes of a cycle so that it does not go off during deep sleep. For further discussion of sleep and body clocks, read the chapter on sleep in *The Owner's Manual for the Brain,* 3rd Ed. (Howard, 2006).

Naps: Naps are also commonly misunderstood. Basically, naps come in two kinds: one where you go to sleep, and the other where you don't. Jane's father and mine both took daily naps, and they actually went to sleep after lunch every day. However, that is not the kind of nap we advocate. The ideal nap is simply a matter of shutting down one's body, much like quiet, still meditation, whereby one's brain waves change from beta waves (normal awakeness and alertness) to alpha waves (the brain state in-between awake and sleep). You know you're in alpha state when you start seeing images in your mind's eye, but images that you can control—you can make them dance, sing, get out of the way, etc. You're still conscious, but you're completely resting, just not asleep. The optimal time for this kind of nap is between 2 – 4 pm in the afternoon, the period when the body temperature is at its lowest during the day, and, incidentally, the period when one is least alert, as evidenced by the high number of accidents (traffic, industrial, and domestic) that occur then. Regardless of what one has or does not have for lunch, one feels drowsy during this period of time as a result of lower body temperature. A meditative type of nap will restore body temperature to normal levels and one's mind to normal alertness. **General Recommendation:** Everyone should find about 10 minutes to be completely still, eyes closed, lying down if possible, when one feels slightly sleepy between 2 – 4 pm in the afternoon. For more discussion of naps, see the chapter on sleep in *The Owner's Manual for the Brain,* 3rd Ed. (Howard, 2006).

Exercise: Aerobic exercise involves moving the large muscle groups repeatedly—and without stopping—for up to 30 minutes with an accompanying elevation of heart rate. This can be accomplished through running, jogging, brisk walking, swimming, aerobic dancing, bicycling, and so forth. For a more complete description of aerobic exercise consult the Internet, or read the description in *The Owner's Manual for the Brain*. The effect of such exercise is to flood the body with endorphins and to flush stress chemicals such as cortisol. An accompanying sense of calmness and relief from stress ensues. **General Recommendation:** Time your aerobic exercise to occur soon after the most stressful time of day, in order to get the maximum benefit of stress relief.

Nonaerobic exercise differs from aerobic by having a start-and-stop quality, such that one's heart rate does not stay elevated for a full 30 minutes or so. Examples are weightlifting, tennis, golf, baseball, and the like. Any exercise increases blood flow, which increases the supply of oxygen to the brain, which enables maximum alertness. All trait levels are heightened by exercise through increased brain efficiency.

Athletic Competition: Winning an athletic competition has the effect of raising males' and females' levels of testosterone. Losing a competition has the opposite effect. So, win a tennis match, and testosterone increases, with an accompanying decrease in A behavior, thus making one feel more aggressive and competitive, as in "Bring me more competition! Who's next! I'm unbeatable." Losing a tennis match lowers testosterone levels, with an increase in levels of A, for a less aggressive stance: "I think I'll go sit in the corner and listen to my iPod!" **General Recommendation:** If you want to pump someone up to be unaccustomedly aggressive, then arrange for them to compete with someone who is beatable; compete just before the time when more aggression is required. On the other hand, if you're trying to calm someone down before a big event where normal levels of aggression might be counterproductive, then arrange for competition with someone who'll beat them!

Summary of Effects of Rest and Exertion on Trait Levels:

	N	E	O	A	C
Poor Night's Sleep	↑	↓	↓	↓	↓
Naps	↓	↑		↑	↑
Aerobic Exercise	↓			↑	↑
Nonaerobic Exercise	↕	↕	↕	↕	↕
Winning an Athletic Competition				↓	
Losing an Athletic Competition				↑	

Media: Television Programming, Music, Cell Phone Use, Computers

First, some general comments about youth and their use of electronic devices in general. In a Kaiser Family Foundation study conducted October 2008 to May 2009 among 2,000 youth in grades 3 to 12, average use of cell phones, computers, television, and so forth was around 7½ hours, which was most of their out-of-school time. Including multi-tasking (e.g., watching TV and texting), the total extended to about 11 hours per day on average. Compared to those engaged for less than 3 hours, the heaviest users, those engaged electronically for more than 16 hours daily, were:

- twice as likely to make Cs or lower in school
- more likely to describe themselves as bored
- more likely to describe themselves as sad
- more likely to report having gotten into trouble
- less likely to like school
- less likely to relate well with their parents

The study didn't indicate whether usage led to problems, or vice versa. Whether usage is cause or effect of such issues, parents and others can and should exert some influence on the amount of use of electronic devices. The study also did not indicate how much of this usage was active (writing a paper, creating a spreadsheet, interviewing for information) versus passive (e.g., listening to music, viewing a video). We hypothesize that active use generally would at least have a neutral effect but likely would not lead to the above consequences.

Television: Research finds that television programming tends to elicit in the viewer the same kind of behavior being viewed. Where it doesn't elicit the same behavior, it tends to establish a sympathy towards it. Viewing violent programming is associated with indifference towards aggressive, violent behavior, and, in some instances, increases in aggressive, violent behavior, or temporary increases in N and decreases in A and C. Viewing sexually promiscuous programming is associated with how early one becomes sexually active and also with unwanted pregnancies; such actions involve higher E and lower C. **General Recommendation:** Avoid violent and sexually promiscuous television programming, or accompany such viewing with activities that offset their effects (family discussions, exercise, and so forth).

Music: Music preferences can affect mood. Faster music promotes positive mood (E+),while slower music is more relaxing (N-). For someone in a sad mood, sad music appears to be more soothing (i.e., matching the mood is comforting, N-). Listening to one's favorite kinds of music is associated with improved mood during the listening and improved mental functioning afterward. Listening to music of any kind interferes with concentration on other tasks (C-), as one simply cannot do two things at once. This is especially true when the two activities employ the same mode (e.g., song lyrics and a reading assignment both involve words). In such a situation, one is under the impression that one is doing two things simultaneously, i.e., multi-tasking, while in fact one is doing two things in alternation, i.e., *semi-tasking*, neither task enjoying complete focus, but half focus, thus increasing chances for errors. **General Recommendation:** When sad, listen to sad music. When neutral in mood and wanting mood improvement, listen to upbeat music. When nervous or stressed, listen to slower music. When trying to concentrate on something that one wants to do well, i.e., without error, do not listen to music.

Cell Phones: Cell phone usage comes in (at least) two modes: talking and texting. Using a cell phone in either mode while alone, i.e., no one else is around, such as in one's own room, has no known impact on self or others (unless usage becomes extreme). In essence, it is no different than using a regular telephone. Cell phones affect behavior primarily in social situations. More extraverted people use cell phones more in social situations, and it bothers them less to be around others using cell phones, while it bothers more introverted people to be around cell phone users (i.e., it temporarily raises their levels of N). Interestingly, N- persons are more upset than N+ persons when they are around cell phone users (probably because N+ persons are soothed by the social intercourse, while N- find it unnecessary and intrusive).

By permitting one to have contact with others who are geographically absent, the cell phone may accentuate traits. For example, having a cell phone can make an introvert more introverted by eliminating the need to be out and in the thick of the action. On the other hand, a cell phone can make an extravert more extraverted by providing an outlet for social connectivity even when physically or geographically isolated. Accordingly, cell phones can make an aggressive person even more aggressive by providing the opportunity for dominance not possible without a cell phone. Cell phones can make an ambitious person more ambitious by permitting action on goal completion when away from the normal work or study area. Conversely, cell phones can make a low-achieving person (C-) even more so by providing a source of distraction not possible otherwise. **General Recommendation:** Cell phones exacerbate N+, E+, O+, and C- behavior. To avoid excessive emotional reactivity (N++), just turn it off when you need to remain calm, as during a class, while driving, and so forth. E+ people need all the help they can get in taking time to be solitary for reading, writing, practice, reflection, and so forth. Turn the phone off to avoid the temptation to end these solitary sessions prematurely. O+ people are easily bored and can use a cell phone to relieve tedium. Instead, consider more satisfying ways to create variety. C- people have a hard enough time focusing on the task at hand, and cell phones are just one more distraction. Turn it off during times when you need all the help you can get for concentrating—doing homework, in class. . .you get the idea.

Computers (including desktops, laptops, phones with computer features, and gaming consoles): Much research has occurred about the amount of computer usage, whether for games, work, entertainment, or social connectivity. A study of 1,102 youth, ages 12-17, conducted by the Pew Research Center's Pew Internet and American Life Project (supported by the MacArthur Foundation), reported its findings in November 2008 ("Teens, Video Games, and Civics"). The report found that practically all early teens play video games, with the percentage decreasing over time, particularly for girls. The thrust of the study was to determine whether gaming was associated with the tendency to be engaged in positive civic activities, such as "following politics, persuading others how to vote, contributing to charities, volunteering, or staying informed about politics and current events."

The study's conclusion was that gaming neither encouraged nor discouraged civic engagement (e.g., participating in charitable, religious, political, etc., activities outside school). In other words, gaming is neither a deterrent, substitute, or promoter of civic engagement. Teens' civic engagement will not change, regardless of their degree of gaming. Also, the research shows that about 1 in 4 teens plays games alone, with no social contact, either face to face or online. This level of solitary gaming is consistent with the fact that about 1 in 4 teens will score strongly E- on the Big Five. So, more introverted teens play games in a more introverted style. Not a big deal.

The satisfying aspect of this finding is that gaming does not increase solitary activity, as many suspected. Gaming is a social activity to the degree that the individuals playing the games are social individuals. Our summer intern research associate, Emily Crowder (a rising sophomore at the University of North Carolina at Chapel Hill), provides an example of how computer games can encourage social connectivity:

> In the summer, when my friends and I can't think of anything to do, we all go to a friend's house. Normally a group of about 15 people ends up coming, and we take turns playing Guitar Hero or Wii Sports (particularly good for being social and taking turns). Playing the games is normally entertaining in and of itself, but even when you are not the one playing, you can sit around and talk and joke with friends. One benefit is that when you run out of things to say, watching others play the video games is normally an entertaining distraction.

Finally, since word processing, email, spreadsheets, database, graphics, and other computer applications enable one to create a large variety of materials at great speed, there is a tendency for individuals not to self-monitor and to create volumes of material or output. The result is a tendency to be more complex and creative than normal (O+), more confrontational than normal (A-), and more spontaneous than normal (C-). **General Recommendation:** Resist the temptation to create output on a computer without proofreading and revising, as is often done during blogging. It is so easy to create volumes of material that it is tempting to be uncritical of what one has created. Also, monitor computer gaming to insure prosocial content (remember, violent/aggressive content elevates levels of violence/aggression in behavior).

Summary of Effects of Media on Trait Levels:

	N	E	O	A	C
Violent TV Viewing	↑			↓	↓
Viewing TV with Sexual Content		↑			↓
Listening to Upbeat Music		↑			
Listening to Sad Music While Sad	↓				
Listening to Slow Music	↓				
Listening to Any Kind of Music					↓
Effect of Cell Usage Socially on E+ Others	↓	↓			
Effect of Cell Usage Socially on E- Others	↑				
Effect of Cell Usage Socially on N- Others	↑				
Effect of Cell Usage on the User	↕	↕	↕	↕	↕
Computer Games		↕			↕
Computer Applications (e.g., word processing)			↑	↓	↓

Environment: Air, Light, Noise, Odor

Air: The more polluted the air, the proportionately less oxygen we breathe, and less oxygen reaches the brain. The result of lower oxygen levels in blood to the brain is less fuel to energize the brain, resulting in drowsiness or suboptimal alertness. When the air is purest, we are most fully alert, and full alertness permits us to use all of our natural energy, whether for traits, talents, or physical endeavors. The way nature has provided to keep the air pure is through negative ions, particles that attach themselves to unwanted particulates in the atmosphere (dust, smoke, germs, and so forth), thus causing the particulates to become heavier and float to earth, with the effect of increasing the proportion of oxygen in the air we breathe. **General Recommendation:** Modern air conditioning depletes the atmosphere of negative ions. To restore them, place an ion generator in your work area. Better yet, find ways of getting plenty of fresh air through opening windows, frequent outside excursions, and so forth. The densest concentrations of naturally occurring negative ions are in the vicinity of rapidly moving water, such as oceanside, whitewater rapids, and the morning shower. That is one reason we tend to feel so invigorated in all three places. Ever wondered why you emerged from your shower with the urge to find a pad and pencil to jot down all the good ideas that emerged while showering? Now you know!

Light: Light from the sun is the purest form of light. When the sun goes down in the evening, the pineal gland detects the absence of natural light around us (whether we are sighted or not) and begins to produce melatonin, the so-called sleep transmitter, ultimately resulting in sleepiness and sleep. We can delay this effect by burning artificial light. At dawn, the pineal gland detects the fresh supply of natural light and shuts down the production of melatonin, eventually resulting in normal alertness. Exceptions are rainy days, when we don't get our full dose of sunlight, and have more trouble gaining alertness. Lack of sunlight is the cause behind "winter depression," or SAD (seasonal affective disorder), that of course can be helped by exposing oneself to light. **General Recommendation***:* If you study or work in an area that does not have access to natural sunlight, you are likely to experience more drowsiness than desirable. To overcome this, get a lamp for your work/study area that has a CRI (color rendering index) of 90 or greater. A CRI of 100 is equivalent to natural sunlight.

Any lamp with a CRI of less than 90 will be missing at least the blue part of the color spectrum and is thus unable to serve the purpose of alerting your pineal gland to shut down melatonin production. Normal hardware and decorating stores do not typically know about the CRI, but you can get this information by talking with a lamp distributor. "Grow lights" and "sunlight bulbs" have, or should have, the full spectrum.

Noise: Noise sustained at the level of 89 decibels (a point determined by OSHA, the Occupational Safety and Health Administration) not only will cause hearing loss, but it is stressful and often leads to depression. As examples, the typical hair dryer operates at approximately 90 decibels, as does a toy xylophone. Listings of the decibel levels of hundreds of different activities are available on the Internet (e.g., http://www.quietsolution.com/Noise_Levels.pdf). Noise tends to increase stress (N+), discourage sociability (E-), prevent idea generation (O-), cause irritability (A-), and distract from the task at hand (C-). **General Recommendation:** OSHA recommends that anyone exposed to sustained noise at 89 decibels or higher should wear earplugs or other appropriate ear protection gear.

Odor: Odor provides effects similar to those of noise. Pleasant odors tend to lead to productivity (E+C+) and relaxation (N-A+). (Much of the perception of "pleasant" depends on what you have been reared with—I [Pierce] particularly like lavender, traceable to my mother's putting drops of oil of lavender in various rooms through our home in eastern N.C.) A thriving new industry based on this premise offers devices for periodically emitting pleasant bursts of a variety of fragrances. Conversely, stress (N+) occurs with exposure to unpleasant odors and overly strong fragrances that are pleasant when weaker.

One particular problem is that 95% of all perfumes are petrochemical based (i.e., not using natural ingredients). Particularly affecting others having to smell them, these petrochemical-based perfumes are highly toxic and cause a long string of problems including nose/throat/eye irritation, stress, distraction, and fatigue (N+C-). An important note to teens as they begin using fragrances, especially thinking that they will attract a partner, is that when you can no longer smell your fragrance, others who have not become used to it (as you have) will still notice it. Frequent re-applications may actually drive away the person you wish to attract. Also, as you enter an enclosed work environment, remember that others may have allergies and that strong fragrances may prevent people from wanting to work with you. Working people really should avoid fragrance at work. **General Recommendation:** Provide pleasant fragrances and eliminate strong or unpleasant odors in work and study areas. Avoid petrochemical-based perfumes. (At concerts, we often end up sitting beside "petrochemical factories" and then have to find other seats!)

Summary of Effects of Environment on Trait Levels:

	N	E	O	A	C
Being in Good Air	↕	↕	↕	↕	↕
Access to Natural Sunlight	↕	↕	↕	↕	↕
Sustained Noise	↑	↓	↓	↓	↓
Pleasant Fragrances	↓	↑		↑	↑
Unpleasant/Strong Odors	↑			↓	↓

A Note on Personality Disorders, or "Diseases" of Personality

In this chapter, we have focused on "states" of behavior, temporary variations of a particular trait's "set point." The purpose of this book is to focus on normal personality and not on diseased personalities. For that, one must consult a different kind of book, such as the *Diagnostic and Statistical Manual of Mental Disorders* (DSM IV; DSM V is scheduled to appear in May 2012).

However, we would be remiss if we were not to at least identify the threshold between normal and disordered personalities. So, what is the difference between a healthy and an unhealthy personality? In brief, an unhealthy personality is one that cannot hold a job or a relationship. An oversimplification? Perhaps. The key to survival, from an evolutionary point of view, has always been making a living and reproducing. Anyone who can't do both is doomed to extinction, or in the case of modern society, to being institutionalized.

So, what causes one not to be able to hold a job and/or a relationship? It occurs when an extreme trait goes rigid. Extreme trait scores are fine. There is nothing wrong with being an 80 on E, for example. Many salespersons are, and they flourish. However, when life takes a turn for the worse (prolonged disease, stress, poverty, or the like), it is possible that a person could lose the availability of BOTH ends of a trait continuum. For example, an E++ person spends a majority of time around other people, comfortable being in the thick of the action. However, even an E++ person needs, on occasion, to be alone, to be quiet, to pay the bills, do homework, and the like. It is when the E++ loses the energy to introvert, to close the door and be solitary, that one is in danger of losing a job or a relationship because unremitting extreme behavior is unbearable by loved ones and employers. Each extreme, N++, N- -, E++, E- -,and so forth, needs to be balanced by at least a small amount of its opposite, or complement. Reactives (N+) need to chill (N-) on occasion, Resilients (N-) need to react (N+) on occasion, and so forth. Reactives who NEVER chill, Resilients who NEVER react, Extraverts who NEVER introvert, Introverts who NEVER extravert, are unbearable, and society deems them unhealthy and in need of help, medication, treatment, or therapy. We mention this here, because personality disorders are, hopefully, a "state," and not permanent. But, they need attention.[1]

Looking Ahead

In the first two chapters of this section, we have focused on describing behavioral traits and their "states." In the next chapter, we will outline the remaining components of personality: abilities, physical states, memories, and values. Then we conclude this section with a chapter that "puts it all together" in a model that describes how we can all experience some form of "happiness," based on our traits, abilities, physical characteristics, memories, and values.

---

[1] For further reading on personality disorders in adolescence, consider *Personality Disorders in Children and Adolescents, by* Paulina F. Kernberg, Alan S. Weiner, & Karen K. Bardenstein. Basic Books, 2000.

3

Rounding Out the Whole Person

Abilities, Physical States, Memories, and Values

> One that reckoneth accounts all the day passeth not a happy moment. One that gladdeneth his heart all the day provideth not for his house. The bowman hitteth the mark, as the steersman reacheth land, by diversity of aim.
>
> --Ptah-hotep, Egyptian official and writer, c. 2400 B.C.E.
>
> All work and no play makes Jack a dull boy;
> All play and no work makes Jack a mere toy.
>
> --Maria Edgeworth, in *Harry and Lucy Concluded* (1825)

Guide to this chapter:

- Mental Abilities: Tools, Talents, and Contexts
- Physical Characteristics
- Memories
- Values: What They Are and How They Develop

We humans are complex creatures with a complex aim. We are not just a bag of behaviors, not just the Big Five traits of N, E, O, A, and C. We are also mental abilities, physical characteristics, memories, and values. The first two—abilities and physical characteristics—are primarily inherited (genetic/nature), as are traits. However, memories and values begin to accumulate at birth and develop over a lifetime (nurture). These four factors won't receive extensive analysis in this book, as they are beyond its scope, but they're worth some discussion because they do affect development of the personality. The section on mental abilities also gives a preview of our new matrix of tools and talents needed for specific careers.

All About Personality

N	E	O	A	C
Need for Stability	**Extraversion**	**Originality**	**Accommodation**	**Consolidation**
N+ Reactive	E+ Extravert	O+ Explorer	A+ Adapter	C+ Focused
N= Responsive	E= Ambivert	O= Moderate	A= Negotiator	C= Balanced
N- Resilient	E- Introvert	O- Preserver	A- Challenger	C- Flexible

Mental Abilities: Tools, Talents, and Contexts

Traditional description of mental ability, or intelligence, has focused on "general" mental ability, or "g." When one is said to have an IQ of 100, it is meant that one has an average amount of "g," of all-purpose intelligence, suggesting that one would be average at every aspect of mental endeavor: language, mathematics, history, competitive sports, entrepreneurship, music, art, philosophy, poker, dance—the list goes on. Someone with an above-average IQ, say 150, would be said to be above average in the same list of mental endeavors. However, this is clearly not the case. Michael Jordan, Yo-Yo Ma, Bill Gates, and J.K. Rowling are all brilliant, but not in the same way. Each has their unique, specific, or "s", form of intelligence. They are not interchangeable. Put them back in the first grade, they could still not magically acquire the others' expertise. Intelligence is not some form of universal modeling clay that can be shaped into whatever one wants. We each are born with our own specially composed modeling clay that each of us shapes into our own unique, special paths.

In this book, we favor the side of the IQ argument that stresses "s," for "specific" abilities/intelligence. We know, that a person can have above-average, even prodigious, ability in any one or more of the list above, while being average, or even abysmal, in other areas of mental endeavor. Having different levels of the many "special" mental abilities could be attributable to one of two causes: different levels of *native ability* (genetic predisposition), different levels of *perfected ability*, or a mix of the two types of ability. One might have above-average native ability in music, yet never develop that ability—no lessons, no choice of instrument, no practice, whether from lack of encouragement, lack of resources, or preference for developing other abilities. To the degree that all differences in ability are due to lack of practice and development, then the "g" theorists might be right. However, we know from studies of twins (e.g., Wright, 1998) that these various mental abilities/talents are just as native as they are perfected, just as genetic as they are learned, as are the various Big Five traits.

Just as we emphasize the importance of building on a person's unique behavioral traits, we also emphasize the importance of building on a person's unique mental ability level. In order to identify an individual's Big Five traits, one can take a simple questionnaire, such as the *SchoolPlace Big Five Profile.* Unfortunately, no single test currently exists that can measure (in one sitting) all of an individual's strengths among the various mental abilities. This is primarily because the "g" theorists have held sway for many years, advocating only the measurement of all-purpose mental ability. This all-purpose mental ability is comprised of verbal ability, mathematical/logical ability, and visual/spatial ability.

As many current scholars have pointed out (cf. Gardner, 1983; Sternberg, 1988; Carroll, 1993; Jacques, 1994), mental ability encompasses far more than verbal, mathematical, and spatial reasoning. Not only are there more than these three abilities that form "g," but every talent/mental ability is subject to different levels of performance depending on context (Ceci, 1990). For example, a math whiz in algebra can fail trying to figure out per-unit prices at the grocery store, while a per-unit pricing whiz can be stymied by the world of academic algebra. The context can make a huge difference in the performance level of a specific ability.

In order for an individual to assess personal areas of strength among the specific mental abilities/talents, we need a kind of map. From that map, an individual can work with a counselor, teacher, parent, or friend to determine personal strengths. As no map currently exists that integrates the thinking of all of the "s" theorists, we have put together our own map. Within five years, we at the Center for Applied Cognitive Studies hope to have completed a new assessment for identifying one's strengths among this broader set of specific mental abilities. So, let's take a look at the "map."

The map—which is actually a matrix, or a row-by-column presentation of the various mental abilities--comprises three dimensions: *tools*, *talents*, and *contexts*. The tools are like components of a computer operating system such as DOS or MAC. The talents are like a computer's application programs such as word processing, drawing, spreadsheets, and databases. By our definition, a "tool" is a function that each "talent" needs in order to do its work. For example, "random access memory" is a function of DOS and MAC that is provided for all of the application programs. Similarly, a person's "short term memory" is a function that is available to mathematicians, writers, artists, athletes, and poker players. Here is a list of the 18 "tools" that our minds must make available to each of our "talents":

The 18 Tools

1. Short Term Memory (Semantic)

Ability to retain factual information (names, telephone numbers, faces, chess board configurations, what cards have been played from each suit, dates, figures, facts, and so forth) for short periods of time, such as over the course of a few hours or even a day.

2. Short Term Memory (Procedural)

Ability to retain procedural (also called "episodic") information (sequences/steps, as in how to open, operate, or shut down a piece of equipment, how to bisect an angle, how to find the way to a new friend's house, how to find something online).

3. Long Term Memory (Semantic)

Ability to recognize and recall semantic information (i.e., facts) for a longer period of time, such as over the course of years, without daily or frequent review (e.g., a phone number, a poem, a friend's birth date, which coin is still missing from your collection).

4. Long Term Memory (Procedural)

Ability to recognize and recall procedural information for a longer period of time, such as over the course of years, without daily or frequent review (e.g., how to tie a bow tie, how to make a proper caramel icing, how to play a card game, how to train a puppy, how to knit, how to ride a bike, how to swing a baseball bat).

5. Organizing (Spatial Arrangement)

Ability to sort (i.e., categorize) various kinds of information into two- or -three-dimensional space. Content could be either

- concrete (e.g., marbles to group by size, recipe ingredients to arrange in order of use),
- abstract (e.g., elements of an essay in preparation for writing, a series of mathematical expressions),
- semantic (e.g., different kinds of marbles—aggies, steelies, etc.), or
- procedural (rules for different kinds of games using marbles).

Organizing includes identifying emergent categories (e.g., conducting triage in an emergency room or disaster scene [who is ok, who is hurt a little, and who needs immediate help] or creating categories of folders for storing emails/IMs. Organizing additionally includes selecting from a list containing distracters (e.g., in studying for a test or preparing for a research paper, sorting available information into "highly relevant," "moderately relevant," and "irrelevant").

6. Planning (Sequential Arrangement)

Ability to sort various kinds of information into a logical sequence—according to time, urgency, hierarchical relationship, linearity, importance, and so forth. Includes both concrete content (e.g., the steps involved in making something) and abstract content (e.g., the steps involved in negotiating).

7. Evaluation of Information

Ability to inspect a body of information (e.g., text, spreadsheet, diagram, photograph) and identify errors, omissions, and changes (e.g., proofreading, editing, comparing an original painting to a copy).

8. Critical Thinking

Ability to examine a body of information (e.g., text, spreadsheet, diagram, photograph) and then identify assumptions, spot logical fallacies, see causal relationships, select logical conclusions, and solve problems (e.g., preparing for a debate, writing a critical review, giving someone feedback on a presentation or performance, preparing a presentation, editing what we have each written in this book).

9. Composition

Ability to create an effective composition on the fly (e.g., speech, spreadsheet, diagram, game plan, improvisational dance, clever excuse for "lost" homework).

10. Presentation

Upon being given the text/script/steps/music/diagram for a presentation (prepared by oneself or by another), ability to present the material effectively (e.g., speech, dance, song, athletic maneuver).

11. Imagination

Ability to come up with an idea that is both novel and effective (e.g., a new way of saying something, as in a slogan; a new mathematical expression to show a relationship among variables, a new movement pattern to accomplish an unusual physical challenge, an interesting way to graph data, a new strategy for trying to persuade a person in power to agree with you).

12. Fluency

Once a novel suggestion has been made for #11, brainstorming ability to generate a number of additional suggestions, regardless of novelty or effectiveness (e.g., come up with a dozen new slogans that express the same meaning, a dozen strategies for persuading a person in power).

13. Elaboration

Ability to take a basic body of information (e.g., text, spreadsheet, diagram) and develop modifications, additions, deletions, and spin-off bodies of information (e.g., take a spreadsheet designed for one purpose and adapt it for another purpose, take a speech written for an all-male audience and adapt it for an all female audience, take a sports analogy and apply it to politics).

14. Learning from Context

Ability to determine the meaning of an unfamiliar symbol or object (e.g., word, phrase, formula, gesture, piece of equipment) by using contextual or environmental clues (e.g., read a description that contains an unknown/unfamiliar word substituted for a familiar word and figure out from context what the nonsense word is, i.e., what the original familiar word was; study a mathematical formula with a novel symbol and figure out its function from context; study a football play or dance movement that contains a novel symbol and figure out its meaning/function).

15. Judgment

Upon being presented with a problem situation that requires the exercise of good judgment, ability to select accurate alternative responses and to exhibit flexibility in selecting types of responses (changing yourself, changing the other person, or changing the situation). For example, you are convinced that a teacher is grading you low for personal reasons; you are given 15 possible strategies to pursue in order to improve the relationship, and you must select the best three strategies to implement.

16. Processing Speed

Ability to complete any of the above mental tasks (1 to 15) quickly, adjusted for accuracy (e.g., how quickly you can think up a new slogan, how quickly you can recall a memory).

17. Time to Mastery

Given a novel skill to learn, how long it takes one to attain mastery (e.g., how long it takes to accurately learn some basic vocabulary and grammar in a new language or to accurately use some made-up mathematical symbols in a college admissions test).

18. Time Span

The amount of time one can work independently without significant help from a boss, teacher, parent, or other expert (e.g., build a computer simulation over a three-year period, start a school club or a business venture and run it for three months before needing major help, design a special community service project/implement it/be interviewed about it in your local newspaper so you can use it for your college application, work alone for one year on a science project, write a novel over a two-year span).

The Eight Talents

As you likely noticed in the examples given for the 18 tools, different areas of ability/talent appeared for each tool. Short Term Memory (Semantic), for example, is a tool available for use with names, chess board configurations, and telephone numbers. Each of these three examples represents a specific domain or area of talent: names are part of the Language, or Verbal, talent domain, chess configurations belong to the Visual/Spatial talent domain, and telephone numbers belong to the Math/Logical talent domain. These are three of the eight talents, or "multiple intelligences," identified through the extensive research of Howard Gardner (1983). While we only cite one book here, a huge literature has grown up around Gardner's MI (multiple intelligences) theory. School curriculum experts have developed programs that use the content of these eight areas to teach basic skills. This approach is based on the understanding that any given child will excel in at least one talent area, or, if not excel, will have at least one talent area that is stronger than other areas. The goal is to use a child's talent, the area of greatest interest/ability, for learning the basic skills. The 18 "tools" that we have just listed are in fact the basic skills, and the research shows us that an individual can have a tool/skill in one talent area that is not necessarily as strong in other talent areas. For example, a child might have excellent Evaluation skills (finding errors) in the Auditory talent area (as in detecting a sour note played by a band or orchestra), but not so much talent in finding spelling errors (Verbal talent) or in balancing a bank account (Math talent).

The goal of introducing all of this material is to help an individual develop an accurate sense of identity based on individual strengths. In Chapter 24, we show how this strength profile (comprised of traits, abilities, physical characteristics, memories, and values) should guide one's choice of a career. For now, let's proceed with identifying all eight of Gardner's "talents." After each definition, we will suggest a famous person who exhibits the specific talent. Then we will offer a map in the form of a matrix that shows how the Tools and Talents fit together. This matrix can be used by any individual to describe personal strengths with respect to mental abilities.

1. Language/Verbal talent

Fluency and comprehension in the use of language involves grammar, phonology (ability to understand and produce shades of difference in the sound of speech—this overlaps with the Auditory talent), rhetoric (matching language to audience), vocabulary, composition, and presentations. Example*:* J.R.R. Tolkien, British author of *The Hobbit* and *The Lord of the Rings.*

2. Numbers/Math/Logical talent

Capability in mathematical and logical operations involves basic computations, use of math and logic symbols, understanding of calculational formulas and how numbers relate to each other in spreadsheets. Example: Bill Gates, founder of Microsoft.

3. Visual/Spatial talent

Accurate perception (detecting similarities, differences, and meanings) of two- and three-dimensional objects involves the ability to rotate them mentally and recognize them from nonobvious perspectives. Example: Steven Spielberg, producer/director of innumerable movies from *E.T.* to *Saving Private Ryan.*

4. Hearing/Auditory/Music talent

Ability to produce and discriminate between a variety of sounds involves sensitivity to pitch, rhythm, timbre, and volume, both in musical and other (e.g., machines) settings. Example: Alicia Keys, rhythm and blues vocalist and winner of multiple Grammy Awards.

5. Physical/Kinesthetic talent

Ability to understand, execute, control, and coordinate a wide variety of bodily movements involves eye-hand coordination, speed, balance, depth judgment, stamina, and principles of physical health and endurance. Example: Lebron James, NBA phenomenon.

6. Relations/Interpersonal talent

Ability to recognize and manage the feelings, needs, and opinions of others involves body language, social graces, techniques to influence, conflict management, and delegation techniques. Example: Oprah Winfrey, television host famous for her ability to empathize with and help others.

7. Thinking/Intrapersonal talent

Ability to recognize and manage one's own feelings, needs, and mental processes involves self-control, objective analysis, blind spots, risk evaluation, and hidden agendas. *Example:* the Dalai Lama, exiled spiritual leader of Tibetan Buddhism.

8. Natural Observer/Taxonomy/Knowledge Building talent

Ability to survey a part of the natural world (e.g., a body of knowledge, an industry, an organization, a type of product or service) and create/understand/manipulate/use a taxonomy that organizes the area in a way that portrays how all of the elements are related. Example: George Washington Carver, Tuskegee Institute professor who, among other achievements, discovered 300+ uses for the peanut.

The Matrix of Tools and Talents

Now that we have identified the 18 Tools and the eight Talents, let's look at how they fit together. Again, imagine the tools as features of a computer operating system, with the talents as application

Table 3.1 Examples of Careers that Draw Upon Specific Mental Tools in Specific Talent Areas

Talents / Tools	Language	Numbers	Visual	Hearing	Physical	Relations	Thinking	Observer
Semantic STM*	Interpreter	Clerk, Accountant	Detective	Sonar Operator	Weight Lifter, Gym Trainer	Salesperson	Therapist	Botanist
Procedural STM*	Debater, TV News	Statistician	Chemist	Mechanic	Dancer	Trial Lawyer	Therapist	Meteorologist
Semantic LTM*	Public -Speaker	Engineer	Art Historian	Musicologist	Sports Writer	Salesperson	Therapist	Botanist
Procedural LTM*	Linguist	Statistician	Intelligence Analyst	Vocalist	NFLQuarterback	Business Consultant	Therapist	Meteorologist
Organizing	Journalist	Budget Analyst	Museum Administrator	Orchestra Conductor	Choreographer	Manager	Philosopher	Archaeologist
Planning	Technical Writer	Project Manager	Graphic Designer	Composer	Athletic Coach	Manager	Researcher	Environmentalist
Evaluating	Magazine Editor	Tax Accountant	Art Authenticator	Audio Engineer	Ergonomist	Drama Coach/ Director	Essayist	OSHA Inspector
Critical Thinking	Book Reviewer	Industrial Psychologist	Art Teacher	Record/ Radio Producer	Athletic Coach	Interviewer	Therapist	Environmentalist
Composition	Writer	Code Writer	Architect Int. Design	Composer	Choreographer	Proposal Writer	News Editor	Naturalist
Presentation	Actor	Software Engineer	Media Producer	Instrumentalist	Athlete	Plant Superintendent	Professor	Environmental Advocate
Imagination	Poet	Architect	Interior Designer	Composer	Choreographer	Advertising Writer	R & D Inventor	Explorer
Fluency	Stand Up Comic	Design Engineer	Graphic Designer	Jazz Musician	Improvisation Dance	Executive Coach	R&D Inventor	Home/Office Organizer
Elaboration	Journalist	Software Engineer	Clothing Designer	Composer	Surgeon	Meeting Facilitator	Columnist	City Planner
Learning from Context	Undercover Cop	Purchasing Agent	Intelligence Analyst	Mechanic Audiologist	NFL Quarterback	Business Consultant	Therapist	Military Strategist
Judgment	Journalist	Market Analyst	Drama Director	Mechanic	Coach Phys. Ther.	Social Worker	Sales	Quality Engineer
Processing Speed	Press Secretary	Broadcast Statisti-Cian	Air Traffic Controller	Jazz Musician	Race Car Driver	Salesperson	Therapist	Military Forward Observer
Time to Mastery	Talk Show Host	Cryptographer	Intelligence Analyst	Instrumental Soloist	Athletic Coach	Salesperson Auctioneer	Spy	Military Forward Observer
Time Span	Book Author	Software Engineer	Architect	Composer	High Performance Athlete	Business Executive	Spy, Wall Street Analyst	Environmental Scientist

* STM = Short Term Memory; LTM = Long Term Memory.

programs on the computer. Just as one operating system might not support a particular application program as well as another operating system (e.g., we've experienced early DOS versions providing better tools for processing numbers, as in spreadsheets, and early MAC versions providing better tools for processing graphics and words), one person's body/brain complex might support a particular talent better than another person's. In short, within a particular person's body, the tools available for, say, semantic long term memory, might not be as effective with numbers as with words and images. In Table 3.1, you will find one example for each cell in this 8 x 18 matrix. We have not tried to be complete—i.e., we have not tried to list EVERY example possible for every cell. For any given cell in the matrix, there might be hundreds, even thousands of examples that we could list. For the sake of introducing this concept, we limited the examples to one per cell.

Table 3.2 Template for Tools/Talents Required for Competency: "Sales Performance"

Tools:	Language	Numbers	Visual	Sounds	Physical Movement	People/ Relations	Internal States	Organizational Schemes
1. Remembering Facts/Things (Short Term Memory--Semantic)	✓	✓				✓		✓
2. Remembering Procedures (Short Term Memory--Episodic)	✓					✓	✓	✓
3. Remembering (Long Term Memory)	✓					✓		✓
4. Organizing	✓	✓				✓		
5. Planning	✓					✓		✓
6. Evaluating	✓	✓	✓			✓	✓	✓
7. Critical Thinking	✓	✓	✓			✓		✓
8. Composing	✓	✓						
9. Presenting	✓	✓	✓	✓	✓	✓	✓	✓
10. Processing Speed								
11. Imagining								
12. Fluency								
13. Time to Mastery								
14. Elaborating		✓						
15. Learning from Context								
16. Judging						✓		
17. Time Span to Act						✓		

All About Personality

Notice that some careers are repeated. We have allowed some careers/jobs to be entered two or more times to make the point that a career is not built on a single tool/talent combination, but is likely based on multiple cells, or tool/talent combinations. In fact, we have done some research on the tool/talent combinations required for the competency of "Sales Performance." In Table 3.2, you will find the results of that analysis. We refer to this kind of table as a "template of tools/talents required for a competency." Currently, we are preparing such templates for over 100 such competencies including leadership skills, listening skills, presentation skills, strategic thinking, conflict management, and on and on. Keep in mind that these "templates" are intended for general use. In other words, "sales performance" is a general competency, and the tools/talents we've identified are for sales roles across a wide variety of contexts. In order to apply this template to a specific context, such as "salesperson for high school yearbook," or "salesperson for large auditorium sound systems," we could use our general sales performance template as a starting point, but we would need to tailor it to the specific context. For example, some of the Auditory talent domain tools would be appropriate for the "sound systems" sales role, but not for the "high school yearbook" sales role.

This completes our discussion of the mental abilities aspect of personality. In a few years, we expect to have written another book that goes into much more detail on Tools and Talents, and how they relate to individual performance/behavior in school and society. Now, let's turn to physical characteristics, the third inherited component (remember: when we say "inherited," we mean "primarily inherited," because everything that is inherited is subject to some degree of environmental influence).

Physical Characteristics

As we mentioned in Chapter 1, physical characteristics are neither behaviors nor skills. They are attributes of our bodies that make us more similar or more different than others. These characteristics don't really cluster into natural groups the way that behaviors and skills cluster into different traits and abilities. In spite of this, we have attempted to group them into characteristics that are more apparent to others (exterior characteristics) and those that are more internal, less visible to others (although such characteristics as speed are, in fact, visible). These physical characteristics are like a geographical map of how our bodies are laid out:

Exterior Characteristics:

- height/weight
- eye and hair color
- skin color/texture/scars/wrinkles
- tooth color/dental work
- nervous tics
- congenital deformities
- voice quality
- nail quality/length/color
- hair quantity/length/baldness/texture
- engineered additions (prosthetics, implants, aids, artificial joints/parts, crutches)

- date of puberty/maturation (early vs. late)[1]

Interior Characteristics:

The Five Senses

- sensitivity of skin to sunlight
- sensitivity of eyes to light/dark/color
- sensitivity of touch—texture/ temperature/pressure
- sensitivity to noise
- auditory acuity
- visual acuity
- sensitivity to intensity/quality of odors
- taste preferences/sensitivities
- taste acuity
- general tolerance for sensory pain/pleasure
- drug tolerance

Muscular/Skeletal

- strength
- dexterity
- sense of balance
- hand-eye coordination
- length of limbs
- reaction speed
- handedness
- tendency to motion-sickness
- flexibility
- endurance
- speed
- strength of teeth/gums

Other Interior

- sensitivity of digestive system to specific flavors, spices, etc.
- allergies
- sleep requirements
- ease of falling asleep, waking up
- genetic predispositions for specific diseases/disorders

---

[1] Nancy Cobb (2007, p. 82ff.) talks about problems associated with early/late maturation. However, research is mixed, e.g., some early maturing teens having an advantage socially while others suffer. An early-maturing boy who has to shave and whose shoulders are broad might have an advantage for being elected or sought for leadership roles. However, such physical maturity could have the dangerous effect of making it natural for him to associate with older boys, though he lacks the social maturity necessary to handle the risky behaviors he might encounter around them. Whether early maturity, for a girl or boy, is a benefit or a problem is clearly influenced by traits. For example, an early maturer low in N and high in C is more likely to resist encounters with alcohol, sex, and drugs more common around older kids, while N+C- early maturers, being more impulsive, could easily have problems resisting temptations when with the older teens.

- sensitivity to weather extremes/air pressure

For a specific career, one or more of these areas of physical characteristics might be relevant. Endurance is more important for soccer players, speed for racers, ease of falling asleep for persons in noisy/stressful environments, sensitivity to extreme weather for outdoor work, quirky palates for work involving much international travel, strength for material handlers, and so forth.

So, how should this list be used? In two ways: 1) to identify remarkable strengths in any of these areas on which it would be natural to build a career, and 2) once having identified possible careers, review this list to see if there are any physical characteristics that could enhance or threaten possible success in one or more of one's chosen careers.

As we will see in Chapter 28, choice of a career needs to take into consideration the relevant traits, abilities, physical characteristics, memories, and values. We will complete our explanation now with brief discussions of memories and values.

Memories

Some nonmainstream theorists maintain that we come into the world with memories—so-called archetypes (memories passed to us from our collective ancestors). We do not adhere to this way of thinking. Our experience and study lead us to conclude that memories form after birth, with one's capacity for remembering relatively well-developed by the age of four. Earlier memories—of experiences before the fourth birthday—can be helped along by parents and other close persons by frequently inviting the child to describe/narrate the experience, as in "Stella, tell Aunt Alle what we did in the park yesterday." With frequent repetition over time, children are able to form and retain such very early memories, but it appears to take concerted effort. At the age of four, such prodigious effort is not required.

Memories are important in personality formation for two primary reasons: First, they shape our personal notions of the various roles we must play in life (how to behave in a particular role, e.g., parent, grandparent, teacher, coach, leader), how to punish bad behavior, how to reward good behavior, how to occupy spare time, how to maintain a house, and so forth). Second, they provide signals for our emotions to activate (e.g., we learn to be scared around snakes, to be angry at intrusions, to be embarrassed or indignant at poor manners). Thus, memories influence our role behavior and our emotional behavior. Memories do not dictate our behavior, they just shape behavior. For example, we inherit the tendency to be patient, but when we finally lose our patience, we are likely to behave in a way that expresses a composite memory (often referred to as a "schema"). For example, we might be patient and let an infant cry for some period of time to see if they will stop crying (others with different genes would intervene much sooner), but, when we finally pick up the child, we would likely treat it in accordance with a memory/schema. So, if we were close to Aunt Sadie growing up, and Aunt Sadie picked up the crying child, sat in the rocking chair, and sang a soothing lullaby while rubbing the infant's back, we would be likely to "reincarnate" or reenact the schema of Aunt Sadie and do likewise with the child.

Important memories, both those that shape roles and those that shape emotions, are formed at different times, different places, and with different role models throughout our lives:

- Times:
    - day care
    - kindergarten
    - elementary school
    - middle school/junior high school
    - high school
    - higher education
    - military service
    - early work experience
- Places:
    - homes
    - neighborhoods
    - schools
    - religious organizations
    - places of work
    - community places (recreation centers, grocery stores, and so forth)
    - vacation spots
    - foreign travel[2]
    - military service assignments
    - club hangouts
    - summer camps
    - friends' homes/backyards
- Roles:
    - parents
    - teachers
    - grandparents
    - religious leaders
    - professors
    - bosses
    - politicians
    - librarians
    - caregivers

---

[2] I (Pierce) remember traveling as a Boy Scout to Sweden as part of an exchange program when I was turning 16. I had thought of Sweden as a socialist, godless society and was mildly apprehensive of what I would encounter. On my first night in my hosts' home, I was tired from travel. They recognized my fatigue and ushered me immediately into my bedroom, not expecting me to stay up with them and talk, and shut the door to give me privacy and rest. As I made my way to the bedside, I found a glass of milk, a peanut butter sandwich, and a bag of M&Ms. I decided on the spot that, if my hosts were atheists and socialists, then it was clearly possible for atheists and socialists to be good people! This continues to be a strong memory for me and shapes how I feel about foreigners, foreign travel, and about being wary of stereotypes. As a person naturally high in O, this experience/memory nudged me a little higher than I might otherwise be—somewhat more comfortable with change and novelty than I might have been.

- coaches
- doctors
- nurses
- students
- writers
- artists
- siblings
- community organization leaders
- police officers
- athletes
- maintenance workers
- hobbyists
- money managers
- gardeners

So, how do we use memories from these times, places, and roles in the formation of our personality, the shaping of our identity, or the choice of our career? We can consciously pick the memories in each of these areas, record the ones for which we have strongly positive and negative emotional associations, and then include this information in determining what to avoid and what to aim for as we make choices about school, career, life partner, major goals, and so forth.

As a young teacher in an inner-city junior high school, I (Jane) came face-to-face with the fact that my first career choice was not meeting my expectations. I loved the students, but most of my colleagues were jaded and thought that nothing could get through to the students because of their environmental challenges. Most of the older teachers were eagerly counting the weeks until they could retire, the shop teacher roamed the halls with a wooden paddle threatening any student if they misbehaved (he also constantly uttered comments to me that would now be considered sexually harassing), and the principal spoke to the entire school over the public-address system every morning using bad grammar.

I found myself remembering and longing to be back working in the office of Dr. John Stewart, the Dean of Fine Arts at my university. As I had worked to support myself through my college years, Dr. Stewart appointed me to run the office my senior year. I made assignments to other working students, planned work schedules, graded papers, ran scholarship auditions, and made preparations for incoming students. After obtaining an M.B.A. degree, I was ultimately able to combine teaching/coaching/training adults into a very satisfying career after starting my own business with Pierce.

On a different front, I (Pierce) have a strong memory of my two commanding officers while stationed with the U.S. Army in Bad Tölz, Germany, in the mid-1960s. The first CO was energetic, cocky, presumptious, and expected me to do most of the grunt work while he schmoozed and conducted "liaison" activities. The second CO was also energetic, but he was humble, thoughtful, personable, socialized with me after work hours, and did his share of the grunt work. Guess who my model for management became? (Well, I *like* to think I am more like the second guy!)

Values: What They Are and How They Develop

Values, like memories, are developed over time. What are values? The word comes from the Latin *valere,* meaning "to be worth something." Today, we use the word "value" in the sense of a set of beliefs focused on a core meaning that is of special importance, or value, to an individual. If someone espouses the value of *materialism*, then they might subscribe to one or more of these materialistic beliefs:

- It is important to acquire many things.
- The things one possesses should be as fine as possible.
- A brand name is a significant indicator of a thing's worth.
- The more things one has, the better.
- It is important to have more things than certain other people.
- It is important to have higher quality things than other people have.
- and so forth

Not all persons espousing "materialism" would have identical sets of beliefs around the core meaning of "possessing things"—some may emphasize quality, some quantity. They as a group, however, would be unlikely to espouse any of the beliefs of an opposite value, such as "spiritualism," with a set of beliefs such as:

- one should only possess things that are essential to basic needs
- less is better
- one should share with others
- one should cultivate nonmaterial pursuits, such as prayer, exercise, hard work, reading, the art of conversation/dialog, the acquisition of knowledge, and caregiving
- and so forth

There is no single, definitive, exhaustive list of values. And, unlike materialism and spiritualism, not all values really have an opposite value. Knowledge is a value, for example, but surely no one espouses ignorance as a value. Many researchers have attempted to develop complete lists of values, but they always seem to leave out something significant to someone. Values are, ultimately, personally defined. One of the more recent efforts to compile a complete list was led by Katherine Dahlsgaard. Her group read over 200 catalogs of virtues and strengths (to us, other ways of saying "values") from the Upanishads to Ben Franklin. Their results (a list of 24 "virtues" are summarized by Martin Seligman (one of the research team) in his book *Authentic Happiness* (2002). We will provide here our own list of values that people commonly espouse. While it is closely based on Dahlsgaard's list, we have added a few we think were needed:

achievement	friendship	professionalism
aesthetics	health	renunciation
affiliation	hedonism	romance
beauty	learning	safety
charity	maintenance	security
compassion	materialism	spirituality

creativity	politics	sport
entertainment	position	tolerance
escape	poverty/asceticism	wealth
family	power	

Any two people espousing the same value would not necessarily express their common value in the same way. Someone espousing "charity" might base it on the belief that giving *money* to worthy causes is important, while another person espousing charity might base it on the belief that giving *time* to worthy causes is important. The core meaning is "to give a portion of one's possessions to others." This does not necessarily include giving to causes that are worthy in society's eyes, only in the charitable person's eyes. And the amount one gives can vary widely among a myriad of people, all of whom espouse the common value of charity: At one extreme, one might give only what one doesn't need personally, another might give a standard percent, and another might give to the limits of personal danger (as in depriving oneself of health-inducing resources in order to give to others).

Values are different from traits, abilities, and physical characteristics. The latter three ingredients of personality start as 100% genetic, and then over time can be influenced somewhat by experience. Values, on the other hand, tend to begin by the urging of one's parents, guardians, family members, religious leaders, peers, teachers, youth workers, employers, and so forth. My dad (Pierce's) said frequently, "Son, do something every day you don't want to do." That was good advice for someone who was not prone to be maintenance-oriented. While maintenance/preservation is not one of my stronger values today, it is sufficiently strong for me to do a modest number of maintenance chores. As I spend a half hour filing, I see and hear my dad saying, "Son, do something every day…." And I smile ever so slightly. We tend to embrace the values of persons we admire, respect, and wish to emulate. I (Pierce) admired two of my parents' best friends, two ladies, one of whom was a voracious reader (and mother of a good friend), the other a fine classical musician (and my piano teacher/youth choir director). Today, these contribute to two of my most cherished values: learning and aesthetics.

However, based on one's experiences, it is likely that some of one's inherited traits, abilities, and physical characteristics will be incorporated into one's unique version of a value. In the two cases just mentioned, Mrs. Peery and Miss Jessie's interests attached themselves to several of my traits, abilities, and physical characteristics to shape my values of learning and aesthetics:

- Learning
    - I was born with high O, with a natural broad range of interests, curiosity, and love of novelty.
    - I was born with good verbal ability (not outstanding, but good), which made reading come naturally.
    - I was born with poor eyesight/myopia (I'm 20/800 without glasses), which made other pursuits, such as sports, less natural.
- Aesthetics/Music
    - Again, I was born with high O, which makes interest in the arts a natural one.
    - I was born with high Auditory acuity: I could easily match pitches tell the difference between instruments, voices, etc., which made it natural for me to learn to read music and enjoy it.

- I was born overly sensitive to loud noise—I've never liked crowds and loud anything. To this day, I have a strong aversion to amplified music—it gives me a headache. This made it natural for me to prefer the more nuanced sounds of chamber music, my favorite.

Had I not been born with high O, weak eyes, aversion to loud noise, good verbal ability, and excellent auditory acuity, then Mrs. Peery and Miss Jessie would not likely have influenced me in the way they did, but they still could have influenced me in other ways, based on other traits, abilities, and physical characteristics that fit with some of their interests. Miss Jessie was active politically, for example, but my lower extraversion leads me away from the political arena (also my dislike of loud noises!).

Your Values: Mature or Immature?

Back in the 1970s, the "values clarification" movement was popular, ultimately to be run out of many schools by parents who thought it "communistic." This school of thought is due for a revival—it is clearly not communistic, and is a helpful way for one to do a kind of self-study of what is truly important. According to the theorists (cf. Simon, Howe, & Kirschenbaum, 1995), values clarification focuses on a seven-step process that encourages one to examine the degree to which one's values are mature (i.e., the result of thoughtful analysis) or immature (i.e., simply accepted hook, line, and sinker from some authority, whether parent, peer, or priest). By asking these seven questions, in sequence, and in a variety of ways (interviews, exercises, journals, and so forth), one can get a sense of exactly how mature a particular value is. Below, we list the seven questions, and briefly examine my (Pierce's) value of "chamber music" in light of these questions. (Note: Chamber music is a specific value that is a part of my larger umbrella value of aesthetics.)

The Seven Steps of Values Clarification:

1. Did you choose the value *freely*?

   Yes. My parents were not chamber musicians, although my mother played piano alone. My father was essentially tone deaf. My high school band director invited me to play in a woodwind quintet for a state contest, and that was the beginning.

2. Did you choose it from *among alternatives*, or were no alternatives considered?

   Yes. I tried playing with a swing band, a large orchestra, a marching band, a concert band, a jazz improvisation group, and a rock group, and none satisfied me like traditional chamber music—solos, duets, trios, quartets, and so forth from the world's historically great composers, mostly with one person playing on a part.

3. Did your choice follow a *consideration of the consequences* that this choice would entail?

   I suspect so. I considered that I might be branded as a "long hair" musician who was not hip/cool. For some reason, being cool was never important to me. I also considered that chamber music is something that is very easy to make happen, in that you do not have to assemble a large group, only a few people. And it didn't require a special place like a rehearsal hall.

4. Do you personally feel really good about your choice?

Yes. I feel like a member of a rather small group. Globally, there are hundreds of thousands of chamber musicians. Locally, the number is rather small. There's something about me that doesn't like moving/being with large groups. I'm also rather impatient with poor musicians; with chamber music, I can choose to play with people at a similar level of expertise. Sometimes I think I would like to play with an orchestra, but the feeling flees.

5. Do you share your strong feelings about the choice/value with others?

Not all that much—it is more of a private thing. Also, from a business relations point of view, I don't think it would be in my best interests to talk about Haydn's London Trios with a business client. Most would prefer talking about Tiger Woods or Britney Spears. My business ideas are likely to be thought strange and not mainstream/valid if they think my personal hobbies are strange and not mainstream. I've heard clients say that about other consultants. So I keep my interests to myself, for the most part. (Kenji Yoshino [2006] calls this "covering" in his book by the same name.)

6. Do you act on your chosen value, i.e., do you walk your talk?

Yes, as I manage to play (or sing) some chamber music at least once a month, and I practice my instrument (recorder) almost daily, as I keep it on a music stand beside my desk, and practice difficult passages by Bach, Vivaldi, etc., while occasionally waiting for my computer to finish some command I've just given it. I also perform frequently with Jane, who has a lovely mezzo-soprano voice.

7. Have you acted only singly, or do you act repeatedly, so as to develop a life style patterning it?

I suppose I act repeatedly, but not as much as I could. I would like to subscribe to one or more magazines, such as the American Recorder Society's, but just haven't done so. Also, I should put more time into maintenance of my instruments, as they are made of fine woods and need annual rubdowns with linseed oil to prevent, or at least forestall, cracking.

It is important to keep in mind that, although a value may be mature, that does not mean that it is a sociably desirable one. A mafia boss could have a mature value about murder. Also, although a value may be immature, that does not mean that it is a sociably undesirable one. A person could volunteer at a homeless shelter without giving it anything like the analytical thought of this seven-step process; yet society would welcome this expression of value. However, this same person could "mature" the value of charity/aiding the down-and-out by subjecting it to this simple but thoughtful analysis in such a way that the value could become even more satisfying.

Putting the Pieces of the Person Together

So, now we have the huge puzzle of personality comprising five [sets of] pieces, three originating in the genes (traits, abilities, and physical characteristics) and two originating in experience (memories and values). Our totality as a person is a mixture of these five sets of ingredients. Our choices of career, lifestyle, our motivators, our spirituality, our hobbies can all be explained as stemming from these five sets of raw materials, the stuff of personality. In the next chapter, we will see how all of these pieces come together to create the possibility for a person to feel a sense of satisfaction with the way his/her life is going—what psychologists call "subjective well being," and what most others call "happiness."

4

Putting It All Together

A Framework for Happiness

> "The Constitution only gives you the right to pursue happiness. You have to catch it yourself."
>
> --Ben Franklin, 18th century polymath and a founding father of the U.S.

Guide to this chapter:

- The Process of Identity Formation
- The Palette of Who We Are
- Happiness Is Goodness of Fit—Between Who We Are and Who We Are Busy Trying to Be
- Human Resource Optimization—the Mechanism for Improving Fit/Happiness

Nancy Cobb (2007) in her text on adolescence writes (p. 136) that the teen years are best understood as a process of making decisions and setting goals for the purpose of increasing autonomy and establishing greater individuation from family and others. In a sense, the teen years are about gaining personal control through establishing how one is unique. "I am a chamber musician." "I am an 'A' student." "I am the fastest thing on two feet." "I am a tech junkie." As we have seen in the first three chapters, the raw material of who we are comprises behavioral traits (the Big Five), mental abilities (Tools and Talents), physical characteristics, memories, and values. It is by discovering these raw materials and building with them, that we develop our sense of self, our sense of identity, and then individuate ourselves from the masses. To acknowledge our raw materials ("I am solitary, creative, competitive...") is the essential task of development. James Baldwin once said that he had to organize his life around "the way my blood beats." He had to acknowledge his native traits, abilities, physical characteristics, memories, and values and give them expression in how he lived his life.

In order to identify our raw materials, the palette of who we are, we must constantly be in discussions with family, peers, and others on the subject of how we are similar to and different from others. Healthy development is associated with open discussion of differences between a teen and those around the young person—discussion in which the teen is open in expressing thoughts about

N	E	O	A	C
Need for Stability	**Extraversion**	**Originality**	**Accommodation**	**Consolidation**
N+ Reactive	E+ Extravert	O+ Explorer	A+ Adapter	C+ Focused
N= Responsive	E= Ambivert	O= Moderate	A= Negotiator	C= Balanced
N- Resilient	E- Introvert	O- Preserver	A- Challenger	C- Flexible

self, as well as receptive to feedback/observation from others. The goal here is "individuation" and open, two-way communication with at least one adult (especially one parent) is critical. Teens need to feel both different from and connected to others. One of the best ways to do this is to understand how someone different from you needs—or doesn't need—your opposite quality.

The Process of Identity Formation

Costa and McCrae (2003) propose (p. 187ff.) that identity begins with biology and is propelled by its daily interaction with social forces. Biology defines our basic tendencies, such as traits and mental abilities. Our basic tendencies run up against the realities, the demands, the constraints, of everyday reality. We get knocked down, encouraged, admonished, blamed, praised, and so forth as we stumble through letting our biology lead. As we run up against reactions to who we are, we begin forming attitudes, values, goals, self-concepts, roles, skills, habits, beliefs, and vocabulary. The dynamic processes that help us adapt in these ways include perception, reasoning, role playing, and coping strategies. All of this happens against the backdrop of events that are local (divorce, gangs, promotions), regional (drought, religious fervor, financial conditions), national (laws, customs, language), or global (war, culture clashes).

"Don't laugh at a youth for his affectations; he is only trying on one face after another to find a face of his own."
--Logan Pearsall Smith,
"Age and Death,"
Afterthoughts. 1931

Cobb (2007, p. 141) writes that Eric Erikson identified three critical areas in which youth need to develop a clear sense of self: gender role, career, and ideology. They, with illustrative examples, are:

- Gender Role:
  - How are girls and boys different, if at all?
  - When is it proper for me as a girl/boy to initiate, criticize, and so forth?
  - Can I engage in activities that are sexually stereotyped—cooking, auto mechanics, sewing, hunting, typing, playing the tuba—without being stereotyped by others or without my feeling stereotyped?
- Career Choice:
  - I am going to be a doctor—a surgeon, probably an orthopedic surgeon, like my dad/mom.
  - I am trying to decide between a career in the military, in government service, or as a missionary.
- Ideology:
  - I am a liberal Democrat.
  - I am a jihadist working for the establishment of the Prophet's law on earth.
  - I am a humanist working for world peace and/or a sustainable environment.

As youth attempt to define themselves in terms of gender, career, and ideology, two processes are at work: "commitment" and "exploration." Commitment is the degree to which one has chosen for eternity where one stands on a particular issue. These are the two levels:

- Low Commitment: Haven't decided, the jury's still out, the book's still open, still doing my research.
- High Commitment: Have made up my mind, have joined the bandwagon, am wearing my belief on my sleeve and taking my stand.

Exploration is the degree to which one is actively seeking information, opinion, feedback, alternatives, and so forth with respect to a particular issue. These are the two levels of exploration:

- Low Exploration: Am not looking for any information, not important for me.
- High Exploration: Am actively seeking information on one or more particular issues.

According to the model developed by James Marcia et al. (1993; reported in Cobb, 2007, p. 142ff.), these two processes form a two-by-two table with four quadrants, each representing a combination of commitment or exploration in its lower or higher forms. Table 4.1 presents this table, along with definitions of the four states of identify formation.

Table 4.1 The Exploration/Commitment Model of Identity Formation

		Exploration	
		Low	High
Commitment	Low	"Moratorium"—Neither actively engaged in exploration nor committed to a definite sense of self/values/etc., often because of fear of making wrong choices.	"Diffused"—Actively exploring with no strong commitment to any permanent sense of self or values, often because do not feel the need to make such a commitment.
	High	"Foreclosed"—Committed to a set of values and not actively exploring; typically this involves accepting, values handed down by parents.	"Achieved"—Committed to a set of values after having undergone a period of exploration; perhaps still able to explore.

According to this model, four typical states are used to describe a youth's position. Those in moratorium are neither exploring nor committed, in a kind of nonchalant "que sera sera" (what will be, will be) state. At the other extreme are youth described as achieved—committed to one or more ways of seeing the world, but not closed to promising new information. In between are the diffused—actively exploring but under no pressure, sense of urgency, or other constraint to make decisions. "Foreclosed" describes those who have made their choices and closed their books. Research (Cobb, 2007, p. 145) shows that teens are seldom in the same quadrant in all domains of identity formation—gender, ideology, and career. For example, a teen could be uncommitted and exploring with respect to career, yet committed and unexploring with respect to ideology. As they age, individuals tend to reach either foreclosure or achievement in gender, career, and ideology.

An individual's behavioral traits can certainly influence where they are likely to stand in this model. "O" (originality) is clearly associated with exploration. In fact, that is how the O trait is defined:

"explorers" at one end and "preservers" at the other. O+ individuals need help making commitments, while O- individuals need help continuing to explore. The same can be said for "C" (consolidation): C+ teens naturally yearn for closure and commitment, while C- teens tend to be more spontaneous, risk-prone, and multi-tasking. Teens low in "A" (accommodation) tend to be tenacious once they've made up their minds, hence more closed to exploration, while those high in A tend to change their views in order to keep the peace and create harmony in relationships.

So, as our biology propels us into the world around us, and we adapt based on what we find, we slowly affirm the basic elements of who we are. Let us now take a look at the complete palette of whom we are.

Figure 4.1 **The Palette Showing Who We Are** (with illustrative examples)

Mental Tools:	
Semantic STM*	Imagination
Procedural STM	Fluency
Semantic LTM*	Elaboration
Procedural LTM	Learning from Content
Organizing	Judgment
Planning	Processing Speed
Evaluating	Time to Mastery
Critical Thinking	Time Span
Composition	
Presentation	

Mental Talents:	
Language/Verbal	Physical/Kinesthetic
Numbers/Logical	Relations/Interpersonal
Visual/Spatial	Thinking/Intrapersonal
Hearing/Musical	Observer/Taxonomies

Physical Characteristics:		
Height	Sensitivity of skin to sunlight	Speed
Skin texture	Sensitivity of eyes to light/dark	Balance
Deformities	Sensitivity to noise	Reaction time
Nail quality	Sensitivity to quality of odors	Handedness
Weight	Sensitivity of touch	Flexibility
Eye color	Sensitivity to intensity of odors	Tendency to motion sickness
Hair color	Taste preferences	Hand-eye co-ordination
Skin color	Ease of falling asleep	Muscular/skeletal
Nervous tics	Predispositions for for diseases	Taste acuity
Hair texture	Sensitivity of digestive system	Quality of teeth
Figure	Sleep requirements	Endurance
Symmetry	Flavor preferences	Allergies
Body hair		
Hair quantity		
Date of puberty		
Visual acuity		
Strength		
Dexterity		

Behavioral Traits:		
N- Resilient	N= Responsive	N+ Reactive
E- Introvert	E= Ambivert	E+ Extravert
O- Preserver	O= Moderate	O+ Explorer
A- Challenger	A= Negotiator	A+ Adapter
C- Flexible	C= Balanced	C+ Focused

Memories:	
Times:	
Kindergarten	Elementary School
Middle School	High School
Higher Education	Military Service
Early Work	
Places:	Vacations
Homes	Religious Orgs.
Neighborhoods	Travel
School campuses	Friends' homes
Work sites	
Roles:	Artist
Parent/grandparent	Scientist
Teacher	Researcher
Caregiver	Maintenance
Religious Leader	Politician
Hobbyist	Financier
Sibling	

Values:	
Achievement	Materialism
Aesthetics	Politics
Affiliation	Position
Beauty	Poverty/Asceticism
Charity	Power
Compassion	Professionalism
Creativity	Renunciation
Education	Romance
Entertainment	Safety
Escape	Scholarship
Family	Security
Friendship	Service
Healing	Spirituality
Health	Sport
Hedonism	Tolerance
Learning	Wealth
Maintenance	

* STM = short term memory. LTM = long term memory.

The Palette of Who We Are

The palette from which we paint our personal identity includes all five sets of raw materials presented in the previous three chapters. In Figure 4.1, we have assembled these raw materials in the shape of a person, with the head comprising mental tools; the right arm, mental talents; the left arm, behavioral traits; the torso, physical characteristics; the right leg, memories, and the left leg, values.

Copy this figure (as long as you include our copyright notice!) and use it as a worksheet for yourself for you and those close to you: family members, romantic partners, teammates, good friends, and so forth. Highlight the areas of the worksheet that represent aspects of yourself that you want to build on, or that you want to keep in mind as you make choices and form goals—about career, about college, about further training, about life mates, about where you will live and/or work. In Figure 4.2, I (Pierce) have prepared a sample of how this worksheet might be filled in. I have grayed out the areas that are less important to me. If I have left an area unshaded, then I think it is a strength, I really like it, or I want to keep it in mind. For example, "sensitivity of skin to sunlight" is selected in the physical characteristics because I sunburn easily, and I have a tendency to get skin cancers. This is something I need to keep in mind as I make choices. It helps explain why I spend so much time indoors. It explains why I do not care to go to the beach in the summer (we go in fall, winter, or spring, and we only walk on the beach in early morning or late afternoon, with hats and sunscreen, and no lying out to soak up rays!). I love being outdoors, but I must stay out of the sun.

I also selected under talents "Thinking/Intrapersonal", "Observer/Taxonomies", and "Hearing/Musical." The first two are very important to me professionally. I really like reading and taking notes, drawing models of my thoughts, and creating taxonomies, building elaborate mental models that show the relationships of many different elements. This has shaped my career, as I have ended up today as a psychologist who constructs tests, does research, writes books, and does many other activities that involve solitary thinking and putting ideas together. But note that in Behavioral Traits I selected "Ambiverted"; so I need a balance of solitary study with something sociable. Again, I have shaped my career to allow about half my time to be spent in more sociable activities: teaching, speaking, consulting, and a small amount of managing others. My music, as you have learned earlier, is very important to me. So important that I did not build my career around it—it is my hobby, my avocation, what I turn to for enjoyment and stress relief. Private Prewitt, in James Jones' novel *From Here to Eternity*, had a similar attitude: "He who loved the bugle had to give it up because he loved it" (p. 68). Prewitt chose not to turn his joy for playing into work by making it a job.

Whether I have chosen from my palette (i.e., what I have shaded out) accurately is important. How do I know that "Critical Thinking" is one of my strengths? I know I enjoy thinking critically, but how do I know I am really good at it? We get feedback on our performance from two sources: objective tests and feedback from others. Tests could include school tests (quizzes, reviews, exams), commercial tests (IQ tests, licensing agencies, tests on specific abilities—such as the Watson-Glaser Critical Thinking Appraisal), contests/competitions (athletic events/games, music contests, spelling bees), and sales (if

I'm able to sell something, that suggests the buyer thinks I'm good at it) Feedback, of course, comes from parents, peers, siblings, teachers, employers, and so on. We suggest that one invite someone knowledgeable of one's overall accomplishments and activities to have a dialog for the purpose of penciling (tentatively underlining) those areas on the worksheet important for making choices and setting goals. And not just one person—use your network to gain a sense of where the truth lies. Do not

Figure 4.2 The Palette Showing Who We Are—Case Study of Pierce Howard

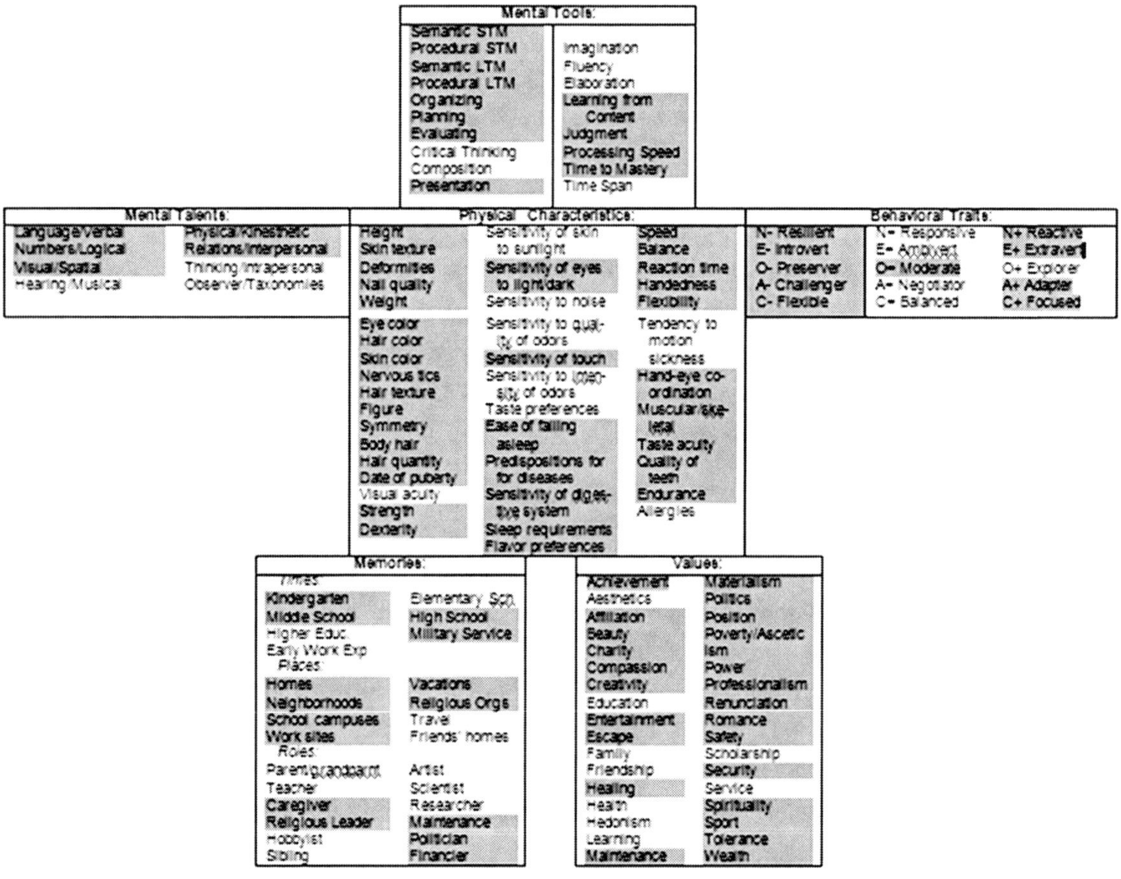

highlight too many areas—it is easy, but not helpful, to highlight lots, or even most, of the areas, but that does not help one to focus on strengths. Not highlighting something doesn't mean you can't do it, or it's not important to you—just that it is not as strong or as important as the highlighted items. Although I (Pierce) am a writer, I didn't select "Language/Verbal"! That is because I don't see myself in the top tier of writers. But I do see myself as strong with Taxonomies (most of the people I know get bored or frustrated with them, but I find them fascinating, both to study and to build). Writing is more like a means to several ends: I write to explain my taxonomies, to affirm my value for Education and Learning, and to revel in thinking, imagining, dreaming, and reflecting.

Once we begin to get a fix on the areas of the palette that we wish to use in composing the direction of our life, we can then make decisions and set goals that result in a life most likely to make us happy or satisfied, or possibly both.

Happiness Is Goodness of Fit—Between Whom We Are and Whom We Are Busy Trying to Be

There are two ways to be happy: One is unintentional, the other intentional. One is unplanned, the other planned. First, the unintentional, unplanned way to be happy. Simply put, it is to be born scoring in the top third of extraversion (E+) and in the bottom third of need for stability (N-). About one person is nine is born with these qualities: full of positive emotions and absent negative emotions (for the most part). In Chapter 1, we referred to the movie characters of Guido played by Roberto Benigni in the movie *La Vita é bella* ("Life is Beautiful"), of Maria played by Julie Andrews in *The Sound of Music*, and of Annie played by Aileen Quinn in *Annie*. We said each character had a set point and could not vary from that set point for a significant duration. They have what we call the temperament of happiness, defined as abundance of positive emotions and absence of negative emotions. Another good example is the character of Evelyn Ryan played by Julianne Moore in the film *The Prize Winner of Defiance, Ohio*. This woman (based on a true story) maintained her positive outlook and mood, rarely succumbing to despair, anger, or terror, in the presence of an alcoholic husband who drank up all his earnings, leaving her to scrape together money for groceries, rent, and clothing for their large family by entering verse and jingle contests. Guido, Maria, Annie, and Evelyn are all characters, people born happy. They are not to be suppressed or derailed. Whatever their situation, they are likely to be happy, to have a positive mood without the negative emotions. They didn't plan it that way—they just are that way. They might suffer brief, temporary, negative feelings without positive ones, but they bounce back with natural resilience.[1]

If 1 out of 9 of us is born that way, then what can the other eight of us do? We (Jane and Pierce) are two of those eight. Pierce is mid range in both N (need for stability) and E (extraversion), and Jane is low in N, mid in E. We both have moments of happiness, but that is the exception. Yet, we love our lives for the most part, and can think of few ways we'd like to change them. How have we, and how can others, plan for happiness when/if it doesn't come naturally? Persons who report greatest life satisfaction tend to be those who engage in roles that are most consistent with their:

- traits, as in
  - selling and high extraversion
  - library work and low extraversion
  - volunteer work and high accommodation

---

[1] Emily Crowder, our editorial research intern and a 19-year-old more conversant with youth culture, suggests these additional examples of happy (i.e., N-E+) temperaments: Isabelle Stevens (in *Grey's Anatomy*), Kate Hudson, Phoebe (in *Friends*), Dori (in *Finding Nemo)*, Kramer (in *Seinfeld)*, Joey (in *Full House)*, Gloria the Hippo (in *Madagascar)*, and Forrest Gump.

- abilities, as in
    - musician and high hearing/auditory talent
    - professional athlete and high physical/kinesthetic talent
- physical characteristics, as in
    - emergency medicine specialist and lower sleep requirements
- salient memories, as in
    - playing chamber music like Pierce used to do with his brother in New Haven
    - emulating characters from musicals while Jane cleaned her room on Saturday morning
- and strongest values, as in
    - making time for exercise for Health
    - able to travel widely for Aesthetics.

McCrae and Costa (2003) call this an undifferentiated sense of self, contrasted with a differentiated self, one in which the individual tends to take on many roles that are not supported by traits (e.g., more introverted persons in a selling role, more creative persons in a repetitive, proofreading role, more considerate persons in a competitive role). These differentiated selves are more likely to have a "shaky and uncomfortable identity." N+ persons appear to have more of a tendency to take on such roles, continuing to experiment in search of the right role, but continuing to be somewhat unfulfilled, "like an insomniac who cannot find a comfortable position in bed" (Costa and McCrae, 2003, p. 229).

So, what we can do is make choices, set goals, plan our lives so that we are able to use our strengths, our values, and our memories as building blocks, as the colors on our palette. The corollary of this approach is that we avoid a way of life that forces us to emphasize our weaker areas, to enter situations for which we have unpleasant memories, or to engage in activities that represent values in opposition to our own strongest held ones (as in a creative person having to proofread for a living). When we attach our strengths and fondnesses to career, family, and social outlets, we are said to be "undifferentiated." We are building on what we are—our personal qualities find expression in the life we are leading. We do not experience a significant discrepancy between who we are and what is expected of us. Csikszentmihalyi and Scheider (2000, p. 13) write about James Coleman's study of young people in the U.S., in which Coleman concludes that the principle responsibility of society toward youth is to

> develop in youth the *capabilities for engaging in intense concentrated involvement in an activity* [emphasis added]. The most personally satisfying experiences, as well as the greatest achievements of man [sic; "humanity" is a better word choice], arise from such concentration, not because of external pressure, but from an inner motivation which propels the person and focuses his or her attention.... It is the concentrated involvement itself, rather than the specific content, that is important.

Such engagement, being totally absorbed in the task at hand, is what Mihalyi Csikszentmihalyi (1990) calls "flow." Flow occurs when what one brings to a task matches the demands of the task. When the task demands more than the individual brings, one experiences frustration. When the task demands less than one brings, one experiences boredom. Hence, the practice of "handicapping" is an athlete's way of staying in flow. When I (Pierce) was bored playing tennis with our younger daughter, I handicapped myself by playing to her singles court as she played to my doubles court. By altering either what we bring to a task (by reading, practicing, taking courses, and so forth) or what the task demands of us (by finding a way to simplify or complicate the task), we can maximize the amount of time we spend in flow. It is with this in mind that we at the Center for Applied Cognitive Studies developed the Human Resource Optimization Model back in the 1990s.

Human Resource Optimization—the Mechanism for Improving Fit/Happiness

In the Introduction, we explained the Trees of Life and how they symbolize the elements of our Human Resource Optimization Model (see p.7). You will recall that this model has two dimensions that interplay: the *resources* that we bring to a task and the *level* at which we perform that task. Now that we have completed the "palette" of who we are, we are in an excellent position to understand the traits, abilities, physical characteristics, memories, and values as "resources" that we bring to any task. They are like the root system in the Human Resource Optimization drawing of the trees. The larger the root system, the more resources we bring to the task. And, not just the bigness of the root system, but the rightness, or appropriateness, of it. The more appropriate and relevant that the resources are that we bring to a task, the more natural it becomes for us. Larger root systems represent better fits between what we bring to a task and what the task actually demands of us, like a math whiz serving as a club treasurer. Smaller root systems represent tasks that demand things of us that are not available, like a five-footer trying to be a team's center against a basketball team comprised of seven-foot players. To the degree that we have the right resources for a task, and we are not doing the task well, that tells us that we need to study, to practice, to find the right teacher/mentor. To the degree that we lack the right resources for a task, we either need to change tasks, or find ways to compensate for our lack of resources, as in the five-footer finding shoes with springs or a jet-powered backpack.

It is clearly possible for one to excel even when lacking the right resources, but it is not natural, and it is not as satisfying as excelling in a task that feels more natural. A man does not have to be courageous when everyone around him is—he can lean on their courage. Sir Winston Churchill described this situation, comparing his own courage to that of his people:

> "I may not be the lion, but it was left to me to give the lion's roar."

All About Personality

Churchill's line expresses well the notion that one doesn't have to have a complete palette to compose a complete life. It is our willingness and our ability to complement our strengths with the strengths of others around us. By knowing our own palette/resources and knowing those of our associates, we can make choices that result in our being fully engaged and having a sense of well-being. In Part 2 of this book, we will go into detail in describing the behavioral traits that we must deal with in understanding our palette and in making decisions that are satisfying.

Part Two

Mapping Out the Big Five Traits

Mapping Out the Big Five Traits

5

Need for Stability

All About Stress

+	*Frank:* Serenity now. Serenity now. *George:* What is that? *Frank:* Doctor gave me a relaxation cassette. When my blood pressure gets too high, the man on the tape tells me to say: "SERENITY NOW" *George:* Are you supposed to yell it? *Frank:* The doctor wasn't specific. -- *Seinfeld,* U.S. sitcom (NBC) from the 1990s
=	I get knocked down, but I get up again You're never gonna keep me down --Chumbawamba, from the song "Tubthumping"
-	Nothing gives one person so much advantage over another as to remain always cool and unruffled under all circumstances. —Thomas Jefferson, 3rd President of the United States

Guide to This Chapter:

- Definitions of the N Supertrait
- Three Case Studies
- Definitions of the Four Subtraits of N
- Implications of N for Your Career
- Implications of N for Relating to Adults in Power (Parents, Teachers, Administrators, Bosses, etc.)
- Implications of N for How You Manage Relationships with Peers
- Implications of N for Your Communication Style
- Implications of N for Your Leadership Aspirations
- Note on the Biological Basis of Behavior
- Biological Basis for Need for Stability (N)

Mapping Out the Big Five Traits

N	E	O	A	C
Need for Stability	**Extraversion**	**Originality**	**Accommodation**	**Consolidation**
N+ Reactive	E+ Extravert	O+ Explorer	A+ Adapter	C+ Focused
N= Responsive	E= Ambivert	O= Moderate	A= Negotiator	C= Balanced
N- Resilient	E- Introvert	O- Preserver	A- Challenger	C- Flexible
N1: Worry				
N2: Temper				
N3: Outlook				
N4: Coping Level				

The three statements that introduce this chapter are samples of how an individual speaks who is thinking and feeling in accordance with the higher, medium, or lower regions of the need for stability (N) continuum. Speaking in this manner doesn't necessarily imply that a person will stay in that area of the continuum all of the time. Thomas Jefferson speaks of the value of cool rationality, but he may not always have been coolly rational. Certainly his rapture with Sally Hemings was proof that he could behave according to *both* ends of the N continuum—in control *as well as* out of control. These quotes are not intended to identify the speaker as definitely possessing the trait expressed in the quote, only to illustrate the meaning of the quote.

All of the quotes are meant to portray positive behaviors. While a quote may *sound* negative or undesirable in some way, that is probably because it differs from how you personally might feel or think. In the proper context, the quotes are all healthy, positive, productive, and desirable. We all demonstrate behavior at both ends of each continuum—we both cry (N+) and reason (N-); to comment on one of the behaviors does not necessarily mean that we endorse that behavior. The statement, "If men could cry, then they could love" doesn't imply that the speaker is N+ or N-, only that the person is talking about an N+ behavior, crying.

Definitions of the N Supertrait and Its Four Subtraits

Let's now take a closer look at the types of behavior associated with the three areas of the N dimension. In general, N is about the degree to which you tend to experience stress. Stress is what you feel when you perceive that something or someone is interfering with your course of action. The "stressor" is whatever does the interfering. There are two important things to understand about stressors:

What stresses one person does not necessarily stress another. Paul may dislike accordion music intensely, while Paulette may love it. With the two sitting in the same waiting room trying to read a magazine, with accordion music playing in the background, one will perceive it as a stressor and feel resentment, anger, or even rage, while the other might pleasantly pat her foot to the music while browsing her magazine. The music interfered with Johnny's concentration because he couldn't ignore it and didn't want it there, but it didn't interfere with Johnette's browsing because a) she welcomed it and b) she wasn't trying to concentrate/read, just browse. Something or someone becomes a stressor only when someone sees it as preventing progress towards one's goal or course of action. In this sense, all stress is a choice. We can choose to view a situation as an interference, or not. The stressor is in the eye of the beholder.

Not everyone reacts to a perceived stressor in the same way, or to the same degree. You might react with fear when your parent asks you to perform a chore when you are studying for a test—fear that time taken away from preparation will affect your grade. Or I might react with anger in the same situation, anger that my parent is putting me in a double bind—damned if I do, damned if I don't, a no-win situation. Or someone else might react with sadness, even depression, at the prospect of not having enough time to make the high grade that one thinks is possible, given more time to study and no chores.

It is the number of stressors we perceive in our lives, and the degree and manner in which we react to them, that places us on the continuum from N+ (many perceived stressors, more extreme reaction) to N- (fewer perceived stressors, mild reaction).

Reactive (N+)

If you are a reactive, you tend to respond to most situations in an alert, sensitive, concerned, attentive, excitable, or expressive way. Under stress, you may be perceived by others as being anxious, tense, restless, depressed, easily discouraged, temperamental, or worried. Typically, you feel the effect of even a little stress more readily than most people and often serve as the "conscience" of those around you. When problems or difficult situations arise, you may tend to take them personally, thinking of them as your problems to solve or as your responsibility even if they really belong to or were caused by someone else. In tough times, you may need plenty of time to vent your frustrations or to get over your concerns before you are ready to tackle the next job challenge. Even though you would benefit from going into problem-solving mode when you experience severe stress, you are more likely to use one or all of the three most common ways of responding to stress: 1) Finding some way to express your emotions and work them through, as in talking with a friend (nurture)[1]; 2) open confrontation and/or aggression (fight); or 3) trying to escape or get away from the source of stress (flight). Eventually, you will need to find a moment of calm (N-) to engage in problem solving, in order to minimize the possibility of the stressor recurring.

---

[1] For most of the 20th century, nurture was overlooked as a response to stress. This is because most of the stress research was done on male subjects. As a result of the Women's Health Initiative (see more at www.whi.org) redoing formerly all-male research, researchers discovered that nurture was a very popular stress management strategy for many females (and some males also). There's nothing quite like grooming other living creatures for soothing one's nerves.

Mapping Out the Big Five Traits

Responsive (N=)

If you are a responsive, you tend to be calm, secure, and steady under normal circumstances. However, surprises, pressures, emergencies, difficult situations, or stressful circumstances can sometimes lead you to worry, anger, depression, discouragement, or other types of stressful responses. Basically, you have a moderate threshold for handling stress. When difficulties arise, you may need a moment or two to blow off steam or get over your disappointment before resuming your regular activities or moving into a problem-solving mode. Stress, like all of the traits, is a continuum of responses, with the two poles being reaction and calmness; you are in the middle of the continuum. This could mean one of two things: 1) Either you are highly contextual in what stresses you (i.e., half of what stresses most people stresses you, and the other half doesn't bother you—one person's storm is another's welcome rain), or 2) Your reaction to stressors is less intense than that of N+ people, more intense than N- people, or some combination of the two. Persons in the first category experience fewer events as stressors than those in the second, but experience them more intensely.

Resilient (N-)

If you are a resilient, you tend to respond to stressful situations in a calm, secure, steady, optimistic, and rational way. Typically, you are stress-free, guilt-free, and urge-resistant. Unless you are very attentive to persons you care about, you may appear to them to be too laid back and relaxed, to be uncaring, lethargic, insensitive, or unaware of the seriousness of problems, or to have tunnel vision. You may not take stressful situations or problems as seriously as you should because you can usually manage without too many difficulties even when the stress is occurring all around you. As problems arise, you usually move into a problem-solving mode rather rapidly and proceed in a rational, analytic way until the problem or the source of the stress has been taken care of.

Here we have defined three levels of need for stability. In reality, it would be more appropriate to define five levels. However, to a certain degree, the extra two levels (Very High N, or N++, and Very Low N, or N- -) are simply intensifications of the High and Low levels. Add the words "very" or "extremely" to the N+ and N- descriptions, and you have descriptions of the Very High/N++ and Very Low/N- - levels of need for stability.

Now that we have introduced the levels of N, let's take a look at three case studies that illustrate how they work in everyday situations.

Three Case Studies

N Case Study 1: Finkelstein's Folly

In a student group such as a study group, project team, or set of club or class officers, some of the dynamics that occur between low-, mid-, and high-scoring team members on the N dimension can be classically illustrated by the following situation. Shortly after breakfast one Friday morning, the reactive (N+), concerned about a problem with a teacher, rushes into the student lounge, where he finds the resilient (N-) and exclaims, "Oh my gosh! We've got a real problem with Dr. Finkelstein! He's threatened to drop our project's evaluation by one letter grade if our first draft is not available for his review next Monday morning. There's no way we can be ready, even if we work nonstop through the weekend. We need to call the team together immediately to discuss what we're going to do!"

The resilient friend (N-) calmly rolls her eyes toward the responsive (N=), who also happens to be in the lounge. The resilient calmly says to the reactive, "Now, you just need to chill a bit. Yes, Dr. Fink has problems at home, and he likes to pull rank with students. His pulling our chain is how he gets to feel better about himself since he feels horrible at home. He likes to see us sweat, to hop when he says 'Jump!' Calm down. One of us will go talk with him after lunch to work it out."

The responsive (N=) student squirms a little uncomfortably in her chair and says, "Well, I think we shouldn't wait too long to respond. One of the main reasons Dr. Finkelstein has these rigid timelines is to teach us, to force us to learn how to organize our time. We do need to take him seriously, but the situation is probably not hopeless. Not letting him know we're probably going to be late could really hit him the wrong way. This is probably a minor problem, but I think we need to deal with it immediately—Dr. Fink would be contemptuous if we waited til after lunch. I think the reactive (N+) is right to bring it to our attention at this time, and we should act on it."

This story emphasizes that people who score in the midrange and higher in N (N= and N+) tend to take the concerns of other students and of adults more seriously. Often people who score lower in N (N-) do not take others' concerns seriously enough. This difference in the level of seriousness can affect how teens interact with parents, teachers, employers, other students, and even intimate friends. In the overall school environment, however, we need both the calming force of the N-, the strong ownership and sense of conscience about problems of the N+, and the equalizing efforts of the N= in order to achieve our goals.

N Case Study 2: Texted in the Nick of Time

At a leadership workshop for student leaders, fifty youth were presented with this situation: "You have just been texted by your best friend: *'Where r u? Prof Mumba ticked. Thinks u r a flake."* You realize that you were supposed to be with your friend in Professor Mumba's office ten minutes ago. You can't get there for 30 minutes, under any conditions. He's threatening to take you off the research project team because he perceives that you have not placed a sufficiently high priority on the research project. Finishing this research project satisfactorily is critical for getting Professor Mumba's recommendation for grad school, which you must have. Without talking to anyone, write down what you are thinking or feeling at this very moment."

An N- - student (very low on the N scale) calmly stood up and endorsed going to Mumba's office and either starting the meeting late, i.e., immediately, or asking Mumba to reschedule.

An N- student (moderately low on N) said she felt a little anxious about the situation but was sure someone had forgotten to tell her about the meeting. However, she would drop what she was doing and go to Mumba's office.

An N= student (moderate N) looked a little concerned but appeared to become more comfortable and spoke more strongly as he continued. He was worried and anxious about how the professor might feel toward him. He also was concerned whether he'd failed to put the meeting on his calendar or whether someone else had made the error. He also decided that the prof was not really upset, just pulling rank. In any event, as soon as he received the text, he decided to grab his information and go to the meeting. After arriving at Mumba's office, he would decide whether he needed to make a verbal apology.

An N+ girl (high on N) looked a little stressed and somewhat ill at ease in front of the large gathering, but her tone of voice was strong and full of the emotion that she obviously felt. Feeling physically uncomfortable after receiving the text message, she used descriptive words such as "very anxious," "very worried," "really scared," and included a few expletives. She thought she had personally erred in not putting the meeting on her calendar. She planned to go immediately to Mumba's office and apologize for being late. She also would probably speak directly to the professor later and apologize again.

The N++ student (very high on N) looked very stressed with the situation. He shifted from foot to foot throughout his presentation and mainly looked down at his notes, yet his verbal comments were full of passion and emotion. He was mortified by the situation with the professor, felt sick, and was sure that his chances for his first-choice grad programs were nil. He knew he'd personally "screwed up" by not putting the meeting on his calendar. He would immediately dash to the meeting and make profuse apologies to Mumba, while telling himself mentally that he should accept the fact that he was going to be pulled off the research project and could kiss the prof's recommendation goodbye.

In reflecting on the different reports, one of the main elements the participants noticed was how personally the higher-scoring students seemed to take the situation. The perception of the communication error shifted from being someone else's fault with the lower-scoring groups to being a personal, life-altering mistake for the higher-scoring students.

Another difference they noticed was the level of emotion or passion that emerged from the speakers as they moved up the scale. In fact, several minutes into the small-group portion of the exercise, the N- - group asked us what was taking the N+ and N++ groups so long. They also had noticed strong gestures and expressions coming from the higher-scoring groups. The lower scorers, N- - and N-, had quickly and rationally handled their discussions of the situation and were ready to present, while the higher-scoring groups needed to vent and talk through their emotional and personal responses to the stressful situation before they could begin to move into a problem-solving mode to determine what they actually needed to do.

The N+ and N++ groups couldn't understand the calm, laid-back approach taken by the N- and N- - groups, while the N= group admitted that they had experienced a combination of the feelings and emotions being voiced by both the N- and N+ groups. During the discussion, one fellow in the N++

group looked at the N- - group and said, "I've got a part-time job with a boss who is just like you guys. He's always calm, cool, rational—really frustrating. One time, when I made a major mistake that inconvenienced him, I sent him an apology card. When he got it, he just laughed and told my coworkers about it. They laughed too, and I felt really embarrassed about the whole situation. Should I have just let the whole situation blow over without doing anything or apologizing?" At this point in the discussion, the members of the N- - group looked back at the N++ person and in unison, without much expression, said, "Yep." The N= group found this very amusing and came up with even more questions about the situation.

N Case Study 3: The Student Body Presidents

Fifteen student body presidents—from public and private schools, and diverse in gender and race—met monthly to discuss common issues faced in their region of the state: behavior at sports events, race relations, bullying, and so forth. While these students formed an intact team accustomed to working together, they were geographically dispersed and lacked the benefit of daily contact. This case describes a team-building session held in the facilities of the regional education center.

Prior to the all-day Saturday session, we had administered the SchoolPlace Big Five Profile to the students so we could provide them with complete, detailed information about their personalities during the team-building session. As the participants entered the conference room where the session was to be held, we greeted each one. In order to facilitate discussion among these students who saw each other infrequently, snacks and beverages awaited them. One of the student leaders was a girl we had been looking for before the meeting so we could talk with her briefly, just to prepare her for her N score. After she had greeted the people who were already there and apologized to them for running late, we unobtrusively asked her to step away from the milling group to talk with us. We explained to her that we just wanted to let her know about one of her scores on the personality assessment before we started the team-building session (her N score was 79, in the very high range). We assured her that she was normal but that she probably experienced more stress than the other team members and probably more than most people she knew. She looked at us strangely and said, "How did you know that? I usually wonder what's wrong with me. I just can't seem to take life and school as casually as other students." After a quick discussion and plenty of reassurance, we returned to the rest of the team.

As we began the session, we went through the usual introductory material and then led the student leaders through the same exercise (Professor Mumba) that we had conducted with the leadership retreat group of fifty (see Case #2). The responses for these student body presidents were similar to those in Case Study 2. After hearing their responses and processing them the same way we had with the earlier group, we asked another leading question of this leadership team: how this scale and their scores related to their leadership position at their high schools. One of the first responses to our question came from a boy who scored N=. He looked at the girl who had received the score of 79 and said, "I had no idea you were that high. I don't see you as stressed at all; you're always taking on extra assignments and responsibilities. You respond calmly and authoritatively to any problem we bring up. So how does this score make any sense to you?"

Shaking her head slowly, N=79 replied, "You just don't know. When we have an emergency or problem at school, I handle it, but I get all tied up in knots. Then my parents have to hear about it when I get home." She then continued and gave one of the best metaphors we've heard to describe what an N++ feels like most of the time. She said, "I feel like I'm a duck sailing across a lake and leaving a smooth wake. All you see is my efficiency, with everything under control above the waterline. What I really feel is that I'm paddling fast and furious below the water just to keep myself afloat and to keep going."

Because we had used the SchoolPlace with this team and because of what this girl told her peers, they suddenly realized that they'd been dumping all kinds of responsibilities on her that they didn't want to do, because she would take it on. In fact, during the discussion that followed, she indicated that she would feel guilty or as if she was letting them down if she didn't take on everything asked of her by her teammates. After that realization in the team-building meeting, the team revised the distribution of the overall team workload and gave the N++ girl some well-needed relief.

A month after the session, the girl telephoned us to thank us for helping to relieve some of her stress. We explained that we hadn't relieved the stress; her teammates had. All we had done in the session was to give them the SchoolPlace as a vocabulary for talking about their individual differences and to facilitate their discussion. By understanding and appreciating the differences in their individual personalities, the team members began to achieve better work performance: Their awareness of this girl's stress helped them to deploy her strengths more effectively. Now, she needed to find a way to share her scores, her "nature," with her close associates back at her school, perhaps with a SchoolPlace team-building session with her fellow student-body officers. Once we can appreciate the fact that diversity is also associated with personality, we can consciously work toward achieving personality diversity in our teams.

Definitions of the Four Subtraits of N

Earlier, we described how three different individuals might react to the same stressor in three different ways: fear, anger, and sadness. This introduces the notion of "subtraits," the specific behaviors that comprise the N supertrait. Keep in mind that supertraits are to subtraits as sections of an orchestra are to its member instruments. Brass, strings, woodwinds, and percussion each have a unique group sound, but within each section are even more unique sounds. At this point, we will look at four aspects of N that we call its subtraits—the four "instruments" that give need for stability its unique qualities.

N1 ***Worry:*** *The amount of fear/anxiety we experience*. Fear results from the perception of impending harm. When we perceive that a stressor is endangering our physical or emotional safety, we tend to be afraid. Unexplained noises in the night, someone approaching us at a high speed, final exam time, a first date, an upcoming game or performance—each of these has the possible consequence of harming us in some way—harming our body, our reputation, our self-image. The N1 subtrait, as do all of the subtraits, has three levels. At one extreme is Marlin, Nemo's frantic, desperate father in *Finding Nemo,* and at the other is the carefree Dory, unaffected by all challenges.

N1+ (High): *Frequent worrying occurs.* Persons high in N1 are highly sensitive to a wide variety of threats. It is as though they are "plugged in" to every outlet in the building, and nothing escapes their attention or concern. These are clearly the "conscience of the group," be it a family, a class, a club, or some other group. These worriers are valuable for ensuring quality, for being completely open to and aware of problems and issues, for wearing their emotions on their shirtsleeve, and for refusing to turn away from dealing with life's hard realities. Anxiety can drive creative production. As actor, director, producer, writer, and comedian Mike Nichols says, "Nerves provide me with energy. They work for me. It's when I don't have them, when I feel at ease, that I get worried." Hermione (from the "Harry Potter" stories) is always worried about grades, classes, homework, and so forth. She serves as the conscience for Ron and Harry when they are about to break rules or do something risky. Elliot (from *Scrubs*) gets so worried about messing up that she does just that. She gets really emotional and holds onto her mistakes. Any time she messes up, she starts crying. Here's Elliot in high N1 mode: "Remember the day when you told me I had pit stains? Well, I have cried every 15 minutes on the half hour since you told me that. I am racked with self-doubt, I have panic attacks, I'm claustrophobic, germphobic, phobiaphobic...."

N1= (Medium): *Some concern from time to time.* Persons in the midrange of N1 either a) worry to a moderate degree most of the time, or b) worry intensely, but not that often. In the first case, the individual becomes a good conscience for the family or group, expressing reservations when others may keep silent. If "fools rush in where angels fear to tread," then in this case the N- are the "fools" who experience no fear, and the "angels" are the N= or N+ who urge caution.

N1- (Low): *At ease most of the time.* Persons low in N1 seldom experience fear. They typically sleep well, have well-functioning digestive systems, and appear impervious to events that others would perceive as threats. On the plus side, this calmness is advantageous in real-time, high-performance situations with low margins for error, such as brain surgery, piloting an airplane, or interviewing for a scholarship. On the down side, this calmness can communicate lack of caring for others and defensiveness arising from being unaware of problems. It can lead to inappropriate risks. In fact, the absence of fear is associated with antisocial behavior. Fearlessness can be a boon when bravery is called for, but can be a demon when a peer group dares a member to engage in a violent, harmful act. Says *Mad* magazine's Alfred E. Neuman, "What, me worry?" Or, more elegantly, from Thomas Jefferson: "Nothing gives one person so much advantage over another as to remain always cool and unruffled under all circumstances."

N2 ***Temper**: How frequently we experience anger.* Anger results from the perception of an impending or actual obstruction—something/someone potentially preventing us from remaining on a desired course of action. Anger typically arises when we feel that someone or something is attempting to take something away from us. This feeling harks back to a time in the jungle when alpha animals staked out their position as number one, when roosters and chickens established their pecking order.

Mapping Out the Big Five Traits

When one has established one's turf and another comes along to challenge one's rights to that turf, anger typically ensues. Whether it is someone trying to take away one's boy/girl friend, one's lead in a contest, or one's home (as in a land developer forcing foreclosure), the threat of impending loss of position or possession has the potential for engendering anger. I (Pierce) get angry with myself (and others) when I (or they) make an error that requires me to stop what I am doing and either redo something I'd earlier done, clean up a mess, or some such.

> **N2+** (High): *Quicker temper*. The high N2s have a short fuse, a quick trigger, living on the edge of anger. This is the meaning of describing someone as a "loose cannon" (e.g., John McEnroe in the 1980s; Newt Gingrich in the 1990s; Terrell Owens today). These are the "bulls in the china shop," capable of explosive anger round the clock. This kind of intensity is productive for defensive linemen on a football team, for actors in a drama, and for pressured project managers needing to crack the whip to get a project in on schedule/under budget. But the intensity isn't very productive for public safety officers who carry a gun or for press secretaries being badgered by the press. The "Incredible Hulk" created a motto for N2+: "You don't want to make me angry!" N2+s are the watchdogs—heightened alertness coupled with instant reactions.

> **N2=** (Medium): *Moderate temper.* Persons mid-range in N2 have either a) a shorter fuse than low N2s, but not as short as high N2s, or b) a pretty short fuse, but don't perceive nearly as many possible losses as do high N2s (i.e., they have a more selective temper).

> **N2-** (Low): *Usually calm*. Persons low in N2 have an unusually long "fuse," or an unusually slow "trigger," in that it takes a lot to make them angry, to get a rise out of them. This could be because they do not care whether they lose what you threaten to take from them, or they choose to remain calm and plot quietly to thwart your efforts to take what is theirs. Whatever the case, N2- is associated with the absence of temper. "Get fired up!" falls on their deaf ears. They just don't get fired up, at least not in the sense of becoming intensely, angrily protective. But that doesn't necessarily mean that you can take from them with impunity. Ronald Reagan exemplified N2- (the "Teflon" president—imperturbable) in his term, as does Barrack Obama today.

N3 ***Outlook****: How we explain situations.* Pessimism and an accompanying sadness result from the perception of an impending, or actual, failure or loss. Furthermore, we attribute the cause of the failure/loss to our own personal qualities that are permanent and pervasive. "I failed the test because I'm not smart, at this, or anything else, and it will always be that way." The other extreme outlook is optimism, whereby one perceives that failures/losses are the result of outside forces that are temporary and limited. "I failed the test because the teacher doesn't like my political views. None of my other teachers are that way; so this is a rare setback. Perhaps I can obscure my views and do better." Optimism is associated with neutral or positive feelings, while pessimism is associated with sadness and related negative feelings. (See Chapter 2, Figures 2.1 and 2.2.)

> **N3+** (High): *Less optimistic explanations.* The pessimistic explanation of how life's events turn out sees setbacks as omens for the future and achievements as one-time occurrences, or luck. This is the opposite outlook in comparison to the optimist. In contrast to the exuberant optimism of "Game, Set, Life!", there is the 180° opposite: "You can't win, Charlie Brown." Charlie, the eternal pessimist. Doom and gloom. Yet, such an outlook has positive value in such careers as tax accountants, quality-control inspectors, and other roles that require an unstinting eye for the down side, a temperament that abhors looking for the silver lin-

ing. Don Quixote and Sancho Panza are a classic pair of opposites on this subtrait, with the former being the optimist, the latter, the pessimist. Don Quixote dreams, and Sancho says the dreams won't work. Similarly, from *Shrek*, Donkey is always optimistic, while Shrek is less optimistic.

N3= (Medium): *Realistic explanations.* Midrange N3 scores suggest one of two profiles: either a) one is rarely extremely optimistic OR pessimistic, but rather more moderate in one's explanations: "Perhaps I'll get more good grades. Perhaps I'll get more bad ones. We'll see." or b) a mid-range score on N3 could be associated with someone who bounces back and forth from optimism to pessimism, highs and lows, depending on the situation. Realism is associated with success in research and other roles that require objectivity.

N3- (Low): *More optimistic explanations.* The optimistic explanation of how life's events turn out sees setbacks as one-time occurrences and achievements as good omens for the future. The popular saying, "You may knock me down, but you can't knock me out," sums up the outlook of the optimist. Also, it's Snoopy's delightful declamation in the cartoon strip *Peanuts*, as he jumps over the tennis net exclaiming: "Game! Set! Life!" The down side of such optimism is that one can be unrealistic about real, serious threats that need attention. Optimism is associated with success in sales roles. Think Luke Skywalker in *Star Wars* or Frodo in *Lord of the Rings.*

N4 ***Coping Level****: The amount of time we require to get over stress.* This subtrait describes the behavior that follows a major crisis, emergency, or other highly stressful situation: death of a loved one, being fired from a job, breaking up with a close friend or partner, failing a course, losing an election, coping with a major illness, loss of income, and so forth. How one copes with such crises is described by a continuum where one extreme bounces back quickly, like being pushed down and jumping right back up and brushing off the dirt, and the other extreme requires considerable time and resources to work one's way to recovery. I (Jane) score very low on this scale. For three years, we had been pursuing work with a very large corporation. Finally, I sold them a pilot project—a half-day team-building session. Two days before the mid-December event, my father died from prostate cancer, but I resolved that I would still lead the session because Pierce was busy with another client. Rescheduling would have been very difficult. I led the session, and they never knew. For me, I was sad, I cried, I missed my dad—yet I was able to compartmentalize that part of my life and keep it from affecting the work with my client. Higher-scoring people have a harder time coping and moving on.

N4+ (High): *Longer rebound time.* Those in the high range of N4 get wiped out by a crisis and need significant time and/or resources to work their way back to normalcy or to move into a problem-solving mode. Whereas a mid-range scorer might need a few hours alone in one's room, those in the high range might require a week, a month, or longer, depending on the nature of the stressor. These people serve clearly as ethical barometers—to the degree that the crisis or stressor they suffered reflected an undesirable state of affairs, the very fact of their extended recovery invites problem solving in order to prevent recurrences. Without such a response to a crisis, one is tempted not to take it seriously—"Well, if you can bounce back from that, it must not be so bad."

N4= (Medium): *Moderate rebound time.* Those in the midrange of N4 tend to exhibit one of two patterns of coping with stressful events: a) They tend to require a moderate amount of time and/or resources to ease their way back from any crisis (as in spending time alone in one's room, and/or talking through the situation with a friend), or b) They are impervious to many crises, but get knocked down pretty hard with others, and, like those in the high range, require much more time/resources for coping.

> **N4-** (Low): *Rapid rebound time.* Those at the low end of the continuum give the appearance of being unfazed by intense stress. While it is possible they feel some inner qualms during an emergency, they tend to maintain self-control throughout and require no special time or activity to help get over it. Calm under fire, cool under pressure, ice in one's veins—these are phrases that have evolved to describe those low in N4, highly resilient, like a coiled spring that is stretched out and, as soon as it is let go of (i.e., as soon as the crisis is over), springs back to its original shape immediately. No time out needed. Good to go. This is the classic sales person who never gets down from being rejected repeatedly by would-be buyers. Or, as the Montreal-based band Simple Plan sings in its album *Shut Up*: "Nothing you say today is gonna bring me down."

We would like to make two points about these four N subtraits. First, when a stressor rears its ugly head, in other words, when something interferes with your preferred course of action, whether a telephone ringing during an intimate moment or interrupting graduate school to care for a seriously sick or needy family member, you will tend to react to the presence of the stressor according to your scores on these four subtraits. Persons scoring low on all four are unlikely to show anxiety, anger, or sadness, but rather will tend to move into problem-solving, as in planning how to minimize the effects of the intrusion. Persons scoring mid to high on N1 will likely become anxious, N2 persons will likely become angry, and N3 persons will likely become depressed. The degree of anger, anxiety, or depression depends on 1) how high the score is, 2) how important the interrupted goal/course of action is, and 3) how much one has in the way of resources (money, time, support, etc.) to eliminate the intrusive stressor or at least to minimize its effects. Persons higher on two or more of these three will exhibit both emotions, either simultaneously or in alternation.

Second, from our study of human evolution, we know that behaviors that help us survive are retained, while those that do not aid in survival disappear. In light of this, it behooves us to remember that each set of opposing traits has survival value—they have each passed the test of time and evolution. Calmness and anxiety, coolness and anger, optimism and pessimism, quick recovery and slow recovery—each has its own unique value in helping us adapt to the demands of our environment. In some situations it pays to be calm, while in others it pays to be anxious. We must avoid the temptation to think of fear, anger, and sadness as negative, bad, or undesirable—they serve an important purpose. In some situations, however, they are not helpful. On the other hand, their opposites—calmness, coolness, and optimism—are also inappropriate at times.

Implications of N for Your Career

If you are N-, you stand out from the pack in your ability to perform calmly in high-stress situations. By volunteering for stressful assignments to the degree that makes sense to you, you will be building on your strengths.

If you are N+, you need to seek out a position or role that is essentially stress-free or has only occasional stress. Celebrate your stressful responses, however, because they tend to serve as a conscience or emotional barometer for your team or organization. Your reactivity, while it can be uncomfortable, is needed.

If you are N=, you will probably be much more satisfied in the long term if your work includes a balance of stressful and restful episodes. One crisis after another or one deadline on the heels of another will probably be unpleasant for you and, in the long term, will be harmful to your health. You need one of two situations: times of intense stress alternating with times of calm or a regular diet of only moderately stressful situations—e.g., the difference between meeting a monthly deadline versus a weekly deadline. You should exercise just after particularly stressful episodes in order to burn up the cortisol (the "fight-or-flight" chemical fuel) that is left in your system from the stress response.

Implications of N for Relating to Adults in Power (Parents, Teachers, Administrators, Bosses)

If a youth who is N- values the relationship with an adult who is N+, the youth needs to take the adult's concerns more seriously. A youth who appears too laid-back, especially to a teacher's concerns, may find the teacher gave a surprising response via grades or other evaluations, mentioning "lack of caring" or "lack of problem ownership."

If a youth is N+ and has an N- adult relationship, the youth may receive evaluations urging the youth to "calm down," "chill out," or "lighten up" because the adult thinks the youth is being far too serious and over-reacting to problems.

If a youth scores N= and is interacting with an adult who is similar, the youth may find that their level of seriousness is exactly right. The same is true if the youth and their boss or associate are both N- or are both N+. People who are similar to us tend to make us more comfortable because they understand how we think and how we approach problems. Of course, if both the youth and an adult are N+, expect interchanges characterized by emotions of anxiety, anger, and sadness, but don't take the feelings personally—each of them is just being natural.

Implications of the N Traits for How You Manage Relationships with Peers

Youths' relations with their peers will be similar to their relationships with adults, in that N- can be misunderstood by an N+ as too cool and uncaring, and an N+ can be misunderstood by an N- as a hothead and negative, rather than simply as expressive. When two N+ are in a relationship, expect fireworks. However, they shouldn't take what is said personally. After the fireworks are over and they can both talk calmly, they should do so.

Implications of the N Traits for Your Communication Style

N- tends to communicate by sharing information, solving problems, making decisions, planning, and being creative. N+ tends to communicate by expressing feelings/emotions—fears, concerns, senses of outrage, despondencies, shame, and so forth. Consequently, the N- may be hard for others to read, emotionally speaking, because the person expresses emotions about almost everything. To make sure others perceive the N- person's strength of feelings, the N- needs to underscore, to emphasize, anything that they feel particularly strongly about. When N+ individuals emote, others want to go into problem solving. However, typically, the emoting N+ wants to stay in expressive mode for awhile.

Sometimes, they don't even want to solve the problem, just to emote about it. The danger here is that the N+ may miss out on opportunities to resolve problems.

Implications of the N Traits for Your Leadership Aspirations

Leadership scholars have written about the "calm, non-anxious presence of the leader." What they mean is that leaders breed confidence in their followers by remaining calm in the face of what others would perceive as stressful situations. Calm in a crisis, nerves of steel, ice in the veins—these are all phrases used to describe effective leaders. Should you aspire to leadership responsibility, this needs to be taken into consideration. Like the girl in Case Study #3 who feels on the inside like a duck paddling desperately under water to stay afloat, the N+ leader will find themselves frequently in positions of having to concentrate on controlling internal feelings and not letting them show, lest they breed fear and concern among their followers, with the resulting lack of confidence in the leader. N+ leaders are most effective in situations with minimal stress. For a leader in a low-stress research laboratory, an N+ could be fine. For a leader on a SWAT team, I would want N-. President Barack Obama illustrates N- in a leader because his continuing calmness breeds hope and confidence among the people. Before him, President Ronald Reagan provided a definitive example of N- leadership, so much so that he acquired the nickname of the "Teflon" president. Barbs just didn't stick to his skin!

A Note on the Biological Basis of Behavior

Before discussing the biological basis of N, let's think for a moment about what we mean by a biological basis for trait behavior. There used to be a school of psychology—Behaviorism—that took the position that all behavior is learned. Just as dogs learn their tricks, so humans learn their behavior—through modeling, conditioning, and so forth. As mother ducks imprint themselves upon their babes, so our idols and heroes can leave their mark on us. I (Pierce) remember a guy in college who walked with his head cocked to the left and with a shuffling gait. I thought he was so cool—Phi Beta Kappa, great musician, handsome, philosophical, respected. As soon as he had graduated and was out of sight, I found myself unconsciously mimicking his walk—head cocked left and shuffling my feet. When I realized what I was doing, I chuckled at myself, and soon abandoned the posing. The Behaviorists would hold me up as an example of how behavior is learned.

But the thinking has changed. Yes, there is an aspect of behavior that is learned, but we are born with certain "predispositions" to certain kinds of behavior. These predispositions are based on combinations of genes, chemicals, hormones, neural pathways, and physical characteristics. Some predispositions are set very early, even in the womb. An example is an embryo's tendency to move and kick, an early predictor of extraversion, or, more specifically, the subtrait E3: Pace, or energy/activity level. Other predispositions emerge later, as during infancy, while others emerge much later, such as a predisposition for alcoholism or post-traumatic stress syndrome. Some of us are more predisposed to certain behaviors than others. It is our scores on the 23 subtraits of the SchoolPlace/WorkPlace Big Five Profile that indicate our predispositions in a variety of behaviors. Over time, as the result of relationships, careers, illnesses, accidents, economic factors, good/bad luck, parenting styles, religious practices, and so forth, our predispositions mature, take shape, and may become more or less intense or extreme. Normally, our experiences change our behavior only slightly, but some experiences (e.g., combat) can change our behavior dramatically. Current research from major studies of twins being conducted globally suggests that approximately 60% of our personalities are inherited.

In each of these five chapters on the five supertraits, we will review what the research tells us are the biological factors that appear to be associated with each of our predispositions. In most cases, it is not clear whether a biological factor is the cause of a behavior, or whether the behavior has caused the biological feature. Just because two things are correlated does not mean that one has caused the other. As University of Michigan neuroscientist Elliot Valenstein (1998) writes:

> Behavior and mental traits, however, are the product of an interaction between anatomical structure and experience—remembered experiences from the past, present experiences, and anticipation of future experiences. Even where there is compelling evidence that some behavioral or mental trait is influenced by genetic factors it is almost always a predisposition, not a certainty.

So, traits are the result of an interaction between our biology and our biography, with both capable of influencing the other. With this in mind, we will summarize now what we know from research about the physical elements that appear to influence our predisposition for need for stability and its subtraits.

The Biological Basis for Need for Stability (N)

Each of the supertraits of the Big Five reflects the physiological activity of an underlying arousal system. An arousal system is one wherein a certain kind of activity proceeds along merrily until it reaches a threshold of some kind. Once that threshold is reached, the kind of activity changes in some way. A smoke alarm is an arousal system: It stays quiet until it senses smoke—i.e., is "aroused" by the smoke—then it begins to buzz or beep. For each behavioral arousal system, a unique type of stimulus triggers the arousal system into new, different, or increased action. For N, the arousal system involved is the autonomic nervous system. The stimulus that triggers it is a stressor, which elicits the *general adaptation syndrome,* or the *fight-or-flight response.* Thus, in a sense, your N score is an estimate of the point at which your fight-or-flight response is triggered and your body moves into autonomic arousal and the activation of the sympathetic nervous system. This period of arousal is eventually counterbalanced by parasympathetic arousal, or a return to normalcy and calmness. Individuals with higher scores (N+ and N++) have a shorter "trigger" and cannot take very much stress before feeling anxious. Those with lower scores (N- and N--) have a lot of "play" in their stress trigger and are able to handle abundant amounts of stress before feeling and showing symptoms of stress: They are often described as having "ice in their veins."

Recent brain-imaging studies reveal that persons with higher N scores tend to have a) decreased volume in the dorsomedial prefrontal cortex and the left medial temporal lobe (including the rear of the hippocampus), and b) increased volume in the mid-cingulate gyrus (DeYoung et al., 2010).

These findings are consistent with the notion of higher N persons tending to have less emotional control, and to being more sensitive to making errors, to experiencing pain, and to goal conflict.

The gene on chromosome 11 that makes BDNF (brain-derived neurotrophic factor) has two variants: If both are one way (the "Val" allele), a person tends to be higher N; the other way (the "Met" allele), lower N; if mixed, mid N. (Ridley, 2003, p. 84) BDNF is sometimes referred to as the "fertilizer of the brain," in that it fosters the growth of new synapses, or nerve endings and connections, that are necessary for new learning and memory. The "Met" allele of this gene is associated with 1) lower N, and 2) increased efficiency of producing and processing BDNF. While it is not clear exactly how increased BDNF production is functionally related to lower N, we do know two related associations: first, that aerobic exercise increases BDNF production, and, second, that aerobic exercise soothes stress by burning up cortisol (the chemical that keeps us in sympathetic arousal). In addition, high N individuals are at risk for depression, and we know that depressed people have less hippocampal volume (the area associated with memory storage). The logical conclusion is that depression hurts memory through unrelieved suppression of BDNF production (since it is critical to forming new synapses for memory), and exercise is both preventive and remedial for this condition. Those with the Met allele are typically protected from depressive tendencies, while those with the Val allele can compensate through a well-planned aerobic exercise regimen. For someone who has had their personal genome analyzed, they could check for the Val allele of the BDNF gene on chromosome 11 as a basis for taking their aerobic exercise more seriously.

Different physiological processes are associated with the four primary subtraits of Need for stability: worry, temper, outlook, and coping level. We will consider each in turn.

N1: Worry

Hamer and Copeland (1998) talk about early predictors of anxiety and shyness: fast fetal heart rate, more blinking, tighter muscles (especially in the face, and having more trouble "making faces"), heart rates greater under stress, higher blood pressure when standing up, saliva with twice the level of cortisol, pupils which dilate more quickly under stress. (pp. 55-62) As these are predictors, when you see them occurring in a child, become determined to make these high priorities: elimination/minimization of stressors, proper diet, and regular aerobic exercise. These priorities are beneficial at all ages.

Underlying these symptoms of fear and anxiety are a family of chemicals. Mice have a gene that produces a protein, stathmin, that is associated with fear (our subtrait N1). With the gene removed, mice exhibit reckless, daring behavior and even show resistance to fears learned through conditioning. Humans have a similar protein. It is likely that at some point in the future, we may be able to control our fear (increasing fear, as in treating sociopaths, who have deficient fear, or decreasing fear, as in treating phobias) through administering doses of stathmin, stathmin enhancers, or stathmin blockers.

In addition to stathmin, levels of oxytocin and prolactin (made in the hypothalamus and controlled by the pituitary gland) tend to decrease N1, while glucocorticoids increase N1. Oxytocin can be increased through breast-feeding, so mothers should place a high priority on breast-feeding exclusively for the first six months of life (i.e., no formula), and then for as long as mother and infant are comfortable with it (a recommendation by the American Academy of Pediatrics). Also, oxytocin, the "cuddle" chemical, is produced through such activities as having meals together. As mentioned elsewhere, teens who eat the evening meal with their family show reduced signs of stressed behavior. The more oxytocin, the more bonding occurs. Glucocorticoids are produced by stress, so it is clear that eliminating stressors can reduce levels of N1.

Specific brain areas are involved in the Need for stability and one's response to stress. S. Whittle, N. B. Allen, D. I. Lubman, & M. Yücel (2005) report in their imaging studies that negative affect (fear, anger, sadness) involves the amygdala, hippocampus, anterior cingulated cortex, and right dorsolateral prefrontal cortex. The amygdala serves the primary role of evaluating stimuli as threatening or not. There is some evidence that larger, more active amygdalas are associated with more inhibited behavior, as increased fear tends to put the damper on venturing out. With pardon to Shakespeare, "Fear doth make cowards of us all." Some studies associate the amygdala more with fear (a reaction to a threat of the moment), and the hippocampus with anxiety (a general state of fear/unease not tied to any concrete threat). Donald Pfaff (in *Cerebrum*, 2007) makes the case that fair play is based on the fear response, in that fears—regardless of whether they are learned or unlearned—of retaliation, punishment, damnation, shame, and so forth limit behavior. This is consistent with why we call N+ "the conscience of the organization," and it is an individual difference variable based on levels of glutamates, CRH (corticotrophin-releasing hormone, a precursor of the stress hormone cortisol), and others that we have just enumerated.

N2: Temper

Anger is associated with the Nr2e1 gene in mice (on chromosome 10) and the NR2E1 gene in humans (chromosome 6). Removal of the gene in mice results in males killing and maiming each other, with females somewhat less vicious, but consequently exhibiting poor mothering. In other words, this gene appears to dampen anger, to be associated with a "slow" trigger. Research is underway to determine how this knowledge might result in medications that could modify anger levels.

Defective versions of the gene that expresses monoamine oxidase A (MAOA) increase the likelihood of violent/aggressive behavior *if* a person was mistreated as a child. Good versions of the gene prevent adult violence even if such mistreatment in childhood occurred. MAOA breaks down serotonin, thus reducing serotonin levels. Optimum levels of serotonin are associated with positive mood, but unusually high *or* low levels of serotonin are associated with temper and aggression. Yes, this appears contradictory, and the precise way that serotonin works is far from completely clear. Yet, it appears that when one has too little serotonin, then MAOA-inhibitor drugs such as linezolid (Zyvox), or turmeric in its natural form, can relieve the aggressive tendencies resulting from low serotonin, and are used for the more resistant instances of depression. In other words, MAOA inhibitors prevent MAOA from breaking down serotonin, thus allowing serotonin to accumulate to a more optimum level. But if one has too much serotonin, then one needs to promote the production of MAOA in order to break down serotonin, thus limiting its accumulation and reducing overall levels.

Anger is also associated with testosterone levels (felt anger) and noradrenalin (expressed anger). Testosterone appears to trigger the actual feeling of anger, while noradrenalin appears to regulate the intensity of the feeling and the degree to which it is overtly expressed. Both of these chemicals are increased as the result of winning a competition, especially winning in a competitive sport. To control someone's temper, try to time their having an athletic competition (tennis, wall ball, etc.) with someone who can beat them (if you want them to limit their temper, as before an important presentation). Or, schedule them with someone whom they can beat (if you want them to increase their temper, as before an important confrontation where meekness would not serve one's interests).

Also appearing to influence levels of violence, at least in mice, are the levels of nitric oxide (nitr*ous* oxide is what we know as "laughing gas" and has been used to put people in a blissful state in the dentist's chair). Mice without nitric oxide are killers. Research is underway to develop medications that elevate nitric oxide levels in humans as a way to minimize violent, aggressive behavior in problem offenders. An implant of some sort, perhaps?

It is interesting to note that the male-to-female ratio with respect to violence and aggression holds across cultures, even if overall rates of violence are dramatically different. Where one country/city may have ten times more killings than another, the ratios in the two locales will still be somewhere around 20 to 1, male to female. All the more reason to encourage males to engage in regular aerobic exercise, proper diet, and minimization of stressors (Hamer and Copeland, 1998, p. 107).

N3: Outlook

The 5-HTT (5-hydroxy-tryptamine, another name for serotonin) gene moderates depression by being a delivery mechanism for serotonin. It is known as the serotonin transporter gene. If one is maltreated as a child, *and* the gene is defective, one is more likely to become depressed at some future time. If mistreated yet possessing the good version of gene, depression is unlikely. If not mistreated while having the defective gene, depression is also unlikely. Having insufficient levels of serotonin in one's system can be offset through diet (tryptophan-rich foods) and exercise. Of course, as we saw earlier, one can have too much serotonin—there is an optimal level.

Another chemical associated with feelings of guilt, depression, and pessimism is Vitamin B12. Low levels of B12 are associated with poor mood. Levels can be determined as part of a regular physical, and supplements are available when a boost is needed. B12 is attached to proteins so meat, fish, and dairy are good dietary sources.

In a sample of 155 12- and 13-year-olds who had taken the Early Adolescent Temperament Questionnaire, N.B. Allen et al. (2006) found the subjects' MRIs showed an association between negative affect and a network in the left dorsal paralimbic area of the anterior cingulate cortex of the brain. Specifically, the researchers were studying frustration in the face of obstacles to goals. Localizing such brain activity associated with a specific behavior is the precursor to developing medications that increase, decrease, or stabilize activity in those pathways.

Finally, low dopamine levels are associated with depression, as well as Parkinson's disease. Higher dopamine levels are associated with a keen sense of seeking rewards. Higher dopamine levels have the peculiar effect of heightening one's curiosity. This comes out in all manner of "what if?" behaviors. What if I winked at him? What if I ran an extra mile? What if I introduced myself to her? Each of these "what if" initiatives is motivated by the anticipation of success, of some kind of reward. Elevate levels of dopamine pharmaceutically through the familiar drug L-dopa or naturally through a lean-protein-rich diet complemented with moderate (unsaturated) fat and carbohydrates.

N4: Coping Level

Autonomic arousal—the so-called "fight or flight" response—occurs when we intensely experience one or more of the negative emotions of fear, anger, and sadness. One of the chemicals that influences how quickly and efficiently a person recovers from autonomic arousal is cyclic guanosine monophosphate. Adequate supplies of this chemical nudge a person back from sympathetic arousal and into parasympathetic arousal, or the normal state of arousal. When the supply of the chemical is inadequate, one tends to stay in sympathetic arousal for prolonged periods. Of course, it is not the only factor that influences the ending of the fight-flight response. Neurons that produce endorphins (natural opiates within our bodies, or the "morphine within") also influence rapidity of recovery—adequate endorphin production, quick recovery; inadequate, stay stressed. Duke University psychiatrist Redford Williams finds that, in addition to these chemical influences, a history of inadequate physical nurture and trust in childhood is associated with staying in sympathetic arousal longer. For a more complete description of the stress response, see Pierce's chapter on stress in *The Owner's Manual for the Brain* (3rd ed., 2006).

You may get the impression that the biological basis of N, or any trait, is a complex affair. You would be right! We have learned much about the physical basis of behavior, and we are learning more daily. One of the major issues of our time is what to do with this knowledge. In Chapter 2, we presented a variety of ways that "states" of a trait might be raised or lowered. Most of the suggestions build on the biological knowledge just presented. A major controversy today revolves around the issue of prescription medications as means for behavior modification (c.f., Valenstein, 1998). In spite of all of this information, and all of the controversy, we all need to remember that every behavior has its opposite, and that each of us has an optimal balance between a behavior and its opposite—our scores on either the SchoolPlace or WorkPlace Big Five Profile are an estimate of where this point of balance is for each of us. Over the long term, that point of balance will not change on average; so we need to arrange our lives according to our need for balance in each of our traits. In the Need for stability dimension, this means that people who score lower can take a lifestyle characterized by more stress, while someone who scores higher should pursue a lifestyle characterized by less stress. And the causes of stress—stressors—are different for each of us. Engage your associates in helping you brainstorm how to neutralize specific stressors. Usually, there's a way. I (Pierce) once worked in a "cubicle farm" without a private office. Unable to get my work done because of interruptions, I came up with the idea of putting a headset on as though I were listening to a (professional) audiotape. Of course, there was nothing coming through the earphones, just silence. But, the interruptions fell to a trickle!

From this discussion of the traits associated with stress, we progress to the traits that govern how we deal with being in the center of the action. Just as Need for stability is associated with the so-called negative emotions of fear, anger, and sadness, we will find that extraversion is associated with the so-called positive emotions of warmth, excitement, and joy.

6

Extraversion

All About Being in the Thick of the Action

+	I want to go where the people dance. I want some action. I want to live. --Alicia Bridges, *I Love the Nightlife*
=	Solitude and company may be allowed to take their turns: the one creates in us the love of mankind, the other that of ourselves; solitude relieves us when we are sick of company, and conversation when we are weary of being alone, so that the one cures the other. There is no man so miserable as he that is at a loss how to use his time. --Seneca, 1st century C.E. Roman philosopher; advisor to the Emperor Nero
-	I lock myself inside my room. I wanna be alone. With you around, you'll only add on. I wanna be alone. --Green Day, *I Want to Be Alone*

Guide to This Chapter:

- Definition of the E Supertrait
- Three Case Studies
- Definitions of the Six Subtraits of E
- Implications of E for Career Exploration
- Implications of E for Relating to Adults in Power (Parents, Teachers, Administrators, Bosses)
- Implications of E for Managing Relationships with Peers
- Implications of E for Communication Style
- Implications of E for Leadership Aspirations
- Biological Basis for Extraversion (E)

In the quotes above, Alicia Bridges reflects the outlook of the more extraverted person. However, keep in mind that not all people with the same trait exhibit the same behavior. Extraversion is a trait, not a choice. Bridges has chosen to use her extraverted temperament through song, while an-

Mapping Out the Big Five Traits

N	E	O	A	C
Need for Stability	**Extraversion**	**Originality**	**Accommodation**	**Consolidation**
N+ Reactive	E+ Extravert	O+ Explorer	A+ Adapter	C+ Focused
N= Responsive	E= Ambivert	O= Moderate	A= Negotiator	C= Balanced
N- Resilient	E- Introvert	O- Preserver	A- Challenger	C- Flexible
N1: Worry	**E1: Approach Level**			
N2: Temper	**E2: Group Orientation**			
N3: Outlook	**E3: Pace**			
N4: Coping Level	**E4: Leadership**			
	E5: Trust			
	E6: Tact			

other extravert might choose volunteering as a candy striper or running for political office. Similarly, the rock trio Green Day nails the essence of what we're like when we introvert. Namely, that we are alone. Aloneness entails, typically, quiet, solitude, stillness. In general, it's the absence of sensory stimulation. However, not all persons with an introverted temperament would choose their closed room as a setting—it could just as well be outdoors, as in "the loneliness of the long distance runner." Many of us find it unpleasant to experience too much of either of these extremes, and we are called more "ambiverted." As Seneca phrases it, these extremes "take their turns." With some ambiverts, the extremes may never occur, as some ambiverts show a preference for moderate stimulation and moderate companionship, rejecting both crowds and solitude.

Definition of the E Supertrait

Traditionally, we have distinguished between extraverts and introverts as those who have many relationships/friends and those who have few. However, current research has expanded our view of extraversion. At its core is a continuum that reflects one's comfort with sensory stimulation. At one extreme is a person who feels comfortable being in the thick of the action—this is the meaning of the phrase "the roar of the crowd, the smell of the greasepaint." Excitement, noise, people—all of these mean sensory bombardment, and people at the other end of the continuum get their fill quickly. Thomas Gray refers to extraversion/introversion in his phrase "far from the madding crowd," one that Thomas Hardy used to entitle his novel about a shepherd's life in rural Dorchester.

Extraversion is a complex trait. While comfort with sensory stimulation is at its core, it also includes warmth (versus coolness), enthusiasm (versus quietness), sociability (versus solitude), active lifestyle (versus sedentary), taking charge (versus leaving well enough alone, or independence), trust of others (versus skepticism), and tactfulness (versus directness, or bluntness). One of the valuable contributions of the Five Factor Model to understanding personality is the notion that, in addition to extraverts and introverts, there is a significant group in the middle we refer to as "ambiverts."

Early in my career—before the Big Five—the tests I (Pierce) took called me an extravert. This never felt comfortable, as I am just as comfortable being alone as I am with others, and I like a balance of the two. In fact, I have a strong negative reaction to being in crowds and an adverse reaction to excess sensory bombardment. I've left concerts before because the lady's perfume next to me felt/smelled like the main production area of a petrochemical factory. And I've left restaurants when the band was amplified so that my ears hurt, and I couldn't hear myself or others talk. The Big Five has rescued me from extraversion by allowing me to be an ambivert! Let's take a look at the three levels of extraversion.

Extravert (E+)

If you are an extravert—scoring above 55 on E, then you typically spend the majority of your time, when you can control it, by being around other people, moving about rather than sitting most of the day, and enjoying being in the center of the action, often as a leader. The higher the score—in the 60s and 70s—the greater the proportion of your time is spent around people, active, in the center of things. With extremely high scorers, precious little time is allotted during the day for "introverted" activity, such as reading, writing, or working with one's hands. Extraverts will often take a solitary, introverted activity, and find a way to make it into a group activity. For example, rather than study alone for a test, an extravert is likely to find one or more study partners to quiz each other, discuss possible questions, and so forth. Extraverts are more likely to read an abbreviated version of a novel (a comic book, a summary in *Wikipedia*, or a movie version), rather than get quiet and solitary with the entire book. Of course, extraverts are different from one another. They all like to spend the majority of their time actively around other people, but they may choose different activities for being extraverted or introverted. For example, one extravert may avoid solitude by joining a study group, yet embrace solitude while practicing the piano. Another extravert may avoid solitude by practicing trumpet with a friend, yet embrace solitude by climbing in bed occasionally with a good sci-fi novel.

> "Good company and good discourse are the very sinews of virtue."
> --Izaak Walton

Your natural style is to be talkative, enthusiastic, assertive, sociable, warm, optimistic, and fun loving. But, as we say, not all extraverts are alike—some will exhibit more or less of these traits than others. It is highly likely that you will be comfortable with strong sensory stimulation—loud sounds such as music or crowd noise, sights such as bright lights, tastes such as those you might encounter during an elegant meal, smells such as those coming from vendors' carts on a city street, or touch, as in the rush of wind past your face when you are skiing. You often become the formal or informal leader of your study, project, sports, club, or work team. However, you may at times come across to others as outspoken, overbearing, aggressive, heedless, or shallow. You may also lack good listening skills because of your tendency to dominate a conversation. *Sesame Street*'s Big Bird typifies extraversion, as does Julie Andrews' character Maria in *The Sound of Music*—she's just too extraverted to stay in a convent. Another example is Will Smith's character "J" in *Men in Black,* especially in contrast to Tommy Lee Jones's "K"—who comes across as more introverted, more humorless. Sharpay Evans, the uppity ingénue in *High School* Musical, typifies unrelenting extraversion, plus, we will revisit her when we need to illustrate "A-." For examples of E+, think of: salespersons, cheerleaders, entrepreneurs, pediatricians, and entertainers, all of whom get precious little quiet time, and are clearly drawn to the action.

Ambivert (E=)

If extraverts run mostly hot and introverts run mostly cold, then ambiverts run either a) lukewarm (a mix of the two that averages out to be even), or b) alternating hot and cold (about half of the time with each). That is another way of saying that ambiversion is the mean between two extremes. But as we have said before, there are two ways to get a mean, or average, score: by adding two extreme scores and dividing by two, or by adding the same mid score to itself and dividing by two. Let's further illustrate the two kinds of ambiverts with Sam Lukewarm and Fran Hotcold. Sam Lukewarm avoids crowds AND solitude, preferring to be around a small group of friends, family, or co-workers most of the time. Fran Hotcold likes to divide time roughly equally between crowds (e.g., clubs, stadiums, auditoriums, cafeterias, and the like) and solitude (e.g., reading, taking walks, computing, driving, hobbying, and the like).

$$(80 + 20)/2 = 50 = (50 + 50)/2$$

We (Jane and Pierce) are more like Sam. We don't care for crowds, although we go to an occasional athletic event (about once every two years), and we get the heebie-jeebies when we have to go to an Expo at a convention (usually about twice a year) and mingle with thousands of conventioneers and exhibiters.

If you are an ambivert, you tend to move easily from being with other people to being alone. If you have to be in an environment with people all the time or be exclusively alone, you will probably find either extreme dissatisfying. Although you have a moderate threshold for sensory stimulation, you will usually get tired of it after a while and will try to get away from it. Because you operate from the midrange, you may come across as an introvert if your peers are strong extraverts or as an extravert if they are strong introverts. Other ambiverts will find you similar to themselves, sometimes wanting to be with others, sometimes wanting to be alone. Kelsey, the accompanist/composer in *High School Musical*, typifies the ambivert, with her introverted side spent in the solitude of composing music and practicing piano, and her extraverted side spent accompanying and helping with theatrical productions.

Introvert (E-)

Introverts have gotten a bad rap over the years. The reason is that they have been perceived as anti-social, as deficient in social skills or values. Marti Olsen Laney in her books on introversion (2002, 2005) attributes this to Sigmund Freud's dislike of Carl Jung and Alfred Adler (they disputed Freud's claims). As Jung and Adler were both introverts, Dr. Freud proceeded to cast introversion in a negative light (Laney, 2005, p. 9). However, recent research has changed our thinking about introversion. Namely, introverts prefer working alone not because it is solitary, but because it is quiet. As a rule, to prefer solitude is to prefer quiet, or absence of sensory bombardment. Marilyn Whirlwind, the nurse-receptionist in the CBS classic series *Northern Exposure*, sits in one episode by the edge of a lake with her would-be boyfriend who is a mime, a 24-7 mime, who has chosen never to talk. She laments the impact of this on their relationship, but understands, as she says gently: "Words are a heavy thing. If birds talked, they couldn't fly."

If you are an introvert, you tend to prefer a quieter environment, which often means being alone. Where possible, introverts will gravitate toward projects where they can work in relative quiet, which again means being alone or with a few people. Typically, you are a serious, quiet, private person who may prefer writing or e-mail to talking with others. To some, you may come across as cold, hard to read, or reclusive. You may also appear to be a loner or even an eccentric to others. Your preferred work environment is in an area where you experience very little sensory stimulation. The "roar of the crowd, the smell of the greasepaint" likely doesn't appeal to you. You would much prefer to be "far from the madding crowd" but not necessarily alone. But alone is OK. Oscar the Grouch in *Sesame Street* plays introvert to Big Bird's extravert: living in a (garbage) can is the ultimate metaphor for getting away from it all. Oscar happens to be a grouch with his anger spilling over, but that is not characteristic of introversion. Think: bookkeepers, programmers, accountants, engineers, researchers, librarians, forest rangers, laboratory technicians, and so forth, all content being productive off stage and away from the action. In football, the linemen are more extraverted, the free safeties more introverted.

Keep in mind that there is no such thing as a pure extravert, ambivert, or introvert. They come in an infinite variety of behaviors, with no two precisely having the same collection. Similarly, the genes, body chemistry, and neural pathways of extraverts (or ambiverts, introverts) are not all the same. Labels such as "extravert" or "reactive" (high N1: Worry) are simply a shortcut to indicate, for example, that one individual has more extraverted behaviors, or more reactive behaviors, in comparison to others. Without knowing the individual in some depth, we have no idea which behaviors those people have. As the French poet Paul Valery writes (in French!), "Truly seeing something is to forget the name of what one sees." The label, or name, such as extravert," focuses your attention and arouses certain expectations, but you have to know the individual to determine which expectations are valid and which are not.

We will now look at three case studies that illustrate how levels of extraversion affect the lives of teenagers.

Three Case Studies

E Case Study 1: The Football Game

We two authors both score as ambiverts. Our favorite ambivert story relates to the first year that the Carolina Panthers played NFL football in Charlotte. In the interest of rallying around the home team and being supportive of this new NFL team in the Carolinas, we had bought tickets with some friends to a home game against the San Francisco Forty-Niners. On game day, after discovering the wonders of tailgating, we headed for what is now Bank of America Stadium with the rest of the crowd.

Mapping Out the Big Five Traits

As we made our way to our seats among the noisy throng, we found ourselves only four rows away from the playing field, seated behind some "TV-wannabe" characters who had come with large prepared signs, blue wigs, and much enthusiasm. The game finally kicked off, and within a short time, the Panthers were winning—a pleasant turn of events! During the first half, we were totally involved in the game and in conversations with our friends. When we scored, we sang the Panther fight song and enjoyed "high fives" with the enthusiasts sitting in front of us during the final high note of the song. By the time the game moved into the third quarter, the overly warm September sun was becoming unpleasant. We caught knowing glances from one another—a grimace here, hands to the ears, slightly audible and disapproving "umphs." With growing concern for our long-term hearing, we noticed that the volume on the stadium music was increasing several decibels with every new song played over the public address system. Even though the Panthers were still winning, the game had begun to drag by for us, and we longed for the end. When at last the final minutes ticked off the game clock, we cheered our victory and made our way out of the stadium with the whooping fans.

At the front gate, one of our more extraverted friends said, "Hey, there are parties with live bands downtown. Let's head there for the celebration!" Our eyes met in silent, pleading assent, signaling escape. We politely declined the offer and told our friends that we would just walk home, since we lived near the stadium and were ready for some exercise. Although we had enjoyed the earlier part of the outing, by the time the game was over, we had had enough—enough of the crowd, enough of the loud music, enough of the sensory bombardment. We had reached our extraversion saturation point and were ready to introvert for the remainder of the day. Quietly, we walked home. The "madding crowd" receded in a most delightful way.

We like to use the image "buckets," or "fuel cans" (see Figure 1.2, "Liam's Fuel Cans for Sociability and Solitude."): For each dimension, two buckets represent the amount of energy an individual has for each end of the continuum. Some people have a large bucket for crowds, a small bucket for solitude. They were the ones who went dancing after the game because they hadn't used up their bucket of "crowd fuel" yet! The people who have a small bucket for crowds and a large bucket for solitude stayed home and watched the game on television with the sound turned down, if not off. We, as ambiverts, have roughly equal-sized buckets for crowds and solitude, and we eventually ran out of crowd fuel—we were running on fumes and desperately needed to switch to our solitude bucket by walking home quietly.

E Case Study 2: Reviewing the Essay

In dormitories, I (Pierce) observed that extraverts tended to enjoy popping into another student's room in situations such as this:

> *E+ (Extravert):* "Hi, Carlos! You look like you're really into that paper you're typing."
>
> *E- (Introvert, flatly):* "I was."
>
> *E+:* "Well, since you've stopped, take a look at this essay for Dr. Goodykoontz for me, will you?"

E-: "OK, leave it, and I will."

E+: "I was hoping you could just look it over and give me your thoughts. I really want to finish it before supper. I've got rehearsals all evening."

E- (sighing audibly): "I really prefer having time to read and digest something before I talk about it."

E+: "I'm not looking for a three-hour speech from you about it. I simply want to hear off the top of your head if you think it hits the main points from Doctor G's recent lectures on narrative technique."

E-: "Take it to Anwar. He's better with fast responses than I am. Otherwise, I need until tomorrow to look it over."

E= (Ambivert, walking by): "What are you guys up to?"

E+: "I need a quick critique of this essay. I want to finish it before supper, and Carlos says he needs until tomorrow to 'read and digest' what I've written before he answers. He suggested you might do it faster."

E=: "Well, I agree with Carlos. You should give us more notice. You've had this assignment for a week already. But I'll do it. Give me ten minutes to read it over and then come by my room. OK?"

E+: "Great!"

Situations like this happen constantly when we don't understand the personalities of our associates. Without knowing how others handle or process information, we often assume that it's the same way we do. When they try to tell us differently, we may incorrectly assume that they're just being uncooperative, they don't care about our project, or even that they don't like us. What appears to be someone else's personal judgment of us is often nothing more than them being them, a matter of personal style.

E Case Study 3: Sweet 16

In a leadership workshop with about 50 high school students, we posed this situation:

> "You have a 16th birthday coming up. Your family has let you know that they wish to help you celebrate in a way that would be most satisfying to you. They ask you to think about how you'd like to celebrate, and they'll do their best to help make it happen. You think about this for a couple of days, and then go to them with your proposal. What do you ask for?"

The students were grouped by extraversion scores. Here's how they responded, from very low extraversion (i.e., highly introverted) to very high extraversion:

E-- (extreme introverts): "I'd like my family to go to the beach for the weekend and just have some nice long walks together."

E- (moderate introverts): "I'd like a dinner for me and a friend at a nice restaurant. It would be quiet and dark and there'd be a fire in the restaurant fireplace. Or if my parents would like to cook us a really nice meal—all my favorites—and have it at home, with a nice fire, that'd be ok, too."

E= (ambiverts): "I'd like a gathering of my friends, maybe a dozen or so, and have a cookout with dancing in our garage."

Mapping Out the Big Five Traits

E+ (moderate extraverts): "I'd want to invite 50 or 60 of my closer friends to a dinner buffet and dance with a DJ at a downtown hotel. And perhaps I could emcee a roast in my honor."

E++ (extreme extraverts): "I'd want to invite all of my friends from school, church, scouts, and work to a dinner/dance at a downtown hotel, and with a live band. I could emcee and call on various people to reminisce about some of our good memories and perhaps talk about our goals for after school. Then afterwards I'd want to take about a dozen friends to our house at the beach and hang out for the rest of the weekend! And maybe have a luau with limbo. And I could organize a volleyball contest."

> *Mother:* "There's more in high school than being well-liked."
> *Charlie Bartlett:* "What do you have in mind?"
> *Mother:* "Nothing, specifically."
> --*Charlie Bartlett*

Interesting truths emerge from these scenarios. Can you spot those that relate to extraversion? One of the most obvious elements is the number of people who are involved in each scenario. As we move from E-- at the low end of the scale to E++ at the high end, the number of people who are included in the event increases, from just the family, to a small group of friends, to a significant segment of the community! One reason for this increase is that additional people contribute to the sensation of the overall experience—the more the merrier/noisier. This relates to sociability, our second element of extraversion. You will also notice that the examples tend to talk more and more about the senses as the E score increases—more sights, more sounds, more tastes, more sensations, more activities for the body to experience. A third element in analyzing the responses has to do with how large a leadership role the person is comfortable taking when being recognized.

Now that we have explored the characteristics of the supertrait itself, let's take a look at the six subtraits of extraversion.

Definitions of the Six Subtraits of E

E1 ***Approach Level:*** *The amount of warmth and enthusiasm we express.* We have often called this the "life of the party" scale or the "cheerleader" scale. At the high end, we tend to see smiles, touching, enthusiasm, laughter, strong sense of humor, and genuine enjoyment. These folks appear to be easy to get to know, or, easy to approach. At the lower end, we tend to see a quieter, cooler person, not necessarily one who prefers solitude, but one who is harder to read, less expressive.

E1+ (High): *Shows a lot of positive feelings.* Persons scoring in the high range tend to be exuberant and are frequently described as "full of life" because of their untiring outward flow of the positive emotions. This quality is often associated with "charisma," that warm, expressive quality that draws like a magnet, like the Pied Piper of Hamelin. Possession of this quality is associated with persuasive ability, as put into practice in sales, politics, reformers (Nelson Mandela had this quality), and the like. A cheerleader who scores high on this quality will be energized by the constant enthusiasm of a football or basketball game, while a cheerleader scoring lower on this quality would likely be drained of energy af-

ter a game. In fact, it is unlikely that someone scoring low on E1 would be attracted to cheerleading in the first place.

E1= (Medium): *Demonstrates some positive feelings.* We are writing this on the Saturday before Barack Obama's inauguration in 2009. It has been interesting to observe his political style. We would describe him as midrange in E1. He does not constantly exude warmth the way that, say, Bill Clinton, Sarah Palin, or even Joe Biden, his running mate, do. However, Obama has enough of this natural quality to be able to turn it on as needed. You can see him turn it on and off during a speech or some other situation when he breaks into a large, genuine smile and then quickly returns to a more serious demeanor. John Kerry, who lost the election four years before, would likely score low on E1, we are sure, as he seldom communicated the warmth we see in Obama. *Note*: Recall that midrange scorers may come in one of two styles, or somewhere in between: either warm/enthusiastic half the time, cool/serious the other half, or lukewarm all the time, somewhere between enthusiastic and serious. Colin Powell strikes us as lukewarm, neither overly serious nor overly enthusiastic, warmer than John Kerry, cooler than Bill Clinton, and relatively unvarying.

E1- (Low): *Holds down positive feelings.* Those scoring low on E1 are typically regarded as serious, perhaps lacking in playfulness or humor, even aloof. This coolness and reserve is a desirable trait for roles that require steadiness and rationality, an even keel. Brain surgeon, nuclear power plant operator, police radio dispatcher, air traffic controller, sniper...you get the idea. It is not that these people lack the ability or interest in having positive feelings—they just lack the natural "amplifier" that takes their feelings up to a sufficient level so as to be noticeable. It is as though their amplifier is unplugged, or turned down real low. Put another way, rather than saying they lack something, they possess exquisite control over their positive feelings. In order to avoid being misread as uncaring/unfeeling, they need to consciously engage in acts of positive regard on occasion, such as sending cards, notes, flowers, giving a hand, and so forth.

*E2 **Group Orientation**: The degree to which we enjoy being with others.* Carol Gilligan (1982) and others, observe that guys see themselves as essentially isolated, while girls see themselves as connected (Cobb, 2007, p. 51). This is likely associated with the fact that girls have higher levels of oxytocin, the "cuddle" chemical that is secreted during mother/infant nursing and also when two people eat together, and that has the effect of forming strong bonds/attachments. While this different sense of connectivity to others appears to form the core of male and female identity, this is different than, for example, scores on E2. High E2 males still see themselves as separated from others, but are nonetheless more comfortable being around people. Low E2 males not only see themselves as less connected to others, but also are also behaviorally more solitary. Females in general simply feel more attached to others, regardless of whether the others are physically present. E2 group orientation is not about this degree of attachment versus isolation, but is about one's personal preference for being around others, versus being alone.

E2+ (High) [1]: *Prefers being around others.* High scorers on E2 are at their most comfortable when they are in the presence of others, be it peers, family, work associates, or some other assortment. As a general rule,

---

[1] D. Dobbs (July 8, 2007) in "The Gregarious Brain" (*The New York Times Magazine,* pp. 43-47) writes about Williams Syndrome (WS). This disorder involves problems with numerical and spatial skills, a strong urge for being with others, and a corresponding love of music, conversation, and storytelling. Those with WS are socially uninhibited, inept at social norms, and often die from circulatory system problems. They have flawed connections to the amygdala, such that they see all faces as friendly, regardless of emotions being expressed at the time—they never develop fear of

these people are more comfortable in crowds or large groups than are lower scorers. And they run out of "solitary fuel" rather quickly. Our (E2+) younger daughter's early career found her alone at home all day working from her home office. Enjoying the work, but displeased with the unremitting solitude, she compensated by turning on the television in a nearby room and a radio in another, as a way of simulating office mates! Plus, she made plans almost every day to meet someone for lunch outside her home. I suppose she's a chip off the old block. While I (Pierce) am on the borderline of medium and high, I clearly have my limits to being alone. When in graduate school, I had to spend uncounted hours in the stacks of the graduate library at the University of North Carolina at Chapel Hill. Plenty of people were there with me, but they were inaccessible, invisible, stuck like monks in their study carrels. In order to provide me with some sense of being around others, I began the practice of using a carrel adjacent to a window that looked down on the university community's many passersby trekking from parking areas along the library walkway and on to various destinations—classrooms, offices, snack bars. Even though I couldn't talk with them, I had active fellows in my midst. Another trick I learned was to use a carrel next to a stairwell, looking up from time to time at peers and other scholars changing floors with books underarm. Where there's a will, there's a way! And awareness is the problem-solver's first step.

E2= (Medium): *Occasionally seeks out others.* Midrange scorers, again, come in two styles: those who like a balance between solitude and society, and those who like neither, preferring something in between being alone and being around lots of people. This latter style, for example, tends to avoid large crowds (like most sporting events) as well as solitude, preferring to be around a few others, such as family, a few close friends, a study group, and so forth. I (Pierce) really like to watch a good basketball game, but I remember in college feeling crowded in the gym during a game. I was much more comfortable going to a cross-country meet—not exactly a crowd-drawing event. I am midrange in E2, the kind who likes small groups and avoids both crowds and solitudes, although I prefer solitude to crowds!

E2- (Low): *Prefers being alone.* It is not that those scoring low in E2 are antisocial, or even without relationships. They are simply content with, and find satisfaction with, studying, working, exercising, cooking, and otherwise going about their business without human interaction or with minimal human interaction. They attend necessary meetings, conferences, conventions, presentations, and so forth, but they use up their "fuel" for such events rather quickly and seek the earliest opportunity to revert to their "fuel tank" for solitude. They

> "The strongest man in the world is he who stands most alone."
>
> --Henrik Ibsen

---

social situations. This is the result of about 25 genes that detach during early cell division (meiosis) soon after conception. "They know no strangers but can claim few friends." (p. 44) The incidence of WS is 1 in 7,500. Apparently the sociability causes the effusive language, as even infants without language but who have WS show the excessive gregariousness, not clinging to a parent, but eagerly going to the outstretched arms of anyone. The WS brain is 15% smaller, mostly attributed to reduced dorsal/spatial areas, thus allowing ventral/language/facial enjoyment areas free rein. This is the opposite of fragile X syndrome, which has similar spatial/numerical problems, but avoids eye contact and social intercourse. In Williams syndrome individuals, the orbitofrontal cortex fails to communicate with the amygdala when encountering threatening faces, but does so when met by nonhuman threats (e.g., rattling snakes and hungry Bengal tigers). WS is E2+ gone awry, while fragile X syndrome is E2- gone awry. WS should also be contrasted with sociopaths: The former cares about people but lacks skill at relating, while the latter has the skills, but doesn't care for others.

will typically feel a sense of relief when the meeting, etc. is over, and they can beat a hasty retreat for their room, office, or other private place. This is one of the failings of the typical school design—too few private places (e.g., lofts, nooks in the library, dark room, weight room, solo music practice studios, shade trees with benches) for the more solitary student. In the typical school, it is easier to find a quiet place than a private place.

E3 ***Pace****: The degree to which we like to be physically active.* This subtrait contains a continuum that is anchored in a preference for sedentary activity at one end and a preference for physical activity at the other, from sitting at a desk to constant movement, like the two extremes of keyboarding at a computer all day versus walking door to door, neighborhood to neighborhood, as a mail carrier. One's activity level is apparent at an early age—in the womb! Infants who move around more during gestation—changing position, kicking, punching, and so forth, end up more active as teens and adults and are typically more extraverted. If infants who move around less, they typically end up more sedentary, more introverted. Conduct your own research! Ask a mother who has had two or more children to identify which kids were more/less active in the womb, and then compare that to the extraversion/introversion levels of her children now.

E3+ (High): *Prefers to be physically active.* High scorers tire when sitting for prolonged periods. The urge to move around, to stand up, to pace or walk, becomes strong, irresistible. The higher the score, the stronger and more frequent the urge. An E3+ who has to sit in class all day with only a handful of minutes in between really needs permission, and explicit opportunities, to stand up periodically during class. Often, high E3s will buy a "stand-up" desk to minimize sitting time. These folks should consider careers in which long periods of sitting are not required, such as teaching, sports, lab work, manufacturing (especially in production areas). At one point In *Wuthering Heights*, Cathy Earnshaw begins to run from the room, and, upon being told not to run, we hear a friend comment: "She's a spirited girl." The speaker was identifying her as E3+, not one to sit reading all the day long.

E3= (Medium): *Maintains a moderate activity level.* Midrange scorers come in two modes: those who like a balance of sitting and moving about, and those who don't like sitting much and also don't like a lot of physical activity. The latter people might prefer a lifestyle that permits standing much of the time but without much moving about, e.g., clerks, doctors, glass blowers, teachers, and the like. Some activities such as instrumental and vocal music performance can be done standing or sitting, according to the preference of the individual.

> ***Remember:*** Extremes for each trait, like sedentary versus active, are not all-or-nothing. Even someone with an extremely high or low score may still have a small amount of energy/inclination for the opposite quality.

E3- (Low): *Prefers a more sedentary way of life.* Low scorers find prolonged periods of physical movement and activity tiring, and begin craving a seat. We once asked an E3- colleague what he did for exercise. He replied, "I sit down until the urge goes away!" It is important to note that low E3 does not mean low mental activity, just low physical activity. For example, this colleague who chose not to exercise was a brilliant psychologist with an extremely active mental life and a very quick wit. "Down time" is very important for both mid and low scorers on E3, especially after spending time around (active and noisy) others.

*E4 **Leadership**: The extent to which we want to lead others.* This subtrait deals with the frame of mind that naturally takes to the responsibility of being the person in charge of others, as group leader, as class or club president, as section leader, as spokesperson, as team captain. At one extreme is the drill sergeant, and, at the other, the independent. The opposite of leadership is not followership, but rather independence—one preferring to go about doing one's own thing rather than having to be concerned about whether others are doing what they are supposed to be doing. Brett Favre has the reputation of a leader willing, even eager, to take charge, while Terrell Owens has the reputation of being, not a leader, not a follower, but an independent.

> **E4+** (High): *Enjoys the responsibility of leading others.* The high E4 likes to be in charge, and the higher the score, the more eager the person is to have leadership responsibility. This does not mean that high E4s are control freaks—that is associated with another trait. One can take responsibility for directing the work of others and still be a good listener open to suggestion. Barack Obama's reputation is built on his appetite for leadership coupled with his openness to others' ideas. Higher scores on E4 are universally associated with leadership. If an individual wants to be a leader, or has to be a leader (as in being told to take charge), and has only mid to low E4, that individual would be well advised to have a trusted teammate to be the take-charge person. I (Jane) have a high score on this scale. When Pierce and I are co-leading a training session certifying people to use the WorkPlace/SchoolPlace Big Five Profile, I tend to give a precise time for participants to return from a break, such as, "Be back in ten minutes." Pierce, with a lower score, often says, "Let's take a break," without specifying a time for participants to return.

> **E4=** (Medium): *Accepts some responsibility for others.* Midrange on the subtrait has two manifestations: one who naturally takes to leadership roles about half the time and then prefers more independent activity the other half of the time, versus one who likes a small amount of leadership all of the time, but not too much at any time, sort of like having one or two people to monitor, but not a throng.

> **E4-** (Low): *Prefers being independent of others.* Low scorers are bored, resentful, fatigued, or otherwise put off by having to take responsibility for supervising the work of others. They like to do their own activity, e.g., a writer, artist, mechanic, or musician who is content to spend day after day being responsible only for oneself. I (Pierce) am a low scorer and have resisted management positions all of my life. When I was a high school teacher, I was encouraged to become a principal; so I left the school system. When I was a consultant, I was asked to manage other younger, new consultants; so I left the consulting firm. In my present company, I am one person in a two-person department. The other person is my research assistant. Thankfully, he is so independent that he requires very little supervision, about one hour every two weeks. I can handle that much!

*E5 **Trust**: The extent to which we trust others.* Trust is the quality of taking other people at their word, of believing that they will do what they say they will do. People who trust tend to assume the best in others, while those who do not trust tend to assume that others will try to take advantage of you, will try to cut corners, will break their promises, or will simply fail to keep their part of the bargain. Trust is important in relationships, but skepticism is equally important in many roles such as security, accounting, law, and air traffic control. Soldiers have to trust their mates and doubt their enemy. A trusting heart can cement a relationship but can also get you killed. In *The Lord of the Rings,* Frodo is trusting of Gollum, whereas Sam is skeptical.

E5+ (High): *Typically takes others at their word.* High E5s tend to be well liked because others feel accepted by them. To be trusted is to breathe freely, while to be doubted can breed anxiety, resentment, and depression. On the other hand, High E5s can be taken advantage of. Sometimes trust amounts to laziness—it takes energy to monitor others, to check behind them, to ask the hard questions, and opting not to be cautious can be either noble (trusting) or ignoble (lazy) in origin. Trusters need skeptics to help them avoid disasters and to make sure they are not taken advantage of by others, especially in business. In attempting to explain the financial crisis of 2008, the analysts have agreed that sufficient controls (policies, procedures, and so forth) were in place, but that the people who were charged with implementing the controls were asleep at the helm. At best, they were too trusting; at worst, lazy.

> ***Keep in mind:***
> About 1 person in 3 scores in each of the high, medium, and low ranges of all of these traits. Or, for every high scorer, there is one medium scorer and one low scorer. The same numbers of introverts populate the planet as ambiverts, and as many ambiverts populate the planet as extraverts. There is no majority trait.

E5= (Medium): *Shows a moderate level of trust.* Midrange scorers on E5 could appear either as someone who is trusting towards about half the people in their world, and doubting towards the others, or as someone who is moderately trusting towards everyone—not blindly trusting, moderately trusting, as in taking the time/effort to ask follow-up questions ("how are you coming on that project?") or by taking the time/effort to personally check on the quality or veracity of someone's claims.

E5- (Low): *Tends to be skeptical of others' intentions.* Low scorers are the skeptics of the world: lawyers, quality inspectors, engineers, construction superintendents (we don't want someone too trusting to supervise building a bridge we're going to cross every day!). While a skeptical nature can be helpful in many contexts, in relationships it can sometimes be toxic. Before doubting someone close to you, one should have convincing evidence, perhaps even corroborated by a third/disinterested/more objective person. People who are very low in trust can be perceived as micro-managing projects, teammates, and situations in general.

*E6 **Tact**: The degree of care we take in speaking.* The modern name for tact is "spin." High scorers on this subtrait typically have a natural tendency to keep other people's sensitivities in mind when speaking. Tact is a social lubricant—it tends to preserve relationships, just as bluntness/directness/lack of tact can be hurtful (even if needed) in relationships. Because extraverts like being around others, tact becomes a means towards that end—be tactful, stay included. But just as tact can preserve a relationship, it can also damage one if certain messages are not sent clearly and with sufficient force. Sometimes, the tactful person needs to be direct, and the direct person sometimes needs to be tactful. Again, none of these traits are all-or-nothing, but rather a matter of proportion. I (Pierce) tend to call a spade a spade (low E6), but I can be tactful on occasion!

E6+ (High): *Carefully selects the appropriate words.* These are the so-called "spin doctors" who take a message and word it carefully to soften its effect. "The king is in his counting house, counting all his money" is "spun" into "The king is exercising his stewardship duties." One form of tact, or spin, is when a direct message is delivered with humor. Relationship gurus have advised, for example, to give unpleasant messages in "baby talk" mode, as when a little sister tells big brother, in baby dialect, "Big pawuhful bobo weft his deodwunt in de gym. Wanna bahwuh mine?" Then she runs away before getting smacked, trusting that big bro will get the message that his natural aroma needs modifying; he will not be offended, but amused and appreciative.

E6= (Medium): *Exerts moderate care in selecting words for a particular situation.* Midrange scorers on E6 will appear as one of two extremes, or somewhere in between. At one extreme is the person who is tactful with about half of their social network (perhaps with specially selected family and friends), yet direct, even blunt, with the other half of their world. At the other extreme is the person who is moderately tactful with most everyone. What is moderately tactful? That is when the message is incompletely "spun," as in, "Thanks for your generous offer of help, but I think I'll do it myself to minimize errors." The zingers slide through the niceties.

E6- (Low): *Tends to speak more directly.* Mass media is full of low-scorers on tact. For every tactful interviewer, host, or reporter, we can find a dozen who are "in your face" with constant, unspun, unsoftened directness. The popular cartoon *Family Guy* has an episode in which Peter Griffin (the father) is kicked out of the yacht club for his blunt language. To go along with his low E6, Griffin is also N- (he doesn't care) and A- (he doesn't think he did anything wrong). Then there is Michael Scott—particularly well known for his lack of tact—in the popular TV show *The Office*. He often puts his foot in his mouth as he inadvertently insults all religions, races, and genders through his lack of tact.

In summary, there is no such thing as the typical extravert, ambivert, or introvert. Some introverts are "take charge" people (E4+). Some extraverts are sedentary (E3-). We are all different mixtures of these ingredients of extraversion. While we are both ambiverts, Jane is warmer (E1+), Pierce is more sociable (E2+ —he'd like to have more parties!), Pierce is more trusting (E5+—Jane will be the one who finds the fiend lurking behind the friend's mask), and Jane is more tactful (E6+—she often says to others, "I can dress him up, but I can't take him out," in reference to Pierce's "telling it like it is"). As Ralph Waldo Emerson writes, "Every individual nature has its own beauty." (If we repeat this quote enough, it should sink in!) We are all different, and the differences are valuable for some situations but irritating in other contexts.

> "Trust in Allah, but tie up your camel."
> --Hand-lettered sign in Skardu, Pakistan

Implications of E for Career Exploration

Someone who is E- will typically be most satisfied in jobs, roles, tasks, and other assignments that provide the solitude and quiet that they prefer. Their strength is in their capacity to shine alone with minimal stimulation—that is, in doing "outpost" work—forest ranger, a one-person satellite office, and so forth. They can be around "madding" crowds for a little while, but they will be eager to get away. Imagine the introverted plumber who loves fixing the plumbing in private homes—quiet, little activity, no or very few people around. One day, he's called upon to help fix the plumbing in a home daycare center with two dozen toddlers beating pie pans unrhythmically and the poor E- plumber yearning for an empty house to plumb. His bucket for crowds would run dry in a matter of minutes!

If one is E+, their strength is in working where all the action is. They would be miserable with a day characterized by solitude and silence. They would yearn for, and look for, sources of sensory stimulation to make them feel alive, just as our younger daughter had TV and radio playing in nearby rooms when working alone at home. McCrae and Costa (2003, pp. 217-227) have determined that the more extraverted people tend to make more money than the more introverted ones. Clearly this is a rule that has many exceptions. However, it does make sense that an attraction to the "madding crowd" would maximize opportunities for selling, networking, and deal-making. On the other hand, the solitary computer geek who designs best-selling video games or makes a fortune by trading stocks could give many an E+ a run for the money title.

If one is E=, then one of two patterns would likely be true. They might prefer alternating episodes of crowds and solitude, as in working a trade show in the morning, then doing paperwork in the afternoon, or they might prefer not to have either crowds or solitude, choosing instead the moderate stimulation of a small group of co-workers.

Implications of E for Relating to Adults in Power (Parents, Teachers, Administrators, Bosses)

An E- youth supervised by an E+ adult must be prepared to ask for meetings, conferences, and other serious conversations the youth desires. Let the adult know that introverts do better when meetings are briefer, when you have an agenda in advance, and when you've been warned beforehand if you personally need to address any items in the conversation—introverts don't like surprises and typically like to be prepared. Extraverts need to be reminded that introverts like to organize their thoughts in writing before appearing in a meeting or other type of discussion. E- individuals need to be understanding and nonjudgmental of E+ individuals' comfort with casual and extended chat sessions, but E- individuals still need to be clear in letting personal limits be known. An extrovert may take an introvert's desire for solitude personally; so the E+ needs to be reassured that it's nothing personal, just a difference in style. To lay the groundwork for the E+ communicating abundantly, the E- would benefit by writing, either through texting, email, or some other form of writing.

An E+ youth with E- adults needs to be aware that it's unnatural for introverts to be productive in the same way that extraverts are. The extraverted youth will likely receive better input by asking the introvert in advance, preferably in writing, giving the introvert time to think about the topic, get organized, and put their ideas on paper before meeting the extravert face-to-face.

If the youth and adult(s) are both E-, they need to be aware of a likely tendency to under-communicate. They need to find a way to touch base with each other on a regular basis, whether through e-mail, texting, or face-to-face. Failure to explicitly commit to adequate communication can lead to miscues, resentments, wrong assumptions, and other varieties of relationship busters.

On the other hand, if the youth and adult(s) are both E+, they should be aware of a tendency to over-communicate, to take too long in meetings, and to put off or otherwise neglect necessary solitary activities such as reading, paperwork, repairs, and practice.

Implications of the E Traits for Managing Relationships with Peers

Managing relationships between a youth and adults is similar to managing relationships between a youth and other youth. However, the other youth may not have adults' grasp of terminology, experience, or other learning that could help in managing the effects of differences. We recommend that a youth with a particularly close relationship with another youth (romantic, work, study group, and so forth) invite the other youth to take the SchoolPlace Big Five Profile and use parts of this book to introduce them to this model. To avoid the mistake of interpreting differences as some kind of personal judgment, relationships should be built around an understanding of trait differences.

Implications of the E Traits for Communication Style

While the two extreme positions on the extraversion continuum use the same grammar and vocabulary, they do have different preferences with respect to the social patterns of communication. For example, extraverts tend to interrupt others. Nothing intentional, they just interrupt. It is their nature. Don't take it personally. On the other hand, extraverts can learn to minimize interruptions through effortful listening, as in the "talking stick" of Native American tradition. For example, a circle of peers has a talking stick, such as a peace pipe, that is held by the person who is currently speaking. Only the person holding the "stick" (it could be an apple or a statue or a baseball or...) may talk. When finished, the speaker may hand the stick to another, or another may reach for the stick. It is considered ill manners to begin speaking before the speaker has explicitly completed their train of thought. Native Americans have developed an assortment of verbal clues (such as "And that's all I have to say about that") and nonverbal clues (such as folding one's arms together) the speaker can use to indicate it is agreeable for someone else to speak.

Extraverts often have difficulty in listening effectively, being so eager to get to their next thought. Tony Hillerman, a mystery writer who specialized in Navajo culture as the setting for his stories, emphasized in his novel *Coyote Waits* that the Navajo place high value on good listening, and that the average white man was considered to be an inferior listener. In one scene, Joe Leapfoot and his sidekick are driving up to a hut to interview a witness. They see an FBI agent leaving the hut for his car. Sidekick says something like, "We don't need to interview her. The FBI has beat us to it." But Joe advises his partner that they will get the information that the white man was too impatient to hear. So E+ and E- complement each other, with the former over-communicating, the latter waiting silently to catch the debris.

Implications of the E Traits for Leadership Aspirations

Not everyone is, or should be, a leader. Various estimates put the incidence of natural leaders in the population at anywhere from 1 in 6 to 1 in 10. However, according to most research, a high score on E is the most significant influence on leadership behavior. If so, the incidence of natural leaders should be 1 in 3 because about that many people score high on E. However, each of the other supertraits plays an important role as well, which causes a more conservative, even drastic, estimate of 1 in 243 (that number is the 1-in-3 likelihood of being in the optimum level for each supertrait: N-, E+, O+, A-, and C+).

One of the more important subtraits of E for leadership is E4, which has to do with a person's willingness to take charge of directing, coordinating, being responsible for, or supervising the work of others. While introverts can lead, they must be aware of their need to compensate for their natural tendency to under-communicate. They can compensate through having a more communicative assistant, through toughing it out and engaging in behavior (e.g., meetings, conferences, and so forth) that is unnatural and fatiguing, and by overusing communication modes that are more natural (e.g., e-mail, written notes, texting, telephone calls, and the like).

The Biological Basis for Extraversion (E)

If the arousal system for N is the autonomic nervous system, with alternating sympathetic and parasympathetic arousal, then the arousal system for E is the peripheral nervous system, with alternating afferent (sensory) and efferent (motor) nerves receiving and sending sensory impulses, plus the interneurons that connect sense perception to motor reaction. The stimulus that triggers this system is sensation (that is, the five senses). Your E score is in fact an estimate of the point at which your motoric nervous system is aroused and, in effect, shouts, "Enough stimulus! Let there be quiet and stillness! Away, now, let me be!" The afferent nerves become saturated with sensation and crave respite. People with higher E scores can take more sensation before becoming saturated; it's a "sock it to me!" outlook. Traditionally, extraversion has been associated with sociability, the tendency to prefer the company of other people. We know now, however, that the underlying reason is the need for sensory stimulation, and other people are the most common source of such stimulation. Yes, we can certainly feel in the thick of things if we are alone in a robotic manufacturing facility full of intense noises, sights, and smells, but if we are on the floor of a convention exhibition with 50 exhibitors and 10,000 conventioneers, ah, then we really *are* in the thick of things.

Recent brain imaging studies (DeYoung et al., 2010) have clarified the aforementioned associations by revealing that persons with higher E scores tend to have increased brain volume in the medial orbitofrontal cortex, an area associated with heightened sensitivity to the promise of and experience of pleasurable rewards. The lower the E score, the smaller this brain area, and the less demand or craving for pleasurable rewards.

Each of the various subtraits of extraversion—approach level, group orientation, pace, leadership, trust, and tact—is associated with its own set of brain and chemical processes. We know more about the biological basis of some processes than of others. At this writing, here is a summary of what we know:

E1: Approach Level

Nicholas Allen and his associates with ORYGEN Research Centre and the University of Melbourne (Australia) studied a sample of 155 12- and 13-year-olds who had taken the Early Adolescent Temperament Questionnaire (Whittle, Allen, Lubman, and Yücel, 2005; Allen et al., 2006). Their imaging studies revealed that positive affect (warmth, positive mood, approachability) is associated with high activity in areas populated with dopamine receptors, including the amygdala, nucleus accumbens, anterior cingulate cortex, and dorsolateral prefrontal cortex. This pathway is sometimes referred to as the Behavioral Approach System. While the precise role of the amygdala in positive affect is controversial, the nucleus accumbens clearly shows high activity in a variety of more extraverted activities (laughter, pictures of joy, sexual pleasure, humor, and so forth). Research is underway to determine how activity in these pathways might be regulated through pharmaceutical or other means.

These studies were corroborated by the Karolinska [Sweden] Institute's Lars Farde, who found that people who score high on "detachment" scales (lack of closeness and warmth in relationships, and a tendency to avoid involvement with other people) have a less dense pattern of dopamine receptors (specifically, the "D2" receptors). It is not clear whether low dopamine receptor density is the cause of such detachment, or whether detachment causes the lower density. Whether cause or effect, however, the two are clearly related and could be part of a larger system, yet to be identified and described. One can compensate for low dopamine naturally (e.g., by following a diet of high protein coupled with moderate levels of unsaturated fats and complex carbohydrates) or artificially (e.g., by taking a prescription drug such as L-dopa).

E2: Group Orientation

Eric Kandel (2006, p. 425) reports that increased sociability or gregariousness (our subtrait E2) are triggered by oxytocin and endogenous opioids (the body's internal "uppers" such as endorphins, as opposed to exogenous [external] opioids such as opium, which originate outside the body). In one species of nematode (c. elegans), there exists one strain that habitually feeds alone, and another that feeds in groups. The difference between these two strains is one amino acid in the protein that defines a specific receptor. If you transplant the loner's protein to the mixer, the latter becomes a loner. If you transplant the mixer's protein to the loner, the loner begins feeding with others. In other words, put the DNA of one into the other and the behavior changes accordingly. Oxytocin levels can be raised or lowered through acts of intimacy such as eating meals together and physical closeness. Opioids (such as endorphins) can be increased through aerobic exercise, hot chili peppers (if you can tolerate them), and physical activities that produce pleasure sensations (pass the chocolates, please!).

The brain mechanisms that are associated with approach level and group orientation appear to be similar and overlapping. Further research is needed to differentiate the two.

E3: Pace

Gamma-aminobutyric acid (GABA) is the major inhibitory neurotransmitter. As such, it is the body's main internal "tranquilizer." That's what inhibition means: keeping cool, chilling out, keeping still. When the body lacks GABA, physical activity increases. The activity covers a broad range of behavior from ADHD to nervousness. Research is under way to differentiate the mechanisms associated with the different kinds of activity levels.

E4: Leadership

Little is known about the biological basis of the tendency to take charge, to assume the leadership mantle, to accept the responsibility for planning and directing the activity of others. More likely than not, it is related to sex hormone levels, which will be discussed at the end of Chapter 8.

E5: Trust

Levels of oxytocin, often called the "cuddle" chemical, are associated with levels of trust. The lower the levels of oxytocin, the less trusting one is; the more oxytocin, the more trusting. Levels of oxytocin are primarily determined by one's genetic makeup. It is interesting to note that when people have a meal together their levels of oxytocin rise. Thus, "doing lunch" is an act of bonding. In related research at the Columbia University Center on Addiction and Substance Abuse, it was found that if teens eat dinner with their family two times a week or less, they are twice as likely to abuse drugs or alcohol as teens who eat dinner with their family six or seven times a week. Eating together raises oxytocin and mutual trust. Of course, base levels of oxytocin are genetic and vary from individual to individual; so some individuals experience less of a rise in oxytocin levels when "doing lunch" than do others.

E6: Tact

Tact is the result of inhibitory processes. We do not know of specific research that links tactfulness to specific chemicals and brain areas. However, we are confident that tact will be linked to some of the same inhibitory processes and chemicals that we have already discussed. Something in the body puts the brakes on when we begin to speak, so that we shape our words in consideration of the effect we want them to have on others. Clearly there is a chemical basis of "spin," whether it is GABA or something else.

From this discussion of the traits associated with sensory stimulation and extraversion, we progress to the traits that govern how we deal with novelty, change, and complexity. In a sense, N and E are complementary, with one covering negative and the other covering positive emotions. O (Originality) takes us down a new path that focuses less on emotion and more on how we behave on the continuum that runs from preference for the familiar to preference for the novel. Curious?

Mapping Out the Big Five Traits

7

Originality

All About What's New and Different

+	Sky's the limit. --Peter Parker, *Spider-Man*
=	"Men of action," whose minds are too busy with the day's work to see beyond it... are essential men, we cannot do without them, and yet we must not allow all our vision to be bound by the limitations of "men of action." —Pearl S. Buck, U.S. writer and first woman to win the Nobel Prize for Literature
-	You know I won't change a thing. --Frankie J, *Won't Change*

Guide to This Chapter:

- Definition of the O Supertrait
- Three Case Studies
- Definition of the Four Subtraits of O
- Implications of O for Career Exploration
- Implications of O for Relating to Adults in Power (Parents, Teachers, Administrators, Bosses)
- Implications of the O Traits for Managing Relationships with Peers
- Implications of the O traits for Communication Style
- Implications of the O Traits for Leadership Aspirations
- Biological Basis for Originality (O)

Peter Parker (the bookworm) and his alter ego Spider-Man (the wall-crawler) peg the essence of high O (originality) with the declaration that "the sky is the limit." This wide-open invitation to change and novelty strikes an abrupt contrast to the Latin pop singer Frankie J's clear rejection of change: "You know I won't change a thing"! The balanced, tempered position is elaborated by Pearl

Mapping Out the Big Five Traits

N	E	O	A	C
Need for Stability	**Extraversion**	**Originality**	**Accommodation**	**Consolidation**
N+ Reactive	E+ Extravert	O+ Explorer	A+ Adapter	C+ Focused
N= Responsive	E= Ambivert	O= Moderate	A= Negotiator	C= Balanced
N- Resilient	E- Introvert	O- Preserver	A- Challenger	C- Flexible
N1: Worry	**E1: Approach Level**	**O1: Imagination**		
N2: Temper	**E2: Group Orient.**	**O2: Range of Interests**		
N3: Outlook	**E3: Pace**	**O3: Innovation**		
N4: Coping Lev.	**E4: Leadership**	**O4: Zoom Scale**		
	E5: Trust			
	E6: Tact			

Buck speaks for the moderate when she insists on a balance between people of "action" (lower O) and "vision" (higher O). These are the central issues that comprise the O (originality or openness) dimension. We begin this chapter with explanations of the three primary levels of the O dimension. Do keep in mind that our use of three levels is arbitrary, chosen to simplify for those learning the model. We could have also chosen four, five, ten, or fifteen levels, but the burden of trying to keep all those levels clearly expressed in everyday language is too great.

Definition of the O Supertrait

Explorer (O+)

Explorers tend to have many broad interests and like to be on the cutting edge of new technology and ideas. O+ individuals are more likely to have artistic hobbies and to prefer watching public television. They typically do not express conservative views and, probably because of their risk-taking and undying curiosity, have a higher incidence of seeing a psychiatrist. Also, associated with this curiosity and being easily bored, they tend to have more career changes than their low-scoring counterparts. They are often curious, introspective, and reflective, seeking new and varied experiences and thinking about the future.

> "When I examine myself and my methods of thought, I come close to the conclusion that the gift of fantasy has meant more to me than my talent for absorbing positive knowledge."
> —Albert Einstein, in his eighties

It is interesting to note that introspection was once associated with introversion. All solitary people were thought to have an active mental life of reflection, imagination, and introspection. However, more current research has determined that introspection is equally characteristic of all levels of extraversion. In other words, higher E is as likely to be introspective as lower E. Put another way, lower E is as likely to NOT be introspective as higher E.

Instead, current studies place the quality of introspection squarely at one end of the O (Originality) dimension. Or, put another way, persons with lower O tend to be substantially less introspective than persons with higher O. Hence, Pearl Buck's persons of "action" (= lower O) and persons of "vision" (= higher O). The down side of being an explorer (O+) is that you are prone to become easily bored when you find yourself engaged in familiar, repetitive activity that does not require effortful reflection. I (Pierce) am rather high in O, yet I must engage in a substantial amount of low O activity, ranging from folding clothes on a Saturday afternoon to proofreading at my office. To offset the natural boredom entailed in such activity, I find ways to make it more interesting. While folding clothes, I watch news, sports, weather, or cooking on TV. For proofreading, I find a proofreading partner and make it a more interpersonal task. I once had a team member who was fluent in French; with her, I would often read out numbers in French (good practice!). That certainly chased away the blahs! Explorers (O+) are likely to be liberal with respect to political views. They also tend to feel comfortable with new theories and complex concepts. They typically describe themselves as creative, imaginative, or artistic. However, others may believe that explorers are living in a fantasy world with their head in the clouds, they are impractical, or they are not in touch with day-to-day, here-and-now reality. Explorers without discipline are like a kid in a candy store—the sky's the limit!

Emily Crowder writes of a friend whose roommate evidenced high O:

> Every time I went to her room, the roommate had completely reorganized her half of the room: she went from having her bed lofted with the desk under it, to moving the desk and putting the dresser there, to completely lowering her bed, then raising it to a middle height, etc. I asked my friend, and she told me the O+ roommate changed her side at least once a week for a whole year. Although she was fine with it at first, she started to get annoyed by the constant change. She just wanted to come back to her room the way she had left it. All the change was discomforting. Although they seemed to get along fine otherwise, they decided not to room together again, and my friend is relieved that she won't have to deal with the constant change.

Moderate (O=)

> "The good news is that while our Haws were initially hesitant, they were open-minded enough to learn something new."
> Spencer Johnson, *Who Moved My Cheese*

Moderates tend to be middle-of-the-road and somewhat down-to-earth, but they will consider a new way of doing something if convincing evidence is available. Although they aren't known for their creativity or curiosity, these qualities will occasionally surface. At times, they may adopt a good idea from someone else and then develop it. They appreciate both innovation (O+) and efficiency (O-). However, they will either 1) never attain those qualities to the same degree as people who are naturally O+ or O-, or 2) it will take a moderate a long time to reach the levels attained by O- and O+.

Midrange Os tend to come in one of two styles: 1) those who are moderate in each of the four component subtraits or 2) those who are high in one or two subtraits and low in the others (averaging out to mid). The former would typically be described as moderately creative, moderately comfortable with complexity, moderately comfortable with change, equally comfortable with the big picture as with the details. The latter might be described as, for example, eager to change, but not coming up with the ideas for change, or comfortable with complexity, but getting lost in the details. Midrange scorers on this supertrait, as in all five supertraits, as a rule are more complex people than more extreme scorers. Sometimes preferring practicality, other times preferring creativity, O= persons are harder to predict than those who more consistently prefer practicality (O-) or creativity (O+). One must get to know them to find out the details of their natural palette of preferences, of their natural sources of energy.

Preserver (O-)

Preservers tend to possess expert knowledge about a particular interest, topic, or subject. They are typically practical and down-to-earth, with a here-and-now, no-nonsense view of the world. Their approach to study, work, and life in general is efficient and prefers to follow established patterns. "If it was good enough for grandpa, it's good enough for me." They tend to be comfortable with repetitive kinds of activity, whether for a class, a project, job, extra-curricular activity, or community activity. I (Pierce) once earned a contract to teach the same two-day class 50 times in one year to a large electric utility client. I dreaded the prospect of this much repetition, even though I had designed the program! So, I hired someone else, someone who scored low in O, to teach for me. It worked out swimmingly.

Preservers are typically seen as conservative, relatively narrow in their thinking, and set in their ways. Where explorers (O+) like to spend money, preservers like to save it. Their hobbies typically include gardening, sewing, and cooking, and they are more likely to watch television game shows than their higher-scoring counterparts are. Most chefs/cooks are lower O, preparing the same meals over and over, but clearly some of the more experimental, creative chefs are higher in O. Preservers prefer tried-and-true approaches and traditional ways of doing things. The typical preserver would rather "fight" than switch. Whereas in its worst aspect, O+ can be intolerant revolutionaries, O- can be intolerant reactionaries. Typifying low O behavior, Hagar the Horrible (the comic strip character) complained to a bartender, "My crew threatened to go on strike unless sweeping changes were made." When asked by the bartender what he did, Hagar retorted, "I bought them all new brooms."

The tension between the two extremes of O—change and permanence—is expressed deafeningly in the film *High School Musical* (here expressly based on the concept of change in social roles). The O+ viewpoint emerges in one of the closing choruses:

> We're breaking free
> To get to the place to be
> All that we can be....

While affirming this commitment to exploration and high O, another chorus challenges with equal firmness:

> Stick to the status quo...

"All that we can be" versus "the status quo": That summarizes succinctly the two poles of energy contained in the O continuum. The tension pulls the typical youth in both directions—to carry on tradition or to forge new paths. William Butler Yeats says it another way in "Sailing to Byzantium" with the phrase "perne in a gyre," which refers to balancing a gyroscope on a string by spinning it back and forth from one extreme to the other, not approaching either end too closely for fear of falling off to a point of no return. The gyroscope is a metaphor for social change: Don't go too far in any one direction, don't throw the baby out with the bathwater, don't embrace all new values and abandon all the old ones. Find a way to establish an appropriate balance between change and stability.

To illustrate how these different levels of O play out in everyday life, let's now take a look at three case studies.

O Case Study 1: Prom as College Application

Three high school juniors are the co-chairs for planning their annual high school prom. Let's listen in as they get started:

> *O+ (Explorer):* "What a great opportunity for us to impress our peers with a far-out prom that's nothing like what has ever been done before: multiple locations, polythematic united by a common theme that only emerges later in the evening, multiple emcees, multimedia shows at various points to highlight our pasts and futures. I'm just brimming with ideas!"
>
> *O- (Preserver):* "No way. Hey, our reputations are on the line. We try something that far out, things we've never done before, and we're highly likely to fall flat on our faces, look like fools in front of our classmates, and be blamed for ruining the prom."
>
> *O+:* "Innovation trumps repetition. This is our only chance to make a statement."
>
> *O-*: "No way. Excellence in execution trumps change for the sake of change. I say we go for preserving our heritage by showing that we can execute with flawless timing and attention to the details."
>
> *O= (Moderate):* "I think there's merit in what you are both saying. We could really screw things up by trying to pull off something that hasn't been done here before. On the other hand, we should use this opportunity to distinguish ourselves in some way—in some way that we can leverage for our own benefit. Why put in all the effort without some payoff?"
>
> *O+:* "Well, I can see your point about the folly of taking undue risks. My venturesomeness sometimes overrides my common sense."
>
> *O-:* "Tell me about it!"
>
> *O+:* "What if we were to try a two-prong approach, in effect, using both innovation and excellent execution. We could plan for a relatively typical prom and focus on perfecting its execution. Then we could document the process with multimedia—video, stills, audio clips. After it is all over, we could edit the documentation of process and execution and call it something like 'A Prom Unfolds.' We could upload it to YouTube! Hey, it might even give us an edge in our college application portfolio."
>
> *O=:* "I like it. We'd have our cake and eat it, too! We could edit all of the video and audio offline and after the fact, with no pressure, and tinker with it until we get it right. Execution AND innovation! And the innovation is essentially risk-free, with lots of margin for error and recovery. Let's do it!"

Mapping Out the Big Five Traits

As our case study shows, the O scale can contribute to conflict when an O+ brings in new ideas or new ways of doing things. Usually the O- will resist these new ideas, preferring to stick to well-proven historical methods, especially if the methods are cost-effective and are working well. Typically, the O= can begin to perceive some value in the O+'s new ideas but may wish to temper these ideas somewhat with the constraints of the day-to-day.

O Case Study 2: Making Sense of Scents

One of the activities we like to do with folks is to line them up in a continuum, according to their scores on a particular trait. We did that for O, with approximately 50 young people arranged from very low scores at one end to very high at the other. When we distribute a brightly colored scented marker and ask people to thoroughly describe the object before time is called, we usually get the following responses:

> *O- - (extreme preserver):* "It's a 5-inch cylinder, 3/4-inch round base, red, shiny hard plastic [plus actual words copied from the marker, such as "Made by….," "Do not shake," and "© date"], 16 smiley faces with fruit shapes, white base, eight ridges inside the base."
>
> *O- (mild preserver):* "It's a 5-inch cylinder, 3/4-inch round base, red, shiny plastic, smiling faces of fruit, "Do not shake," white base with ridges, take off the cap, look, the cap fits in the base, chiseled point on writing tip, smells like cherry."
>
> *O= (moderate):* "It's 5 inches long, has a little round base, it's kind of a cherry-colored red, shiny outside, take off the cap, listen, it makes a nice popping sound when you take off the cap, it writes red on flipcharts."
>
> *O+ (mild explorer):* "It's cherry-colored, about 6 inches long, it's shiny and glistening, take off the cap, hey, that's a good sound, umm—smells good, kids could use it for a clicker, you can draw fat and skinny lines with it, hey look, it rolls like a rolling pin, teachers can use these to liven up classrooms, kids would love to color with these things."
>
> *O++ (extreme explorer):* "It's bright, smooth, take off the cap, it's a pretty color to look at, it's kind of pointy on the end. [What are you doing?] I'm tasting it to see if it tastes like cherry, yuck! they definitely didn't pick this cherry off the tree, the cap looks like a crown, or a space capsule zooming around the Earth, you could connect a bunch of these together to make a colorful pointer, you could stand 10 of them up like bowling pins and then bowl them down, we could paint our fingernails with it."

Notice that you hear more specific details about the marker from the lower-scoring groups, and that the higher-scoring groups basically ignore the details as they come up with their zany ideas. With one student leadership group, a low O accused the very high group of not following the rules. What emerged from the discussion was that, the lower the O score, the more people tended to stick with the object, focusing in on it, whereas, with the higher O score, people tended to view the object in a much larger context and look at its possibilities; O= people did some of both with the object. This discussion led to a new appreciation for what different people on the team brought to the table. As it turned out, the O- people were content doing repetitive roles in study, project, or other groups—proofreading, practicing, rehearsing, assembling, and so forth. The O+ people, on the other hand, were not content with constant repetition. They became bored and started to look for new and possibly improved ways of doing the task. Some of their creative ideas and experiments were not as high-quality as the proven methods, but if they developed a better way of doing the same task, it was appreciated and adopted by the O- and O= people. I (Pierce) can remember a time when I volunteered to help get out a mailing for a political campaign: folding, inserting, moistening, and sealing letters into envelopes. Boring! I found myself every five minutes or so coming up with a modification of our assembly line process that hopefully would result in getting the job done quicker so I/we could get on to more challenging matters!

O Case Study 3: Choosing the Lab Assistants

A science teacher in a small high school was responsible for teaching biology, chemistry, and physics—a one-teacher science department. She had requested last year that the school system allot her a senior—someone who had taken biology and chemistry the previous two years and was currently enrolled in physics—to serve as a lab assistant. Having a responsible student in charge of lab setups, monitoring safety procedures during lab, and insuring proper storage, would take a tremendous load off her back. Of course, she couldn't have just one student for all five periods—it would have to be five students, each for one class period.

The good news was that the school system had approved her request. The bad news was that now she had to choose from among 15 applicants. What criteria should she use in selecting the five lab assistants? Clearly grades and attendance record were important. Hmm, what else? She recalled that she had administered the SchoolPlace Big Five Profile to all of her biology students several years ago. The purpose was to teach them the five basic dimensions of behavior and to show how they permeated the animal kingdom as well as humans—well, all but C (Consolidation), which was only to be found in chimpanzees among the animals. But that would be a good teaching point with respect to how evolution worked. Could she use the Big Five information as an aid in selecting lab assistants? Certainly. So, what trait(s) should she look for? In considering the O dimension, she considered the desirability of having someone who was creative and innovative. Yes, that was always delightful company for her, as she was a rather creative and innovative individual herself. We love people like ourselves—Narcissus at work!

In discussing her dilemma with a friend who taught sociology and psychology, the friend pointed out that the lab assistant role required anything BUT creativity and innovation. In fact, it appeared to require the opposite—strict attention to safety procedures, careful attention to details such as labels, comfort with insuring that equipment was clean and operational. She could get into real trouble if she had assistants who were curious and tried to vary the procedures as a way of satisfying curiosity or relieving boredom. She had better look for students with good grades, good attendance, and low O—subject specialists who knew their thing and enjoyed practicing and perfecting until all was a smooth running system with zero defects, malfunctions, or surprises. This was not a role for an explorer. This was a role for a preserver. No change-master here—a status quo, steady-as-she-goes senior shall rule the lab.

Mapping Out the Big Five Traits

Definitions of the Four Subtraits of O

Now that we have seen how the O supertrait operates on a general scale, we shall take a look at the more specific aspects of O. We have identified four important subtraits of Originality: imagination, range of interest, innovation, and zoom scale. Their definitions, along with anchors (descriptive phrases) for the high, midrange, and low ranges of each subtrait's continuum, follow:

O1 ***Imagination****: Our preference for inventing plans and ideas.* This subtrait deals with the two extremes of active fantasy life versus living in the here and now. At the one extreme, we find the people who see what is there and stay focused on it. At the other extreme are individuals whose imagination seldom quits working. These are people who are good at making puns, or who are good at jazz improvisation, who are constantly rearranging or ornamenting, in short, the temperament for seeing what is not there. We like to call it reading the lines (O1-) versus reading *between* the lines (O1+)—proofreading versus writing poetry, playing a recital versus composing a new piece. Contrast, for example, the live-in-the-present Danny (O1-) and the fantasy-obsessed Augie (O1+) in the 2008 film *Role Models.* Or if you prefer, contrast the imaginative, jousting, would-be squire Will Thatcher and the more down-to-earth Alan Tudyk in the 2001 movie *A Knight's Tale.*

O1+ (High): *Creates new plans and ideas.* The difference between persons who are high in O1 and persons who are high in O3 (how we accept change) lies in the origin of the change idea. Persons who are O1+ tend to be the originators of change—they come up with the idea in the first place, e.g., the prom planner in Case Study 1 who wanted the multi-site, polythematic prom to beat all proms. In *High School Musical*, Kelsey, the accompanist/ composer in *High School Musical,* whom we identified as an ambivert in the previous chapter, now typifies the high O1+. She is not content to play the compositions of others—she yearns to write new compositions of her own and arrange the works of others to suit the needs of the current production. High O1 individuals are often day-dreamers who have difficulty buckling down and keeping their eye on the detail. They have the unremitting urge to act on their unrelenting question of "What if...?" What if I tried it this way? What if I started at the end instead of the beginning?

O1= (Medium): *Creates and implements equally.* Midrange scores for O1 come in one of two modes (or somewhere in between the two). In the pure O1= mode, we find individuals who are moderately imaginative. The imagination originates in responding to some trigger. We may see a bird pecking at seeds on the patio, and my imagination is triggered to think of the universe raining on the earth, and the fecundity of Mother Nature providing seeds for her birds. The difference in a midrange O1 and someone higher is the higher scorer tends to stray farther from the "trigger" or stimulus. Rather than be limited by Mother Nature raining on the earth, the very high O1 might be taken to asteroids or galaxies long, long ago and far, far away, while the mid O1 might simply move mentally from the bird nibbling seeds to animals searching for food in the primeval forest; then the mid O1 might use the imagery in writing a short-story assignment for English class.

The other mode of mid O1 is the individual who might have just as wild an imagination as the high O1, but on fewer occasions, instead balancing vivid fantasy with the comfort of staying in the here-and-now. These mid O1s have imaginations that are more situational. They could be susceptible to triggers in history class, but not in physics because they are too ab-absorbed in the latter to dream. Or they may dream while working on a weekend job, but not during sports practice, again too absorbed in the here-and-now to dream.

O1- (Low): *Implements plans.* This is the no-nonsense person who typically lives in the moment, totally absorbed in the demands of the current task, seldom finding their mind wandering to other climes. This individual can proofread for relatively long stretches of time without tiring, as the task comes naturally to them. Low O1 prefers implementing plans to thinking them up. They are generally known as tacticians rather than as strategists. High O1 likes to think up strategy. Low O1 likes to take the strategy and make it happen, get the job done, execute, take the hill, plow the land, move the product out the door, get the homework completed.

O2 ***Range of Interests****: The extent to which we make things complex.* This subtrait comprises the two extremes of keeping things narrower versus broader, simpler versus more complex. Higher scorers are like Troy Bolton in *High School Musical,* who is not content just to be a basketballer, but wishes to complicate his life by also being a thespian. This is in contrast, to Sharpay Evans, content to play the ingénue, over and over, not branching out, resentful of competition, lest she might be forced out of her comfort zone. This subtrait can be mistaken for a mental ability, but it is different. High and low O2 individuals can have the same mental horsepower—it is just that one prefers exercising it on more complex issues spanning a variety of bodies of knowledge, whereas the other tends to prefer exercising mental horsepower on a more narrowly defined area. The polymath versus the mathematician, the generalist versus the specialist.

O2+ (High): *Seeks complexity.* The high O2 is drawn to theories and knowledge in a variety of fields. If you were to test the students who opt for "humanities" or "interdisciplinary" curricula in college or graduate school, they would likely score high on O2. In balancing breadth versus depth, the high O2 usually succumbs to breadth. That is not to say that high O2s are not capable of depth knowledge in a particular field, it is just that they more commonly will sacrifice depth for breadth. A mathematician higher in O2 might read a new economics book or a new book of poetry rather than taking on yet another proof. These are the people who have to be reminded to "dumb it down" before trying to communicate with others, not because lower O2s are dumb, but because higher O2s "over-complexify" things. I (Jane) recently received an emailed question from a client. In response, my high O2 wrote a seven-page white paper to explain every possible way to look at the question. Fortunately, the client was also high in O2 and greatly appreciated my effort. For a low O2 client, this would likely have been far too much information. I (Pierce) am high in O2, and I can recall an old friend and fellow consultant, Win Lail, who used to respond to every new idea I ran by him with this phrase, "I like it, and it has great promise, but it'll never work unless you find a way to simplify it." Horrors! Simplify? It was Einstein who once said something to this effect: "It is wise to express things as simply as possible, but not too simple." Persons high in O2 need to be aware of the need to simplify, to live with the tension of complexity and simplicity. Basketballer Troy Belton's father was also his coach (in *High School Musical*), and at one point dad/coach says to son/Troy, "You're a playmaker, not a singer." Of course, Troy replies, "Did you ever consider I could be both?" Ironically, he's a playmaker in two senses!

O2= (Medium): *Prefers a balance of simplicity and complexity.* Midrange O2 scorers come in two types (or a combination of both). First is the individual who likes a moderate amount of complexity, like studying math and physics, rather than studying either alone on a more in-depth level. The second type is the individual who likes complexity in some areas of life and simplicity in others. The latter individual might like complexity in sports, as in training for the decathlon rather than just being a runner, yet prefer a simpler, narrower approach in hobbies, as in making and flying model airplane kits rather than designing race-winning planes.

O2- (Low): *Prefers simplicity*. This person's credo is the KISS principle—keep it simple, stupid! This is the subject specialist who prefers going into depth in one particular field, such as poetry, rather than following possible leads into other fields such as history, psychology, art, sociology, anthropology, or any other field that could relate to the content of a poem. Whereas high O2s are typically known as good problem-solvers because they can bring lots of diverse information and perspectives to bear on a problem, low O2s are equally good problem solvers in their own field because of their level of expertise, their specialized knowledge, makes them able to spot causes that are typically only apparent to persons who are highly trained in that special field. Sometimes a problem calls for a specialist, sometimes for a generalist—both have their value. The specialist (O2-) is like the engineer who was called to an ocean liner to fix a mechanical problem. After spending five minutes poking around, he took a wrench and tapped a pipe, with the result that the ship's mechanical systems returned to a proper state of performance. Sending his invoice some time later, the ship's captain was stunned to find a charge of $500. He demanded that the engineer explain such a large charge for five minutes of work. The engineer responded with an itemized bill: "For tapping on pipe: $5. For knowing where to tap: $495." That's low O2 at work!

*O3 **Innovation**: How easily we accept change.* This subtrait is all about the two opposing tendencies of resistance to change versus acceptance of change. On the one end of the continuum, we have the energy devoted to maintaining the status quo, to doing things the way they've always been done, to valuing efficiency over innovation. At the other end, we have the energy devoted to being the innovation leader, to being open to suggestions for new or different approaches, to exploring. Resistance to change was typified by President George W. Bush in his stances towards global warming and embryonic stem cell research. Contrast this with the Barack H. Obama campaign theme of "Change We Need" and his promise of a cabinet composed of a "team of rivals" to identify and execute necessary change.

O3+ (High): *Readily accepts changes and innovations*. As we pointed out earlier, it is the high O1 who dreams up opportunities for change, and the high O3 who embraces the idea and moves forward with it. The good news is that high O3s are famous as agents or sponsors of change, but the bad news is that they can embrace change for the sake of change, to relieve boredom, or to mask serious problems with the distracting power of change. A high O3 with problems in a relationship might embrace the opportunity to take up a new hobby or activity with that person as a way of taking their minds off deeper problems. As Shakespeare's Macbeth says, "The labour we delight in physics [cures] pain." A high scorer on this scale also typically looks for more variety in the week, wanting every day to be different. Higher O3s are usually willing to try different foods. On our first trip to Malaysia, we thoroughly enjoyed the incredible taste of the very smelly durian fruit (sort of a combination of junior-high locker room and a sulphur bomb). And on a recent trip to Mexico, we enjoyed fried grasshoppers. We have low O3 friends who were delighted to find a McDonald's to eat in during their first trip to Europe.

O3= (Medium): *Is somewhat accepting of changes*. Midrange scorers on O3 typically are more like one of two types: The person with a pure midrange score is moderately comfortable with most any kind of change: change in family routines, change in study habits, change in decorations, change in politics, and so forth. But the person prefers not too great a change. Change from 50-minute class periods to 60-minute periods, not to 3-hour periods. Change from singing in a quartet to singing in a quintet, not to singing in a 50-voice chorus. Change from playing middle linebacker to playing outside linebacker, not to playing free safety. Increments, not giant steps. Creep, not leap. The second type of midrange O3 is one who is up for change in some aspects of life and not in others: Change my wardrobe any way you want, but don't change my room. Change the way we take family vacations, but don't mess with the meal schedule. Change the church we go to, but don't change the neighborhood. For these individuals, willingness to change is situational—sometimes a go, sometimes the status quo.

O3- (Low): *Wants to maintain existing methods.* The low O3 resonates with the old cigarette slogan about "we'd rather fight than switch." Go with what works. Love me, love my stuff. If it was good enough for grandma, it's good enough for me. The positive aspect of this resistance to change is that it conserves energy and resources and enables one to focus on high performance, undistracted by novelty. The negative side is that one can get left behind, can fail to take advantage of promising opportunities because of being wedded to the past. They can be victims of the "BGOTO" syndrome, failing to see the "blinding glimpse of the obvious." In all things, we need to understand the tension between O3+ and O3-. One should never dominate the other. Most O3+s will break the bank, and most O3-s will die on the vine. That is why in the U.S. we have Republicans and Democrats, conservatives and liberals, counterbalancing each other, trusting the people to sense when it is time to change or maintain the status quo.

O4 ***Zoom Scale****: Our tolerance for handling details.* The final subtrait of O (Originality) is about perspective, with one end of the continuum involved in the details, the other flying in the clouds. Some have said that God is in the details, others that the devil dwells there. As necessary as details are to most ventures, the big picture is necessary for correcting our wanderings and shaping our goals and vision. People who can't "see the forest for the trees" need people who "live in ivory towers," and the two need to appreciate the tension between the one getting the job done and the other making sure that the job stays in focus. Zoom in, zoom out. Too much focus on the details and the overall shape of the statue is problematic.

O4+ (High): *Prefers a broad view and resists details.* The high O4 is concerned with the overall shape of things. "What is the purpose of the expenditure?" is more important than the details of how each penny will be spent. "Are our goals the right ones?" is more important than the details of how much progress we are making toward our goals. Without high O4, we risk losing our way. With too much O4, we risk not having enough money left in the budget at the end of the month. High O4 asks how a relationship is going and is less concerned whether all of the details get taken care of (Did the card get sent on time? Have the flowers been ordered? Did I send a thank-you note?) High O4 asks, "Why?" while Low O4 asks, "How many?" As part of my job, I (Jane) need to attend planning meetings where we prepare and plan for the next versions of our online assessments with Pierce, Caryn Lee (our business partner), our system programmer, and our system tester. With my high O4 score, I'm very comfortable when we are looking ahead. When we start delving into the details, the pages of system documentation, and the steps to make the next version reality, I struggle to stay involved in the conversation after just a few minutes. Intuitively, I know the details make all the difference in the quality we offer, and I sincerely appreciate the efforts of those who make them reality. Yet, my personality craves an "overview," not an in-depth review of all the steps. Fortunately, this meeting occurs infrequently.

O4= (Medium): *Attends to details if needed.* There are two possible ways to be midrange in O4. One is the "pure" midrange who keeps the zoom focused about half-way between close and far. Impatient with too much detail as well as too much theorizing, this individual is like the sports team leader who lets others handle the details and lets the coach handle the strategy, preferring neither extreme. The other way to be mid-range in O4 is to obsess about the details in some areas of life (i.e., zoomed in), while staying at a higher level (i.e., bigger picture, zoomed out) in others. This might be someone who likes to do orienteering courses or historical reenactments, focused on the details of executing the plan. Yet in other areas of life, such as room decorating or personal dress, the person cares little about whether every little detail of clothing is just so, but is more concerned with whether the overall effect is making the right statement about who they are. "What does wearing black say about me?" versus insuring that every string is removed, every button stitched, every wrinkle removed.

O4- (Low): *Is attentive to details.* These low O4 individuals are the ones who enjoy making sure that nothing falls between the cracks, the ones who save you from embarrassment by making sure that all the details are taken care of. They have their checklists, and they check them twice. They make sure you don't overpay, that you don't get overcharged. They take pleasure in finding errors while proofreading text or reconciling balances. My (Pierce) preference is for the big picture. I like to stay zoomed out, knowing that from time to time I need to zoom in and make sure the details are right. When I was in 8th grade, my father, who was a wholesale grocer, invited me to work in his office after Saturday morning choir practice was over, then ride back home with him for lunch. While at his office, he offered to pay me double the absolute amount of any "carrying" entry in his books that had an error. This was before computers. I had an adding machine with keys and a lever. I checked his invoices, e.g., four boxes of chewing gum @ $1.48 = $5.92. Every time I found an error, either over or under the right amount, he would pay me double the amount. Not my cup of tea! I'm a big picture kind of guy. I did it for a few Saturdays, then managed to find something that required less attention to detail.

Now that we have defined all of the subtraits of O, let's take look at how the O dimension affects various aspects of one's life.

Implications of O for Career Exploration

Low O individuals tend to take pride in tasks that require efficiency, precision, and thorough attention to detail. Repetition provides the opportunity to increase performance quality, as in "practice makes perfect." Use comfort with routine to advantage in jobs and tasks that require a no-nonsense approach to high production and demanding quality standards. Avoid roles that require you to deal with uncertainty, ambiguity, lack of structure, and figuring out the future for prolonged periods. Low O is a practical, here-and-now, get-the-work-out-the-door kind of worker. As a trainer or teacher, low Os are able to teach the same training seminar or classroom subject week after week, taking pleasure in continuing to polish their performance and delivery.

High O individuals need to avoid jobs or roles that require repetition, because they easily become bored doing the same thing more than once. They require a job with great latitude or job autonomy so that they can play what-if scenarios in their head, try to imagine what tomorrow will bring, and create new products and services for both new and old markets. They also need people around them who are low in O to balance their perspective, to provide a reality check.

Individuals who are O= will likely find that one of two situations will be more likely to satisfy them—either a balance of two extreme types of activity or more moderate activity that does not become extreme in either direction. On one hand, they may like to switch between more creative tasks and more repetitive tasks, as in big-picture conversations (O+) in a morning meeting followed by proofreading and paperwork (O-) in the afternoon. Or, on the other hand, they may prefer activities throughout the day that are neither particularly creative (O+) nor particularly repetitive (O-), such as writing memos or handling customer service issues.

Implications of O for Relating to Adults in Power (Parents, Teachers, Administrators, Bosses)

When one is O- and others around them are O+, build on the preserver's value as a producer who gets things done. The O+ don't care so much for implementing plans and taking care of the details; instead, they would rather dream things up and solve problems. The O- preserver will endear themselves to explorers by doing what the explorers see as drudgery. Conversely, the explorers can take away the tasks that frustrate the preserver—the cerebral, vague, what-if game of scenario/future planning.

When one is O+ and others around them are O-, realize that they may tire of O+ suggestions and prefer that you put more effort into production. If you thrust your ideas on them too frequently, they'll begin to see you as a dreamer, a spender—as overhead rather than profit. They don't like idea generators, of course, until they are in need of one! Be selective in your imaginative initiatives. Pick your visionary battles!

Implications of the O Traits for Managing Relationships with Peers

Lower O peers do not typically share the degree of curiosity characteristic of higher O. Consequently, the suggestions of higher O to "explore," whether the exploration is intellectual, physical, territorial, social, or whatever, will often be met with "Nah" or "I'm not in the mood" or "Get real" or "Not my cup of tea." The danger here is that the higher O will take these discouragers as a sign of personal rejection or that the lower O is finding fault with the higher O's judgment, values, or common sense. However, the lower O is simply expressing a natural preference, one that would be expressed around others, not just a higher O. So, we cannot take such rejections personally. Of course, exceptions abound. The O- individual may suspend their natural preferences in order to serve a higher priority. Or the O+ individual might do the same. I am reminded of a friend's midteen O+ son (athlete, musician, scholar, spiritual, hobbyist, pilot) who had fallen head-over-heels in love for the first time. His mother illustrated the intensity by commenting, "He even stays with her to watch a movie a second or third time through, and he NEVER does that! He hates to see a movie twice. But not with her!" Here the O+ typically eschews repetition in favor of new exploration, but in our friend's case repetition was embraced in hopes of another kind of embrace.

Implications of the O Traits for Communication Style

The way O comes out in everyday communication is in the "leaps." Because low O tends to focus on the here-and-now, their conversation tends to be relatively easy to follow, like a narrative or description in which all of the detail is present. The low O style tends to stay focused on the subject and provide sufficient detail to get the picture across. This contrasts with the higher O who tends to make leaps from element to element, omitting transitions, linkages, connections, preferring instead to jump from interesting point to interesting point, feeling no interest or responsibility for providing "road signs" to help others follow their line of thought. Often you will hear an O+ saying things like "Are you with me?" or "Am I making sense?" because they often have a sixth sense that they are difficult to follow. Frequently, they need to back up and make connections for the listener.

But just as the O+ needs to provide road signs, the O- needs to provide the destination. The O- can get so caught up in the details of the story that the point is lost. It can be like a "shaggy dog" story that goes on for so long that at one point someone will comment, "Where is this going?" or "What's this about, anyway?" Road signs and destinations. The O- needs to remember to talk about "why," and the O+ needs to remember to provide links. I (Pierce) remember once being on stage and getting a question from my audience. After my five-minute answer, they said, "Interesting, but that has nothing to do with my question!" Well, I had thought it did; so I had to go back and make the connection. Recently, a lower O associate reviewed the manuscript for Chapter 5 of this book and commented that I needed to do something about the "bullets" in the final section on the biological basis of N (need for stability). "What's the problem?" I retorted. She explained that I had simply provided a list of facts without explaining how they related to N or what use might be made of the information. I had simply jumped from point to point, without taking time to explain how they related to each other or how they related to the larger purpose of the book, relying instead on the reader to connect the dots. "Can't do that," she reminded me! In rewriting that section while keeping her advice in mind, this will be a better book for having made this high O take time to be low-ly. I (Jane) often have to explain Pierce's O+ puns to O= and O- friends and associates. When Pierce makes a clever pun during lunchtime conversation in our break room, I usually laugh first and then have to make sure that others "got it."

Implications of the O Traits for Leadership Aspirations

There are (at least!) two kinds of leaders: strategists and tacticians. Strategists create the overall vision, mission, goal, or objective. They think big-picture and come up with the rough outline of a plan that will accomplish the purpose, whether it is winning a battle, game, sales contest, or art competition. Tacticians provide the details that will cause the plan to work: how to supply the troops, how to deal with various forms of resistance, and so forth. Strategists ask, "What and Why," and tacticians ask, "How, When, Where...."

Leaders who are higher in O tend to be strong in creating a vision, in coming up with interesting and unusual ways to accomplish their goal, but they tend to get bored with developing the intricate plans necessary to realize their vision. This is where the O+ leader needs lower O teammates and followers to handle the details. Similarly, O- leaders can come up with highly detailed and intricate plans, but they need higher O teammates to remind them what the purpose of it all is. Once I (Pierce) was driving in rural North Carolina and emerged at a crossroads with signs pointing in two different directions to my destination. A fellow smoking a corncob pipe and rocking in a porch chair decorated the porch of a country store nearby. I got out of my car and approached the old man with, "Sir, does it matter which road I take to get to Hickory?" He quipped, "Nope, not to me it don't [*sic*]." When the goal is vague and ill defined, it doesn't matter much how to go about trying to accomplish it!

The Biological Basis for Originality (O)

The arousal system that provides the basis for the O set of behaviors is a combination of the dopaminergic system and the general state of arousal of the cerebral cortex. Dopamine is proving to be the "creativity" chemical, with levels of dopamine and dopamine receptors related to one's capacity to hold visual images in one's mind, whether they are visionary, futuristic images or hallucinations. The stimulus that triggers this system's switch from curiosity-seeking back to familiar territory is novelty—that is, anything unfamiliar, whether in the form of ideas, foods, theories, values, art, skills, hobbies, or words. Your O score, then, is an estimate of when you will use up your available dopamine in your pursuit of novelty, and your system then says, "Whoa! No more novelty or complexity. Take me back to the simple and familiar, the tried and true."

The brains of higher O individuals appear to be more prone to handle greater quantities and kinds of information in short-term memory. Recent brain imaging studies (DeYoung et al., 2010) support this notion by revealing increased volume in the parietal cortex of individuals with higher O scores.

The four subtraits of O have some chemistry and brain structure in common, yet each has its own unique physiology. Here is a summary of what we currently know about the subtraits of O:

O1: Imagination

As a general rule, levels of dopamine are associated with levels of imagination. Although it is folly to identify any one single chemical as the sole cause of a set of complex behaviors, especially the set we call "imagination," all studies find elevated levels of dopamine present with creative, imaginative behavior. Neuroscientist Candace Pert reports having worked on a "creativity pill," a cocktail of dopamine and other agents that would enable a person for a short period of time to find it more natural to ask "what if" questions. Over the next few decades, many such pharmaceutical agents will become available for temporarily or permanently modifying one's level of energy for particular behaviors--. This will be a brave new world with ethical and personal consequences and unknown ramifications and possible side effects. The chemistry of imagination is certainly more complex than a hit of dopamine, but like alcohol, whatever else you might add to dopamine, it consistently has its effect!

O2: Range of Interests

One reason for persons with higher O scores being more inter-disciplinary and the lower O more single-subject focused is that the neurological underpinning for the two is different. The many neurological pathways associated with different bodies of knowledge and skills are more interconnected in the higher O individual, while the same pathways in lower O individuals are more distinct, less interconnected. As a consequence, it is less natural for the lower O to make quick and easy connections between perceptions. This leads to greater efficiencies among O-, and greater problem-solving tendencies among O+. There is some evidence (DeYoung et al., 2009) that high O2s, persons who are more comfortable with complexity, tend to have better short-term memories—more dense hippocampal areas of the brain. That makes sense, as complex scenarios become frustrating if you can't hold elements of the situation in working memory. Persons unable to do so would naturally have a preference for simpler phenomenon.

O3: Innovation

S. Whittle, N. B. Allen, D. I. Lubman and M. Yücel (2005) report from their imaging studies that the amygdala serves the primary role of evaluating stimuli as threatening or not. There is some evidence that larger, more active amygdalae are associated with greater inhibition with respect to novel stimuli. As we pointed out in Chapter 5, some studies associate the amygdala more with fear and the negative emotions. The dorsolateral prefrontal cortex appears to inhibit negative affect, such that this area is under-active during experience with negative emotions, compared to the same area in other individuals who are not experiencing them. What this suggests is a neural network in which the negative emotions tend to suppress interest in novelty, in preference to the more familiar. Under stress, we prefer our favorite ice cream, rather than exploring the exotic fruits of Mandalay. Being N+ does not entail one's being O-. Rather, when one experiences the N+ states of fear, anger, and sadness, it is uncharacteristic to be interested in novelty and the unfamiliar. In one study whose source I cannot recall, it was determined that during stress the brain shuts down its higher thinking powers in the frontal cortex by a factor of some 80%. Under stress, then, we revert to our training and are not prone to explore new options. That is why pilots are trained so extensively: during emergencies, they can revert to their training without having to think. For example, look to now-retired U.S. Airways Captain "Sully" Sullenberger, who landed his disabled plane on the Hudson River in New York City on January 16, 2009, creating the now famous Miracle on the Hudson, in which every person survived. And when pilots have their training to fall back on, they tend not to get so stressed; so they retain a greater portion of their frontal-lobe thinking ability. The lesson here is that, when one wants to be able to use their mental resources for planning, creativity, problem solving, or decision making, they need to get rid of all immediate stressors, as well as take some aerobic exercise to clear their system of cortisol (see Chapter 5). Even just a brisk 10-minute walk, especially outdoors, can do wonders to reset your system.

O4: Zoom Scale

The Zoom Scale describes a continuum that has "big picture" at one end and "comfort with the details" at the other. The former is clearly associated with the abundance of dopamine and lower amounts of testosterone. Higher testosterone levels are associated with perseveration and focusing on details for long periods of time. Along with lesser levels of dopamine, higher testosterone would tend to squash the imagination and aid in focusing on the here and now.

We have now covered three of the five supertaits. We turn now to the fourth of the Big Five: A (accommodation). Whereas N dealt with stress, E with sensory bombardment, and O with novelty, A deals with power and how we behave around it. Fasten your seatbelts.

8

Accommodation

All About Power and Dominance

+	Atticus Finch: If you just learn a single trick, Scout, you'll get along a lot better with all kinds of folks. You never really understand a person until you consider things from his point of view, until you climb inside of his skin and walk around in it. -- Harper Lee's *To Kill a Mockingbird*
=	There's a time when a man needs to fight and a time when he needs to accept that his destiny's lost, the ship has sailed and that only a fool will continue. -- Young Ed Bloom (Ewan McGregor), *Big Fish* (2003 film)
-	What are you writing? I'm trying to come up with my own personal motto...something I can live by. Oh I have a few...'Love your neighbors as yourself'...'Laugh and the world laughs with you'... What did you write? 'Crush the little people.' I'm trying to be realistic. -- *Pearls Before Swine* (comic strip)

Guide to This Chapter:

- Definition of the A (Accommodation) Supertrait
- Three Case Studies
- Definitions of the Four Subtraits of A
- Implications of A for Career Exploration
- Implications of A for Relating to Adults in Power (Parents, Teachers, Administrators, Bosses)
- Implications of A for Managing Relationships with Peers
- Implications of A for Communication Style
- Implications of A for Leadership Aspirations
- Biological Basis for A

Atticus Finch is teaching his daughter, Scout, one of the finer points of high A behavior, that of being empathetic, i.e., focusing on the needs, interests, and point of view of others. High A is all about

Mapping Out the Big Five Traits

N	E	O	A	C
Need for Stability	**Extraversion**	**Originality**	**Accommodation**	**Consolidation**
N+ Reactive	E+ Extravert	O+ Explorer	A+ Adapter	C+ Focused
N= Responsive	E= Ambivert	O= Moderate	A= Negotiator	C= Balanced
N- Resilient	E- Introvert	O- Preserver	A- Challenger	C- Flexible
N1: Worry	**E1: Approach Lev.**	**O1: Imagination**	**A1: Service**	
N2: Temper	**E2: Group Orient.**	**O2: Range of Int.**	**A2: Compliance**	
N3: Outlook	**E3: Pace**	**O3: Innovation**	**A3: Humility**	
N4: Coping Lev.	**E4: Leadership**	**O4: Zoom Scale**	**A4: Speak Out Level**	
	E5: Trust			
	E6: Tact			

being agreeable, or accommodating, an attitude that is characterized by subordinating one's will to that of someone else. It is reminiscent of the sayings of Ruth in the *Old Testament* ("Whither thou goest, I will go"), of the early dialog by Nora in Henrik Ibsen's *A Doll's House* ("I have been your doll wife" and "Whatever you say, Torvald"), and in the *New Testament* concept of "turn the other cheek." The other extreme is expressed in the comic strip *Pearls before Swine* by "crush the little people," an extreme and antisocial (and hopefully tongue in cheek) version of the *Old Testament* view of "an eye for an eye and a tooth for a tooth." In fact, by the end of *A Doll's House*, Nora realizes she must draw upon her A- resources when she musters the courage to tell her husband, Torvald, that "I must learn to stand alone. That's why I can't stay here with you any more...I have another duty equally sacred...my duty to myself," as she slams the door on the repression of women. In *Big Fish*, young Ed Bloom espouses the wisdom of the midrange as he urges the more balanced view, suggesting that there may be virtue in knowing when one needs to back away and let the other prevail. These two polar views are often expressed through justice (A-) and mercy (A+).

Let's now take a closer look at the types of behavior associated with the three areas of the continuum associated with the A (accommodation) dimension.

Definition of the A Supertrait

Adapter (A+)

The A dimension is really about how we relate to power, authority, and positions in a hierarchy, both when we have it and when we are faced with others who have it. Adapters tend to relate to authority by being tolerant, magnanimous, and accepting. Often, they defer to other people and are seen as helpful, easily moved, and team players. Typically, they may allow others to win or be right more than they allow themselves to. At times, they may come across to others as spineless, naive, submissive, conflict-averse, gullible, dependent, or even unprincipled (because they keep yielding their position). In the U.S., not many high A players roam the turf in the National Football League because pigskin paradise is flooded with testosterone, big egos, and diehard competitors. However, one tough dude has the reputation of knowing

when to defer to the needs of others: quarterback Brett Favre. Even though Favre enjoys his accomplishments, he shows respect for others' needs to achieve greatness. For example, in order for Michael Strahan—an opposing defensive end—to establish the record for most sacks in a season, Favre assumed the fetal position to enable the clinching sack. In another example of selflessness, when the Packers were losing 47-3, Favre took himself out of the game for the sake of team, acknowledging that he just didn't have it that day, even though his streak of throwing for a touchdown 36 weeks in a row would be broken. Contrast this behavior with receiver Terrell Owens' reputation of "all about me" (understandable, given a tumultuous upbringing). It is not so much that "T. O." is more selfish on the field—that is more controlled by the coach and quarterback. One sports writer says T. O.'s "all about me" reputation comes from drawing attention to himself out in the community.

Negotiator (A=)

> The generous who is always just, and the just who is always generous, may, unannounced, approach the throne of heaven.
>
> —Johann Kaspar Lavater

Negotiators tend to be able to shift between competitive and cooperative situations fairly easily, usually pushing for a win-win strategy. They normally have a comfortable sense of personal identity, neither excessively dependent nor excessively independent, as expressed by the 18th century scholar Johann Lavater. Just, but generous; tough, yet kind; respectful of both the letter and the spirit of the law. Typically, negotiators (A=) can work well either as team members or as independents. At their worst moments, they might be regarded by others as sitting on the fence between opposite views as you try to help both sides to compromise. I am reminded of a client's office with a hanging needlework saying, "And the lion and the lamb shall lie together, and the lamb shall not get much sleep." The negotiator attempts to help the lion (A-) and the lamb (A+) co-exist, even thrive.

As with the other supertraits, midrange A comes in two modes: 1) The pure negotiator is unconcerned with either winning or with promoting others' winning. Instead, the pure negotiator goes along merrily taking life in stride. Que sera, sera. Whatever will be, will be. There is something of the fatalist in this mode. 2) Someone with a situational attitude toward the exercise of power clearly prefers to win in some situations; while in others, they like to see others win. This might be the athlete who needs to win on the field or court but who gladly paves the way for friends or family who might be competing for resources, as in, "Sure, you take the car tonight. I'll walk or catch a ride with someone."

Challenger (A-)

Challengers tend to relate to authority by being skeptical, tough, guarded, persistent, competitive, or aggressive. Often, they are independent in their thoughts and ask questions, especially to protect their self-interests and to make sure they win. Challengers are the classic salespeople, the classic wheeler-dealers. In their extreme form, challengers espouse the philosophy of the Green Bay Packers' ex-coach, Vince Lombardi: "Winning is not everything, it is the only thing." At times, they may come across to others as hostile, rude, aloof, self-centered, proud, haughty, hardheaded, or combative.

Mapping Out the Big Five Traits

These "my way or the highway" stereotypes are easy to parody in popular as well as classical culture. In the comic strip *The Lockhorns*, Leroy and Loretta attempt effortlessly to out-insult each other day after day. Or in the film *High School Musical*, Sharpay Evans typifies the A- who stops at nothing to get her way. She and her fraternal twin brother are both in the final production number. At one point, both climb a ladder, and she reaches over to push him down lower so she can be higher. You go, alpha girl! We will hear more from Miss Evans when we discuss the subtraits of A. Her character is a rich case study in low A. Very low A! Actually, such examples are not hard to find. Consider Miranda from *The Devil Wears Prada*, who drives family and employees away through her demanding, competitive nature: "Bore someone else with your questions."

> I believe in the brotherhood of man, all men, but I don't believe in brotherhood with anybody who doesn't want brotherhood with me. I believe in treating people right, but I'm not going to waste my time trying to treat somebody right who doesn't know how to return that treatment.
>
> —Malcolm X

The two lead characters in the Pixar film *WALL-E* provide a delightful illustration of higher and lower A interacting. WALL-E is the high A, showing his consideration of others early on by screeching to a halt as he is about to run over a grasshopper, then gently commanding it to move aside for his own protection. EVE is the no-nonsense, higher-evolved robot who destroys (A-) anything that displeases her with a zap from her bionic arm/wing. WALL-E in his friendly, playful manner (A+) shows her all of his toys and goodies, while her competitive (A-) nature solves a Rubik's cube in a matter of seconds. At one point, WALL-E tries to shake her hand/wing, but she clamps it shut. As soon as she accomplishes her mission of finding a sign of plant life on Earth, she shuts down with no thanks or goodbyes and returns to her base. Of course, she eventually allows enough A+ in her behavioral repertoire to develop a pleasing relationship with WALL-E.

Emily Crowder, in her hunt for trait examples in popular culture, suggests these with contrasting A:

- Paula Abdul (higher A) and Simon Cowell (lower A) on *American Idol*
- Harry Potter (higher A) and Hermione Granger (lower A) in the J. K. Rowling series
- The Caretaker (higher A) and Dad (lower A) in *The Kite Runner*
- Mom (higher A) and Dad (lower A) in *That 70s Show.*

Now that we have explored the three most common levels of A (accommodation), let's see how they play out in everyday scenes through three case studies.

Three Case Studies

Case Study 1 of A: The Lamb in the Lions' Den

A group of girls started a social club at a private high school. The club, Entré, was comprised of wealthy girls who had not outgrown their status consciousness. They saw themselves as the crème de la crème of their school's society. Unknown to them, most others saw them for what they were, spoiled rich girls whose pride bordered on arrogance and who were uninterested in mingling with peers of more modest means. What they lacked in intellect they made up for in attitude. What they lacked in social consciousness they made up for in fashion consciousness. What they lacked in interior beauty they made up for in show. These were the girls of low A (hmmm, rhymes with Entré!).

One year, during the early part of the school year in which new members were recruited, the leaders of Entré reviewed the list of eligibles (rich sophomores). Their collective eyes stopped on Clara Nett's name. Clara was the sister of a recently graduated Entré girl, in other words, a "legacy." With some reservation, Clara was issued a bid. Why the reservation? The reason their eyes stopped on her name was that, while clearly eligible, she was undesirable inasmuch as she was plain (didn't use makeup), humble (she was a volunteer for several organizations in the community), and studious (she wanted to be a doctor). Out of their long-standing policy of issuing bids to legacies, they overrode their better judgment and issued the invitation.

Clara did not particularly want to be in Entré, as it threatened to take time from her already well-developed interests and commitments. Plus, social clubs just didn't have that much appeal to her. However, in chatting with her parents and her older sister, she decided to accept the bid. Reluctantly. Overriding her better judgment.

Well, what would you imagine it is like for one A+ to join the company of 20 girls with low A? We're talking a lamb in the lions' den. One independent girl joining a cohesive group of 20 snobs. Not pretty. Having done their duty, they essentially proceeded to ignore her, perhaps hoping that she would not survive initiation, that she would drop out. High A that she was, she took all that they gave. Passing her initiation was important to honor her sister's previous involvement.

But after a couple of months of membership, having passed initiation, Clara had enough. Tired of being left out of meetings, of being the butt of gossip, of being on the receiving end of snide remarks, she sat down with her parents and discussed her plight. Rather than just quit, they came up with the idea of forming a new group, the Putnam Society, as a tribute to the author of *Bowling Alone*. Robert Putnam has pointed out a 33% decrease in social capital (measured in part by social service) during the last 50 years of the 20th century. This new group would also be for girls, but it would have no financial background restrictions, and it would include only girls interested in a coordinated effort to provide service to the local community. Initiation would consist of successfully participating in a group service project such as cleaning, painting, wallpapering, and landscaping a group home for special-needs kids. Clara left the lions' den to join, not a flock of sheep, but a delightful mixture of humanity. Rich and marginal, beautiful and otherwise, fashionable and frumpy, scholarly and getting by, but all committed to social service. Their motto: "Service is the rent we pay for the privilege of living on this earth." (Sister N. Eldon Tanner)

Mapping Out the Big Five Traits

In reflecting on this episode, it is normal to find that one person with extreme behavior rarely thrives among a throng of other persons who exhibit the opposite extreme, e.g., one introvert with 20 extraverts or vice versa; one creative type with 20 no-nonsense types or vice versa. Such lopsided groups are difficult to manage. Possible, but difficult. Everyone must want to make it work. In the case of Entré, such desire was absent.

Case Study 2 of A: The Know-It-All

When working with our student leadership group of 50, we presented this situation: "A 'know-it-all' on your class study team has really bummed you out by stealing your idea, taking it to the professor, and getting credit for it. What are your thoughts and feelings? What do you do about it?" The 50 students were distributed according to their A scores along a continuum from 0 to 100. They clustered into about five clearly different groups, from very low A to very high A. Here is how they responded to the situation:

> *A++ (very high adapters):* "We don't want to stir the water; we'd let well enough alone but be wary of working with that student anymore." "We would modify the idea and submit it to the professor. No need to confront anyone. Eventually what goes around comes around."
>
> *A+ (moderately high adapters):* "We would ask the know-it-all where he got the idea. If he didn't fess up, we'd let it pass." "We would submit the idea to the teacher anyway, and let her deal with it. We didn't do anything wrong and shouldn't have to suffer from his actions."
>
> *A= (negotiators):* "This wrong must be redressed. We would approach the know-it-all privately and say he can't get away with claiming ownership of the idea. We would negotiate some way for him to keep his self-respect and restore the authorship to us."
>
> *A- (moderately low challengers):* "No problem. The idea is ours, and the professor will more than likely recognize this as a pattern of his behavior. We would go to the professor, establish our claim, and let her deal with his plagiarism."
>
> *A- - (extremely low challengers):* "We would be outraged. Cut him off at the knees. We would insist that he go with us to discuss this with the professor. The most important thing here is to put him in his place. We would come up with some way that we could embarrass him in the eyes of the teacher and the class. This is not a clear honor-code violation, but it is close. We should submit it to the Honor Council just to make a point."

People with a high score (A+) tend to accept the existing situation without question. While they are not necessarily "doormats" (i.e., people who let others step on them), they often have trouble looking out for their own interests. As we move down the scale to hear from other groups, there is a growing sense that they could (A=) and ultimately will (A-) do something that restores their authorship of the idea. The A= group begins to negotiate options that allow the perpetrator to save face, while the A-- group threatens to take him to court. A+ people will often give in for the good of the community; they are the ultimate team members. That is, they promote harmony and good feeling. However, they may fail to ask the tough questions that are crucial to team viability. Conversely, A- people rarely can take a situation as it exists without asking questions or pushing back. A= people are capable of responding either way.

Case Study 3 of A: Cut in the Yearbook Budget

To hear the A scale in action on campus, let's listen to the following conversation taking place during a three-person editorial team meeting (the facilitator of the meeting is the A= member):

A= (Negotiator): "Our next agenda item is what we should do about the problem of producing our yearbook with the 10% increase in costs from the publisher. We can't have the same number of pages or color options as last year's product unless we go up in price."

A+ (Adapter): "I think we should all share the burden, and ask every department to find a way to reduce their space requirements by 10%."

A- (Challenger): "Nah, that's capitulating. I say we go up in price and keep the same page and color scheme."

A+: "Well, that is certainly a possibility. It would really be nice not to have to change."

A-: "There you go again—caving in to me without standing up for your own idea."

A+: "I'm really ok with your suggestion."

A=: "Franco (A+), there's merit in your idea of space reduction. At least that way, everyone could still pay what they are expecting to pay. There's the possibility that less-well-off students couldn't pay the increase, and the resulting lower sales would compound the problem. And Molly (A-), I do wonder if some kind of increase in fees might work. Maybe not the cost to the student but the costs for advertising space?"

A-: "That'd work. Or we could concentrate on selling more ads than last year. Or some combination of more ads, higher fees for ads, and slightly higher costs to the student."

A+: "Times are tough. We can sell more ads and more expensive ads, but we'll have to work hard and figure out some benefit for the advertisers above and beyond what they've normally expected."

A=: "I think we're on a doable track here. Let's draw out a couple of scenarios and go to our faculty advisor for a final resolution."

This script highlights some of the clear distinctions between the A- and A+ points of view. The defiant stance that comes as second nature to an A- (challenger) may be perceived as conflict to an A+ (adapter). In order to preserve the "peace" of the team, the A+ selflessly yields his position for the "good" of the team. Meanwhile, the A- loses respect for the A+ because she can't get a good argument from him. The A=, the facilitator in this case, becomes the translator between the A+ and A-. By explaining the needs and positions of the high and low scorers, the A= helps them to reach a compromise in which they both get their needs met, and the team accomplishes its goal of providing the kind of yearbook that their students have come to expect, while keeping it at a reasonable price for students to purchase.

Now that we have seen the A supertrait in action, let's take a look at four specific subtraits of accommodation.

Definitions of the Four Subtraits of A

A1 ***Service****: The relative emphasis on personal versus others' needs.* This subtrait is comprised of two opposite points of view that might be described as "It's all about me" and "It's all about thee." This is the subtrait most associated with 1) one's relative preference for mercy (A1+) or justice (A1-) or 2) whether one is more likely to drop what one is doing to help others or instead to persist in one's own activities.

A1+ (High): *Focused on the needs of others.* The higher end of A1 is more focused on others' needs, thus making it more likely that someone high in A1 will show a fairly consistent pattern of showing mercy, i.e., forgiving and forgetting and letting bygones be bygones. This behavior is also associated with naturally attending to the mental and emotional states of others, known as "theory of mind." (Nettle, 2007, pp. 158-163) Nettle identifies two aspects of theory of mind: mentalizing and empathizing. The former attempts to identify what a person is thinking; the latter, what they are feeling. While all humans exhibit this capability, lower A1 individuals find it less natural, while higher A1 tend to thrive on practicing it.

> For when the One Great Scorer comes
> To write against your name,
> He marks—not that you won or lost—
> But how you played the Game.
> --Grantland Rice, sportswriter

A1= (Medium): *Balances own needs with others'.*
The midrange of A1 is likely to resemble one of two patterns. On the one hand, the "pure" A1= is someone who is neither totally selfless nor totally selfish, but rather more focused on finding mutually agreeable options, as in, "Let's do something we both enjoy." Shall we say someone prone to the art of compromise? On the other hand, the "polarized" A1= is someone who defers to others about half the time, while holding out for self the other times. This is a more complex mid A1, and it's harder to predict their behavior. They may, for example, defer to one parent and not the other.

A1- (Low): *Focused on the needs of oneself.* The lower end of A1 is more focused on satisfying one's own needs, interests, or goals. This would include a very strong preference for doing things "my way," i.e., "my way or the highway," as suggested earlier. In *High School Musical*, pianist and composer Kelsey comments to Gabriela concerning Sharpay Evans' A1- behavior: "If that girl could figure out a way to be Romeo AND Juliet, her own brother would be out of a job." She is referring to the fact that Sharpay's twin brother is also an actor. Typically when a low A1 is accommodating to others' needs, the low A requires a large amount of energy to do so, sort of like taking one's medicine or eating one's greens because you know they're good for you, not because you like them.

> The young always have the same problem, how to rebel and conform at the same time. They have now solved this by defying their parents and copying one another.
> --Quentin Crisp (English writer and gay activist)

A2 ***Compliance****: Our relative emphasis on competition versus cooperation.* The difference between A1 and A2 is subtle but important. Whereas A1 is about my needs versus your needs, A2 is about the need to win, period, and the degree to which one is comfortable engaging in the conflict and competition required to win, as opposed to backing away from argument or competition and allowing others to win. It is possible, for example to be selfish (A1-) and noncompetitive (A2+), as well as unselfish (A1+) and competitive (A2-). With the former, we could have someone who is the classic "passive-aggressive," as in backing out of an argument about how to do something, then going about doing it howsoever one pleases. With the latter, unselfish (A1+) and competitive (A2-), we would find someone who takes up a friend's cause and then fights to the finish.

A2+ (High): *Prefers cooperation and harmony.* The high range of A2 is all peace and harmony. At least, that is what is preferred. In order to achieve it, this individual typically backs away from arguments, deferring to the position of others who wish to fight or challenge. The classic image of the high A2 is that of the supplicant, e.g., two hands in prayer or the Muslim prostrate towards Mecca. Even taking a bow when being introduced to someone is a token of (at least temporary) submission. Phil Hanes, noted philanthropist in Winston-Salem, NC, had the reputation of terrorizing (A- -) all who approached him. At a dinner honoring outstanding teachers in the University of North Carolina system, President C. D. Spangler asked James Houlik, saxophone instructor at the N.C. School of the Arts, what his secret was for getting along so well with Hanes. Houlik related that the first time Hanes tried to engage him in an argument, the teacher brought it to a halt with this remark: "Mr. Hanes, I refuse to engage in a battle of wits with an unarmed man." Is that an insult or a backing away? Probably both but certainly a forceful way of behaving in a high A2 manner. The risk of being high A2 is that one will be perceived as weak, as a "doormat" as pointed out earlier; so having such phrases as Mr. Houlik's can help one appear more forceful. Perhaps the ultimate credo of the high A2 is that penned (in Latin, of course) by the 15th century German Catholic monk Thomas à Kempis: "As thou wilt; what thou wilt; when thou wilt." In other words, "you the boss, what you say goes, no argument from me. Period."

A2= (Medium): *Prefers negotiating for the win-win.* Midrange scorers on A2 come in two modes. The first is the "pure" A2 who doesn't care to win at the expense of others, yet does desire to win. This is the "win-win" approach. Let's see if we can find a way for you to win AND for me to win. I want the car tonight and you do also. We can't both have it. I also want an extra $20 from the parents. How 'bout you take the car, and I take the $20? I win, you win. Besides, with my extra cash, I'll have no trouble finding a bud with wheels. The other mode of mid A2 is the situational variety, in which one insists on winning half the time, while allowing others to win the other half. This individual picks their battles, and it is typically more complex and more difficult to predict when they'll fight/compete and when they'll back off from the argument. This individual does not have the energy, the temperament, to try to be persuasive all the time, just part of the time. At other times, they just shrug and give in.

A2- (Low): *Comfortable with competition and conflict.* As we mentioned earlier, the low A2 is the most easily caricatured in all of literature, from the Godfather to the Lockhorns. Well, the low A2 is the primary exemplar of this target for caricature! In extreme form, they not only have to win—they have to kill their rivals. We once negotiated with a publisher in England who told us, "I not only want to beat the competition, I want to drive them out of business, out of house and home, slay them." We decided to take our business elsewhere! We have put Sharpay Evans (from *High School Musical*) on the pedestal as a prize-winning example of low A. Well, here she is, with lyrics sung to her brother, Ryan, that exude very low A2:

> Kicking and scratching, hedging all my bets, to climb the ladder of success.
> Bop to the top, don't let it stop.

This is in sharp contrast to the character of Gabriela Montez, whose higher A2 bows out to keep harmony when the going gets rough at one point. One of many mottos of the low A2 is: "If you can't take the heat, get out of the kitchen." Or, if you are unwilling to battle with me, don't get started. Don't start what you aren't willing to finish. Gabriela decided that the "heat in the kitchen" from Sharpay was too great for her to continue, given her values/temperament.

A3 ***Humility:*** *Our tendency towards pride versus humility.* There is a touch of A1 in A3. That is to say, humility involves a degree of focus on the needs of others, whereas pride involves a degree of focus on the needs of self. Though related, these two subtraits are different. They are like sausage and avocado—both have fat in common, but protein fills out the one and carbohydrates the other. Accordingly, both A1 and A3 have selflessness in common, but altruism fills out the first one and humility the other.

> **A3+** (High): *Tends to be humble and deflect credit.* The defining characteristic of the high A3 is the tendency to deflect credit. This is the "Aw, shucks, tweren't much" attitude, or "My teammates deserve this more than I do." My (Pierce's) mother liked to tell me the story of my older brother, Lee, who had been at Camp Yonahlossee in the North Carolina mountains one summer. Several months after his return home, she learned that he had won a major award there and had been given a rather nice trophy. She'd seen nothing of it. When asked about it, Lee told her that he had hidden it under his bed. This is high A3 behavior. It is the opposite of the "let your light shine" philosophy or the "if you've got it, flaunt it" attitude that characterizes low A3. High A3 is epitomized by the New Testament's (Mathew 5:5): "The meek shall inherit the earth," or as Ben Franklin writes, "To be humble to superiors is duty, to equals courtesy, to inferiors nobleness."

> **A3=** (Medium): *Balances pride and humility.* The "pure" mode of mid A3 believes in just enough humility to avoid arrogance, but not so much as to risk reverse snobbery. As author Helen Nielsen writes, "Humility is like underwear, essential, but indecent if it shows." Toned-down humility, or soft-spoken pride. Like the half-full or half-empty conundrum. The more complex mode of mid A3 is someone who takes easy pride and recognition in some aspects of life and not in others. Proud of accomplishments in golf but deflecting of accomplishments at work. Proud of winning an election but humble about having acquired the wealth to finance it.

> **A3-** (Low): *Tends to be proud and accept credit.* This is the "if you've got it, flaunt it" temperament. There was the touch of pride, if not arrogance, in televangelist Jim Bakker's response to a journalist's probing question about the riches (e.g., gold-plated faucets) adorning his home: "God doesn't like junk." Proverbs 16:18 advises that "pride goes before destruction, a haughty spirit before a fall." And in this case, Proverbs was right! Jim Bakker's kingdom—built on greed, arrogance, and the contributions of his followers—came crumbling down. The danger of excessive pride peppers literature from its beginnings. After Odysseus blinded Cyclops, pride led the journeyer to boastfully reveal his name, thus enabling Cyclops to call on his father, Poseidon, and point him to the right perpetrator on whom to take revenge. We talk here of extreme pride. Pride in and of itself is fine. In fact, our research shows that a healthy dose of pride is associated with success, for example, in the field of sales. Salespeople don't typically succeed with an "aw, shucks" attitude. Rather, they tend to exude,"I'm good. My product is good. My company is good." I (Pierce) am reminded of a line from one of the "elocution" poems that my sister, Nancy, used to recite, both in and out of school: "The police officer said to me, 'Are you lost, little girl?'; 'No, nice officer, but where can nursie be?" A3-, like A2-, is the butt of caricature: "Why does it take millions of sperm to get one egg fertilized? Because they never stop to ask directions."

*A4 **Speaking Out:** The preference for the foreground or the background.* This subtrait is a blend of two qualities: the tendency to be assertive and the degree of comfort being in the foreground, e.g., being on stage. At one end of the continuum, we have people who express their opinions readily, are not particularly self-conscious around others, and are not easily embarrassed. At the other end are people who are more reticent, who prefer to let others do the talking, and tend to be relatively easy to embarrass.

A4+ (High): *Naturally more reserved and in the background.* Persons scoring higher in A4 tend to be quieter in groups and thus harder to "read." They tend to keep their opinions to themselves. It is not that they do not have opinions, just that they are reluctant to espouse them openly, whether because of self-consciousness, a lack of knowledge or experience, a sense of status differences, a fear of being laughed at or judged, a discomfort around people in power, or some other reason. If you don't know what an A4+ is thinking or feeling, it is because you haven't asked them. If you don't know what an A4- is thinking or feeling, then you haven't been listening! High A4s are not necessarily introverted. Not all extraverts are talkers, and not all talkers necessarily are quick to reveal their thoughts. Many talkative people prattle on about their weather, fashion, and so forth, without ever revealing much about themselves. It is this reluctance to self-disclose that is associated with A4+.

A4= (Medium): *Comfortable with a moderate degree of visibility and engagement.* Mid A4 comes in two principle styles. The pure A4= is one who is likely to speak their share of the time, no more, no less. In a 60-minute meeting of 10 people, this person will likely speak about six minutes, with high scorers speaking far less and low scorers speaking more than six minutes each, i.e., more than their logically "allotted" time. The other style of A4= is more situational, whereby an individual might be highly assertive in some situations, say a study group on political issues, and more reticent in others, say a study group on solving simultaneous equations.

A4- (Low): *Comfortable being the center of attention.* For the low-scoring A4, all the stops are pulled out, like an organ playing full blast! Lack of knowledge or experience is no reason for an A4- to keep silent. If you've got an issue, the A4- is likely to have something to say about it, whether factual, evaluative, or otherwise. Assertiveness is an important ingredient of leadership, just as is the ability to listen. Leaders must communicate, but communication is two-way. You must know what a leader is thinking, but the leader must also know what you are thinking. The leader must be comfortable standing in front of most any kind of group and talking about the vision, about the plan, about how to solve the problem, about important issues facing the group. The danger of extremely low A4 is either insufficient listening or insufficient time for others to get their input on the table.

We have now described four important subtraits of accommodation. We know the behaviors associated with being more, or less, accommodating to others. Let's take a look now at how these behaviors relate to specific aspects of our social world.

Implications of A for Career Exploration

For challengers (A-), their strength and their liability are one and the same: They tend to question everything as a matter of course. Although this minimizes the possibility of "groupthink," they continually risk resentment and alienation from others. They prefer jobs based on pushing back, such as accountant, courtroom lawyer, or drill sergeant.

For adapters (A+), again, their strength and their liability are identical: They tend to subordinate their needs to the needs of others as a matter of course. They will therefore always be valued as a team member, but they should be wary of situations in which they are responsible to someone with whom they do not share the same values. In such situations, they will find it next to impossible to stand up to that person when necessary. These individuals also tend to feel at home in various kinds of service work (McCrae and Costa, 2003, pp. 217-227), e.g., a customer service representative or jobs in the hospitality, education, health care, retail, food service, or social service agencies.

Mapping Out the Big Five Traits

Negotiators (A=) will tend to be valued as a peacemaker and as a negotiator, one who strives to achieve the win-win situation. They are well advised to build on their natural ability to see both sides of a question or situation.

Implications of A for Your Boss and Associates

If you are A- and your boss or peers are A+, be prepared to find little resistance to your thoughts, because they will probably tend to submit to your strong questioning and opinions. Be sure to take the time and effort to find out what they truly think; if you don't, they will build up resentments over time and leave you. You may not respect their lack of "backbone," but trust that they really do have opinions, even if they don't have the courage to battle with you.

If you are A+ and your boss or peers are A-, you are in danger of seldom getting your interests met unless you share the same values. Take the time and effort to put your thoughts and needs in writing, and use your notes as a form of muscle with which to approach them and stand up for your needs. Plan the arguments you will have to make ahead of time, so that you will have a script to use when words don't come naturally. If you can't respond during a strong discussion, A- people will lose respect for you and might ignore you.

Implications of A for Relating to Adults in Power (Parents, Teachers, Administrators, Bosses)

The A dimension is important for all relationship management, whether youth to adult or youth to youth. One of the classic profiles that can lead to unhealthy relationships occurs when one person is lower A, the other higher. Lower A is associated with persons who tend to have, and exercise, more power, i.e., persons who tend to be higher in a hierarchy. It is typically the A- behaviors that get people to the top of a hierarchy: principals, heads of departments, bosses, and so forth. As a general rule, bosses, or people in charge, tend to be lower A—it is their nature to enjoy the dominant role. Young people who are higher in A stand the chance of being taken advantage of by these persons in dominant roles because A- superiors like agreeable A+ students who volunteer, who tend not to speak back, and who like to avoid arguments. In these cases, the A+ student needs to know their limit and to develop some standard lines (remember James Houlik's retort: "Sir, I refuse to engage in a battle of wits with an unarmed man?") that help them state their limits or needs without being confrontational. These lines could be something like: "I'm uncomfortable doing that." Or "I'm concerned about over-commiting—my time is pretty much maxed out right now." Or "I'll think about it" (and then hope it goes away). Young girls, as described earlier in the writings of Mary Belenky (*Women's Ways of Knowing*, 1997), are especially prone to conceding to the dictates of authority figures. Using such "distancer" phrases with authorities can help these young women in finding their own voices at an early age.

The A- youth interacting with A- adults is likely to lock horns, to butt heads, to engage in disagreements, even arguments, with some frequency. This is not necessarily a bad thing, as those low in A tend to respect those who argue their case well, who stand their ground. On the other hand, when an A- youth interacts with an A+ adult, the youth can get their way, in spite of the adult's possession of valuable information, because the adult is reluctant to be unpleasant. In these cases, the youth is well advised to have some standard questions to ask when they feel that an adult is backing off too quickly, such as: "Can you help me think this through?" Or "What would you do if you were in my situation?" Or "What do you see as my possible options?"

Whatever the trait similarities or differences between a youth and an adult, it is important to remember to state one's opinions, to listen to the other person, and to ask good open-ended questions beginning with "how, when, where, what, and who." However, once the youth has asked the question, they need to listen to the response without interrupting.

Implications of the A Traits for Managing Relationships with Peers

Peer relationships get their dynamic from A scores, just as the youth-adult relationships we just described. The difference is that youth tend to want to emulate the behavior of peers who are "salient" at specific times in their life. This point is discussed earlier (in Chapter 2, "States") in relation to the work of Judith Rich Harris. So, whether lower or higher A, young people will tend to accommodate to those in their most significant peer group. The important thing to remember when this identity formation is happening is for the young person to have close family or friends to discuss what is happening. How do they feel about the changes that are happening as a result of feeling close to this peer group? Are there other peer groups that would build more satisfyingly on how I am developing as a person?

As a general rule, young males who are higher in A tend to have "more effective social relationships in middle age" (McCrae and Costa, 2003, p. 218). How does this happen? In other studies, it has been found that women find one particular trait to be the most important determinant in a relationship with a man, and that is the willingness to apologize, to say "I was wrong." This trait is clearly associated with higher A. It is not that low A men cannot have satisfying relationships with women. It is just that low A men need to have the presence of mind to know when to back off their pride and say, "I was wrong." I (Pierce) had a friend who once drove his family to Myrtle Beach, South Carolina from Charlotte. When he arrived at highway 17, he turned right, when in fact he should have turned left to get to the Grand Strand. After a mile or so, his wife said, "Shouldn't we have turned left back there?" Unable to swallow his pride, unwilling to admit he was wrong, he covered his error with, "No. Brookgreen Garden is just down the road. I thought we'd all enjoy stretching our legs there and seeing the nice statues." This behavior is not endearing!

Challengers (A-) who can admit that they are wrong (when they *are* wrong, of course), and adapters (A+) who can resist inappropriate deference to authority figures—ah, bliss. Or, spoken somewhat irreverently by a friend some years back: "World peace will break out when men learn to cry (A+) and women learn to burp (A-)." Here's a more enlightened version: "World peace will break out when challengers learn to listen and adapters learn to speak up." But it is difficult to act in ways that are not natural or genuine for us.

Mapping Out the Big Five Traits

Implications of the A Traits for Communication Style

Communication is getting accurate information from one person to another without becoming distorted by the "noise" surrounding them. Noise, in the communications sense, is anything that alters the precise meaning of a message. Noise could include actual noise, such that loud noise prevents hearing the message accurately. But noise can also be more subtle things, such as differences in values and experiences of the two persons trying to communicate. Words can have remarkably different meanings to persons of different backgrounds. In England "turnover" is cash flow, as we discovered to our surprise several years after the fact, being accustomed to understanding it as referring to the rate of employee departures and replacements. "Boot" is the trunk of a car, versus boot is the big, tall shoe. One of the problems that lower the A has in communication is that they have an unnerving tendency to assume that their usage is the correct one, and that the other guy is wrong. The lower A needs to make it a common practice to allow the possibility that they are in error.

The higher A has the reverse problem in communication. They have a disappointing tendency to assume too readily that the other guy is right. Not always, but enough for it to be problematic with regard to getting the point across. For both extremes of A, an effective practice is to ask the listener to say, in their own words, what the speaker has just said. Not always, just when the stakes are high. You don't say, "Will you marry me?" immediately followed by, "Now, what do you think I meant by that?" Rather, something like, "No sleepovers while we're out of town. Now, tell me what that means to you." When our younger daughter was in the 11th grade, we agreed to chaperone 10 teenage girls during spring break at Myrtle Beach. Just before the car began to pull away, one of the parents gave us each a pin to wear on our chests that shouted in big letters, "Just what don't you understand about NO?!"

Just as two people with low A can lock horns, two with high A can kill each other with politeness! The classic cartoon depiction of the high A is "Alphonse and Gaston," Frederick Burr Opper's early 20th century depiction of two friends who were so polite to each other that their best interests were not often served. Upon seeing a truck barreling down the street, one would say, "You get out of the way first, dear Alphonse!" Then, "No, dear Gaston, certainly you should go first!" And so on until, neither having moved for fear of being impolite to the other, both are run over by the truck!

Implications of the A Traits for Leadership Aspirations

Neither extreme of A is conducive to effective leadership. High A can result in insufficient toughness, being taken in by fast-talking subordinates and being too nice a person to insist subordinates toe the line where it counts. Traditionally, leadership has been associated with lower A, but not too low. Just low enough to be tough enough, aggressive enough, to get a job done. A recent movement has advocated a "kindler, gentler" kind of leader called the "Level 5" leader (see various books by Jim Collins), one who takes less pride in one's own accomplishments and abilities, and more pride in that of others, one who is humbler, a servant leader. However, if the leader can't handle the essential tough tasks of a leader, they will not be effective in that role. We have found that it is rare to find an effective leader who is high in A within a traditional organizational culture. Some cultures permit a high A to lead effectively. In such cultures, aggressive, fierce, take-no-prisoners competitiveness is shunned. They are the exception. Higher A leaders should insure that they have someone close to them to whom "tough tasks" can be delegated.

Emily Crowder points to a character in *The Office* as portraying the perils of excessively high A for leaders. Michael Scott, earlier cited for typifying low E6 (low tact), also exhibits extremely high A. He is ineffective as a leader because he won't stand up for himself or his employees. When people talk back to him, he tries to act tough but eventually always backs down. Some of Michael's pearls: "I'm friends with everybody in this office.... I love everybody here." "What is the single most important thing for a company? Is it the building? Is it the stock? Is it the turnover? It's the people." "The most sacred thing I do is care."

Emily contrasts Michael's high A in leadership to Margaret Tate in *The Proposal*. Tate is flawed because she is too aggressive and competitive. Her grandma quips, "Do you prefer Margaret or Satan's Mistress?" Aware of others' negative perception of her, Margaret casually asks Andrew Paxton, her assistant, "Was that your family?" Andrew: "Yes." Margaret: "(Do they) tell you to quit?" Andrew: "Every single day."

The Biological Basis for Accommodation (A)

The arousal system that governs the A set of behaviors consists of the sex hormones, along with the serotonergic system. The stimulus that triggers this system into action is the dominance challenge. For people with a higher ratio of the male hormones, such as testosterone, to the female hormones, such as estrogen and progesterone, defiance is the norm. As the balance of sex hormones shifts, whether in males or females, the norm shifts from defiance to submission. Your A score, then, is an estimate of the point at which you tire of being defiant and turn to acts of submission. Serotonin levels affect this trigger point: Higher levels are associated with relaxation and peacefulness; lower levels with aggression (and in some conditions, depression). Note that this is a ratio and not the absolute quantity of the hormones.

Recent brain imaging studies (DeYoung et al., 2010) reveal that individuals scoring higher on A tend to have accordingly greater or lesser volume in brain areas associated with nurture, altruism, and understanding of others. Specifically, A+ individuals tend to have greater volume in the posterior cingulate cortex (associated with understanding others' ways of thinking) and the fusiform gyrus (associated with recognizing faces), while having less volume in the posterior left superior temporal sulcus (associated with evaluating what others' actions mean).

Each of the four subtraits of A is in its own way related to this androgen/estrogen balance, yet there are some interesting strands of research that identify separate biological associations with each subtrait.

A1: Service

Nurturing others (higher A1) and serving self (lower A1) fall under the category of what are typically referred to as "gender roles," with the stereotypical female being more nurturing, the stereotypical male more self-serving. Our research challenges the stereotype while supporting the continuum of behavior from nurture to self-service. Research reported by Lerner and Steinberg (2004, pp. 233 ff.) concludes that gender role characteristics are determined by a combination of genetic and environmental influences. Gender roles have to do with the way males and females are "supposed" to behave in various situations—whether they behave the same or vary according to their sex. Boys shouldn't cry, girls shouldn't fight, that kind of thing. The particular environmental influence found by the researchers is called "nonshared influence," which means environmental influence that one sibling might have experienced that other siblings did not. I (Jane) took Spanish in high school with Graciela Vallvé, while my two sisters studied Latin. That is "nonshared" influence. There is a slight difference in the degree of each source of influence according to sex—for males it is about 1/4 genetic, 3/4 nonshared influence, and for females, about 1/3 genetic, 2/3 nonshared influence. In other words, males are slightly more influenced by their environment than females are in how their gender roles are formed.

The development of specific schemas, such as what to do when a child is crying, is nonshared environment (e.g., Aunt Milly likes to say "let me kiss the booboo" and then puts me in her lap and rocks) built on an underlying temperament that is genetic (i.e., higher or lower levels of oxytocin, vasopressin, estrogens, and so forth). So the schema one develops could be 1) kiss the booboo immediately upon hearing/seeing the crying and rock the kid (this assumes higher levels of "nurture chemicals", e.g., A1+), or 2) see if the kid can/will ride it out for a while, and if that doesn't work, then kiss the booboo and rock the kid (lower levels of cuddle chemicals, e.g., A1-).

A2: Compliance

Studying a sample of 155 students, ages 12 and 13, who had taken the Early Adolescent Temperament Questionnaire, Nicholas Allen et al (2006) report that magnetic resonance images (MRIs) showed that the behavior called "affiliation" (desire for harmony with others, hence averse to conflict) is associated with two areas of the brain, areas in the left ventral limbic anterior cingulated cortex that are smaller than areas of the right rostral limbic anterior cingulated cortex. Research is underway to determine how this knowledge might be used in developing pharmaceuticals to modify the "affiliative" needs, either upwards (e.g., for individuals who are self-defeatingly antisocial) or downwards (e.g., for isolated individuals stationed in outposts with little human contact).

A3: Humility

Pride goeth where the spotlight is. In one experiment, a high testosterone person put in a low status position performed worse on cognitive ability measures, while low testosterone persons performed better in low status positions. The effect worked independent of gender. The lesson from this is that high testosterone persons experience stress when put in low status, or subservient, positions and consequently do not have their full mental resources available to perform tasks. Perhaps this is the unfortunate basis of the U.S. criminal justice system. It certainly should not be the basis of the educational system. High testosterone students in submissive relationships with instructors will likely resort to habitual patterns of performance that do not reflect their full mental potential. Her first year in college, our A- younger daughter recognized this in herself. She realized that she tried harder and received better grades from professors she liked and respected.

A4: Speak-Out Level

The same Nicholas Allen and others (Whittle, Allen, Lubman, and Yücel, 2005) found that the behavior called "constraint" involves areas with higher serotonin activity (but not too high), including the dorsal anterior cingulate cortex, the dorsolateral prefrontal cortex, and the lateral orbitofrontal cortex. Activity in these areas is associated with effective inhibition control and greater social awareness/empathy, with less activity associated with uncontrolled inhibition, as in attention deficit hyperactivity disorder (ADHD) and schizophrenia. "Uncontrolled inhibition" is a behavioral pattern related to quite a few different kinds of undesirable activities in addition to those just cited, including violent aggression and substance abuse. Research is underway to develop pharmaceuticals that increase activity along this well-defined neural pathway in hopes of increasing prosocial behavior. As it relates to A4, the greater the inhibition, the less speaking out/more reticent, while the less the inhibition, the more speaking out/more assertive.

We have now been introduced to four traits of the Big Five. In the next chapter, we turn our attention to the final dimension, the dimension that evolved most recently in the evolutionary chain, C (consolidation), the dimension that dreams big and goes for the gold.

Mapping Out the Big Five Traits

9

Consolidation

All About Focusing on Goals

+	The trouble with being number one in the world—at anything—is that it takes a certain mentality to attain that position in the first place, and that is something of a driving, perfectionist attitude, so that once you do achieve number one, you do not relax and enjoy it. —Billie Jean King (winner of 39 Grand Slam tennis titles; founder of three tennis organizations)
=	Captain: Fraulein Maria, did I say that bedtime is to be strictly observed in this household? Maria: Yes, well the children were scared of the thunderstorm and... You did, sir. Captain: And do you or do you not have trouble following these simple instructions? Maria: Only during thunderstorms. -- *The Sound of Music* (1965 film)
-	I like to mix it up.... You know...be spontaneous. --Earl Pickles, in *Pickles* (comic strip)

Guide to This Chapter:

- Definition of the C Supertrait
- Three Case Studies
- Definitions of the Four Subtraits of C
- Implications of C for Career Exploration
- Implications of C for Relating to Adults in Power (Parents, Teachers, Administrators, Bosses)
- Implications of C for Managing Relationships with Peers
- Implications of C for Communication Style
- Implications of C for Leadership Aspirations
- Biological Basis for Consolidation (C)

Tennis great Billie Jean King (holder of 12 Grand Slam singles titles, plus 27 doubles) captures the essence of high C (consolidation) when she refers to "not relaxing" in the pursuit of being "number one." That, in a nutshell, is the meaning of the high end (C+, "Focused") of the personality dimension

Mapping Out the Big Five Traits

N	E	O	A	C
Need for Stability	**Extraversion**	**Originality**	**Accommodation**	**Consolidation**
N+ Reactive	E+ Extraverted	O+ Explorer	A+ Adapter	C+ Focused
N= Responsive	E= Ambiverted	O= Moderate	A= Negotiator	C= Balanced
N- Resilient	E- Introverted	O- Preserver	A- Challenger	C- Flexible
N1: Worry	**E1: Approach Lev.**	**O1: Imagination**	**A1: Service**	**C1:Thoroughness**
N2: Temper	**E2: Group Orient.**	**O2: Range of Int.**	**A2: Compliance**	**C2: Structure**
N3: Outlook	**E3: Pace**	**O3: Innovation**	**A3: Humility**	**C3: Ambition**
N4: Coping Lev.	**E4: Leadership**	**O4: Zoom Scale**	**A4: Speak Out Lev.**	**C4: Concentration**
	E5: Trust			**C5: Methodicalness**
	E6: Tact			

we call C. At the other extreme, the cartoon character Earl Pickles in the comic strip "Pickles" exudes the essence of low C by avowing his love for "mixing it up" and being spontaneous. In other words, avoid slavish devotion to the task at hand. Or as Ralph Waldo Emerson once put it (in "Self-Reliance"), "A foolish consistency is the hobgoblin of little minds." I do not think that Emerson was advocating low C, however, but rather urging moderation in C behavior. A "foolish" consistency would be an excess of discipline and focus, which paves the way for Maria's encounter with the Captain in the *The Sound of Music*. Here, the Captain, who is clearly high C, is reprimanding the governess for lack of focus on his rules, while in response she suggests that thunderstorms should be an exception to the rules. Otherwise, the Captain (and Maria) would be guilty of a "foolish consistency" by enforcing bedtime rules in spite of the children's fear of the thunderstorm. Maria's gentle reproof of the Captain is a reminder of Sophocles' comment on Creon's stubbornness in *Antigone,* that the tree that does not bend in the wind, breaks.

Let's take a closer look at the types of behavior associated with the three levels of the C dimension.

Definition of the C Supertrait

Focused (C+)

Focused individuals tend to work toward their goals in an industrious, disciplined, and dependable fashion. We call this dimension "consolidation" because it provides a nice metaphor of all of one's energies working together for a common purpose. Those scoring high on C are in their element when they are totally focused on making progress towards a high priority goal. Their mind is like a serial processor, proceeding in a linear, sequential manner. They typically have a strong will to achieve and do so with hard work, good preparation, a well-thought-out plan, and extensive organization. When they promise to deliver, they deliver; their word is money in the bank. They typically consolidate their time, energy, and resources in pursuit of their goals. High Cs tend to consume less alcohol than lower Cs—they are more consistent enforcers of their self-imposed limits. High Cs also tend to visit psychiatrists less than lower scoring individuals. This is not because high Cs are necessarily more healthy mentally but rather because their discipline leads them to be more

> I'm determined to reach my goal
> --Missy Elliott, *Higher Ground*

effective and consistent in implementing therapeutic regimens; so they require fewer follow-up doctor visits. Accordingly, while higher Cs have first heart attacks at the same rate as lower Cs, the higher Cs have far fewer second and subsequent heart attacks, again because it is more natural for them to follow the regimen that the doctor prescribes (McCrae and Costa, 2003, pp. 217-227). At times, they may be perceived to be workaholic, overly demanding, compulsive, meticulous, or stubborn. Many an extremely high C has been poked fun at by being described as someone who schedules time for spontaneity!

Of all of the Big Five dimensions, this C trait is the one that is most related to traditional measures of success: being number one and making piles of money. C scores correlate positively with grades, class rank, income, and level in an organizational hierarchy. This does not mean that mid- to low-C individuals cannot get ahead, but rather that it is more common for higher C scorers to be characterized by wealth and status. It does take discipline to achieve great things, and discipline comes naturally to the high C. Low Cs must typically find some external resources to compensate for the lack of natural focus and discipline. We will discuss this below. But meanwhile, I must be disciplined and finish discussing high C!

Leonard Bernstein once said that, to achieve great things, two things are needed: a plan and not quite enough time. I suppose that Bernstein latched onto the time element for this reason: Having abundant time to accomplish a task tempts one to procrastinate, much like the fable of the tortoise and the hare, with the hare resting while in the lead and ultimately losing. Perceiving that one does not have the luxury of abundant time for a task has the effect, particularly in the C+ person, of putting all distractions aside and bearing down on the task at hand. Forget food, television, hobbies, and small talk—stay on task and get it done. This is what happens when some students put off work on a term paper until just before the deadline, or put off working through much of the course material until just before an exam. Comedian Dan Bennett must have been hinting at the same phenomenon when he wrote that "There's nothing wrong with the younger generation that becoming taxpayers won't cure." April 15's approach has a way of forcing one to focus one's energy on the task at hand.

The positive aspect of high C is its productivity and achievement, but the negative side lurks as a threat to personal happiness—too much focus on tasks can dry up relationships. Anna Karenina's husband was that way, and Anna drifted away from him as a result. Here is Tolstoy's description of him:

> "Every moment of his life was filled up and apportioned, and in order to find time to perform all the tasks allotted to each day he observed the strictest regularity. 'Without haste and without rest,' was his motto." (p. 100, from the Maude translation, W.W. Norton)

This is clearly a description of a man of accomplishment with an overabundance of high C, yet also of a man neglecting his important relationships.

Balanced (C=)

> All work and no play makes Jack a dull boy.
> —James Howell, 17th century English historian

Balanced individuals, those scoring in the mid range, come in two general patterns. First is the "pure" form of balanced that is characterized by moderation in the various markers of consolidation. Whereas C+ is perfectionistic and C- is casual, the midrange is neither—attentive to getting it right but comfortable at a point short of perfection. The same for planning: respectful of and a user of plans and planning but retaining plenty of wiggle room for the unexpected or spontaneous. Ambitious but not necessarily ambitious to be number one in the nation—number one on campus would do. C= individuals are focused on goals but are comfortable veering off goal with some frequency. Phi Beta Kappa (the prestigious scholastic honorary society) is probably not a goal for the pure mid C, but Dean's List might be.

The second pattern is more polarized: extremely ambitious in some areas of life, but unambitious in still other areas. This could be someone who wants to be editor of the school newspaper, but is content to sit on the bench in basketball. Or someone whose study area is as neat and well organized as can be, but whose clothes closet and drawers are post-Hurricane Katrina.

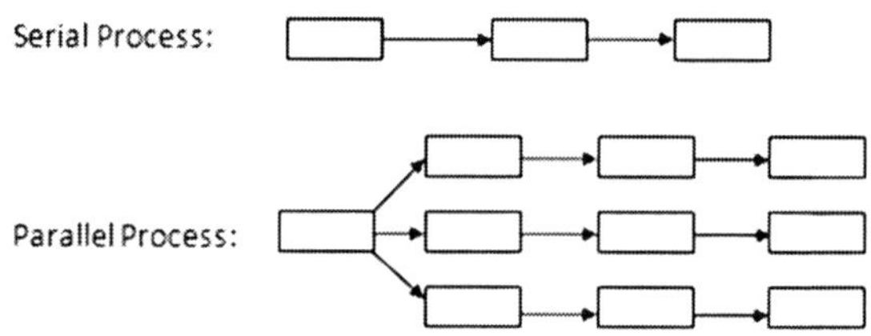

Both patterns of C= tend to keep study/work demands and personal/social/family needs in good balance. Their mind operates at times like a parallel processor and at times like a serial processor, both switching tracks and proceeding linearly. They are probably more ambitious than a flexible (C-), yet more prone to enjoy leisure than a focused (C+). From time to time, they are able to interrupt their focus on goals with some spontaneous diversions.

Flexible (C-)

Flexible individuals tend to approach goals in a relaxed, spontaneous, and open-ended fashion. Their mind is like a parallel processor, able to switch tracks on the run. They are likely to be a procrastinator. They are able to multitask easily, becoming involved in many projects at the same time. However, they may be perceived as being casual about their responsibilities or as being unorganized, unproductive, or irresponsible.

> There is nothing insignificant.
> —Samuel Taylor Coleridge, English romantic poet

Marshall McLuhan once described people as varying on a scale from more goal-oriented to more role-oriented. According to that perspective, the flexible person would tend to be more role-oriented (cooking, writing, gardening, studying, parenting, managing, proofing, and so forth), switching back and forth between the many different areas of responsibility and interest, while the Focused person tends to zero in on one superordinate goal and to ignore, or give short shrift to, any pursuit that they perceive as unrelated to that goal.

The poet Samuel Coleridge captures the lack of discipline and goal focus of the low C when he speaks of nothing being insignificant. By implication, when nothing is insignificant, no stone may be left unturned, every lead must be followed up, every idea must be chased. In short, it becomes impossible to focus or establish priorities. When everything is important, nothing is central. As a character on the *Route 66* television program back in the 1960s once commented on someone with a "hippie" life style: "By loving everything, you end up truly loving nothing." [A reviewer of this book's first draft recalled an incident in which her ex-High-C-husband commented to her: "Why can't you just do one thing and do it well?"]

In a later chapter, we will discuss mental health and how personality traits relate to personality disorders. In a word, when people lose their flexibility, their ability to draw on both ends of a continuum, such as solitude and society, we call that lack of flexibility "rigidity." Being rigid at one end of a continuum is unhealthy and requires therapy to restore flexibility. It is OK to have a preference for one end of a continuum over the other, so long as one is able to use the lesser preference as needed.

Two personality disorders (Nettle, 2007, pp. 146-7), Attention deficit hyperactivity disorder (ADHD) and obsessive-compulsive personality disorder (OCPD, commonly called OCD), illustrate the opposite extremes of C when they go rigid. ADHD is associated with the lower extreme of C gone rigid, and OCD is associated with the higher extreme of C gone rigid. Being high or low on C does not mean one has ADHD or OCPD, but the behavior of extremely high or low C individuals can resemble the features, both good and bad, of the two disorders. ADHD (associated with rigid C-, coupled with rigid N+ and often rigid A-) is disadvantageous for making scholarly grades, yet a boon for those living in unpredictive, quick-changing situations. Thus, soccer players and stock floor traders benefit from having a temperament that naturally shifts attention rapidly. OCPD (C+ gone monomaniacal) is disadvantageous for building relationships, yet clearly benefits those in pursuit of big dreams. However, lest we make things too simple, consider that the July-August 2009 *Harvard Business Review* cautioned that the future would be characterized by "permanent change," a condition that will clearly challenge high C CEOs.

Now that we have described the three levels of the C supertraits, let's take a look at how consolidation (C) plays out day-to-day.

Three Case Studies

C Case Study 1: An Impromptu Meeting is Called

A team of four has been working on a class presentation. Each member of the team serves in a different role: Two conducted the basic research, the third wrote it up, and the fourth will prepare the PowerPoint slideshow and present it to the class. It is 8:50 A.M., and the presenter is calling team members on their cell phones. As it is close to the end of the semester, all three are working on reports with imminent deadlines for other classes. Here's how the dialogue might occur with each C type:

> *Presenter:* "I need to call a meeting for 9:00 to discuss several issues in our presentation sequence and format. Can you join me? My computer is set up with a projector in the media lab so you can view the slides."
>
> *C – (Flexible):* "Sure. I'll grab my notes and come right now."
>
> *C= (Balanced):* "Uh, OK. Give me about 10 minutes to finish the first section in this report I'm writing, and I'll be there."
>
> *C+ (Focused):* "No, not right now. I'm in the middle of this report I have to finish this morning. I have an opening on my schedule at noon and could join you then."

All three people who were asked to join the meeting were working on reports due soon, yet they responded in three distinct ways, depending upon their scores on the C scale. People who are lower in C tend to be more spontaneous and manage multiple tasks during their day, although they sometimes lose track of their top priorities. People who score in the midrange stick to their tasks a little more easily but are still capable of being spontaneous. People who score in the high range stick to their goal or to the top priorities that will lead them to their goal, if at all possible. They do not like surprises or interruptions. They prefer to finish what they're working on before starting another project. They also like to finish projects ahead of schedule.

C Case Study 2: The To-Do List

We sometimes ask people the following questions: "Think back over last weekend. Recall everything you planned to get done during the weekend. What percentage of what you planned to do did you accomplish? Did you add in extra items? Did you have a written list?" The answers typically are as follows:

> *C- - (extreme flexibles):* "Why should we have a plan for the weekend? We just let things happen." "I usually have a few things I want to get done going into the weekend. I feel pretty good if I get 20 to 25% of them done." "I have some things that I think about wanting to do for a long time before I finally get around to them, like painting my room. I've been talking myself out of that one for about six months now."
>
> *C- (moderate flexibles):* "Going into the weekend, I usually know what I'm going to do and almost always add in some extra things." "I feel good if I get about half the things done that I want to get accomplished." "There are a couple of usual things I plan to do and know I'll get done, like going shopping for stuff I need or getting my hair cut/fixed. But I like to be flexible to allow for anything unexpected that may come along." (Sometimes, about one person in a group of five will make a written list for the weekend, just to organize his or her thoughts, but may not follow it.)
>
> *C= (balanced):* "Most of the time I get half to two-thirds of my list accomplished on the weekend." (About half of the small group will consistently have a written list. All of them will say that they have a mental list for the weekend.)
>
> *C+ (moderately focused):* "I usually accomplish at least 80 - 90% of my list during the weekend." (Most of the group will use a written list and will admit to adding extra items to the list just for the joy of being able to cross them off afterward.)
>
> *C++ (extremely focused):* "It's rare for me not to accomplish everything on my list for the weekend." (Most of these people say that they accomplish 100 to 120% of what they plan to do during the weekend, since a family member can usually get them to add in something extra.) "I often stay up later just to finish the items on my list before the school week begins again." "If an item or an event isn't already on my to-do list or my schedule before Friday evening, it won't be added."

The important thing to remember is that the C- is not necessarily unproductive. Rather, people who score C- are just not as methodical as those who score C+. At times, C- people may actually accomplish more than C+ people, though in a less organized fashion. The C- person may also have to be reminded about the goal, since she or he may get sidetracked by the many tasks and responsibilities that compete for attention during the day.

The C+, on the other hand, may get so focused on the goal and on staying with the assigned task that they may fail to flex around important opportunities that come up unexpectedly. We like to say that lower O's get six projects done in six months, finishing all of them at about the same time, while higher O's get six projects done in six months also, but they finish one project before beginning another. Parallel versus serial processors.

C Case Study 3: The Three Producers

A large university has a well-established campus radio station. The programming is accomplished by three producers with differentiated roles. As you read about each producer's role, try to estimate where you think each producer scores on the C scale.

> *Producer 1:* He is the senior producer. In his position, he has final say on all programming,. In addition, he oversees the day-to-day operations and the staff of eight people. He is known as a good delegator. Even with his many responsibilities, he makes time to speak with guests and visitors. The programs that he personally produces are well-researched and professionally executed, even though he delegates most of the research to Producer 2, and he relies heavily on Producer 3 to keep him organized and on schedule. One of his productions has been picked up by the national network to which they belong, and he has submitted another program in hopes of its getting picked up by the network.
>
> *Producer 2:* He is the jack-of-all-trades among the production staff. The other two producers delegate to him, primarily because he enjoys jumping from one thing to another. His research skills are prodigious, and he enjoys using Internet, telephone, personal visits—whatever it takes to track down the necessary information or resources. He doesn't complete very many productions, but his portfolio is bulging with projects that he has been a part of.
>
> *Producer 3:* She is the younger of the three producers and is in charge of organizing and coordinating the annual (and ongoing) fund drive. In this capacity, she develops and manages a very elaborate calendar of activities and a large cadre of volunteers. She is also in charge of getting out the monthly programming guide sent to thousands of alumni, subscribers, and interested community members. She never misses a deadline and consistently stays within her budget. She keeps organized through a system of color-coded files and labels, and she has a reputation for allowing nothing to slip through the cracks. She sets the goals for both fundraising and volunteer recruitment and tracks them regularly. She rarely meets with people who just drop by; rather, she schedules them at a more convenient time.

Now, you must decide. What C scores would you likely find for each of the three producers?

If you assigned Producer 1 the C=, you are correct. He is sometimes capable of being spontaneous and flexible with people who drop by, yet he can delegate well and seems to maintain a well-run organization without trying to do it all himself.

If you placed Producer 2 in the C- range, you are correct. His gift is in multitasking, whether he is making phone calls, surfing the Internet, texting a resource, or going out to do interviews. When he is needed, he is there. Unfortunately, when his turn comes to prepare and finish a production, his quality does not match the polish of his colleagues. He is always energetic and full of life, if not all that well thought-out and detailed.

If you said C+ for Producer 3, you are correct. She is known and valued for her organizational skills, and she keeps the campaigns going and growing, constantly setting new goals to achieve. However, the spontaneity of people dropping by is not something she handles well, scheduling them for times that better suit her schedule.

Definitions of the Four Subtraits of C

C1 ***Thoroughness****: The degree to which we strive for perfection.* One important element involves whether someone is more casual or more compulsive about getting it exactly right. While on the surface, this scale might appear to be the same as the O4: Zoom Scale (it measures the continuum that ranges from preference for details to preference for the big picture), an important distinction separates them. While both are concerned about details, one is about details for details' sake, and the other is about details in the service of a standard. For example, a low score on O4 might be reflective of someone who thoroughly enjoys proofreading, but the person could proofread for spelling and grammar only and perhaps not realize that the document was worded in such a way that it not address the interests and needs of the intended audience. That is the difference between, for example, proofreading and editing, where the editor needs not only to focus on details, but also needs to focus on other journalistic standards. In other words, a person could stay focused on the details but ignore overriding quality requirements. In this dimension, high C1 is focused on quality, on the standard, and is sworn to get it exactly right, even if they do not perform the work themselves. They might not like wading through the details and might delegate them to someone else, but they would review the work and insure conformance with the stated standards.

C1+ (High): *Continual need to refine or polish.* The high scorer on C1 remains focused on quality, day and night, sometimes to a fault. Their motto: "If it is worth doing, it is worth doing right." When everything has to be perfectly executed, however, one finds that one is unable to get it all done. Perfectionism takes time. And not everything needs to be perfect. The aforementioned motto is just that, a motto, not a law. Every omelet does not have to be perfect—sometimes it is OK to cut corners. But this is a hard thing for a C1+ to swallow. I have found that it is helpful to sit down with high C1 people from time to time and review their To Do list with them, helping them identify the items that would benefit from their perfectionistic attention and those on whom it would be wasted. Swarthmore psychologist Barry Schwartz in his 2004 book *The Paradox of Choice* calls these folks "maximizers." They who make every decision momentous, examining all possible choices before painfully choosing. They are indiscriminate about prioritizing decisions—all are highest priority and entail scrupulous investigation and analysis.

C1= (Medium): *Occasional need to refine or polish.* The two modes of C1= are: 1) the pure midrange scorers who are more attentive to quality standards than the low C1, yet who do not obsess over getting it perfect like the high C1, and 2) the situational midrange scorers, who obsess on getting it perfect on some things and not on others. The latter type of C1= is like me (Jane), when I got up in the middle of the night shortly before our younger daughter's wedding and typed up a 20-page, minute-by-minute script for the wedding weekend and the week leading up to it in order to insure that nothing went wrong. Yet in other areas of my life, striving for perfection is out of the question.

C1- (Low): *Low need to continually refine or polish.* Low scorers are reflective of the "good enough for government work" attitude. Too bad, as much government work is excellent and, in fact, perfectionistic. But what is meant here is that, if it works, it is OK. Don't obsess about perfection, just satisfy the basic requirements. Barry Schwartz contrasts these "satisficers" with the previously mentioned maximizers. Satisficers are primarily interested in just getting by, not sweating the small stuff. The good news for them is that they can make a lot of decisions in a given time period, but, for lack of preparation, they make many bad decisions.

C2 ***Structure****: The degree to which we stay organized.* One can learn organizational skills such as the color-coded scheme of Producer 3 in the third case study for C. But knowing how to organize is different than having the temperament to exert energy on organizing. Knowing how to organize, and executing it well, is a competency, while actually enjoying the process and naturally choosing to do it without coercion is a trait. Intellectually, I (Jane) know how to organize, but I hate doing it. I score low. As an adolescent, I took hours every Saturday to clean my room, a task my mother thought should have been done quickly. Yet, with my door closed, I was acting out my favorite artist's songs while staring at myself in my dresser mirror, rather than engaging in the drudgery (to me!) of cleaning.

C2+ (High): *Keeps everything organized.* This person just naturally thinks about getting and staying organized. They get the heebie-jeebies if their affairs, or the affairs of persons around them, are bordering on disarray. I had a friend in college—we took many of the same classes, sang in male chorus together, and lived one year in the same dormitory. Jim's room was between my room and the main stairwell; so I frequently passed it. His study carrel had three shelves of book above his desk, with each book precisely aligned like Prussian soldiers about one inch back from the edge of its shelf. Jim was C2+. I wasn't and still am not. Whenever I passed his room, and the door was open, and he wasn't in sight, I would slip in and punch two or three books out of alignment. Of course, the devil made me do it!

C2= (Medium): *Maintains some organization.* The two forms of midrange C2 are 1) the pure, who is moderately well organized—there is a system, but things don't always get put back in their places; 2) the situational midrange who is well-organized in some areas of life (perhaps their books are orderly, even grouped alphabetically by author and/or subject) but is chaotic in other areas (perhaps their clothing storage is haphazard).

C2- (Low): *Is comfortable with little formal organization.* I like to describe the difference between high and low C2 as "files and piles," with the higher C2 faithfully filing everything, and the lower C2 throwing everything into its rightful pile, with some piles having more internal integrity than others. Ah, the delight of going through a long-neglected pile only to discover a long-missed or forgotten-but-loved item. Not having the temperament for organization does not mean that one cannot place value on it. I once worked with an architect who was managing partner of a large, regional architecture firm. We did a team-building session, and everyone shared their Big Five scores. When his teammates saw his C2 score (it was VERY low), they said, "Something's wrong with this test! He's the most organized person in the company." He turned beet red and fessed up. "No, the score is right. When I began with this firm, I knew that my sloppiness was a threat to my career. So, I hired an assistant and told her to keep me organized, and in return I'd look out for her. I gave her carte blanche—she had permission to interrupt meetings, even, if it took that to keep me organized. And she's still with me!" They said, "But your house—it's spotless, too!" He laconically replied, "Yeah, that's my wife's doing. If you want to see the real me, go look at my workshop in the garage. It's a war scene, and that's where I feel most at home." One last gasp, "But your car—it's spotless." He retorted, "That's my assistant's doing. I gave her keys to my car a long time back, and she keeps it cleaned up for entertaining clients. Check my trunk, though, she stays out of it, and it shows the real me: a mess." This architect's way of acknowledging and dealing with a trait needed for his work but missing from his temperament is an excellent example of Human Resource Opti-

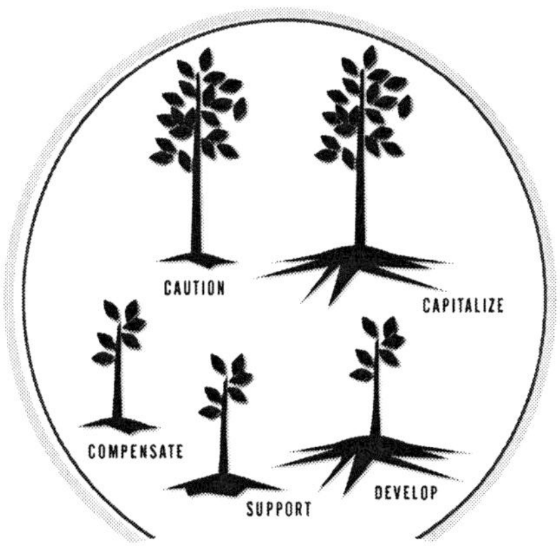

HUMAN RESOURCE OPTIMIZATION

mization (HRO). Remember the five trees? His would be the one with shallow roots (poor infrastructure) and stunted branches. Caution: He didn't really improve his performance by using this strategy, as it was his assistant who was actually performing! However, he got the credit.

Frans de Waal (2005), primatologist at Atlanta's famed Yerkes Primate Center, provides a delightful description of low C2 and shows how behavioral disorganization does not necessarily entail mental disorganization:

> "Listening to Ludwig van Beethoven's perfectly structured music, one would never guess what his poorly heated apartment looked like. Visitors complained that the composer lived in the dirtiest, smelliest, most disorderly place imaginable, strewn with wasting food, unemptied chamber pots, and filthy clothing, his two pianos buried under dust and papers. The maestro himself looked so slovenly that he was once arrested as a vagrant. No one asks how Beethoven could have created his intricate sonatas and noble piano concertos in such a pigsty. We all know that wonderful things can originate under atrocious circumstances, that process and product are separate things, which is why the enjoyment of a good restaurant is rarely enhanced by a visit to its kitchen." (pp. 32-33)

Nancy Cobb (2007) points out that, for teenagers, "A messy room and a busy phone may be signs of a young adolescent moving toward autonomy rather than of innate sloppiness or irresponsibility." (p. 214) In other words, a teen's sloppiness may be temporary, and then again....

C3 ***Ambition****: How pushed we feel to achieve.* This subtrait is all about the degree to which one feels the desire to be on top, to be the alpha male/female, to be Numero Uno, to be president/CEO, to be first in any the field of endeavor. This is the subtrait that builds civilizations. This subtrait also has an interesting relationship to the other four subtraits of C: It is like the main actor, with the other four subtraits like the supporting cast. C3: Ambition is about wanting to be number one, while the other four—perfectionism, organization, concentration, and methodicalness—are the means to get there. Higher C3 with low scores on C1, C2, C4, and C5 are what we call the "spoiled brat"—wanting the prize but lacking the discipline to earn it. Higher scores on C1, C2, C4, and C5 with a low score on C3 are like the bureaucrat—a well-oiled machine with little thought of a destination. Note: This subtrait would, on the surface, appear to be the same thing as A2: compliance, which is about competition. Ambitious people are often competitive, but necessarily so. Similarly, competitive people are often, but not always, ambitious. Like the father who always beats his kid at ping pong (A2-) but who is content with his level of responsibility and achievement at work (C3-), or the CEO (C3+) who dislikes competitive sports, preferring jogging or weightlifting (A2+).

C3+ (High): *Craves even more achievement.* High scorers on C3 do not rest on their laurels. When former president of Bank of America Hugh McColl retired, he had begun three new businesses by the end of the year. I don't know his score, but it would have to be way up there. These C3+ have a yearning for continually greater achievement. Not continual improvement, but continual achievement—newer, bigger, and greater goals than those just achieved. These are goal-setters. They dream the (im)possible dream, then wake up and pursue it.

C3= (Medium): *Needs some additional achievement.* Midrange scorers tend towards one of two kinds: 1) the pure C3= has goals that are more intermediate than the high scorers. Where a C3+ might want to be president of the country, a pure moderate C3 might settle for being a senator or congressional representative. Then there is 2) the more polarized midrange C3, who would have lofty goals in one aspect of their life, but they would be more accepting of things as they are in other areas. For example, this latter C3= might want to take a Little League team to the World Series, yet might be content to ply their woodworking or gardening skills without entering any contests. I once coached a pharmaceutical sales manager who scored 53 on C3. He supervised 18 sales representatives in New England. I guessed that he had no interest in becoming vice president of sales for the entire country, i.e., he didn't want his boss's job. He said, "You've got that right. How'd you know?" I said his moderate C3 score suggested he didn't have enough "fire in the belly" to want to be number one, and that usually people with his score wanted more balance in their life. He laughed and agreed, sharing that he was an amateur rock climber, and he wouldn't have time for his climbing if he were vice president. So, yes, balance was very important to him.

C3- (Low): *Is satisfied with current level of achievement.* It is very important to understand something about low C3 scores. They do NOT mean that these individuals have no goals. They may in fact have very challenging, very difficult, and complex goals. It is just that the goals do not typically have to do with becoming number one at anything. If that happens, it would not be rejected. It is just that it was not sought after. I (Pierce) am moderately low, about 40, on C3. But I have goals—writing books, developing new tests and other products, learning new music to perform in public, learning to cook new cuisines. I have many goals, but none of them involve becoming number one at anything. And I don't remain totally focused on any one goal at any one point in time—I like to mix them up and turn from one to another. Low C3s tend to have lots of goals, or no goals, but what distinguishes them from high C3s is the lack of a monomaniacal, tenacious focus. If my publisher wants to make me a number one bestseller, I won't object. But that would be his goal, not mine. But I'd cooperate!

*C4 **Concentration**: How sustained our attention is.* I (Pierce) never could figure out how my older brother Lee could sit in the sunroom of our eastern North Carolina home at holidays (he visited from New Haven) and quietly read his (usually thick) book with the television on and multiple conversations babbling all around him. Surely, he would score very high on this scale. It is as though he could "unplug" himself from everything around him and concentrate, never yielding to distractions.

> "It is discipline, not desire, that determines your destiny."
> —Lebron James (2009) quoting Coach Dru

C4+ (High): *Prefers to complete one task before starting another.* These people have the temperament of my (Pierce's) brother Lee. They have internal "blinders" that make it possible for them to focus their attention on whatever they desire and to tune the rest of the world out. This is a gift. I find it impossible to read with a television or radio dialog in the background. I envy high scorers.

C4= (Medium): *Can shift between tasks before completion.* Midrange C4s come in two forms: pure (they can concentrate in the midst of mild distractions for short periods of time) or polarized (they can concentrate amid some kinds of distractions, say, children playing gleefully, but not amid other kinds of distractions, say, a band practicing nearby). I (Pierce) am of the latter type. I can't concentrate with words coming from a TV or radio. I always take a book to read in doctors' waiting rooms, and I am always thankful for those who have either only instrumental music or no music or TV. For me, words compete with words for my attention. But I can read with wordless music, even though I prefer it quiet. My biggest distractions are auditory, as I find it easier to resist visual distractions (e.g., people walking by).

C4- (Low): *Shifts easily between ongoing tasks.* These are people who find it easy to multitask, primarily because their attention is easily distracted; engaging in a variety of tasks is natural for them. They typically turn from one thing to another without resentment or frustration, eager for the change of attention. However, in order for these people to minimize errors, as in trying to concentrate on homework, they would be well advised to eliminate all distractions for short periods of time (e.g., 30 minutes), then take a nice break, then resume, and so forth until finished. Troy Bolton, basketballer and thespian in *High School Musical*, found himself unable to concentrate on his basketball play because of the double distractions of trying out for a musical role and being head-over-heels in love. So, his dad/coach admonishes him: "Without you completely focused, we're not gonna win next week....Get'cha head in the game."

C5 ***Methodicalness****: How much planning we need to do.* Remember making models as a kid? Did you plunge right in and start gluing parts together with occasional (at best) reference to the plans? Or did you follow the plans, step by step? The former typifies C5-, the latter, C5+. Another name for this dimension might be "planfulness," the degree to which we conduct our lives according to plans, whether they are plans of our creation (associated with O1+ and A12-) or are created by someone else. The patience to stick to the plan—or not—is a part of our inherited temperament.

C5+ (High): *Develops plans for everything.* High scorers on C5 live by the plan, by the schedule, by the procedure. Not only do they respect plans, but they are comforted by having them. The higher the score, the more areas of one's life are governed by plans. Even time for spontaneous play (e.g., with a child) is planned. If it is not in the plan, forget it. The good news about such adherence to structure is that the C5+ produces impressive efficiencies and gains the reputation of finishing things on time and within budget. The danger of being so wedded to plans is that one may miss out on valuable opportunities because they aren't allowed for in the plan. One business thinker opined that Texas Instruments (remember them?) failed because they developed elaborate strategic plans and then followed them to a "t." The problem with that was they failed to adapt their plans according to changing market conditions.

C5= (Medium): *Does some planning.* The midrange scorer in C5 could be either 1) more of the "pure" type, whose plans lack detail and leave lots of wiggle room to accommodate changing situations, or 2) more of the "polarized" type, who might have detailed plans for some areas of their life similar to those of the C+ but no plans at all in other areas. I am more like the latter. I built a model railroad (from a kit) for our grandchildren, and I followed the plan to a "t." However, in my cooking, while I do typically cook new dishes after consulting a cookbook, I resist following a recipe, relying on a combination of memory and spontaneity.

C5- (Low): *Operates in a more spontaneous mode.* Low scorers on C5 are the people for whom the expression "shoot from the hip" originated! No such thing as a "game plan." Vacations? Just hop in the car and head somewhere. Grocery shopping: "Hmm, how about one of these, and, oh, yes, that looks interesting also." What list? People who are comfortable engaging in activities without prior planning are known as ad-libbers, as stand-up comics, as press secretaries (they do their homework, but you can't plan everything that you are going to be asked). Rabbi Jerome Tolochko used to speak to our (Pierce's) high school student body once each semester. When he took the podium, he asked what people would like for him to talk about. Several possible topics were shouted out, like "horses," "hot rods," or "football." Rabbi Tolochko would pick one topic and then proceed to give a 30-minute homily aimed at extending the moral education of Kinston's youth. We were all in awe of him. I don't know what his score would be on C5, but his behavior was clearly C5-.

Now that we have defined each of the five subtraits of C, let's take a look at how the C dimension influences various aspects of our lives.

Implications of C for Career Exploration

C- individuals will likely find management responsibility an unnatural fit. They will be frustrated by others' expectations that they be disciplined, focused, ambitious, and methodical, when their true nature enjoys jumping from one task to another. Interruption is their middle name. Two pieces of advice: First, prefer staff to line positions. By staying away from management responsibility, they can emphasize their strength, which is jumping from the priorities of this moment to those of the next. Second, find jobs that have minimal job freedom, or autonomy. Research (Bigazzi, Kello, and Marciano, 1999) has shown that people who are low in C achieve higher performance ratings when they are in jobs with low freedom or autonomy, and they get lower performance ratings in jobs with a high degree of freedom, discretion, or autonomy. In other words, more highly constrained jobs give C- workers less opportunity to make counterproductive decisions, while highly autonomous jobs expose the weakness of C– workers—distractibility. Give them enough rope and they'll hang themselves. Keep in mind, however, that other trait scores can influence how one feels about constraints: A high C who is lower in O will be comfortable with constraints, while a high C who is higher in O will feel a great deal of tension—wanting to be disciplined, but craving exploration and variety.

C+ individuals possess a discipline, ambition, and focus that will be sought after to perform management duties. If they choose to be entrepreneurial, their chances of success are high, because they possess the tenacity both to persevere until they have accomplished their goal and to resist tempting distractions that can dilute and delay their efforts. Of course, being high in C is not sufficient, alone, to insure job or study success. You also need the knowledge, ability, values, and experience that are required for any particular endeavor. I once investigated a vice-president of finance and administration who was extremely disliked by his people. It turned out he had all of the desirable traits to do the job, including C+, with high scores in all five subtraits, and he also had a master's degree in business administration (MBA), but he lacked the mental ability to do the work required. His people and his boss needed someone who could think 25 years into the future while handling a multiplicity of variables, such as availability of resources, varying costs of labor, fashion changes in market demands, and so forth. It turned out that he had been a successful manager in the past in jobs that did not require such complex mental analysis, while this new challenge was simply more than he could handle. I asked how long it typically took someone to be able to understand their complex financials; they said it typically took about 18 months into the job. This guy had been there four years already.

C= individuals will find that management is a viable option for them, but only in a nonworkaholic culture. In a workaholic setting, they are likely to feel pressured to put in the extra hours that violate their sense of balance between their personal and private lives. Of course, they can compensate for lack of this compulsive quality by having people close to them who provide that sort of natural energy. It really depends on the specific culture in which these individuals find themselves. Higher-C managers are attracted to, and do well in, jobs such as project management and sales and industries such as finance, real estate, insurance, pharmaceuticals, and chemicals. Lower C individuals typically are attracted to jobs such as consulting, teaching, and material distribution, and industries such as information science, agriculture, communications, religion/not-for-profit, and education. But remember, context is all-important. Look carefully at any job's requirements to insure that what it expects in the way of trait behavior is a good match for what you bring to the job.

Implications of C for Relating to Adults in Power (Parents, Teachers, Administrators, Bosses)

If you are C- and your boss or associates are C+, they represent a resource for keeping you organized and on schedule. Learn not to resent their focus and discipline, but rather to lean on it. For their part, they need to value your spontaneity and willingness to shift priorities in order to help them reach their goals. When you feel overwhelmed with multiple tasks, sit down with your C+ boss or associates and ask them to help you set priorities. And do it often, even daily!

If you are C+ and your boss or associates are C-, you are often going to feel like a stranger in a strange land, with the two of you having your roles reversed—bosses are supposed to be disciplined, workers flexible. A boss who is low in C will need you to keep him or her and the office organized and focused. Offer your services; without them, your boss or associates will likely flounder, and you will look bad by association. Eventually, your contribution to team effectiveness will be rewarded. If you make it a competition in which you resist helping your boss or associates, you will be regarded as a maverick who only looks out for number one and is not a team player.

Implications of the C Traits for Managing Relationships with Peers

Differences in C scores provide much opportunity for misunderstanding, blame, and resentment in relationships. A high C1 person resents the low C1"s lower standards and often feels the necessity of coming along behind the low C1 in order to fix things up to standard. On the contrary, the low C1 often resents the high C1's obsessive strain for everything to be perfect. I have a friend whose wife was so high in C1 that she could not have guests into the house unless she had worked for days, even weeks, to get everything perfect in readiness. This became such a source of stress to my low C1 friend that they ended up divorcing. He was unable to live with such behavior, and it got to the point that he never asked anyone to his home. Instead, he started seeing people away from home, and seeing his wife less frequently naturally caused problems in the relationship.

This same sort of misfiring occurs in the other four subtraits of C, with highly organized individuals resenting low C2 partners who are viewed as slobs who *intentionally* leave messes for the C2+ to clean up and restore to order. Where large gaps in subtrait scores appear, it is important that the individuals understand each other's behavior as fixed. It has always been that way. it will likely always be that way, and the behavior is not something that is done just to annoy or take advantage of the other person. The low C2 does not leave the wet towel on the bathroom floor because they chuckle at the knowledge that the higher C2 will pick it up. They leave it there because they are temperamentally that way. Put them in another relationship in another country, and the same behavior obtains. You can go crazy thinking that someone just being themselves actually means to drive you crazy. It is best to be amused at the differences, as in, "There goes Jane again, seeing a thief behind the bush!" Or even better, "There I go again, assuming the coast is always clear!"

Implications of the C Traits for Communication Style

The most salient way that the C dimension influences communications has to do with the issue of distractibility. The focus of the high C typically results in their doing what they say they will do. Their word is "money in the bank." Distractions typically result in bouncing back immediately to the task which was at hand before the interruption. With the lower C, distractions can often mean that the task which was at hand at the time of the interruption has become history, out of mind, lost and gone forever, until such time as something or someone redirects the low C's attention to the interrupted, now-forgotten, task. So, what does this mean for communications? The low C needs a series of reminders: notes stuck on mirrors, calendars, PDAs, notes in one's pocket, to-do lists with priorities assigned. The low C needs also to make arrangements with others to remind them gently from time to time of high priorities. A student low in C, who really wants to get a paper in on time, had best ask a parent, a sibling, a friend, or a roommate, to help them return to the task when distracted. In order not to be reluctant to provide the reminder, these friends or family need the explicit permission of the low C. Few people like to be the one who has to nag; so explicit permission helps. Jane will be working on a high priority, say, a new solo to sing for early service at church, when the phone rings. She takes the call, then goes to the kitchen, and before you know it, the new solo sits abandoned at the keyboard. So, about 10 p.m. or so, I say gently, "Did you want to work any more on that solo before bedtime?" Then, typically, "Omygosh, it completely left my mind. Thanks." Then back to the keyboard.

Implications of the C Traits for Leadership Aspirations

Greg Mortenson, coauthor and main character of *Three Cups of Tea* (Viking, 2006), tells the story of building the first school in Korphe, Pakistan, though the community had survived for 600 years without one. Mortenson promised to build the school in gratitude for Korphe's citizens who saved his life after a disastrous attempt at climbing Pakistan's second highest peak, K2. At one point soon after the beginning of construction, Greg's local mentor, the elder Haji Ali, beckoned him to leave the work site for a moment. After walking uphill for an hour, the elder began to reveal his reason for the work interruption:

> "These mountains have been here a long time," he said. "And so have we....You can't tell the mountains what to do....You must learn to listen to them. So now I am asking you to listen to me. By the mercy of Almighty Allah, you have done much for my people, and we appreciate it. But now you must do one more thing for me."
>
> "Anything," Mortenson said.
>
> "Sit down. And shut your mouth," Haji Ali said. "You're making everyone crazy." (pp. 149-150)

They then walked to the elder's house, where his wife served tea:

> "If you want to thrive in Baltistan [their region in northern Pakistan], you must respect our ways," Haji Ali said, blowing on his bowl. "The first time you share tea with a Balti, you are a stranger. The second time you take tea, you are an honored guest. The third time you share a cup of tea, you become family, and for our family, we are prepared to do anything, even die," he said, laying his hand warmly on Mortenson's own. "Doctor Greg, you must make time to share three cups of tea. We may be uneducated. But we are not stupid. We have lived and survived here for a long time."
>
> "That day, Haji Ali taught me the most important lesson I've ever learned in my life," Mortenson says. "We Americans [here, he really means A-C++ folks] think you have to accomplish everything quickly. We're the country of thirty-minute power lunches and two-minute football drills. Our leaders thought their 'shock and awe' campaign could end the war in Iraq before it even started. Haji Ali taught me to share three cups of tea, to slow down and make building relationships as important as building projects. He taught me that I had more to learn from the people I work with than I could ever hope to teach them." (p. 150)

Haji Ali was saying, in essence, the same thing Ringo Starr said in his album title "Stop and Smell the Roses." Karenin would have done well to make time for three cups of tea, or to stop and smell the roses, with his wife, Anna. So, while it is important for leaders to have some focus/discipline, it is also important to form relationships with coworkers who may not appreciate such driven work.

Mapping Out the Big Five Traits

The Biological Basis for Consolidation (C)

The arousal system that supports the C set of behaviors is the attentional focus system. This system is affected by levels of testosterone: Higher levels are associated with a greater capacity to focus one's attention on sustained, repetitive, goal-focused behavior. Distractions are the stimuli that trigger the attentional system; they cause the individual to lose focus, or attention. Your C score, then, is an estimate of the point at which you finally say, "That's enough focusing for awhile. It's time to take a break, to play, to have a change of pace." Very high C scorers (the higher testosterone level) seldom act on that message. The lower the score (the lower testosterone level), the more frequent the message.

Recent brain imaging studies (DeYoung et al., 2010) have identified this focus system as comprising a large area of the middle frontal gyrus in the left lateral prefrontal cortex. This area is associated with the capacity to hold information in working memory, including the capacity to continue with a task to its conclusion. Persons scoring higher in C have greater brain volume in this area, and they also show an increased tendency to focus, or conversely, a decreased susceptibility to distractions. Decreased volume in this area would logically make concentration/focus less natural, leading to a tendency to move from one activity to another.

While C is generally rooted in the property of testosterone to foster perseverance and the property of inhibitory chemicals such as GABA to foster focus and avoid distraction from goals, each of the five subtraits has its own biological peculiarities. Research is spotty, but here is our attempt to relate recent findings to the five subtraits of C (consolidation): thoroughness/perfectionism, structure/need for orderliness, ambition/will to achieve, concentration/resistance to distraction, and methodicalness/ planfulness.

C1: Thoroughness

Perfectionists are more vulnerable for depression. This is clearly related to the previous finding of lower serotonin among OCPD individuals. Perfectionism is associated with a fear that one must be perfect, or else.... It is likely that what softens perfectionism would also soften depression and anxiety. Perhaps some of the methods we know for raising serotonin levels, whether pharmaceutical (as in anti-depressants) or natural (as in eating/drinking dairy products and foods with fat content) could ease the urge of otherwise perfectionistic individuals to lighten up from time to time. Obsessing over the details? Have a chocolate milkshake! Or perhaps something not quite so caloric. A yogurt?

The inhibitory mechanisms involving GABA and other chemicals are clearly at work here in C1. The essence of the compulsion to be thorough at everything is clearly linked somehow to an inhibitory process that supports persevering at a task until it is perceived as perfect. The weaker that inhibitory process in an individual, the more likely the individual is to discontinue effort on a task short of perfection. The trick is to know the difference: When a task would benefit from perfectionism, go for it! When no significant benefit would accrue from perfectionism—other than personal satisfaction—then back off shy of perfection. By eschewing unnecessary thoroughness, you will have time for activities you would otherwise have insufficient time for.

C2: Structure

Obsessive-compulsive personality disorder (what can happen when high C becomes rigid) is associated with 40% lower serotonin levels than normal, which suggests that one reason some people are so driven to achieve is that they don't have as much of the "chill" neurotransmitter. Interestingly, persons reporting themselves as deeply in love, obsessed with a romantic other, also have substantially lower serotonin levels.

The compulsion to organize everything is a close relative of the compulsion to get everything perfect, and both are rooted in lower serotonin and elevated GABA. The primary difference between these two subtraits is that C1 emphasizes adherence to some kind of standard, while C2 emphasizes neatness and structure, regardless of the standard. Together, they create a formidable force.

C3: Ambition

When we discussed the biological basis of need for stability (N) in Chapter 5, we mentioned a genetic pattern that also happens to apply to consolidation (C). Here it is, again. The gene on chromosome 11 that makes BDNF (brain-derived neurotrophic factor) has two variants: If both are one way (the "Val" allele), one tends to be higher N and lower C; the other way (the "Met" allele), lower N and higher C; if mixed, mid N and C. (Ridley, 2003, p. 84) BDNF is sometimes referred to as the "fertilizer of the brain," in that it fosters the growth of new synapses, or nerve endings and connections, that are necessary for new learning and memory, both being the driving forces behind ambition and the will to achieve. The Met allele of this gene is associated with 1) lower N/higher C and 2) increased efficiency producing and processing BDNF. While it is not clear exactly how increased BDNF production is functionally related to lower N (particularly N1, N3, and N4) and higher C, we do know three related associations: 1) Aerobic exercise increases BDNF production, 2) aerobic exercise soothes stress by burning up cortisol (the chemical that keeps us in sympathetic arousal), and 3) the BDNF produced by aerobic exercise is associated with greater learning and memory, a characteristic associated with higher C (i.e., C+ make higher grades but are not necessarily smarter than lower Cs). So BDNF levels are negatively correlated with N and positively correlated with C. This explains the higher correlation of N and C in most Big Five tests, especially the NEO PI-R, where the correlation between N and C is around .5. BDNF levels are not correlated with the other three supertraits, E, O, or A. So, regular exercise can lessen N and strengthen C. For someone who has had their personal genome analyzed, they could check for the val allele of the BDNF gene on chromosome 11 as a basis for taking their aerobic exercise more seriously.

C4: Concentration

Nick Allen (University of Melbourne, Australia) has correlated MRI brain images of 153 12- and 13-year-olds with their answers to survey questions dealing with their frustration at being interrupted or blocked from completing a task and also their voluntary regulation of behavior and attention. One of his findings is that activity in the larger dorsal anterior cingulated cortex is associated with stronger control of behavior and attention, and individuals who have ready access to activity in this brain area are less likely to be frustrated. This kind of research will result in discovering appropriate methods for helping both with increasing concentration and with softening the emotional edge associated with being interrupted or blocked.

Mapping Out the Big Five Traits

C5: Methodicalness

In a related study, N. B. Allen et al. (2006) found, in MRIs of 155 12- and 13-year-olds who had taken the Early Adolescent Temperament Questionnaire, there is an association between a network in the left amygdala and hippocampus, left dorsal paralimbic area of the anterior cingulate cortex, and left and right areas of the orbitofrontal cortex. The researchers called the behavior pattern called "effortful control" (capacity to plan, focus, shift attention, and suppress inappropriate responses). Activity in these areas is associated with effective inhibition control and greater social awareness/empathy. Less activity is associated with uncontrolled inhibition, as in ADHD and schizophrenia. This research should lead to methods of exerting appropriate control of these subtraits, particularly in treating unhealthy forms of rigidity in these traits, such as ADHD and schizophrenia.

Hamer and Copeland (1998) suggest that "self-direction" is the best predictor of overcoming addiction. They relate it to C, particularly C5, i.e., methodicalness, which is associated with caution and thinking before acting. (p.135) This research promises to help develop methods to help addiction-prone individuals by using known methods of increasing C, such as aerobic exercise and any other methods of raising levels of BDNF.

This concludes our presentation of the five supertraits of the Big Five. But just like the dimensions of nutrition (fat, carbs, and so forth), the dimensions of personality do not exist in isolation. Just as nutritional elements come in combinations (e.g., beef steak = protein + fat), personality supertraits and subtraits also come in combinations (e.g., friendliness = E+ and A+). In the next chapter, we will discuss many more of the "blends," or combinations, of these traits.

10

Blends

The Interactions of Traits

> "We're all in this together!"
>
> --*High School Musical*, grand finale

Guide to This Chapter:

- Definition of Blends/Interactions
- Simple 2 x 2 Interactions
- Complex Multi-Trait Interactions
- Complex Trait-Nontrait Interactions
- Interactions with One's Environment

Not only are *we* all in this world together, interdependent for the survival of the planet, all of the 28 supertraits and subtraits are also in this together, rarely, if ever, acting singly. More commonly they are *inter*-acting, not just with each other, but with abilities, physical characteristics, memories, values, and the features of one's current environment (family, peer groups, school, neighborhood, and so forth). Pioneering social psychologist Kurt Lewin put it this way, in one of the field's most famous theorems: B = f(P + E), or "Behavior is a function of the person and their environment." To paraphrase: The way we respond in a situation is a combination of what we bring to the situation (our traits, abilities, memories, values, and physical characteristics) and the characteristics of the situation itself (noises, smells, demands, opportunities, privacy, supervision, the personality[ies] of the other person[s], novelty, and so forth). In this chapter, we will take a look at these interactions from several different points of view:

1. Simple 2 x 2 interactions, or what we call "style boxes"—simple, but powerful, combinations of two supertraits interacting with each other.

2. Complex multi-trait interactions, including anywhere from 2 to all 28 traits working together in such a way as to lead to a predictable result.

Mapping Out the Big Five Traits

N	E	O	A	C
Need for Stability	**Extraversion**	**Originality**	**Accommodation**	**Consolidation**
N+ Reactive	E+ Extraverted	O+ Explorer	A+ Adapter	C+ Focused
N= Responsive	E= Ambiverted	O= Moderate	A= Negotiator	C= Balanced
N- Resilient	E- Introverted	O- Preserver	A- Challenger	C- Flexible
N1: Worry	**E1: Approach Level**	**O1: Imagination**	**A1: Service**	**C1:Thoroughness**
N2: Temper	**E2: Group Orientation**	**O2: Range of Interests**	**A2: Compliance**	**C2: Structure**
N3: Outlook	**E3: Pace**	**O3: Innovation**	**A3: Humility**	**C3: Ambition**
N4: Coping Level	**E4: Leadership**	**O4: Zoom Scale**	**A4: Speak Out Level**	**C4: Concentration**
	E5: Trust			**C5: Methodicalness**
	E6: Tact			

3. Complex trait-nontrait interactions, in which traits, abilities, memories, values, and physical characteristics, and the current situation all interact to guide behavior in a particular direction.

But first, let's get a little more precise about what we mean by "interaction."

Definition of Blends/Interactions

Have you ever eaten a graham cracker? If so, you know that the taste is mildly sweet. Have you ever tasted an apple? Similarly, depending on the age and variety of the apple, it may be more tart or moderately sweet. But, and here's one of our favorites, have you ever eaten a bite of a Nabisco Graham Cracker and then followed it immediately, before chewing, with a bite of a sweet/tart Fuji apple, and then chewed the two together? Wow, it is a veritable dance (or ballet, circus, party, celebration) in one's mouth, with an intense sweetness that is different both in quality and in intensity than either the graham cracker or the apple alone. The cookie and the fruit interact to create something that is different than the two taken separately. That is not the same, at least for us, as putting peanut butter on a piece of bread—it just tastes like peanut butter and bread. While technically they are blending in our mouths, we still experience them separately because they do not interact the way graham crackers and apples do to form an emergent and new taste.

In a similar fashion, warmth (E1+) and organization (C2+) can occur together in the same person, but they do not necessarily *interact* in such a way that they create something more than the two traits alone—a smile and a neat room. On the other hand, when warmth (E1+) and competitiveness (A2-) occur together, they interact to create an impression different than either trait alone. Competitiveness by itself is often perceived as heartless and intimidating, while warmth by itself is often viewed as guileless and innocent. But put the two together, and you have *persuasion*, that quality that can seduce a grandparent into sacrifice, that can talk twenties out of a parent's purse, that can hoodwink a peer into taking a dare or agreeing to take on an unpleasant chore. The warmth is the spoonful of honey that helps the medicine (e.g., getting the short end of the deal) go down. It is these kinds of combinations of personality characteristics that we want to explore in this chapter, and we begin with the simplest kind of blend: the 2 x 2 stylebox (this is read as "two by two").

Simple 2 x 2 Interactions

We coined the term "stylebox" back in the 1990s to refer to the unusual effects of taking certain combinations of supertraits two at a time. For example, the research tells us that O (originality) and C (consolidation) interact in an academic context such that five unique academic styles emerge. You can follow our brief discussion of these styles visually by referring to Figure 10.1. The vertical axis represents the originality supertrait scale, while the horizontal axis stands for the consolidation supertrait scale. When a person has both high O and high C (this would be the upper right area of Figure 10.1), curiosity and discipline/ambition interact to form what we call the "High Honors" style. This is the person who is naturally motivated to achieve high marks in a variety of subjects, based on their love of complexity and desire for achievement. Those with the highest scores (i.e., over 65 in both O and C) are most likely to make highest honors, e.g., Phi Beta Kappa (oldest national academic honor society in the U.S.) for universities and the National Beta Club for elementary and secondary schools, while those with the next highest level of scores (e.g., 55-65) likely to make "Dean's List" or "Honor Roll." These are individuals who tend to make the highest grades in any subject they attempt. Then there is the Subject Specialist. They who tend to do very well in one particular subject or area, such as physics, and perhaps in a closely related area, such as mathematics (e.g., in its close relation to physics). Other examples include French history and French language, psychology and biology, and so on. These subject specialists are more likely to be lower in O and higher in C. They tend to be selected in honorary organizations that recognize achievement in specialized areas, such as Pi Kappa Lambda or Tri-M for music, Sigma Pi Sigma for physics. Then there is the "Extracurricular" style that is characterized by modest grades and wide-ranging involvement in nonacademic endeavors, much like someone with a "C" average accompanied by participation in chorus, newspaper, a sport or two, a social club,

Figure 10.1 **Stylebox: Academic Performance Styles**

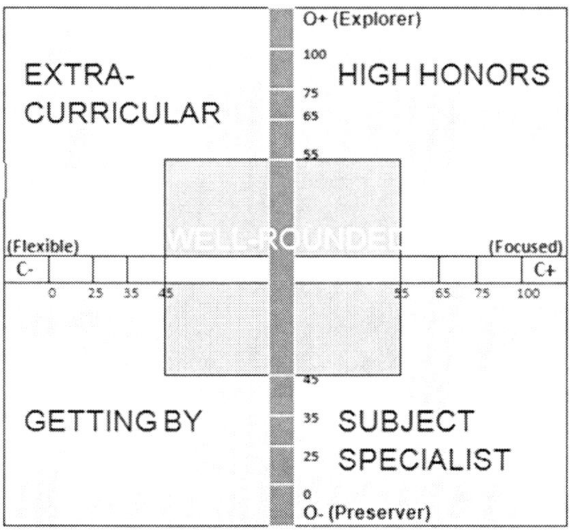

and a service organization. These people are higher in O (expressing their curiosity and love of variety through diverse extra-curricular opportunities) and lower in C (their comfort in jumping tracks frequently). The "Getting By" style characterizes those lower in both O and C, who perhaps have one major interest but who are not particularly concerned about achievement—the business major who looks forward to being a manager some day, or the jock who hopes to land a job hanging around a gym, or the English major who plans on working in the family business. These want the credential, the status, as a minimal ticket to a modest career. Finally, the "Well-Rounded" style comes from one who is mid-range in both O and C. These are the individuals who follow no extreme: neither geek nor nerd, scholar nor slouch. Good grades, but no honors. Studious, but not to the exclusion of a social and extra-curricular life. When our friend John Kello talked of the A students who would be his colleagues (as fellow professors) some day, he was referring to the High Honors and Subject Specialist styles. When he talked of the B students who would be his doctors and lawyers some day, he was referring to Subject Specialists and Well-Rounded. When he talked of the C students who would endow his university some day, he was referring to individuals from Getting By, Extra-Curricular, and Subject Specialist.

One note about these styleboxes: What if an individual scores high or low on one trait (say, high C) and midrange on the other (i.e., mid O)? In this case, the likelihood is that this individual would exhibit characteristics of the two styles associated with the one extreme score. So, for high C, you can see in Figure 10.1 that both High Honors and Subject Specialist would apply. An example of this interaction would be someone who earns Phi Beta Kappa AND the Physics Prize. By being midrange in O, they are comfortable both with specializing in one subject and giving focused attention to other subjects. In Figures 10.1a and 10.1b, we show two sample plots of possible scores on this stylebox. The first shows one who is 75 on C and 25 on O, thus clearly landing in the "Subject Specialist" area. The second shows one who is 50 on C and 75 on O, thus sharing the "Extracurricular" and "High Honors" areas.

Figures 10.1a and 10.1b Sample Plotted Scores of Two Extremes (a) and One Extreme/One Midrange (b)

a. **C = 75, O = 25** b. **C = 50, O = 75**

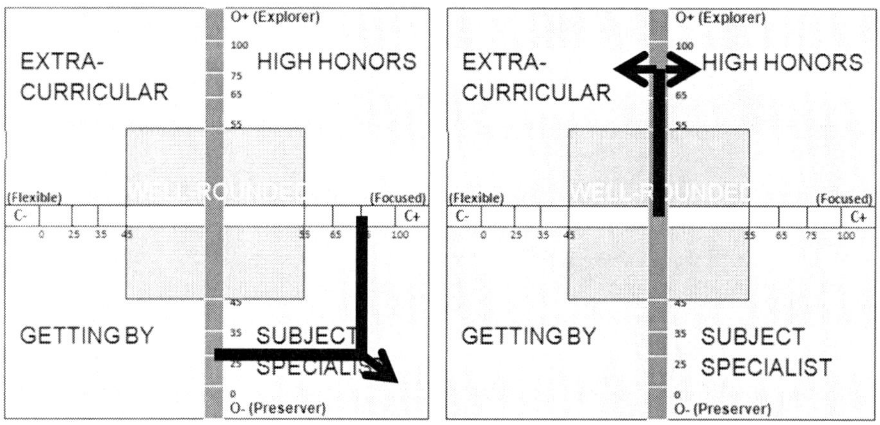

Another stylebox example is what we call the "Social Learning Style." Follow along by referring to Figure 10.2. The two traits interacting here are N (need for stability, on the vertical axis) and E (extraversion, on the horizontal axis), such that N is associated with one's dependence/independence on a facilitator of learning, and E is associated with one's dependence/independence upon a structured approach to learning. Those higher in N tend to prefer having a facilitator (teacher, trainer, coach, consultant, mentor, and so forth), while those lower in N tend to prefer being more on their own (reading, experimenting, researching, observing, practicing, and so forth). Those higher in E tend to be comfortable with a more open-ended, less structured approach to learning (trial-and-error, moving from topic to topic with no necessary sequence or logic), while those lower in E tend to prefer a more structured approach (step-by-step, lesson plan). The four styles that emerge from the interaction of these

Figure 10.2 Stylebox: Social Learning Styles

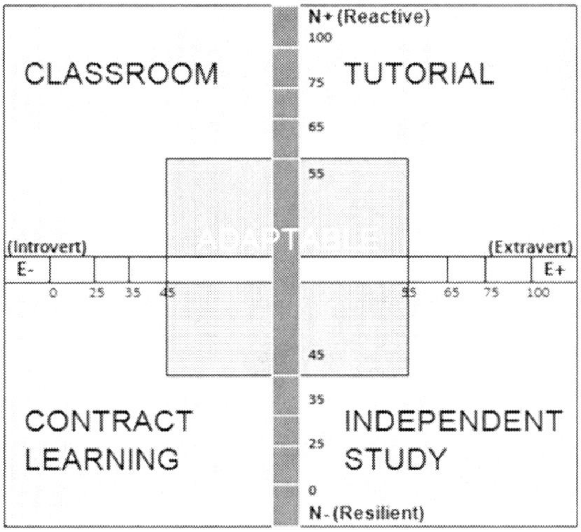

two dimensions are Traditional Classroom learning (N+ preference for a facilitator, combined with E- preference for structure), Contract Learning (a package provided to the learner, based on E- preference for structure, combined with N- comfort being independent of a facilitator), Independent Study (self-designed approach, stemming from N- independence of a facilitator and E+ comfort without a plan), Tutorial (the classic Oxford don guiding an otherwise independent study, based on the learner's being higher on N/preferring a facilitator and higher on E/comfortable without a plan, letting one thing lead to another), and Adaptable (midrange on both N and E and comfortable moving back and forth among all four of the styles).

One stylebox that involves behavior familiar to everyone is that of Emotional Temperament. This simple pairing involves N and E, with higher N associated with the negative emotions (particularly worry, anger, and sadness) and higher E associated with the positive emotions (which don't differ in kind but rather in degree). Following along with the stylebox in Figure 10.3, N-E+ is associated with happiness or warmth, the absence of negative emotions and the presence of positive emotions; N+E+ with being excitable or emotional, or alternating between negative and positive emotions; N-E- with being cool, or showing neither negative nor positive emotions; and N+E- with being reactive or distressed—this is the conscience of the group who is a barometer for foul weather, for sensing when things are awry. Blonde bombshell Sharpay Evans in *High School Musical* exhibits the volatile emotionality of the Excitable (N+E+), contrasted with the abiding happiness of Gabriela Montez (N-E+)—the new girl in town/onstage with the abounding positive emotion (excitement, enthusiasm, warmth, curiosity) of E+ coupled with the absence of negative emotion (N-).

We will look at other "styleboxes" in individual chapters yet to come, e.g., the "Kolb Learning Styles" in Chapter 13 and "Conflict Management" in Chapter 17. Here, we simply wish to introduce the subject and explain how styleboxes work, so that when you encounter them later, they will be familiar. Now let's turn to blends that are a bit more complex—multi-trait interactions.

Figure 10.3 Stylebox: Emotional Temperament

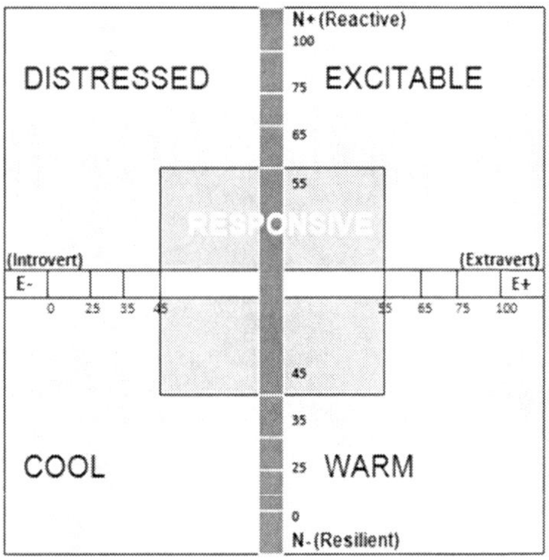

Complex Multi-Trait Interactions

In this section, we want to introduce three classes of multi-trait blends: everyday behaviors, common vocational tendencies, and personality disorders. Our goal here is to show how two or more traits can combine in such a way that their emerging behaviors are like alloys in which the individual ingredients, or traits, lose their separate identity in the service of the emergent behavior. In each case below, one does not have to score in all of the areas indicated in order to exhibit the behavior: It is just more likely that an individual who *does* score in all of the areas will exhibit the identified behavior. Also, a person who scores in *all* of the indicated elements is likely to exhibit the associated trait to a more extreme degree. As an example, I (Pierce) am high in O, but moderate in N, A, and C, yet I exhibit the "aesthetic" behavior," but not as much as a friend of ours who is N-O+A+C+.

Everyday Behaviors

Aesthetic: Persons who are N-O++A+C+ tend to value, as well as exhibit, high standards for beauty, design, art, and appearance.

Aggression: Normal, everyday aggression is the result of N2+A2-, whereby anger interacts with competitiveness and self-interest to lead to some form of hostile striking out. Lerner and Steinberg (2004, p. 26) point out that modes of aggression tend to differ by sex. Females' aggression is more relational and verbal (e.g., spreading lies or "back-stabbing"). Males' aggression is more physical (e.g., shoving or stabbing in the gut). This is the pattern of behavior in about one of every nine individuals (i.e., the 1/3 who score high on N2 times the 1/3 who score low on A2 yields 1/9). As the sexes age, the severity of aggression increases—giving rise to the Italian proverb, "Little children, headache; big children, heartache." While the pattern never goes away, we can learn to deal with our aggressive impulses in a more socially acceptable manner.

Born to Serve Others: The disposition to devote one's life to serving others, e.g., through health sciences, social work, or volunteerism, is highly likely to emerge from one who is N+E+A+C-. Such a profile would be sensitive, outgoing, other-directed, and spontaneous.

Consensus Builder: Persons who are midrange on E2, high on E4, and midrange on A (i.e., moderately gregarious, prone to take charge, and having a negotiating manner that prefers to go for the "win-win") are typically known by others as consensus builders, those who tend to guide discussions in such a way that everyone supports the decision. These individuals like everyone to be "on board" and will make the effort to help form a consensus.

Hard to Read: Persons tend to be rather hard to read if they are N1234-E12-A4+ (low in negative and positive affect, solitary, and reluctant to be assertive or take center stage). It is difficult to know what they are thinking or feeling. That does not mean that they are thinking and feeling nothing—one must open the door for them with gentle questions such as "What's on your mind?" or "Whatcha feeling now?"

Initiator: An initiator is someone who naturally makes suggestions to have a meeting, to pursue a particular activity, or the like. They typically do not wait for others to initiate such actions. Alabama football coach "Bear" Bryant referred to these people when he said, "Make something happen!" These are the people who are most likely to make suggestions when the plan is not working or is slowing down. Folks who are E+O+C- (outgoing, creative, and spontaneous) are highly likely to exhibit this behavior.

Micro-Management Tendency: Some individuals can't leave well enough alone, and they have the tendency to hover over one's back after delegating a task. Sometimes that is a good thing, but sometimes it is not. Those who are E5-O4-C1+ (skeptical, comfortable with details, and perfectionistic) are highly likely to exhibit this behavior. If the person to whom they delegate is competent, then these delegators need to try to resist micro-managing them, lest the delegatee resent the unnecessary oversight, intrusions, suggestions, and reminders.

Sensation Seeking (SS): Robert Cloninger (2004) divides SS into four parts: thrill seeking, experience seeking, susceptibility to boredom, and disinhibition (i.e., uninhibitedness). Persons with this behavioral pattern exhibit curiosity, excitability, impulsiveness, enthusiasm, extravagance in their tastes, disorderliness, risk taking, craving for variety and novelty, and an appetite for intense feelings and sensations. The opposite of a person high in SS tends to exhibit indifference, a reflective/introspective demeanor, frugality, orderliness, a regimented lifestyle, a preference for the familiar and the conventional, and a preference for less intense sensations and feelings (Hamer and Copeland, 1998, pp. 30, 53). The researchers report that Israeli scientists found a relation between SS and variations in the D4DR gene (it generates the dopamine receptor D4). High SSs have longer D4DR genes; low SSs, shorter. The increased dopamine in a high SS's system incites the what-if behavior associated with dopamine. But dopamine is only one component (Hamer and Copeland, 1998, p. 46). Upwards of a dozen other genes are suspected of influencing SS behavior. The SS construct involves the interaction of N+E+O+A-C-, or what we call the "Calvin" profile (of *Calvin and Hobbes* fame). Reactivity, extraversion, creativity, self-absorption, and spontaneity are the ingredients of this "stew."

Temper Prone: Those who are likely to feel anger and to show it in frequent outbursts are exhibiting a behavior associated with being N2+E6-A124- (blunt, self-serving, competitive, assertive, un-self-conscious, and prone to feel anger). The more extreme the N2 and A2 scores, the more likely the person is to exhibit so-called "Type A" behavior, which psychiatrist Redford Williams of Duke University describes as an unrelenting antagonism. This behavior, particularly in its extreme forms, is not heart-healthy, and steps should be taken to offset its effects, e.g., aerobic exercise and restraint techniques (such as the familiar "count to 10 before losing your cool"). Remember the earlier client who chomped down on his imaginary corncob pipe to prevent angry outbursts? Read Williams' book that he wrote with his historian wife, Virginia, for more ideas (*Anger Kills*).

These are just a few of the thousands of blends that have been identified through research. We have a database called *The Offspring of the Big Five* that contains all of the blends that we know about. Contact us if you would like information on how to gain access to this database.

Common Vocational Tendencies

Many jobs are associated with specific Big Five profiles. This does not mean that an individual must have that profile in order to be successful in that job, but it does mean that persons with that profile would likely find that they have the natural energy to do that job. For example, extraversion provides energy for sales jobs, while introversion provides the sedentary energy for desk jobs. More introverted people can sell, but the sociability required will tire them. We have known sales people who were more introverted and who redesigned their jobs so as to use the telephone and Internet for 90% of their selling activity. This way they didn't feel so exhausted at the end of the day. Similarly, more extraverted people can succeed in desk jobs, but they need to find ways to incorporate their higher activity level into the role, such as using "stand-up" desks (as was done by Winston Churchill, Virginia Woolf, Karl Marx, Thomas Jefferson, and Leonardo da Vinci). This practice of finding ways to offset the effect of lacking the optimal trait for a job is what we have called "Human Resource Optimization." As a reminder of the five parts of the HRO model, we print again the icons that show the relationship between the different sizes of trees (i.e., levels of performance) and different sizes of root systems (i.e., degree of fit of one's trait infrastructure). For more explanation of HRO, see "The Tree of Life" in the Introduction.

Now, here are some of the more common blends of traits that support specific jobs or roles. They are based on a study conducted by the Center for Applied Cognitive Studies that analyzed the correlations between Big Five traits and Edgar Schein's eight "career anchors." (Johnson, Howard, Roebuck, Lesesne, and Brock, In Press; Schein, 1993)

Autonomy: Able to do things one's own way, on one's own terms; success comes from achieving independence (sample jobs: independent consultant, independent contractor, small business owner, private practice doctor/lawyer/architect). The profile that most commonly yearns for autonomy is N+N234+E5+O+O1++A3-C4-.

Challenge: Overcoming complex circumstances in order to beat out the competition; success comes from the challenge—if it's easy and repetitious, it is boring and not challenging. (Sample jobs for challenge lovers: "big ticket" salesperson, product manager, athletic coach, project manager). The profile that tends to crave this kind of personal challenge is N-1- -34-E23+O2++A-C+3+++14+ (the number of pluses or minuses indicates how strongly that trait contributes to the blend).

Entrepreneurial: Building one's own business/organization from zero to a point of financial success; success comes from using one's ability to build an organization (sample jobs: business owner, entrepreneur (starting a new business within a larger corporation). The profile most likely to spawn the entrepreneurial urge—and be successful at it—is N-E+O+A-C+.

Lifestyle: Flexibility to balance work and personal life; success associated with perceiving self as a whole person, not one-sided (sample jobs: any that expect a regular eight-hour day, with no overtime; normally associated with nonmanagement jobs such as clerk, bookkeeper, or [in some cases] teacher). Those who prefer such balance tend to have most of these traits: N+4+O2-A+++123+C3-.

Mapping Out the Big Five Traits

Managerial: Being responsible for leading others towards successful goal attainment; sense of success is tied to the organization (sample jobs: supervisor, coach, manager, executive, business owner, principle, superintendent). Managerial aspirations tend to be associated with N-3-E+23+O2+
A- -123-4- - -C13+.

Security: Achieving predictability and stability in employment and income in exchange for loyalty to the employer; success comes from feeling needed by the organization (Sample Jobs: tenured teacher/professor, government employee, soldier/sailor/marine/air force pilot, employee in a large corporation with a track record of no layoffs) Those preferring secure positions over the other seven qualities tend to have many of these traits in common: N1++O- -124-A4+C2++45+.

Service: Making a contribution to a cause, a community, or some other entity; success associated with sensing that one's work makes a difference for someone (sample jobs: missionary, ombudsman, teacher, minister, nurse, politician). The motivation to serve tends to stem from these traits: N3-E+12+A+12+.

Technical: Being an expert in one's chosen skill area; success associated with being perceived as highly knowledgeable/skilled (sample jobs: tenured professor, consultant in a technical specialty, corporate trainer, published technical writer). Those aspiring to be known as experts tend to exhibit N+23+E15-O-A-1-C4+.

Clearly, there are exceptions to all of these "rules." For example, many psychologists would espouse the notion that they would like to be "autonomous," as in starting their own private practice or having free reign to pursue their research interests in an academic setting. However, while both clinical psychologists (i.e., therapists) and experimental psychologists (i.e., laboratory researchers) could have a strong desire for autonomy, the former tend to be higher in A, the latter lower in A (McCrae and Costa, 2003, pp. 217-227). Here is an example where the demands of a person's specific job would override the traits associated with their more general role.

Personality Disorders

The possession of a specific trait profile reveals nothing about one's mental health. We repeat (and will again!) Ralph Waldo Emerson: "Every individual nature has its own beauty." Two persons—one mentally healthy, the other mentally sick—can have the identical trait profile. The difference between the two is that the unhealthy person's profile has gone "rigid" in one or more traits. Recall that each trait comprises two opposing kinds of energy, such as solitude and sociableness for E2. When a trait goes rigid, one of the two opposing traits becomes unavailable to that individual. So, a catatonic schizophrenic would go rigid with solitude and lose the energy for socializing, while one suffering from histrionic disorder would go rigid in socializing and lose the energy for solitude. One tends to go rigid when one or more of their support systems fails them: financial, family, health, environmental, and so forth. What might cause a trait to go rigid, i.e., for a person to begin preferring one extreme to the exclusion of the other, of taking refuge in one's comfort zone? Causes include prolonged stress, malnutrition, abuse, lack of support, poverty, illness, and other prolonged adverse living conditions. The symptom of having gone rigid is one or both of 1) not being able to hold a job, or 2) not being able to hold a relationship.

We emphasize this point because there is no such thing as an unhealthy profile. However, if a person with a given profile *were to ever become mentally sick,* we have some idea of what that sickness, or disorder, is likely to be. Read more about the relationship between traits and disorders in Costa and Widiger (1994). Meanwhile, here are several familiar disorders and the likely profile from which they would typically emerge.

Attention Deficit Disorder (ADD): Under normal conditions, persons with the profile N+O+C- would be characterized as reactive, curious, and spontaneous. Under stressful circumstances, when the individual's props fall out, this normally healthy profile, although lacking in discipline, becomes rigid, with the consequence that the person loses the normally small reserves of calmness, stability, order, and discipline, and the person exhibits ADD. Add E+ to the mixture, and you have ADHD, or inability to focus coupled with the inability to sit still.

Avoidant Personality Disorder (APD): Through one's daily routine, a person with the profile of N134+E1=23-O3-A4+ would tend to be somewhat reactive, solitary, conservative, and quiet. Should the props fall out and some of these traits go rigid, then this individual is likely to withdraw from public contact and be diagnosed with APD.

Dependent Personality Disorder (DPD): From day to day, an individual with the profile of N134+E6+A1234+C3+ would be described as reactive, pleasant, friendly, deferential, and ambitious. Should the props fall out and these traits go rigid, this individual's inability to make decisions that serve their own welfare would help lead to a DPD diagnosis.

Histrionic Personality Disorder (HPD): The typically spontaneous, emotionally excitable, and outgoing individual is associated with the profile of N24+E12356+O13+2-A1-4+C14-. Should the props fall out and they go rigid, the person would be unable to be comfortable alone, would become "hyper" around others, and would likely diagnosed with HPD.

Narcissistic Personality Disorder (NPD): The profile N24+3=E6+O1+A134-C13+ under normal conditions thinks well of themselves on their way to success, but should the props fall out and their traits go rigid, they likely would be diagnosed with NPD because they would become irresponsibly obsessed with a sense of entitlement entailing no need to be personally responsible.

Obsessive-Compulsive Personality Disorder (OCPD): Under normal circumstances, a person with the profile N23+E1-A124-C235+ would be described as a hard-working and focused individual. Should their props fall out and several of these traits go rigid, then this individual is likely to be diagnosed with OCPD.

Mapping Out the Big Five Traits

Paranoid Personality Disorder (PPD): The normally cautious individual with the profile of N12+E125-6+O3-A123-C1+, should the props fall out and their traits go rigid, would become constantly fearful of betrayal, attack, disloyalty, and other forms of paranoia, and likely be diagnosed with PPD.

Temper Disregulation Disorder (TDD): We have mentioned earlier the "Calvin profile" of N+E+O+A-C-. We have also mentioned that the developmental task of growing up has been identified by Costa and McCrae (2003) as decreasing N, E, and O, while increasing A and C. So, growing up is becoming calmer (N↓), more comfortable with solitude and quiet (E↓), accepting the need for repetition and practice (O↓), becoming concerned for others (A↑), and becoming more disciplined and ambitious (C↑). When this developmental process is thwarted, and when an individual's props fall out and they go rigid at higher levels of N, E, and O and at lower levels of A and C, it is likely to be recognized as Temper Disregulation Disorder (formerly known as Conduct Disorder), a "pattern of behavior in which the basic rights of others or major age-appropriate norms are violated." In order to be diagnosed as TDD, one's school, job, or social performance must be adversely affected. This pattern of aggression and delinquency occurs among boys at a rate of about 1 in 10, in girls, 1 in 20 (Lerner and Steinberg, 2004, p. 627 ff.).

Again, please recall that these profiles *do not* indicate either mental sickness or the degree of risk for poor mental health. Rather, they indicate what a person's mental illness might look like should they, in fact, become ill. It is like saying that if a person is Italian, then, if they ever get physically sick, it would likely be from a germ, bacteria, or virus commonly found in Italy.

We have focused up to this point exclusively on the interactions of traits with one another. Now let us take a look at traits as they react with other personality elements.

Complex Trait-Nontrait Interactions

Every behavior, be it goal-setting, planning, exercising, problem-solving, acting, schmoozing, or making small talk, is the result of a complex interaction of the traits, cognitive abilities, physical characteristic, values, and memories that one brings to the situation, PLUS their interaction with the characteristics of the situation itself. In Figure 10.4, we diagram the personality ingredients that Horace Hornblower activated when he drove home from summer music camp. Horace (E=O+C+), first French hornist in his high school orchestra, had spent three weeks at Eastern University's summer band, orchestra, and choral music camp. While there, he met the girl of his dreams, Viola Stradivare, a violinist from a distant city. During their spare moments, they enjoyed pizza and soda, hand-in-hand walks around the extensive campus, an occasional swim, and frequent chamber music sessions such as the Brahms Horn Trio for piano, French horn, and violin (the piece from which the 50s tune "I'll Never Stop Loving You" was taken). He deeply in love, head over heels. Both Horace and Viola swore fealty to one another and promised to return to the camp next summer.

Horace's dreaminess was interrupted by an unsettling thought: "What if Viola progresses in her music to a greater degree than I do? She will drift away, seeing me as stuck at my current level. I must commit to the goal of making significant progress in my horn playing over the next 11 months." Horace knew his greatest weakness as a hornist was the inability to execute a "lip trill." Trills are normally accomplished on the horn by rapidly depressing and releasing a valve. Lip trills, on the other hand, are executed exclusively by the lips, as rapid contortions of one's lips, in coordination with diaphragm support, move the sound between two adjacent notes that have the same fingering, thus not requiring the movement of valves. The problem was that Horace had tried lip trills before, only to encounter the unsatisfying, uncontrollable flutter of his stiff lips. He lacked the natural limpness of his lips to bring off a satisfactory lip trill, and lip trills were a signature of an accomplished horn player. He was determined to return to Eastern University's camp with an impressive lip trill. He set out to find training resources including teachers, books, and the like. He would use the Mozart horn concertos, full of lip trills, as his practice material.

Now, take a look at Figure 10.4, "The Behavioral Processing System." This diagram shows how the qualities that Horace brings to his goal will either inhibit his progress or facilitate it. Clearly his high C trait will be critical, thus supporting him in setting an ambitious practice regimen and sticking to it. However, his high O trait (note the dashed line to his C+ trait) suggests that he is bored with repetition, and that will work against his efforts to stick to the practice schedule. On the other hand, his Hedonism values will support his desire to solidify the relationship with the girl of his dreams, in anticipation of pleasures without end. Although his Auditory cognitive ability insures his success at summer camp, his stiff lips inhibit his Auditory learning ability. On the other hand, his mid E trait suggests that he has equal amounts of energy to practice (E-) and to take care of other social commitments (E+). All in all, he

Figure 10.4 The Behavioral Processing System

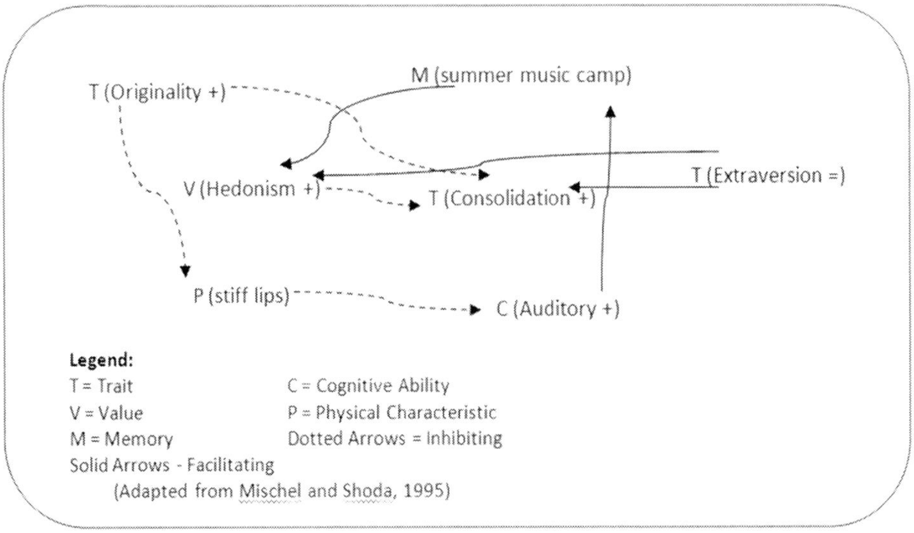

is in a reasonably good position to accomplish his goal, with the two exceptions of 1) being easily bored with repetition and 2) having stiff lips. He can increase his chances of success by making his memory of

Viola and the camp experience ever present, through putting pictures in his practice area and the like. And, of course, he needs to find an instructor/coach who has successfully led a horn player through this particular problem.

The value of knowing one's traits, abilities, and so forth is that it enables one to identify strengths and weaknesses, facilitators and inhibitors that relate to important goals. Without such knowledge, progress towards goals tends to be hit-or-miss.

Interactions with One's Environment

In the beginning of this chapter, we introduced Kurt Lewin's formula of B = f(P + E). We have been focusing this entire chapter on the "P" of the formula, what the person brings to a situation. But personalities do not act in a vacuum. Students of literature have often had to interpret a story in terms of whether the conflict therein illustrated Character versus Self, Character versus Character, or Character versus Nature (or Machine, Supernatural, and so forth). That is another way of saying that we struggle internally among our many traits, abilities, memories, values, and physical characteristics/limitations (Person versus Self), we struggle externally in our many relationships (Person versus Person), and we also struggle externally with the demands of our environment (Person versus Nature). Rather than deal with these contexts here at the end of Chapter 10, we will devote the remainder of the book to showing how we, as individuals, behave as the result of our personal characteristics interacting with the demands of our relationships (parents, peers, romantic partners, teachers, employers...) and our environment (geography, culture, institutions...). In the next chapter of this section, we will present an extensive case study, one that shows an individual moving through the preteen years, through university, and how personal qualities and the environment work together to shape the individual's goals and their path for attainment. For, after all, that is what life is about—getting where we want to go. What's the comment by the Cheshire Cat in *Alice in Wonderland*? "If you don't know where you are going, any road will take you there!"

11

Ripeness Is All

A Case Study in Development of Traits Over Time

> "Adolescence is a period of rapid changes. Between the ages of 12 and 17, for example, a parent ages as much as 20 years."
>
> --Author Unknown

Guide to This Chapter:

- Case Study: The Book of Me: My Life from 12 to 22
- Introduction: Mama's Boy and Church Rat
- Chapter 1: (Junior) High School Initiation
- Chapter 2: First Chair at 14
- Chapter 3: Estelle McClees and the Reign of Science
- Chapter 4: From Transylvania to Stockholm
- Chapter 5: The Summer at Phillips Andover Academy
- Chapter 6: Yet Another Initiation
- Chapter 7: Double Whammy: Wes Tilley and Transylvania II
- Chapter 8: Enough School, Let's Experience the World
- Epilogue: Settling in for a Lifetime

What is maturity? What is growing up? How can you tell whether a teen is on the trajectory towards greater maturity, or whether they are stagnating or even regressing? Paul Costa and Jeff McCrae (2003) in their classic study of human development provide a relatively simple guideline: N, E, and O decrease somewhat as A and C increase. In plain English, that means that, as we mature, we become calmer (N↓), more comfortable with ourselves (E↓), more comfortable with our chosen path (O↓), more interested in maintaining long-term relationships (A↑), and more disciplined in the pursuit of our goals (C↑). On the contrary, a young person who is stagnating or even deteriorating would show signs of growing more reactive (N↑), more dependent on peer groups (E↑), less committed to possible paths of interest (O↑), more self-absorbed (A↓), and less disciplined with fewer goals (C↓). In each of these instances, we are not talking about major shifts of 30 to 50 points or shifts, for example, from

Mapping Out the Big Five Traits

N	E	O	A	C
Need for Stability	**Extraversion**	**Originality**	**Accommodation**	**Consolidation**
N+ Reactive	E+ Extraverted	O+ Explorer	A+ Adapter	C+ Focused
N= Responsive	E= Ambiverted	O= Moderate	A= Negotiator	C= Balanced
N- Resilient	E- Introverted	O- Preserver	A- Challenger	C- Flexible
N1: Worry	**E1: Approach Level**	**O1: Imagination**	**A1: Service**	**C1:Thoroughness**
N2: Temper	**E2: Group Orientation**	**O2: Range of Interests**	**A2: Compliance**	**C2: Structure**
N3: Outlook	**E3: Pace**	**O3: Innovation**	**A3: Humility**	**C3: Ambition**
N4: Coping Level	**E4: Leadership**	**O4: Zoom Scale**	**A4: Speak Out Level**	**C4: Concentration**
	E5: Trust			**C5: Methodicalness**
	E6: Tact			

being an extrovert to being an introvert. Rather, we are talking of small shifts of 10 or so points. A good example is my (Pierce's) shift from being moderately extraverted in high school to being ambiverted in college and beyond. The practical effect of this shift is that it made more time for reading, for study. In high school, in fact, I disliked reading, so much that I would read a "Classics Illustrated" comic book in order to be able to write a "book" review on, say, *The Last of the Mohicans* or *David Copperfield.* In high school, the energy I might have spent on reading and studying was spent in hanging with the guys, playing basketball, listening to music, having jam sessions, or building something together. Today that energy has become transmogrified into time for reading and writing.

Some argue (cf. Cobb, 2007, p. 245) that a healthy group identity precedes a healthy individual identity—that one must feel accepted, valued, wanted by one or more groups in order for one to feel safe in exploring/affirming one's sense of self. Nancy Cobb (2007) in her text on adolescent psychology cites the work of Barbara and Philip Newman of the University of Rhode Island. The Newmans hold that the primary task of preadolescence is achieving comfort in the group through the tool of "gossip," whereby values and norms are clarified and confirmed. Later, the primary task of adolescence is achieving personal identity through the tool of self-disclosure. So, in early adolescence, we are hoping for a child's peer and other groups to establish one's identity through the affirming course of gossip:

- "That Smith kid can really play the guitar."
- "Have you seen that Jordan kid play hoops? Awesome!"
- "Isn't Martha the smoothest talker you've heard in a while?"
- "You can really trust that Wigand kid to let you know when something's not quite right, can't you?"
- "I bet that Clinton kid will be president some day!"
- "The Palin girl sure can hold her own around all the guys—she's going places, you wait and see."
- "I think Obama is going to make quite a lawyer, don't you—the way he thinks calmly on his feet?"

These themes find their way back to us through the gossip networks and lay the groundwork of our evolving identity in adolescence. As we gain confidence and clarity in our traits, abilities, values, and physical characteristics, we let our networks know that we are on track by revealing our personal thoughts and feelings about who we are and what we are becoming:

- "Playing the guitar is so soothing—it takes my mind off of everything, and I'm totally into the world of six strings and an acoustical box."
- "Basketball makes more sense to me with each hour of practice."
- "I get a charge out of connecting with an audience."
- "Standing up for what is right is often scary but never regrettable."
- "I never entered an election I didn't passionately want to win."
- "I really enjoy being a player in traditionally male arenas—it energizes me."
- "When someone challenges me in public, I become totally focused on composing my dialog—the rest of the world recedes."

Through these acts of self-disclosure, our networks nod among each other in tacit approval.

Now let us take a look at this process of the adolescence, of subtle shifts in traits; of subtle peer group nudges that bring out some traits, abilities, and values (and suppress others); of events that emphasize our strengths and reveal weaknesses. In order to present a case with sufficient realism, I use as my subject someone I know intimately—myself (Pierce). In accordance with the approach of John McAdams (1993), I have organized the story by chapters, each having its own theme (in this case, the salient peer group will be the theme) and principal characters. I will quickly summarize the high points that established my personal characteristics by the age of 12 and then show the tapestry of circumstances that modified my traits, abilities, values, memories, and physical characteristics through my 10 years of adolescence. I will close with a summary that illustrates the stability of where I was at age 22.

The Book of Me: My Life from 12 to 22

Introduction: Mama's Boy and Church Rat

My first 12 years were those of an only child, yet an only child with six siblings, all of whom had left home by the time I was born in 1941. We lived on Queen Street hill, site of the annual soapbox derby, in Kinston, North Carolina. Eastern North Carolina was tobacco country. My father owned his business, an independent wholesale grocer, one of a dying breed that has yielded to the national and regional chain stores. His N-E=O-A=C+ profile compares closely to my adult profile, with the exception that my mother's O= displaces his lower O in my inherited traits. Mother's higher E influenced me early on until I mellowed to an E= in adulthood. While both were readers, I didn't pick up the habit until my 20s, but I have fond memories of them with books: dad in his rocker, mom on her sofa or in bed. Dad was on the school board; so school achievement was fostered early on. Dad was tone-deaf, but mother was an active musician—her energetic Saturday morning piano patter was my alarm clock, warning me that youth choir practice was imminent. We were in and out of the church building constantly—we didn't miss a service, meeting, or event, and I LOVED those eastern N.C. covered dish dinners. Gordon Street Christian Church was like an obstacle course that had to be navigated.

With six older brothers and sisters whom I didn't get to know until later, I filled my life with their 18 offspring, a veritable circus of nieces and nephews that made holidays a constant party. When I turned 8, mother organized a Cub Scout den composed of all of my "friends," and I began my love of exploration, from learning how to make a brick oven in the backyard to making and decorating wooden bed trays to give to shut-ins. My frequent ride-alongs with mother delivering food, gifts, and the like to the less fortunate formed an early habit of charity—she urged me never to take a job that I didn't absolutely have to have to survive, because someone more needy could be deprived of meaningful work. I wanted to sell greeting cards during one holiday season, but she convinced me that it would take precious dollars away from a woman that mother knew whose only source of income was door-to-door greeting card sales. Instead of letting me work, she upped my allowance. Mother used fear and guilt to motivate me—"Eat everything on your plate, lest the starving children of China...", "If you do that again, I'm sending you to reform school," "You should ask X to come to your party, even if you don't like him, and he's not your friend, because his dad's been suffering several business reverses and he needs support," and such.

With the need to wear glasses arriving when I was 7, sporting achievement became increasingly difficult. Poor depth perception and an anxious temperament led me to avoid high-risk sports—I lived in Bavaria for two years with Uncle Sam's army in my 20s and never tried to ski. I tried out for "termite" football when I was 11, but was 3 pounds overweight, so I turned my uniform in rather than suffer the denial that comes from dieting. Then I tried out for basketball and broke my foot—a greenstick fracture, but enough to derail my abortive sporting career. I wouldn't try out for another sport until my summer at Phillips-Andover Academy, where I learned at age 17 to enjoy track and field, specializing in discus, hammer, javelin, and shot put. But when I returned to my high school and tried to join the newly organized track team, I discovered that I couldn't do both track and band; so guess what won? My three years of piano lessons began in 4th grade, with Miss Jessie starting the lesson by sitting me on the couch and playing middle C, then asking me to identify subsequent notes without looking. From this early training, I developed proficiency in reading music.

My parents were relatively old (mom 45 and dad 55 when I was born), and I was a handful (especially during the summers with school out of session so summer camps filled every summer from first grade on—sailing, archery, riflery, assorted crafts, dancing, music, designing worship services, baseball, swimming. I have a vivid memory of driving through New England with my folks and visiting my brother Lee, who was a counselor and instructor at Camp Greenwood in Cummington, Massachusetts, nestled in the Berkshires. It was there at the age of 10 that I sat in with the youth orchestra and fell in love with the French horn, which I made up my mind to begin playing when I started 6th grade in the fall.

So, here's the profile with which I entered 7th grade:

Traits: N+E++O++A+C-
Abilities: Auditory/Musical
Values: Service, Spiritual, Aesthetic
Physical Characteristics: myopia, fragile feet
Memories: Cub Scouts, boy soprano, Daddy's store, Camp Greenwood, Camp Morehead, Camp Caroline
Role Models: Mother, Miss Jessie (choir director, piano teacher, and intellectual), Clint Bradshaw (preacher)

Chapter 1: (Junior) High School Initiation

Kinston had only five schools, three for Caucasians (and the occasional Middle Easterner, Latin American, or Asian) and two for African Americans. The Caucasian "high school" was actually six grades, 7 through 12, with about 100 students at each level. On the first day of 7th grade in the fall of 1953, this recently-turned-12 boy met up with several other new 7th graders and walked to school together, finding strength in numbers, knowing that we would be "initiated" into high school, mostly by the 8th graders. The numbers did no good, as upper classmen swarmed on us with lipstick and shoe polish, covering our faces, hair, and hands with black and red. We suffered the indignity of being painted/branded through the day and walked quickly that afternoon to my house, just two blocks from the school, where mother helped us remove the various pigments with cold cream and any other removal agents she could rummage. Cleansed, we were no longer kids—we were now officially teenagers.

My courses were the obligatory English, math, history, science, and art, and I chose band as my elective. At the tender age of 12, I managed to win the "assistant first chair," leaping over several upperclassmen who didn't care as much for the instrument as I did. The first chair, or principal hornist, was Henrietta Swain, a lovely senior whom I idolized. This was quite a leap into adolescence, with hormones mixing with music making (I discovered 20 years later that she had a crush on me but squelched it for fear of being stigmatized for "rocking the cradle"). Our school had no string program; so band was it—no orchestra. But our repertoire was more than that of a traditional band. While we played the traditional Sousa marches and English suites for winds, we also played the symphonic literature of Strauss, Gershwin, Tschaikowsky, Elgar, all arranged for wind band. Our director, Mr. Shipman, offered private lessons, which I took a couple of afternoons a week after school. We played for football games, and during football seasons I learned to detest marching. My low C and high O was fit to be tied with the repetitive drills of counting steps and playing the same tunes over and over again. But I had to persevere with "marching band" during football season in order to be able to play with "concert band" the rest of the year. I think one reason I hated marching band so much was that the horn parts were mostly "oom-pahs" that involved incessant short notes played on the offbeat in a bouncy back and forth with the tubas and bass drums, who played on the downbeat. Music fit for O-.

So my peer groups in the 7th grade were the band, especially my closer friends who were band members (Charles, Mark, Annette, and Robert), my youth group (Chi Rho) at church, the youth choir at church (where my newly changed voice sank from soprano to bass), the kids in my immediate neighborhood, Boy Scout Troop 41 (I had graduated from Cub Scouts), and my closest nieces and nephews (close both in age and in friendship)—Bobby, Joe, and Curt. While Cub Scouts had been my salient peer group for the previous two years, my new salient peer group was Chi Rho, where I became extremely active in a leadership role and tried my skills at preaching, designing devotional services, religious theatre, singing, and most important of all, socializing. Our church youth group was big into socializing with each other: dancing, partying, recreating, service projects, and the like. This was the context in which I had my first dates: going to the movies, having dances in my garage, and using my dad's delivery trucks for hay rides. Mother, partly wanting me not to be idle on the weekend, started a Saturday night dance class, where she and a couple of dozen other parents chipped in and paid Jackie Hale, a dance teacher, to train us in ballroom dancing (box step, shag, waltz) and folk dancing (square, among others). For most of the 7th and 8th grade, Chi Rho and concert band were my salient peer groups, with Chi Rho edging out band for having the strongest influence. (Band would take on more importance later.) I think Chi Rho was the most salient of all my peer groups because it engaged my O+ through its diversity of activities. There was opportunity for interaction in Chi Rho, but band was all "work" with little interaction, and I was a social creature. Also causing Chi Rho to be salient for me was the advisor, D. L. "Pete" Warren, a youth minister extraordinaire, who used humor, sports, and a stinky cigar to wrap us burgeoning teenagers around his little finger. It was Pete who first encouraged me to take the Bible less literally, to take life less seriously (i.e., to lighten up), and to enjoy doing research (through encouraging me to design activities for our youth group).

My art teacher tried her best to lead my eyes and hands in concert for producing likenesses, all to no avail. The good news is that I discovered at an early age that I had no talent for drawing, but I still yearn to be able to produce a likeness of someone/something. My growing interest and ability in making music offset my lack of talent in art and athletics. And with my increasing involvement with the French horn, I abandoned piano lessons, mostly because I resented my mother's close supervision thereof. She didn't know enough about the French horn to supervise me; so stopping the piano was a ticket to greater independence. It also protracted my low C by encouraging exploration over discipline.

One strange theme of my junior high years was a friendship with Edward Hill, son of an impoverished seamstress. Their home in "south Kinston" was drafty and smelled otherworldly, certainly not the same fragrance of lavender and magnolia that gently filled our home on Queen Street hill. The Hills were poor, and we were well-to-do, and I think my mother engineered our friendship as a way of keeping me grounded. As I grew older and more socially self-conscious, Edward and I drifted apart, but similar relationships have filled that void ever since. Somehow, mother instilled in me a desire to avoid having an "upper crust" identity. Mother and Dad were members of the local country club, but only for me to go swimming with my friends. They never attended events at the club, and I grew to have a strong distaste for private club membership, as I came to learn that my Catholic and Jewish friends could not belong there. To this day, I have never joined a private club. And to this day, I count several "Edward Hills" among my friends. This pattern caused my A+ to stay elevated until I reached college and started having to make some tough decisions. My mother's influence on my high A is reflected in a letter I received my junior year of college, in which she wrote in response to something I had written earlier: "Don't judge until you know all the facts, and when you know all the facts, you won't judge." I wrote back, "What about Hitler?" By that time, my A score had moderated, no longer deferring to her.

So, here's my profile when I entered 9th grade, the first official year of high school:

Traits: N+E++O++A+C- *(stayed pretty much the same)*
Abilities: Auditory/Musical, Interpersonal *(Chi Rho brought this out)*

Values: Service, Spiritual, Aesthetic
Physical Characteristics: glasses, fragile feet
Memories: Cub Scouts, boy soprano, Daddy's store, Camp Greenwood, Camp Morehead, Camp Caroline, Chi Rho, marching band (yuck), concert band (yum), Boy Scouts and their camps
Role Models: Mother, Miss Jessie, Pete Warren, Harry Shipman

Chapter 2: First Chair at 14

By the beginning of 9th grade, Henrietta had graduated, and I was playing first chair. This was a special event because it opened the door to chamber music. Mr. Shipman encouraged his first chair players to be in chamber ensembles and to prepare pieces to play in the state contest conducted each spring at Duke University. With this introduction to chamber music (which included playing Mozart, Beethoven, and other French horn sonatas and concertos), my salient peer group shifted to band. We began playing away from school—I recall fondly having jam sessions in Dan Wooten's garage, experimenting with jazz, swing, and various classical idioms. That year we persuaded Mr. Shipman to start a "big band" group, playing the repertoire of Benny Goodman, Tommy Dorsey, and the like.

Also with 9th grade came the study of Latin, a decision that would lead me down a more serious path. I regret that I did not study French or Spanish, the only other languages offered at our school. While Latin helped me feel more aristocratic, a "living language" would have made me a better citizen of the world, which would soon be opening its doors to me. The study of Latin perpetuated my O++C- tendency to explore with minimal commitment to particular goals. Besides, Latin was considered harder and a better preparation for college, with French and Spanish being considered "crip" courses, so Latin led to greater status. I also discovered the world of higher math with the study of Algebra I. My teacher, Agnes Freeman, was also the school counselor. She was kind, loved teenagers, and made learning a joy. Modulating from serious to smiling, she rarely succumbed to anger or even a frown. Her nurturing manner kept her calendar full with student appointments. We would take the Kuder Preference Test just to have time with her. I remember her comment when one of our peers became pregnant: "You don't always love what teens do, but you always love them nonetheless." Ms. Freeman became a model of learning, of love and acceptance, and of making the most of life.

The 9th grade marked two significant events: my first romance and my first travel out of the country. Vicki Griffin was a soprano in our youth choir and a soloist with our high school chorus. Vicki and I "went steady" for the next two years. Our dating grew out of Chi Rho hayrides, etc., and we planned to build on our mutual love of the church and music to be missionaries to Africa. Vicki was very much like me and encouraged me in all of my natural tendencies: emotionally volatile, curious, deferential, spontaneous, undisciplined (I remember those passionate interludes in Elizabeth City), musical, religious, and so on. She was not a student, in that life was not in books for her but in other people. We formed a peer group of our own, and our mutual judgment became the arbiter of what was in or out. Along with this romance, my Boy Scouting was progressing steadily towards the rank of Eagle. The plethora of merit badges required for this goal appealed to my O+, while the specific requirements for completing Eagle's standard nudged my C- ever so slightly upwards. During the summer after my freshman year of high school, I joined a dozen or so scouts from eastern N.C. in attending the World Jamboree in Quebec. This was my first contact with people from other continents. My personal love of cooking and fine dining was heightened during this festival, as each group of scouts put on display its finest regional dishes. We from eastern N.C. cooked apple cobbler and hush puppies, dishing out samples to passersby, as we passed by fellow scouts from around the world and sampled their crepes, yams, and fried grasshoppers. My interest in cooking had taken a giant step when I learned that one of my friends (now a retired psychiatrist) LOVED to wash dishes. We made a mad pair, with me dirtying pots and pans with fried chicken and mashed potatoes and him furiously keeping up with me by washing, scrubbing, and drying. The odd couple, huh? Again, this encouraged my O+ while holding down my C- (in that I was able to avoid cleaning up after my messes!).

Here is my profile as I entered 10th grade:

> *Traits*: N=E++O++A+C- *(romance and growing acceptance in various groups was causing my N+ to settle somewhat)*
> *Abilities*: Auditory/Musical, Interpersonal
> *Values*: Service, Spiritual, Aesthetic, Environment *(Boy Scout activity was bringing me closer to nature)*
> *Physical Characteristics*: glasses, fragile feet, motion sickness (got sick on one of Dad's fishing trips)
> *Memories*: Cub Scouts, boy soprano, Daddy's store, Camp Greenwood, Camp Morehead, Camp Caroline, Chi Rho, marching band (yuck), concert band (yum), Boy Scout camporees and camps, prepping for state music contest, making out in the back seat
> *Role Models*: Mother, Miss Jessie, Pete Warren, Agnes Freeman *(notice that the preacher has dropped out, and no preacher will ever replace him)*, "Sparky" Hood (scoutmaster)

Chapter 3: Estelle McClees and the Reign of Science

Tenth grade was significant in two ways: achievement in Boy Scouts and the arrival of Miss McClees. In scouting, being selected to the Order of the Arrow was one of the first assaults on my E++. To achieve the first level of recognition in the Order of the Arrow, I had to remain silent (no talking) for 24 hours, beginning by sleeping alone under the stars at Camp Croatan on the banks of the Neuse River with only a poncho for protection, and then waking to a Spartan breakfast consisting of a piece of bread and juice, then performing grueling physical labor (stump removal), relieved by a dry bologna sandwich and a cup of milk, followed by more grueling work throughout the afternoon. When one's guard fell and you uttered one or more words, the supervisors put a notch on a stick carried with you. Three notches and you were sent home, as happened to several. I found a new respect for solitude, silence, reflection, and discipline. I survived the ordeal and, a year later, achieved the next level in the Order of the Arrow, this time through a day of memory work, a sort of evolution from silence, as we were permitted to practice recitations to one another before being examined at the end of the day. Also, this emphasis on silence, study, and restraint began to form a new slant on my experience of the spiritual, which would become manifest some 15 years later when I joined an ongoing "unprogrammed" (i.e., silent) Quaker meeting in Winston-Salem. Order of the Arrow was not really a new peer group, as my involvement with it was only periodic, but the principle effect was to provide me with a sense of achievement, status, and new sense of maturity. During this year, I also completed requirements for Eagle Scout, the process of earning 21 merit badges appealing to my O++ as I delved into areas ranging from coin collecting to fishing. Concurrently, I earned the "God and Country" award, again demanding much memory work. I did more memory work in scouting than I did for my high school classes! These demands prevented my C- from falling any lower, though my love of spontaneity and multi-tasking kept me steady at low levels of C. The end of the year brought recognition to me as a part of the "Report to the President" program, whereby each Boy Scout regional council selected an honor scout to report to the state's governor, and then each state selected one of these to report to the President. I made it to the governor, but not to the President. However, as a runner up, I was selected with three other scouts from the southeastern U.S. to be flown to Sweden for two weeks to study their culture and to associate with their scouting program. More of that later. While I was flattered at being chosen, I never caught the bug to become ambitious by entering lots of other contests, either political or otherwise. The environment certainly should have fostered the C3+ spark to achieve, but it just didn't ignite in me, probably due to genes (lack of testosterone?). I just never did have the appetite for the self-promotion and rah-rah behavior associated with electioneering and negotiating hierarchies.

Estelle McClees, "Miss McClees" to us, was the new arrival in our high school faculty. A bright, middle-aged, unmarried science teacher who lived and breathed education, she turned our science department from a sleepy, underachieving college requirement into an energetic, aggressive quest for knowledge and understanding of what makes things tick. She taught biology, chemistry, AND physics; so my friends and I studied with her for three straight years. I will never forget one day in her class when it started to snow. As we all focused on the increasingly larger flakes, she stopped her lecture and posed a question to the class: "Students, what causes snow?" She made an impromptu lesson out of what would in the past have simply been a distraction. That year, Miss McClees organized the school's first science fair, and the scholarly competitive juices flowed. Thanks to her energy, enthusiasm, knowledge, and caring for student, our small high school class of about 115 produced some 20 doctorates, including Ph.D., M.D., J.D., and Ed.D. Miss McClees caused my O++ to remain in the stratosphere by encouraging curiosity, experimentation, exploration, and independent study.

Meanwhile, I wanted to be a preacher more than ever. I asked "Santa Claus" for books that would help me be a good preacher. I got the multi-volume *Interpreter's Bible* and *Bartlett's Familiar Quotations* and preached in my church on youth Sunday. The old folks in the congregation would come up afterwards and comment that I reminded them of my grandfather, a popular minister in eastern N.C. in the late 19th century. The magic of being a part of this legacy was supporting my career choice in spite of the secular allure of Miss McClees, Mr. Shipman, and Sparky Hood. One factor that impelled me in this religious direction was my romance with Vicki Griffin, as we made plans to be medical/musical missionaries to the Belgian Congo. In support of my chosen career, I collected stories and pithy quotations to use in sermons. I wrote brief devotionals for use in various church publications and services.

Mapping Out the Big Five Traits

Of all of the peer groups during the 10th grade—scouts, church youth group (now CYF, Christian Youth Fellowship, as I had outgrown Chi Rho), church youth choir, band, an increasing number of service clubs sponsored at the high school, my salient group shifted from band back to church youth group, partly because Vicki was there and not in band, and partly because of the leadership of Pete Warren in encouraging a wide variety of activities that appealed to my E+ and O++. And, of course, my A+ had me pegged as a "do-gooder," and my identification with the church was solid and pervasive.

This is what my profile looked like during the summer before 11th grade:

Traits: N=E+O++A+C- (*notice that the Extraversion is beginning to decrease)*
Abilities: Auditory/Musical, Interpersonal, Intrapersonal *(heightened by the Order of the Arrow experiences)*
Values: Service, Spiritual, Aesthetic, Environment
*Physical Charac*teristics: glasses, fragile feet, motion sickness
Memories: Cub Scouts, boy soprano, Daddy's Store, Camp Greenwood, Camp Morehead, Camp Caroline, Chi Rho, marching band (yuck), concert band (yum), Boy Scout camporees and camps, prepping for state music contest, making out in the back seat, science fair, Order of the Arrow ordeal, Report to the Governor
Role Models: Mother, Miss Jessie, Pete Warren, Agnes Freeman, "Sparky" Hood (scoutmaster), Miss McClees, Mr. Shipman

Chapter 4: From Transylvania to Stockholm

The summer after 10th grade contained three milestones: six weeks at Transylvania Music Camp (TMC), my 16th birthday and the attendant driver's license, and two weeks in godless, socialist Sweden. For many, attendance at TMC was the prelude to being a music major and having a career in music. For me, it was the solidification of my primary hobby. I experienced my first taste of playing with an orchestra, of singing with a highly talented small choral group, of performing with world-class conductors, of studying music theory and taking private horn lessons with highly qualified instructors, and of exposure to the complete world of classical music, from early to current. I learned the joy of chamber music with string players, as there were none in Kinston. My horn repertoire stretched to include more difficult pieces by Hindemith and Strauss. Near the end of the six weeks, I was notified that I had been selected to stay on for a couple of weeks to sing and play in the festival, an honor I intensely wanted to enjoy. However, I was slated to go to Sweden for two weeks in the Boy Scout exchange program. I weighed the two, and making my first trip across the ocean won out. This was the first of several decisions that clarified for me that music was not going to be a career, but a hobby. After six weeks at TMC, I was hooked on classical music and particularly chamber music.

Sweden was an eye-opener, and the first challenge to my essentially fundamentalist eastern N.C. religious tradition. I had heard that Sweden was a godless country (for the most part) and that their socialist system was un-American. Two weeks in Swedish homes and scout camps led me to new respect for socialism and a society without God as its core. My first night in Stockholm after flying over the ocean in a military transport, my host family, knowing I was tired, ushered me straight to my bedroom and wished me a good night's rest. They closed the door, and I wandered over to the bed, where on the side table was a glass of milk, a peanut butter sandwich, and a small bowl of M&Ms. So much for godlessness! These people, who did not go to church and did not spout religious sayings, were kind, thoughtful, cheerful—anything but the self-serving, offensive, immoral louts I had expected. The world was becoming a curiosity, and I was becoming less provincial. My O+ was being nurtured, tickled, expanded.

Driving through Swedish cities, countrysides, highways, and villages had promised to be my introduction to the evils of socialism, but instead I found cleanliness, no signs of poverty, no street people, no slums, and pleasant people throughout who, for the most part, spoke English and regarded me as family. So much for the evils of socialism. Nudge that O++ score up a few more points. And take away one of the supports for my unquestioning value for the Spiritual.

My 16th birthday had passed while in Sweden, and my driver's license awaited me when I returned home. (Mother taught the examiner in her Sunday School class, and she had talked him into examining me before I went to Sweden but holding my license for my return.) Beginning the 11th grade with a driver's license, a car, a summer in the mountains with music, and an eye-opening trip to Sweden, suggested that my junior year might be a dull one of low significance. Far from it, for the year was filled with tragedy and triumph. To begin the year, only a month after I had embraced my independence through such feats as picking up Vicki in my car and going to choir practice together (we were singing with the adult choir now, on Wednesday nights), I experienced my first death of a loved one. Vicki died suddenly from a cerebral hemorrhage. Her incompetent doctor had prescribed, by phone, an aspirin and bed rest for her bloated tongue and headache. Mother called me at school during mid-morning with the news. I went home, closed myself in the music room, and played the Verdi *Requiem* from beginning to end. Our dream of being a missionary team to the Congo was smashed. My optimistic, accepting, A+ outlook that characterized my churchiness was dealt a blow. I was to retrench, ask more hard questions, and ask why.

My friend Mike Mitchell, who was my preacher's stepson, and I began a spree of questing, of looking for answers, of experimenting with new behaviors. We had an act called "Frank and Earnest," whereby when we were double-dating with two unsuspecting girls, one of us would refer to the other as Frank (or Earnest), and from that point on, we were honor-bound to speak only what came to mind—total honesty and directness, no sugar-coating, no holding back.

When Mike and I weren't intimidating our dates, we were meeting at the local DuPont plant after school, where Miss McClees had talked several of their Ph.D. researchers into teaching a once-weekly, after-school seminar in advanced laboratory techniques, demonstrating equipment to us that was not available in our high school lab. This was my newest peer group, and it was to become the salient group for that academic year. While I was not prominent within that group (as it was full of kids wanting to be science majors), the group itself was a source of pride, energy, exploration, and excitement. Adding to my renewed interest in school, my geometry teacher, Gladys Sutton, recognized my ability in math and asked me one day to do some substitute teaching! The Algebra I teacher needed to take a couple of days off, and a substitute was unavailable, so she asked if I would be interested in teaching the classes, with the understanding that they would provide me with a lesson plan. Sure, I said, why not? No problem for this O++C-. What's another distraction?!

Well into the year, Mr. Shipman nominated me for the N.C. All-State Orchestra. I made it and traveled to Greensboro and the W.C. (Woman's College, as it was called then; it's now the University of North Carolina at Greensboro) for four days of playing French horn with the finest possible assembly of orchestral players in the state. My love of classical music was cemented. As a follow-up to this experience, I started taking private French horn lessons with Mel Parnell at East Carolina University in Greenville, about a 25-mile drive from home. After a few lessons, Mr. Parnell invited me to play fourth horn in the university orchestra. I leapt at the chance; so I began commuting twice weekly after school for practices and then joined them when they went on the occasional tour, playing at venues around the region. While deepening my involvement with the aesthetics of music, this did nothing to mature my scholarly side. The love of reading would have to spawn in a different stream, a different time.

At the end of the 11th grade, my profile had grown in this way:

Traits: N=E+O++A=C- *(ever so subtly, fostered by Vicki's death, the A+ has toughened)*
Abilities: Auditory/Musical, Interpersonal, Intrapersonal *(heightened by Vicki's death)*
Values: Service, Spiritual, Aesthetic, Environment
*Physical Charac*teristics: glasses, fragile feet, motion sickness
Memories: Cub Scouts, boy soprano, Daddy's store, Camp Greenwood, Camp Morehead, Camp Caroline, Chi Rho, marching band (yuck), concert band (yum), Boy Scout camporees and camps, prepping for state music contest, making out in the back seat, science fair, Order of the Arrow ordeal, Report to the Governor, orchestral playing, DuPont science demonstrations, "Frank and Earnest" shenanigans, chamber music in the mountains, peanut butter sandwich in Sweden, enclosed with the Verdi *Requiem*
Role Models: Mother, Miss Jessie, Pete Warren, Agnes Freeman, "Sparky" Hood (scoutmaster), Miss McClees, Mr. Shipman, Thor Johnson (*internationally known visiting conductor at TMC*), Ms. Sutton, DuPont scientists

Chapter 5: the Summer at Phillips Andover Academy

Mother, concerned for my academic welfare, wanted me to go off to private school. We had visited several prep schools in the region, including Woodberry Forest, where one of my friends was enrolled. I didn't want to go. I was convinced that Miss McClees was as good as could be had. Perhaps mother was afraid I'd be persuaded away from being a minister (although I really wanted to be a medical missionary), or perhaps she was just worn out from being 67 years old and trying to parent a teenager—she had been a parent nonstop now since 1916; that's 42 years! Time to retire. She talked me into attending Phillips Academy in Andover, Massachusetts, just for the summer session before my senior year, so I could have a taste of what a more challenging curriculum was like. I agreed, with the understanding that I could return to Grainger High School for my senior year if I still wanted to at the end of the summer.

Three eye-openers occurred for me that summer. First, I took a course called "The Study of Man," which was a combination of literature, anthropology, philosophy, linguistics, and history. The reading assignments were demanding, stretching, and definitely appealing to my O+. In one paper, I wrote for Mr. McCarthy, I had used the expression "right knowledgeable" to refer to someone. He red-lined it, writing in the margin, "provincialism!" I approached him after class and wanted to know what was wrong with that expression, as everyone I knew back home used it. He said, "Well, you make my point. They use it in eastern North Carolina, but you'll find that it is regarded as nonstandard usage elsewhere." I grumbled, not fully understanding, but definitely feeling something akin to an inferiority complex, like a stranger in strange land. A week later, I was reading *King Lear,* and came upon Shakespeare's line that "our graces are *right* honored"! Aha, I had proof that my usage was NOT provincial, after all. Showing this passage to Mr. McCarthy, he retorted, "Howard, I can't help it if you Carolinians are 450 years behind the times!" Mr. McCarthy was the first instructor to show me the joy, wonder, and consternation of taking language seriously. At home, the only concern was for misspellings, comma splices, and run-on sentences, with little attention to subtlety. I credit this summer stay in Massachusetts with lighting the spark of my interest in language and beginning the slow, sometimes painful, process of improving my ear for the right word.

Second, each student was required to take one sport. My O+ was drawn to something I'd never experienced—track and field. For the next two months, I shot the put, heaved the javelin, threw the hammer, and heaved the discus. That summer was the beginning of my preference for individual sports over team sports. It's similar, I suppose, to my preference for chamber music (with one on a part) over large group music. Something stirs in me at the thought of an individual holding one's own among others, like a character in a play. This preference further fed my reduction from A+ to A=. I have never become a radical individualist, for my interest is more in avoiding boredom than in being unique. And the pattern that by now has become established is that I basically enjoy the pressure of holding down my own part, whether in music or in life at large.

Third, I began to experiment with music. They had no orchestra, and the band had no trumpeter. Becoming bored with playing French horn in bands, I volunteered to play first trumpet with the summer school band. That was a hoot, and it served to lighten me up a bit, as we played everything from marches to rock-and-roll. But I didn't abandon the classics. I had my horn with me and worked on Brahms' Horn Trio with two faculty members who played piano and violin. Lovely. In fact, so lovely that I made a decision that I would not play in the band my senior year back home. Enough with the oom-pah-pahs. When I returned to Kinston, I signed up for World History and dropped band.

It worked for a semester, but I missed playing daily. Having managed to avoid playing with the marching band and being herded around like cattle, I sheepishly went to Mr. Shipman and asked if he would let me play in the band second semester. He agreed; so I was back on track and had escaped football band. I managed another participation with N.C. All-State Orchestra, and I played in woodwind quintet and brass quintet for the state music contest in Durham. And when we unexpectedly had to play in a parade that spring, I volunteered to be the drum major so I wouldn't have to play oom-pahs.

Mapping Out the Big Five Traits

All of this emerging evidence suggested that I was beginning to get a feel for looking out for myself while still being a team player (A=).

Maturation was bringing to my attention more resources than what was available just in my neighborhood. I discovered that the organist at the local Presbyterian church had a harpsichord; so I made the acquaintance of Buford Goodman, and for the next several years we enjoyed chamber music together. We also began singing madrigals and other small group songs apart from church and school, just sitting around our music room or in Buford's office. When my brother Lee (voice, cello, recorder) and sister Virginia (voice—she had sung grand opera) would visit for the holidays, we would invite Miss Jessie and Buford to the house and have a musical soiree for our own enjoyment. My parents and any others visiting took great delight in these events, in the tradition of grand soirees of the palaces of Europe, much scaled down. To this day, my favorite entertainment is an evening of making music with friends.

For the speaker at our high school graduation, we decided to have four students speak on the topic of "The Educated Heart." I was one of the four, and for the first time, my preaching style was transferred to a secular podium. In the next year at college, my English professor was to set me firmly on a more secular style of composition. Mother had asked me where I wanted to go to college. I wanted a small, church-related college relatively close to home and with a good academic reputation. The school that best fit that bill was Davidson College, four hours away but a world apart, as I would soon discover. That is the only college to which I applied, and, fortunately I was accepted.

For my senior year, the salient peer group was my church youth group, CYF. I was a leader and very active member. I was going to become a preacher/missionary, and the church took a keen interest in assisting with my preparation. Pete Warren asked me to join him in weekly discussions with a young, African-American minister in Kinston and some of his flock—we saw it as laying the groundwork for eventual school desegregation. However, this was the last year that church groups were salient for me. College would prove the ultimate seductress. And, scouting had been over for a year, as I had outgrown it, there being no more awards to earn or new experiences to try. However, I would remain a lifelong camper and lover of the outdoors. So, here is my profile as I entered my freshman year of college:

> *Traits*: N=E+O++A=C-
> *Abilities*: Auditory/Musical, Interpersonal, Intrapersonal, Verbal/Linguistic, Math/Logical *(Ms. Sutton spotted this)*
> *Values*: Service, Spiritual, Aesthetic, Environment
> *Physical Charac*teristics: glasses, fragile feet, motion sickness
> *Memories*: Cub Scouts, boy soprano, Daddy's store, Camp Greenwood, Camp Morehead, Camp Caroline, Chi Rho, marching band (yuck), concert band (yum), Boy Scout camporees and camps, prepping for state music contest, making out in the back seat, science fair, Order of the Arrow ordeal, Report to the Governor, orchestral playing, DuPont science demonstrations, "Frank and Earnest" shenanigans, chamber music in the mountains, peanut butter sandwich in Sweden, enclosed with the Verdi *Requiem*, evening musical soirees at home, shot put and Brahms at Phillips Andover, being labeled "provincial"

Role Models: Mother, Miss Jessie, Pete Warren, Agnes Freeman, Miss McClees, Mr. Shipman, Thor Johnson, Ms. Sutton, DuPont scientists, Mr. McCarthy, Buford Goodman

Chapter 6: Yet Another Initiation

This time, school initiation featured "Beanies," the red and black short-billed caps required of all Davidson College freshman. With the abrupt change of the relatively casual demands of high school to the burn-the-midnight-oil expectations of a rigorous college that had produced among the highest numbers of Woodrow Wilson scholars, Rhodes scholars, and the like, my low C took a hit. My multitasking, spontaneous high school days were over. Now it was five classes, and maybe one outside activity, two at most. Right out of the chute, my intention to become a medical missionary was challenged. My advisor, Henry Lilly, a beloved English professor, urged me to delay taking freshman chemistry until I had adjusted to the rigors of college academics: "It is so hard on the boys," he lamented, "and the failure rate is quite high." He didn't have to tell me twice, as my A=C- quickly bowed to his suggestion. By the time my sophomore year came around, I felt the pre-med train had left me at the station. I tried biology, but the emphasis on bugs and frogs left me cold. My attention had turned to the wonders of philosophy. Taking a sophomore survey, each chapter introduced a new school of philosophy, beginning with the stoics and epicureans and ending with the existentialists and positivists. I was hooked, each school of thought being more attractive than its predecessor. My O+ was dizzy with delight, and my church youth group receded, feeling irrelevant in comparison to such profound/unique philosophical beliefs. Not being sure quite why, my attitude towards religion and church was balancing between aloof and unappreciative. I took two years of Bible under Max Polley, my new role model. Dr. Polley taught the difference between vertical and horizontal relationships in religion, with the vertical being theological and the horizontal being ethical. I came to the conclusion that vertical religion had no value without the horizontal, social/ethical dimension. I would later begin to wonder whether a theological life was, in fact, necessary for leading an ethical life. Values were shifting under foot.

Keeping me sane throughout all this was my first cousin, Nancy Howard Smith, a fine musician and piano teacher and wife of the Student Union Director, C. Shaw Smith. She had her own dormitory of kids upstairs, from newborn through junior high, five altogether, and a full-time cook. In exchange for babysitting, I got delightful home-cooked meals weekly. Growing up with 18 nieces and nephews, babysitting was a natural for me. Importantly, the Smith family taught me that being a classical musician did not mean that one had to be a snob. While Nancy did mazurkas and three-part inventions with aplomb, she joined her husband's love for musical comedy with alacrity. At first, I scorned their lowbrow leanings and thought Lerner and Loewe, as well as Gilbert and Sullivan, to be beneath me. Over four years, I unlearned this view and grew to admire Nancy's moving back and forth between the sublime and the ridiculous, allowing that the ridiculous had its own element of the sublime, and the sublime its own element of the ridiculous. Admiring her made me lighten up and become more well-rounded.

Mapping Out the Big Five Traits

My favorite subject was mathematics, and I was mesmerized by the intricacies of symbolic logic. I had always understood math as numbers, not realizing that it involved a much broader symbol system. Yet, still wanting to be a preacher, my heart was in literature, philosophy, history, Bible, and French, as they would help me be a better preacher, and I would need the French language in the Congo (as a missionary). I still kept notes for sermons, and I bought paperbacks by the dozen, confidently underlining passages that I wanted some day to use in a sermon. So, even though the math came easy, freshman math was my last math course, and I never took on calculus and beyond. My mistake. Had I been less intent on being a minister, which was my "bliss" at the time, my passion would have been in math. Today, it is expressed in my work with statistics and computer programming. I recognize today that math/logic is my strongest suit, as evidenced by higher scores on both the SAT and GRE quantitative tests.

At Davidson, I encountered love of learning daily. My freshman history prof, Brad Thomson, was a brilliant lecturer who made western civilization vivid, using only words. I went to his office one day to ask what he had written, not meaning to flatter him, but genuinely wanting more of his verbiage. It was feeding my soul. He said he had not time to write books and articles, that all he had time for was to read enough to keep his lectures up to date. He pointed to a stack of newspapers by his door, maybe two feet tall. He said, as though tired from it, "That stack is replenished daily from all over the world, and I must read it daily, or I fall behind." Now I knew the secret of the freshness of his tri-weekly holdings-forth. And, to this day, I commit to at least one newspaper a day, to help keep staleness at bay, although the "paper" is more frequently electronic.

Davidson had no orchestra, and its band promised an unwanted share of oom-pah-pahs. Now was the time to shift my musical focus to choral singing and to explore the marvelously rich repertoire of the male chorus. At the time, Davidson was an all male school, and I was to come close to forgetting the close-up sound of sopranos and altos. We explored the Russian male chorus literature for starters and then spread around the world for gems of the unique, all-male sound. But chamber music was to rise in importance. My brother Lee, afraid that I would abandon instrumental music altogether, gave me a wooden recorder for Christmas that year. I learned to play by being accompanied by "Music Minus One" records, as I played Telemann, Mattheson, and Bach with New York pros. Two daughters of my biology professor, Tom Daggy, were gifted string players, one a violinist, the other a cellist. We would meet, as time permitted and their home visits from college allowed, to explore the trio and quartet sonatas of the 17th and 18th centuries. I learned the incredibly physical, even erotic, intimacy of making music with attractive young women. We had to pace our breathing so that we felt the music as one, and that is intimate. We had to maintain eye contact, to sense each other's next move, a release here, an attack there, a crescendo and accelerando followed by diminuendo and ritardando. This was not mechanical stuff, this was intimacy! While thinking my music had settled at a new level, a new chapter began. I discovered that Dale Higbee, a nearby psychiatrist, had a trio of recorder players at Catawba College and would like to make it a quartet. For the rest of my four years of college, I played with his group and occasionally traveled in the region to play concerts.

My peer groups during the first two years of college were my classes; the Higbee Consort; the male chorus; the Smith family; my three friends from Kinston who matriculated with me at Davidson, Charles, Bobby, and Tommy; my immediate roommate and neighbors in the dormitory; and the fraternity that I had joined, ATΩ (at the time, 85% of all freshman joined fraternities, which were primarily eating places and social outlets, not residential facilities). The salient group was the fraternity, as it was comprised of an impressive cross-section of college life that helped shape my undergraduate experience—swimmers and scholars, pre-med and pre-ministerial, rich and poor, aesthetes and philistines, locals and internationals, Yankees and Rebs. Mealtime was a lively analysis of current events, from race to religion, from sports to politics. The ongoing bridge game provided temporary relief from the stress of study, day or night. I was voted "best pledge" my freshman year, as my relatively high A made being subservient to the demands of upperclassmen somewhat natural. I didn't resent the demands on my time as a pledge because the learning bug had not yet bitten. I was smitten with the intellectual life and enjoyed being around intellects, but it had not become a way of life in terms of "walking the talk," putting in the "sweat equity," doing the reading that would eventually take over my eastern N.C. root system. So, with the fraternity as my salient group, here was my profile entering the fateful summer of 1961:

Traits: N=E+O++A=C-
Abilities: Auditory/Musical, Intrapersonal, Verbal/Linguistic, Math/Logical *(Notice that Interpersonal has dropped off the radar—I felt like a leader and organizer in high school, but it turns out I was a big fish in a small pond; at Davidson I abandoned my interest in leadership and began the slow process of moving towards being a professional. It seemed that I had Interpersonal talent in high school, but the college years put that in sharper perspective—I paled in comparison to the Interpersonal genii who would one day populate the workplace.)*
Values: *Intellectual, Aesthetic, Justice (Service and Spiritual took a back seat to Justice and Intellectual—this was the era of school integration and lunch counter demonstrations.)*
*Physical Charac*teristics: glasses, fragile feet, motion sickness
Memories: Cub Scouts, boy soprano, Daddy's store, Camp Greenwood, Camp Morehead, Camp Caroline, Chi Rho, marching band (yuck), concert band (yum), Boy Scout camporees and camps, prepping for state music contest, making out in the back seat, science fair, Order of the Arrow ordeal, Report to the Governor, orchestral playing, DuPont science demonstrations, "Frank and Earnest" shenanigans, chamber music in the mountains, peanut butter sandwich in Sweden, enclosed with the Verdi *Requiem*, evening musical soirees at home, shot put and Brahms at Phillips Andover, being labeled "provincial," chamber music with the Daggy girls, babysitting the Smith kids, playing recorders with three college professors, mealtime at the ATΩ house, playing bridge in the (empty) dorm on weekends *(Davidson was a "suitcase" school, with mass exodus that flooded regional girls' colleges on the weekends)*
Role Models: Mother, Brad Thomson, Dale Higbee, Dr. McGavock (math prof), Max Polley, Shaw and Nancy Smith *(notice that the high school role models have now been replaced—not gone, just now in the background; out of sight, but not entirely out of mind)*

Chapter 7: Double Whammy: Wes Tilley and Transylvania II

I drove back to Kinston for the summer of 1961, ready to rest after two grueling years of college. First on my agenda was home cooking, then off for a spin with Mike Mitchell and a couple of girls with whom we could continue our "Frank and Earnest" routine. But our reunion turned serious. Mike was concerned that I was staying too close to home, that I was still too provincial in my outlook, that I had not seen enough of the world. He threw down the gauntlet, challenging me to risk abandoning my innocence by joining him for the summer at Transylvania College in Lexington, Kentucky. TC was a flag-ship college sponsored by our church, the Disciples of Christ, so he and I felt that mother would view my request to spend the summer there as further preparation for the ministry. Well....

She bit. Off we drove to the land of blue grass. During the trip, Mike and I planned the strategy for an all-out frontal attack on my provincialism:

- I had never held a job—I would look for a job doing hard manual labor just to see what it felt like. (I ended up washing dishes at the YWCA cafeteria in Lexington.)
- I had never taken even a sip of alcohol (although it was legal for my age at that time)—Mike would arrange for a keg party with some of his classmates. (My first encounter with beer resulted in, well....)
- I had never studied just for the sake of studying, in and of itself, but always for grades—I would audit three courses taught by the prominent Austrian psychologist, Dr. Hans Hahn, known for his experimental work on empathy. (I sat in on his classes in child psychology, abnormal psychology, and experimental psychology, doing wide reading related to the classes but taking no tests and writing no papers.)
- I had never kissed a girl without first feeling I was "in love" and was "going steady" with her—Mike would set me up with a girl at the aforementioned keg party. 'Twas a brief encounter but surely a revelation.
- I had always belonged to the same church—I would attempt to join a very different kind of church just to see what it felt like. (I joined St. Paul's Episcopal Church in Lexington, telling them, at the time in earnest, that I planned to become a priest.)
- I had never smoked—I would try cigarettes, cigars, maybe even a pipe, just to see what it was like. (I ended up a sporadic smoker for about the next 20 years—Luckies, Winstons, the occasional ci-gar, and several pipes [with, of course, Heine's Blend, in honor of Dr. Polley].)

The result of all of my summer experiments was a kind of empty feeling. All of the prohibitions of my youth, all of the warnings of the evils of the ways of the world, proved to be groundless. I felt no different having worked for pay, having joined another church, having "sinned" in my own eyes. It seemed to be mostly my mother's judgment I was trying to avoid, not God's (as I had perceived). Thus, I stopped capitalizing "god," demoting him to an element of my past/youth. I realized that my chosen career had evaporated. Not only that, I came to the realization that the basis of my moral behavior for 19 years had vanished underfoot. The swarm of life questions which flooded my mind gave me a new reason to study, to learn. I began to read everything I could get my hands on that purported to establish bases of moral behavior. This was scary. I was worried/confused as to whom I would become. I wrote my Davidson girlfriend, who was fully planning to be this preacher's wife, and broke off the relationship, telling her that I was a different person now, and that I did not feel it right to continue our relationship, that she was free to find another pre-min. I said it not lightly, but in despair. My level of N rose for the moment.

Returning home briefly before starting my junior year, I tried to be honest with my mother, but I still hid some truths/realities/actions from her. I still feared her scorn, her pouting disappointment at my behavior. It would be several more years before I could be honest with her about my lost faith. At school, I researched my moral questions and search for meaning with books and philosophy courses. Several years later, I finally discovered a book that, for me, provided some answers. In short, my life since the summer of 1961 had become a search for meaning, and my appetite for Learning only increased. No more easy answers. This lonely quest firmly entrenched me at the mid A level. I no longer lived in dorms, preferring the solitude and quiet of living in rooms off-campus. I would emerge for classes, for male chorus, for the Higbee consort, for meals, then back to reading—that year I spent much of my time as E- (Introvert). That junior year, I had a course in Literary Criticism with Dr. Wes Tilley, a new hero. One night at his home, while entertaining a group of students, Dr. Tilley described what had happened to him as an undergraduate at the University of Chicago. The first semester, he completed all course requirements and sent his parents a report card with all A's. Then, he made up his mind that he loathed sticking to the course syllabus and wanted to try an experiment. He would read the first assignment of each course, but then he would follow his nose, letting the current text suggest the next one. Read *Hamlet*, then read a history of Denmark, then read the works of Kierkegaard, and so on, with the content of today's book providing clues for follow-ons. He read at least a book a day for the next 3.5 years and ended up Phi Beta Kappa. That became my ideal: a life of learning, in which the content of today's reading entails tomorrow's. This very morning, I read Gladwell's *Outliers* and learned of Annette Lareau's recent book *Unequal Childhoods*—it will be next on my list!

Desperate to find a basis for meaning and right behavior, I not only read, I searched out other resources. Princeton University's chaplain (I recall his name as Dr. Wayne Buttress) spoke at the college Vespers service (which we were required to attend) one night, and what he said made sense to me. He was holding a Q and A in the college union afterwards, and sensing the importance of his presence, I scurried to the union, consciously choosing not to attend a fraternity meeting that was scheduled for immediately after Vespers. The next day, I was slapped with a $100 fine for the unexcused absence. There was no way I could justify spending my parents' money on such a fine. So, I informed the fraternity that I was going "inactive," that I was quitting. It turned out that several of my friends went inactive also around the same time, and so we formed a new peer group, heading up the road to the Anchor Grill for a few laughs and heady discussions. This group, including Dick, Walt, Bill, and David, remained my salient peer group through graduation. We were renegades of a sort, finding comfort together in the way of A. E. Housman, who suggested that "Malt does more than Milton can to justify God's ways to man."

Mapping Out the Big Five Traits

This is the profile with which I emerged from undergraduate school, to join the Army:

Traits: N=E=O++A=C- (*the extravert in me made room for the introvert to cohabit on an equal basis*)
Abilities: Auditory/Musical, Intrapersonal, Verbal/Linguistic, Math/Logical *(Intrapersonal is maturing with my intense search for meaning.)*
Values: Aesthetic, Justice, Learning *(Intellectual replaced with Learning, from appearance to hard reality)*
*Physical Charac*teristics: glasses, fragile feet, motion sickness
Memories: Cub Scouts, boy soprano, Daddy's store, Camp Greenwood, Camp Morehead, Camp Caroline, Chi Rho, marching band (yuck), concert band (yum), Boy Scout camporees and camps, prepping for state music contest, making out in the back seat, science fair, Order of the Arrow ordeal, Report to the Governor, orchestral playing, DuPont science demonstrations, "Frank and Earnest" shenanigans, chamber music in the mountains, peanut butter sandwich in Sweden, enclosed with the Verdi *Requiem*, evening musical soirees at home, shot put and Brahms at Phillips Andover, being labeled "provincial," chamber music with the Daggy girls, babysitting the Smith kids, playing recorders with three college professors, mealtime at the ATΩ house, playing bridge in the (empty) dorm on weekends, (many) evenings at the Anchor Grill, Sunday evenings with Dr. Tilley, varieties of experience at Transylvania College
Role Models: Mother, Brad Thomson, Dale Higbee, Dr. McGavock (math prof), Max Polley, Shaw and Nancy Smith, Wes Tilley, Earl MacCormac (logic prof)

Chapter 8: Enough School, Let's Experience the World

With my spiritual crisis and ensuing search for meaning, course grades took a back seat in my priorities, likely due to my N=C-. A calmer, more disciplined nature would likely have taken the loss of faith in stride and pumped out decent grades. However, my focus on meaning caught me a few hours short of a bachelor's degree. Being tired of school, I decided to join the Army, get married, and see a little of the world, in that order. By taking six weeks of official leave after Basic Training and Advanced Training, I was able to return to Davidson as a Military Intelligence Specialist. That was enough to get the hours necessary to graduate. Finally, weeks before my 22nd birthday, I had finished my degree, was engaged to marry, and was preparing for two years in Germany with Uncle Sam. The first year in the Army solidified my love of chamber music and libraries, as I spent much time in Enoch Pratt Free Library in Baltimore and further explored the baroque chamber music repertoire with local musicians. This was a year of getting comfortable with the personality I had become. My O++ got cut down to size, as the humdrum demands of military life forced my practical, everyday, maintenance side to sprout wings and develop. My Verbal/Linguist abilities got a boost at U.S. Army Intelligence School (at Fort Holabird, near Baltimore) by their expectation that I learn how to 1) type efficiently, 2) write clear, objective reports, and 3) conduct effective interviews. Three decisions along the way were significant: I was offered a chance to go to Army Language School in Monterrey, California, to become proficient in the foreign language of my choice. Being tired of school at that point, I declined. In some ways, I regret that decision, for I have never developed real fluency in a foreign language. Had I been lower N, higher C, I likely would have accepted the offer. I also was offered a paying job in Baltimore singing alto, yes, that's right, alto—sung in falsetto voice, in St. Paul's Episcopal Church in Baltimore. None of their altos could read music at the time, and the choir director just wanted me to help them make entrances and get through difficult passages. I declined. I also tried out for the U.S. Army Band and Chorus and was offered a position singing bass (at last!). Had I accepted that offer, I would only have had to "work" for a few hours a week and would have been able to finish my master's degree while in the Army. However, an officer at Fort Holabird sort of shamed me into declining the offer, urging me to use my final two years to see something of the world. I declined the chorus and spent the two years in Bavaria, southern Germany, instead.

During this last year of adolescence/first year of adulthood, I don't feel like I really had a peer group. I was moving around from one base to a campus to another base and so forth. I was rootless geographically and socially, but feeling stronger with the person I had become. In Chapter 4 of this book (as opposed to Chapter 4 of this Case Study!), we presented the Commitment/Exploration model of identify formation (refer to Table 4.1). We made the point that a person can be in different parts of the model in different areas of their life. This was true for me. In the area of my private life, I was in "Moratorium"—a high commitment with low exploration in terms of seeing myself as a chamber musician. This has remained true through today. But in my spiritual side, I was clearly in "Diffusion"—high exploration with low commitment to any one source of meaning in my life. I would not reach "Achieved" until my 27th year, 1968, the summer I taught in the N.C. Governor's School and studied F. S. C. Northrop. No new role models for my 22nd year. No real peer groups. A year of consolidation.

Here's where I was at the end of adolescence:

Traits: N=E=O+A=C- *(My excessively high O was now cut down a notch, primarily as the result of military life.)*
Abilities: Auditory/Musical, Intrapersonal, Verbal/Linguistic, Math/Logical *(The Intelligence Corps would emphasize the development of my Verbal/Linguistic Ability.)*
Values: Aesthetic, Justice, Learning *(Read all I could get my hands on, from Dostoevsky to Camus.)*
*Physical Charac*teristics: glasses, fragile feet, motion sickness
Memories: Cub Scouts, boy soprano, Daddy's store, Camp Greenwood, Camp Morehead, Camp Caroline, Chi Rho, marching band (yuck), concert band (yum), Boy Scout camporees and camps, prepping for state music contest, making out in the back seat, science fair, Order of the Arrow ordeal, Report to the Governor, orchestral playing, DuPont science demonstrations, "Frank and Earnest" shenanigans, chamber music in the mountains, peanut butter sandwich in Sweden, enclosed with the Verdi *Requiem*, evening musical soirees at home, shot put and Brahms at Phillips Andover, being labeled "provincial," chamber music with the Daggy girls, babysitting the Smith kids, playing recorders with three college professors, mealtime at the ATΩ house, playing bridge in the (empty) dorm on weekends, (many) evenings at the Anchor Grill, Sunday evenings with Dr. Tilley, varieties of experience at Transylvania College, Basic Training, nights in Baltimore
Role Models: Mother, Brad Thomson, Dale Higbee, Dr. McGavock (math prof), Max Polley, Shaw and Nancy Smith, Wes Tilley, Earl MacCormac (logic prof)

Epilogue: Settling in for a Lifetime

At age 22, I had two areas of unfinished business: career and the meaning of life. I was blindly following the career path of becoming an English teacher. First, I wanted to be a professor, but then I decided that I wasn't the Ivory Tower type; so I decided to get my doctorate in English education and become a trainer of high school English teachers. The education department was my first introduction to research, and my advisor suggested that I take all of the statistics and research courses, for that would make me more marketable. I did, and that proved excellent advice, as it formed the basis of my current and forever career: psychological research.

I did not achieve peace spiritually until reading F. S. C. Northrop and the life of Leo Tolstoy in 1968. Through some integration of their writings, I came up with the notion that life in its purest, unadulterated form was the right of every person. Anything that maximized the quality of life in its purest form was good, and anything that detracted from life in its purest form was evil. I then had an answer to my question of how a person could be ethical and not theological. Armed, I engaged life. This Intrapersonal struggle had left me a very serious person, even to this day I get the advice to lighten up. In my late 20s, I learned to enjoy mystery novels, at first because I thought they were good for me (i.e., they would help me lighten up), but now because I really like them. While not any more a theological person, I consider myself a good Presbyterian and an active member of the choir at our neighborhood church. Being steeped in church music as a child and teen, I just can't close that door. I go to church for the music—that is my "higher power." My form of religious experience is to render Bach, or Lauridsen, or Biebl, or Byrd with others, all trying to sound as one.

I trust that this case study has illustrated how everything works together to form the person and their identity: traits, abilities, physical characteristics, values, memories, and their interaction with other people and the environment in which we find ourselves. For the remainder of this book, we will examine how the Big Five influences our behavior in the many environments we find ourselves inhabiting: school, home, community, and beyond. First, we will look at traits in school.

Part Three

Traits in School

Traits in School

12

The Big Five and Natural Learning Strategies

How Each Trait Behaves in a Learning Situation

> "The teacher's task is not to talk, but to prepare and arrange a series of motives for cultural activity in a special environment made for the child."
>
> —Maria Montessori, *The Absorbent Mind*

Guide to This Chapter:

- Learning Strategies and the Big Five
- How N (Need for Stability) Expresses Itself in a Learning Situation
- How E (Extraversion) Expresses Itself in a Learning Situation
- How O (Originality) Expresses Itself in a Learning Situation
- How A (Accommodation) Expresses Itself in a Learning Situation
- How C (Consolidation) Expresses Itself in a Learning Situation

The sculptor Michelangelo spoke of "discovering" the implicit shape contained within a block of marble, then chipping away until it was finally revealed. In much the same manner, the educator (trainer, teacher, coach) must discover a learner's unique set of preferred behaviors that relate to the task of learning. While it is true that you can just set out to teach someone any old way you wish, if you take the time to identify a learner's natural tendencies, the learner (as well as the teacher) will experi-

Traits in School

N	E	O	A	C
Need for Stability	**Extraversion**	**Originality**	**Accommodation**	**Consolidation**
N+ Reactive	E+ Extraverted	O+ Explorer	A+ Adapter	C+ Focused
N= Responsive	E= Ambiverted	O= Moderate	A= Negotiator	C= Balanced
N- Resilient	E- Introverted	O- Preserver	A- Challenger	C- Flexible
N1: Worry	**E1: Approach Level**	**O1: Imagination**	**A1: Service**	**C1:Thoroughness**
N2: Temper	**E2: Group Orientation**	**O2: Range of Interests**	**A2: Compliance**	**C2: Structure**
N3: Outlook	**E3: Pace**	**O3: Innovation**	**A3: Humility**	**C3: Ambition**
N4: Coping Level	**E4: Leadership**	**O4: Zoom Scale**	**A4: Speak Out Level**	**C4: Concentration**
	E5: Trust			**C5: Methodicalness**
	E6: Tact			

ence less stress, will exhibit less resistance, will typically require less time, and will retain the learning longer. Learning is an active process in which learners must take information from the outside and make it a part of themselves, internalizing the information. And, just like work, when the learning process builds on their natural behaviors, things go more swimmingly.

Each level of the Big Five traits contains behaviors that are helpful for learning. In the next chapter, we will describe learning "styles." Learning styles are combinations of traits expressing themselves in a learning situation. In this chapter, we only focus on the learning strategies associated with each specific Big Five trait. Whether we are learning how to strengthen a skill or a body of knowledge—referred to in the business world as "development"—or how to offset the effect of our limitations—known as "compensation"[1]—our appropriate learning style must be engaged in order to learn effectively.

Learning Strategies and the Big Five

Each of the Big Five personality dimensions has implications for how we learn best. The remainder of this chapter spells out the ways in which the natural behaviors associated with the three areas of each trait continuum (high and very high, midrange, low and very low) express themselves in learning situations. Whether you're a teacher, a coach, a counselor, a curriculum specialist, an administrator, a designer of learning materials and programs, or an individual learner who wants to be more effective, these strategies will be of interest to you. In order to form an ILP (Individual Learning Plan) for a specific individual, you'll need to know his or her Big Five scores. If they aren't available, you can estimate them by referring to Appendix A or by reviewing the range descriptions for the three ranges of the scales in Chapters 5-9. In either case, this would be a "guesstimate" of their actual levels for each of the Big Five. You would be well served to administer the full SchoolPlace Big Five Profile™ so that your planning is based on the most accurate information and more comprehensive scoring algorithms.

In addition to forming ILPs for individuals (including yourself!), you may also need to form GLPs, or Group Learning Plans. For example, say that you're preparing two learning modules for two

[1] See the Introduction for a discussion of the relation between development and compensation as a part of Human Resource Optimization (HRO).

different, but homogeneous groups of students. Because each group is behaviorally homogeneous, it is likely that most, if not all, members of the group would respond favorably to the same set of learning strategies. For example, one group might be composed of athletes who are all likely to have a high activity level, while the other group might be composed of computer enthusiasts who are more seden-sedentary. Clearly, common sense tells us to use more E+ strategies for the first group and more E- strategies for the second one. Having such homogeneous groupings is clearly not the norm. However, there are quite a few special circumstances where an instructor or coach would have a relatively homogenous group that would benefit from a common strategy—e.g., cheerleaders, computer club, brass band, and service clubs.

How N (Need for Stability) Expresses Itself in a Learning Situation

The overall consideration for how N affects learning has to do with minimizing stress for higher N, while building on the ability to withstand stress for lower N. Learners who are high or very high in N (N+ or N++, with scores over 55) would benefit from these learning strategies:

- Ensure that the learning environment is free of stress for the learners. If they are bothered by something, talk it through, and get it out in the open and dealt with. If a learner has just left a stressful episode, allow him or her to engage in something physical to relieve the symptoms, such as taking a ten-minute brisk walk, doing some jumping jacks/pushups, hitting a punching bag, shooting some basketball, or pitching horseshoes. Learners who are visibly stressed have relatively little of their cerebral cortex available for learning, creating, planning, problem solving, and so forth.
- Consider having learners use a journal, either on paper or on a computer, to express what is bothering them, what they are feeling, what is on their mind. Such a "mental dump" helps to focus, to get intrusive thoughts off their minds and out of the way of effective learning.
- Typically, these learners appreciate having access to an instructional leader or facilitator.
- Be sure to process failure. For example, ask, "How will you approach this differently next time?" Minimize ways to fail so that they don't take it personally and become unmotivated. For example, simplify the task, divide it into smaller/simpler segments, provide opportunity for safe (i.e., away from prying eyes) practice.
- In the immediate environment, protect the learners from potential sources of stress such as noise, an extremely hot or cold room, deadlines, or judgmental peers.
- Because they are generally fearful of failure, many strive harder to achieve, especially those who are also higher in C. When you sense this, help them form a plan for success.
- Be liberal with genuine praise and encouragement; celebrate small wins periodically; let them know when they are on the right track.

Traits in School

- When they do something wrong, have them talk through exactly what they were thinking while doing the task, and listen carefully for errors in their approach.

The following strategies are for learners who score in the midrange of N (N=, with scores between 45 and 55):

- Generally speaking, people who score in the middle range prefer a balance of learning strategies drawn from the two extremes—for example, not too much praise and encouragement (this can become tiresome) but not too little either (they need a certain amount of praise).
- On the other hand, some people in the middle range have a need for strategies of truly moderate intensity, rather than just a balance of the extremes. For example, rather than giving effusive and frequent praise or minimal, restrained praise, try giving recognition in a moderately inflected voice—that is, don't say either "That's fantastic!" or "Ho-hum, you've excelled again," but rather "Good job."
- Rather than being constantly available or, on the other extreme, simply there when they need you, try making "rounds" with them, just passing by from time to time and occasionally asking how things are going.

These strategies would be appropriate for learners who are low or very low in N (N- or N--, with scores below 45):

- As a general rule, these learners need a minimum of leadership. Be available to them, but let them work independently as much as possible.
- Speak calmly to them; they tend to be put off by emotional or threatening appeals, especially if they are also low in A.
- These learners can handle more stress than most; so find ways to build on this. For example, let them manage activities that have time limits and deadlines, as well as activities that have small room for error, as in precision work, and also activities that normally stress others, such as making presentations in front of others.

How E (Extraversion) Expresses Itself in a Learning Situation

The guideline here is that the more extraverted one is, the more one is comfortable around lots of sensory bombardment such as the use of media, discussion groups, noisy machinery, and the like. The more introverted tend to process information better in situations characterized by low sensory stimulation (quiet, not bright/smelly). These strategies should be effective with learners who are high or very high in E (E+ or E++, with scores above 55):

- Employ learning activities that bombard the senses with colors, light, wind, smells, textures, tastes, and fragrances; emphasize physical activity.

- Employ physical rewards such as food, picnics, or sports.
- Try to match their high energy in an authentic way—for example, by following their tempo of talking and walking.
- Provide opportunities for them to exercise leadership roles. Don't assume that they want or need privacy; being in the thick of activity is the norm for them.
- Have them engage in a dyad (a relationship between two people) as a helpful way to learn to be more comfortable with solitude.
- Assign or encourage tasks that are by nature active and social, such as discussing, demonstrating, interviewing, acting, role playing, collaborating, leading, investigating, reporting, or working on a committee.

Consider these strategies for learners who are midrange in E (E=, with scores between 45 and 55):

- Generally speaking, those who score in the middle range prefer a balance of learning strategies drawn from the two extremes—for example, loud, boisterous activity followed by quiet seatwork.
- On the other hand, some people in the middle range have a need for strategies of moderate intensity, rather than just a balance of the extremes. For example, instead of just balancing large-group activity with solitary activity, try using mostly small- to medium-sized group activity. Instead of alternating between loud and quiet, employ a moderate background rumble.

Try these strategies for learners who are low or very low in E (E- or E--, with scores below 45):

- More introverted learners can function well in groups, as long as two precautions are taken. First, allow them to prepare for group discussion by making notes, getting organized, developing a plan, preparing visuals or demonstrations, making a script, preparing a written agenda or plan ahead of time, and so forth. Second, limit their discussion in groups, both full and small, to a relatively small part of the day—it will drain their energy.
- Try to match their lower activity level by talking quietly, walking or talking more slowly, and so on.
- Assign or encourage tasks that are calm and quiet by nature, such as reading, writing, drawing, organizing, keyboarding, collecting, sorting, or observing.
- Appeal to their uniqueness as a person, as more introverted individuals tend to have the sense that no one else experiences the world quite as they do. Help them identify and build on that uniqueness.

Traits in School

How O (Originality) Expresses Itself in a Learning Situation

The essence of O in a learning situation has to do with repetition (-) and novelty (+), simplicity (-) and complexity (+), practice (-) and exploration (+). For learners who are high or very high in O (O+ or O++, with scores above 55), try these strategies:

- They have a twenty-four-hour-a-day curiosity, so feel free to use diverse examples and metaphors to illustrate a concept; for instance, you can use a technical example even if the person isn't technically proficient.
- Don't expect these learners to continue with a particular kind of activity for too long: they like variety and change.
- Verbally recognize them when they persist in a particular activity for an extended period; they may become uncomfortable staying with a single experience for a long time, but their long-term success will depend on their being able to defer the need for variety on occasions when they need to deal with monotonous and repetitious details.
- Remember that their interests may be chaotic and lack integration, coordination, and a clear sense of priorities.
- Because they tend to think about and plan for the future, emphasize how their detailed work today will lay the groundwork for future courses and areas of interest.
- Take the opportunity to help them to establish priorities and get organized, or encourage them to take time out to do it for themselves. If they are lower in C, prioritizing does not come naturally; so they appreciate assistance, which needs to be refreshed periodically!
- In a team context, have them perform roles such as designer, creative writer, brainstormer, artist, interviewer, or interpreter. Appeal to their interest in theory and aesthetics.

Following are considerations for learners who are midrange in O (O=, with scores between 45 and 55):

- Generally speaking, people who score in the middle range prefer a balance of learning strategies drawn from the two extremes—for example, some exploration of new and different topics balanced with practice and development of expertise in the more familiar ones.
- On the other hand, some people in the middle range have a need for strategies of moderate intensity, rather than just a balance of the extremes. Here are some examples:
    - When introducing unfamiliar concepts or subjects, emphasize the elements that are familiar. Build on their identification with the familiar elements.
    - When planning a learning episode, provide just enough structure to help the individual get started—too much structure may bore them by failing to involve their imagination in the

planning process, while too little structure may frustrate them because of their need for a minimum level of guidance or structure.

These strategies should be effective for learners who are low or very low in O (O- or O--, with scores below 45):

- Because people who are low in O have a narrower range of interests, build on their existing interests; for example, use baseball, cars, computers, or cooking examples to explain mathematical concepts.
- They don't possess a strong curiosity, especially about unfamiliar subjects, so present them with questions and options rather than expecting them to come up with their own.
- Introduce new learning in small steps, linking each step to the next before putting a whole model together.
- Since they are so grounded in the present, help them ask "what if" questions to help them think "outside the box" and about the future.
- In a team context, encourage them to perform in such roles as counter, assembler, calculator, builder, copier, technical writer, describer, or observer. Appeal to their typical interest in financial and economic values.

How A (Accommodation) Expresses Itself in a Learning Situation

The A supertrait manifests itself in learning situations through activities that are more competitive (appeals to A-) or more cooperative (A+), more aggressive (-) or more nurturing (+), more on center stage (-) or more offstage (+). These strategies should be effective for learners who are high or very high in A (A+ or A++, with scores above 55):

- Remember that they have very little appetite for competition and prefer cooperative methods. This does not mean that they are not motivated by achievement, but rather that they typically are uncomfortable with activities that involve winners and losers. Getting elected president is for A-, while coming up with a plan to save the environment is for A+.
- In a disagreement or argument, they tend to submit, defer, or otherwise give in to the desires of others; pair them with a midrange scorer who can serve as a negotiator.
- These people tend to be more reticent than most; encourage them to develop a healthy skepticism, ask questions, and look out for their own needs in other ways.
- Emphasize what they have accomplished in and of itself, rather than whether it is better or worse than what others have done.
- Avoid too much praise of them in front of others since they tend to be more humble and often are uncomfortable when praised.

Traits in School

Following are considerations for learners who are midrange in A (A=, with scores between 45 and 55):

- Generally speaking, people scoring in the middle range prefer a balance of learning strategies drawn from the two extremes—for example, taking part in some activities that are highly competitive but also some that demand cooperation.
- On the other hand, some people in the middle range have a need for strategies of truly moderate intensity, rather than just a balance of the extremes. Here are some examples:
    - Group work where groups cooperate internally but compete with other groups; so the individual doesn't really win or lose.
    - Provide multiple kinds of awards (originality, utility, attention to detail, humor, insight, and so forth) so that everyone scores relatively well on something.
- Build on their natural inclination to favor win-win situations; so use them as negotiators and facilitators; they do less well in either arguing a singular point of view or in passively observing the debate.
- These people tend to be genuinely androgynous and don't identify with solely feminine and nurturing or masculine and aggressive roles; avoid relying on them in either a "bad-guy" role (as in a class monitor, time-keeper, or sergeant-at-arms role) or "teacher's pet" role (as in being pointed out as the best example, or spending excessive time in dialog with them).

These strategies should be effective for learners who are low or very low in A (A- or A--, with scores below 45):

- They have a heavy appetite for competition and a strong need to win; they enjoy debate, simulations, and other activities in which there are clear winners. Their ability to cooperate will increase if you precede the activity with aerobic exercise.
- They identify with traditionally "masculine" values, behaviors, and attitudes such as aggressiveness, competition, dominance, and hierarchy. Attempt to involve them in learning strategies that build positively on these values, such as debate, competitive simulation games, and evaluative activities.
- In an argument or disagreement, they tend to dominate or beat the other person down; pair them with a midrange scorer who will serve as a buffer, or negotiator, between them and others.
- Give them plenty of praise and/or recognition (verbal, written, and awards) since this will likely help them thrive.

How C (Consolidation) Expresses Itself in a Learning Situation

The C supertrait is related to the way individuals regard their goals, with higher Cs preferring to concentrate on a single goal until it is achieved, while lower Cs are fine moving back and forth between activities, whether or not they are related to specific goals. These strategies should be effective with learners who are high or very high in C (C+ or C++, with scores above 55):

- They are motivated by traditional indicators of achievement: rankings, awards, status symbols or titles, high grades or scores, breaking records, winning elections.
- They prefer to set one or more goals and to pursue them without being distracted by unrelated activities; assist them in establishing appropriate goals; otherwise, they may ferociously pursue goals that are nonproductive.
- Because of their tendencies to be highly organized and/or perfectionistic, help them to avoid getting bogged down in cleaning, straightening, polishing, proofreading, and other repetitive activities.
- They can delay their need for rewards or recognition until completion of the work; resist the temptation to specify rewards or incentives in advance, for that could stifle their imagination.
- They naturally prefer and work well with structure, rules, and guidelines. When structuring would be premature, they must be encouraged to resist their need to structure things and just examine the situation instead.
- When conducting research (whether book, Internet, interview, and so forth), insure that they do not cut short their information gathering in preference for completing the assignment. Help them pace the research phase, for they will want to push for closure in order to accomplish their goal.

Following are considerations for learners who are midrange in C (C=, with scores between 45 and 55):

- Generally speaking, people who score in the middle range prefer a balance of learning strategies drawn from the two extremes—for example, taking part in highly structured and focused activities as well as unstructured, spontaneous ones.
- On the other hand, some people in the middle range have a need for strategies of truly moderate intensity, rather than just a balance of the extremes. Here are some examples:
    - Rather than providing a complete plan or structure or none at all, try providing the bare outlines of a plan and let them fill in the details.

   - Rather than focusing on only one activity for long stretches or on pure spontaneity, try working for a moderate amount of time on one activity, then switching to a second activity, alternating between them.

These strategies should be effective for learners who are low or very low in C (C- or C--, with scores below 45):

- These people typically resist activities that require them to proceed from beginning to end without interruption; they are "parallel processors," who enjoy being involved in several processes simultaneously.
- Because they typically are not organized, provide suggestions, crutches, or other specific ways to help them organize their learning activities and work space. Pair them with a C+ in order to facilitate organization. Recognize their small victories.
- Divide their work into smaller segments in order to minimize their (and your) frustration at not getting to closure.
- To help them focus on their priority goal(s), use progress charts, a visible reminder of not only what they have accomplished, but what remains ahead, and what actually comes next.
- Practice time is critical in many learning situations, and C- (as well as O+) individuals tend to be bored with practice. For C- learners who really want to become expert at something, you will need to help them find crutches to use in supporting the many daily hours of practice required. For example, do shorter but more frequent practice sessions, spread throughout the day. Also use rewards, and provide relief from practice by mixing it up with other activities. I (Pierce) keep my alto recorder (early wood instrument similar to the flute) by my computer, so that I can practice while I'm waiting on the computer to do its thing—a classic strategy for an O+ (relieves boredom) and C- (multitasking).
- Because of their more spontaneous nature, it is not as easy to delay gratification with them. Provide small, frequent treats to encourage meeting deadlines and not procrastinating.

In summary, learning style is nothing more than building on a person's natural behaviors and values in order to help them acquire new information, skills, and concepts. Excessive reliance on an individual's weaker behaviors is stressful, and stress interferes with learning. Of the two opposite behaviors, practice and creation, our (Pierce's and Jane's) weaker is practice, our stronger, creation. To ask us to spend much time in practice is stressful; we would be more motivated and more effective in a role in which we could be more creative. We're writers, not poofreaders! (That was intentional. ☺)

Recall that this chapter has been focusing on the unique learning strategies associated with each of the Big Five Supertraits. If you were to have the long-form scores of the SchoolPlace Big Five Profile™ that include the 23 subtraits, it would be a relatively easy process to look at each of the subtrait scores and to determine the natural learning strategies associated with it. For example, more solitary assignments for E2-, more group work for E2+, and a balance of the two for E2=; similarly, more multitasking for C4-, more single-tasking for C4+, and a balance for C4=. Using this depth of analysis is helpful for the subtraits that are more extreme (i.e., below 40 or above 60), as they reveal strong preferences. On the other hand, we need to encourage all learners with extreme scores to understand the importance of their distasteful, under-preferred opposite traits. Creators need to proofread, trusters sometimes need to doubt, loners sometimes need to work with a group, and so forth.

Before we move on, let's think for a moment about the logistics of assigning trait-based strategies. Two schools of thought are relevant:

a. *Teacher-assigned groups*. This method assumes that the teacher has Big Five scores for all of the students in a class. Accordingly, assign students to activities that build on their salient traits. For example, for a history class preparing for a debate, assign students who are both higher in E and lower in A to be the actual debaters, those who are lower in E and higher in A to do the research and prepare notes for the debaters, and those who are mid E and mid A to be judges or jury.

b. *Self-selected groups*. In this method, you assume that students will select a role that feels natural to them. You can offer the same roles/strategies offered in the previous example, but simply permit self-selection. If a high A student elects to be a debater and ends up having a miserable experience because they are too timid to challenge their opponents head-on, that becomes a learning point for them in future tasks—either to self-select into less aggressive roles or to plan strategies to bolster their energy for aggression.

Whichever method you prefer, the important consideration here is to provide a balance of high and low strategies for each of the Big Five.

In the next chapter, we will expand our treatment so that we can see how blends of traits work together to form common learning "styles." To use an analogy, Chapters 5-9 are to Chapter 10, as this chapter is to the next. In each case, the first of the pair focuses on pure traits, and the second of the pair focuses on blends.

Traits in School

13

The Big Five and Learning Models

How Traits Blend to Form Styles

> "You have to develop a style that suits you and pursue it, not just develop a bag of tricks. Always be yourself."
>
> --Jimmy Stewart, 20th century American actor
>
> "Style is an easy way of saying complicated things."
>
> --Jean Cocteau, 20th century French writer

Guide to This Chapter:

- Definition of Learning Styles
- The Learner Alone with Their Own Styles: LASSI, Academic Goals, Social Modes, Task Mastery versus Performance Ability, Problem Solving Styles, Kolb
- The Learner in Groups: Cooperative Learning, Tuckman, Leadership, Johari Window

Jimmy Stewart uses the word "style" in the sense that we use it in this chapter and in this book. He sees style not just as a trick here, a trick there, a different trick today than tomorrow. Rather, style is a pattern of individual "tricks" that tend to occur together. As Jean Cocteau remarked, the word "style" is easier to use than to define. Sending chocolates to apologize for poor behavior, that is a trick; sending chocolates, offering to mow the yard, to paint the shed, to clean up one's room, to babysit kid brother this weekend, and to wash dishes for a week, now, that is style (perhaps we could call it the "getting oneself out of the doghouse" style! Or the "un-doghouse" style, for short).

Traits in School

N	E	O	A	C
Need for Stability	**Extraversion**	**Originality**	**Accommodation**	**Consolidation**
N+ Reactive	E+ Extraverted	O+ Explorer	A+ Adapter	C+ Focused
N= Responsive	E= Ambiverted	O= Moderate	A= Negotiator	C= Balanced
N- Resilient	E- Introverted	O- Preserver	A- Challenger	C- Flexible
N1: Worry	**E1: Approach Level**	**O1: Imagination**	**A1: Service**	**C1:Thoroughness**
N2: Temper	**E2: Group Orientation**	**O2: Range of Interests**	**A2: Compliance**	**C2: Structure**
N3: Outlook	**E3: Pace**	**O3: Innovation**	**A3: Humility**	**C3: Ambition**
N4: Coping Level	**E4: Leadership**	**O4: Zoom Scale**	**A4: Speak Out Level**	**C4: Concentration**
	E5: Trust			**C5: Methodicalness**
	E6: Tact			

A Caveat Regarding Learning Styles

For quite some time, educators have urged teachers to match the styles of their students as a way of "individualizing" instruction. Be concrete with a concrete student, and so forth. Although a multi-million dollar industry has emerged to support implementation of learning styles in classrooms, precious little research is available to support this practice. In a quest to find some justification for it, the journal *Psychological Science in the Public Interest* commissioned four psychologists to review the literature (Pashler, McDaniel, Rohrer, and Bjork, 2010). In essence, they set out to find proof for the "meshing" hypothesis—the notion that the teacher should match the student's style for maximum learning. In short, they found no support. Rather, they found that students learn, or fail to learn, in spite of the style used by the teacher. Moreover, they found the most powerful predictor of student performance to be, not "meshed styles," but ability: "The basic result was that the students with higher ability performed better than the students with lower ability regardless of instruction." (p. 114)

So why even include this chapter on learning styles? For this reason: There is no one right way for students to approach learning, nor one right way for teachers to teach. The point of this chapter is for all of us to appreciate individual differences, to see individual strengths and preferences, and to resist the urge to hogtie teachers into being a different person with each student. The data doesn't support that, and until such time as researchers present data in support of the "meshing" hypothesis, the message is for teachers to be themselves, incorporating what research has proven to be effective in the classroom, and also allowing students to use their natural energies in the pursuit of mastery.

Definition of Learning Styles

Merriam-Webster's Collegiate Dictionary (11th Ed.) defines style as "a distinctive...manner...of behaving" or "a particular manner...by which something is done." We think of style as a combination of strategies that tend to occur together. In this sense, taking a house gift when visiting someone for dinner is a strategy, an individual strategy, something too simple to be called a style. However, if, in addition to taking a house gift, one also offers to set the table, to help serve, to help wash dishes after dinner, and among all the helping, one also helps keep the conversation going by telling jokes, inquiring about others' recent history, and discussing world affairs, then this combination of strategies which typically occur together on the same visit would be called the "Loquacious Helper" style. OK?

In the previous chapter, we identified *strategies* associated with each of the Big Five supertraits that have to do with the ways that people with certain traits tend to learn best. However, each strategy was associated with only one trait at a time. In this chapter, we will see how combinations of traits result in identifiable *styles* of learning and teaching. First, we will explore the styles which characterize individual learning patterns regardless of whether an individual is working alone or in a group. Second, we will look at learning patterns, or styles, that characterize situations in which individuals, for whatever reason, are learning as a part of a group, or team, effort. Most of the styles that we will discuss apply equally to learners/students and teachers. For example, just as a student could be described as having an "energetic, active, exploratory learning style," a teacher could also be said to have an "energetic, active, exploratory teaching style." So, first, let's take a look at six different ways of looking at individual learning style.

The Learner Alone with Their Own Styles: LASSI, Academic Goals, Social Modes, Task versus Performance Motivation, Problem-Solving Styles, Kolb

The style of the individual learner may be described in hundreds of ways. Many different scholars have attempted to identify what they think to be the most common learning styles. Probably the most well-known model of learning styles is that developed by David Kolb. His will be one of six different models presented here. We don't pretend that these six are an exhaustive list, but rather that they represent a variety of perspectives on how learners approach the task of learning—of reaching understanding, acquiring mastery, and committing to memory. Learning by its very nature is a process of change—by acquiring new learning you are no longer the same person. And the different styles that learners use to understand, to master, and to retain, are as varied as personality itself. First we present a model of how students tend to study.

Learning and Study Strategies Inventory (LASSI)

Dr. Claire Ellen Weinstein has made lemonade from lemons. Dr. Weinstein was a Brooklyn teacher who found that her father and siblings were inefficient learners. In her efforts to teach them strategies they could use in improving their learning efficiency, she identified 10 specific study patterns that are necessary for learning. While she calls them "strategies," we think she means them in the sense that we use the word "style." In fact, the best term to describe these 10 study areas would be "competencies," a term we introduced in our Introduction. Competencies are combinations of traits, skills, and abilities.

At the University of Texas at Austin, Weinstein ultimately earned a Ph.D. based on her model of the way students study. Students who are taught in her model show remarkable improvements in high school and college course outcomes. Among the University of Texas, Austin's at-risk students who experience her model, graduation rate is 71%, compared to 55% for the student body at large (as reported in the *APA Monitor*, April 1998, p. 36). In fact, we understand that the model is so successful for at-risk students that the university is now administering it to all entering students. Her instrument, LASSI (Learning Attitude and Study Strategy Inventory), has been translated into more than 30 languages. The 177-item assessment yields a score on 10 competencies divided into three categories: skills, will, and self-regulation. The higher the score in an area, the more the student appears to be proficient in that competency. Ideally, students need to be proficient in all 10 learning competencies.

What we have done is to identify the traits that appear to support each of the 10 competencies. What this means is that, if a student has the supportive traits for a competency, and they are not doing well in that competency, then it should not be too hard for them to improve in that supported competency. However, if a student is not doing well and does not possess the supportive traits, special effort must be made to compensate for the missing traits. The learner, along with their teacher, counselor, or parent, simply needs to discuss how they can overcome the lack of natural behavior for a specific competency. After presenting all 10 strategies and the traits that support them, we will provide examples to illustrate how to plan activities, policies, or other ways to offset the lack of a trait.

Skills:

1. **Information Processing**: Using visual and verbal elaboration, reasoning from hypotheses.

   Supportive Traits: **N-E12+O12+A4-**

2. **Selecting Main Ideas**: Ability to stay focused on key points.

   Supportive Traits: **N-C1245+**

3. **Test Strategies**: Prepare appropriately, integrate diverse material.

   Supportive Traits: **N134-C145+**

Wills:

4. **Attitude**: Clarity on goals and eagerness to learn all subjects.

   Supportive Traits: **O+C+**

5. **Motivation**: Accepting responsibility for doing the specific tasks necessary for success.

   Supportive Traits: **N-C134+**

6. **Anxiety**: Able to study, take tests, and participate in class and groups without counterproductive worrying.

   Supportive Traits: **N134-A4-**

Self-Regulation:

7. **Time Management**: Managing time in order to complete test preparation.

   Supportive Traits: **C2+**

8. **Concentration**: Able to focus on the task at hand without succumbing to distractions.

   Supportive Traits: **N-E-O1-C+**

9. **Study Aids**: Willingness to use and invent study aids, from text gimmicks to study groups.

Supportive Traits: **E2+O1+A23+C15+**

10. **Self-Testing**: Taking personal responsibility for checking out one's level of understanding of the material before the test itself.

Supportive Traits: **C145+**

Let us say that a student has trouble with #7, Time Management. The critical subtrait that supports this competency is C2, Organization. Organization includes keeping things put in their place, having clear priorities, and staying focused on the most current priority. Those high in C2 find it natural to keep everything put up, to know what imminent priorities are, and to avoid being distracted and pulled away from one's current priority. Some of us just don't have this trait in sufficient quantity to help us manage our time, with the result of seldom having sufficient time for us to do the learning task properly, whether it is writing a paper; practicing a presentation or performance; reading, reviewing and reorganizing our notes; or doing memory work. Persons low in C2 who would like to stop running out of time could benefit from several compensatory strategies. As we pointed out in the Introduction, compensatory strategies are what you do when you lack the necessary supportive traits or abilities for a competency. In this case, compensatory strategies might be:

- In each class, identify a study partner who has no trouble with time management and contract with them to put you through the same schedule of study that they undergo.
- In each class, identify a study partner who has the same trouble as you and agree to create schedules together, to monitor each other, and even possibly to have a competition such that one or both could get a pizza (or whatever) from the other by "winning"—if both achieve the goal, say a particular grade, or at least completing the study protocol as agreed upon. Then come up with some kind of reward that both would enjoy.
- Ask a parent, roommate, sibling, friend, or associate to monitor your intended schedule, particularly for critical tasks.
- Establish a "study hall" for yourself, one or more periods of time in which you attempt to eliminate all distractions, and solicit your family, friends, etc. to prevent interruptions or distractions (phone calls,

etc.) during those times, i.e., ask them to be "gatekeepers." When I (Jane) was a college freshman many years ago, we had an imposed study time in all dorms for freshmen—7 until 10 p.m., Sunday through Thursday nights. During that time all freshman had to be signed out to the library or in their rooms with their doors closed. At the end of the first semester, if a freshman achieved a certain grade point average, they no longer had to participate in the imposed study time. Only one other freshman on my hall and I met the requirement.

- Find ways to isolate yourself from distractions/interruptions, whether by going to the library, or simply another location. When I (Pierce) need time to review my notes before a speech and maybe think of a couple of jokes/stories to tell, and there are too many people milling around for me to do it, I will go to the nearest bathroom, sit in a stall with the door closed, and review my notes while sitting on the otherwise unnecessary potty.

The problem of poor time management is amplified when one is also mid to high in N (Need for stability)—not only do these individuals run out of time, but their stress increases, and their efficiency and quality suffer. I (Pierce) am like this (N=C2-), and I hate the feeling of being nervous when I'm running out of time. The way I avoid this is to use "false deadlines." If a project is due on the 15th, I give myself an earlier target. I just won't let myself work up to the last minute—I get too nervous, and I don't like the feeling. Over time, I have learned to give myself false deadlines, and it is rare today that I experience the last minute jitters. My temperament hasn't changed—I'm still N=C2-, but I've changed my behavior for the most part. You can't change your genes, but you can change your jeans! (More on this relationship between genes and the environment is in Chapter 2.)

Or a student may have trouble with #6, Anxiety. It is very important to be free of intense worry when studying. A little worry is OK—Hans Selye called that "eustress," or healthy stress. But intense stress—when your heart beats faster, palms get sweaty (you know the feeling)—interferes with learning efficiency and memory storage. The traits that support freedom from anxiety are N134-A4- . The important thing here is timing. The effects of stress, that fight or flight feeling, need to be dissipated before you can study effectively. So, you need to do something *after* the stressful situation has occurred and *before* your study session. If your study session is in the evening from 7-10 pm, then get some aerobic exercise (30 minutes of elevated heart rate from jogging, bicycling, stair-stepping, brisk walking, swimming laps, and so forth) just before that. You should find that preceding study with an aerobic workout helps clear the mind from worry. If the worry begins to creep back, take a break and go for a 5-10 minute brisk walk. If you're in the middle of something (test, presentation, class discussion), try deep breathing exercises (as in yoga or natural childbirth training) or isometric exercises.

Professionals may request a sample of LASSI from H & H Publishing Company Inc. in Clearwater, Florida, by calling 800-366-4079, or by e-mailing your request to hhservice@hhpublishing.com. Or visit their web site at www.hhpublishing.com and order LASSI in the quantity desired. If you are a parent or student who would like to get a copy of the test, see your school counselor, psychologist, or other education professional to obtain a copy and to assist in administering and interpreting the results.

Academic Performance Goals

We have already presented this model in Chapter 10. If you will turn back to Figure 10.1, you can refer to the "stylebox" for academic performance goals while we do a brief recap of the model. Costa and McCrae (1992) found an interesting relationship between O (originality) and C (consolidation) that relate to the style with which one tends to formulate goals relative to completing an academic experience, whether it is a high school or a college degree. The five styles that emerge in this stylebox reflect the interplay between O and C, between the competing impulses for exploration/preservation and for discipline/spontaneity. The former is reflected in one's scope of interests, the latter in one's grades. The five styles that reflect blends of these two tendencies are:

- **Extracurricular** (O+C-): more emphasis on variety of involvement than on degree of achievement, as in average grades accompanied by sports, arts, social, club, and other activities.
- **High Honors** (O+C+): equally high emphasis on variety of involvement and on degree of achievement, usually resulting in highest honors, such as Phi Beta Kappa, Dean's List, National Honor Society, or Beta Club.
- **Getting By** (O-C-): emphasis on pursuing a narrow set of interests without particular regard to achievement levels, such as being a "lab rat," "a "computer geek," a "jock," or a "theatre groupie."
- **Subject Specialist** (O-C+): emphasis on high achievement within a narrow set of interests, as in winning the math cup/prize or the music scholarship.
- **Well-Rounded** (O=C=): moderate grades and moderate variety of activities, usually with participation in a variety of activities and respectable grades across many subjects.

Knowledge of these tendencies is not the same thing as being fated or destined to exhibit them in a particular student's academic career. It is possible, for example, that one could achieve highest honors without being C+, but it would be unusual. Highest honors require focused discipline. Sure, there is the rare case where brilliance alone can achieve without discipline, but it is uncommon. On the other hand, a student who lacks extraordinary natural discipline could, with knowledge of this relationship between discipline and achievement, increase the likelihood of achieving highest honors by submitting themselves to external forms of discipline. For example, they might join a community-based after-school study program, find an associate who would take responsibility for nudging them in the necessary paths, or select a school that is known for enforcing such discipline (such as a military school).

All of these styles can be associated with fulfilling careers. It is just that certain styles tend to be associated with particular careers. For example, "getting by" is highly unlikely to get into medical school (or most graduate schools for that matter), but the person could very likely be a promising successor to run a small family business. Keep in mind that "getting by" is based on behavioral traits, not mental abilities, and could be accompanied by a prodigious intellect, just not a disciplined one.

Traits in School

Social Modes of Learning

Costa and McCrae (1992) found another interesting relationship between the Big Five dimensions and approaches to learning, this time between N (need for stability) and E (extraversion). (This model was also introduced in Chapter 10, so turn back to Figure 10.2 for a visual guide to this brief recap.) This has to do with what we call the social mode of learning, or the way the learner tends to prefer organizing the learning experience, both with regard to the involvement of other people and with regard to the degree of spontaneity in the learning process. Those with higher N scores tend to prefer that a facilitator or teacher be in charge, while those lower in N tend to prefer learning independent of a teacher or facilitator. Those higher in E tend to be more comfortable in relatively unstructured learning situations that are characterized more by dialog and exploration (i.e., like the prototypical extraverted experience—a party), while those lower in E tend to prefer a more structured, sequential process. This results in these five social styles of learning:

- **Classroom** (N+E-): This learner is likely to be more comfortable when in a traditional classroom experience, which is a blend of being led by a teacher through a relatively sequential, orderly process.
- **Tutorial** (N+E+): This learner is likely to be more comfortable when working with a tutor who guides the learning experience, but it could lead anywhere the tutor and learner choose to go.
- **Contract Learning** (N-E-): This learner is likely to be more comfortable when working according to a contract that specifies how to accomplish the learning objective(s) step by step and then proceeding without a "teacher" (but certainly a teacher is available if needed).
- **Independent Study** (N-E+): This learner is more likely to feel comfortable when pursuing a topic of study with no initial plan provided by anyone and with no specific teacher serving as a guide (but perhaps available if needed).
- **Adaptable** (N=E=): This learner is more likely to be comfortable switching among each of the above four styles.

Task Mastery versus Performance Ability as Motivators

Nancy Cobb (2007, p. 302) and others (cf. Dweck, 2006) have written about two broad patterns of motivation with respect to the kinds of goals people take on. These two pure motivational forms are like poles of a continuum. At one end is the style called "task mastery" (Dweck calls it "growth mindset"), while at the other is one called "performance ability" (Dweck calls it "fixed mindset"). The former focuses on taking on a challenge, something that represents a stretch, something that is not a "sure bet," and doing it well. Performance-ability style focuses on committing to a goal based on the sense of what one's limits/capabilities are, i.e. a "sure bet." This is like risk taking versus playing it safe, learning something new versus riding on one's laurels. For me (Pierce), a task mastery goal would be to learn to speak a foreign language fluently, which I have never done (although I have studied four foreign languages over the years), and this would be a stretch for me. I *think* I could do it, like the little engine that could, but I don't know for sure. On the other hand, a performance ability goal for me would be to agree to play a Telemann sonata on my recorder in a public performance, but only after reviewing the sheet music to insure that the key signature is agreeable and that no tricky passages lurk therein. The task mastery kind of goal involves more interest in learning, i.e., in taking on something that not only is a new experience, but that contains some elements that do not promise easy mastery. There are many sonatas that I have never played, but agreeing to learn them would not be a "mastery" goal because they are easy for me—I have learned many just like them. On the other hand, there are sonatas out there that are very difficult, and mastering them is not a given. In fact, I am working right now, and have been for a year, on a sonata by Vivaldi that is *very* challenging, at least for me. It may take me another year or two to get to the point that I'd be willing to play it in public.

To always play it safe (the performance ability goal) has its benefit: We know that we will excel, that we will wow the audience, that we will make an A (as in electing to take a "crip" course, not to learn, but to perform/make a good grade). However, the down side of always playing it safe is that we stagnate, we do not grow, and that over time we become boring to ourselves and to others, and we provide decreasing value to those around us. There are few roles in life that do not demand some learning, some growth, from year to year. Perhaps raking leaves is such a role. The point of describing these two kinds of goal-setting approaches is to make individuals aware that it is advisable at an early age to set "mastery" goals at least in one or two areas of one's life. We might wish to play it safe and risk stagnation in many areas of our lives, but surely each of us has at least one area of our life in which we could agree to take on challenging goals. For me, exercise is important for maintaining health, but I do not care about doing more than the minimum that I know I can do and that meets my and the doctor's objectives: Walk briskly for 30 minutes at least five times a week. I'm happy to keep that a performance goal. Now, with cooking, music, research, writing...those are birds of a different feather! Bring on the stretch goals!

The Big Five traits most likely to be associated with persons who engage in mostly performance goals ("playing it safe") are N+ and O-. These individuals tend to be more easily stressed and less desirous of novelty. That is not to say that someone who is N+O- would not try mastery goals, but only that they might try fewer and would need more encouragement, support, reward in so doing.

Persons who are N-O+ have nerves of steel and an exploratory outlook, a combination that is ideally suited for the stretch goals of mastery. Those traits could be the reason that I (Jane) transitioned so easily from my undergraduate degree in education into the field of training and organizational development. I entered the field by joining a consulting firm, earned an M.B.A. while working full time, started a consulting company with Pierce, volunteered on a committee with our local chapter of the American Society for Training and Development, and became president of the chapter within six years. Of course, as a general rule, persons who are higher in C tend to set more goals than others do, but just being a natural goal-setter, a natural go-getter, does not mean that one will set stretch goals.

Traits in School

Problem-Solving Styles

Costa and McCrae (1992) identify another blend, called problem-solving styles, that relates to learning. They found that the supertraits O (originality) and C (consolidation) yield a stylebox similar to the ones we have already viewed. In Figure 13.1, you will see the stylebox for problem solving. A problem occurs when something has gone wrong, and solving it involves identifying the cause of the problem, as well as identifying a way to restore the condition to normal. The O dimension relates

Figure 13.1 **Stylebox: Problem-Solving Styles**

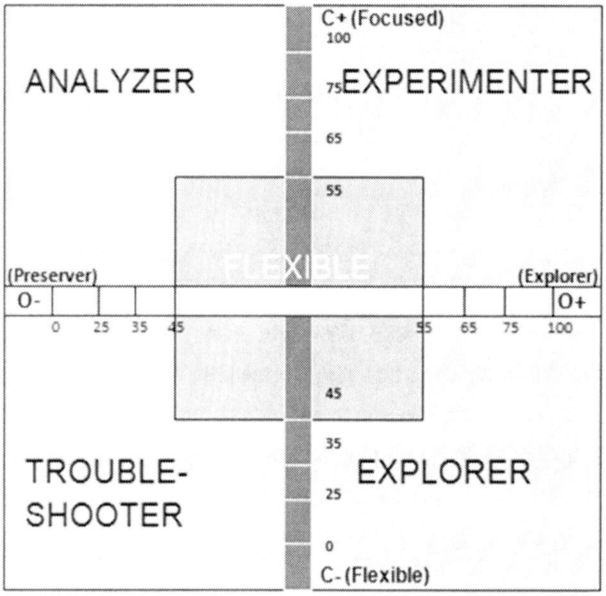

to problem solving by influencing whether a person is more likely to use common explanations and to try traditional solutions (O-), or whether they are more likely to find hitherto unfound causes and to try innovative solutions (O+). The C dimension relates to problem solving by influencing whether a person is more likely to be systematic, methodical, in their approach (C+), or whether they are more likely to use a more spontaneous, trial-and-error approach. Here are the five resulting styles:

- **Analyzer** (O-C+): Prefers to use a step-by-step method that has achieved results in the past.
- **Experimenter** (O+C+): Prefers to form hypotheses and then perhaps design a new method especially addressing the features of the current problem.
- **Troubleshooter** (O-C-): Prefers to randomly apply hunches in a trial-and-error manner and based on approaches that have worked in the past.
- **Explorer** (O+C-): Uses a trial-and-error approach similar to the Troubleshooter, but with the difference that new, unusual approaches are tried.

- **Flexible** (O=C=): Comfortable switching back and forth among the above four styles, depending on the nature of the problem and the situation.

It is helpful to know our own tendencies in approaching a problem and to compare that tendency to a partner who may be trying to solve the problem along with us. For example, if Fran is O-C+ and Ollie is O+C- and they are lab partners (or siblings, or parent and child, or student leader and faculty advisor), then, without prior consideration or planning, they are likely to approach solving a problem at cross purposes. Fran will plunge into a stepwise method that has worked before and plug along unrelenting towards a solution, while Ollie will tinker around looking for data, gathering evidence; likely he will be resistant to and contemptuous of Fran's methodology. The two need to get their heads together and see how they can create synergy, with Fran's system taking advantage of Ollie's data gathering—both are necessary but need to work in concert. Each needs to value the other and to see one's own style is often deficient by itself.

Figure 13.2 Stylebox: Kolb's Learning Styles

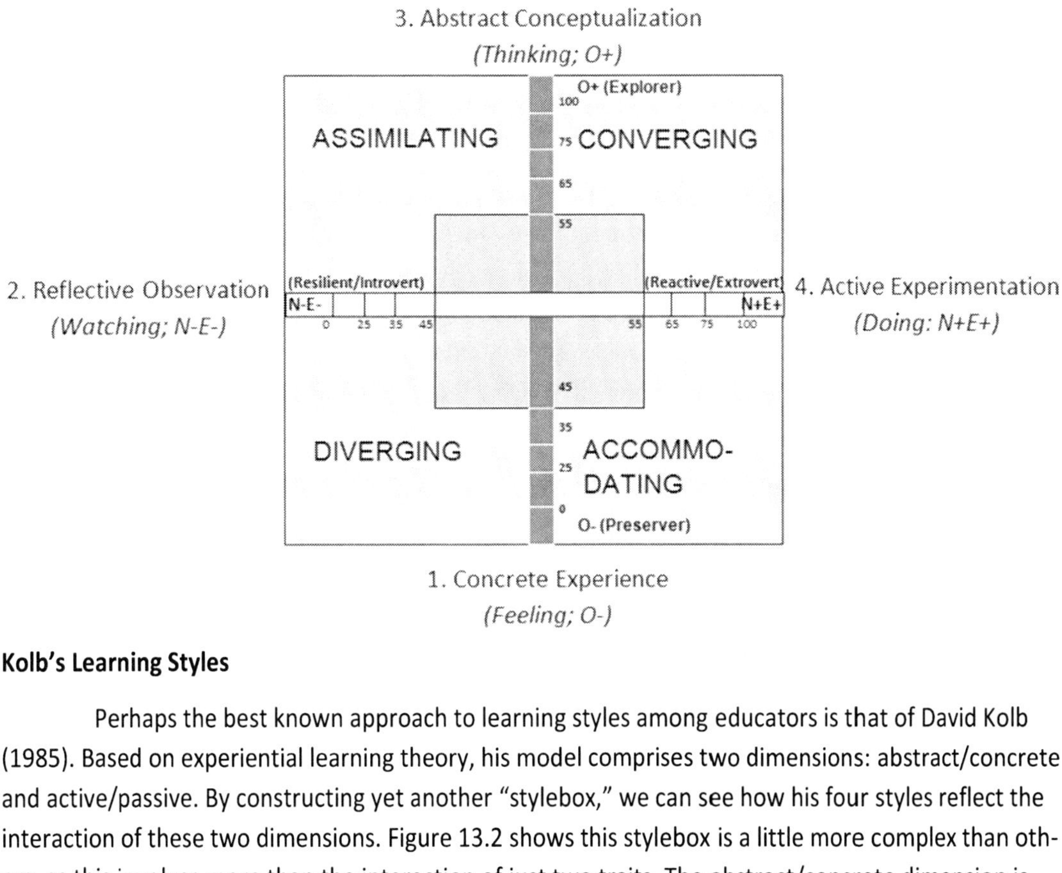

Kolb's Learning Styles

Perhaps the best known approach to learning styles among educators is that of David Kolb (1985). Based on experiential learning theory, his model comprises two dimensions: abstract/concrete and active/passive. By constructing yet another "stylebox," we can see how his four styles reflect the interaction of these two dimensions. Figure 13.2 shows this stylebox is a little more complex than others, as this involves more than the interaction of just two traits. The abstract/concrete dimension is based on the O (originality) trait, with the higher end supporting a more abstract approach to learning, and the lower end supporting a more concrete approach. The active/passive dimension is based on the blend of N (need for stability) and E (extraversion), with the active approach to learning being supported by the blend of emotional reactivity and extraversion, and the passive approach to learning being supported by the blend of calmness and introversion. The four extremes of these two dimensions form the four phases of his theory of experiential learning:

1. **Concrete Experience** (O-; also called "feeling"): All learning, all discovery, begins with pure perception, in that we immerse ourselves in data and experience of the moment, whether it is Charles Darwin observing fauna in the Galapagos Islands or it is coach Roy Williams observing miles of video recordings of the upcoming opponents for his University of North Carolina at Chapel Hill men's basketball team.
2. **Reflective Observation** (N-E-; also called "watching"): Observation is followed by the detection of patterns, as in Darwin's seeing systematic relationships between changes in physical characteristics within a species according to the physical features of their habitat, or Coach Roy's finding that the upcoming opponent's point guard has a strong tendency to look left before passing right.
3. **Abstract Conceptualization** (O+; also called "thinking"): Observation is followed then by forming a kind of hypothesis and coming up with a plan to test it, as in Darwin's looking for examples of variation in other, different species, or Coach Roy's looking at additional tapes to see if the pattern holds.
4. **Active Experimentation** (N+E+; also called "doing"): Hypothesis formation is followed by hypothesis testing and subsequent real world implementation. Here Darwin formulates his theory and writes his book, and Coach Roy formulates his game plan and executes it.

Four styles emerge from combinations of these four pure phases of the experiential learning process. Kolb describes the process of moving from phase 1/pure perception to phase 2/pure reflection as "Diverging." He describes moving from phase 2 to phase 3/pure creativity as "Assimilating." He describes moving from phase 3 to phase 4/pure experimentation as "Converging." Finally, he describes blending phase 4 (testing) and phase 1 (observing it being tested in the real world; so back to pure perception) as "Accommodating."

Each phase of the process has typical, if not unique, learning activities associated with it:

- **Concrete (O-):** Case study, reading biographies, reading stories, examining visuals, participating in various movements, using the five senses
- **Passive (N-E-):** Reading, hearing lectures, Internet and other research, proofreading, numerical analysis, drawing
- **Abstract (O+):** Theory, debate, interdisciplinary approaches, symbol systems, exposition, essays, diagrams, charts, tables, formulas, process redesign, organization design, systems thinking
- **Active (N+E+):** Physically the learner, experiments, interviews, group work, role plays

The point of Kolb's model is that each of us tends to have favorite phases of the learning cycle; yet the complete learning experience requires all four phases. We need to examine our own individual "prejudices" with respect to learning activities. Then we either accept our limitations and compensate by finding partners with complementary styles, or we suck it up and intensify our efforts at employing the styles that our traits don't naturally support. In my (Pierce) personal case, my blind spot is the "concrete" phase, as I naturally prefer the more abstract, and I must exercise great patience to allow sufficient time and effort in doing the initial data gathering and observation.

Up to this point in this chapter on learning styles, we have focused on the individual learner, whether working alone or with others. The remainder of the chapter focuses on groups charged with a learning task.

The Learner in Groups: Cooperative Learning, Tuckman, Leadership, Johari Window

By a group, we don't mean a traditional classroom of 20 and up to hundreds in a lecture hall. Rather, we mean a small group with anywhere from two to six people (it could accommodate somewhat larger groups). These small groups are sometimes referred to as cooperative learning groups, project teams, or study groups. With each of the models presented, the individual still acts singly, but always in the context of interacting with others. We want to show how a group can, and should, build on the different traits that individuals bring to it. We do not wish to dictate what roles a person should play because of their traits. Rather, we want to suggest the kinds of roles a group members would find to be most natural, based on traits. By knowing one's natural energy for particular roles, an individual may avoid unnecessary stress or inefficiency by finding opportunities to employ their strengths.

Team Roles for Cooperative Learning

Much has been written about cooperative learning (cf. Johnson, Johnson, and Holubec, 1993). Put simply, it is using the unique abilities and temperaments of individuals to create a strong group learning experience. In classic design, a cooperative learning group begins with concrete data collection and basic observation and progresses through some kind of presentation. What we have done here is to identify some of the more common roles used in these cooperative learning groups and have identified the traits that most naturally support each of these roles. When a student knows and understands which roles should come most naturally, then it becomes commonplace for such students to volunteer for the kinds of roles where they have the natural energy and are more likely to succeed. Again, we do not intend here to dictate which roles a student must or should play, but rather which roles are likely to be more comfortable, natural, and, hence, successful.

Here are eight roles found commonly in cooperative learning groups, along with the traits that naturally support them:

- ***Presentation Deliverer*** (E+A4-): This is the individual who stands up and guides the audience through a Power Point presentation, a series of charts, and other media aides; who narrates a production; or otherwise is the "up front" person.
- ***Critic/Editor*** (O+A-): This critical role (pardon the pun!) can make the difference between an ordinary presentation and a polished one. This person keeps the audience in mind and makes suggestions as to

how to shape the presentation so that it has optimal impact. Makes recommendations on what to leave out, what to change, what needs adding.

- ***Manuscript/Visual Copy Prep*** (O-C1+): This is the person who enjoys polishing the presentation until it is absolutely perfect, whether it involves paying close attention to graphic design details or checking for consistency in layout.
- ***Project Leader*** (N-E+A=C+): The leader helps set goals, lays out the steps of the plan, provides suggestions along the way, monitors the work of individuals to see if they need extra resources or assistance, holds the group to a high standard, and takes responsibility for timely completion.
- ***Proofreading*** (E-O1-C+): This individual keeps the group from being embarrassed by handing in work with misspellings, wrong words, and the like.
- ***Research*** (E-O+C-): This is the one who likes digging up facts and other material through library or Internet research, interviews, correspondence, and other data-gathering procedures.
- ***Project/Report* Design** (O+): This is the dreamer, the creative one who conceives the overall visual design concept that appeals to the audience involved.
- ***Discussion Facilitator*** (N=E=O=A=C=): This individual leads all group meetings and facilitates the discussion in such a way that each individual gets adequate "air time." Also leads the question and answer session after the final presentation is over.

Tuckman's Four Stages of Team Formation

Bruce Tuckman (1965) made his fame by identifying four stages that all groups tend to go through as they progress from day one through completion of their task. He calls them forming, storming, norming, and performing. Based on an individual's traits, one stage may be more natural than the others. And, if the entire group has a similar trait profile, then the group itself might have a tendency to get stuck in one of the four phases. One's trait infrastructure predisposes them to linger in or regress to one or more stages that are natural for them. The list below indicates which traits are associated with each stage.

- Stage One: *Forming* (N-,E+,A+). This is the initial stage in which individuals get to know each other. They swap stories, tell jokes, and generally are unconcerned about the group's actual task.
- Stage Two: *Storming* (N+,A-,C-). At some point, conflict emerges with one or more persons serving as the "conscience" of the group and challenging others to get to the task.
- Stage Three: *Norming* (N-,O+,A=). In this stage, the group gets serious about formulating its plans in order to get the job done. This is when they get analytical, do brainstorming, and establish guidelines and procedures for effective functioning.
- Stage Four: *Performing* (C+). This is the stage in which the team is engaged in producing what it has been charged to come up with.

Clearly, this is a cyclical process, and a group can jump from one stage to another. If too many of the group have the "forming" profile, they may spend too much time in "feel good" activity and avoid the task of hard work. On the other hand, if too many have the "storming" profile, they may spend all their time arguing and bickering about turf and other matters. If too many have the "norming" profile, then they may spend all their time considering possibilities (ever heard of "paralysis from analysis"?) and avoid getting the actual work done. If too many have the "performing" profile, then they may be prone to jump straight to finishing their assignment with inadequate attention paid to thinking through their plan. As Peter Drucker, the management theorist, is said to have advised, "Time spent on the front end is saved in the back." Or, time spent in planning reduces the time needed for execution. Taking too little time for planning tends to result in more errors during executing, hence more time required for doing corrective patchwork.

Leadership

In any group there must be at least one leader. The leader is the one who takes personal responsibility for identifying what needs to happen to get the job done and for insuring that it gets done. We have created an excellent, and simple, model for leadership that we call the "SEA" model. It identifies three roles that the leader performs:

- **Scan** (O+C-): The leader must insure that the entire domain is scanned so that all possible relevant information is brought to bear on the issue at hand—checking for library and Internet resources, identifying individuals who could be helpful, and generally insuring that the team is well-informed about its options.
- **Evaluate** (N-A=): Once all the relevant information has been brought to bear on the task at hand, the leader insures that the team evaluates and prioritizes the information: deciding what to leave out, determining what is missing, specifying how to arrange things, planning how to proceed, solving any problems, and so forth.
- **Act** (E+C+): The leader insures that, once all information is brought to bear, and has been evaluated, the team gets right to work doing the various tasks required to complete the team's task effectively. This is where the leader monitors, supervises, coordinates, encourages; in short, insuring that everyone does what is needed to achieve a high-quality completion.

As is plain to see, this process is cyclical, continuing to repeat itself through the life of the team. Scanning, for example, is a continual process, always checking to see if new information or resources might be available for the benefit of the team. Also, note that scanning and acting call on two opposite qualities: scanning uses C- and acting uses C+. Hence, no single leader possesses all of the natural energy for getting the job done; so they must identify other persons in the group to share certain roles with. Since I (Pierce) am low in C, for example, a high C leader could lean on me to take responsibility for the scanning function. And since I (Jane) am low in N, a high C leader might ask me to help evaluate options and prioritize next steps. Leaders need to be aware of their natural propensities, whether to scan, to evaluate, or to act—and not to over- or under-do any one of the three leadership roles. The leader needs to recognize the areas where they need to lean on others for support.

The Johari Window

This final learning style model is about personal learning, about learning about oneself in the presence of others. Two psychologists—Joe Luft and Harry Ingham (hence, the name "Joe-Harry," or "Johari," pronounced like the two first names)—set out to define the way individuals grow into maturity. They concluded that the ultimate test of maturity is that everything about an individual is known both to that individual and to those around them. In essence, no secrets, no blind spots, what you see is what you get. They developed their model into a square, or window, as illustrated in Figure 13.3.

Figure 13.3 The Johari Window

	Known To Me	Unknown To Me
Known To Others	"Public Self"	"Blind Spot"
Unknown To Others	"Hidden Agenda"	"Untapped Potential"

The goal of the Johari Window is to enlarge the "Public Self"—the area of information about ourselves that is known to everyone, ourselves included. The way to enlarge this area is by reducing the other three areas:

- The "**Blind Spot**" comprises things that others know about us that we do not know about ourselves (e.g., that we have bad breath, or are overbearing, or talk like a baby, or use bad grammar, or whatever); we reduce this area by asking for feedback from those close to us.

- The "**Hidden Agenda**" comprises things that we know about ourselves that others do not know—our private self (e.g., that we are insecure in certain situations, that we crave chocolates, that we want to be president some day); we reduce this area by self-disclosure and by sharing information about ourselves with those around us.
- The "**Untapped Potential**" comprises things that we have never tried, hence, we don't know, and others don't know, whether we could do them (e.g., could I learn a foreign language?, could I snow ski?, could I take so-and-so out on a date and feel good about it?); we reduce this area by taking appropriate risks, by trying things for the first time.

In our judgment, this is how traits relate to the four panes in the Johari Window:

- Public Self: N-,E+,A+,C-
- Blind Spot: N-,E-,A-,C+
- Hidden Agenda: N+,E-,A-,C+
- Untapped Potential: N+,E-,O-,A+,C+

In each case, the traits that we have identified are the traits that are most naturally associated with keeping, or maximizing, information in that pane of the window. For example, Untapped Potential is associated with O-, as persons low in O tend to be less curious, and so would be prone to take fewer risks, than someone higher in O. Similarly, Hidden Agenda is more likely to be characteristic of someone lower in E, who is more solitary and typically less self-disclosing. Blind Spot is associated with A- in that persons lower in A are less likely to ask for feedback, seeing themselves as more often right than wrong. The Public Self is associated especially with low C, as these folks are more spontaneous, and hence, more prone to let it all spill out.

Before leaving this chapter, we suggest that you review the various sections and make notes about the styles most natural to engage in for you or someone you have in mind. In the next chapter, we will explore a variety of behaviors that are typical of the school environment, and how they relate to traits.

Traits in School

14

The Big Five and Natural School Behavior

Common Expressions of Traits in Various Daily School Activities

> "Education is neither writing on a blank slate nor allowing the child's nobility to come into flower. Rather, education is a technology that tries to make up for what the human mind is innately bad at. Children don't have to go to school to learn to walk, talk, recognize objects, or remember the personalities of their friends, even though these tasks are much harder than reading, adding, or remembering dates in history. They do have to go to school to learn written language, arithmetic, and science, because those bodies of knowledge and skill were invented too recently for any species-wide knack for them to have evolved."
>
> –Steven Pinker, *The Blank Slate (2003, p. 222)*

Guide to This Chapter:

- The Four "Campuses"—Classroom, School, System, and Community
- Common Student Behaviors in School: Goals, Practice, Performance under Autonomous Conditions, Safety, Energy Level, Diversity

The mission of school, according to Steven Pinker, is to help us learn what we are not evolved to learn in other, more natural ways. As a natural accompaniment to the everyday rhythms of life, we have evolved to teach each other to talk, but not to teach other physics. So, we must be off to school (or for some, schooled at home). In the two previous chapters, we have looked at how individuals

Traits in School

N	E	O	A	C
Need for Stability	**Extraversion**	**Originality**	**Accommodation**	**Consolidation**
N+ Reactive	E+ Extraverted	O+ Explorer	A+ Adapter	C+ Focused
N= Responsive	E= Ambiverted	O= Moderate	A= Negotiator	C= Balanced
N- Resilient	E- Introverted	O- Preserver	A- Challenger	C- Flexible
N1: Worry	E1: Approach Level	O1: Imagination	A1: Service	C1:Thoroughness
N2: Temper	E2: Group Orientation	O2: Range of Interests	A2: Compliance	C2: Structure
N3: Outlook	E3: Pace	O3: Innovation	A3: Humility	C3: Ambition
N4: Coping Level	E4: Leadership	O4: Zoom Scale	A4: Speak Out Level	C4: Concentration
	E5: Trust			C5: Methodicalness
	E6: Tact			

approach learning based on their individual trait profiles. In this chapter, we are going to look at what the research tells us about the kinds of school environments that are associated with maximum student learning and positive development. We will begin with an overview of the four "campuses" that students experience during their school years: classroom, school building, school system, and the community at large. Each impacts student learning in its own way. To round out the chapter, we will describe common behaviors expected of students and how they relate to Big Five traits.

The Four "Campuses"

A citizen of the Bronx (a borough of New York City, as well as a county of the state of New York) is also a citizen of New York City, New York State, New England, the United States of America, North America, and of the greater planet. Just as the person is influenced by the culture and conditions of each of these frames of reference, so do Lerner and Steinberg (2004) describe (pp. 126 ff.) the typical student's school as having four frames of reference. We refer to each of these four as a campus, inasmuch as each frame of reference has its own kind of influence on an individual's education. Each of us involved in education (whether we are a student, parent, teacher, administrator, politician, or voter) needs to understand how each contributes, so that our expectations of each "campus" are clear and consistent.

The Classroom

Research shows that the *degree to which teachers perceive themselves as effective* is directly related to levels of student achievement and morale. This finding is independent of grade level or subject matter—simply being convinced of one's own effectiveness gets better results. This would appear to be a combination of the teacher sensing when they are getting results, as well as having self-confidence in one's ability to get results even before the teaching process has had a chance to work. This sense of high "self-efficacy" (as it is called by many) is more common among teachers in the elementary grades than it is among teachers of adolescents. It is also more common among teachers in wealthier communities. This suggests that we need to focus on hiring more teachers with a strong sense of their effectiveness to work in secondary education and poorer communities. The feeling of being effective is primarily cognitive and is not related to traits. In other words, the sense of being effective as a teacher is the result of perceiving meaningful results among one's pupils. It is the "Aha!" the teacher feels upon seeing a student's body language say, "I understand, I get it, what you're doing here is working."

In addition to the effectiveness of self-efficacy, research by Wayne State University classroom management theorist Jacob Kounin (1970) reveals that the *quality of "withitness"* (with-it-ness) is crucial for maintaining order in the classroom. Arguing that discipline and instruction are linked like shrubs and kudzu, the "withit" teacher knows what is going on at all times in their classroom. They accomplish this by arranging all seats to permit constant eye contact and by continually scanning for instances of behavior that needs to stop, that is counterproductive, distracting, and so forth. These "withit" teachers appear to have eyes "in the back of their head" as they nip these behaviors in the bud through cease-and-desist orders. Kounin's research found that it was the desist orders themselves that maintained order, so important for learning, and not the style or manner in which the order was given. In other words, it is the act of saying, verbally or nonverbally, "Enough, be quiet already," in a timely manner, regardless of tone of voice, choice of words, or underlying attitude, that maintains order, a major prerequisite for learning. The quality of withitness may be more natural for a teacher who is sufficiently extraverted to be comfortable taking it all in, sufficiently low in A (accommodation) to be tough when it is called for, and sufficiently low in C (consolidation) to be comfortable multitasking (focusing on both the lesson and the learners).

Along with self-efficacy and withitness, research beginning with Ned Flanders (not to be confused with the animated character of the same name on the TV program *The Simpsons*). His research at the University of Minnesota (1970) identified *verbal interaction* as a critical precursor to academic achievement. In fact, recent research by a group of Virginia researchers led by Bob Pianta identified extended, continual feedback of teachers to students as the best predictor of academic success. Student comments that are ignored or dismissed with an abrupt single word (e.g., yes, no, right, wrong, try again, etc.) simply don't have the positive effect on learning that extended teacher comments do:

> Teacher: "What does 'survival of the fittest' mean?"
>
> Student: "The ones that exercise the most will live longer."
>
> T: "So, you're saying it means that those with strong muscles live longer than others?"
>
> S: "I suppose so."
>
> T: "Well, that is certainly one possible meaning of the term, 'survival of the fittest.' What might be another meaning?"
>
> S: "Hmmm. You mean that it could mean something other than being strong?"
>
> T: "Well, there are many ways to be strong: muscular strength, intellectual strength, emotional strength, and so forth. How could these other kinds of strength relate to survival?"
>
> ...and so on

Traits in School

This kind of extended interaction between teacher and student serves both as feedback to the quality of the student's contribution and as a way to help the students begin to organize their thought processes. The benefit is not just to the student in the interaction—other students following along with the interaction also benefit. Another benefit of this kind of extended interaction is that it tends to create a safe environment that encourages students to participate without fear of being shot down. Teachers higher in O (originality) will find such extended interactions more natural, as they enjoy exploration, imagination, and complexity. Teachers who simply believe there are right and wrong answers (O-A-C+) tend to be less patient with such extended interactions and will likely have to try harder to be patient in drawing students out through paraphrasing, open-ended questions, and descriptive, thoughtful feedback.

Pianta's research group found another important set of teacher behaviors: *understanding, recognizing, and accepting a student's perspective* without trying to make them into adults or clones of oneself. There is a somewhat tricky difference between classroom behavior that is inappropriate (passing personal notes back and forth) and appropriate (being fidgety is normal for some teens). But teachers who try to have students desist in every behavior, other than eyes and hands riveted to the task at hand, not only tend to lose control but also end up with students who achieve less. Teenagers do not all exhibit attention and engagement in the same way that the teacher wishes, and the teacher needs to develop the knack of knowing when to issue desist commands and when to go with the flow. CentACS intern Emily Crowder relates that when she is listening to a lesson, she needs to be doing something with her hands. Normally that means that she is either doodling or messing with her fingernails. Although it seems like she is not listening, she says it actually helps her to stay awake better and absorb the information. Says Emily: "Often times, teachers would see this, assume I wasn't paying attention, and ask me a question to try and catch me daydreaming, but it never worked. If someone had forced me to stop, I would have just gotten frustrated with the teacher, not been able to focus as well, and would have performed worse."

Also, students achieve more when teachers are *well-organized and in control* (C+), insuring good monitoring, feedback, and structured interactions in small groups. Even though research shows that *mastery goals* (Dweck's "growth mindset") lead to higher levels of achievement over the lifespan than do performance goals (Dweck's "fixed mindset", or playing it safe, not biting off more than one can chew for the sake of always looking good),[1] both kinds of goals are more likely to be achieved by students when their teachers are well-organized and in control. On the other hand, public feedback whereby student performance is compared openly is harmful for many. Girls especially have been shown to do better in math and science when cooperation is emphasized over competition.

Another characteristic of the classroom that is associated with high achievement is a phenomenon referred to as *high versus low "flow"* (Csikszentmihalyi and Schneider, 2000, pp. 148 ff.).

---

[1] These are discussed in more depth in chapter 13, in the section "Task Mastery versus Performance Ability as Motivators."

According to this line of research, each classroom activity can be characterized as to the degree it fully engages the student so that they actively participate with their minds maximally attentive (i.e., high flow), versus the degree to which the student is passively participating and minimally attentive. Examples of high flow are tests, quizzes, group work, and individual work, while typical low flow activities include listening to lectures and watching videos or television. In general, individual work produces maximum flow (e.g., writing a paper, creating an art work, conducting a lab experiment/procedure, writing a computer program, engaging in a physical activity/sport). In each case, the student has a goal and is actively trying to reach it. Another ingredient of flow involves whether the activity matches the temperament of the learner. A low O (originality) student following a rigid procedure is more likely to be in flow than a high O student (who is more likely to get bored or to try it another way). While a high O student is more likely to be in flow trying to write a rhymed verse, a low O student less likely to be in flow (probably out of frustration with finding rhyming words).

One strategy that can be effective either in the individual classroom or in larger contexts (school-wide, community at large) is *peer tutoring* (also called peer coaching; e.g., Kleiner, Porch, and Farris, 2002). In its traditional form, older students (one or two years older) who have learned a specific skill (e.g., solving simultaneous equations) help a younger student learn that skill in a one-on-one setting. This practice has been used primarily with students who are at risk of failure and dropping out. In addition to coaching academic skills, a very effective practice has been using high-status students to coach high-risk students in, for example, techniques for resisting drugs (Lerner and Steinberg, 2004, p. 649).

The School Building(s)

Remember students wear four hats, in the sense that they learn and develop in four contexts. It is as though they suffer from multiple-personality disorder as they negotiate their way through classroom, school, system, and community—the four "campuses." The most time consuming campus is the classroom itself, as the student deals with the various expectations of four or more instructors. The second campus is the school itself—the administrative staff, support staff, custodial staff, cafeteria staff, counselors, parent-teacher organization, security staff, student government, student publications, athletic programs, arts programs, social clubs, service clubs—with each aspect of the school's program influencing the quality and quantity of learning. To the degree that the overall school program is guided by sound research and best practice, the school can have a positive influence on student development. Let's now take a look at what some of those practices are.

One of the simplest things that school administrators can do is to *provide a safe and structured environment* for learning. Lerner and Steinberg (2004, p. 645) write: "Schools with clear, fair, and consistently enforced rules tend to have low rates of student misbehavior." What constitutes "clear, fair, and consistent"? We suppose that these qualities can vary with the community that the school serves. What is clear in one context may not be clear in another. Same for what is fair. The challenge here is for the school administrator to keep their communication channels open with parents, staff, students, and peers for feedback on the clarity, fairness, and consistency of their policies. One way to do this is to administer an annual survey that asks the kinds of questions relative to positive school atmosphere. Google the phrase "school climate surveys" to see current examples; then consider adapting them to your own school. Discuss results of the survey with your school leadership team and take action where needed.

Tracking students by ability levels appears to benefit high ability students, whether the tracking involves grouping within a class, or having multiple sections of a class differentiated in their enrollment by ability level. On the other hand, lower ability students do not appear to benefit from tracking, for a variety of reasons (poorer teachers, resources, peer groups, etc). In one study (Lerner and Steinberg, 2004, p. 144), a comparison of Catholic schools (no tracking—all take the same demanding curriculum) and public schools (with tracking) showed higher levels of overall student achievement at the former, after controlling for relevant differences. The lesson here is to expose all students to a demanding curriculum, with the understanding that natural learning strategies must be kept in mind whether grouped or not, e.g., low A (accommodation) students responding better to competition as a learning strategy, and so forth (the details of this are presented in Chapter 12). Students high in C (consolidation) are likely to achieve regardless of the tracking practices—it is the lower C students who need more monitoring/supervision in order to achieve.

Extracurricular activities, those official school programs other than required classes, are associated with higher levels of achievement, higher graduation rates, and more positive self-concept, regardless of a teen's social class. Sports, while also associated with some of these positives, also carry a greater risk for substance use, mostly attributable to stress and physical-performance demands in the high pressure of interscholastic/intercollegiate sports programs. The student athletes who are moderate to high in N (need for stability) AND also lower in C (consolidation) tend to be more impulsive, lack the natural discipline to achieve competitive results, and tend instead to rely on the unnatural support of drugs and steroids. Appropriate coaching and counseling of the impulsive student athlete should be aimed at supplying both stress relief (e.g., one-on-one dialog) and structured discipline (e.g., study halls, individual study plans). Much of the research points to the value of smaller schools, where fewer candidates for extracurricular positions (including sports, drama, and the like) means a larger proportion of students can be involved.

The School District

The third campus is the school's administrative district or region and the policies that guide day-to-day operations and decisions. The tendency of students to drop in achievement from elementary to middle school is associated with moving from a single group that stays together all day long to multiple groups and classes, such that fewer strong relationships are possible both among students and between students and teacher, and teachers, now only one authority among many, experience less control. Attempts at maintaining student relationships and teacher control into middle school have been shown to minimize the typical drop in achievement from elementary to middle school. *Middle school is an ideal time for teachers to encourage increasing student self-management and decision-making/planning/problem-solving.* Interestingly, the drop in middle school classroom test scores is not paralleled by a drop in standardized achievement test scores, leading to the conclusion that the drop in class achievement is more related to teaching practices (especially socially comparative, competitive ones) than to anything having to do with student ability or even behavior. Also, elementary teachers use more mastery-type goals with students, while middle grade teachers deemphasize them, preferring easier-to-manage performance goals and their inevitable public social comparisons (i.e., seeing each other's grades). In general, what is true for middle schools as written here is also true for high schools. The lesson here is to focus system-wide on self-management and mastery goals at the middle school level.

Most school districts require teaching certificates, master's degrees, and relatively high scores on standardized teacher examinations for their teaching staff. When establishing such requirements for employment, the wise leader must ask a basic question: Do the employee selection requirements actually *predict* future performance of teachers? Robert Gordon (Center for American Progress), Thomas J. Kane (Harvard), and Douglas Staiger (Dartmouth) designed research to answer these questions (Gordon, Kane, and Staiger, 2006). They found that the *possession of a master's degree, possession of a teacher's certificate, and high scores on standardized tests of teaching ability or knowledge fail to predict success as a teacher*. Their recommendation: Design a way to hire prospective teachers for a probationary period and then look for the kinds of effective teacher behaviors identified above in the section on "The Classroom." The school system could develop ways to:

- Observe candidates who are already teaching elsewhere.
- Observe candidates in a laboratory or summer camp type of setting.
- Ask favored teacher education universities to provide evidence of new teachers' having mastered the core competencies identified above in "The Classroom."
- If pre-qualifying the teachers is not possible, then offer a probationary contract only. Then offer a combination of training in the core competencies with evaluation in the classroom setting.
- Develop trait profiles of high performing teachers and use the profile as an aid in teacher selection.

In 2007 a blue-ribbon committee (National Center on Education and the Economy, 2007) of educators and business people joined in writing *Tough Choices for Tough Times,* subtitled "the report of the new commission on the skills of the American workforce." The thrust of this extremely significant report is that work varies according to creativity and routineness. At present, the U.S. and other developed countries have been able to keep most of the creative work for themselves, while moving most of the routine work offshore. The problem, as they see it, is that our schools, from elementary through university, emphasize routineness by using traditional true/false, multiple choice, fill-in-the-blank, and essay testing as the primary methods for determining a student's grasp of a course of study. While these methods evaluate a student's retention reasonably well, they fail to test the higher-order skills of divergent and critical thinking. The blue-ribbon committee called for an equal, if not higher, *emphasis on methods of evaluation that check for a student's ability to use their knowledge gained in a course in a creative manner*, one that could possibly translate into the ability to be competitively innovative in the world of work. In addition to a factual test on the contents of *Hamlet,* have students come up with novel ways of staging the play's scenes to provide insight or entertainment in a fresh way. In addition to memorizing the periodic table of elements, have them invent new products (much like science fair projects). In addition to solving problems in Boolean algebra, have them invent their own number or logic system and create a game to teach it. In short, school systems need to direct all their educators to find ways for encouraging higher-cognitive encounters with course material, not just lower-cognitive encounters.

The school system is responsible for developing programs that can be used system-wide. One such kind of program is *"teaching for peace,"* an approach that has proved to have multiple positive effects including improved attendance, reduced bullying and fighting, and improved grades (Cobb, 2007, pp. 289 ff.). Programs that fall under this category include cooperative learning, conflict resolution training, dealing openly and constructively with controversy, mediation programs, and bullying programs (see Olweus' program in Norway).

One thing that these programs need to emphasize is that certain traits tend to be more prone to nonpeaceful behavior. Accordingly, these programs need to be prepared to help students learn how their traits help or hinder their striving to be peaceful, how they can offset the effects of certain traits, e.g., like the guy I trained to bite down on his imaginary corncob pipe when he wanted to control his temper. Traits most associated with nonpeaceful leanings are those associated with impulsiveness: higher N, higher E, lower A, and lower C.

In his book *Outliers,* Malcolm Gladwell draws attention to a little known fact: Most people think the school *performance gap between richer and poorer students* gradually increases over time. True, and not true. The pattern he reports is that richer and poorer are in a dead heat with respect to gains in school achievement from September to May, i.e., during the regular school year. It is only during the summers that the gap widens. So, when you only look at year-end numbers, over time the gap widens. The explanation is that richer kids are around books, book readers, and book advocates during the summer months, while poorer students are typically around neither books nor readers. And they typically are not encouraged as readers. Gladwell relates this to "rice cultures" in Asia that produce high-achieving students because of long school days and year-round school attendance. Gladwell describes the KIPP (Knowledge is Power Program) programs in some U.S. cities that are modeled after the hard-working rice cultures. KIPP has poorer kids going to school year round from 7:30 a.m. to 5 p.m. and later, and their achievement is excellent. Having more time in class allows taking more time to understand and solve problems, takes the pressure off, removes the necessity to be speedy, and provides better nutrition. "America doesn't have a school problem," Gladwell writes. "It has a summer vacation problem…." (p. 260)

One of the more controversial findings from the tons of school research has to do with *same sex schools*. Lerner and Steinberg (2004, p. 253) report that same sex schools have relatively little effect on boys, who show minimal improvement in academic performance and other developmental variables. Girls are another story, as they show greater achievement, espouse more ambitious aspirations, take harder courses, and avoid delinquency and gender stereotyping. They conclude that girls need two things to be delinquent: puberty and boys! Similar positive effects have been found in all-girl classes (i.e., within a mixed sex school). While not true for all girls, many of them open up more in all-girl classes and take more academic risks, with the result of higher achievement.

University of Michigan professor Richard Nisbett (2009) contributes a significant summary of the research on increasing intelligence (in his book *Intelligence and How to Get It*). He suggests several system-wide policies that could influence the overall IQ development of a school district's population:

- Class size makes a difference. Elementary and middle school students in smaller classes (15 versus 22, on average) averaged 10 points higher on achievement tests than students in larger classes. Poor and minority students showed greater gains from smaller classes than did middle-class and white students. (p. 61)
- Voucher programs and charter schools do not get significantly better results than regular public schools. (p. 72-3)
- Certification/credentialization of teachers does not impact student achievement. (p. 72-3)
- Experience does count—first-year teachers get better results in second and subsequent years. But after several years of experience, the students' benefit from increased teacher experience levels off. (p. 72-3)
- Students benefit from a policy of rewarding excellent teachers. (p. 73)
- Computer instruction in math and science gets better student results than other methods that do not incorporate computers. (p. 73)
- Cooperative Learning programs get better student results. (p.73)
- Students who go hungry show improvement in intelligence when taking food supplements. (p. 80)
- Students who were fed breast milk (with its unique fatty acids) through their ninth month of life averaged 6 points higher on standard IQ tests than those not breast fed.
- Nisbett encourages everyone interested in quality education to study and follow the reports of the U.S. Department of Education's "What Works Clearinghouse" at http://ies.ed.gov/ncee/wwc/ .

New York University education professor Diane Ravitch (2010) has prepared a summary of school system do's and don'ts, with special warnings against excessive use of choice and testing.

The Larger Community

The final "campus" is the larger community in which the student exists outside of school, during afternoons, evenings, weekends, and summer. Internships, apprenticeships, community-based youth organizations (CBYOs), community service, youth memberships in civic organizations (e.g., Junior Civitan/Rotary/Kiwanis), and other, wider-reaching programs (Boys' State, foreign student exchange, and so forth) all play a significant role. Sociologists, psychologists, and educators all report that *involvement in such community activities* positively affects youth development, academic as well as social and emotional (Cobb, 2007; Lerner & Steinberg, 2004). Just "Google" the phrase "community based youth organizations" for an introduction to not only to the myriad kinds of youth organizations, but also to governmental and private funding sources.

Common Student Behaviors in School: Diversity, Energy Level, Goals, Performance under Autonomous Conditions, Practice, Safety

Now that we have defined the contexts that students live in—that they have to deal with, let's take a look at some common school behaviors that go beyond the various learning strategies and styles described in Chapters 12 and 13.

Diversity

"Diversity" currently means "the various races" or ethnic groups for most people. However, here we use a broader meaning. The degree to which a student is comfortable with diversity refers to the student's comfort level being around students of other sexes, races, religious beliefs, first languages, sexual orientations, ability levels, income levels, physical characteristics, developmental timelines (i.e., earlier/later maturing), values, and, yes, personality traits. In other words, those who are comfortable with diversity are comfortable with all manner of individuals who differ from them in one or more ways. They are not only *comfortable* with these differences, but *curious* about differences in an accepting way. Today's students are expected to be able to work and study side by side with persons of different backgrounds. Those who are accepting and curious about differences have an advantage in being able to adapt and succeed in the many educational and career contexts that face them throughout a lifetime.

Our research suggests that the traits that most naturally support this comfort with diversity are N2- (absence of a temper), O23+ (wide range of interests and innovative), and A123+ (oriented towards being of service to others, towards avoiding conflict, and towards being somewhat modest). Students with the opposites of these qualities (N2+, quick to anger; O23-, fewer interests and a preference for the status quo; and A123-, tendency to focus on self needs, competitive, and proud) would be well-advised to understand situations in which their natural behavior would not serve them well. In other words, when they find themselves in situations in which they must work with students who are significantly different from them in one or more ways, they need to understand how their natural tendency to get angry, to reject complexity, to resist change, to look out primarily for one's own interests, to need to win, and to boast of one's achievements, might not be productive for them. They need to learn to use their opposite qualities in these situations—be calm, explore the complex before judging, consider the reasons for different approaches (and also their possible advantages), consider the other person's point of view and background, and respect the other person's need to have their way on occasion, as well as the other person's need to receive positive recognition.

Energy Level

Learning requires different kinds of energy. Energy, or activity level, might be best described as a continuum that ranges from the extremes of completely sedentary (i.e., sitting down at every opportunity) to completely up and about (i.e., standing and/or moving about at every opportunity). The best single measure of where an individual would be on this continuum is the subtrait E3 (Pace). The higher one's score, the greater the need to be up and about and the less comfortable that individual is with staying seated much of the time. To the degree that a high E3 needs to be active much of the day, it would behoove that individual to find ways to accomplish "seated" tasks (e.g., reading, computer work) in an "unseated" manner. As we mentioned in the chapter on extraversion, one option is to use a standup desk. Other options are the "treaddesk," with which you can walk/run on a treadmill while doing deskwork, as well as a stationary bike with a reading stand. Those with lower scores on E3 have the opposite issue—if they must be active for much of the day, they need to find ways to be active in a sedentary manner. For example, if a low E3 student must stand for long stretches in a laboratory situation, obtain a collapsible tall stool for support (i.e., either lean against it or actually sit on it). Of course this mode of activity becomes very important when planning for a career (or a mate, for that matter!). The less that one has to engage in nonnatural behaviors, the better. We do not try to eliminate our opposite, or less preferred behaviors, but we certainly need to find ways to minimize or offset them. We'll never take naturally to proofreading, but we can delegate whenever possible, and we can find ways to make it more pleasant (e.g., by having a proofreading partner).

Goals

J. D. H. M. Vermunt developed (1994) the ILS (Inventory of Learning Styles) in order to describe the learning styles of college and university students. What he calls learning styles is not the same thing that we have called learning styles (e.g., in Chapter 13). He writes, not so much about learning, but about the various kinds of academic goals. In other words, what are the kinds of goals that university students set for themselves? (Note: While Vermunt's research was with students in higher education, it would appear to apply to many secondary school students.)

His research yielded four distinct goal-setting styles (subsequent research identified the Big Five supertraits associated with each style—see Busato, Prins, Elshout, and Hamaker, 1999). Vermunt's styles are:

1. **Undirected**. These students do not set goals. As a consequence, they tend to have problems handling volumes of material, as it is difficult to set priorities when there are no goals to guide one's decision making. These students tend to have this profile: N++O--C- (very emotionally reactive, a strong preference for the simple and traditional, and spontaneous/multitasking).

2. **Reproduction Directed**. These students are primarily interested in achieving high grades; so they tend to reproduce information collected in class at exam time in order to score well. We have seen this style referred to as the "regurgitation" style! The associated Big Five profile is: N-E+A++C++ (calm, sociable, very adaptable, and very disciplined).

3. **Application Directed**. For these students, neither the desire for high grades nor pure love of learning provides the driving force, but rather the practical utility of a course of study: Can I make a living with it, will it contribute to solving the world's problems, does it make a difference in society? These people want to apply their learning to real-world settings. This reminds me (Pierce) of a friend in medical school who decided to go into surgery. He quipped, "If you can't cut it, you can't cure it." Yes, application directed was he! This profile is: E++O+A++C++ (very sociable, moderately innovative, highly adaptable, and highly disciplined).

4. **Meaning Directed**. These students are the inventors, the artists, the innovators, the professors, who want to find out what the material means, how it interrelates with other material, and then develop their own personal synthesis of what it means and what to do with it. Their profile tends to be: N-E+O+++C+ (calm, somewhat sociable, extremely creative and comfortable with complexity, and somewhat disciplined and ambitious).

A person does not need to score in each of the associated traits to exemplify a particular pattern of academic goal setting. Rather, the closer their profile is to that of a particular goal setting style, the more likely they are to follow it in their academic decision making. Our primary style is #4, meaning directed. I (Pierce) remember one college semester in which I ignored a professor's syllabus and started reading everything I could get my hands on about the first unit of his course, because I had found it so interesting and full of personal meaning. Our secondary style is #3, as we have a strong bias towards material that has some practical utility. We are not likely to find happiness in an ivory tower.

Performance under Autonomous Conditions

Two academic behaviors that can make the difference between minimal mastery and expert mastery are the capacities to 1) be disciplined in the absence of a disciplinarian, and 2) practice daily for hours without significant tiring. The supertrait C (consolidation) is associated with discipline, the personal temperament for resisting distractions, for being comfortable following a particular process or methodology, for adhering to perfectionistic standards, and for staying organized in the pursuit of one's goals. Those who score high on C are their own disciplinarian, their own enforcer, their own schedule keeper, their own slave driver. Those who score low on C lack the natural discipline to stay on task unless a taskmaster is at hand. When the cat's away, the mouse will play. The solution for the low C student is to find a crutch to compensate for the lack of natural energy for discipline. This is why some students go to military schools, an environment that specializes in ever-present taskmasters. This is why many athletic programs offer study halls to athletes. This is partly why boarding schools have dorm counselors, house parents, and big brother/sister programs. The cause of the problem is autonomy. It does not matter whether high C students have autonomy or control over their behavior—they will be disciplined regardless. However, low Cs tend to engage in self-defeating behavior when they are in an autonomous environment. This is why so many college freshmen drop out after a quarter, a semester, or a year. It is not because they can't do the work—it is because they cannot discipline themselves to get the work done thoroughly and in a timely manner. Low C students need crutches in order to succeed academically. Whether it is a study hall or a roommate/taskmaster with permission to nag, the low C student needs to be aware of this need and to act on it.

Practice

The second task critical to becoming an expert is practice. Hours of practice. Florida State University professor Anders Ericsson has made famous his rule of 10,000 by 20: practice something for 10,000 hours by the time you reach age 20 and you'll be an expert, world class, whether it is in sports, the arts, or computer programming. This phenomenon has recently been highlighted in Malcom Gladwell's bestseller *Outliers: The Story of Success* (2008). Such practice makes the difference between a concert pianist and a teacher of concert pianists. Well, some individuals are more naturally comfortable engaging in practice than others. The fact is that there are different kinds of traits at work in both supporting and interfering with the need for practice. Three traits are of critical importance in supporting practice: E2- (comfort being alone), O3- (comfort with repetitive activity), and C4+ (self-discipline and willingness to submit to a regimen). Practice is typically a solitary activity. One way for more extroverted learners to be comfortable with practice is to employ group practice. Of course, not all practice is solitary. Duo pianists and basketball teams must practice together. But even pianists must do their scales and basketballers, their foul shouts. And then there's the repetition—hour after hour of the same thing. That's hard on someone who is O+. They will need to figure out a way to vary their practice routine in order to avoid boredom. Do it with your eyes closed, with your ears covered, with one hand behind your back, do it backwards, start in the middle, try it at different speeds, time yourself and keep records, find a partner to compete with, try it wearing different kinds of outfits, wear silly hats.

Safety

Safety is not a universal requirement for learning. However, in the chemistry lab, on the athletic field, in the tool shop, walking down the stairs, and even in the school orchestra (unsafe playing postures can lead to lifelong injuries), safety is an important ingredient for success. The traits associated with safety are: N-E-O-A+C+. This is none other than the ultimate grown-up! If you recall, earlier we talked about N, E, and O decreasing over time; A and C increasing over time. We also talked about the comic strip character "Calvin" of *Calvin and Hobbes* being the typical child, N+E+O+A-C-. Calvin, safety-wise, is a living time bomb. Don't let him loose in the chemistry lab! Safe behavior involves being calm, not reactive; still, not active; no nonsense, not curious; compliant, not challenging; disciplined, not spontaneous. Anyone with an unsupportive trait for safety who must study/work in an environment that requires safe behavior needs to dig deep and build on their limited reserves for calmness, stillness, repetitiveness, compliance, and methodicalness.

Generally, behavior that supports safety is controlled behavior, as opposed to impulsive behavior that is out of control or on the verge of it. Unsafe behavior is walking by someone operating a band saw and slapping them on the back, conversing or texting on a cell phone while driving into a busy intersection, showing off acrobatically while chasing a fly ball on the baseball diamond, or satisfying one's curiosity in the chemistry lab about what would happen if something from one vial was added to the contents of a boiling beaker without reasonable precautions. To compensate for traits that do not support safety, the N+ must learn to take frequent breaks and to breathe deeply and regularly during a delicate procedure; the E+ must learn to zip their mouth and imagine oneself in a straight jacket; the O+ must defer curiosity until the conditions are conducive; the A- must muster what energy they have available to comply with standard procedures; and the C- must wear mental blinders and resist being distracted by other events in the vicinity.

A Final Word on the Behavior of Learning

Throughout one's lifetime, one must learn thousands, millions, trillions of facts, faces, concepts, vocabulary, skills...well, the list is endless. Each learning episode, whether brief (as in learning a vocabulary word) or extended (as in learning a new language), begins with ignorance. At the beginning of every learning episode is a feeling of anxiety, uncertainty, confusion, or dread, with some beginnings' feelings more fleeting, some more protracted. I (Pierce) may feel a slight headache coming on at having to stop and master a new statistics formula, but after I get into the learning episode, the negative feelings typically yield to the positive feelings associated with eventual mastery. Or I may put off having to master a new computer software program out of the dread of having to plow through a poorly written manual, like the time I bought a scanner and left it in the box for two months before finally setting aside time to plunge in. Chaim Potok writes about these feelings in his 1975 novel *In the Beginning*, the story is about David Lurie's coming of age in his yeshiva and New York City neighborhood between the two world wars. As the novel opens, Potok has David set the tone for us:

> "All beginnings are hard.
>
> "I can remember hearing my mother murmur those words while I lay in bed with fever. 'Children are often sick, darling. That's the way it is with children. All beginnings are hard. You'll be all right soon.'
>
> "I remember bursting into tears one evening because a passage of Bible commentary had proved too difficult for me to understand. I was about nine years old at the time. 'You want to understand everything immediately?' my father said. 'Just like that? You only began to study this commentary last week. All beginnings are hard. You have to work at the job of studying. Go over it again, and again.'
>
> "The man who later guided me in my studies would welcome me warmly into his apartment and, when we sat at his desk, say to me in his gentle voice, 'Be patient, David. The midrash says, '"All beginnings are hard.' You cannot swallow all the world at one time."'
>
> "I say it to myself today when I stand before a new class at the beginning of a school year or am about to start a new book or research paper: All beginnings are hard.... Especially a beginning that you make by yourself. That's the hardest beginning of all." (pp. 9-10)

A lifetime of learning is one beginning after another. The better we get at the behaviors of learning, the less difficult learning can become. But it will never be easy. Remember, all beginnings are hard, with some not as hard as others, and with some becoming less hard over time. What do they say, no pain, no gain? In the next chapter, we will explore some of the myths of learning: Things that people think are true about learning and schooling but which in fact are false.

15

Myths About Learning

How the Big Five Helps to Explain Some of the Myths

> *How We Know What Isn't So*
>
> --title of book by Thomas Gilovitch
>
> *The Demon-Haunted World*
>
> --title of book by Carl Sagan

Guide to This Chapter:

- What We Mean by Myths About Learning
- An Alphabetical Listing, from Accelerated Learning to Speed Reading, with Some Comments on How the Big Five Relates to Many of Them

The dictionary typically provides two principle definitions for "myth." On the one hand, a myth is a traditional story, often based on historical events, that is thought to explain something (e.g., Penelope's nightly unraveling to explain or illustrate loyalty, in this case to her husband, Ulysses). A myth also is a false belief that is maintained uncritically, especially by groups that have a special interest in perpetuating the belief (e.g., the "world is flat" society). We are interested at this point in the second kind of myth—false beliefs held uncritically. In this chapter, we will identify myths about learning, beliefs that research has determined to be without foundation. Tom Gilovitch's book cited above is all about everyday myths in this sense: things we believe that have no factual foundation, such as the belief in so-called "hot streaks" in basketball (read his book to find out why they do not exist). Carl Sagan's book cited above is also about this kind of myth, which he calls "demons," beliefs held strongly by some but which research finds baseless, such as horoscopes.

In 1984, the U.S. Army Research Institute asked the National Academy of Sciences to form a committee to evaluate "nonordinary" techniques for improving human performance. This request followed the urging of some who felt that "New Age" educational technologies that had been developed outside

Traits in School

N	E	O	A	C
Need for Stability	**Extraversion**	**Originality**	**Accommodation**	**Consolidation**
N+ Reactive	E+ Extraverted	O+ Explorer	A+ Adapter	C+ Focused
N= Responsive	E= Ambiverted	O= Moderate	A= Negotiator	C= Balanced
N- Resilient	E- Introverted	O- Preserver	A- Challenger	C- Flexible
N1: Worry	**E1: Approach Level**	**O1: Imagination**	**A1: Service**	**C1:Thoroughness**
N2: Temper	**E2: Group Orientation**	**O2: Range of Interests**	**A2: Compliance**	**C2: Structure**
N3: Outlook	**E3: Pace**	**O3: Innovation**	**A3: Humility**	**C3: Ambition**
N4: Coping Level	**E4: Leadership**	**O4: Zoom Scale**	**A4: Speak Out Level**	**C4: Concentration**
	E5: Trust			**C5: Methodicalness**
	E6: Tact			

the mainstream might have some basis for their claims of achieving high results. The defense establishment was willing to consider any technique that might provide a competitive edge in the armed services. They wanted to know, however, which beliefs had merit (i.e., evidence that they really worked) and which were myths. John Swets, a consultant from Cambridge, Massachusetts, was appointed chair of the committee, and Daniel Druckman, formerly of the consulting firm of Booz Allen Hamilton, was appointed study director. Their results were published as *Enhancing Human Performance: Issues, Theories, and Techniques* (Druckman and Swets, 1988).

During the next two years, reaction was intense and widespread. As a result, the committee reformed in 1990 to evaluate areas that had not been included in the earlier study and to address concerns raised by that study. Robert Bjork was brought in as committee chair and Druckman was retained as study director. Their findings were published as *In the Mind's Eye: Enhancing Human Performance* (Druckman and Bjork, 1991). This extensive effort directed towards separating myth from fact formed the basis of a section in my (Pierce's) book, *The Owner's Manual for the Brain* (2006, 3rd Ed.). For more on the role of the teacher and on what we know about effective learning practices, try my book!.

The list beginning in the next paragraph reflects the proceedings of these National Academy of Sciences investigative committees, plus the result of other independent investigators. We list here myths about learning—learning methodologies that have claimed positive results but haven't stood up to the scrutiny of scientific investigation.

Alphabetical List of Myths About Learning

Accelerated Learning. This much publicized approach to teaching and learning has a following of true believers. However, it appears to be more of a marketing technique than anything else. We say this because it is nothing but old, tried-and-true techniques repackaged to look like something new—a classic marketing ploy. Repackage it, and you can sell more books, curriculum material, workshops, consulting hours, and so forth. We are aware of two well-designed studies (cited in the National Academy of Science books) that took on the claims of acceleration advocates (Bush, 1986; Wagner and Tilney, 1983). They identified 11 defining elements for accelerated learning. Of these 11, only two were nontraditional and therefore "unique" to accelerated learning as a part of their approach: the use of relaxation techniques and the use of music as an accompaniment to learning drills (as in reciting verb conjugations). Their research found that comparison groups that did not use music and relaxation performed at a higher level than the music and relaxation groups. They found that the music interfered with attentional focus—it was a distraction and interfered with moving from consciousness to memory. As evidence of this finding, I (Jane) recall being a participant in a training session where music was played during a group activity. As a singer, I was very distracted and found myself more engaged in humming harmony with the music than in participating in the group activity.

In addition to finding the music counterproductive, they found that the relaxation exercises caused learners to be excessively relaxed—a moderate level of tension, or arousal, such as that provided by a small caffeine hit or some brief exercise, is required for optimal learning. No basis was found for the high claims of accelerated learning's superior results. Good accelerated learning is basically no different from good teaching, generally. Claims of 5- to 50-fold improvements were based on poor research designs. The two best studies cited earlier found that SALTT (Suggestopedia Accelerated Learning and Teaching Technique) produced 40-50% lower results than traditional methods. The other nine elements of accelerated learning were all deemed to be traditional characteristics of effective teaching already in mainstream use: advance organizers, dramatic presentation, spacing, practice, mnemonic aids, student-generated elaborations, tests, imagery, and cooperation in groups. It would be interesting to conduct a study to see if the use of music is more effective with E+ students (who like sensory bombardment), O+ students (who like variety), and/or C- students, who enjoy shifting attention. In a similar vein, it would be interesting to conduct a study on the use of relaxation techniques to see if it is more effective with N+ students (who have a higher-than-average response to stress).

Achievement Tests. A number of studies that culminated (2006) recently with the research of Robert Gordon (Center for American Progress), Thomas J. Kane (Harvard), and Douglas Staiger (Dartmouth) discredit the notion that the myriad of achievement tests used for both college admissions and teacher selection predict future success as a student or as a teacher. These tests include the Scholastic Achievement Test (SAT), the Miller Analogies Test, the Law School Admission Test (LSAT), the General Management Admission Test (GMAT), and the Graduate Record Examinations (GRE), among others. For students, these tests predict grades on lower-level courses, such as survey courses, that primarily test for lower-level cognitive skills such as memory (recall and recognition), understanding of formulas, and basic reasoning. Hence, they predict grades in the first year of college rather well, second-year college grades less well, and third/fourth year grades not at all. The same goes for graduate school: They predict first year (i.e., survey courses) grades, but not the second and subsequent years that require sophisticated synthetic, analytical, and creative ability—the higher cognitive skills. They also do not predict success in a career (e.g., publishing) as measured by salary, position, or achievement. As for teachers, these tests do not point to future success in teaching.

Altered Consciousness. The notion here is that by using either exercises or devices one can alter an individual's consciousness to improve learning rates (e.g., time required for acquisition and mastery, effectiveness of long-term memory storage). The goal is to assist the individual in attaining an optimal level of arousal for learning. While continued research on these techniques is worthy, the evidence to date is that they do not significantly enhance learning. Devices such as "Hemi-Sync" that stimulate a specific brain area apparently do not affect learning effectiveness. As pointed out earlier, relaxation techniques can adversely impact learning by reducing attention and arousal to such a degree that insufficient attention is focused on the new learning, and material fails to become established in long-term memory. Satisfactory methodologies are apparently unavailable for researching these claims. There is one exception here: Persons who are high in N may require some amount of relaxation (such as aerobic exercise) after a particularly stressful episode and before trying to learn. Excessive stress levels (that include increased blood pulse rate, perspiration, acid in the stomach, dilation of the eyes, and so forth) interfere with learning, and they should be reduced by aerobic exercise before engaging in effortful mental activity.

Asian Mathematics Superiority. Malcolm Gladwell (2008; also see Dehaene, 1997) explodes the myth that Asians are genetically superior to Westerners in mathematics ability. It has nothing to do with ability, but with language and culture. Western languages (and some Eastern) have words for numbers that do not reflect the logical structure of numbers, thereby making calculations unnecessarily cumbersome, especially mental calculations (e.g., adding numbers in your head). In many Asian languages (Chinese, Japanese, Korean), the words for numbers are substantially shorter (e.g., Chinese *qi* versus English *seven*) than their English (and German, French, Spanish, and so forth) equivalents. As a consequence, students who speak European languages average remembering 7 numbers learned in two seconds, while Chinese remember 10. In addition, Chinese words for numbers follow a consistent logical pattern, where 21 is "two-ten-one," 17 is "ten-seven," and 4,321 is "four-thousand-three-hundred-two-ten-one." With all numbers aligned consistently in this manner, not only are mental calculations easier and quicker, but written ones are as well. The performance gap becomes significant when these two features—shorter words and more logical structure—combine with what Gladwell calls the "rice paddy" culture and its support for persistence and long, hard work (i.e., longer school days and longer school years). Therefore, the gap is not due to individual ability, rather to the evolved nature of the language and the cultural norm for hard work/study. Western (and Eastern, for that matter) learners who are higher in A (more obedient) and C (focused work ethic and style) will have an edge.

Equipotentiality. This is the notion that every person has the same potential as every other person in the world. Or, as the military recruiting poster exhorted, "You can be anything you want to be." This notion is drummed into young children through such characters as Chipper Chipmunk, and it is plain false. However, in one sense it is true. I (Pierce) can be a school principal if I choose to be. In fact, I once interviewed to become one. However, I realized at the time that I didn't have the temperament for it. I am too high in N to be effective in handling the high stress load of the typical principal. I am insufficiently extraverted, preferring to spend longer stretches of time in solitary work than would be advisable for a school principle. I lack the knack for organization and methodology that is so necessary for effective administration. It would not be a natural fit for me, but I could do it. I might get ulcers or high blood pressure, but I could do it. But why do it if I lack the natural temperament? Human evolution has resulted with people who have thousands of different temperaments, each suited for different work. If everyone had the same temperament, then everyone would want to be the "principal." Imagine that! This entire book is based on the assumption that we each have different gifts, different personalities, and that our personal satisfaction is dependent on recognizing our uniqueness and finding outlets that build on our strengths.

Full Brain. Ever heard someone say, "My brain is full!" No known record exists to our knowledge of a brain that has been used to capacity: a brain that cannot remember another fact or face, a brain that cannot learn another language or skill. What is happening when one says their brain is full is that they are fatigued from learning new material. Estimates are that the typical person spends only about 15% of their awake time engaged in what is called "effortful learning"—that is, mentally engaged in something that is challenging, such as memorizing new vocabulary words (especially in a non-native language), struggling with a new vocal technique or dance step, or reading the technical manual for a new piece of software. This effortful activity—effortful in the sense that you have to try hard, you can't just coast on past learning accomplishments—is tiring. To have talent in an area makes it less tiring, but tiring nonetheless, assuming it is really effortful. The rest of our waking hours we spend in practice, or in taking what we already know and perhaps experimenting with it, as in trying slight variations with a new serving technique we have learned for our tennis game. Some have estimated that our brains have the capacity of 10,000,000 books of 1,000 pages each. We are nowhere near capacity. How about you? Dig in, dig deep! N+O- individuals are most likely to lament that they've reached their capacity, as they tend to be more stressed by the frustration that accompanies new learning, and less interested as a general rule in learning material that is noticeably different from what they have already acquired along the way. All that is required for them to continue "filling their brains" is to take a nice break from study, get some exercise, do something familiar for a time, and then get back to "effortful engagement."

Graduate Degrees. Educators, licensing agencies, government bodies, school systems, and especially universities have long maintained that teachers who possess a Master's degree make more effective teachers than those who have only a Bachelor's. What this means is that teachers who have taken more advanced courses in their subject area (e.g., English teachers who have taken such courses as Shakespeare's histories, the poetry of Wordsworth and Coleridge, and the plays of the Restoration; or, science teachers who have taken courses in optics, particle theory, and cloning techniques) and who have written a research paper (or thesis) are thought to be more effective than teachers who have taken mostly survey courses (e.g., English teachers who have taken American Literature, British Literature, World Literature in Translation, and History of the English Language; science teachers who have taken general physics, general chemistry, qualitative analysis, general biology, and history of science). As mentioned in the last chapter, this isn't so. Robert Gordon (Center for American Progress), Thomas J. Kane (Harvard), and Douglas Staiger (Dartmouth) designed research to ascertain the validity of the traditional claim that teachers with Master's degrees were better teachers (Gordon, Kane, & Staiger, 2006). They found that the *possession of a master's degree fails to predict success as a teacher*. Their recommendation: design a way to hire prospective teachers for a probationary period, and then look for the kinds of success behaviors identified in the previous chapter.

IQ is a Single Number. We have already discussed the issue of intelligence as a single, versus a multiple quality, in Chapter 3. It bears repeating here, although only briefly. People are smart at different things. There is no single number that can adequately reveal a person's mental ability. A person with an "IQ" of 120 sounds like someone who could be mentally above average at everything, but while that is occasionally the case, it is usually not the case. A person can be smart with words and inept with interpersonal skills, smart with music and inept with spatial analysis, smart with mathematics and inept with emotional acuity. To treat IQ as a single number is like treating basketball ability as a single number: to say a person was 90th percentile overall in basketball ability could mask, for example, poor speed, poor rebounding, or poor defense, while excellence in many other areas would compensate. However, if you want a rebounding specialist at a critical point in a game, you don't put someone in the game who is 90th percentile overall—you want/need someone who is very high in rebounding, forgetting the rest for the moment. Look for a person's mental strength and build on it. Forget using single numbers as estimates of mental ability. When you hear someone say, "Sam is smart," retort, "Smart at what?" For the different "kinds of smartness," review Chapter 3.

IQ is Unteachable. Intelligence has long been thought to be entirely inherited. That is no longer the case. Clearly, there are elements of mental ability that are largely inherited and relatively impervious to change, such as tone deafness and color blindness. However, as Anders Ericsson has demonstrated, practice can make more perfect (see discussion under "Practice" in Chapter 14). Malcolm Gladwell (2008) reminds us, "Working hard is what really successful people do...." (p. 239). He relates how several individuals and groups that were thought to be merely talented, in fact, got their 10,000 hours of practice in by the time they needed to enter professional status. The Beatles got their 10,000 hours of practice during gigs in Hamburg. Bill Gates got his 10,000 hours of programming in through a combination of fortunate opportunities in academic and other early computer labs. One difference on math tests globally is that cultures that teach persistence do better. Gladwell, in his book *Outliers* (2008), relates an experiment in which successful completion of a long, boring, demographic-type questionnaire was found to predict math achievement—the more missing items on the demographic survey, the lower the math achievement. Perseverance and practice are key for developing expertise. Yale University psychologist Robert Sternberg calls intelligence "mental self-management," and persistence and practice are certainly aspects of mental self-management. Such persistence comes more naturally for lower O (who are not bored so much by repetition) and higher C people (who naturally take to concentrating and being methodical). Sternberg, a specialist on intelligence, once accepted a contract that challenged him to design a program that would raise the "IQ" of Venezuela, a country that had suffered an intellectual drought under a long, malevolent dictatorship. It worked! You can find more about it both in Sternberg's writings (e.g., 1988) and by searching "Venezuela Intelligence Project" on the web. Other factors known to positively affect intelligence levels include nutrition (both during and after gestation), birth weights, adequate verbal interaction with parents/caregivers, and, of course, the opportunity to experience well-designed formal education.

Multitasking. Essentially, there is no such thing as multitasking. The mind cannot pay attention to more than one activity at one time. When a second activity is introduced, the mind's attention shifts to the second activity. To the degree that the initial activity is automatic (i.e., has the benefit of extensive practice, as in riding a bicycle), then the automatic activity may go on along with the new activity that requires attention, like reading a book while riding a stationary bike. However, should the automatic activity require attention, the mind would shift from the new activity/reading back to the previous activity. An example would be riding a bicycle down an untraveled country road, and reading something while riding, only to come upon a section of the road with potholes. Avoiding potholes is not automatic and would require attention. So, multitasking is never doing two things at once that both require full attention—at best, it is alternate-tasking, where one's attention moves back and forth between/among two or more activities. This practice increases the chance of error—riding the bike down an untraveled country road while reading or talking on a cell phone is fine, but it increases the chance that you will miss seeing the broken glass that will puncture your tire.

Ergonomics researcher Christopher Wickens, director of the University of Illinois Aviation Research Laboratory, says (see *APA Monitor,* January 1994, pp. 16 ff.) that when one must pay attention to multiple inputs or tasks, it helps if the inputs involve brain resources that are different ("noncompeting"). For example, if one must pay attention to two visual inputs, that is more difficult (and more error prone) than paying attention to one visual and one auditory input. He has identified three "dimensions"—i.e., sets of resource trade-offs common throughout a variety of workplace settings: visual vs. auditory, verbal-linguistic vs. spatial-manipulative, and response vs. perception-cognition. In each of these cases, alternating between each member of a pair (i.e., watching a child swimming while talking to a friend, talking to a friend while knitting, and driving a car while observing traffic) is safer—and easier—than alternating between two mental activities in the same mode (i.e., watching a child swimming while watching another child diving, talking to a friend while listening to the radio, driving a car while working a Rubik's cube), but just because it is easier does not mean that it is safer than focusing on a single activity (i.e., watching a child swimming, driving with no—or little—traffic, knitting).

There is a sex difference with respect to multitasking, or alternate-tasking. Male-differentiated brains find it easier to handle multitasking, such as talking while building something. The typical male brain has brain areas for these functions that interfere with each other less than they do in the typical female brain (see more about this in *The Owner's Manual for the Brain,* 3rd Ed., Section 31.4). Still, it is an illusion to think one is actually multitasking. When you are attempting to do two things at once, you increase the chance of error involving the activity that is not occupying your full attention but is on autopilot—watch a basketball game while folding laundry, and you'll either miss a good play or mismatch your socks! And don't even think about talking or texting with a cell phone while negotiating a busy intersection. The solution is to focus on one task until you reach an agreeable stopping point, and then shift to another task if you like. This is not multitasking, but alternate-tasking. If you insist on simultaneously engaging in two or more tasks, make sure only one involves full attention and/or is high risk. This is easier for C+ individuals who find it easier to focus and concentrate on one thing. It is also easier and more natural for E- individuals who prefer lower levels and fewer kinds of sensory stimulation. O+ individuals are also more tempted to multitask in order to avoid boredom. Individuals who are E+, O+, *and* C- are clearly prone to multitasking and should take special precautions to avoid serious errors. Namely, they need to identify activities that require full attention, either for safety or quality reasons, and allocate their small amount of energy for focused attention on those activities, one at a time.

Photographic (Eidetic) Memory. Research on memory has taken a significant turn in recent years. Memory used to be regarded as a structure; now it is seen as a process. A memory was thought of as a single unit with an identifiable place of residence somewhere in the brain that could be recalled when necessary. Now a memory is viewed as a reconstruction from many different chunks stored redundantly throughout the brain (see more in Pierce's chapter on memory in *The Owner's Manual for the Brain,* 2006, 3rd Ed.). This new view of memory was brought dramatically to the public's awareness after John Dean's testimony at the Watergate hearings. Viewers were initially impressed with Dean's avowed excellent memory for detail. But when his testimony was later compared with accurate records of conversations, viewers (and Dean himself) were flabbergasted to learn that most of his testimony was at best flawed and at worst made up. So, memory is not photographic. Some people have better, more reliable memories than others, depending on their body chemistry, their nutritional habits, their exercise patterns, their stress levels, their techniques for remembering, and the degree to which they practice their retrieval. Every remembrance is a rapid reconstruction of elements, some more accurate than others. The more one practices a memory (as in telling a joke, reciting a poem, singing a song, and so forth), the more consistent one's reconstruction will be. Of course, if you practice a faulty reconstruction, then you will be consistently wrong! Be humble about memory, and understand that random elements can cause retrieval to be faulty. Use a memory partner, acknowledging that two or more retrievers are better than any one. Traits have a role here, as those low in A tend to be more confident in their memory because of their intrinsic competitiveness, yet they are as likely as others to have flawed retrievals. What makes them less reliable is they are as less likely to admit errors in reconstructing a memory. Those high in O are tempted to embellish, to supply missing elements, just to make it interesting. On the other hand, O+ individuals are more likely to be adept at creating pneumonic aids because of their vivid imaginations. Those higher in E are plagued by their high degree of sensory bombardment and its associated propensity for including irrelevant elements from the myriad of sensory data surrounding the event being retrieved. A+ and C+ individuals have a memory advantage--the former try harder out of wanting to please, and the latter try harder because of their disciplined ambition.

Sex Differences. Traditionally boys have been thought to excel in math and girls in language, and that these differences were innate. Early research attempting to clarify these differences suspected that they were caused by cultural practices (e.g., not buying erector sets and Legos for girls, not buying dolls for boys) rather than heredity. More recent research has confirmed that, with the gradual elimination of cultural sex discrimination, the differences in math and language performance are disappearing (Lerner and Steinberg, 2004, p. 241). Math differences are at their greatest in grade 1 but approach parity by grade 12. Verbal ability is equal in grade 1, but girls are superior by grade 6, then the gap gets smaller around grade 12. However, the sex gap in sports favors boys throughout. Apparently society has placed a higher priority on eliminating sex biases in math and language but not in sports. As girls find their "voice" (recall Mary Belenky's [1997] observation that the traditional American girl is not encouraged to develop her own "voice," but to defer to others), these inequalities melt. The degree to which a girl has her "voice" developed is associated with her level of A (accommodation), with lower A girls having stronger opinions and demands. I (Jane) am a low A, yet I grew up in a conservative family with parents who were 38 and 45 when I was born. Throughout my youth I heard such maxims as "Don't talk back," "Pretty is as pretty does," and "Children should be seen and not heard." Around age 30, I finally found my "voice" to allow my challenger free rein, anda life partner in Pierce who could accept that voice. Interestingly, the two countries with the most legislation aimed at eliminating sex discrimination (Sweden and the U.S.) have the smallest academic performance gaps on the world scene.

Sleep and Learn. The National Science Council investigated the notion that persons can learn while asleep. For example, place an audio learning program (e.g., a CD with vocabulary, verb conjugations, and so forth) in your iPod or other playback device that you can program to start playing after you've fallen asleep. They found no evidence that this practice results in learning gains while an individual is engaged in verified sleep. There is some evidence that one can learn during light sleep, as opposed to deep sleep, but the gains are minimal compared to what one can learn after a refreshing night's sleep. Disturbing sleep raises ethical, as well as medical, issues. We know of no evidence that traits make a difference in one's ability to learn while asleep. Sleep is the time for new learning from the previous day to become established. Don't interfere with it!

Speed Reading. Back in the 1950s, the U.S. Department of the Navy studied the effectiveness of so-called speed reading programs and found that they were neither more nor less than skimming techniques. Students were trained to read topic sentences (the first and last in the paragraph), and the comprehension tests used to evaluate the training only questioned the content in these sentences. When students were tested on material that was scattered randomly throughout the reading passages, comprehension plummeted. More recently, University of Missouri at Kansas City educational psychologist Ronald Carver (1990) published a review of research on reading speed. Several findings emerged:

- The normal reading speed is 200 to 300 words per minute.
- Faster speeds involve skipping words.
- Skipping words results in decreased comprehension.

We suggest you follow these guidelines:

Traits in School

- When you are reading only to find new information on a subject you are already familiar with, then skimming (reading faster than 300 words per minute) makes sense.
- When you are reading for detailed understanding of a more unfamiliar subject, you should slow down your reading, probably below 200 words per minute.
- For most other reading, accept the typical rate of 200 to 300 words per minute.
- Don't claim to read at a thousand or more words per minute. That's not reading, according to research; it's skimming. Calling it "speed reading" is like referring to microwaving a dinner-in-a-box as "cooking." It's not; it's nuking or warming.

Speed of reading is clearly related to the Big Five traits. Those most able to focus, concentrate, not get distracted, and read in the most efficient manner possible are most likely to be N- (calm, at ease, stress resistant), E- (solitary, quiet), A+ (obedient), and/or C+ (disciplined, concentrating). The opposites of these are more likely to be inefficient readers. However, they can find ways to compensate for the trait that decreases efficiency. For example, someone who is N+ and aroused as the result of a stressful episode could first engage in some aerobic exercise, and then try reading, now that their bodies have returned from parasympathetic to sympathetic arousal. Someone who is E+ and wanting to be active could try reading while exercising on a stationary bicycle. Someone who is A- and is resisting the assignment could make a contest out of it, and see if they can read the assignment within an arbitrary time limit. Someone who is C- could try eliminating all distractions for a set period, say an hour or more, until the task is complete: no TV, no music, closed door, cell phone off. The latter instance will find that they finish their assignments more than twice as fast as when they try to read with distractions. Whether an O+ is an efficient reader depends on whether the material is different, new, complex, appealing to the imagination—otherwise, they are likely to be bored, will find their mind wandering, and will lose efficiency. They would be well advised to read in shorter spurts, taking breaks to relieve the monotony. O- readers will be more efficient when reading familiar material—if it is too different or complex, they are likely to become frustrated. Again, read in shorter spurts with frequent breaks.

Transfer of Learning. In their landmark book *Transfer on Trial*, Detterman and Sternberg (1993) explode the myth that more intelligent individuals are better at transferring new learning to remote situations. They talk about near and remote transfer (or proximal and distal transfer). The former involves learning a principle such as the proper way to prune a pear tree, and then applying the same principle to pruning an apple tree. Whether or not this transfer is appropriate, people do commonly engage in this kind of transfer. The nature of near transfer is that the contexts in which you apply the learning are extremely similar. However, the other kind of transfer, remote transfer, is the one that has been thought to be unique to the highly intelligent. Remote transfer involves applying a principle to a new situation that does not resemble the context in which one learned the principle originally. Once I (Pierce) solved a problem for a company that had baffled their experts for a year. They had taken the same problem-solving course that I had, but they had not practiced the technique since leaving the workshop in which they learned it. On the other hand, I had been teaching the technique for five years and had tried it on several dozen different kinds of problems. I had developed a deep sense of the *kind* of situations that could be solved by the technique. When I encountered this company's problem, I recognized the underlying structure of the problem and its relevance to my technique. Their experts were unable to make the remote transfer because they had not developed a feel for the kind of context in which it was appropriate. They were only able to use the technique on problems that closely resembled the original problem presented in the workshop, and no problem that they had encountered since the workshop was close enough to the original, in terms of its surface characteristics, for them to recognize the technique's applicability. Detterman and Sternberg argue that, if you want people to be able to transfer principles, formulas, concepts, and the like from one situation to another, then you have to give them extensive practice in using the learning in a wide variety of contexts. Individuals higher in O are more likely to find remote transfer interesting. On the other hand those higher in O are less likely to want to practice the same technique repeatedly, while those lower in O would be comfortable with extensive practice. Those lower in A, out of pride and/or competitiveness, could be resistant to using someone else's technique until such time as they make it their own.

Now that some of the main myths that interfere with learning have been exposed and thrown over, the next chapter will take a look at how we can use our knowledge of traits in the development of curriculum, lesson plans, and, in general, making instruction more personally meaningful.

Traits in School

16

The Big Five in Class

How Teachers, Students, and Parents Can Use the Big Five to Enliven Coursework

> "Know Thy Self"
>
> --Socrates, Shakespeare, and Na'im Akbar (African-American psychologist)

Guide to This Chapter:

- How the Big Five Relates to Curriculum
- How the Big Five Relates to Specific Programs in the Arts
- How the Big Five Relates to Specific Programs in the Sciences
- How the Big Five Relates to Specific Programs in the Vocations

Most of us have been exhorted to "know thyself" since first hearing that advice as a youth. Know one's limits, one's weaknesses, one's strengths, one's priorities, one's goals, one's values, one's loyalties. While certainly held as a core value in many cultures for eons, the priority of knowing oneself can mean so many different things that it can quickly lose its center, its compelling force. On the one hand, knowing oneself could be as trivial as knowing one has an allergy to peanuts and that peanuts are a no-no in one's diet. On the other hand, knowing oneself could be as momentous as declining a plumb appointment because one has a conflict of interest.

In this chapter, we have a special meaning for this phrase: To "Know Thyself" is to know your behavioral preferences, to know your traits, to be able to give a name to the various elements of your behavioral repertoire. To know oneself is to know that one has little energy for repetition (if one is O+), for example, and that in order to gain expertise one must find ways to practice without being depressed, distracted, or otherwise vanquished by boredom bred of one's aversion for repetitive practice. Knowing where one's energy is abundant, and where it is in short supply, is what we mean by "Know Thyself." If we know ourselves and are true to ourselves, we cannot then be false to anyone. The best

Traits in School

N	E	O	A	C
Need for Stability	**Extraversion**	**Originality**	**Accommodation**	**Consolidation**
N+ Reactive	E+ Extraverted	O+ Explorer	A+ Adapter	C+ Focused
N= Responsive	E= Ambiverted	O= Moderate	A= Negotiator	C= Balanced
N- Resilient	E- Introverted	O- Preserver	A- Challenger	C- Flexible
N1: Worry	**E1: Approach Level**	**O1: Imagination**	**A1: Service**	**C1:Thoroughness**
N2: Temper	**E2: Group Orientation**	**O2: Range of Interests**	**A2: Compliance**	**C2: Structure**
N3: Outlook	**E3: Pace**	**O3: Innovation**	**A3: Humility**	**C3: Ambition**
N4: Coping Level	**E4: Leadership**	**O4: Zoom Scale**	**A4: Speak Out Level**	**C4: Concentration**
	E5: Trust			**C5: Methodicalness**
	E6: Tact			

way to gain a sure understanding of where we stand on each of the Big Five dimensions is for it to be integrated into school curriculum. How?

How the Big Five Relates to Curriculum

For the sake of convenience, we will organize secondary school and university curricula—the courses for which they grant credit—into three clusters: the arts, the sciences, and the vocations. Every course, or program, relates to the Big Five in three ways:

1. *The Course Content Itself*. The course content, to differing degrees, contains examples of Big Five traits. To wit, in a literature class, a character in a story may be portrayed as more extraverted or more introverted, or perhaps as balanced between the two (i.e., more ambiverted). These examples are instructive, both as a way of teaching students the Big Five dimensions themselves, and as a way of giving students a way to understand, criticize, evaluate, and grapple with the course content. For example, one writer might be said to be superior at describing characters because the traits are more apparent, while another writer might describe characters in such a way that their traits remain hidden. Another writer might write only about one or two traits of a character, thereby creating a stereotype rather than a realistic character. Thus, students can use their knowledge of the Big Five as a tool for actively evaluating course content.

2. *The Way the Course is Taught/Learned*. The teacher and the students together can discuss and plan around how different traits on the part of both the teacher and the student affect how the material is taught and how the student attempts to learn it. For example, a more extraverted teacher might emphasize lecture and group work, while a more introverted teacher might emphasize seatwork, independent study, or laboratory work. This could help or hinder in teaching course content. For example, a more extraverted teacher might hesitate to assign sufficient writing for students to gain writing skills, as grading papers tends to be a more introverted activity. Such a teacher would be well-advised to understand such a tendency and to plan how to compensate for it. For example, that same teacher might consider using small groups of students to engage in peer reviews of each other's writing. From the student's perspective, a more extraverted student might give short shrift to writing assignments, preferring instead to engage in a more social activity. Such a student would be well-advised to find a

way to spend more time writing in a way that is quasi-social, such as going for a walk with a notepad and jotting down a mindmap or some other outlining technique while walking, then sitting somewhere (park bench, train station, library, beauty salon) and writing fast and furiously from the outline (writing tends to flow when such "prework" is done).

3. *The Way the Student Relates to the Course Content*. Pretty much every course under the sun will relate to one or more of each student's traits. As the student figures out, for example, which characters in a story share the same traits as they do (e.g., "I'm more introverted, just like Holden Caulfield" in J. D. Salinger's *The Catcher in the Rye*). They can wrestle with how the character's handling of the trait can identify how the student could adopt, modify, or avoid that behavior in their own life and career. In this case, the student might write an essay or journal entry on the subject of "How My Introversion Is, and Will Be, Similar to and Different from Holden Caulfield's."

So, for each course or curricular area, we want to explore how the content, the teaching/learning process, and the personal learning might be addressed. The goal here is not to be exhaustive, for that would constitute a book in and of itself! (Hmmm, maybe next year....) Rather, the goal here is to say enough to begin dialog in these many areas. Each curricular area will be treated by proposing some questions and activities that could address our three aspects.

How the Big Five Relates to Specific Programs in the Arts

1. Composition

Content: What traits are revealed about each character in the piece? If no traits are apparent, how could the piece be revised to include more revelatory detail about traits? Should additional characters be introduced to provide contrast or support for existing characters? Could elements in the background (plants, furniture, and so forth) be personified with traits to add conflict or interest to the piece? How do you think the piece will affect readers of different trait profiles? Is the piece written in such a way that it will appeal to the kind of reader (traitwise) that the writer intends to appeal to? How could the tone of the piece be modified in order to achieve the desired effect on readers with a specific trait profile?

Method: Which traits provide the most natural energy for specific kinds of writing (e.g., O1+ and creative writing, O4- and technical writing, A2- and polemic writing/debate)? Do the teacher's traits cause a preference for assignments based on these relationships? If so, how should the teacher identify and avoid the preference? Are students able to select writing tasks that build on their natural energy/stronger traits? If given an assignment that involves a weaker trait (e.g., an O1- student being asked to write poetry), does the teacher assist them in finding satisfactory ways to adapt to the assignment (e.g., in this case, writing a poem about something familiar, not imagined)?

Personal: Which characters in the piece have traits similar to the student's? The opposite of the student's? How can the student manage their life so that they get results similar to, or different from, the results associated with the character of interest to them? How can I build on my natural trait energy to make my writing more interesting, more concrete, more real? If I am writing about a character that has a trait opposite from mine, do I know someone with that trait who could critique my depic-depiction for its realism?

2. Dance

Content: What are the various movements that could be used to convey particular traits? What traits appear to lie behind the various movements that you see in the dance segment? How can a movement sequence be modified to communicate a trait differently or more intensely? How can opposing traits be communicated through movement in order to heighten the drama of the dance?

Method: Do the traits of the teacher and the student connect in such a way that the teacher emphasizes aspects of dance that build on traits that both teacher and student share (e.g., both are N+ and emphasis is on expression of negative emotions). Or is there a mismatch with the teacher emphasizing a set of expectations based on the teacher's trait that the student does not share? If the latter, is the teacher able to help the student understand the student's lack of natural energy for this aspect of movement and figure out ways to compensate?

Personal: The student will choreograph a piece that expresses a strong trait, with movements for other dancers that provide contrast (if the student is A3-, and programs their piece to express pride, then include movements for other dancers that provide contrast with the opposite trait, humility). In order to get to know your weaker traits, choreograph pieces, or perform pieces choreographed by others, that explore these weaker traits.

3. Economics

Content: How do different economic theories, systems, or policies reflect different traits? Do some appeal, for example, to higher A, others to lower A (altruism versus greed)? How can a person low in C manage to bring sufficient discipline, organization, and focus to bear on their financial dealings so as to be a financially successful in a traditional sense? Study the biographies of various economic theorists, determine their traits using content analysis, and explain how features of their theories might have been influenced by specific traits. How can individuals with various traits make economic decisions that will be satisfying, given their traits? For example, certain traits would be more comfortable with low risk investments, others with high risk.

Method: Teachers who are lower in O and A are more likely to have a preference for more traditional, more conservative economic models and policies. How can they insure that they do not give short shrift to schools of thought with which they are uncomfortable? They could hold debates within the class as a way of encouraging the exploration of both sides of issues. This would aid both students and teachers in learning about both sides of things. To help students overcome bias about various economic issues, conduct stereotyping exercises in which they cover the board with phrases they think are true of adherents of a particular economic theory. Then conduct research to determine whether any of the attributes are, in fact, valid.

Personal: Conduct research with family and friends to find out how many different economic systems, theories, or policies have been experienced by persons in each student's network. Interview at least one friend or family member for each different economic experience, and determine how they see the strong points and weak points of each one. Have the student compare their personal views with the views of their close family or friends. Are there traits they have in common with these friends or family members that might explain their common likes or dislikes with respect to economic matters?

4. Foreign (Second or Third) Languages

Content: For all of the countries that speak the language you are studying, review each country's mean on the Big Five traits (cf. McCrae and Allik, 2002). Are the countries similar in the way they differ from other language/country means? How can characteristics of the language and/or culture explain the differences in means, such as many Asian countries having higher means on A, Latin countries having higher means on E, Scandinavian countries having lower means on E, India's lower means on O, and so forth. Have groups compete in translating Big Five trait names from English into the foreign language and critique the nuances of meaning in the various translations. Initiate class discussion on how best to describe the various traits in the foreign language. Discuss cultural equivalents and how you cannot use literal translations much of the time. For example, some cultures are OK with talking back to parents or bosses as a measure of A4, while others would universally avoid it. How would you describe an equivalent behavior—"talking back" in English is equivalent to what phrase or idiom in Spanish? Compile a list of synonyms in the foreign language that expresses levels (low, medium, and high) of each of the Big Five traits—make a display of some sort and keep adding to it as more vocabulary is acquired.

Method: One's personality can affect one's vocabulary in a language, as well as the kind of reading material and writing assignments that are suggested. The teacher needs to insure that a personal preference for material reflecting preferred personal traits (e.g., an E-O+ teacher assigning Proust) is balanced with material that appeals to students with different profiles (e.g., "action" stories for E+O- students). All too often, foreign language curriculum is biased towards the traits of the curriculum developers.

Personal: Have students keep a journal in which they build vocabulary in the foreign language that they can use to describe themselves in each of the Big Five dimensions. Develop a pen pal or social networking friend who is a native speaker of the language and introduce each other using the trait words. Then expand to writing about family members and friends who have different traits, learning to use the trait words associated with traits that are different from one's own. Take care that students do not use pejorative words to write about persons with opposite traits. Learn about nuances in the foreign language, such as the difference in English between "loner" and "preference for solitude" for persons low in E.

Traits in School

5. Geography

Content: There is a sizable literature that describes the relationship between climate, terrain, agriculture, and other geographical features on the one hand and behavioral temperament on the other. Some of these relationships are suggested in the earlier section on "Foreign Languages." Create a trait map of the world, such that each country's level of a particular trait is color coded for quick identification. Country means for traits are available in a variety of places (cf. McCrae and Allik, 2002), as well as levels for each trait for the 50 states of the U.S (cf. Rentfrow, Gosling, and Potter, 2008).

Method: Teachers must take care to avoid personal bias towards certain geographical areas and their strong traits. Instead, celebrate different climes for different traits. Have maps that show the geographical backgrounds of class members and explore the degree to which individuals from those cultures reflect their different trait levels or not.

Personal: Interview all family and friends to determine the countries of their ancestors and prepare a map based on the countries of their ancestors. Indicate each country's level of each trait, whether individuals differ from their ancestors, and which countries most fit the student's own profile. Then make a study of the country(ies) that most resembles the student's profile and explore how it would probably feel to live in such a country, where a larger proportion of the citizens are more similar (or less similar) to the student in temperament.

6. History

Content: A country's history is the story and study of its leaders, inventors, artists, revolutionaries, workers, laborers, writers, teachers, philosophers.... Through the study of biographies of representative persons from a country's past/present, do content analyses and come up with trait profiles for each leader. Use their trait profiles to assess how a different trait level might have influenced the course of history differently. For example, what if Abe Lincoln had been lower in A, or if Stalin had been higher in A? Compare and contrast famous pairs/trios/etc. with respect to their similarities and differences on traits. Analyze how that contrast explains success, failure, and general achievement (e.g., the Wright Brothers, Juan and Evita Peron, Rasputin/Nicholas II/ Alexandra/Alexei, Nelson and Wini Mandela, Hitler plus one or more around him).

Method: It is terribly easy in teaching history to show favor for personages like oneself. I (Pierce) had a high school American history teacher who was E+A-C+. He was a football coach and admired military leaders, most all of whom were E+A-C+, i.e., just like him (sociable, proud, competitive, and focused). I grew to dislike the course and the teacher, as 95% of what we were accountable for was names of generals and dates of battles and the like. History teachers must take care to achieve balance in the personages they highlight and to invite students to explore figures both similar to themselves and different, traitwise. Assign passages containing concrete trait descriptions of historical personages; identify the persons' traits and discuss their implications. Here is an example from Jeffrey Rosen's *The*

Supreme Court: The Personalities and Rivalries that Defined America (New York: Times Books/Henry Holt and Company, 2006. pp. 12-13):

> The most successful chief justices, in other words, have shared a particular style of judicial temperament. They have been modest, likable, efficient, deft at finding common ground, and at least as smart as their colleagues without being overtly brilliant or intensely academic. Some of the most effective chiefs have been former politicians or politically minded executive officials who had a knack for bringing together colleagues of different minds. By contrast, the less successful chiefs have been insecure, heavy-handed, and more concerned with being recognized as the symbolic head of the Court than providing leadership behind the scenes.

It is relatively clear from this passage that the most successful chief justices are N-E+A=, while the less successful are likely N+A-. Agree? Sounds like a good discussion! Based on each student's profile, how would they likely fare as a chief justice?

Personal: Compile (on one's computer, on a wall poster, in a journal, or whatever) a list of historical personages you've studied whom you admire or revile; indicate how each appears to be similar or different from you on each of the Big Five traits. Read biographies of historical personages you admire, reflect on how they are similar and different from you on the Big Five, and speculate on how the course of your life might be similar or different from theirs based on your similarities/differences in temperament.

7. Literature

Content: The world's literature—poetry, essay, drama, fiction, television, film, storytelling, lyrics—is of course a treasure trove for exploration of the Big Five personality traits, and the Big Five model is a powerful tool to use in literary criticism. At the lowest level, one can simply identify the traits of characters based on the language used to describe their behavior. This can be extremely simple as when Iago reveals that "I follow but myself" (I.i.58), whereby we nod in tagging him as A-. Or when Othello rails at "the tyrant custom"(I.i.230), whereby we recognize the tension between higher and lower O. It is also fun to find contrasting passages, where two characters reveal themselves to be polar opposites. Here, Iago and Roderigo:

> N-A-: "Ere I would say I would drown myself for the love of a guinea-hen, I would change my humanity with a baboon." Iago, I.iii.314-317
>
> N+A+: "I confess it is my shame to be so fond, but it is not in my virtue to amend it." Roderigo, 318-19

In Willa Cather's *Death Comes for the Archbishop*, Father Latour comes across as a complete and well-drawn character:

> N- calm and unflappable, even in the presence of evil; always patient and full of plans
> E+ daily lunches with all of his stakeholders
> O+ longs for a beautiful cathedral; explores the territory; aesthetic, enjoys art, wine, fine foods
> A= goes for the win-win
> C+ focused on his goal and self-disciplined

Traits in School

In fact, we propose that this is one of the primary values of the Big Five for Literature—to serve as the basis for critiquing character development. If characters are flat—all you hear are witticisms, jokes, stories, gossip, and the like, with no self-revelatory information, those characters tend to be less interesting, less compelling, than those whose five, full-trait dimensions come across, whether subtly or hard-hitting.

Method: For a reading assignment, have students keep a log of trait-revealing words for each character that interests them, and at the end, attempt to construct the characters' trait profiles based on all of the words and phrases. Then, have them use these profiles as a way of explaining why characters do or do not get along (Anna Karenina and her husband are an excellent case study for this). Also discuss other aspects of characters' relationship (e.g., contempt arising from an A- interacting with an A+, boredom from an O+ with an O-, oppression from an E- with an E+, frustration from a C+ with a C-, and amicability from an A= with another A=). Suggest they rewrite, or retell, a story by giving one or more characters different/opposite traits than the ones in the original. For poems, traits are often hard to see, so have small groups imagine what the traits are, and support their conclusions. Have students create card games based on their reading in which other students try to identify the trait(s) behind a particular quote on each card.

Personal: Ask family members and friends to describe some of their favorite characters from all of literature. Have discussions with them for the purpose of agreeing on the characters' trait profiles and what they might mean, as in, "Do you think one of the Lockhorns [the cartoon characters] is lower in A than the other? Is their mutual antagonism what attracted them to each other, or do you think it is an evolution from their years together? Do they really mean it when they insult each other, or are they just being themselves with no regard for what they're saying? How does all this relate to how we interact with each other and with our friends?"

8. Music

Content: Have a discussion about which traits particular instruments express more naturally, such as trumpets expressing E+ and A-. What would trumpets have to do in order to express the opposite? Is that what mutes are for? There is a literature on the ability of music to express different emotions, moods, and behavioral patterns—prepare charts and the like of how to compose, and recognize compositions, so as to conjure specific Big Five traits. A good start for a reference is the work of McGill University music neuroscientist Dan Levitin (2006, 2008). Also, see the chapter on music in *The Owner's Manual for the Brain* (Howard, 2006, 3rd Ed.). Examine the personality traits reflected by one's choice of instrument. Read the biographies of musicians, identify their trait profiles, and explain how their traits are reflected in their compositions, performances, and/or repertoire. How might their music be different if they had exhibited different traits?

Method: In teaching and studying music history, be aware how personality can influence choices and preferences. Teachers should insure that their own strong traits do not cause their choices to overwhelm students with opposite traits. Assist students in identifying how their preferences in music relate to traits. For instrumental or vocal music majors, make sure that their goals are linked to their traits and that they understand how certain traits support certain kinds of goals more than others. For example, to be a solo concert performer, it takes far more practice than to teach or play with a larger group.

Personal: Much of what one prefers in music depends on what one has listened to growing up. However, I (Pierce) listened to Little Richard and the Beatles growing up, and they are currently not on my playlist. How has one's trait profile influenced one's music preferences? For example, I am moderately high on N and am prone to nervousness when stressed. I think this explains why I often turn off the radio when they are playing music I describe as "nervous" music. Jangly music jangles my nerves even more. Give me some Mozart, some Bach, to restore order to my soul. Keep a journal of music preferences and how they might relate to traits.

9. Philosophy

Content: Study the biography of a philosopher. How does their trait profile explain their philosophy? Is stoicism proposed by low Ns, Epicureanism by E+C-, logical positivism by O-? By reading a philosopher's biography and then attempting to describe their trait profile, one can gain insight in the way traits influence philosophical outlook.

Method: Of course the philosopher is typically known for objectivity, but clearly many philosophy teachers allow traits to influence who their favorite philosophers are: The teacher who is N+ may prefer the tortured pessimism of Schopenhauer, while the N- teacher may prefer the mental coolness of Epictetus. Student and teacher alike need to be alert to the fact that no philosophy is intrinsically superior to another and that one's take is heavily influenced by one's traits.

Personal: Read the biography of your favorite philosopher(s), determine their trait profile, and see how they and you are similar and different. How does their philosophy relate to their traits? How does your admiration for this philosopher relate to your traits? Every time I (Pierce) read a philosopher who writes eloquently and stirringly about the need for order, I feel pangs of guilt, knowing that I'll never be that way. Yet I value those who are. I prefer the philosopher who urges me to accept the small, mad world called home.

10. Political Science

Content: True or False: Political theories, systems, institutions, and the people who lead and espouse them, especially those we call politicians, tend to reflect the traits of those who thought them up and keep them politically alive. Study the lives of political theorists and profile them by analyzing the content of the language used to describe their behavior. Perhaps you will find the laissez-faire theorists, for example, tend to be lower in C. Are welfare state theorists higher in A? Can political parties be identified by differing trait levels? What does the literature have to say about the traits of the ideal leader? Are there different kinds of leaders with different trait profiles? Evaluate the traits of current leaders against this ideal profile. For leaders who lack a particular trait, how do they compensate for the lack, if at all? (For example, Nixon lacked N-, Gerald Ford lacked E+, Jimmy Carter lacked A-, Bill Clinton lacked C+, G. W. Bush lacked O+, and Barack Obama lacks N+: Did each compensate successfully? If so, how?)

Method: Individual teachers and students are likely to judge political systems and theories based on their personal values (and traits). Insure that all theories, systems, and institutions are evaluated based on a) the goals they strive to realize, and b) universally agreed upon standards (such as the Universal Declaration of Human Rights). Teachers and students who are lower in O and A are least likely to be objective with respect to political ideas significantly different their own. They would be advised to rely extensively on such open forums as debates and compare-and-contrast.

Personal: Compare your personal trait profile to that of a political theorist with whom you agree and also one with whom you disagree strongly. Are your traits and values more similar to one than the other? Are your traits the result of your political views or vice versa? Study the relationship between traits and political views of other members of your family and personal network. Do you personally aspire to be a leader? If so, how does your profile compare? Are there traits you lack? How might you plan now to compensate for that lack, given the type of leadership aspirations that you have? (cf. Chapter 22 on leadership).

11. Psychology

Content: Psychology is the homeplace for study of the Big Five Model of Personality. Study the origins and history of the Big Five by going back to the work of Gordon Allport and Harold Odbert in 1936. How can you explain earlier personality models (Freud, Jung, and so forth) by using the Big Five? Get both the competitive (A-) and cooperative (A+) juices flowing by having small groups see who can create the most impressive collection, quality- and quantity-wise, of names, pictures, and quotes from popular culture (TV, movies, music, politics, sports) that illustrate each level of the supertraits. Think up interesting research questions, design experiments aimed at answering them, conduct the experiments, and report the results (e.g., Do extraverts walk more briskly than introverts? Is there a particular trait that best predicts how healthily one eats? Do particular clubs or sports appeal to different traits? Are traits related to patterns of cell phone use? To what degree are brand names associated with specific traits [e.g., Do A- prefer Red Bull? Does a particular trait tend to shop at the Gap, as opposed to J. Crew?]).

Method: To illustrate that "there is no one right way to be," begin and maintain over the years a chart (on the wall and/or online) that shows the jobs/careers/roles that tend to be associated with a particular level of each of the five supertraits. Begin with the careers that students in the class are currently considering. Also start with a list of careers that psychology majors typically consider. Have students help fill out the chart by researching specific careers/jobs/roles of interest to them by using the O*NET (they do not, at this writing, use the Big Five nomenclature, but they do use trait names that can be translated into the Big Five framework) and other online research resources (such as our website at www.centacs.com). Have students take multiple Big Five assessments and then evaluate the results in terms of accuracy, utility, and so forth.

Personal: Have each class member do a family tree wherewith they show the supertrait levels for as many generations as possible. (We've analyzed six generations of Howards by using newspaper clippings, obituaries, and interviews with the living who remember stories about deceased ancestors.) Make a chart comprised of all extended family members and friends and where they score on each of the five supertraits. Make journal entries based on that chart about how you are similar to and different from other family and friends. Using the above methods, write a biography of a deceased ancestor and estimate their most likely Big Five profile (I [Pierce] wrote one about my grandmother, who died before I was born).

12. Religious Studies

Content: Conduct content analyses of the biographies of religious leaders from around the world and throughout time, representing different cultures, different religions, and different roles (e.g., those who started a religion, such as Jesus, Abraham, or Mohammed, and those who are considered prophets or typical advocates today, such as a priest, rabbi, or mullah). Examine the biographies of leaders of different sects within a religion (e.g., more fundamentalist versus more progressive) and determine whether there is a trait similarity across religions that differentiates the more fundamental from the more progressive. Find quotes from religious literature that involve a particular trait (e.g., Ruth's statement in the Bible to her mother-in-law Naomi, "Whither thou goest, I will go" reflects high A). Determine whether any one religion emphasizes any one trait level more than another.

Method: Each teacher and student should examine whether or not there is a personal trait that influences their religious preferences or practices. For example, a very high A is more likely to place a high emphasis on service and/or charity, while a very high O is more likely to place a high emphasis on theological theory. With this understanding, knowing that there are others who have opposite traits, and likely opposite views, show that the two can co-exist. Have ongoing dialog about the essential impossibility of the notion that there is any one right way to be religious that is extrinsically superior to any other way of being religious, based on the diversity of traits and motives that exist in the world. Discuss the Jesuit notions (also very common in the East) that individual differences in traits are to be minimized and that any one person should be able to do anything, as opposed to persons having "differing gifts" and thereby should not be expected to do anything except what is natural, i.e., to engage in their gift, their bliss (as Joseph Campbell calls it). Keep a gallery of religious and mythical figures that illustrate different traits (the Hindu gallery of thousands of deities is a good starting point, with various ones having distinct traits). Over time, this should illustrate the ubiquitous presence of all levels of all traits.

Personal: How does one's unique trait profile suggest that one might most naturally express themselves in their religious affiliation, organization, or practices? How can one's unique "gifts" (i.e., traits) serve as a part of the totality of religious experience? Energy for organizing the study of religious texts (C+), energy for designing new religious programs (O+), and so forth. Are there current roles one is performing (e.g., being a leader of a youth group) that may or may not be based on natural trait energy? Might there be other roles that one could perform that would be more natural? (I [Pierce] used to be "president" of youth groups at church, but I've since come to realize that I'm much better outside of leadership roles, doing things like "program designer").

13. Sociology

Content: One of the major themes in sociology today is the role of resiliency in the ability of young people to prevail over difficulties in their upbringing and early environment. Studies indicate that resilience, the ability to rebound from setbacks quickly and without major loss to personal drive and motivation, is primarily inherited. Have the class investigate what people can do to compensate for not being born with this genetically based quality. What are techniques, exercises, policies, values, and so forth that can be learned that offset the effect of not being naturally resilient? Then apply all of this learning to the class with respect to their individual scores. In class, have those with higher N understand both their most natural roles and what they can do to personally compensate for lack of resiliency. Have individuals with low N understand their natural resilience and what it suggests about the kinds of roles and challenges they can take on more comfortably than those with higher N. For example, I (Jane) am N-. When my dad died, Pierce and I had been trying to work with one major corporation for several years. I was scheduled to deliver an introductory session to a group of managers the second day after my dad died. Pierce had another client, and I was the only person who could do it. Rather than cancel the morning session, I delivered it. No one there knew that my dad had just died. I then drove my mother home for the funeral. I was sad, I was grieving, but as a low N, I can compartmentalize my emotions. In a crisis, my rational self emerged. I had to deliver this program, and I did. My actions would have been very difficult for someone high in N.

Method: Be aware that sociologists typically prefer social forces as an explanation of behavior, while abundant evidence supports the notion that traits—mostly inherited, partly learned—are a strong determinant of behavior. Be prepared to continually ask the question about how traits might alter the effect of social forces. For example, with the classic study that Stanley Milgram conducted on obedience to malevolent authority, how might subjects with different traits explain who did and didn't obey.

Personal: Have students keep a journal in which they write down each new sociological principle studied in class. Then have them consider how their personal trait profile might make them more or less likely to exhibit that principle in their own lives. Encourage them at some future point, either during the course or later in their lives, to review this journal and observe the accuracy of their predictions and conjectures.

14. Theater

Content: Whether acting, reading, or writing a play, have students identify the Big Five profile of each character. Then, for one or more of the characters, list the kinds of behaviors that typically come from those traits. Then suggest how these behaviors might help understand how to act out the role. Learn prototypical stances (e.g., low O could be someone looking through an imaginary magnifying glass at the details, low E could be reading, and so forth) for each level of each trait, and then have students role-play a variety of differently traited characters. Critique plays based on the identifiability of traits of the main characters. For example, Nora in Ibsen's *A Doll's House* is clearly high A who eventually musters enough low A to stand up for herself. Based on his behavior and language, what are Torvald's traits? To the extent that students can identify the traitedness of characters, those characters can be said to be more well-rounded, more robustly developed.

Method: Drama teachers are perhaps singularly least likely to show a preference for one trait over another, inasmuch as their very job involves exploring the value and dynamics of all behavior. On the other hand, most of us are prone to prefer persons like ourselves: Creatives like creatives, neatniks like neatniks, and so forth. The drama teacher stands in an ideal role to assist students in understanding differences based on the Big Five and how they are not chosen by the individual but rather evolved. Much of life's drama comes from not understanding that differences are impersonal. Neatniks think slobs are sloppy just to spite them—they take it personally. Should we all understand that personality differences are not to be taken personally, much of the conflict in drama would disappear.

Personal: Students of drama could practice assuming different levels of traitedness for periods of time; they could record their feelings about the experiences. More extraverted persons should practice introversion, as in going camping alone, and more introverted persons should practice extraversion, as in volunteering at a Special Olympics (full of sensory bombardment), so that they learn how to be comfortable in a variety of roles by drawing upon their own experience with opposite traits. To be unfamiliar with opposite traits makes one end up being typecast, always playing the same person, like Bruce Willis and Meg Ryan, while the really great actors are able to play opposing traits convincingly, like Phillip Seymour Hoffman and Rene Zellweger, so much so that they are often physically unrecognizable from role to role.

15. Visual Arts/Architecture

Content: Develop an iconography for the prototypical visual depiction of different levels of the Big Five: List the visual images associated with each level of N, E, O, A, and C. Then, critique existing works of art in terms of the practice of artists in revealing the traitedness of their subjects, such as medieval artists' use of icons to depict the seven deadly sins and that sort of thing, or Frans Hals' use of clearly "extraverted" props as seen in his well-known portrait of *The Merry Lute Player,* or Caravaggio's *Bacchus*. Also, architects have known for some time that persons with particular traits tend to have strong preferences in the design of the space in which they live, work, and play. Consider how building design can support traits, such as Jefferson's bedroom/study combination at Monticello that satisfied his high O.

Method: Teacher and student alike can develop an encyclopedia of images that depict different trait levels. Consider the possibility that teachers' or students' profiles may influence the kind of visual art preferred. More extraverted persons may undervalue art that exudes peace and quiet, preferring the clanging boisterousness of a Jackson Pollock dripped painting or a Breughel bacchanal, whereas a higher O might delight in the improbability of an Escher or a Dali. List one's artistic preferences and examine them for the possibility of trait bias.

Personal: Develop your personal iconography of traits so that when, for example, you portray someone you intend to be high in A, you have some "signature" ways of portraying them, such as a nearby lamb, suppliant hands, a veil, or shadows. Also, develop your own encyclopedia of visual design ideas: colors, proportions, shapes, and general environmental features preferred by different levels of traits, such as red typically being preferred by the more extraverted, and blue its opposite.

How the Big Five Relates to Specific Programs in the Sciences

1. Biology

Content: At least three Big Five applications exist for the biologist: neurological pathways, genetics, and ethology. Identify the brain areas, neuronal pathways, and neurotransmitters/hormones associated with different traits (such as dopamine with O+; see the latter portions of Chapters 5-9 for additional detail from ongoing research on the biology of behavior). Conduct experiments aimed at examining the effects of various chemicals and dietary regimens on the behavior of animals (such as the effect of fats in increasing A). Study the relative degree of heritability of the various traits (A appears to have the lowest heritability rate). Teach formulas for determining the degree of heritability of traits, and apply them to students' own family trees. Identify how various animal species illustrate the Big Five—all, from chimps to guppies, exhibit variation in each of the Big Five dimensions, with the exception of C, which is only found among chimpanzees, the latest and closest evolutionary species next to humans. Observe live animals and photographs for examples of various trait behaviors. Jane Goodall's photos of chimpanzees are a great starting point (e.g., grooming behavior—looking for and picking nits off another—is illustrative of A+).

Method: The old Skinnerian notion that all behavior is learned is dead. Sure, some behavior is learned. But much is inherited. Use this truth to enrich the teaching of biology to include variations in the Big Five traits. Find ways during a semester or quarter to show the effects of breeding for behavior, perhaps with guppies or some other small fish or animal.

Personal: Have students experiment on themselves with diet and observe the effect on various traits. For example, what happens if I eliminate sugar for one month? Caffeine for one month? Fat for one week? Meat for one week? Dairy products for one week? Make predictions and observe results.

2. Chemistry

Content: The chemistry of behavior is alive and controversial, from Candace Pert's powerful story of her (reportedly stolen) discovery of the endorphin receptor in her *The Molecules of Emotion* to Elliot Valenstein's exposé of psychiatrists and the pharmaceutical and insurance industries in *Blaming the Brain.* As a way of appealing to the less quantitatively oriented students and broadening the more quantitative students, develop a reading list of books that deal with the chemistry of behavior (aggression, love, monogamy, and so forth), and award some kind of credit for reading and reporting based on this list. Over time, compile a chart of some kind that depicts the role of different chemicals in various behaviors, with full appreciation for the complexity of these relationships.

Method: Using the results of the next section (Personal: student self testing), keep records on neurotransmitter and hormone levels and their relation to trait scores. Work in cooperation with biology and psychology teachers.

Personal: Include opportunities for students to explore their own body chemistry and how it relates to behavior. Use salivary testosterone testing, blood analyses, and the like.

4. Environmental Science

Content: Have students explore the relationship of various Big Five traits to behaviors as they affect one's stance towards environmental protection and degradation. Particularly, ask students to interpret various kinds of data and then show how individual interpretations can be influenced by one's traits. For example, how lower O interpret data as benign out of distaste for change and to maintain the status quo, while higher O may be too eager to interpret data as toxic out of their eagerness for change. Or how higher A may be more swayed to one interpretation out of a desire to avoid conflict and how lower A may resist an interpretation out of sheer ego protection.

Method: Show how meta-analytic tools can get beyond these previously identified biases based on individual traits, such as using rational decision analysis and root cause analysis problem-solving models.

Personal: Have each student identify personal goals for managing their own local environments. Most of the goals could be based on reducing personal, familial, neighborhood, or community "footprints." Discuss goal-setting in terms of how their individual traits should shape the kinds of goals they embrace. For example, more extraverted students should use their outgoing energy to pursue goals that involve energizing groups of people in a concerted activity, while more introverted students might be better served by coming up with goals that build on their comfort with quiet and solitude. Help them value diversity in behavior, just as you are trying to get them to appreciate biodiversity in the environment.

Traits in School

5. Health

Content: Cover the literature on the relation of the Big Five to health behaviors. The UNC-Chapel Hill Alumni Behavioral Health Study has correlated the Big Five scores of thousands of college alumni to specific health behaviors such as coronary heart disease proneness, length of hospital stay (more extraverted patients have shorter stays as a rule—they want to get back into the action), likelihood of adhering to a course of treatment, and so forth. Conduct your own class research on the relation of traits to health issues and diseases. Do extraverts catch more colds (because they have more contacts)? Are higher N students (and teachers) more likely to smoke or drink? Pose such questions, collect data that could lead to answers, and discuss the implications of the results. Where a particular trait is associated with a kind of health risk, discuss ways of compensating so as to minimize the risk.

Method: Aim for fairness and objectivity here: Emphasize the up side and the down side, health wise, of every extreme trait, and how persons with extreme traits might compensate.

Personal: Keep a personal journal in which each student identifies the health behaviors to which they are prone, based on their traits, and how they feel about that. Then set goals based on these feelings. Invite them to use all available resources in coming up with strategies to achieve their health goals. Expect periodic evaluation of progress towards goals and possible reformulation of strategies or goals.

6. Mathematics

Content: Conduct research on the probability of particular traits exhibiting specific behaviors. Collect data on trait scores and the specific behaviors in question. For example, track the number of times they are tardy to class, the number of minutes they are tardy, the number of verbal contributions they make per class hour, the length of the verbal contributions they make, and so forth. Analyze data and come up with prediction models. Show how the use of multiple regression techniques can improve prediction.

Method: Consider word problems and/or field studies that will appeal to a wide variety of traits. For example, don't use all competitive examples, such as sports averages, that appeal to low A students, but also include math problems that would appeal to higher A students—for example, showing the improved efficiencies based on synergy/cooperation. Use the Prisoner's Dilemma exercise to show the calculation of game theory outcomes, and show how traits could influence decisions. Introduce students to various rational decision models as a way of minimizing the effect of traits on their decision making.

Personal: Become a trait statistician. Collect frequency data on specific behaviors of family members and show relation to traits: language usage (repeated words, types of repeated words), attire (formal, informal, jeans, wearing clothes for a second/third/etc. day without washing/cleaning), time spent on practice, time spent on maintenance (from brushing teeth to cleaning room/house), television viewing habits (length, type of program), cell phone habits, how a computer is used. Attempt to demonstrate which of all these behaviors show a clear relation to trait scores.

7. Physics

Content: Teach Festinger's concept of JND (just noticeable difference). Conduct class research to establish JND for various perceptual phenomenon. Include cases of behavior, using Big Five scores on more observable behaviors (e.g., sociability and assertiveness) and less observable behaviors (e.g., anxiety and level of trust). Discuss the implication of students' findings. There is a literature on this area (i.e., the JND for levels of trait behavior).

Method: Consider the possibility that different levels of some traits may find some areas of physics of more natural interest than others. Higher scorers on O2: Range of Interests, for example, may wish to study astrophysics as a whole, while lower scorers may find one specific area of astrophysics, such as optics, of more interest for going into depth.

Personal: Select aspects of physics for in-depth study based on your natural trait energy. For example, some areas require more attention to detail while others are more theoretical and big picture.

How the Big Five Relates to Specific Programs in the Vocations

At this point, if you have been reading each curriculum area, you will have sensed that 1) there are some general underlying principles behind all of the suggested activities, and 2) the suggestions are becoming a bit repetitive. So, rather than continue with the format of *Content...Method...Personal*, we will simply make some comments appropriate to each of the vocations listed below.

1. Auto Mechanics. More extraverted mechanics will tend to be uncomfortable working in solitude and silence; they will tend to provide themselves some "action" by having radio, television, iPod, and the like going in the background. While entertaining, this can increase error proneness, as one simply cannot focus on two things at once. One suggestion: After completing segments of one's work, turn off the music/talk, and review the work for completeness and accuracy. Better yet, save the music/distractions until you are engaged in a task that is more tolerant of errors.

2. Business. Running a business relies on low O, while entrepreneurial activity/business startups benefit from higher O. O+ individuals frequently start a business and then neglect to turn over the running of the business to lower O managers who are comfortable with repetition and details. Low C business managers need to learn early on to have a partner who is higher in C in order to keep organized and focused on goals.

3. Construction Management. Three Big Five-related issues are critical to construction management: safety, project management, and quality control. Students of this trade need to be aware of how their traits do, or do not, support these three, and plan how to compensate. Safety is associated with N-E-O-A+C+ (calm, quiet, focused on the here-and-now, deferential to authority, and disciplined). Project management is optimally supported by E+A-C+ (outgoing/active, tough, and disciplined). Quality control is associated with N+O-C+ (anxious, here-and-now, and disciplined). Observe that, while many construction managers are responsible for all three roles, they are supported by contradictory traits. Hence, one must either compensate or delegate. Learn early that one simply can't do it all alone and will need to rely on others with complementary traits.

4. Driver Education. The critical traits associated with DE are those associated with safety: N-E-O-A+C+ (calm [*especially for instructors!*], quiet, focused on the here-and-now, deferential to authority, and disciplined). Impulsive drivers take more chances and have more accidents. The safe profile defined here is the opposite of an impulsive one. Drivers with opposite traits to those defined here need to learn when to suppress their natural traits. For example, extraverts may be fine carrying on a conversation while driving down a lonely country road, but they should zip it when approaching a busy intersection or when passing in traffic.

5. Electricity. The comments about safety under Construction Mgmt. and Driver Ed. apply here as well.

6. Engineering. The prototypical engineer is patient, disciplined, and focused on detail (N+O-C+), with some exceptions (e.g., design engineers tend to be more creative and big picture, i.e., higher O). Engineering students who lack patience, discipline, or attention to detail need to learn when it is important to use their sparse reserves. They also need to learn techniques to increase these qualities, such as deep breathing, aerobic exercise, taking frequent (if short) breaks, changing tasks, and so forth.

7. Furniture Making and Woodwork. See Engineering; the comments all apply here, including the comments about design.

8. Home Economics. The culinary and other "home arts" are populated with two kinds of workers: creative and production. From early in one's education, one needs to learn one's nature in this regard and find ways to cope when one is expected to engage in the opposite role for any appreciable length of time. For example, a caterer who is creative needs an assistant to help with the production side, and a chef who enjoys turning out large volumes of product needs an idea person around to help make sure menus don't get "stale" over time.

9. Information Technology (IT). This field is part knowledge and part execution, like pretty much all vocations. Again, it is helpful here to know whether one is temperamentally better suited for creative, complex tasks (O+) or more cut-and-dry, grind-it-out tasks (O-) such as detailed programming. Distractibility is a killer here, as losing focus while writing code or designing systems can result in oversights that involve many hours of investigation and rework. Easily distracted IT students need to learn how to curb their E+, O+, or C-. N+ IT students need to learn techniques to combat anxiety by regaining their calmness through deep breathing, taking breaks, aerobic exercise, and so forth.

10. Journalism. Are you going to pursue a journalism career that is characterized by "Just the facts, mam" or one that is characterized more by complex investigative reporting? Journalism has plenty of room for the former (O-) and the latter (O+). Extraverted, or even ambiverted, journalists need to learn tricks to make themselves more comfortable with solitude and silence so as to stay in their inner world of composition. Many make a conscious shift to change their frame of mind, as well as to signal others, that now is the time for writing (e.g., I (Pierce) burn a candle, wear a hat, or position a prism to defract light). Before "onstage" activity, whether an interview or a broadcast, higher N journalists would be well served to learn a regimen that is calming (again, deep breathing, aerobic exercise, jumping jacks, mental rehearsal/visualization).

11. Military Science. Are you a leader, a follower, or possibly neither, but rather an independent? Those aiming for leadership responsibility in the military are best served by having the prototypical leader profile: N-E+A-C+, with O dependent on whether the leader is more responsible for strategy (O+) or tactics (O-). (See Chapter 27 on Leadership.)

12. Physical Education. There is a fairly sizable literature on the relation of traits to sports and exercise. Because there is such a concern about the paltry amount of exercise that most youth get in developed countries, physical education departments would be well advised to create charts and other resources for students to consider the kinds of physical activity that their traits most naturally support. Much of this information appears in Chapters 18 and 20 on sports and health, respectively.

13. Planning. Planning is associated with C+: methodical, focused, organized, and perfectionistic. Other aspects of planning draw on opposite ends of the O dimension: Higher O is associated with the creative aspect of planning as well as the aspect that entails complex interfaces, with lower O being associated with the detailed, concrete, step-by-step aspect that can test the patience of a high O. Know your temperament and find ways to compensate if you must engage in a kind of planning that draws on a trait opposite to what is most natural for you.

14. Secretarial Studies. The larger portion of administrative and secretarial work draws upon E-O-A+C+ (quiet, detail-oriented, deferential, and focused). More extraverted persons in this field may aim towards greater responsibility such as office management or be drawn towards more sociable roles that involve less pure secretarial work, such as that of a receptionist. More creative persons in this field may search for opportunities that entail more imagination and complexity, such as learning new kinds of computer applications and taking on ambitious projects.

15. Social Work. The natural profile for much of this work is N+E+O-A+C- (worrying over others' welfare, comfortable in the thick of the action, living in the here-and-now, being untiringly altruistic, and juggling many different responsibilities). Study your traits to determine how they do, and do not, support the demands placed on the social worker. Either find a niche that suits your individual temperament or find ways to compensate.

16. Teacher Education. The prototypical teacher is upbeat, optimistic, and untiring (N-E+). Early-grade teachers tend to be higher in O (enjoying complex interdisciplinary activities—a little bit of everything), higher in A (don't need to be as tough as the typical high school teacher), and higher in C (a premium placed on being, and staying, organized). In the higher grades, there is need for greater toughness (A-) and greater focus on a singular subject (O-). While organization (C+) is important at higher grades, it is less so than in the earlier ones. Those interested in administration should read Chapter 22 on leadership. The high O secondary teacher who becomes bored with repetition after some years can find new energy by finding outlets for curriculum design, coaching new teachers, working with publishers, and taking on extracurricular responsibilities. Know your profile and find ways to build on your trait strengths.

A Suggestion for Introducing Students to the Big Five

In order for all teachers (plus counselors, administrators, and so forth) to be able to use the Big Five with students, yet not have to worry about taking the time to define the concepts to them, the school should introduce all students to the Big Five at the beginning of the school year, e.g., in an advisory group or residence hall "getting acquainted" activity. Then throughout the school year, all teachers would need is some device to briefly remind students of the definitions (such as a wall poster) when wishing to apply the Big Five as part of a lesson plan. Such a beginning-of-the-year introduction to the Big Five could be easily accomplished in several hours over several days, with some homework aimed at personalizing the Big Five for students by involving family and others who are in their social networks. Suggested guidelines for lesson plans are available from the Center for Applied Cognitive Studies, along with the associated testing and materials for qualified people.

In lieu of a school-wide introduction, individual teachers may work individually or as a group to introduce students to the concepts by a simple combination of administering the SchoolPlace Big Five Profile and then using either this book or the SchoolPlace Big Five Workbook (a much briefer version of this book!—32 pages), plus some card sorts, posters, and other materials available from the Center for Applied Cognitive Studies.

In the chapters of this section, we have focused on using the Big Five to help maximize student learning and academic success. In the next and final chapter of this section, we will explore how the Big Five can help us understand some of the major distracters, or derailers, from school success.

17

Distractions from School Success

How Traits Relate to Stress and Conflict in Their Many Forms

> "Cry, the beloved country, for the unborn child that is the inheritor of our fear. Let him not love the earth too deeply. Let him not laugh too gladly when the water runs through his fingers, nor stand too silent when the setting sun makes red the veld with fire. Let him not be too moved when the birds of his land are singing, nor give too much of his heart to a mountain or a valley. For fear will rob him of all if he gives too much."
>
> --Alan Paton, *Cry, the Beloved Country* (1948/1987, p. 111)

Guide to This Chapter:

- The Nature of Distractors
- The Nature of Flow and How to Manage It
- The Nature of Conflict and How to Manage It
- The Nature of Stress and How to Manage It
- Major Distractors: Situations that Cause Stress, Disruption of Flow, and Conflict in the School Experience
- Coping
- Spotting Failure: The Risk Factors

Alan Paton describes a point of view in a country held captive by apartheid—what greater source of distraction from school success can be imagined? His solution seems to be detachment—don't become so enamored of the good in your life that fear of losing it leads you to compromise your principles in order to retain it. This is akin to a shopkeeper paying the mafia in order to keep the business open without being hurt or vandalized, or to a boy who abandons a friend in order to keep his girlfriend, or a girl who chooses not to earn good grades in order to maintain her popularity

Traits in School

N	E	O	A	C
Need for Stability	**Extraversion**	**Originality**	**Accommodation**	**Consolidation**
N+ Reactive	E+ Extraverted	O+ Explorer	A+ Adapter	C+ Focused
N= Responsive	E= Ambiverted	O= Moderate	A= Negotiator	C= Balanced
N- Resilient	E- Introverted	O- Preserver	A- Challenger	C- Flexible
N1: Worry	**E1: Approach Level**	**O1: Imagination**	**A1: Service**	**C1:Thoroughness**
N2: Temper	**E2: Group Orientation**	**O2: Range of Interests**	**A2: Compliance**	**C2: Structure**
N3: Outlook	**E3: Pace**	**O3: Innovation**	**A3: Humility**	**C3: Ambition**
N4: Coping Level	**E4: Leadership**	**O4: Zoom Scale**	**A4: Speak Out Level**	**C4: Concentration**
	E5: Trust			**C5: Methodicalness**
	E6: Tact			

among non-achieving partiers. Actually, I (Pierce) knew a Catholic boy in high school who stopped dating a Protestant girl in order to please his priest. I also knew a girl in college who hid her tests and papers so no one could see her (good) grades. Then there was the girl I dated when we were undergrads—she wore a stage mustache when I took her to dinner one weekend. The explanation: she did not want to become too enamored of her beauty (she was stunning without the mustache!), lest it cloud her judgment.

In this chapter, we want to examine some of the forces that would rob us of our deserved success: decent grades and developing into positive citizens. All of these forces fall somewhere under the heading of stress and conflict, so we will begin with coming to an understanding of how they work, and the common strategies for dealing with them.

The Nature of Distractors

Stress, conflict, and flow—these three form the core of what keeps us from attaining our goals. Recall the quote: "Faith, hope, and love, but the greatest of these is love." Well, stress is the mother of all distractions. Conflict and flow are major aspects of stress. But what is stress? When something gets in the way of your goal (immediate or long term), that is a stressor. If you're trying to get to class and a bully stops you, that is stress. If you're trying to solve a complex math problem and you can't think because of a conversation going on nearby, that is stress. The bully and the conversation are stressors. However, they are not intrinsically stressors. Something acquires the status of a stressor only when you decide that it is preventing you from pursuing your goal. Bullies are bad, conversations are benign, but both can be stressors, but only if you decide that that they are obstacles, or only if you let them distract you from your focus, your objective. When your romantic interest comes up from behind, gives you a hug, whispers in your ear, and wants to cuddle, that is a good thing. But if, at that moment, you are trying to hold together something delicate that you have glued and must hold for a while, then the invitation to cuddle or hang out is a stressor. Unless, of course, you decide that the gluing isn't important, say "What the heck," and join in the cuddling. Stressors are all in the eyes of the beholder, and that is one of the major keys to managing stress—we often have the power to defuse a stressor, sometimes by something so simple as changing our goal.

Conflict and flow relate to stress in this way: Conflict by its very definition means that two or more persons each want something that neither can have fully except at the expense of the other. So, by definition, conflict is stressful. I want quiet, you want music. Conflict. And stress. However, I can change my goal of being with you, leave the room, and find a quiet space away from you. Now you have your music, and I have my quiet. No more conflict, no more stress. Flow is total engagement: being so absorbed in your task that you lose all sense of time, place, temperature, hunger, and so forth. Two things take you out of flow: having insufficient resources (whether financial, mental, physical, or whatever) to successfully complete the task, or having so many resources that the task becomes trivial, a slam dunk. The former leads to frustration, the latter to boredom. Both states are "out of flow," unsatisfying, and typically stressful. The goal of self-management is to maximize flow, minimize conflict, and eliminate stressors.

The Nature of Flow and How to Manage It

We'll begin with flow. When you are bored, you are not challenged. Things are too easy. You need to perceive that you have at least a 50-50 chance of succeeding, and not much more than that, in order to stay in flow. Less than that, you're frustrated. More than that, bored. To stay in that flow zone there are two things you can do: increase/decrease your resources or increase/decrease the challenge. To relieve boredom, increase the challenge or decrease your resources. If you are bored listening to a class lecture, make note-taking more of a challenge, as in making mind maps, outlines, writing without linking verbs, writing in a second language (either totally or in phrases), creating diagrams or models of the lecture content, and so forth. Or engage in unnoticeable physical activity that engages your attention, such as yoga deep breathing, isometrics, or relaxation exercises. If you are frustrated reading a passage because it uses words you don't know, make a list, look up the definitions, and reread. I (Pierce) was bored in a graduate statistics class because other students didn't know basic arithmetic, and the teacher took time to explain it to them. Boring. I asked the prof if I could take the class as independent study. He agreed. Back in flow! So, much of the time, we are in control of staying in flow, whether by altering our personal behavior or by attempting to modify our environment or those people around us. We are rarely bored and usually have earbuds to catch National Public Radio when we're walking or riding the bus, or we make conversation with passengers. We always have a notepad and pencil, so if nothing's on the radio, we can make to-do lists, outline projects, and other things. Or we can record thoughts on our iPhones. Lance, the cracker baker, says, "Never go 'round hungry." We say, "Never go round out of flow!" With respect to traits, flow has to do with being engaged in your most natural traits for most of the time. For us, that is high O activity—working on complex, new problems that require some imagination. For someone else, it might be low A, such as being involved in some form of competition most of the time. Athletes and salespeople find this state natural and energizing (but would leave us cold and out of flow).

Traits in School

The Nature of Conflict and How to Manage It

Students of conflict management have identified two aspects that must be managed: preserving the relationship and gaining one's objective. In every conflict, one must ask these two questions: How much do I want to preserve my relationship with the person with whom I am in conflict, and how strongly do I want to hold out for getting what I want? The former is associated with A, the latter with C. Those who are higher in A tend to place a higher value on preserving the relationship (recall from the Bible the Book of Ruth's "Whither thou goest, I will go"), while those lower in A can be more cavalier about the relationship (recall from *Gone with the Wind* Rhett Butler's, "Frankly, my dear, I don't give a ...."). People higher in C tend to be more persistent in the pursuit of their goal, their object, their stake in the conflict, while those lower in C are more likely to let themselves be distracted by other matters. These relationships have been visualized in the form of a "stylebox" (see our explanation in Chapter 10), as you can review here in Figure 17.1.

Figure 17.1 Stylebox: Conflict Management Style

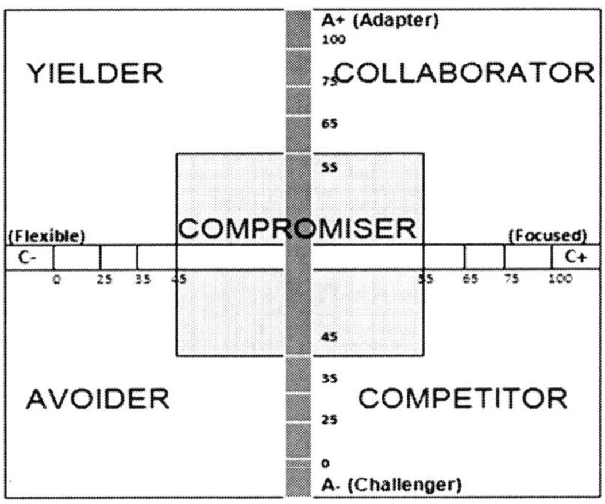

Persons with extreme scores on these two traits are likely to have one strongly preferred style of managing conflict. In conflict, one high in A and low in C is likely to be a "Yielder" who gives in to the other in order to preserve the relationship; A-C-, an "Avoider" who escapes for the moment hoping for a better day; A-C+, a "Competitor" fighting for their stake; A+C+, a "Collaborator" who negotiates for a win-win solution; and A=C=, a "Compromiser" who tries to meet the other half way, not holding out for their original stake, but not abandoning it altogether. Research shows, however, that all five styles can be beneficial in different situations. Anyone who uses any one style consistently will come across as a bully, or spineless, or cowardly, or thoughtless. If you feel that you rely on one style to the exclusion of others, perhaps you would find it helpful to keep a journal of how you behave in conflict situations. Think about how you might handle conflict differently next time and which of the styles might have been more productive, more satisfying for you and the other person(s). Discuss these styles with those close to you, and invite them to think through which style would be appropriate when you enter a conflict with them or with others. They will realize the value in avoiding the exclusive use of any one style.

Some say the "Collaborator" style is best and could be used exclusively, but, in fact, sometimes you just have to avoid, or yield, or compromise, or stand up for yourself, and not always insist on taking the time and emotional energy required for the collaborative win-win.

The Nature of Stress and How to Manage It

For the remainder of this chapter, we want to present some of the specific stressors that tend to distract students from school success. They are all potential stressors, in the sense that they all have the potential to prevent us from making progress towards a goal, whether a small, immediate goal, such as hearing what the teacher is saying, or a large, remote goal, such as winning a scholarship. Some of these stressors can be managed by manipulating the situation for return to the flow state. Some can be managed by using one of the conflict management strategies. For the others, there are really only two things that can be done to offset a stressor: eliminate the stressor itself and/or eliminate the effects of the stressor.

There are four ways to turn a stressor into a benign event: 1) Eliminate the stressor itself; 2) Change your goal, so that the event is no longer an obstacle; 3) Find a way to buffer the stressor, to soften or mask its effects; or 4) Reframe the stressor so it becomes benign. Let us say the stressor is caring for an elderly relative. It is a stressor because it keeps you from putting adequate time into your studies or into some other worthy pursuit. You could eliminate the stressor by placing the elderly relative in a nursing home, by hiring an at-home nurse, by going to boarding school, or by just refusing to accept the caregiver role. Or you could change your goal several ways, for example: 1) Defer the goal to a later time and not worry about it until the need for caregiving is over; 2) Modify the goal (rather than going for top all-around GPA, go for a subject award, such as a math or creative writing cup); 3) Eliminate some other goal of lesser importance to make more time for studies (such as stopping involvement with a club, a team, a performance group, or a job that does not have as much meaning for you as the grades or the relative); 4) You could modify other goals in order to give you more time for study, such as, instead of running outdoors, run in place on a mini-trampoline (or some other apparatus) in the room with your relative; so you exercise and attend at the same time; 5) Buffer the stressor by moving your study area into the relative's bedroom, or wherever much of your time would be spent with them, so you can easily switch from study to caregiving; 6) Use study methods that do not require isolation and quiet, such as audio devices, flash cards (have the relative call things out to you, if possible, making them a study partner), studying with a peer while caregiving, either by inviting the peer to be with you while caregiving or by communicating with the peer on the telephone or computer while caregiving. Or you could reframe the stressor and just simply decide that it isn't stressful, that it is just another item on your list of responsibilities, and that you'll get it all done, prioritizing as usual and not doing the things with lower priorities (e.g., makeup, gardening, or watching television).

Traits in School

When the worst happens, as the stressor grabs you, and you feel the full effects of the fight-or-flight syndrome, it is imperative that you get aerobic exercise as soon as possible after the stressful episode is over. The toxic effect of stress—the cortisol pumped into your system as the result of sympathetic arousal aimed at enabling you to run from the "Bengal tiger" (i.e., the stressor)—will stay in your system for up to 2 ½ days. Unless flushed by aerobic exercise, these toxins will do damage to your body over time.

Now let's take a look at some of the stressors specific to the school setting.

The Major Distractors:
Situations that Cause Stress, Disruption of Flow, and Conflict in the School Experience

After-School Jobs

When a student must work for pay outside school hours, three factors are particularly important in whether the work experience is helpful or harmful with respect to school success: the number of hours worked, the reason for working, and the quality of the work itself. Fifteen hours a week seems to be the threshold, with fewer hours associated with generally positive school performance, and more hours with negative. When the hours crawl above 15 a week, above three a day, high school students tend to experience lower grades, increased absences from school, greater substance use, and a preference for more "crip" courses (taking easier courses is one way to compensate for their long work hours that make homework difficult). When the reason for working is to save for further studies, the effect is more positive on school performance, while working for money to buy new media is not. Finally, the quality of the work experience is a factor. To the degree that the work expectations match the basic temperament of the student, the experience will not be as stressful, and more energy will be available, e.g., for doing homework. N+ students should have low stress work, E+ should have lots of activity and people contact, E- should have relatively quiet and solitary work, O+ should avoid work that is too repetitive and prefer work that allows a certain amount of judgment and imagination, O- should find comfort in routines, A- enjoy competitive work, A+ cooperative work, C- like work that enables them to switch back and forth among different tasks, and C+ prefer to set goals and achieve them in an orderly fashion. When job expectations match these qualities, minimal fatigue ensues. While in college, I (Jane) needed to work part-time (20 hours a week) to cover my expenses. As I mentioned in an earlier chapter, I made good grades, was on the Dean's List, and graduated with honors. I regarded students as slackers if they took their college experience less seriously than I did. As they slept late, sat around talking and listening to music, or played bridge, I was working or studying. Because I had less free time, I had to make the most of my time outside of work and class. Even though I score low in consolidation, I applied myself since I realized that my available study time was so valuable. Now I know that my low score on Chapter also helped me handle the stress of working.

> Teenagers complain there's nothing to do, then stay out all night doing it.
> --Bob Phillips,
> Texas journalist

Bullying

Bullying is a conduct disorder, a form of aggression whereby one intentionally desires to harm another person. The bullying may be verbal, physical, or psychological "attack or intimidation that is intended to cause fear, distress, or harm to a victim" (Lerner and Steinberg, 2004, p. 360). Bullying is at the maximum in elementary school, decreasing up through the high school years and leveling off at around 1 in 10 boys, 1 in 40 girls (that is a global average). What makes a bully a bully? The research points to two causes: genetics and environmental models (a "bully pulpit" as it were!). Bullies appear to adopt a kind of "cognitive script" (p. 361) from persons in their family or neighborhood. The trait profile that is primarily genetic and that makes one more susceptible to adopting the bully role is an impulsive profile: N+E+O+A-C- (reactive, sociable, curious, challenging, and unfocused; pp. 636-7). Two subtraits are especially common among bullies: motor restlessness (E3+) and poor concentration (C4-). Research has found that levels of testosterone are related, but in an interesting way. Individuals with high testosterone (that is the primarily genetic part of the equation) who feel marginalized by society are more prone to become bullies, while those with higher testosterone who feel a sense of flourishing and success tend to become leaders. Lerner and Steinberg (2004, pp. 650-651) cite two programs that have effectively addressed bullying: the Norwegian Olweus Bullying Prevention Program (see http://www.clemson.edu/olweus/) and one designed by G. R. Patterson (1982). The most effective anti-bullying programs are bimodal, teaching skills to both students and parents. Another option is for schools and communities to create organizations that can channel these marginalized students into responsible leadership roles. An increasingly effective constraint on bullying is the School Resource Officer (SRO), campus-based police officers who are both friend and authority (see more at www.nasro.org).

Depression

Julia Graber (in Lerner and Steinberg, 2004, pp. 587 ff.) writes about the problems associated with teens' tendency to internalize problems (i.e., ruminating, daydreaming, and otherwise obsessing, as opposed to talking about them, expressing them through music and art, journal writing, and so forth). The more youth internalize, the more likely they are to experience moodiness at the mild extreme, and depression and other disorders at the serious extreme. By the 15th year, the incidence of depression is similar to adults', and it is about twice as frequent among girls as boys. Caucasians have a higher incidence than African American teens, and poverty puts Caucasians at greater risk for depression than it does African Americans. Over half of the teens experiencing major depression have another disorder (having two such linked disorders is called comorbidity), and the other disorder is more likely to have appeared before the depression. For example, sustained general anxiety often precedes depression. In addition, early physical maturing is associated with depression in both sexes. Depression is associated with several different forms of negative cognitive processing such as negative self-views, faulty attributions, and expecting the worst. Ruminating on these negative thoughts makes it all the worse, with girls being more likely to ruminate than boys. These faulty cognitive processes have likely been inherited from parents, picked up from peers, and so forth.

These negative cognitive processes can be modified through cognitive behavioral therapy. One of the more effective techniques is one developed by Martin Seligman. Perhaps you recall our explanation of his approach in Chapter 2 (see Figure 2.1 and Table 2.2). As a reminder, when a youth explains a bad event (e.g., a poor math grade, a broken date) in terms that are *internal* ("I am dumb at math"), *permanent* ("I'll never do any better"), and *pervasive* ("I'll fail at everything else too"), then we must encourage them to consider alternative explanations that are *external* ("You had to work the night before, and had no time to study"), *temporary* ("You can find more time to study for the next test and do better"), and *limited* ("You have done and will do better on your other subjects"). Conversely, when they discount a good outcome (e.g., a good grade in math) with an explanation that is external ("I was lucky"), temporary ("That's the last good math grade I'll ever get"), and limited ("I won't get that good a grade in any other subject"), then we need to encourage them to consider alternative explanations that are more healthy and, hopefully, accurate (Internal: "I earned it by studying hard", Permanent: "I can keep up this pattern indefinitely", and Pervasive: "I can do this well in my other subjects if I apply myself"). Students who are higher in N, lower in O, and lower in A may resist thinking through such alternative explanations. Such changes in thinking don't come quickly. Be persistent and supportive in inviting them to consider more optimistic explanations for both bad (external, temporary, and limited) and good outcomes (internal, permanent, and pervasive). Consider modeling this behavior yourself in the presence of your teen. Think through the possible explanations for good/bad things that have happened to you; have a conversation with your teen about possible explanations; try to find internal, pervasive, and permanent explanations for good outcomes and external, limited, and temporary explanations for bad outcomes. Follow political, sports, television, and other popular personalities in the news, study their explanations of successes and failures, and then characterize them as more optimistic or pessimistic.

Dropping Out

Of course, dropping out of school is the ultimate distraction from school success. The risk factors for dropping out have recently been summarized by Schargel, Thacker, and Bell (2007). We list them here:

Previous School Experience:

- Absent 20 or more times during the previous school year
- Retained in at least one grade
- Low grades (Cs and Ds or below)
- Disciplinary problems or disruptive behavior
- Attended five or more schools during a lifetime

Personal or Psychological Characteristics:

- External locus of control (i.e., being in agreement with others' perceptions of their individual abilities, worth, or value—believed or actual)
- Low self-esteem
- At least one disability (e.g., ADHD, learning disabilities)
- Poor peer support
- Depression or other emotional problems
- Early sexual activity or promiscuity
- Substance abuse

Adult and Family Responsibilities of Student:

- Has a child
- Must work to help support the family

Family Background and Cohesion:

- Single-parent home
- Permissive parenting
- Poor parent-child relationships
- Family receives public assistance
- Neither parent nor guardian is employed
- Primary language of the family is not English
- Sibling has dropped out of school
- Parent(s) did not graduate from high school

School-Caused Risk Factors:

- Ineffective discipline system
- Overburdened school counselors
- Negative school climate
- Retention and/or suspensions used to control discipline (rather than addressing causes in other ways)
- Disregarding student-learning styles
- Passive instructional strategies
- Lack of relevant curriculum
- Low expectations of student achievement
- Fear of school violence

Parental discipline, monitoring, concern, encouragement, and consistency have also been linked to academic achievement. Children whose parents consistently set high standards work harder and do better in school. Additionally, an authoritative parenting style, characterized by warmth and concern coupled with boundaries (i.e., clear rules and limits), has been shown to have a positive effect on academic achievement. I (Jane) experienced this my entire school career from my parents, who did not have much education. Good grades were insisted upon, especially by my dad, who grew up in a rural area, finished the 8th grade, and was self-taught thereafter. Even when I went to graduate school at age 32 to get my MBA—taking out a student loan to pay for it, he asked me what my grades were at the end of the first semester. I had received three A's and a B+. Upon hearing this, he said, "You'd better get that 'B' up!" And I did!

Early/Late Maturation

The timing of puberty is strongly related to adolescent mental health (Lerner and Steinberg, 2004, pp. 29 ff.). Here, there is a strong sex difference. Specifically, girls suffer from early puberty by the tendency to associate with older youth while lacking the discipline to handle the older kids' risky behavior. Early maturing girls tend to get pregnant earlier, have more abortions, attain lower educational levels, and achieve lower employment status. Boys, on the other hand, are more likely to benefit from early puberty, as they tend to find themselves more popular and self-controlled. Early maturing boys tend to make better grades than other boys, while late maturing girls tend to make better grades than other girls. Early maturing girls who live in the city are more likely to use drugs. In general, kids who mature earlier OR later than their peers tend to experience more stress. Early maturers have the equipment without the experience, while later maturers have the experience but not the equipment. Both are stressful situations for adolescents. We have not seen research on this subject, but it would make sense that early or late maturation will have less effect on boys or girls who are lower in N and higher in C, as these individuals tend to be naturally rational, methodical, and oriented towards problem solving. It is the teens who are higher in N and lower in C who would likely benefit from particularly authoritative parenting that helps with goal setting, planning strategies to meet goals, changing schools to avoid toxic peer groups, and providing ongoing support for making progress towards goals.

Finding One's Voice

Mary Belenky (et al, 1997) writes about the stereotypical girl in the U.S. who is discouraged by parents and other elders from developing her own "voice." Instead, she is encouraged to defer to the judgment of others (e.g., teachers, elders, religious leaders). This is discussed at greater length in Chapter 2. Suffice it to say here that failure to develop one's independent sense of judgment and decision-making ability delays maturation and discovery of the true self. While boys and girls can both suffer from this practice, it is clearly more of a problem for girls—not all girls, clearly, but for many of them. The role of adults in all kids' lives should be to help them develop their independent sense of judgment through such techniques as the "T-bar" analysis, whereby you simply draw a line down the page and list the benefits of a course of action on one side, the concerns on the other. When trying to decide among multiple courses of action, do one T-bar for each possible course of action, and then select the action that has the most significant benefits, the fewest significant concerns. Teens most susceptible to being discouraged from developing their voices are high in N and A and low in O —they want to please and to honor tradition; so they need special support in learning to think for themselves. Dr. Craig Nelson, prize-winning University of Indiana expert on how to teach critical thinking, has primarily spread his suggestions through faculty workshops. Some of his material is now available online (such as http://ctl.csudh.edu/SpeakerSeries/Nelson05.htm). Also, check out his list of published writings at http://www.bio.indiana.edu/facultyresearch/faculty/Nelson.html.

Gender Role Stereotypes

This day and age, mainstream culture purports to keep all options open for both boys and girls. In practice, however, much gender-role stereotyping goes on privately in the homes of our youth, in their neighborhoods, and in their peer groups. Teens most subject to gender role stereotyping tend to be N+ and O-. They tend to worry about doing anything that doesn't fit the mold. Youth must be encouraged to consider school subjects and activities with an open enrollment where everyone has an equal right and opportunity to try for success in any area in which they have an interest. The only way to discover that one has talent (in music, cooking, foreign languages, math) is to try it.

Another, and insidious, form of stereotyping is that of blaming African-American males for being under-represented among high school and college graduates. African-American females are more likely to graduate from high school and college. In 2005, the black female:male ratio for college degrees was 1.69 to 1. These differences can be explained only by the effect of stereotyping, not innate ability (Nisbett, 2009, pp. 102-103). It is the responsibility of everyone who works with young people to consciously show equally positive expectations to everyone.

Media

This is a tough one! The media—television, movies, radio, computers in their many forms, MP3 players, telephones, smart phones, Kindles, iPads—are the ultimate metaphor for life in general. In every area—food, art, sports, politics, education, construction, and on and on—there is much of high quality and usefulness side-by-side with much that is of poor quality and little or no usefulness. The exercise of judgment in the use of media, alas, is not much superior to the exercise of judgment in food and sport. Excesses in each field leads to its own special forms of abuse: in food, overweight; in sport, neglect of family; and in the media, addiction. In an interesting article in *Time*, March 2, 2009, about the problem of Internet abuse in mainland China, writers defined Internet addiction as non-work-related Internet activity for six uninterrupted hours daily for six years. To overcome the addiction, the Chinese send teens and adults to boot camps of about three months, where a regimen of military-style drill, exercise, reading, and discussion groups (and NO Internet access) weans them.

If we were to use the Chinese guideline as a standard for media in general, that would suggest that six hours a day of non-school or non-work media for six years constitutes addiction and requires attention. This would include not just the Internet and its social networks, but watching television, IM-ing, telephone conversations, blogging, listening to music, and so on. In Chapter 2, we discussed media use at some length, especially with respect to how it affects trait levels. Below we provide a summary of how media could relate to chances for school success (much of this repeats what we wrote in Chapter 2):

- Needless to say, time spent with non-school or non-work media is time not spent studying for class.

Traits in School

- Viewing violent programming is associated with indifference towards aggressive, violent behavior, and, in some instances, increases in aggressive, violent behavior.
- Viewing sexually promiscuous programming is associated with how early one becomes sexually active and also with unwanted pregnancies.
- Faster music promotes positive mood (E+), while slower music is more relaxing (N-).
- When one is sad, sad music appears to be more soothing (i.e., matching the mood is comforting and tends to move one towards the lower end of N).
- Listening to one's favorite kinds of music is associated with improved mood during the listening and improved mental functioning after the listening.
- Listening to music of any kind interferes with concentration on other tasks (C-), as one simply cannot do two things at once.
- Using a cell phone while alone, e.g., in one's own room, has no known behavioral impact on self or others (research suggests it may have a physical effect, as holding the cellular unit up to one's ear has been tentatively linked to brain tumors—so use the speakerphone feature whenever possible). In essence, it is no different than using a regular telephone. Cell phones affect behavior primarily in social situations. More extraverted people use cell phones more in social situations, and it bothers them less to be around others using cell phones, while it bothers more introverted people to be around cell phone users. Interestingly, N- persons are more upset than N+ persons when they are around cell phone users (probably because N+ persons are soothed by the social intercourse, while N- people find it unnecessary and intrusive). In a social setting, texting can be detrimental to relationships. If you're texting, then you cannot focus on the conversation, and you decrease interaction with the group.
- Computer use (including desktops, laptops, phones with computer features, and gaming consoles) has spawned much research on the health of its degree of use, whether for games, work, entertainment, or social connectivity. A study of 1,102 youth ages 12-17 (a project of the Pew Research Center) reported its findings in November 2008 ("Teens, Video Games, and Civics"). The report found that practically all early teens play video games, with the percentage decreasing over time, particularly for girls. The thrust of the study was to determine whether gaming is associated with the tendency to be engaged in positive civic activities such as "following politics, persuading others how to vote, contributing to charities, volunteering, or staying informed about politics and current events." Their conclusion was that gaming neither encouraged nor discouraged civic engagement..
- Also, the research shows that about 1 in 4 teens plays games alone, with no social contact, either face-to-face or online. This level of solitary gaming is consistent with the fact that about 1 in 4 teens will score strongly E- on the Big Five. So, more introverted teens play games in a more introverted style. Not a big deal. The satisfying aspect of this finding is that gaming does not increase solitary activity, as many suspected. Gaming is a social activity to the degree that the individuals playing the games are social individuals.

- Finally, because computer applications such as word processing, email, spreadsheets, database, graphics, and so forth enable one to create with abandon at great speed and great variety, there is a tendency for individuals not to self-monitor, but to create volumes of material or output. The result is a tendency to be more complex than normal (O+), more creative than normal (O+), more confrontational than normal (A-), and more spontaneous than normal (C-). For example, a young woman at Duke University in 2010 created a PowerPoint presentation for a friend in which she rated all the young men with whom she had had sex. Her friend forwarded the presentation, and it ultimately became a global, viral phenomenon
- As a general rule, the more television watched, the greater the tendency to embrace stereotypical gender roles (Lerner and Steinberg, p. 254).

Natural Trait-Related Distractions

Each of the Big Five supertraits has a type of distraction associated with it. Here, we recap what they are:

Need for Stability (N): This trait is about susceptibility to stress. One's score on N is an estimate of the amount of stress one can experience before experiencing the "General Adaptation Syndrome," the fight-or-flight response. When this happens, the brain shuts down most of its ability to learn, to remember, plan, solve problems, or make decisions. One reverts to one's training or is on "autopilot," as it were. The lower the N score, the more stress one can handle before shutting down. The higher the score, the less stress one can handle. Students with higher scores need to learn how to remove a source of stress from their minds and to flush the cortisol out of their system with as much aerobic exercise as possible (though even a 10-minute brisk walk helps)—all of this before trying to learn new materials or skills.

Extraversion (E): This trait is about the amount of sensory stimulation one can handle without being distracted by it. Higher scores, i.e., more extraverted individuals, in fact like more noise, more activity, more hustle and bustle, and find it relatively natural to learn in the midst of such stimulation, while lower scores, i.e., more introverted students, find it harder to ignore such stimulation. Learning environments need to provide both kinds of spaces—quieter for more introverted students, more bustle for more extraverted ones. I (Pierce) am an ambivert (in the middle); so when I was in graduate school and had to spend most of the day in the library, I tried to find a study space near a stairwell and/or a window so there was at least a little activity going on! I like it quiet, but if it is too quiet, I get jittery. Our younger daughter, when she worked alone in her home as an insurance agent, turned on the radio and television in nearby rooms so it felt more like there was hustle and bustle nearby, thereby simulating an office environment—she has a much higher score on E than her parents!

Originality (O): This trait is about how much novelty and complexity one can experience before it becomes unpleasant and the need to return to doing something more familiar and simple takes over. So, with the lower the O score, too much new material becomes frustrating, uncomfortable, and stressful, while for the higher O score, too much practice and repetition leads to boredom and a strong need for diversion. To avoid the distraction of boredom, higher O students need the opportunity to experience novelty and complexity. And to avoid the distraction of frustration, lower O students need the opportunity to practice, polish to perfection, and simplify complex material.

Accommodation (A): This trait is about the spirit of competition versus cooperation in a learning environment. The lower the score, the more that competition is welcome, while higher scores are typically associated with an aversion to competition and a preference for cooperation. An emphasis on competition is not as conducive to learning for the higher A as it is for the lower A. It distracts their attention from learning and onto the unnaturalness of the competition itself. Learning environments should provide both kinds of opportunities, so that higher and lower A learners can participate to their level of comfort in either kind of activity.

Consolidation: (C) This trait, with respect to learning environments, is about being allowed to finish something before starting something else. Higher scorers on C really like to get to a stopping point before moving to another kind of activity, and are annoyed by disorganization, lack of methodology, and lack of a plan. Teaching/learning plans that are characterized by lots of jumping around from topic to topic, rather than following a clear sequence and logical development, are disconcerting to these students, and students tend to hold the teacher in lower esteem as a result. Students lower in C tend to find such unstructured and spontaneous experiences more comfortable, more natural. They find highly structured learning experiences too constraining and yearn for spontaneity.

Neighborhood/Socioeconomic Status

The socioeconomic status of neighborhoods is directly related to school achievement and other indicators of positive development, but more so for boys than for girls. This suggests that parents may be more permissive for boys, who through greater independence are more subject to neighborhood influences (Lerner and Steinberg, 2004, p. 476ff.). In poor neighborhoods and families, kids are exposed to dramatically less use of language. In families on welfare, children hear, on average, only 600 words daily, while the children of professionals hear 2,000 words daily on average. This gap produces a dramatic difference in language exposure and learning at home by the time school begins for a child. Similarly, children of professionals receive six encouraging comments for every reprimand, while children of welfare families receive two reprimands for every word of encouragement. (Keep in mind Carol Dweck's finding that praising kids for their effort is more motivating than praising them for being smart—the latter tends to lead to backing off of challenges and playing it safe.) These are not only distractions, but also major deficits that are compounded as the child grows older. They can be compensated for by community programs, longer school days, and year-round school.

Peer Pressure

Review the longer treatment of this subject in the discussion of peers in Chapter 2. In summary, during the ages of 8 to 25, the strongest environmental influence on the formation of personality is the "salient peer group"—the one peer group among one's many peer groups at any one time that stands out as the group with which an individual most strongly identifies, most strongly wants to be like and be accepted by. This salient peer group can be a positive contribution to school success, or it can be a major distraction, or somewhere in between. Counselors, teachers, administrators, and parents have some power in removing students from toxic peer groups, whether through changing schools, changing neighborhoods, changing classes, or by imposing consequences on continuing association with the peer group. In one case we know of, a child was in a toxic peer group, and the parents cut off her financial allowance until she stopped associating with the group. That did the trick, fortunately.

Physical School Atmosphere (air, sun, ions, smells, noise)

The physical learning environment can distract the learner in many subtle ways. In rooms/buildings with air handling systems that recirculate air, the ratio of negative to positive ions is suboptimal. When negative ions are depleted, about 1 in 3 individuals will become drowsy because of less oxygen getting to the brain (negative ions, the kind generated by "smoke eating machines" and popularly sold by gadget stores, pull particles out of the atmosphere and permit a greater proportion of oxygen to enter the body with each breath). The solution is for these students to go outside into fresh air with some frequency, to open windows to the learning areas, or to put ion generators in the air handling system.

Natural sunlight also makes a difference. Sunlight causes the pineal gland to stop producing melatonin, the sleep neurotransmitter. This results in increased arousal and alertness. Lack of sunlight in the morning results in many individuals' never awaking fully. In some, this results in "winter depression," or SAD (seasonal affective disorder). In many countries of Europe, buildings are required to be designed in such a way that every room has access to sunlight. The solution for classrooms/learning areas with no windows to let in sunlight is to light the rooms/areas with lamps that have a CRI (color rendering index) of 90 or higher ("grow" lights have this property). A CRI of less than 90 results in at least the blue part of the spectrum of light being missing, resulting in a drop in alertness. This principle, of course, applies not just to classrooms, but dormitory rooms, bedrooms, study halls, and the like. Once nighttime has set in, it becomes less important, UNLESS one wants to stay up for a long time, i.e., beyond a normal bedtime, as in an all-nighter or late-nighter. In this case, it would be wise to have a lamp with CRI > 90 for maximum alertness and learning efficiency. Of course, this could then lead to another serious problem, sleep deprivation.

Other aspects of the physical environment can also distract from learning. Many times we have sat in a classroom with noisy lawnmowers or leaf blowers nearby. Ideally, such noisemakers should be limited either to areas where instruction is not happening or to hours when classes are not being held. Strong smells also distract from learning: strong fumes from paint, cleaning materials, and the like cause headaches and learning inefficiency.

Traits in School

Pregnancy

Teenagers who watch television programs with sexual content are more likely to become pregnant or get someone pregnant (*Pediatrics*, November 2001). RAND Corporation surveyed 2,000 teens ages 12 to 17 about their television viewing and sexual activity. In a follow-up survey three years later, 700 of the teens reported having had sex. Those with more extreme viewing (the 90th percentile) were twice as likely to have been involved with a pregnancy. Those living with both parents were less likely to become pregnant. The study authors recommended putting a cap on teens' viewing of television with sexual content. Also, as these programs tend to show sex without its consequences, they recommended that the television industry should write into its scripts the effects of unprotected sex.

That said, professional home visits to poor, unmarried teen moms reduced their arrest rate by half and decreased the risk of their abusing their children by a factor of around 5. Other programs aimed at mental stimulation, parenting instruction, and emotional support (e.g., the Perry preschool project in Michigan and the Child Parent Center in Chicago) are equally successful (Lerner and Steinberg, 2004, pp. 646-7). An interesting finding is that teens who get their sex education in school from health professionals are more likely to start having intercourse later than those who get it elsewhere. "School sex education delayed the age of intercourse." (Graham, 2004, 142)

How do traits relate to sexual behavior? In several ways. Beginning with higher curiosity (O+) (curiosity tends to get us interested in sex in the first place), boys who are higher in N and lower in C (a classic impulsive profile) tend to be more curious about sex, while girls who are higher in E tend to be more curious. While lack of constraint may get boys started, and excess of sociability may get girls started, it is low C that keeps both sexes going—both boys and girls who are lower in C, once having started sexual activity, are more likely to continue with the most frequency. At the college level, females higher in both E and A tend to show more sexual activity. How do parents, advisors, and teens use this information? Well, it depends primarily on your philosophy. However, given the inevitability of sexual activity, two strategies appear wise, at a minimum: First, encourage formal exposure to sex education, and second, do whatever possible to prevent unprotected sex. Focus on students whose traits put them more at risk.

Substances (drugs, alcohol, caffeine, tobacco)

Laura Chassin and her coresearchers (in Lerner and Steinberg, 2004, pp. 665 ff.) report that the risk profile for substance abuse includes temperamental deviance, mental shortcomings (especially verbal and analytical), and suboptimal parenting, the three of which combine to increase the likelihood that teens experiencing them will come under the influence of drug using peers (p. 675). They cite (p. 676) these terms associated with temperament problems (from which it is easy to construct a Big Five profile, which we have inserted in parentheses):

- Unconventionality (O+)
- Low ego control (N+, A+, A-, C-)

- Sensation seeking (E+, O+)
- Aggression, impulsivity (N+, A-, C-)
- Inability to delay gratification (C-)
- Reactivity (N+)
- Emotionality (N+, E+)
- Slow adaptability (O-)

Positive schooling (clear rules, etc.) and authoritative parenting can reduce the risk of substance use in young people with this profile.

The mental shortcomings come under the head of executive function—mental abilities that are associated with self management. Specifically Chassin cites (p. 677) these abilities, or the lack thereof:

- Goal/future orientation
- Planning
- Organizing
- Focused attention
- Ability to form hypotheses
- Mental flexibility
- Decision making
- Judgment
- Inhibition control
- Self regulation
- Poor retention

She points to the need for continually assisting these kids in setting goals, planning steps to achieve, monitoring progress, providing feedback, modifying the plan as needed, and rewarding progress.

In many, if not most, cases, teen drug use is a form of self-medication for stress (p. 681). Stresses resulting from depression and poor anger management are better predictors for substance use than is the stress that results from anxiety (p. 683). Emphasize anger management and treatment for depression.

Summer Vacation

In Chapter 14, in the section "The School District," we identify summer vacation as the major reason that the children of poor and working class families fall behind in school achievement. Programs such as KIPP have reversed this trend.

Coping

Each of the distracters that we have just now identified is a significant source of stress for teens. When one or more of these distracters/stressors emerges in one's life, one must decide how to cope. The word cope comes from the French *coup* or *couper* (and from earlier Greek and Latin words) meaning a "blow' or "to strike out" (not in the sense of baseballs three strikes and you're out, but in the sense of attacking). So, to cope means to protect oneself from stressors by attacking the problem either at its root cause or by some other method. Coping strategies emerge from the interaction of two variables: 1) the amount of personal control the individual exhibits (using an intentional, voluntary, controlled behavior, versus engaging in an instinctive, involuntary behavior), and 2) the amount of involvement the individual exhibits in the coping behavior (active engagement versus passive disengagement). The four kinds of coping strategies that appear in the four quadrants resulting from plotting these two dimensions are presented in Figure 17.2.

Figure 17.2 The Four Kinds of Coping Strategies

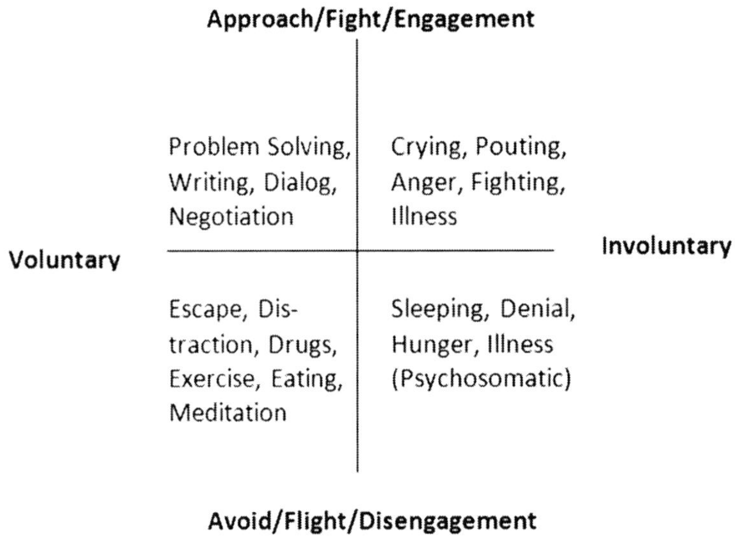

Typically, involuntary responses predominate in the younger years, with voluntary responses accompanying maturity (Lerner and Steinberg, 2004, p. 276). This is related to the fact that the frontal cortex matures later than the limbic system. From an evolutionary perspective, this is likely due to forced earlier maturity/puberty in modern society, and teens of long ago most likely experienced a closer synchrony in the development of the two systems (p. 283). As a general rule, engaged strategies (i.e., those in which the individual is actively participating, such as talking the situation through) result in more positive development (i.e., they tend to make one more resilient) than disengaged strategies (i.e., the individual's mind is not actively addressing the situation, such as listening to one's playlist). Such disengaged strategies tend to put one more at risk (p.278). These coping strategies, while they can be taught to youth with any trait profile, tend to be more natural for some traits than others. The engagement strategies tend to be more linked with E+A-, whereas the unengaged tend to be linked with the opposite of this, E-A+. The voluntary strategies tend to be linked with N-O+C+, whereas the involuntary tend to be linked with the opposite of this, N+O-C-. We recommend that students, parents, school, and community members get together in formal or informal settings and share ideas on how to maximize the use of voluntary, engaged coping strategies. Especially important in these discussions is understanding that using a particular coping strategy is more natural for certain trait profiles than for others, and that one would benefit from figuring out how to adapt a coping strategy so that it builds on one's natural trait energies.

Spotting Failure: The Risk Factors

As a way of summarizing this chapter on distracters from school success, consider that all of the risk factors may be grouped into two categories. It would be helpful in every family, and for every student, to be aware of how they stand with regard to these two categories of risk factors, and what could be done to reduce the risk. Research has identified *moderators* and *mediators* (Lerner and Steinberg, 2004, pp. 263 ff) as the two broad categories of risk factors. Moderators are conditions that exist before stressors/distracters begin to threaten: age, gender, temperament, autonomic reactivity (your N scores, or how intensely you react to stress), supportive relationships, and effective cognitive style (such as the Kolb learning styles discussed in Chapter 13). When each of these conditions is optimal with respect to a particular stressor, then the effect of the stressor is minimal. For example, we mentioned that early maturation is more stressful for girls than for boys. So, if an early adolescent begins to show signs of physical maturity earlier than their peers, the effect will be more "moderate" for boys than for girls. It will also be more moderate for N- girls than for N+ girls. If both parents are present and they follow an authoritative parenting style with strong support and open channels of communication, then the effect will be more moderate. If the adolescent has learned problem solving strategies (or other procedures to use in a crisis or stressful situation) and has a successful pattern of using them as a coping device, then the effect will be more moderate.

These moderating factors are, in essence, preventive, like eating right and exercising are preventive with respect to health. The other factors are said to mediate, and in that sense they are like a contingency plan—when the stressor/distracter occurs, the mediating factors go into action, much like when one suffers a health problem, the hospital and its staff are there as a contingency, as a medium through which the stressor passes and its effect softened. These mediators include: coping strategies initiated by a concerned family, processes such as family councils that go into action when needed, and, again, cognitive style. The latter strategy, cognitive style, is both preventive and contingent, moderator and mediator. It softens the effect of a stressor by way of one knowing one will have some mental control over the situation, much like the religious attitude of "death, where is thy sting." Religious faith and practice in this same sense are both moderator and mediator, by dulling the edge and also by addressing the pain.

Here is an example. Should an individual be approached by a bully, how the teen handles it will be a function of moderators (Does the school have an ongoing bullying program that the student can call into action? Do the parents of the victim have a pattern of being supportive and following through? Has the teen learned routines that they can employ when bullied? Do the teen's traits help or hinder, given the type of bullying?) and mediators (Can appropriate tactics be implemented to stop or soften the effect of the bullying? Are the normal resources available [as opposed to being out of town, for example] at the time of the bullying?)

In the six chapters of this section, we have explored how the Big Five relates to what happens to adolescents during the school day. In the next section, we will explore how the Big Five relates to what happens after school: extracurricular activities, the family, personal health, and how we fit in with the diverse cultures of the world.

Part Four

Traits After School

Traits After School

18

The Big Five in Extra-curricular Activities

Sports & Exercise, Fine & Performing Arts, Social & Service Organizations

> "Since I was two years old, I haven't wanted to share."
>
> --Bobby Frasor, UNC-CH basketball guard, on the prospects of sharing the ACC title with Duke

Guide to This Chapter:

- How Traits Influence Students' Choices Outside the Classroom
- The Big Five in Exercise (in general) and Sports (in particular)
- The Big Five in the Fine and Performing Arts
- The Big Five in Social and Service Organizations

Life is about means and ends. The ends in our lives are our goals, and the means are planning, making decisions, and solving problems. The emphasis in the classroom is on acquiring the skills and knowledge necessary for embracing sound goals, and for the planning, decision-making, and problem-solving necessary en route to achieving our goals. Bobby Frasor was a senior at the University of North Carolina at Chapel Hill when, early in March 2009, he gave an interview to the press in anticipation of the upcoming basketball rematch with the Blue Devils from Duke University, just a few miles down the road. To win the game was for his Tar Heels to win the regular season Atlantic Coast Conference men's basketball championship, to win it outright, the kind of victory where you hold your head high. To lose the game would be for Chapel Hill to tie for first place with Duke. Bobby's goal was clear—he had no interest in sharing first place—he wanted first place for him and his team. He got it, with the Tar Heels beating Duke for the second time that season, and going on to win the NCAA national men's bas-

Traits After School

N	E	O	A	C
Need for Stability	**Extraversion**	**Originality**	**Accommodation**	**Consolidation**
N+ Reactive	E+ Extraverted	O+ Explorer	A+ Adapter	C+ Focused
N= Responsive	E= Ambiverted	O= Moderate	A= Negotiator	C= Balanced
N- Resilient	E- Introverted	O- Preserver	A- Challenger	C- Flexible
N1: Worry	**E1: Approach Level**	**O1: Imagination**	**A1: Service**	**C1:Thoroughness**
N2: Temper	**E2: Group Orientation**	**O2: Range of Interests**	**A2: Compliance**	**C2: Structure**
N3: Outlook	**E3: Pace**	**O3: Innovation**	**A3: Humility**	**C3: Ambition**
N4: Coping Level	**E4: Leadership**	**O4: Zoom Scale**	**A4: Speak Out Level**	**C4: Concentration**
	E5: Trust			**C5: Methodicalness**
	E6: Tact			

ketball championship a month later in Detroit versus the Spartans of Michigan State (after momentarily losing their momentum in the conference tournament). Young Bobby Frasor was clearly focused on his goal.

Sports participation has often been described as a laboratory, a training ground, for life. We would expand that notion to describe the entire spectrum of extracurricular activities—what students do outside of the classroom (excluding the intimacy of family life). To the extent that the classroom primarily provides skills and knowledge, extracurricular activities provide the opportunity to practice their applications to setting and achieving goals—winning games, setting records, earning a starting position on the team, besting one's time, winning an election, entering a competition, trying out new roles (secretary, treasurer, sergeant-at-arms, speaker, statistician, trainer, mascot, editor, sales rep).

How Traits Influence Students' Choices Outside the Classroom

Research (Csikszentmihalyi and Schneider, 2000, p. 14) shows that U.S. teens spend more time around peers and less time around adult role models. The consequence of this imbalance is a disadvantage with respect to having opportunities for observing positive role models in concentrated engagement. More precisely, American teenagers spend about 12 more hours weekly with peers, in comparison to teens in similar societies who spend proportionately more time around adults. One principle reason for this imbalance is the U.S. emphasis on school-sponsored activities that are nonacademic: sports, clubs, yearbooks, and the like. This makes the wise selection of extracurricular activities that much more important for students.

We will see throughout this chapter that the energy provided by one's traits makes some activities more natural than others. What we want to make clear is that, just because a particular trait provides natural energy for an activity, that does not mean that one has to have a certain score on that trait in order to excel in that activity. For example, persons who are more extraverted tend to be more attracted to being interior linemen in football—those high in E tend to like being in the thick of the action, where it is noisy, muddy, hard-hitting—full of sensory bombardment. However, being extraverted doesn't mean you'll be a good lineman, and being introverted doesn't mean you won't. All other things being equal (skill level, weight, age, gender, experience, and so forth), an extraverted lineman is likely to feel more natural spending long stretches of time in practice, while an introverted lineman is likely to begin yearning for something quieter with less sensory bombardment. In other words, when the natural energy for an activity is present in suboptimal levels, one is likely to be more fatigued or more stressed by that activity.

One may want to be an interior lineman but not have the natural traits for it. Why? Because Dad was. Because big brother was. Because Uncle Merv was. Because it is the only position left that I have a chance starting at. It could be for any of thousands of reasons. One of the things that extracurricular activities can do is allow us to learn which kinds of activities are supported by our natural trait energy (as well as by our abilities, values, and so forth), so that by the time we hit the workforce full-time and, perhaps, start a serious relationship or even a family, we have a good sense of who we are, what comes naturally for us, and how we can set smart goals that are consistent with what we bring to the table.

If one has the ideal profile for a given activity, however, that does not mean that you will be good at it. Feeling natural in the role is not the same thing as being good in it. You may lack experience, you may lack a requisite skill, you may have the wrong values, you may have other activities on which you place a higher priority and put in more practice there, you may have had poor instruction, you may lack critical physical characteristics, and so on. We once were asked to help a young manager who supervised 20 customer service representatives. We tested her, and her trait profile was ideal for leadership: N-E+O-A-C+. However, she had no control over her people, and conflict was rampant. After a 30-minute lunch conversation trying to understand what was going on, we asked her, "What kind of training have you had in management skills?" "None," she quipped. Well, we enrolled her in a management training class, and within a year the problems all went away. Sort of like trying to be a physician solely on the basis of having the right temperament (good bedside manner, careful decision maker, calm in crisis, and so forth), but without ever having gone to medical school!

These principles apply to every role in life. Having the natural traits for a role doesn't mean you'll automatically be good at it, nor does not having the ideal trait profile mean you'll be bad or inept. Having the ideal traits for something makes you a natural for the role, but, like the physician with the good bedside manner, you also need skills and knowledge. And, if you lack one or more traits for a role, you can find a context in which your deficiency is offset, or you can find a way to compensate for your deficiency. It can be as simple as high N persons selecting situations that are less stressful, or low C persons having a colleague who helps keep them organized. Now let's take a look at how traits play themselves out in several different extracurricular arenas.

The Big Five in Exercise and Sports

So, let's begin with a look at physical activities in both forms—exercise (noncompetitive) and sports (competitive) forms. In one sense, both are competitive, whether it is trying to best one's opposition or whether one is competing solely against one's own past best performance. In one sense, noncompetitive exercise is the same exercise time after time, with no intention of adding some challenge, of increasing the goal. If it is 100 pushups, 50 sit-ups, and a 30-minute run daily five days a week, with no interest in varying the pattern, then perhaps that could be described as purely noncompetitive. Nonetheless, here we will first discuss essentially noncompetitive exercise and its relation to traits; then a similar discussion of competition follows. We treat exercise first because it applies to a larger group—all sports participants exercise, but not all exercisers engage in sports.

> ***Caution:*** Research findings that associate traits with behaviors do not mean to claim that all persons with those traits exhibit those behaviors, but rather that many do. E+ folks *tend* to be leaders, but not all are, and likewise for other associations.

First, why do people exercise? One study (Courneya and Hellsten, 1998) identified six common motives for engaging in some kind of exercise regimen: appearance, enjoyment, health, socializing, stress control, and weight management. Those who identified appearance as their primary motive tended to score very high in need for stability (N++) and high in extraversion (E+). That makes sense, as these individuals tend to prefer staying in the thick of the action, which means being around people much of the time, and they are worriers who get concerned and anxious when they don't look as good as others. Being N++E+ certainly doesn't mean that you will necessarily exercise very much. And if you are an N++E+ who exercises but does it for some other reason, that is perfectly normal. All we are saying here is that many people who say they exercise in order to improve or maintain their physical appearance score N++E+. Those who list enjoyment as their motive for enduring the sweat and pain of exercise tend to be lower in N, very high in E, and high in O. These are people who tend to be unaffected by stress in general (not just the stress of exercise), who are active by their very nature (exercise is almost a way of life for them), and who are curious and imaginative (and so are likely to entertain themselves mentally while enjoying the endorphin rush). Those who claim improving their health as the exercise motive tend to be higher in E, A, and C. They are "people people," sociable and thoughtful of others. They tend to feel a sense of responsibility for keeping up their health for the sake of those relying on them, and their higher C sense of discipline feeds into that sense of responsibility. Next are those who state that their motive for exercise is social. Guess who? E+. Exercise as a way to meet and be with people. Enough said. Then there are those who exercise primarily as a way of offsetting the stress in their lives: N+E+O++. These individuals are by nature active, so an active coping strategy makes sense. In addition to being active, they enjoy the life of the imagination and are likely to use the time while exercising as an opportunity to escape into other worlds—reading or listening to books, music, talk radio, or even appreciating the changing seasonal beauty of nature in their neighborhood. Finally, weight management is the exercise motive for those who are N++E+, the same profile as those who list appearance as their motive. Weight = Appearance. Simple! Here is a summary of the motives for exercising:

Appearance:	N++E+
Enjoyment:	N-E++O+

Health: E+A+C+
Social: E+
Stress: E+O++
Weight: N++E+

It is interesting to note that E+ is a component of all six motives! Active people exercise. This suggests that the key to encouraging a more introverted teen to exercise may perhaps be to identify a motive other than these six, and to support that motive. What might be some motives for those who are more introverted other than these six? One certainly would be that exercise clears the mind, gets rid of the cobwebs that ensue from hours with books, computers, and hobbies. Regular exercise reduces mental errors. Aerobic exercise enhances memory and learning ability. Exercising is being responsible. These and other motives could spur the E- to start exercising. Also, note that O-, A-, and C- individuals do not tend to claim these motives for exercising, so either they don't exercise so much or they perhaps have other motives, such as

- it's being a change of pace (C-)
- a spur of the moment idea (C-)
- a competitive venture (A-)
- something to give one a competitive edge by being more mentally alert and physically developed (A-)
- enjoying the sheer repetitiveness of much exercise (O-; we have one O- friend who exercised so much that his body turned against him in the form of an immune system disorder, and he had to stop exercising altogether).

Traits have their reasons for exercising. That's good to know. What about the converse—do traits have their reasons for *not* exercising? Yes, they do. The same study that found the six motives also found four obstacles: embarrassment, lack of energy, lack of motivation, and lack of time. It is interesting that the profiles uncovered here are extremely similar. N++C- individuals listed embarrassment as their reason for not exercising (self-consciousness about one's body, about one's degree of physical coordination, about the quality of one's workout outfits, and so forth). This profile makes sense: Those who are naturally worriers and who lack the goal focus are more likely to use embarrassment as a reason to stay off the Jazzercise floor. Their commitment to goals that would profit from exercise is just not present.

Those with a profile of N+E-C- identified lack of energy. Think about it: E- individuals tend to be sedentary anyway, and lack of energy for intense activity is their nature. The typical introvert must rise above their nature to engage in serious exercise (of course, introverts who happen to be high in the subtrait E3, Pace, would be an exception to this "rule"). Couple introversion with worrisomeness and spontaneity, and you have even less energy for activity. Worry is fatiguing in and of itself, and a disciplined approach to exercise (the opposite of C-) tends to breed energy, while irregular exercise is less sustaining.

Traits After School

Lack of motivation ("I just don't care about exercise—it is not important to me, neither it, nor its supposed benefits") was the reason for not exercising given by those with a profile of N+C-. This combination—reactive and spontaneous—is typically associated with impulsive behavior. Exercise is typically a commitment to a regimen, and impulsive people just by their nature get their fill of regimen quickly. The last thing an impulsive N+C- student wants to do after a day of schedules, bells, class periods, deadlines, and prolonged periods of efforts at concentration, is to submit themselves to more. They would typically prefer to be free to follow their impulses and not be tied down to a course of action or an exercise regimen—maybe some reading, maybe some music, maybe text some friends maybe some room cleanup (nah!), maybe write a letter, maybe surf the net, and so on. But not more of the same C+ behavior—they've used up all of their natural fuel for that and are "riding on fumes."

The fourth obstacle given was lack of time. No particular trait pattern was associated with that obstacle/excuse for exercising. This means that those who exhibit one end of a trait are as likely to claim they don't have the time for exercise as those at the other. Here is a summary of the four obstacles:

Embarrassment:	N++C-
Lack of Energy:	N+E-C-
Lack of Motivation:	N+C-
Lack of Time:	No Significant Relationships

Notice that the three obstacles for exercise with traits associated all share the common profile of N+C-, what we call the "impulsive" profile. This is a high-risk profile for not exercising. These individuals and those close to them would be well-advised to explore unusual, uncommon motivators that might nudge these impulsive individuals to get needed exercise. If they are E+, make it a social affair. If they are O+, make it unusual (such as never biking/walking/running the same path twice, or in an unusual area, such as a botanical garden or mountain climbing). If they are A-, make it a matter of pride and competitiveness. Find some overriding motivator that trumps the desire to remain free and uncommitted. Perhaps find a way to relieve them of some of their existing commitments to "C" behavior (schedules, etc.) by alternatives that are more spontaneous (e.g., doing independent study rather than taking a class).We've known N+C- high school students who were home-schooled and did fine, so long as they lived up to their weekly goals, with minimal supervision.

So, once someone commits to exercise, how are they likely to conduct themselves while actually exercising? Regardless of whether the exercise is a team sport or a run around the track, how do their traits suggest that they might approach the activity? Here, we will simply list the results of several studies (Courneya and Hellsten, 1998; Paunonen and Ashton, 2001; Wang, 1997) and then discuss a few of the more interesting findings.

Accident-prone:	N+E+
Adherence:	N--E+O-C++
Air of Self-Confidence:	A--

Believes in Own Abilities:	E-A--
Dedicates Self to Improve Game:	E-
Ease Adapting to New Suggestion:	A+
Enthusiasm for the Sport:	No Significant Relationships
Exercises Routinely:	N14-E3+C4+
Ideal Overall Profile:	E-O-A+
Moderate:	O++C+
Outstanding Work Ethic:	E-O-
Plays for Team, Not Self:	A+++
Positive Attitude in Practice/Game:	O-A+++
Regularity:	N-E+C+
Sacrifice Other Things for Sport:	A+
Safety-prone:	N-E-
Strenuous:	N-E++O-C++
Supports Teammates:	A++
Willing to Listen to Criticism:	A++
Works Hard to Improve Weakness:	E-

As was the case with the motives and obstacles just discussed, most of these relationships have a kind of "face validity" to them. For example, "works hard to improve weakness" is associated with low E (introversion). Working hard to improve a weakness involves long stretches of (usually) solitary practice. You don't improve your free-throw percentage by hanging out with other players at the gym: You do it by spending long sessions alone, or with a friend/parent as a rebounder, taking hundreds of shots, one after another. This does not build on one's energy for sociability or leadership, but rather on one's comfort in spending time alone, away from the action. Of course, not all practice is like that, but much of it is.

Then there's the "ideal overall profile" for an athlete: E-O-A+. This individual keeps their mouth shut, is comfortable practicing until perfect, and aims to please by being obedient and deferential—for many coaches, a dream player. Keep in mind, though, that a coach's dream is not necessarily a winner or an achiever. Pleasing to coach, but not necessarily a winner. We are complex individuals, and we have a variety of strengths and weaknesses. By knowing our trait profile or the profiles of our teammates (or of those we coach or love and support as family members), we can study these relationships and understand which sports behaviors come more naturally for them, and which might benefit from special understanding, encouragement, and compensatory strategies.

In one study that attempted to understand the difference between girls who did and did not participate in school sports (Stoner and Bandy, 1977), they found that girls who participated in team sports tend to have a higher need for deference, which means the kind of attention associated with low A3 (pride and the enjoyment of being praised in public), in comparison to girls who did not participate in sports at all. Compared to the same group of nonparticipants, girls participating in individual sports tended to have higher needs for change (O3+) and intraception (a mixture/blend of imagination/O1+, feelings/N+, and aspirations/C3+; "intraception" is typically contrasted with "down to earth"). There were no significant trait differences between preference for team versus individual sports among girls who did participate in sports. In other words, there are three points here:

1. The trait differences between individual and team female athletes are negligible.
2. The team-sports girls are much lower on A3 than nonparticipating girls, yet only negligibly lower than individual-sports girls.
3. The individual-sports girls are much higher on O3 and intraception than nonparticipating girls, yet only negligibly higher than team-sports girls.

So what do these differences suggest? First, humble girls who are not attention-seeking (they tend to be A+ in general, A3+ in particular) may need special support in order to get sufficient exercise. Depending on a girl's actual trait profile, abilities, values, and other factors, girls who are especially likely to be in need of special encouragement and/or arrangements are both A+ and N+E-C- (recall that the latter profile is particularly prone to find excuses not to exercise). Special arrangements, for example, could be membership in a gym, a social approach, a buddy system, or a formal class (e.g., Jazzercise).

In closing this section on exercise and athletics, let's think for a moment about how traits relate to several specific sports. The principles at work here could apply to any team or individual sport. For example, we know (Piedmont and Blanco, 1999) that actual game performance in soccer (as measured by goals scored, saves, accuracy of passes, area coverage, and the like) is predicted rather accurately by one's score on C (consolidation). Soccer, more than many sports, entails constant concentration—eternal vigilance—with few timeouts, or very rapid ones, such that one's mind simply cannot wander the way it can during lulls in baseball, football, cricket, basketball, tennis, golf, and volleyball. With inning/side changes, pauses between pitches/serves/plays, and timeouts, one's powers of disciplined concentration are not so strained as they are in soccer. The soccer player, like the Secret Service agent, must constantly scan for movement and positioning, and this behavior comes most naturally for those higher in C. Soccer coaches tend to rate as their best all-round players those who are low in N and high in C: cool (N-) and focused (C+), seldom anxious or angry, and very quick to get over a crisis, letdown, or failure. They rarely have temper issues, and as we discussed with C+ and overall game performance, they stay focused and don't get distracted by irrelevant activity.

Also we know that basketball players with a reputation for winning tend to be givers, in that they are willing to pass until the best shot is found, and that requires higher A behavior than that of takers, those who take every shot they can get, an indication of lower A. One way for a lower A ballplayer to become natural at giving the ball up (i.e., passing it to a mate) is to become competitive and proud of being the best passer on the team. While the act of giving the ball up doesn't come naturally, the competitiveness and pride does! In football, quarterbacks tend to be O+ (more creative, can improvise, comfortable with complexity and reading patterns on the field), interior offensive and defensive linemen tend to higher in E (comfortable in the thick of the action) and lower in O (living in the here-

and-now and comfortable with repetition), and free safeties tend to be lower in E (comfortable being alone, quiet, and away from the action for the most part).

The Big Five in the Fine and Performing Arts

Research on the association between musical preferences and traits (Buttsworth and Smith, 1995; Howard, 2000; McCown, Keiser, Mulhearn, and Williamson, 1997; Paunonen and Ashton, 2001) has produced some interesting results. First, what traits tend to be associated with those who "see themselves as musicians"? These self-described musicians tend to have this profile: O+13+A4-. In plain English, they tend be oriented towards novelty and the future, have a vivid imagination, are comfortable with change, and assertive/expressive/comfortable being in front of people. No surprises there—creative and out front. It would be hard to imagine a musician who prefers staying in the background, as the very act of making music is front and center, for the most part. Exceptions abound, for sure.

What about a musician's preferred method of expression? Are instrumentalists of a different temperament than vocalists? Yes and no: Vocalists tend to be worriers (N1+) who are distrusting (E5-), while instrumentalists tend to be particularly strong at concentrating (C4+). Both, however, score high on imagination (O1+), as do musicians in general. These defining characteristics do make sense: Vocalists are plagued by a myriad of variables that appear to be out of their control—colds, sniffles, coughs, perfume/smoke of others, scratchy throat, so many variables that, in fact, a commitment to singing might even tend to push one's N score somewhat higher than might otherwise be the case. The instrumentalist doesn't have to worry about so many variables. However, they do have to concentrate on many aspects of their instrument simultaneously in a way that singers don't: arm position, breath support, embouchure, posture, vibrato, temperature of the instrument, condition of the reed/bowhairs, fingering, pitch, saliva control. For the instrumentalist, lapses in concentration spell catastrophe, or at least embarrassment.

Listed below are some additional associations between traits and specific musical pursuits:

Ability to Play "By Ear":	E2+O2-A1-3--
Brass:	N1-E+
Keyboard:	N-E1+A-
Performers:	N-O-A+
Preference for Exaggerated Bass:	E+C-
Sight Reading Ability:	E-
Wind Players:	N1+E1-C+A1-2+

Some of these interrelationships are fascinating. For example, playing "by ear" (i.e., being able to improvise without printed music, as in making up a harmonic line while someone else is singing or playing the melody) is a more extraverted characteristic, while "sight reading ability" (i.e., being able to look at printed music and correctly render it with one's instrument of choice, including voice) is typically the result of extended solitary practice, a more introverted mode.

Traits After School

What about the flip side of the coin? Music appreciation? Do different traits like different kinds of music? Dr. Adrian North, head of the applied psychology department at Heriot-Watt University in Scotland, has identified 104 distinct types of music and has set out to find out what personalities are drawn to each kind. After surveying over 36,000 people globally, North reports his results using adjectives rather than Big Five trait names, but the translations are rather straightforward (at ease = N-, outgoing = E+, creative = O+, gentle = A+, hardworking = C+). He also reports on the self-esteem (high or low) of the respondents. Some preliminary findings (we list the music type first, followed by the traits associated according to North's research):

- Blues: N-E+O+A+ (and higher self-esteem)
- Bollywood: E+O+
- Chart Pop: N+E+O-A+C+ (and higher self-esteem)
- Classical: N-E-O+ (and higher self-esteem)
- Country & Western: E+C+
- Indie: O+A-C- (and lower self-esteem)
- Jazz: N-E+O+ (and higher self-esteem)
- Opera: O+A+ (and higher self-esteem)
- Rap: E+ (and higher self-esteem)
- Reggae: N-E+O+A+C- (and higher self-esteem)
- Rock/Heavy Metal: N-E-O+A+C- (and lower self-esteem)
- Soul: N-E+O+A+ (and higher self-esteem)

Note that a preference for "indie" music tends to be associated with lower self-esteem. We have tried to find a clear definition of "indie" music, to no avail. This makes sense, that hard-to-define music would appeal to young people actively engaged in searching for personal meaning and definition. However, we would imagine that, as some of these young people with lower self-esteem begin to improve in their sense of self-worth, perhaps they might be nudged into a different musical preference with more positive associations. Of course, this is just a hypothesis, not an absolute. Clearly there are plenty of indie music lovers who have positive self-esteem, just as there are many indie musicians and fans who are very clear what indie music is. We look forward to hearing more from North's interesting research.

At this point, it becomes tricky to divide all of the music/personality research into neat categories. Below is a grab bag of associations that come primarily from a survey by G. D. Wilson (1994), plus a few other sources, as found in Pierce's *The Owner's Manual for the Brain* (2006, 3rd Ed.):

- Conservatives (e.g., O-) tend to prefer simpler, more familiar music.
- Liberals (e.g., O+) tend to prefer more complex, less familiar music.
- E+O+ tend to prefer more complex, less familiar music.
- The higher the singer's vocal range (i.e., sopranos and tenors), the greater their emotionality (e.g., N+E+), the more variable the quality of their performance over time, and the greater their stage fright.
- Basses have higher testosterone, more love affairs (E+C-), and higher ambition (C3+).

- Tenors miss the most cues (C4-), sopranos the fewest (duh—they have the melody!).
- Compared with singers, nonsingers are lower in E, higher in A, and more intelligent (Guess we better stop singing in order to improve our intellectual reputation! Not! Remember, these are averages, or trends, not absolutes. ☺).
- Compared with instrumentalists, noninstrumentalists are higher in E, lower in N.
- Jazz musicians are higher in N and O, lower in A and C (more creative and spontaneous).
- The higher the pitch, the more positive the effect on the mood of the listener (N-E+).
- Slower tempos coupled with minor keys warm the brain, which leads to greater cortical arousal/increased alertness.
- Faster tempos coupled with major keys cool the brain, which leads to more positive mood (N-E+).
- Classical period composers (e.g., Mozart, Beethoven, Haydn) and mid/late Baroque composers (e.g., Vivaldi, Handel, Scarlatti, Corelli, Telemann) are considered to be "universal donors" in that they offend the fewest listeners (except for J. S. Bach, who attracts a more limited set of admirers).
- Across all cultures:
    - High frequencies are associated with joy, low frequencies with sadness, and varied frequencies with excitement.
    - Strong melodic variation is associated with joy and excitement, and slight variation with sadness.
    - Rapid tempos are associated with joy, slow tempos with sadness, and moderate tempos with excitement.
    - Loud volume is associated with joy, soft with sadness, and varied volume levels with excitement.
    - Irregular rhythms are associated with joy, regular with sadness, and very irregular with excitement.
    - Tonal patterns that alternate between going up and down are associated with joy, mostly descending patterns with sadness, and mostly ascending patterns with excitement.
    - Complex use of overtones (as in using a variety of instruments) is associated with joy, fewer overtones with sadness, and minimal overtones with excitement.
    - Repetitive rhythms (such as Ravel's *Bolero* and the music of Philip Glass) can induce a trance-like state close to ecstasy.
    - Music that slows gradually has a gradual relaxing effect.
    - Lullabies around the world mimic the breathing rhythm characteristic of deep sleep.

What is clear is that plenty of room exists for all kinds of trait combinations in the world of music, as is true also of all the arts. If you take a specific profile, and think through how that profile could express itself in a particular artistic mode, there will inevitably be a good fit.

The Big Five in Social and Service Organizations

As a general rule, it would appear that social and service organizations (e.g., fraternities/sororities and Habitat for Humanity) would draw from opposite profiles. Organizations promising more social engagement (mixers, dances, parties, initiations, and the like) would seem to appeal to N-

Traits After School

E+O-A-C- students—those who are calm, gregarious, traditional, somewhat self-absorbed, and spontaneous. Organizations promising more service engagement (helping those in need, volunteering in health care settings, internships in government and business, tutoring other students, and the like) would seem to appeal to N+E-O+A+C+ students—those who worry about others' welfare, who are more solitary, who are curious and like variety, who are basically altruistic, and who are disciplined. We are sure many social organizations and many service organizations appeal to their own narrow audiences. However, we would propose that the ideal after-school or community organization would do both: meet both the social and service needs of young people. Who says that a crew that builds a Habitat for Humanity House can't have a hot dog roast and a pizza event mixed in with building homes? Or that a fraternity/sorority can't have a service project along with a party? The social part is the easy part. It takes virtually no creativity or planning to have impromptu dances, meals, and parties. Meaningful community service is another matter—it takes planning. We suggest that all organizations that are primarily social have a service component, and that all service organizations have a social component. That way, both social and service organizations will appeal to a wide variety or personalities.

In the September 22, 2008, issue of *Time* magazine, a feature on "21 ways to serve America" identified a variety of ways to approach the mandate to engage in service, and they appeal to a variety of traits. Here are some of them:

- Sponsor and plan a tour that combines fellowship and service, as in taking a group to New Orleans for post-Katrina cleanup or to Haiti to help after the earthquake.
- Rethink holidays (Christmas, Hanukkah, Eid al Fitr, Diwali, Thanksgiving, Easter, Passover, and so forth) to decrease emphasis on personal acquisition of gifts and calories, and instead to think up and carry out appropriately seasonal service projects (e.g., singing Christmas carols in nursing homes and hospitals, staffing soup kitchens and homeless shelters, and doing cleanup work in parts of the city/region that would benefit from a facelift).
- Find a government or non-government service coordinator in your area and make yourselves available.
- Arrange free caregiver relief and babysitting services for the families of military personnel deployed overseas, for long-term caregivers for the elderly, for single parents, and so forth.
- Begin a tutoring program where older students tutor younger students who need assistance.
- Visit www.volunteer.gov and browse their database containing millions of different kinds of organizations and service opportunities. Do it individually or with good friends and find agreeable ways to serve (and be social, and learn).

Sports, the arts, and service form a core of after-school engagement that keeps its participants away from the "devil's workshop"—idleness. In the next chapter, we will explore how the Big Five can help understand and manage the dynamics of home life.

A Case Study in Team Dynamics: The Chemistry of Volleyball

Contributed by Emily Crowder, UNC-Chapel Hill student and CentACS Research Intern

In understanding the dynamics of this team, it's helpful to know the traits of the players and the leaders.

Coach Patterson:	N= E= A+ C=
Captain 1 (Tracey):	N+ E+ A= C+
Captain 2 (Amy):	N- E= A+ C+
Average traits of team:	N- E= A+ C=
Player 1 (Jill):	N++ E+ A- C+
Player 2 (Becca):	N+ E+ A-- C+

Tracey and Amy had both been playing volleyball since sixth grade, and finally, as seniors, they were elected captains. Amy was excited to be captain. She had put all her heart into encouraging and supporting her team throughout the years, and she was eager to begin her final season. Tracey, who had been captain the previous year as well, was glad that Amy was joining her in leading the team. Though they were quite different, they got along well, and Tracey appreciated Amy's drive. The majority of the team was seniors, so everyone expected a good year. But before the official start of the season, problems had already begun to arise. The girls all had the skill to do well, but the team was tainted by drama. At team camp, Jill and Tracey got in a fight. Tracey had critiqued Jill's playing, and she broke down. She began crying and accused everyone of judging her. While Coach Patterson comforted her, the rest of the team began to see the flaws in the team makeup. The team was already distracted by unnecessary drama. Most of the players thought that Jill had overreacted. What Tracey had said was not that harsh, and already Jill was crying to the coach, who gave her all his sympathy. Immediately, the team began pushing her away.

Unfortunately, the problems only deepened as the season progressed. Tracey and Amy did their best to lead the team. While Amy tended to react calmly to problems and tried to encourage everyone to get along, Tracey counterbalanced her and would take problems more seriously and speak up about them. It was typically Tracey's job to tell the team what was wrong and be more assertive because Amy was uncomfortable confronting them. Most of the team responded favorably to their leadership styles and did as they were told, even accepting less playing time to allow others a chance; however, Jill and Becca were not as accepting. When they were taken out of the game because of an off day, they would confront Coach Patterson. They would raise their voices at him and get emotional about losing their spots. Although his original decision had been for the good of the team, Coach Patterson would give in to their tears and let them walk over him. He would put them in positions they wanted, taking out others who deserved the spot. As this continued, the usually calm team started getting frustrated. They didn't think it was fair that Jill and Becca acted so selfishly and dramatically, and still got what they wanted. Soon, the frustration among the team became obvious to both team leaders and spectators.

Coach Patterson realized he couldn't appease Becca and Jill without hurting the overall team; however, he didn't want to confront them. Instead, he made the captains explain his decisions to sit them out. Knowing that Becca and Jill would yell at Tracey, Amy decided that she would take the job. She uncomfortably stood in front of the team and announced the line-up for that day. As furious as Becca and Jill were, Amy knew it was for the good of the team. But the damage was already done. The team still felt walked on by the two girls and were furious that their coach had let it happen. The team fell apart. The majority of the team was so upset that they ostracized the other girls and stopped trying in practice and games. Meanwhile, Jill and Becca felt hurt by their team and would get emotional or yell at the other players during games. Amy and Tracey tried their hardest to keep the team together, but nothing worked, and they too grew frustrated with their disappointing season. Parents, players, and captains all wondered, "What happened?"

The trait makeup of the team drastically affected its well-being. The main problems in the team resulted from the differences in need for stability (N) and accommodation (A). To the majority of the team (low in N), the two girls high in N were viewed as overreacting, too sensitive, and too likely to take things personally. Meanwhile, Becca and Jill thought that the others didn't care enough about the game and would get upset. Unfortunately, neither of the captains was able to connect the two extremes. The only person naturally prone to negotiating between the two groups was the coach. He would listen to the N+ girls complain, trying to calm them down, and he would try to inspire more urgency in the rest of the team; however, he also tended to give in to the girls' complaints as he listened. This made the rest of the team lose respect for him, which resulted in their ignoring his talks. By ignoring him, the team failed to hear the worries and opinions of the other girls. The only bridge (the N= coach) between the two extremes on need for stability was not enough for the team.

The drastic variations in accommodation also were a source of adversity for the team. To the A- players, the rest of the team appeared submissive and too weak to successfully compete. Meanwhile, the majority of the team was high in accommodation and viewed these girls as selfish and not team players. They felt walked on by the girls, but they failed to stand up for themselves, which enabled Becca and Jill to continue their behavior. Worse, the coach failed to stand up for himself and the team. With his high accommodation, he gave in to the girls' complaints, which upset the others who wanted him to do what was best for the team. Unable to voice their frustration, they took it out on the game and stopped trying. What the team really needed was a leader who was low in accommodation. While Tracey's A= enabled her to be persuasive and direct with her team sometimes, she was uncomfortable doing it continuously. Even when she would confront Jill and Becca, she would not persist in her argument because they were too defensive and competitive. Amy was even less apt to confront people and avoided raising her voice, hoping not to start a conflict. The coach, who needed to be A- was the complete opposite, making him seem weak. The whole team lost respect for his lack of backbone. The team looked to him for discipline, motivation, and strength, all of which he failed to deliver. Overall, the team needed an N=A- leader who could balance the personalities of the N scale and who would not shy away from confrontation when the team's best interests were at stake. Without this leader, the team crumbled.

It is also important to note that the previous year, there had been a second coach. Although she was the assistant coach, she had an important role. She was low in N and in A. Under her lead, the team still had some small setbacks, but she was able to stand up for the team's needs and say no to those who confronted her. She would calmly talk to them and stayed firm in her decisions, no matter what occurred. With her departure, the team needed to find a replacement for her leadership and failed to do so. As a result, the team's strongest force was gone, and no one remaining was able to effectively lead the team.

19

The Big Five at Home

How Knowledge of Traits Helps Family Members Understand, Accept, Manage, and Influence Each Other

> "It's quite possible to be so influenced by the ideals and commands of your neighborhood that you don't know what you really want and could be. I think that anyone brought up in an extremely strict, authoritative social situation is unlikely ever to come to the knowledge of himself."
>
> --Joseph Campbell, *The Power of Myth*, p. 176

Guide to This Chapter:

- Genetics and the Family: Like Parent, Like Child?
- How Traits Influence Parenting Style
- The Effects of Modeling
- The Development of Language
- The Management of Time and Space in the Home

In his *Antigone*, Sophocles has Haemon warn his father Creon, King of Thebes:

But for a man to learn, though he be wise,
Yea, to learn much, and know the time to yield,
Brings no disgrace. When winter floods the streams,
Thou seest the trees that bend before the storm,
Save their last twigs, while those that will not yield
Perish with root and branch. And when one hauls
Too tight the mainsail sheet, and will not slack,
He has to end his voyage with deck o`erturned.
Do thou, then, yield. Permit thyself to change.

(Part IV; translation not identified; http://sophocles.classicauthors.net/Antigone)

Traits After School

N	E	O	A	C
Need for Stability	**Extraversion**	**Originality**	**Accommodation**	**Consolidation**
N+ Reactive	E+ Extraverted	O+ Explorer	A+ Adapter	C+ Focused
N= Responsive	E= Ambiverted	O= Moderate	A= Negotiator	C= Balanced
N- Resilient	E- Introverted	O- Preserver	A- Challenger	C- Flexible
N1: Worry	**E1: Approach Level**	**O1: Imagination**	**A1: Service**	**C1:Thoroughness**
N2: Temper	**E2: Group Orientation**	**O2: Range of Interests**	**A2: Compliance**	**C2: Structure**
N3: Outlook	**E3: Pace**	**O3: Innovation**	**A3: Humility**	**C3: Ambition**
N4: Coping Level	**E4: Leadership**	**O4: Zoom Scale**	**A4: Speak Out Level**	**C4: Concentration**
	E5: Trust			**C5: Methodicalness**
	E6: Tact			

Over two millennia later, Joseph Campbell, forearmed with the wisdom of Sophocles, describes the classic conundrum of parenting and growing up: how to provide solid local roots while simultaneously providing strong wings for exploration and identity formation. This theme peppers the history of literature, from Sophocles to the present. Sophocles compares the old man, stuck in his ways, to a tree that will not bend in the storm, thus risking a break, and to a ship's sail held too tight, thus in risk of capsizing. More recently, Rahim Khan cautioned the father of Amir that "Children aren't coloring books. You don't get to fill them with your favorite colors." (From Khaled Hosseini's *The Kite Runner*; see full quotation at beginning of Chapter 2 in this book.) And southern U.S. journalist Hodding Carter writes that "There are two lasting bequests we can give our children: One is roots, the other is wings."

One of the ways that this paradox plays out in the home is through the daily confrontation of one family member's personality traits with another's. When two family members exhibit opposite ends of a trait continuum (say, trust [E5+] versus skepticism [E5-]), the first reaction tends to be, "Why can't you be more like me? Why can't you be more trusting/skeptical? Why do you have to be the opposite of what I stand for?" This is one more variation of the tree that will not bend in the storm, the sail held too tight, the parent wanting to dictate the colors on the child's palette, wanting to nourish the roots and hide the wings. It is the reason that Mary Belenky (as described in Chapter 2) attributes to the tendency of many young girls (and some boys) to have no "voice" until they leave home. How can the family nourish roots *and* wings? How can one promote both stability *and* change?

One way is to understand that, while we certainly pass certain genes onto our offspring, no one parent passes 100% of the genes. Rather, no parent can expect more than 50% similarity to themselves. This cold fact insures misunderstanding and its ensuing conflict. In the first section of this chapter, we will explore how genetics insures diversity in every family, and how each family faces the challenge of taking that diversity as a personal affront, or of accepting it and building on it.

Genetics and the Family: Like Parent, Like Child?

Let's keep it simple. This is not going to be a textbook lesson in genetics. Rather, it is going to be a concrete illustration of how traits run in families. Well, at least in one family—mine! I (Pierce) have had the opportunity to administer a brief version of the Big Five to four generations of my family: my parents, their seven children (including me), their 17 grandchildren, and their 32 (and counting) great grandchildren. The results of these 54 profiles covering four generations appear in Table 19.1. The first generation—my mother and father, Eleanor Cross Johnson Howard and Curtis William Howard—appear on the first and second rows, and their Big Five trait levels are repeated at the head of each of the seven columns, each column representing a "blood line" of three succeeding generations. No in-laws/spouses are included. If the popular adage "like father, like son," or "like mother, like daughter," holds true, then we would expect the traits of the second generation to match perfectly with the traits of the corresponding gender parent of the first generation. In other words, the unshaded (female) children should match my mother's profile in the first (unshaded) row, while the shaded (male) children should match my father's profile in the second (shaded) row. A simple inspection reveals that my three sisters share traits with my mother at rates of 2 out of 5, 1 out of 5, and 3 out of 5. On average, the women of the first generation share two out of five traits. The men are about the same: 1 out of 5, 2 out of 5, 2 out of 5, and 2 out of 5, for an average of just under 2 out of 5.

Table 19.1 **The Curtis and Eleanor Howard Trait Bloodline through Four Generations**

	NEOAC	NEOAC	NEOAC	NEOAC	NEOAC	NEOAC	NEOAC
1-Mother	=+==+	=+==+	=+==+	=+==+	=+==+	=+==+	=+==+
1-Father	-=-=+	-=-=+	-=-=+	-=-=+	-=-=+	-=-=+	-=-=+
2-7 Kids	+++=-	+--==	-+++-	-+=++	==+=-	==+=-	==+==
3-Grandkids	+=+--	--=-=	+=+=-	-=+=-	-==-=	-=+=-	=++--
	+=+++	+++=-		++===	---++	=====	+-+-=
		--=-+		++==+	-++--		
				-+==-			
4- Great-grandkids	=++==	-+=++		-+++-	-+===	=----	+====
	-+++-	-+-++		=---+	-=+=-	+=-+=	-++=-
	----+	-++=-		-=-++	====-	+=-+=	=+===
	+++-=	==++-		-++=-		++-==	
		=+++-		-++==			
		+---+		++++-			
		+++=-		-+-++			
		-+--+		=+++-			
		=++==		=++--			

Notes: The Mother's and Father's scores of the first generation are copied to be above each of their seven children. The bloodline descendents are listed below each of these seven second generation children. No spouses/in-laws are included. Females are unshaded; males shaded. Scores obtained with the Big Five Locator (Howard, Howard, and Medina, 1996), either through self-reports (of the living) or multiple raters (of the deceased). The score ranges for N, E, O, A, and C are shown in that order, with "-" indicating low range scores, "=" indicating medium range scores, and "+" indicating high range scores. The children within a family are not listed in birth order, so as to provide anonymity.

Well, as each of us gets 50% of our genes from our mother, and the other 50% from our father, the rate of similarity for same sex descendents one generation apart of 40% (2 out of 5) would seem about right. What if we looked to see the rate of similarity of each second-generation child (i.e., my siblings and me) with *either* of our parents, regardless of gender? The rates are, understandably, somewhat higher: 2 out of 5, 2, out of 5, 2 out of 5, 3 out of 5, 3 out of 5, 4 out of 5, and 3 out of 5, for an average of just under 3 out of 5, or 54% similarity. How likely is this rate of similarity to have occurred by chance? To answer this question, we need to know the probability of a member of the second generation having the same score as any one parent, and then of either parent. The first probability is 1 in 3 that I would match either parent on any one trait, while to match any one parent on all five traits would be 1/3 x 1/3 x 1/3 x 1/3 x 1/3, or 1 in 243. In plain English, we would expect, if the relationship is random, only 1 person in 243 would match their parent on all 5 traits. That relationship holds here, in that *none* of my generation matches either parent completely. Supposedly, if my parents had birthed 243 children, one of the kids would have matched one of the parents trait-for-trait! What about the actual rate of similarity that we see: that the average child is similar to 40% of the same sex parent's traits? The probability of having two out of five traits the same as one parent's is 1/3 x 1/3, or 1 in 9, or about 11%. In other words, a chance relationship would yield 11% similarity, so our 40% similarity suggests a strong genetic relationship. The chances of any one child matching *either* parent on any one trait would be 2 out of 3. So, the chances of matching on three of either parent's traits (which is in fact the case here) would be 2/3 x 2/3 x 2/3, or 8/27, or about 30%. The fact that the rate is actually 54% again emphasizes that this is not a random relationship, that something is being passed down.

> "Heredity is what sets the parents of a teenager wondering about each other."
> --Laurence J. Peter

So, one generation passes some of its traits to the next, but not all. Three out of five of our traits are likely to resemble our parents'. But let's back away from the first and second generations and look at the larger picture. Does the Howard family across four generations resemble the progenitors, or have they strayed from the fold? For this, we need to look at Table 19.2. The result here is intriguing: a clear pattern (i.e., the bolded numbers) describes the family: N-E+O+A=C- (calm, outgoing, creative, negotiable, and spontaneous). How does this compare to the first generation progenitors (mom and dad)? From Table 19.1, you can see that, as a couple, they were N-/=, E=/+, O-/=, A=, and C+. Their influence is apparent for N, E, and A. However, something happened to their low O and high C! What happened to their no-nonsense, conservative sense of practicality and their disciplined focus on achieving their goals? Some might suggest that the O-C+ could have "skipped" a generation. However, an inspection of the four generations reveals that the pattern is rather consistent. While affirming their calm, outgoing, and negotiable temperament, we siblings struck out into new trait territory with our creative longing for variety.

How could this be explained? Perhaps by several factors: the influence of provincial eastern North Carolina (first generation) versus the fact that five of the seven children moved to more metropolitan areas, the influence of being part of a family business with traditional sex role models (first generation) coming into contact with the various liberating influences of the latter half of the 20th century, and the conservative religious tradition of the progenitors (essentially O-C+) meeting up with the effects of liberal education, the city, and modernity.

Table 19.2 **Frequency of Trait Level Scores across Four Howard Generations** (n = 58)

	Low	Midrange	High
Need for Stability	**25**	16	17
Extraversion	9	18	**32**
Originality	14	14	**30**
Accommodation	14	**28**	16
Consolidation	**26**	17	13
Expected:	**18**	**22**	**18**

The point here is that, yes, we do resemble our parents in some ways, but we have both genetic and cultural influences that lead us in new directions. We cherish the roots provided by our ancestors and affirm the right to try out our wings. David Rowe (1994) in his book *The Limits of Family Influence* writes:

> The implication is that parents are often given too much credit for children who turn out well, and too much blame for children who turn out poorly.... Feeding a well-nourished but short child more and more will not give him the stature of a basketball player. Feeding a [child with a] below-average intellect more and more information will not make her brilliant. Exposing a shy child to socially demanding events will not make him feel less shy. (p. 92)

In short, the task of the family is to take stock of how each of its members is similar to others, how each is different, to celebrate both the similarities and differences, and to build on them, never thinking twice about wishing that a family member were different, or "more like me."

How Traits Influence Parenting Style

What do we mean by "parenting style"? A style is a pattern. To say one has "style" means that one pursues their own individual approach to consistency, be it in clothing, language, sports, or academics. Even lack of consistency is a style: Unpredictability is its own pattern. We have looked at several different kinds of styles in other chapters: conflict management (Chapter17), coping (Chapter 17), problem solving (Chapter 13), and learning (Chapter 13). While those four style patterns are certainly relevant to parenting and family life, there are three roles that are particularly applicable to the home: control, intimacy, and coaching. Now we want to look specifically at them.

Approaches to Control

Clearly the most constant issue the generations run up against in a family is that of control: the degree and manner (i.e., "style") to which parents attempt to exert control over their teens. Researchers (e.g., Cobb, 2007; Csikszentmihalyi and Scheider, 2000) have identified two dimensions of control: the degree to which parents have expectations for their youth, and the degree to which they support their youth in pursuit of those expectations. We refer to these two dimensions as Demanding/Undemanding and Supportive/Unsupportive (see Figure 19.1 for a visual depiction of these relationships). These two dimensions form a "stylebox" with four natural styles (for each style, we have indicated which traits would most likely exhibit that style):

Traits After School

1. **"Authoritative"—**Here the parent combines high expectations with high support, as in "study/practice hard, rest when you need to, and let me know how I can be helpful." It is like the business practice of complete delegation: Assign the goal and monitor progress towards the goal, offering assistance as needed. This style builds most naturally on the trait energy provided by A-C+ (demanding) and N+E+ (supportive). Having these traits is not necessary for exhibiting this style, but these traits tend to be associated with this style. A more introverted parent clearly has reserves of extraversion and can dig deep to draw on these extraverted reserves, for example, when the need comes to be supportive.

2. **"Authoritarian"**—Here the parent combines high expectations with low support, as in "study/practice hard, and I'll get out your way." This style tends to be associated with the trait energy of A-C+ (demanding) and N-E- (unsupportive).

3. **"Indulgent"**—Here the parent combines low expectations with high support, as in "you do what is important to you, and let me know how I can help you." This style is known by some as permissiveness and is associated with the trait energy of A+C- (undemanding) and N+E+ (supportive).

4. **"Neglectful"**—Here the parent combines low expectations with low support, as in "go do your thing." In essence, the parent abdicates, assuming either consciously or unconsciously that the youth has the motivation and resources necessary for satisfactory development and doesn't need much of anything from the parent(s). This style tends to be associated with the traits N-E- (unsupportive) and A+C- (undemanding).

(5.**"Situational"—**This is not really a style, but rather a condition where parents score in the midrange and are likely to use one style with one child and a different style with another, as would be the case in "playing favorites." Or the "situational" parents could vary the styles used in different aspect of a single child's life—they might be authoritative in sports but neglectful in academics, or vice versa. Which style a parent uses with a child here would depend on what energy the parent has available.)

Csikszentmihalyi and Schneider (2000, p. 116)) write about a questionnaire—The SCQ (Support/Challenge Questionnaire)—that measures the degree to which parents exhibit each of these styles. Their research found that almost half of the families surveyed reported high support/high challenge styles that are characterized by maximal parental engagement. Almost a third reported low support/low challenge styles (disengaged parents), and roughly 1/10 reported the each of the other two types. The high/high condition was associated with youth who exhibited the most positive school performance and the most positive self-development.

Simplified, this is a matter of whether the parents are in charge (authoritarian), the youth is in charge (indulgent), no one is in charge (neglectful), or control is negotiated (authoritative). Teens' degree of interest in current and future schooling is related to the degree of their parents' involvement in the teen's schooling, whether it is with homework, projects, PTSA, volunteering, working with interns, or other activities (Cobb 2007, p. 283). This kind of engagement is the natural outcome of the authoritative style. An important determinant of whether parents and their youth can achieve the more interdependent pattern of the authoritative style is whether or not true intimacy can be achieved. So, now we turn to the nature of intimacy.

Figure 19.1 Stylebox for Parental Control

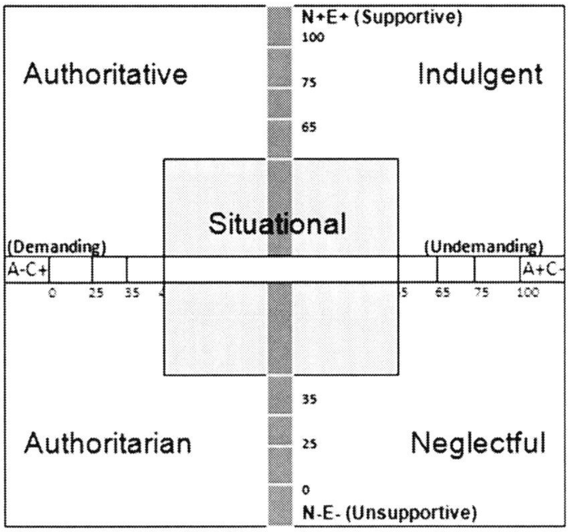

The Nature of Intimacy and the Importance of Learning a "Facilitative" Style

Nancy Cobb (2007) defines intimacy as "sharing of one's feelings and thoughts in an atmosphere of caring, trust, and acceptance." (p. 159) So, what traits are associated with such sharing? We propose that the role of the parent that elicits intimacy is that of the "facilitator"—one who brings out the concerns, feelings, insights, observations, information, and hopes of those around them. A facilitative person is one who makes it easy for others to say what's on their minds. Our research has found that the traits associated with facilitation are all in the midrange: no extremes. The facilitative person is neither too reactive (N+) nor too calm (N-), too outgoing (E+) nor too silent (E-), too full of ideas (O+) nor too comfortable with the status quo (O-), too deferential (A+) nor too defiant (A-), too structured (C+) nor too flexible (C-). In short, the facilitative person makes others comfortable by not exhibiting any extreme behavior. I (Jane) have facilitated many groups in my career. I am either in the midrange or close to the midrange in all traits but two: N- (low need for stability) and O+ (high originality). The more challenging things for me to do while facilitating a group are to keep from suggesting my ideas and to make sure I let people have adequate time to vent and express their feelings before leading them into problem solving. The danger of having lots of ideas is that others around me may stop expressing their own ideas. In order to achieve intimacy, I (we) must resist our extremes while facilitating discussion:

- The anxious, temperamental member must submerge their feelings to a degree.
- The calm member must show some feelings as evidence that they care.
- The sociable member must keep their mouth shut and let others talk.
- The taciturn member must express their thoughts and feelings.
- The creative member must bring out the creativity in others.

Traits After School

- The traditionalist member must be open to appropriate change.
- The deferential member must on occasion stand up for themselves.
- The defiant member must on occasion defer, say they're sorry, listen.
- The focused, disciplined member must on occasion be spontaneous.
- The spontaneous member must on occasion provide and embrace structure.

The general rule for facilitating intimacy is: Know your extremes, and refrain from exhibiting them while trying to be facilitative, as in leading a family meeting or checking base with another family member. This is true for a parent with a youth, an older sibling with younger, or a parent with a spouse or other family member (grandparent, etc.). Nancy Cobb says it this way: "Families that allow members to express their ideas, even when they differ from those of others, communicate that it is safe to disagree. Once adolescents have this safety, they are able to examine how they really feel." (p. 159) This is not an easy task. Judith Rich Harris (2006) reports that studies show that over 80% of both fathers and mothers say that they favor the younger of two children (p. 91). Such natural prejudices must be understood and resisted. Don't let the shine of number-one child dull—keep it polished and fresh. Further, Andrew Collins and Brett Laursen (in Lerner and Steinberg, 2004, pp. 331 ff.) note that teens report the greatest incidence of conflict with mothers, then siblings, then friends, then romantic friends, finally fathers (conflict with the mother is somewhat stronger for girls than for boys, but conflict with the mother is the most prevalent regardless of sex). This underscores the importance of mothers and older siblings making a concerted effort to practice and master the facilitative role. This is not to say that one must *always* be facilitative, but rather that one must have a sense of when the stakes are high and then consciously assume the role of a facilitator submerging one's personal needs, deferring their expression until a later time.

The Role of the Coach

One of the frequent roles of both parent (or parent surrogate) and older sibling is in coaching a youth in academic or other tasks. Whether helping with homework, assisting in the planning of a project, or advising on major choices, the coaching role is of highest strategic importance in positive development. Mark Lepper has identified what he calls the five Cs of tutoring (in Nisbett, 2009, p. 191):

1. Control—Develop the learner's sense of being in control of the process, rather than just obeying others' orders.
2. Challenge—Encourage the youth to set goals that may be out of their comfort zone, not just goals that are a "slam dunk."
3. Confidence—Communicate your confidence both in your ability to be helpful, as well as your confidence in the youth's ability to master the task/achieve the goal.
4. Curiosity—Encourage the learner's expression of curiosity, as in wanting to understand the "why" behind the "how"—not just how to solve a problem, but why it originated in the first place, what other approaches might be, and so forth.

5. Contextualize—Relate a youth's learning to the context of their current, past, and future lives; show the relationship of a particular learning or activity to memories, realities, and dreams that have personal meaning for the learner.

Richard Nisbett writes (2009, pp. 188-9):

> It is crucial for parents to teach children that their intelligence is under their control.... It is important to teach children that if at first you don't succeed, try again harder.... It is probably a bad idea to praise children for being intelligent. Instead, praise hard work, which is under their direct control.

Phillip Graham's (2004, p. 83) Eight Guidelines for Parenting Teens:

1. Respecting individuality
2. Finding a lifestyle that gives enough time for your teenager
3. Providing a model of love, caring, and good communication
4. Trying to understand the world from the viewpoint of your teenager
5. Remembering to tell teenage children you feel pleased with them
6. Empowering teenage children to the greatest degree possible
7. Being sympathetic to reasonably safe experimentation but making it clear that dangerous behavior is foolish and unacceptable
8. Trying to get help when teenage confidence is lost and it is difficult to know what to do

This advice is related to Carol Dweck's mastery vs. performance goals, which we discussed at some length in Chapters 13 and 14. She found that kids who are praised for hard work will actually work harder and persevere longer than kids praised for ability. It is far more demotivating to think that failure results from lack of ability than from lack of effort, as it is easy to convince most people that you can always try harder. "Praise for effort, not smarts." (Nisbett, 2009, p. 190) Only use rewards when kids are unmotivated. When they enjoy doing something, resist confusing them by rewarding them, as it tends to "turn play into work."

The Effects of Modeling

We can model behaviors many ways for other family members. Positive behaviors are catching—they spread. Studies (Cobb, 2007, p. 211) using beepers tracked the relative reports of feeling very happy versus very unhappy by both teens and their parents, with teens reporting very happy feelings five times more frequently than their parents, very unhappy three times more frequently—i.e., more highs *and* lows. While it is important to be authentic, e.g., to show concern when one is concerned, it is also important to model positive emotions. While one may be feeling discomfort, it is still possible to give a smile to a returning family member. While one may be seething with rage over an incident not involving a family member, it is still possible to submerge it and have a good laugh with loved ones.

Conflict is normal and in itself does not damage relationships. Continual fighting is another matter, as it leads to adjustment problems. Continual fighting models negative behavior. Where possible, understand the source of the fighting and do one of two things: Accept the cause and stop fighting, or do some problem solving so that the cause of the fighting is addressed. In other words, fix it or accept it. Recall the Serenity Prayer: "Give us the courage to change what we can, the patience to accept what we cannot change, the wisdom to know the difference."

Conflict decreases between teens/parents throughout adolescence, but the anger accompanying specific episodes increases (Lerner and Steinberg, 2004, p. 339). This points to needs for both withholding unsolvable conflicts and for making the effort to solve problems where possible. Certain traits find this easier said than done. N-O+ are more likely to enter into problem solving, while A- are more likely to hold onto a grudge. When conflicts do emerge, boys are more likely than girls to disengage, and mothers are more likely to compromise than fathers. This highlights the importance of following up with boys to insure their issues are getting addressed, of moving into facilitative mode with those girls tenacious in conflict, of following up with mothers to insure that compromise does not result in resentment, and of challenging fathers to consider acceptable alternatives to their originally staked-out position.

The home needs to foster a "hard work" culture. Studies show that the reason certain groups have the reputation for outstanding achievement (e.g., Asians, Ashkenazi Jews) is not attributable to genetic superiority, but rather to coming from cultures that value and encourage hard work, perseverance, second effort, and the like (Nisbett, 2009, p. 181). The KIPP (Knowledge Is Power Program) approach to schooling is an attempt to implement this core value of hard work, both at school and in the home. This approach is characterized by (Nisbett, 2009, 136-137):

- 7:30 a.m. to 5:00 p.m. school day
- Extra time for the arts, museums, etc.
- Three extra weeks of class in summer (usually July)
- ½ day every other Saturday
- Home visits
- Insistence on "kindness and good behavior"
- Hire/fire power for the principal
- Teacher cooperation
- Reward/punish system for behavior and performance

In essence, the KIPP approach attempts to model hard work around the clock, and is specifically designed to overcome the summer drop in performance among working class youth (see more on this in Chapter 14). Financially sustained by Don and Doris Fisher (of the Gap), KIPP schools outperform other schools in their areas.

Finally, the importance of modeling good health cannot be understated. Richard Nisbett summarizes in this way:

> The effect of exercising thirty minutes or more per day on fluid intelligence-based tasks is .50 SD [standard deviation] across all studies. Strength training plus cardiac training is better than cardiac training

alone. People who exercise regularly in middle age are one-third as likely to get Alzheimer's disease in their 70s as people who do not exercise. You can start exercise in your sixties and reduce the likelihood of Alzheimer's by half. (pp. 184-195)

The Development of Language

Parents who are professionals use around 2,000 words per hour around their kids. This compares to working class parents' use of 1,300 per hour. By the age of 3, the children of professionals have been exposed to 30 million words versus 20 million for working class. These professional kids have 50% more words. One reason for this dramatic difference is that professional parents tend to assume that kids are a natural part of family events such as dinnertime; so parents do not restrict their conversation to the adults at the table. Working class parents do not show the same tendency, tending instead to ignore children in their conversation. In addition to the quantity of conversation, the quality of conversational content is dramatically different. Professional parents make six positive comments for each negative, while working class parents make only two positives per negative. This gives the kids of professionals a threefold advantage with respect to the amount of encouragement received at home. Schools, religious groups, and others must place a priority on helping all parents realize the importance of including young people in their conversation and the importance of maximizing encouraging comments while minimizing discouragers. Society tends to worsen the matter, as bookstores located in college graduate markets have 1,300 children's titles for every 100 children in the neighborhood, while shelving only 30 children's titles per 100 children in working class markets. (Nisbett, pp. 86-69)

For children born to African Americans on welfare, however, the story is even more dramatic. These young people hear only about 600 words per day. Thus, by the time they are 3 years old, they have only heard around 10 million words in comparison to the 30 million words heard by kids with black/white professional parents. (Nisbett, 2009, p. 111ff.) These African American welfare children have an even starker exposure to encouragers, as they hear on average two negative or discouraging comments for every positive/encouraging comment. When they reach the age of 3, professionals' children have experienced a half million encouragers to only 80,000 discouragers, while the same age black child of a welfare mother has experienced 200,000 discouragers to only 75,000 encouragers.

> "The best way to keep children at home is to make the home atmosphere pleasant, and let the air out of the tires."
> --Dorothy Parker

The Management of Time and Space in the Home

Home life is defined by time and space: by how much time is spent doing what, and by how space is used. Csikszentmihalyi and Schneider (2000, p. 69) report on a study that followed how teens spent their time in two categories, work and play, with the following results. Out of every ten hours, three are spent in work, three in play, three in neither, and one in a combination of the two. This pattern was true for both boys and girls. Work included such things as school and jobs, while play included discretionary leisure such as hanging with friends, television viewing, and listening to music. The category of neither work nor play included meals and personal care, and both work and play included extracurricular activities at school and hobbies/other activities (such as Scouting) at home and in the community. The researchers found that the combination of work and play together resulted in maximum engagement on the part of the youth. These activities, such as debate, orchestra, service activities, newspaper, and athletics, provide the greatest payoff—reports of highest self-esteem, pleasure, and greater perceived importance to their future. The minimum engagement associated with the neither-work-nor-play activities were associated with the lowest ratings of self-esteem, pleasure, and perceived importance to their future. The task of the family is clear: Find ways to minimize activities that are neither work nor play, and maximize those which are both.

The quantity and quality of time that young people spend with adults highlights a need for change. Compared to teens worldwide, U.S., teens spend far more time with their peers, in comparison to the time spent around adult role models. In fact, studies show that American teens average 12 hours more each week in time spent with their peers versus adults than do their international counterparts (Csikszentmihalyi and Schneider, 2000, p. 14). Also, the typical U.S. teen spends only 30 minutes alone with their father (regardless of their parents' marital status), and much of that time is spent watching television. This is a call for increasing time spent with adult role models in general (whether in private lessons, internships, community service, and so forth) and time spent with the father (whether in help with homework/school projects, household maintenance, exercise, and so forth).

Donald Roberts, Lisa Henriksen, and Ulla Foehr reported (in Lerner and Steinberg, 2004, pp. 487 ff.) on a survey by the Pew Internet and American Life Project. They found that U.S. teens average over six hours daily involved with some form of media. Here's how it breaks down:

- For younger teens, three of the six hours involve watching television.
- For older teens, about two of the six are for television, music/audio media gaining ascendancy over television.
- Boys watch more TV than girls.
- Girls listen more to music than boys.
- Teens from higher socioeconomic status homes and whose parents have more education spend less time with media.
- Teens from single parent homes tend to spend more time with media.
- One's television viewing habits tend to stick with you for life.
- As a general rule, as the computer in its many forms takes on more functions, it will capture more of the typical teens' time.
- Most media use is in one's bedroom.
- Time spent with music tends to pay off with respect to friendships, as kids knowledgeable of the current music scene typically have more friends and higher social status.

- Time spent watching violent TV programming and/or playing violent video games is directly related to levels of violent behavior later in life. It appears to desensitize teens/people to the effects of violence. Clearly, some trait profiles are more susceptible to this effect that others. The statistical relationship between hours spent watching/using violent media and subsequent violent behavior approximates the cause-and-effect relationship between tobacco use and cancer.
- Watching TV with sexual content, particularly between unmarrieds (which is mostly what networks offer), is associated with casual attitudes towards sex, decreased insistence on remaining a virgin, and increased sexual activity.
- Body dissatisfaction is associated with reading fashion magazines and watching TV programming featuring slender heroines, particularly soap operas and music videos.
- In a fascinating naturally occurring experiment, after television was introduced in Fiji, eating disorders skyrocketed. They were essentially non-existent when TV appeared in 1995 but rose around 11% three years later.
- Teens smoke the cigarettes that advertise the most.
- If a teen's favorite movie star smokes, the teen is more likely to smoke. And, film/TV smoking incidence is increasing.
- Alcohol use is related to TV/music-video viewing, with drug use being related to listening to heavy metal music.
- Kids who do not use drugs report lower interest in all forms of popular music.

Here is a summary of the summary:

- Encourage moderate listening to popular music; discourage heavy metal listening.
- Avoid violent programming (TV, games, and music/other).
- Avoid programs with sex among unmarrieds.
- For girls, avoid TV/media content with toothpick-figured heroines; encourage normalcy as the preference for the figures of heroines.
- Avoid programming that has smoking (no more *Mad Men* for Junior!).

In closing, let us talk about the importance of every family member having a "sacred place." This was proposed by Joseph Campbell (1991) in *The Power of Myth*. Originating in a dialog with television host Bill Moyers, here's what Campbell had to say:

> Moyers: "What does it mean to have a sacred place?"
>
> Campbell: "This is an absolute necessity for anybody today. You must have a room, or a certain hour or so a day, where you don't know what was in the newspapers that morning, you don't know who your friends are, you don't know what you owe anybody, you don't know what anybody owes to you. This is a place where you can simply experience and bring forth what you are and what you might be. This is the place of creative incubation. At first you may find that nothing happens there. But if you have a sacred place and use it, something eventually will happen....You are always doing something that is required of you. Where is your bliss station? You have to try to find it. Get a phonograph and put on the music that you really love,

> even if it's corny music that nobody else respects. Or get the book you like to read. In your sacred place, you get the 'thou' feeling of life..." (p. 115)

Our sacred place is sitting in our living room with views to the outdoors. Where's yours? In the next chapter we will look at how traits relate to physical, mental, and spiritual well-being.

A Case Study in Family Dynamics: The Banner Family

Contributed by Emily Crowder, UNC-Chapel Hill student and CentACS Research Intern

In order to examine the interactions within this family, see if you can observe how their traits come into play:

Gordon (the father, 57 yrs):	N- E+ O++ A- C-
Debbie (the mother, 54 yrs):	N+ E= O- A+ C=
Matthew (21 yrs):	N+ E= O= A= C+
Grace (19 yrs):	N- E= O- A+ C+

Thanksgiving has finally arrived, and the Banner household is preparing for the whole family to come over. Though it's only Wednesday, Debbie Banner is already in a panic. She is worried over every detail. Every single part of the house must be clean just in case someone wants to walk around. Her husband, Gordon, and the rest of the family try to convince her that no one is going to care about small things like the dog toys in the corner of the room, but she refuses to believe it and snaps at the rest of them for not being helpful. Matthew, her son, gets frustrated with all the stress and makes a snippy comment towards his mother, then storms up to his room, slamming the door, and turning his music up as loud as possible until his father yells at him to turn it down. Grace is left in the room, trying to figure out what she can do that would calm her mother down. She offers to help make a dish so that her mother can have a break. Gordon decides to help arrange the table instead of helping in the kitchen because he prefers cooking without a recipe, just throwing basic ingredients into a pan, which would drive both Debbie and Grace crazy as they put together the usual Thanksgiving recipes. As Grace and her mom cook, Grace is still uneasy with all the yelling and arguing that has been going on, and she tells her mother to go relax for a bit, hoping to ease her anxiety. Grace, always one to devote herself to others, remains alone cooking, hoping that everyone will eventually calm down enough to enjoy the meal the next day.

Fortunately, by the next day, everyone seems to have gotten over their tension. At dinnertime, the grandparents and cousins begin to arrive, each bringing a delicious-looking dish to add to the feast. The meal is filled with many different conversations. Gordon is telling everyone about his newest "great idea." Grace and Matthew laugh when they hear it, but he insists it will work. He tries to defend his idea by bringing up the time he wanted to invent a liquid hamburger, which everyone naturally mocked, even though years later the army started using a similar idea to provide on-the-go food. With the mention of the army, the conversation quickly turns to politics, and Matthew and his father start a heated debate over economic policies. Matthew gets upset with every position his father supports, while Gordon refuses to back down on his beliefs. Grace, uncomfortable with the arguing, asks if they can refrain from politics and discuss something else, much to the agreement of her mom. As the conversation changes direction, Grace tries to tell a story. After starting a sentence three times and being interrupted by her father, she finally gives up and sits back quietly, annoyed at the frequency with which her father does this. Gordon, however, takes no notice until Debbie eventually lets him know what he's doing. Once the conversation changes topics again, Grace gets up to help her mother clear the dishes and get them out of everyone's way.

After the meal, Gordon goes to the living room with the other guys to watch some football, while Matthew and Grace head upstairs to finish some postponed schoolwork and emails. After a while each wanders back downstairs to join those who are still there. Gordon continues chatting and watching football for a few hours, while Debbie sits down with her sisters to enjoy a cup of coffee. Ready to get out of the house, Matthew, Grace, and their cousins pick out what to see for their traditional Thanksgiving movie, which will give them all a chance to finally sit back and relax.

How individual traits come into play:

It is easy to see Debbie's N+ behavior in this situation. As hostess of the celebration, she is worried and tense. And not only was she stressed to begin with, but her focus on small details (O4-), which seems insignificant to the others, gives her even more that she feels she has to do. Along with her anxiety about the upcoming dinner, her higher intensity level on N2 contributes to her snapping at the others. After this lashing out, Matthew's reaction is the strongest due to his even higher need for stability. Meanwhile, Grace, who is high in accommodation (especially A1 and A2) and strongly dislikes conflicts, offers to chip in to help ease her mom's nerves.

Traits After School

At the dinner table, the conversation immediately illustrates the differences in originality within the family. Gordon, with his large imagination (O1+), tells of new ideas, while his children, who are lower in originality, see them as ridiculous and even comical. After discussing his innovative ideas and moving on to politics, Gordon's competitive spirit (A-) comes into play. While he argues with his son, Matthew's higher N (need for stability) comes through as he gets more emotional in the debate. Unfortunately, the rest of the family, being high in accommodation, is uncomfortable with the divisive topic and ensuing argument which prompts them to stop this conversation. After switching topics, Gordon continues to dominate the conversation at his daughter's expense, as he is low in A (accommodation) and high in E4 (Taking Charge). Meanwhile, Grace is high in A and low in E4, making her even less likely to speak up in the first place.

Following the meal, it is easy to observe the family's varying extraversion levels. Gordon, the Extravert, continues hanging around the guys and watching television, while his kids take a little time to themselves (E=) upstairs to get things done (C+) before rejoining the group in a more relaxing setting. Debbie, who is more extraverted than the kids though still an Ambivert, surrounds herself with fewer people and less noise than Gordon and his TV-watching group. And the children, who have had enough stimulation for one day, escape the noise of the house by going to a movie where they can just watch the screen without exchanging any chatter.

20

The Big Five and Health

Physical, Mental, and Spiritual Wellness

> "Who sees all beings in his own Self, and his own Self in all beings, loses all fear.... When a sage sees this great Unity and his Self has become all beings, what delusion and what sorrow can ever be near him?"
>
> --*Upanishads* (Isa Upanishad, verses 6-7, in Mascaro, *The Upanishads,* 1956, pp. 49-50)

Guide to This Chapter:

- Health as the Highest Good
- Some Guidelines for Physical Health
- Some Guidelines for Mental Health
- Some Guidelines for Spiritual Health
- Some Guidelines for Relational Health
- A Suggested Checklist for a Periodic Personal Health Check-Up

The passage above that is taken from the collection of Hindu scriptures called the *Upanishads* points us toward the key to a sense of subjective well-being: the sense that each of us is made of the same ingredients and that, like cookies and cakes, we only differ in degrees. All cakes have flour, sugar, eggs, salt, and milk (cut us some slack here!), just as all humans have N, E, O, A, and C. Some cakes have more sugar, some have less, but no cake is all sugar or no sugar, just as no human is all extraversion or no extraversion. Knowing our commonality is humbling, amusing, enlightening, and puzzling. But most of all, it should get us off any high horse and increase our level of mutual acceptance.

Health as the Highest Good

Happiness is a false god. Books abound that claim to reveal the key to lifelong, 24-7-365¼ happiness. As we have said earlier, happiness is the abundance of positive emotions and the absence of

Traits After School

N	E	O	A	C
Need for Stability	**Extraversion**	**Originality**	**Accommodation**	**Consolidation**
N+ Reactive	E+ Extraverted	O+ Explorer	A+ Adapter	C+ Focused
N= Responsive	E= Ambiverted	O= Moderate	A= Negotiator	C= Balanced
N- Resilient	E- Introverted	O- Preserver	A- Challenger	C- Flexible
N1: Worry	**E1: Approach Level**	**O1: Imagination**	**A1: Service**	**C1:Thoroughness**
N2: Temper	**E2: Group Orientation**	**O2: Range of Interests**	**A2: Compliance**	**C2: Structure**
N3: Outlook	**E3: Pace**	**O3: Innovation**	**A3: Humility**	**C3: Ambition**
N4: Coping Level	**E4: Leadership**	**O4: Zoom Scale**	**A4: Speak Out Level**	**C4: Concentration**
	E5: Trust			**C5: Methodicalness**
	E6: Tact			

negative emotions. With only one in three persons scoring high on E (thus endowed with a steady supply of positive emotions), and only one in three scoring low on N (thus normally without feelings of fear, anger, or sadness), only one in nine persons (1/3 x 1/3) is born truly happy. The rest of us are happy at times, but that is not our natural state, as it is for the one in nine born that way, like Maria in *The Sound of Music,* like Guido in *La vita é bella (Life is Beautiful)*, like Evelyn Ryan in *The Prize Winner of Defiance, Ohio*. For the other eight out of nine to wish we were Maria, Guido, or Evelyn is like a short person wishing to be tall. The healthier outlook is to accept our innate differences from them and to embrace our own special ways of achieving inner satisfaction, the sense of well-being that we call "health"—a good, old-fashioned, Old English word that means simply to be flourishing and absent of pain. This sense of well-being does not require ecstasy (although it is nice on occasion), joy (also tasty every now and then), or bubbly-giggly euphoria (which we often experience when playing with children). Rather, it simply requires the absence of pain and the sense of being on a path, making progress. In our final chapter, we will discuss in some detail what this path is all about, and how to maintain this sense of progress. For now, we want to focus on what we can do to maintain the sense of being in good health—physically, mentally, spiritually, and socially. And we will see how the wisdom from the *Upanishads*, the acceptance that we are all somehow alike, is the prerequisite for flourishing without pain.

Some Guidelines for Physical Health

> "In order to know whether a human being is young or old, offer it food of different kinds at short intervals. If young, it will eat anything at any hour of the day or night."
> --Oliver Wendell Holmes

In her biography of her father, Count Leo Tolstoy, Alexandra describes the ethic of love that he embraced in his 40s. Tolstoy's ethic was humanistic, in that he began with the assumption that the natural state of being alive was the best of all states. Hence, anything that altered that state was evil. Both coffee and killing, alcohol and poverty, tobacco and disease, were evil in Tolstoy's mind, as they, each in their own way, altered the state of being fully alive, the state of normal, everyday alertness and consciousness that permitted planning, problem solving, decision making, creativity, and the enjoyment of life, liberty, and the pursuit of happiness.... Anything that promoted or maintained the natural state of consciousness—

education, sufficient income, appropriate freedom, nutritious diet, loving relationships—was then defined as good. Count Tolstoy, the once profligate spoiled brat, acted upon his newfound ethic by becoming vegetarian, by abstaining from caffeine, nicotine, and alcohol, and by becoming a proponent of progressive education for all. He called it the ethic of love—love of all living things, in their natural form. Once an invited guest, who knew of the Count's recent conversion to vegetarianism, requested before attending a planning meeting at Tolstoy's estate that the Count provide him with meat for his meal, otherwise he'd be unwilling to attend. The Count obliged, tying a living hen to the chair reserved for the guest, with the instruction that, if the guest insisted on flesh, he could kill and prepare it himself!

Tolstoy's stringent ethic of love places top priority on maintaining one's body in its natural state of functioning. While we do not recommend abstinence from caffeine and her cousins (thought we'd better say this, lest you quit reading!), we do recommend adhering to doses of everything such that we do not deviate from normal alertness in a way that would endanger the health of others or ourselves. Here is our set of guidelines for maintaining this sense of optimal physical health:

- *Get a good night's sleep*. This is different for different people. We sleep in cycles that average 90 minutes. The only way to know how many cycles you need is to sleep for several nights in a row in which you go to bed at a reasonable time and wake up naturally, and refreshed, without setting an alarm. One person may sleep for five 90-minute cycles, for a total of 7.5 hours, while another may sleep for four 2-hour cycles, for a total of 8 hours. You can figure the average length of your cycles by finding the common denominator of all of your sleep episodes. Teens require more sleep than those younger or older—about nine hours a night. However, only about 1 in 5 gets that much sleep—here's the kicker: 80% of teens who get 9 hours of sleep get As and Bs. Read more about this in Pierce's chapter on sleep in *The Owner's Manual for the Brain* (2006, 3rd Ed.).
- *Limit yourself to no more than one dose of caffeine in the morning, and one in the afternoon*. One dose equals approximately 1 milligram of caffeine per pound of body weight. With a 2-ounce espresso weighing in at 100 milligrams, that's the limit/dose for a 100-pound person. It takes about seven hours for the dose to metabolize/wear off. I (Pierce) have one dose early in the morning, switch to water, then another dose in the afternoon after my "nap." [(Jane) Yes, he takes a short one almost every day, even at the office in his recliner.] Many teens love Red Bull—80 mg in an 8-ounce can. Research shows that more than a dose 1) does not increase alertness (the feeling that it does is deceiving), 2) increases errors, and 3) maintained over time, leads to addiction. Also, caffeine is dehydrating, and excessive use over time will affect mental efficiency, including moods, learning, and memory.
- *Prefer a moderate, balanced, natural food diet.* Candace Pertt, a Georgetown University physiologist, once wrote that the best diet is not to eat anything that hasn't been around for at least 3,000 years! That eliminates processed foods, and that's a good start! As they like to snack, make sure teens have plenty of fresh vegetables, fruits, whole grain breads, and unsalted nuts available. They need to be able to grab and chew with no prep time; so keep snacks in ready-to-eat form, as in carrot sticks, celery pieces, and the like. A great alternative to chips is sliced jicama or toasted lavash. They go great with hummus.
- *If alcohol consumption has begun (hopefully at the legal age), limit to two servings daily.* Subject to body size and sex, of course, with smaller bodies and females allowed less.

Traits After School

- *Exercise, both aerobic and anaerobic.* Aerobic exercise cleans the body of cortisol, which, if allowed to accumulate through lack of aerobic exercise, will damage the body by aiding the buildup of plaque in veins and arteries. Exercise is best done after the most stressful time of day. And find ways to maintain muscle tone throughout the body with anaerobic exercise. These exercises counteract the effects of stress, as well as stimulate new neuronal growth that is necessary for learning. Also, the increase in obesity globally is attributed to two factors: diets increasingly high in fats and decreasingly active lifestyles (more true for urban than for rural areas). (Lerner and Steinberg, 2004, p. 574)
- *Tobacco and its more potent inhaled cousins have no place in the healthy lifestyle.* Period.
- *Maximize fresh air.* Recirculated air is depleted of negative ions and causes drowsiness over time, due to insufficient oxygen. Negative ions remove pollutants, thus maximizing available oxygen. If a young person must remain for long periods in recirculated air, then get them a room ion generator (they are not expensive, but make sure they have been approved with respect to not emitting ozone).
- *Maximize exposure to natural sunlight.* Natural sunlight shuts down the production of melatonin, the sleep neurotransmitter, thus maintaining maximum alertness. If a youth is in a space that has no windows, then they are not getting natural sunlight. Unless, that is, they have lamps with a CRI (color rendering index) of 90 or higher. Any less than that and a lamp will be missing at a minimum the blue portion of the spectrum, and drowsiness is likely. Grow-lights used for indoor vegetation have CRIs of greater than 90.
- *Causes of Death and Physical Harm.* Boys are at greatest risk for death by vehicle (Lerner and Steinberg, 2004, p. 559), while girls who give birth and have not reached physical maturity are three times more likely to die from childbirth-related causes than are older, more mature females (p. 565). These young people need special attention to understand their risks. Both boys and girls who are N+ (emotionally reactive), E+ (desirous of strong sensory bombardment), O+ (easily bored and seeking variety), A- (competitive and self-assured), and C- (spontaneous and multitaskers) are at higher risk for being risk takers, whether with cars, skateboards, or with their bodies. Conversations with them about their special susceptibilities for highway and sexual accidents should focus on understanding the nature of the risk and what they can do to minimize it (e.g., absolutely no cell phone use or other forms of multitasking while driving; if they are sexually active, insure appropriate precautions are in effect and that they fully understand the damage of sexually transmitted diseases).

> I never expected to see the day when girls would get sunburned in the places they do now.
> --Will Rogers

Now, who's going to adhere to these guidelines!? For one thing, those who are N-C+ are more likely to do so because they are more naturally rational and disciplined. Those who are N+C- would benefit from externally imposed restrictions, similar to those imposed by being in a boarding school or by serving in the military! Short of that, they should invite their parents, siblings, or other significant relations to help them adhere, as in, "Hey, dude, don't offer me a second Red Bull—one's my limit for the time being! OK?" Put up signs that reinforce these guidelines. Have intrafamily contests, dormitory contests, etc., to help reinforce them. Also, those higher in O crave variety, and variety can be the enemy of physical health. Those easily bored end up with less sleep, extremes in diet, and so forth. High O individuals, especially those who are N+ and C-, will have an especially tough battle and need the understanding and cooperation of their family and friends to stay the course.

Some Guidelines for Mental Health

The key to mental health is to acknowledge both ends of every trait continuum. Even though we may be extraverted, sometimes we need to introvert. Make this a general rule: While you may prefer one end of a trait continuum, you should never completely neglect the other end. When one begins to embrace one end of a trait continuum and neglect the other, one risks becoming rigidly fixed at that end. One who celebrates their perfectionism, for example, must not be perfectionist at everything, lest they become obsessive and compulsive, never able to lighten up and be casual about something. Barry Schwartz wrote a book about this, in fact, called *The Paradox of Choice*, in which he described *maximizers* and *satisficers*, the former being those high in C1 who make every decision/project/task and so forth the subject of maximum effort and highest standard. One must keep Haemon's warning to his father Creon in mind, that he who does not bend in the wind, snaps (for complete citation, see our introduction to Chapter 19).

> "Most people would sooner die than think, in fact they do."
> --Bertrand Russell

And snap they do. In fact, the cause of most mental disorders is this very condition of losing one's access to *both* ends of one or more trait continua. Machiavelli in *The Prince* recognized this relationship, arguing that the ideal leader must never commit to any one extreme, always balancing one extreme with another. The leader who is all courage, for example, is feared, not admired, and thus must, on occasion, show humility. Such rigidity in behavior—all trust/no doubt, all doubt/no trust, all society/no solitude, all talk/no silence, all change/no stability, all leading/no following—tends to lead to one or both of two consequences: failure to maintain a relationship and/or failure to hold a job (or maintain adequate grades to stay in school). Failure to keep a job (or maintain grades) and/or maintain a relationship is thus symptomatic of behavioral rigidity of some sort. When this occurs, the individual needs professional help in restoring behavioral flexibility. The best insurance against reaching this point is encouraging appropriate balance. Be aware of one's tendencies toward a strong preference for any one trait or more, and discuss/monitor the importance of paying adequate attention to its complementary or opposite trait. Use the example of the wind breaking the tree that will not bend. To know one's strong behavioral preferences is to be forewarned of the dangers of ignoring their opposites. You can't have one without at least some of the other!

Some Guidelines for Spiritual Health

We need to be careful here and make sure that our preaching doesn't lead to meddling! What is it that all spiritual activity has in common? Well, first, we must make a distinction between spirit and religion. Most commonly, the spiritual life is contrasted with the material life, with the material life defined as the pursuit of concrete possessions (art, money, clothes, beach house, stamp collection) and the spiritual life defined as the pursuit of abstract possession (knowledge, skills, moral reasoning/behavior, attitudes, wisdom, service/altruism). Religion, then, by definition, can be more spiritual or more material or both. Religious organizations that focus on bricks and mortar are by definition more material, while those focusing on helping the poor are more spiritual. The most spiritual religious organization I (Pierce) ever participated in was an unprogrammed Quaker meeting that met in peoples' living rooms—absolutely no bricks and mortar, just meditation and social service. The most materialistic religious organization I (Jane) ever heard of was Rev. Jim Bakker's PTL (Praise the Lord) ministry at Heritage USA in Fort Mill, SC. Bakker fraudulently bilked followers and ended up with a lengthy prison sentence (he's out now, living in Branson, Missouri). His most famous quote was: "The Lord don't [sic] like no junk!" in response to press allegations of his spending his faithfuls' donations personally on items such as actual gold plated faucets in his bathroom. And of course, there are those religious organizations that manage a blend of the two.

Here we are not talking about religion, yet not excluding it. Rather, we are talking about the life of the spirit, with or without religion. Spiritual behavior undergoes stages of development. These stages have been described by numerous scholars (Lawrence Kohlberg, Jean Piaget, James Fowler). What these descriptions have in common are the following stages, each associated with a chronological period of development:

1. *The Selfish Stage*. This is the "you scratch my back, I'll scratch yours" outlook that is characterized by reciprocity and selfishness. This stance is best described by the so-called Golden Rule: Do unto others as you would have them do unto you. This is moral/spiritual behavior at its most primitive. Many religious organizations foster this basic, give-and-take approach for a lifetime—they get stuck there. Jim Bakker's PTL Club described above comes to mind.
2. *The Organization Stage*. Typically individuals mature into this stage during adolescence, wherewith they abandon the egocentric reciprocity of the first stage for a system of rules that lead to thinking about the principles involved in responsible personal and social behavior, such as "have compassion for the poor" (the Koran), "self-denial and material surrender" (Hinduism), and "love one another" (Christianity). These principles become codified into systems (the Ten Commandments) and organizations (World Council of Churches).
3. *The Doubting Stage*. In late adolescence and early adulthood, typically as the result of formal education or hard experience, individuals question the assumptions of their codes and organizations and undergo some form of withdrawal, either publicly and explicitly (e.g., by discontinuing their membership/followership and exploring other approaches) or privately and implicitly (e.g., Mother Teresa's journals that questioned her beliefs while continuing to serve with the Missionaries of Charity). I (Jane) had such an experience in my late teens when I read *Siddhartha* at a friend's urging shortly after starting college. It represented an entirely new way to view the world than my rather traditional Protestant Christian upbringing had provided.
4. *The Universal Stage*. At some point in adulthood, some individuals gain the insight that all of the world's religions and philosophies share a core set of concerns, issues, and assumptions. This has been described by some as the stage of mysticism, the stage of epistemology, and the stage of science. It is characterized by comments like this one by Michael Gazzaniga, author of *The Social Brain*: "If believers

could come to realize there isn't ten cents worth of difference in their substantive plans, perhaps they might then begin to see the magical part for what it is." People who reach this stage are likely to embrace documents such as the "Universal Declaration of Human Rights" adopted by the General Assembly of the United Nations in 1948 (http://www.un.org/en/documents/udhr/). These individuals may pursue their spiritual life independent of a religious organization, or they may embrace an organization (church, mosque, temple) with the understanding that no religious organization is complete in itself but is part of a more universal community. People at this stage embrace the notion of the universal humanity of all people, cultures, religions, political systems, and so on.

Moving through the stages of spiritual development does not happen inevitably as do the stages of physical development. Men will grow beards, and women will grow breasts, but not all will move to stages two, three, or four of spiritual development! Spiritual development is the result of education and experience. One of the oft-stated goals of liberal arts education is the attainment of stage four thinking. On a more personal family level, Lerner and Steinberg (2004, pp. 155 ff.) point out that moral reasoning and growth is best facilitated by Socratic-type dialog, in which parents, peers, and others engage young people in thinking through moral issues, forcing them to consider causes and alternative courses of action, form opinions, and use their reasoning skills. This approach is more effective in forming moral character than one-way strategies such as supplying information, direct criticisms, and strongly urged courses of action. Prefer warm dialog to cold or hot criticism. One example would be the student conflict/arbitration groups found in some high schools.

Some Guidelines for Relational Health

We will be discussing relationships in some depth in a later chapter. For now, suffice it to say that the quality of relationships in one's life is strongly related to overall personal health. Harvard sociologist Robert Putnam in his classic *Bowling Alone: The Collapse and Revival of American Community* (Simon and Schuster, 2001), made a distinction between material capital, personal capital, and social capital, i.e., money/possessions, knowledge/skills, and relationships/social connectivity. He traced a 30% national decline in social capital in the U.S. over the last half of the 20th century with an accompanying downturn in positive development (increases in crime, decreases in school performance, and so forth). He measured social capital by a variety of indicators: membership and positions held in civic, social, religious, political, etc. clubs and organizations; voting frequency; holding public office; having dinner with friends; and so on. Each of these indicators pointed to the number of high-quality relationships in every geographical area of the country. He found clear relationships between deficits in social capital and incidents of violence, poor school performance, and poor health (including an increased incidence of Alzheimer's Disease).

In a summary of global research on teen health (pp. 578-80), Lerner and Steinberg (2004) found that, across all criteria studied, the causal factors most associated with positive teen health results are:

1. Positive family connections
2. Positive school connections/attendance
3. Positive peer connections

Traits After School

4. Personal resilience
5. Positive youth development activities in the community
6. Spirituality—belief in higher power than self

It is interesting to note that, of these six causes of teen health, four have to do with relationships! All of the six are protective against undesirable development, and their opposites are risk factors. So, if relationships are so important, how do we encourage them short of pushing kids out of the door?

Constance Flanagan has addressed this issue (see Lerner and Steinberg, 2004, pp. 721 ff.). She reports that the more connected that teens are to other people through family, school (especially extra curricular), or community (church, temple, mosque, community-based youth organizations [CBYOs]), the more likely they are to be active in politics and community affairs as a young adult, including the frequency with which they exercise their right to vote in elections. Teens' degrees of student achievement and community involvement are directly proportional to their teachers' and administrators' explicit expectations and encouragement for young people to get involved in extracurricular activities. Getting involved takes urging. Involvement in CBYOs serves to inoculate youth against risky behavior, such as antisocial activity and substance use/abuse. One exception to this glowing report on the positive effects of extracurricular activities comes from University of Michigan psychologists Jacquelynne Eccles and Bonnie Barber (1999 and subsequent studies). They found that high schoolers' participation in sports, and especially team sports, was associated with significantly higher incidences of drinking alcohol and getting drunk than for non-athletes. This was true regardless of the sex of the athlete, their intellectual aptitude, or the educational level of their mother. Even though athletes tend to drink more, apparently their positive educational attainments were not diminished as a result. They drank *and* succeeded in school. Eccles and Barber did not report on the relation of traits to this relationship, but we would strongly suspect that the more impulsive (i.e., N+C-) and more aggressive (i.e., E+A-) profiles would be more likely to exhibit the excessive drinking and hence would be more in need of monitoring.

One insight into the value and impact of non-academic engagement comes from the French historian Alexis de Tocqueville (1805-1859), who referred to CBYOs in their many forms as "schools of democracy." He saw them as places where youth get experience testing/experimenting with leadership skills in a context where risk is shared by all and with minimal risk of negative impact on one's future outlook (i.e., you can't really get a failing grade being committee chair in a recreation center). Such involvement appears to have a special benefit for African-American male teens, who reportedly feel safer in programs that are away from their school campus (Lerner and Sternberg, 2004, p. 728). For these organizations to be maximally effective, adults need to be in the background, supportive, and available, but not in charge. In addition, the adults and teens must adhere alike to the same set of rules (p. 730). A promising development in this arena is "service learning" programs. These initiatives couple community volunteer work with an academic component, such as volunteering with the cancer society and studying aspects of cancer, or volunteering with a police department and studying causes of aggression. Although these programs are relatively new, they appear to be having excellent results. However, there is little longitudinal evaluative data to provide definitive judgment (pp. 731 ff.).

A Suggested Checklist for a Periodic Personal Health Check-Up

Most people, at least those who can afford it, or who have the service available for free, get an annual physical check-up. Many popular "self-help" writers (e.g., Steven Covey, Janet and Chris Attwood, Peter Benson) recommend something like that for life in general. Covey writes about "sharpening the saw" by insuring that one is engaged in a balance of activities (exercise, spiritual activities, and so forth), Benson says find your "spark," while the Attwoods suggest that you identify your top five "passions" and make sure that you are consistently engaged in all of them, but not necessarily all at the same time. Of course, if something better (i.e., potentially more satisfying) than your five passions comes along, by all means take advantage! Although I (Pierce) didn't care much for the Attwoods' book (full of fluff, in my humble opinion), I really do like the basics of their approach. They suggest that you identify up to 15 passions: activities, processes, skills, or other things than engage you so thoroughly that you could do them forever. They give your life meaning, intensity, satisfaction, and they are intrinsically energizing. From this list of 15, you select your top five, and then make sure you manage your life in such a way that you rarely leave any of them unattended. I did this exercise after (quickly) reading the book, and came up with this list (I'm sure yours would be different!):

- Translating research into practice
- Working on a book
- Helping people gain insight
- Making chamber music
- Experiencing sensory pleasure
- Learning something new
- Reading for pleasure
- Engaging with family
- Developing friendships
- Being close to nature
- Developing new products
- Searching for meaning
- Dining with friends
- Being stimulated intellectually

I carefully meditated on this list and narrowed it down to the top four (they recommended the top five, but I found that all 15 were somehow included in these four). Next, I listed specific activities that related to the four passions and then gave myself a grade (1 to 10, 10 being highest) on how well I was living the four passions on daily basis:

1. Translating research into practice (10)

Traits After School

- Designing programs (training courses and speeches)
- Writing books
- Developing tests and reports
- University teaching, internships
- Preparing miscellaneous materials (handouts, workbooks, spreadsheets, newsletters, bulletins)

2. Learning something new (10)
   - Professional associations
   - Studying adolescence
   - Researching mental abilities
   - Publishing software
   - Exploring item response theory
   - Computer adaptive testing
   - Keeping up with the happiness literature
   - Experimenting with Facebook, Linked In, Twitter
   - Learning miscellaneous new statistical analyses
3. Developing friendships (5)
   - Professional associations
   - Dinners/cooking together
   - Making chamber music
   - Camping
   - Maintaining house/yard
   - Reunions
   - Model railroading
4. Experiencing sensory pleasure (10)
   - Reading
   - Television/movies
   - Playing or listening to chamber music
   - Experiencing various ethnic cuisines
   - Attending concerts
   - Good health
   - Spending time in the great outdoors

Table 20 Autopilot Restart Checklist, or How to Find What Has Caused the Blahs

Step One: Quick Restart. Check through the five categories to the right, and see if you can spot the culprit responsible for feeling de-energized. If so, it should be obvious what to do to restart. If not, continue with step two below. In general, the blahs are relieved by a change of pace, like stopping reading to work with your hands.	1. One or more of my **passions** is unsatisfied 2. My **physical** condition is out of whack 3. My **mental** life is out of whack 4. My **spiritual** life is out of whack 5. My **relational** life is out of whack
Step Two: Extended Restart. Peruse the detailed sources of the blahs below, and find the one that you think is the most likely cause of your current condition. Then check to the right for an idea on what to do about it.	
One or More of My Five Passions is Unsatisfied: • #1 (enter them here) • #2 • #3 • #4 • #5	**Suggestions:** • Back off of an overattended passion to make room • Back off of non-passion activities; delegate where possible • Rethink non-passion activities so they become one of your passions (e.g., housework could become relationship development) • Think up new activities for the underattended passion that would be compelling
Some Aspect of My Physical Condition Needs Attention: • Been eating too much • Too much sugar • Too much caffeine/jittery • Too much alcohol • Too little sleep • Too little exercise • Sexual restlessness	**Possible Remedies:** • Take a nap; go for a walk • Nap; sleep; walk • Walk; calisthenics; drink water • Drink water; walk; nap • Nap; sleep 1 cycle; exercise; fresh air; sun • Exercise of choice • Find your partner
Some Aspect of My Mental Condition is Out of Balance: • Priorities are unclear/feeling overwhelmed • A problem needs solving • A decision needs to be made • A project needs to be planned out • Too much stress • Too much/little socializing • Too much/little sensory stimulation • Too much/little physical activity • Too much/little leadership responsibility • Too much/little creative effort • Too much/little complexity • Too much/little change • Too much/little work with detail • Too much/little perfectionism • Too much/little structure • Too much/little focus on goals • Too much/little concentration • Too much/little adherence to a schedule • Too much/little active engagement (e.g., practicing) • Too much/little time spent in my comfort zone	**How to Restore Balance:** • Update my To-Do list/focus on top priority for now • Find help to identify cause/solution • Establish criteria; evaluate options • Identify the steps required • Get away from/remove source; aerobic exercise • More/less time alone (e.g., with hobbies) • More/less time quiet and low key • More/less sedentary activity • More/less time engaged in personally meaningful work • More/less time engaged in routine, practical matters • More/less time spent simplifying, or with simpler matters • More/less time spent with what is familiar • More/less time away from the details • More/less activity that requires only casual effort • More/less pure exploration and spontaneity • More/less time in sheer relaxation unrelated to goals • More/less activity that does not require mental effort • More/less unplanned, unscheduled time alone or w others • More/less passive involvement (e.g., listening to music) • More/less challenging/stretching goals
Some Aspect of My Spiritual Life is Out of Balance: • Too much/little focus on others • Too much/little physical pleasure • Too much/little time on lower level/maintenance • Too much/little time spent on my possesions/things	**How to Restore Balance:** • More/less focus on self • More/less focus on the intellectual • More/less time on higher level/production • More/less time/energy/resources spent on material things
Some Aspect of My Relational Life is Out of Balance: • Too much/little time with family/friends/others • Too much/little time with closest friends/family • Too much/little time spent preparing my legacy	**How to Restore Balance:** • More time with those ignored; less with those doted on • More time with ignored; less with those doted on • Either get busy on your legacy, or chill for awhile!

Traits After School

I keep an abbreviated list (just the four passions) in my wallet and taped beside my computers at the office and at home, as constant reminders, lest I should allow lesser priorities to usurp my passions. This approach makes sense to me, and I recommend it as a simple but powerful way to stay fo-focused, to communicate with others about what is really important to each other, and to define how we can be mutually understanding, accepting, and supportive of each other's core values and passions.

Now, that said, what happens when you feel blah? Or as our grandson Liam said as a little boy, "All out of puff" (learned from Thomas the Tank Engine programs). The feeling that your "get up and go" has somehow "gone down and went [sic]." It is the feeling that your autopilot is not functioning properly, that you are stymied as to what to do next, such that you end up kind of staring into space. For some of us, this feeling comes more frequently than for others. What can we do to shake off this feeling, to rid ourselves of the "blahs"?

For some of us, we have old, familiar remedies that work most every time: going for a brisk walk, listening to some particular kind of music (for us, Bach's Brandenburg Concertos!), taking a nap, brewing a cup of tea, having a chat with a close friend/family member, cleaning/organizing the house/office/room, and so on. Surely you have your "old reliable" blah-busters. But what do you do when none of these seem to work? I have developed an "Autopilot Restart Checklist" to keep by my work and rest areas (desk, bed, reading chair, car) so that, if I'm feeling blue/blah, I can review the list in hopes of identifying the cause of the blahs and then quickly figure out something to do so I might emerge rejuvenated and engaged. I encourage you to take this checklist (Table 20), study it, and modify it in such a way that it makes sense for you.

As a low N (resilient) person, I (Jane) very rarely have anything like the "blahs." However, it is important to respect and respond to a partner or child who is experiencing them. When that person is dissatisfied, it affects their demeanor and overall relationship with you and the rest of their world. Take time to discuss these checklist items with the person.

So far, we have focused in this book mostly on the trait culture in the U.S. In the next chapter, we will take a look at how traits work around the world.

21

The Big Five Across Cultures

How Traits Relate to International Similarities and Differences

> "What evolutionary biology also tells us is that all humans, belonging as they do to the same species, have the same phylogenetically given human nature, with their differing cultures having come into being during quite recent times, through the varying exercise of choice."
>
> --Derek Freeman, *The Fateful Hoaxing of Margaret Mead* (1999, p. 215)

Guide to This Chapter:

- The Big Five Trait Structure is Universal
- Variations are in Means, Not in Standard Deviations
- Major Cultural Differences Are Related to Differences in Trait Means

Derek Freeman (1999) is known for having exposed Margaret Mead for bending over backwards to prove her mentor's thesis that culture was the sole determinant of personality, and that genetics was not a factor worth serious consideration. In the quote above, Freeman summarizes his proof that the human genome contains clear markers for personality traits, such that all humans share the same dimensions of personality. However, he points out, as we have been saying repeatedly in this book, culture or the environment (peers, school, the family, the community) can shape these traits so that they may become expressed somewhat differently from culture to culture. Aggression is universal, but it is expressed differently in New York City and Tokyo. The typical American and Japanese could have identical genetic structure, yet differ on how they express equal amounts of genetically based aggression, based on how their respective cultures have trained them to express it. While the typical American can talk back to their boss or parent, the typical Japanese, while having the same aggressive feelings, would need to find a different way to express them. It becomes "You don't know what you're talking about, Dad!" versus "Honorable father may wish to rethink his honorably stated position."

Traits After School

N	E	O	A	C
Need for Stability	**Extraversion**	**Originality**	**Accommodation**	**Consolidation**
N+ Reactive	E+ Extraverted	O+ Explorer	A+ Adapter	C+ Focused
N= Responsive	E= Ambiverted	O= Moderate	A= Negotiator	C= Balanced
N- Resilient	E- Introverted	O- Preserver	A- Challenger	C- Flexible
N1: Worry	**E1: Approach Level**	**O1: Imagination**	**A1: Service**	**C1:Thoroughness**
N2: Temper	**E2: Group Orientation**	**O2: Range of Interests**	**A2: Compliance**	**C2: Structure**
N3: Outlook	**E3: Pace**	**O3: Innovation**	**A3: Humility**	**C3: Ambition**
N4: Coping Level	**E4: Leadership**	**O4: Zoom Scale**	**A4: Speak Out Level**	**C4: Concentration**
	E5: Trust			**C5: Methodicalness**
	E6: Tact			

The Big Five Trait Structure is Universal

McCrae and Allik (2002) have amply demonstrated that the Big Five trait structure is a human universal. In over 60 language and cultural groups, they have shown that the five dimensions of N, E, O, A, and C appear strongly worldwide, in collectivist as well as individualist cultures (e.g., China and the U.S.), and in all language groups, whether alphabetic or pictographic. What is of particular interest to the reader of this book is how traits might vary around the world among teenagers.

In a partial answer to that question, Allik, Laidra, Realo, and Pullmann (2004) administered a five-factor assessment (in Estonian) to 2,650 Estonian adolescents (1,420 girls, 1,230 boys) ages 12 to 18. This was compared to an adult sample of 793 men and 1,112 women with an average age of 37.5 (and a range of 19-60).

In the 2004 Allik (et al) study, IQ (measured according to the traditional "G" model) increased more than one complete standard deviation, while the traits seemed "to be practically frozen." (p. 454) This relationship was true for both boys and girls. In another finding by Allik and his associates, they report that, around the world, people tend to be more extraverted between ages 14 to 17 than at any other time of their lives (p. 455). On the other hand, O (originality) scores are highest for all individuals around the world in their 20s, with some cultures peaking earlier/later than others (p. 455). Finally, the fluctuations in individual test scores tends to settle down by age 16, with one exception: During the first year of college, N (need for stability) scores tend to increase, evidence of the increased stress associated with (typically) leaving home and engaging in increased academic and career competition.

In our development of the norm group for the SchoolPlace Big Five Profile at our Center for Applied Cognitive Studies in Charlotte, NC, we found that, while different age groups from 12 to 22 might have different means from year to year, and that individuals might show some significant variation from year to year, the overall trend is neither up nor down. Some theories attribute the ups and downs of individual scores to the natural "storm and stress" of the teen years, but with no clear rise or fall over time, rather just hovering around a kind of set point. Quick tempered this year (maybe a provocative teacher or peer group), calmer next (maybe a new, satisfying relationship), then quick tempered the following year (maybe some hormone issues, plus family troubles), and so forth, varying around a set point. However, we found that adolescents as a group are rather stable traitwise until they begin to start a family and career in their 20s, at which time N, E, and O tend to decrease slightly (they become somewhat calmer, less prone to party, and more practical), and A and C tend to increase slightly (i.e., they become somewhat more cooperative and focused).

There is a tendency globally for teenage girls to increase in N (need for stability), while boys tend to remain stable. Much of this increase comes in the subtrait N3, which is associated with depression, inasmuch as it deals with a pessimistic explanatory style. Girls' increase in N tends to reach a maximum around age 15, and then to moderate. Overall, however, changes are minimal throughout adolescence globally. Allik, Laidra, Realo, and Pullmann (2004) concluded (p. 446) from their study: "Age trends in personality traits during adolescence are generally rather small."

Variations are in Means, Not in Standard Deviations

Table 21.1 presents the standard scores (mean is 50, standard deviation is 10) on the Big Five supertraits for 26 countries. In this table, we use the U.S. as the principle point of comparison, with the U.S. assigned a 50 on all five supertraits. We can then easily see how other cultures score relative to the U.S. Notice that most of these countries score lower than the U.S. on E (extraversion), with some (e.g., Hong Kong) scoring a whole standard deviation or more lower than we do. This helps to explain the image of the "ugly American," the reputation Americans have for being "in your face," or boisterous, loud, and insensitive in many parts of the world. It is not so much that we are necessarily uneducated rubes who don't know any better—it is more that we are accustomed to experiencing a higher level of sensory bombardment on a daily basis. It is possible that our original colonists brought with them the genetic and cultural propensity for higher extraversion. Known to be outspoken in religion, exploratory in spirit, and often criminally driven to escape punishment abroad, our ancestors easily represent a more extraverted element of their former populations.

So, what does a young person do with this information? First, as a general rule, know that others tend to perceive us Americans as loud and insensitive. When interacting with exchange students and others from different cultures, practice restraint in speech and keep the volume down generally. Of course, there are many differences among individuals in the U.S. and abroad. Hence, it is possible for a quieter American to encounter a noisier outsider, but that is uncommon. Second, when a young person has the opportunity to travel or live abroad, either as a tourist, an exchange student, or as part of their family's move to another country, for whatever reason, it would behoove that person to study the chart below and see where opportunities for cross-cultural misunderstanding might lie. For example, let us say that a young person—we'll name "Sandy—with a profile of N=60, E=60, O=45, A=40, and C=60 is going to spend a year in France as a student (our older daughter did that for her senior year of high school). By referring to the table, you can see that Sandy's 60 on N compares favorably with the French norm. Sandy is 10 points higher than the typical American, while the French are 5 points higher than the typical American. This suggests that Sandy's reactivity should find sympathetic reception among most of the new relationships made in France. On the other hand, Sandy is a 45 on O, 5 points lower than the typical American, while the French as a group are about 4 points higher than the typical American. This makes Sandy about one standard deviation *lower* than the typical French young person. This suggests that Sandy may be in situations that call for greater comfort with change, exploring what is new and different, dealing with complex issues, and valuing creativity more than is normally comfortable. Sandy will need to take care to be uncharacteristically accepting in these situations. The normal impulse might be to insist, "We don't do it that way," or to say, "Our way is better." Perhaps a more sensitive response would be "I am used to doing it in a different way; be patient with me as I try this new approach." This could be true of everything from academic/school procedures to how one behaves at mealtime. Showing a willingness to try new ways typically earns respect in other cultures, while insistence on having it the accustomed way from your home country or region often breeds overt or covert negative judgment from others.

Table 21.1 Big Five Trait Scores across 26 Countries
(based on NEO PI-R scores with diverse college and adult samples; adapted from McCrae, 2001)

Country:	N:	E:	O:	A:	C:
Americans	50	50	50	50	50
Belgians	53	47.7	51.8	50	46.6
Croatians	52.8	45.1	49	47.5	53.2
Dutch	48.6	43.9	55.7	54.6	48.6
Estonians	49.7	49.9	52.6	50.8	49.6
Filipinos	50.8	43.8	51.8	52.9	51.5
French	55.4	47.3	54.1	52.1	47.4
Germans	52.8	47.3	56.7	49.1	46.7
Hispanic Americans	49.5	47.5	51.2	47.1	51.6
Hong Kong Chinese	53.3	37.6	49.2	54.6	49.2
Indians (Marathi)	49.1	40.7	51.4	56.7	55.7
Indonesians	48.6	43.3	49.9	51.9	50.3
Italians	55.6	46.6	52.6	48.9	50.4
Japanese	55.3	41.7	51.7	47.7	42.6
Malaysians	54.2	42.5	46.6	58.5	54.2
Norwegians	47.4	53.6	51.5	49.9	45.7
Peruvians	50.8	45.5	50	48.6	49
Portuguese	55.5	46.3	49.2	51.2	50.3
Russians	53.6	45.2	49.1	46.7	46.5
South African Blacks	49.1	41.4	47.7	50.4	47.9
South African Whites	51.9	47.2	54.4	52.2	47.9
South Koreans	53.6	40	51.4	52.3	48.8
Spaniards	57.1	48.3	48	49.4	48.3
Taiwan Chinese	51.5	42	50.2	54.5	48.1
Yugoslavians	51.1	47.6	56	48.4	51.7
Zimbabweans	50.9	42.3	47	51	51.8

If you have a friend from another country/culture, or plan to spend significant time around another country/culture, try comparing your scores to their country's norms, or to a country that you think is similar. Incidentally, we are collecting country norms continually, so if you do not see a country of interest to you here, email us (info@centacs.com) at the Center for Applied Cognitive Studies to see if we might have norms for the country of interest to you. Interestingly, for our neighbor to the south, Mexico, we have collected excellent norms from our partner in Mexico City. Guess what? They are significantly more extraverted as a country than the U.S., about one whole standard deviation higher. When we travel there, we have to be prepared to grin and bear it with respect to the high volume in many of the eateries. In one cantina we visited recently, there were 20 televisions blaring, three different bands playing, and about three different chug-a-lug contests going on. In order to carry on a conversation, we had to pass around a PDA with our written comments!

In the next chapter we will discuss leadership. However, there is some interesting research on leadership across cultures that we want to mention here. Dr. Colin Silverthorne (2001) from the University of San Francisco psychology department studied leadership effectiveness in three countries: the United States, Taiwan, and Thailand. As you will see in the next chapter, effective leaders tend to score somewhat higher on E, O, and C, and somewhat lower on N and A, with respect to the population averages. In other words, effective leaders, compared to their country's norm, tend to be calmer, more outgoing, more visionary t, more tough-minded, and more disciplined and ambitious. Or, simplified, they are N-E+O+A-C+. In Silverthorne's study, he went to senior executives in about 30 diverse public and private businesses in the three countries and asked them to identify the names of mid-level managers whom they regarded as particularly effective or ineffective. In Table 21.2, you will see the standard scores for each of the six groups (i.e., the three countries, with an effective and an ineffective group within each).

Table 21.2 **Leadership Across Three Cultures** (adapted from Silverthorne, 2001)

	N	E	O	A	C
US Effective	**47**	**53**	**55**	**43**	**56**
US Ineffective	*66*	*42*	*41*	*34*	*38*
Taiwan Effective	**47**	**54**	**50**	**46**	**58**
Taiwan Ineffective	*70*	*43*	*48*	*34*	*40*
Thailand Effective	**53**	**53**	**47**	**46**	**44**
Thailand Ineffective	*63*	*38*	*48*	*38*	*40*

For us, there are five very interesting patterns here:

1. N, E, and A behave exactly as we would expect, and in all three countries: Effective leaders are higher than the norm (i.e., higher than 50) in E, and lower than the norm in N and A. Thailand shows a small exception on N, where effective leaders are slightly above 50 on N, but the ineffective leaders, true to the global pattern, are much higher on N than the effective leaders.

Traits After School

2. Since N scores are different in Thailand, where the effective leaders score slightly higher than the U.S. norm, we suspect that the country mean for Thailand needs to be set higher on this dimension. As you will note from Table 21.1, Malaysia scores about one half of a standard deviation higher than the U.S. on N, and it is likely that Thailand would show a similar pattern.

3. In the case of N and E, ineffective leaders in all three countries score in the opposite direction: higher than the norm on N and lower than the norm on E. However, note the exception for A: Ineffective leaders in all three countries don't score in the opposite direction, but rather they score to a more extreme degree in the same direction as the effective leaders. In other words, effective leaders are tough-minded, while ineffective leaders are *too* tough-minded.

4. The U.S. is the only country in which effective leaders score significantly different from ineffective leaders on O, with the more effective leaders scoring higher than the norm and ineffective leaders scoring lower than the norm. This suggests one of two possible scenarios for Taiwan and Thailand: Either the sample is too small, hence biased, but a larger sample would show the same U.S. trend, or businesses in these two countries might want to consider the advisability of identifying higher O candidates for leadership positions.

5. While C behaves for U.S. and Taiwan as we expect, with effective leaders scoring higher than the norm and ineffective leaders lower than the norm, that is not true for Thailand, where effective and ineffective leaders score only four points apart. Again, we suspect that this can be attributed to a small and/or unrepresentative sample.

Now, one final comment about differences in means between countries. Even though two countries might have different averages on a trait, such as the 12 point difference on E between Hong Kong (HK) Chinese and U.S. citizens, that does not mean that, within the boundaries of either country, there is any less or more variation in that trait in comparison to other countries. While the HK Chinese, as a group, are less extraverted, less noisy, than Americans, within the HK Chinese community there are individuals who are seen as very noisy in comparison to other HK Chinese. These noisy HK Chinese would not seem so noisy in the U.S. In other words, the genetic makeup that influences extraversion is the same in Hong Kong and New York, but New Yorkers don't try to dampen their natural temperaments as much as do the HK Chinese. And, among the HK Chinese, who've learned as a culture to suppress their natural extraversion, some suppress it a lot more than others! The result is equal amounts of variation across all cultures, but with different averages or set points. It would be like two geographical areas with different average year-round temperatures, say, 80° and 70° F, yet with both areas having the same range of daily variation in temperature from high to low of 80 degrees (e.g., 30° to 110°, and 20° to 100°, respectively). Different means with a similar amount of variation are the norm.

Major Cultural Differences Are Related to Differences in Trait Means

Dutch anthropologist Geert Hofstede (2001) has made a major contribution to cross-cultural understanding by identifying dimensions that differentiate cultures. Each of the dimensions is related

Table 21.3 Hofstede Dimension Scores for 26 Countries

(Countries are ranked from highest score to lowest; the American/U.S. scores are bolded/italicized solely as a point of reference. Adapted from McCrae, 2001.)

Country:	Power Distance:	Country:	Uncertainty Avoidance:	Country:	Individualism:
Malaysians	21.8	Norwegians	25.3	Norwegians	28.5
Indians (Marathi)	21.1	Belgians	24.9	Germans	27.1
Hong Kong Chinese	18.4	Russians	24.4	Belgians	24.8
Zimbabweans	17.4	Peruvians	22.5	Yugoslavians	24.6
Filipinos	15.6	South African Whites	22.1	French	24.5
South Koreans	15.4	Germans	21.9	South African Whites	24.4
Taiwan Chinese	15.4	Estonians	21.9	***Americans***	***24.0***
Indonesians	15.3	Japanese	21.7	Estonians	23.9
Croatians	15.0	South African Blacks	21.6	Italians	23.7
South African Blacks	14.8	Spaniards	21	Russians	22.6
Portuguese	14.0	Italians	20.9	Hispanic Americans	22.6
Dutch	13.0	***Americans***	20.9	Dutch	22.6
Peruvians	12.3	French	20.9	Japanese	21.4
Hispanic Americans	12.1	Hispanic Americans	20.8	Portuguese	21.3
Italians	11.9	Croatians	20.1	Filipinos	21.0
Spaniards	11.6	Filipinos	19.5	Spaniards	20.5
Americans	***11.5***	Yugoslavians	19.5	Peruvians	20.2
Yugoslavians	10.9	Taiwan Chinese	19.3	South Koreans	19.9
Estonians	10.7	Indonesians	19.1	Taiwan Chinese	19.2
South African Whites	10.7	Zimbabweans	18.2	Croatians	19.2
Russians	10.4	Portuguese	17.2	South African Blacks	19.1
French	10.4	South Koreans	16.6	Indonesians	18.4
Belgians	9.7	Dutch	16	Zimbabweans	17.5
Japanese	8.9	Hong Kong Chinese	13.8	Indians (Marathi)	17.1
Germans	7.9	Malaysians	13.4	Malaysians	16.2
Norwegians	6.7	Indians (Marathi)	12.6	Hong Kong Chinese	13.8

to Big Five traits. The three dimensions that we will present here are as follows:

- *Power Distance*. This has to do with the degree to which inhabitants of a culture tend to defer to those senior in a hierarchy, and to accept differences in status. To exhibit power distance is to "know one's place," and is associated with these traits: E-O-A+C+ (and lower power distance cultures are associated with the opposite of this trait profile).
- *Uncertainty Avoidance*. Cultures high in uncertainty avoidance like things to be clear, black or white, cut and dry, right or wrong, and tend to have lots of laws, procedures, standards, and traditions. It is asso-

ciated with N++E+A--C- (and lower uncertainty avoidance cultures are associated with the opposite of this trait profile).

- *Individualism/Collectivism*. Cultures high in individualism celebrate self-determination and making one's own way without necessarily taking into consideration one's family or reference group, while collectivist cultures place a premium on one's family or reference group as the primary decision making and approval granting authority. High individualism is associated with E+O+A-C- (and collectivist cultures are associated with the opposite of this trait profile).

In the same study (McCrae, 2001) that listed the trait means for 26 countries in Table 21.1, the researchers also computed the scores on these three Hofstede dimensions for the same 26 countries. They are listed in Table 21.3. This table may be used similarly to Table 21.2, in that one would find it useful to compare the Hofstede scores for one's own country to the country of an exchange student friend, or to a country that one might be visiting as an exchange student, tourist, new resident, etc.

Knowing the scores for one's own country in comparison to that of another country can give a clue how to interpret a variety of behaviors, reactions, policies, and so forth. Americans as a group tend to be lower on Power Distance, moderate on Uncertainty Avoidance, and higher on Individualism. Said another way, Americans tend to de-emphasize status differences and to make decisions without particular regard for what one's reference group thinks. We tend to go it alone and see unlimited opportunity. So an American traveling in India (high Power Distance—think of the caste system there) should be mindful of titles, degrees, and the like: "Yes, Doctor (or President, or whatever) Ramachandran, I understand the important point you are making. Could we also consider…." In such a culture, one also would be expected to pay attention to one's own trappings of status. For example, in the U.S. I (Pierce) don't typically refer to myself as Dr. Howard, but in a high Power Distance country it would be expected. On the other hand, in France (low Power Distance), we should be relatively comfortable treating status differences pretty much the same way we do at home. We would ignore them. With respect to Individualism, Americans (high Individualism) should again be on my guard in India (low Individualism) and take care to be mindful of the needs and wishes of our hosts and associates there. Yet while in France (high Individualism), we could once again relax and do our own thing. During travels in India (very low Uncertainty Avoidance), we (moderate Uncertainty Avoidance) should just suck it up when experiencing the utter lack of rules and structure, with multilane highways characterized by no sense of what a lane is, and with a virtual circus of animals meandering along and on the roads. Just view such lack of structure as interesting or amusing, but not get indignant about it.

In the next section of this book, we will look at how the Big Five influences three of our major life decisions: how we do or do not exert leadership qualities, how we manage our relationships (including marriage), and how we choose and manage our careers.

A Case Study in Cross-Cultural Differences: Erin and Sofia
Contributed by Emily Crowder, UNC-Chapel Hill student and CentACS Research Intern

Erin: N- E= O- A+ C+ Sofia: N= E- O= A+ C+

In Erin's sophomore year of high school, her mom decided to host a Chinese exchange student, Sofia, for two weeks. Erin was hesitant at first because her school was having a dance the first weekend of Sofia's stay, and she didn't want to back out on her date. However, her mother convinced Erin that she could take Sofia along to the dance, and they would both have a good time. When Sofia arrived, she got along well with the family. After a week of visiting local sights and going to classes, it was time for the weekend dance. When they arrived, Erin immediately joined her friends on the dance floor and hoped that the group of exchange students would do the same. But to her disappointment, she noticed that none of the Chinese exchange students were joining in. They were all huddled together near the doors, looking a bit uncomfortable. Erin didn't want them to feel excluded, so she went over to Sofia and asked her to come dance. Looking embarrassed, Sofia quickly shook her head and said, "In my school, we are not even allowed to hold hands with guys." Erin instantly understood. The exchange students were way out of their comfort zone. The American acceptance of teenagers dancing so close together was drastically different from the strict rules on guy/girl social interactions in Sofia's home city in China. Erin knew that regardless of how much she insisted Sofia dance, it wouldn't happen. There was too much of a cultural difference.

The situation of these two students, one American and one Chinese, is a perfect example of how different cultural practices may result in different trait levels across countries. In relation to the average extraversion level in the United States, the Chinese students are much lower on the extraversion spectrum and are shocked by the Americans' passionate dancing. But in relation to the Chinese population, where it's unacceptable for youth to interact so closely, some of these students might be more extraverted and could be viewed as ambiverts or extraverts. Various cultural differences affect norms on all supertraits. However, knowing these differences is essential to accepting and understanding others from different backgrounds. For example, an American traveler, aware that China is typically lower in extraversion, could be more respectful and try to speak more quietly when visiting. On the other hand, a Chinese onlooker might understand that a loud American isn't being rude; it's just normal to be more vocal in the United States. Understanding cultural differences, like those Sofia and Erin encountered, can help make everyone more comfortable or accepting when interacting with people from different cultures.

Traits After School

Part Five

The Big Five and Major Life Choices

22
Big Five and Leadership

To Lead, to Follow, or to be Independent

> Leadership occurs when someone takes responsibility for effecting a necessary action.
>
> --Pierce and Jane Howard

Guide to This Chapter:

- What is Leadership?
- Leaders and Followers: The Options for Behavior in Groups
- Three Case Studies in Leadership: Optimal, Suboptimal, and Antagonistic Fits
- Summary of Adaptive Strategies for Leaders

Some time ago, we had the opportunity to give advice to the author of a book on leadership. An editor had read his manuscript and praised it for the splendid variety of stories, anecdotes, and illustrations that emerged from the author's personal knowledge of some 50 well-known leaders. However, the editor was concerned that the episodes lacked an underlying theory of leadership that connected all of the leadership examples in a way that made clear what leaders have in common. We read and reread the manuscript. The theory we came up with was succinct, yet, in our humble opinion, powerful. We defined leadership with the statement that heads this chapter and went on to identify three behaviors that had to happen for leadership to occur: Leaders *scan* their environment to find things that are in need of change, they then *evaluate* the results of their scan, and then they *act* on the results of their evaluation. Scan, evaluate, act. We called it the SEA model. It is a change-based model of leadership.

What is Leadership?

We like our model of leadership! However, let's take a moment to put it into a larger perspective. In the previous chapter, we introduced a study by Chuck Silverthorne that showed the common structure of effective leadership in three different countries. That study is reflective of many studies that we have done at the Center for Applied Cognitive Studies, as well as studies done elsewhere. All of these studies find that effective leaders tend to be calm, outgoing, visionary, appropriately tough, and focused on achievement. Leaders are calm (N-) in order to breed confidence among followers during a

The Big Five and Major Life Choices

N	E	O	A	C
Need for Stability	**Extraversion**	**Originality**	**Accommodation**	**Consolidation**
N+ Reactive	E+ Extraverted	O+ Explorer	A+ Adapter	C+ Focused
N= Responsive	E= Ambiverted	O= Moderate	A= Negotiator	C= Balanced
N- Resilient	E- Introverted	O- Preserver	A- Challenger	C- Flexible
N1: Worry	**E1: Approach Level**	**O1: Imagination**	**A1: Service**	**C1:Thoroughness**
N2: Temper	**E2: Group Orientation**	**O2: Range of Interests**	**A2: Compliance**	**C2: Structure**
N3: Outlook	**E3: Pace**	**O3: Innovation**	**A3: Humility**	**C3: Ambition**
N4: Coping Level	**E4: Leadership**	**O4: Zoom Scale**	**A4: Speak Out Level**	**C4: Concentration**
	E5: Trust			**C5: Methodicalness**
	E6: Tact			

crisis. Leaders are outgoing (E+) in order to know what is going on by staying in the thick of the action, as opposed to staying in the quiet of one's office or other private space. Leaders are visionary (O+) in order to see what is not there, to see what things could be but not yet are, to dream dreams of a better life or world. Leaders are appropriately tough (A-, possibly A=) in order to have the courage to give constructive criticism and to stay the course as needed, rather than to yield in deference to dissenting voices, but leaders are not so tough as to resist the give and take of negotiation, the interplay of dialog, and the need to listen to the opinions and ideas of their people. Leaders are focused on achievement (C+) in order for the group to meet its obligations and achieve its dreams, without being distracted by seductive lesser opportunities.

This is not new. This formula, N-E+O+A-C+, can be seen in descriptions of great leaders in literature. Alfred, Lord Tennyson summarized the character of Ulysses in the closing lines of the eponymous poem in this way:

> ...and tho'
> We are not now that strength which in old days
> Moved earth and heaven, that which we are, we are,--
> One equal temper of heroic hearts,
> Made weak by time and fate, but strong in will
> To strive, to seek, to find, and not to yield.

If you read carefully, you will see the formula for leadership imbedded in the key words of the last three lines:

> One equal temper (N-) of heroic hearts (E+),
> Made weak by time and fate, but strong in will (C+)
> To strive (A-), to seek (O+), to find (C+), and not to yield (A-).

Many other passages from the world's great literature support this model of leadership. Remember our reference to Sophocles' *Antigone,* where son Haemon warns his father, King Creon, that he is being too low in A; that he will break because he is being a tree that will not bend in the storm. This is a subtle point—we don't interpret "bend in the storm" as an admonition to submit to one's detractors. Rather, we interpret it as being willing to listen, to consider, to negotiate, yet still to hold out for the "win-win." The opposite, in other words, of "my way or the highway."

More recently, Jeffrey Rosen (2006) describe the difference between the most effective chief justices of the U.S. Supreme Court, in contrast to those chief justices who have gone down in history as unsatisfactory:

> The most successful chief justices, in other words, have shared a particular style of judicial temperament. They have been modest, likable, efficient, deft at finding common ground, and at least as smart as their colleagues without being overtly brilliant or intensely academic. Some of the most effective chiefs have been former politicians or politically minded executive officials who had a knack for bringing together colleagues of different minds. By contrast, the less successful chiefs have been insecure, heavy-handed, and more concerned with being recognized as the symbolic head of the Court than providing leadership behind the scenes (pp. 12-13).

By examining the language that Rosen uses to contrast successful with unsuccessful chief justices, we can see the Big Five pattern emerging. The successful justices were modest (A= or +), likable (N-E+A=), efficient, (C+), deft at finding common ground (clearly A=), and had a knack for bringing together people of different minds (O+). Put all this together, and you get N-E+O+A=C+, dead-on with our definition. The unsuccessful chief justices, on the other hand, were insecure (N+), heavy handed (A--), low in Tact (E6-), and attention seeking (A--, especially low in A3/Humility).

This leads to a need for clarification: Our definition of leadership could be for anyone: tinker, tailor, soldier, or spy. Teacher, manager, football tackle, street cop, hospital nurse, CEO, or secretary. When we say someone is a leader, we typically mean that they take responsibility for getting things done. Non-leaders are those who essentially sit back and wait for leaders to get going and tell them what to do. At the simplest level, when the temperature is too warm, the non-leader will sweat and suffer until someone with leadership characteristics takes responsibility for cooling things down. However, this act of leadership does not have to come from the "titular" leader (chair, director, coach, manager, supervisor, president, superintendent, team leader). This is the point we need to clarify. Leadership is a behavior, not a job. Anyone can engage in leadership behaviors. Many titular leaders, in fact, engage in very few leadership behaviors. Surely each of us has encountered titular leaders (boss, etc.) who fail to take responsibility for effecting necessary changes. Instead, they see their role as basically following a script that has been established over time. This leads us to define these roles:

- Manager: one who directs the work of others; may tend towards one of two extremes:
    - *Strategic Manager:* one who envisions new possibilities and forms the necessary strategy for achieving those possibilities. We also call this a "Leader Manager."
    - *Tactical Manager:* one who accepts the strategy/vision of others and implements the strategy, policies, and procedures required to achieve the vision. We also call this a "Maintenance Manager."
- Leader: one who shows initiative in taking the responsibility for identifying, advocating, and achieving necessary changes to the status quo; may be a manager or may be an independent contributor who works alone or as a member of a team.

The Big Five and Major Life Choices

When you go into a new situation, if you want to know who the "leader" is, you can ask who the boss is, or who the person in charge is. However, that doesn't mean that the boss or the in-charge person is actually a "leader." They may, in fact, be anything *but* a leader. We hasten to add that leadership behavior is contextual, in that a person may lead in one aspect of their lives and not in others. A football player may lead teammates to show more emotion in a game, while shying away from creating new strategies to thwart a pesky foe. A president may lead in going to war, but not in greening the planet. A student may lead in de-escalating conflict among peers, but not in blowing the whistle on a teacher's unethical behavior. As leadership behavior varies according to context, the causes of the variation could be manifold: different traits at work, different values, past history, differences in skills, and so forth.

Bertolt Brecht got at the heart of this matter in his play, *The Life of Galileo.* In that story, Galileo yields to the pressure of the pope, who has insisted that the scientist recant his "heretical" view that the earth is not the center of the universe. Andrea, the son of Galileo's housekeeper, laments the scientist's reluctance to be a "leader" by quipping, "Unhappy the land that has no heroes." Galileo's response, "No. Unhappy the land where heroes are needed" (Scene 13, Willett translation). Said another way, so long as things are going well—the family is getting along fine, grades are acceptable, the teachers are being humane and even engaging, the football team has a respectable record, the chorus is singing like cherubs—there is no need for leadership. All we need are maintenance managers. It is when things go awry that the need for leadership emerges, and things can go awry in many little ways (like the room being too warm) or in some big ways (like climate change). The 43rd U.S. President, George W. Bush, chose not to be a leader with respect to climate change, but rather to continue the status quo—maintenance manager. Former Vice-President Al Gore chose to be a leader with respect to climate change and ended up winning the Nobel Prize. Unhappy the land that needs a hero. Unhappy the land that needs a leader. The evidence is that pure maintenance of planet Earth will result in, not the status quo, but, rapidly deteriorating quality of life ending in extermination. That is a pity. Too bad. We can't just do business as usual. Someone, please, do something! We need leadership, whether from titular leaders (e.g., presidents) or from individual leaders who take responsibility and do something needed (e.g., the homeowner who installs solar panels and goes off the electrical power grid).

Leaders and Followers: The Options for Behavior in Groups

Now we know what a leader is. Or, at least, we know what leadership is. You don't need leadership when things are trucking along fine. Everyone is doing their job; systems are all go. Who needs a leader?

Well, sometimes you need a *leader* (i.e., someone who has a hefty appetite for scanning, evaluating, and acting). Other times all you need is some *leadership* (i.e., someone who'll take responsibility *now*, but not necessarily for very long—just long enough to get us through this problem). Persons with profile of N-E+O+A-/=C+ tend to have the natural energy to be a *leader* in the first sense, while *anyone can be leader for a moment!* The difference between momentary leaders and permanent leaders is the degree to which their trait structure (and, or course, their experience) is naturally suited to handling the demands of leadership. One of the critical tasks of youth is to understand how one is suited for leadership responsibility. Because society places such high status and rewards (i.e., high salary) on those with leadership titles (editor, coach, president, manager, and the like), young people often commit themselves to the goal of attaining one of those titles for the wrong reasons. They want to be president (or boss, coach, director) for the prestige, the money, to make Mom and Dad proud, to wow the opposite sex, whatever. Most institutions are set up, in fact, to encourage such misguided goal setting. How do you get a raise in most organizations? By being promoted to a management position, by becoming the boss, the leader. Over and over again, organizations promote good technicians (computer programmers, bookkeepers, architects, and so forth) into management positions solely because the person is a good technician, and the good technician accepts the promotion because of the increased pay and prestige. Sadly, they often fail, because they lack the natural trait energy to carry out the demands of leadership day-in and day-out. They are worrying, solitary, comfortable with the status quo, submissive, and multitasking, when they needed to be calm in a crisis, in the thick of the action, visionary, appropriately tough, and focused on a priority goal. N+E-O-A+C- versus N-E+O+A-/=C+. Fortunately, some organizations now have "dual career tracks," such that technicians can remain as technicians and still get promoted (senior technician, senior consulting technician, special projects technician, and so on) and make more money without having to take on management duties.

High school and college are the times to understand one's trait infrastructure and the kind of group role that it supports. Someone with the ideal leader profile—N-E+O+A-=C+—can pretty much count on targeting any titular leadership role compatible with their technical interests. They do not need to worry about not having the energy to be successful as a titular leader. However, there are not very many of these people—roughly one person out of every 121 has this ideal profile (i.e., 1 in 3 is N-, 1 in 3 is E+, 1 in 3 is O+, 2 in 3 are A- or A=, and 1 in 3 is C+, or, 1/3 x 1/3 x 1/3 x 2/3 x 1/3, which equals approximately 1/121). The rest of us will be deficient from the ideal in some way. Whether or not our deficiency is a significant handicap depends on the context of our desired leadership. If you want to be a leader of accountants (who are mostly E-), and you are E=, then that is a good fit, for ideally the leader is not that much more extreme in a given trait that the majority of the followers. But if you are E- with E- followers, you run the risk of losing touch, of not having sufficient information to make good decisions.

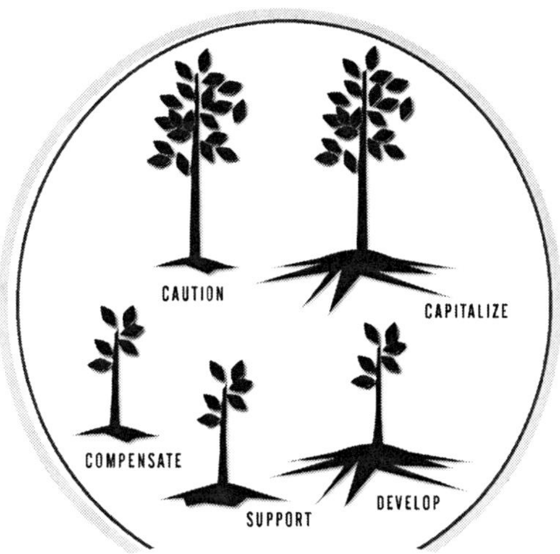

HUMAN RESOURCE OPTIMIZATION

The Big Five and Major Life Choices

However, that does not mean you should not be a leader. After all, there are few who are ideally suited for the leader role. However, in order to be successful, you will need to find ways to *compensate* for the lack of fit. Remember our HRO image? Where the roots are inadequate for the tree to flourish, you need to compensate. This could take the form, in this case, of 1) finding a teammate who is somewhat higher in E who would be willing to chair meetings and do other more extraverted tasks necessary to effective team functioning or 2) creating technology-driven, information-gathering devices so that you can maintain your solitude while keeping in touch with what is going on, of scanning the environment for things that need changing or improving.

I (Pierce) realized in my 20s that I was not temperamentally suited for titular leadership. However, I am a *leader* from time to time. I can chair a project for a finite period of time. I can take the initiative to fix something that needs attention. Just don't make me, or expect me, to do leadership stuff all day every day. I would not be a happy camper. I am an independent contributor like Mozart, like James Michener, like all of the creative or hard-working practitioners out there who just want to do their thing and not have to be responsible for other people. To have daily responsibility for other people would make me too nervous and even angry (my N is 56). I would resent having so many meetings, conferences, and phone calls (my E is 51). I would get bored and resent having to deal with details and quality control (my O is 67). I would avoid giving necessary constructive criticism (my A is 49). I would find it next to impossible to remain focused on the current priority (my C is 42). My O score (very high) is the only one suited for titular leadership of the visionary variety. But it is next to impossible to be an effective visionary leader without the discipline, drive, and "go-get-em-ness" to subordinate personal needs to those of the group on a daily basis.

On the other hand, I (Jane) have gravitated toward leadership and management roles throughout my career because I have more of a fit for the role than Pierce, although I am missing some elements. Like Pierce, I am very high in O (71) and lower in C (40), thus prone to be more of an innovator, creating new business strategy being more natural for me than paying attention to the bottom line. My lower C has helped me easily tolerate frequent interruptions from employees with questions, and my very low N (32) has provided me with rational calmness during tough times. My lower A (38) has enabled me to stick to my agenda during negotiations and make tough decisions that Pierce would have preferred to avoid. Both of us are ambiverts, lacking the natural energy to spend extended time in the meetings and individual conferences so necessary to run an organization, both preferring a balance of meeting and greeting with solitary time at our mutual desks working on our individual projects.

So, what is your profile? How does it compare to the ideal leader profile? And if you want to be a leader some day, does the context of your envisioned leadership match the demands of the ideal leader profile, or is it an exception? If your profile differs from what would be required to do an effective job as a leader, then you must make a decision whether you want to do a lifetime job of compensating, or whether instead you want to be a lifelong individual contributor. Incidentally, being the titular boss is not the only way to get prestige, money, and the attention of the opposite sex. You can also be a lawyer, a doctor, an inventor, musical performer, an athlete, an artisan, an artist, a writer, an architect, an engineer, a professor, a counselor, and so on. Two chapters from now, we will explore the world of careers and how to find the best match between your trait profile and your career choice.

Summary of Adaptive Strategies for Leaders

In closing this chapter on the Big Five and leadership, we present Table 22.1 that identifies the optimum supertrait score for leadership in most situations, plus the benefits, concerns, and remedies that are associated with being below the ideal, above the ideal, or right on target. This table is based on the following assumptions:

- Everyone can be a leader.
- There is an ideal level of each supertrait that provides the kind of behavioral energy required for leadership in most situations.
- Individuals who score close to the ideal will find most leadership roles energizing, assuming that they have the proper technical knowledge, mental abilities, and experience required for a specific leadership role.
- Individuals who score above or below the ideal can benefit from knowing that they have too much or too little of a trait for leadership to be natural for them; they can form adaptive strategies based on that knowledge.
- While the ideal levels that we have identified hold true for most leadership roles, there are a considerable number of leadership roles that require a different level than the usual ideal.
- When a specific leadership role's trait requirements differ from the ideal (e.g., a leader of people who are more introverted than the norm should ideally be around a 50 in extraversion, rather than the suggested score of 60), the benefits, concerns, and remedies should be modified to reflect the shift downward or upward.

Every individual has the option to be a leader, a follower, or an independent contributor. The closer one's personal trait profile is to the ideal, the easier it is to make the decision to accept leadership roles. The more one's profile departs from the ideal, the more important it becomes to consider whether one chooses to be a follower most of the time, or rather to be independent. These are the three social roles that everyone must balance, must find the optimal level for. One person might prefer them evenly divided, while others prefer mostly one to be characteristic of how they spend their days. Clearly, Henry David Thoreau preferred to spend most of his time as an independent contributor, while Martin Luther King, Jr., preferred to spend most of his time as a leader. The majority of the population has chosen to be followers, many of whom literally followed Dr. King on foot by marching behind him during his lifetime. To lead is to set goals for oneself and one's followers. To be an independent contributor is to set goals for oneself only. To be a follower is to set goals primarily in service to one's leader. And, of course, there are many people who elect to do all three. In the final chapter of this book we will deal specifically with the nature and practice of goal setting.

Table 22.1 Summary of Adaptive Issues and Strategies for Leaders

(Reprinted from Howard and Howard, 2010)

To the Left of the Optimum Score Range	*Optimum Leader Score Range (Note: Score ranges change.)*	*To the Right of the Optimum Score Range*
N: Need for Stability Note: The following are general statements and need to be examined along with the leader's subtrait scores on the WorkPlace 4.0.Profile.		
Score Range: 0-39	**Score Range: 40-45**	**Score Range: 46-100**
Benefits: Many. Very resilient, perceived as eternally calm and unflappable, extremely difficult to unnerve, rational in a crisis, your extreme calmness can inspire high confidence in others.	**Benefits:** Borderline resilient and responsive, calm, cool, and collected when needed, recovers quickly from crises, inspires confidence with subordinates that you are durable and will prevail, will show appropriate concern from time to time. Can typically think of what to do next in a crisis.	**Benefits:** Responsive and reactive, likely to become somewhat or very concerned about internal or external clients/customers; your responsiveness/reactivity will show subordinates that you are human and care.
Concerns: Occasionally could communicate coolness or indifference to others looking for leadership, can move on to other matters while team members may still need direct leadership help from you.	**Concerns:** None.	**Concerns:** Many. Wariness, your tendency to worry, and/or your temper could tend to eat away at the confidence of colleagues in your leadership ability. Occasional bursts of anger could damage relationships. Apologize soon afterward.
Options: Make it a point to communicate, by speaking or in writing, all positive and negative feedback to your followers so they will know where they stand. When a problem occurs, involve everyone in avoiding future problems by scheduling a time to revisit the matter, after N= and N+ people have calmed down. Allow people to express feelings.	**Options:** None needed.	**Options:** Learn the arts of meditation, isometrics, deep breathing; aerobic exercise helps manage the stress; deal aggressively with sources of stress at work and at home.
Notes: When someone tells you about an issue or problem, your first instinct is to correct it, coolly and rationally. Many times an N= or N+ person simply needs to vent or emote without your solution.	**Notes:** While this is a "typical" leader scoring range for N, it may not be the profile for a successful leader in all parts of the organization.	**Notes:** If you work in a customer service area, it could help to be a leader with a midrange or slightly higher score on N so that you can: a) work with or lead others who score higher on this scale and b) gravitate toward serving internal and/or external customers for your organization.

Table 22.1 (continued)

<table>
<tr><th>To the Left of the
Optimum Score Range</th><th>Optimum Leader Score Range
(Note: Score ranges change.)</th><th>To the Right of the
Optimum Score Range</th></tr>
<tr><td colspan="3">E: Extraversion
Note: The following are general statements and need to be examined along with the leader's subtrait scores on the WorkPlace 4.0 Profile.</td></tr>
<tr><td>Score Range: 0-54

Benefits: Introvert and ambivert, excels in a quieter, paperwork-intensive leadership position; more accepted in highly introverted cultures such as accounting, engineering, IT, and R&D; tends to listen very well.

Concerns: Many. Tendency to under-communicate, minimizes the number of meetings that might be needed, may not take charge easily. Could prefer written communication to spoken communication. Quietness may be mistaken for aloofness or smugness. May not tell others about thoughts unless asked.

Options: If uncomfortable, delegate meeting facilitation to another, more extraverted team member; increase use of verbal and written communication (even delegating it to an assistant who uses your name), especially for informal matters (recognition, constructive criticism, reminders).

Notes: In area of an organization where IT, engineering, accounting/ bookkeeping, and/or research/ development are going on, a middle to lower E leader may be more successful because the leader will probably be more like most of the other people in the department and relate better than a strong extravert.</td><td>Score Range: 55-60

Benefits: Borderline ambivert and extravert, friendly, approachable, outgoing, enthusiastic, natural communicator in face-to-face situations; comfortable taking charge of the work of others. This leader's extraversion does not preclude listening to others.

Concerns: None.

Options: None needed.

Notes: This is a "typical" E score for a leader, but it may not be the score that is needed in some specialized sections/departments/ areas of the organization.</td><td>Score Range: 61-100

Benefits: Many. Strong extravert; comfortable leading by wandering around; enjoys being in the thick of things; handles a heavy meeting schedule well; enjoys meeting and greeting; likely has an extensive network of contacts inside and outside the organization; good in a highly extraverted culture such as sales, entertainment, or politics.

Concerns: Few. Resists closing the door and churning out the necessary deskwork; can tire out teammates if they are more ambiverts or introverts by insisting on longer, face-to-face meetings; more comfortable with phone calls than with email. Avoid popping into offices of introverts to get a quick reaction to some written document. Give them time to think and prepare.

Options: Establish a "quiet hour" in which you are protected from interruptions, resist interrupting others during a meeting discussion, avoid holding side conversations or phone calls during a meeting when someone else is talking.

Notes: In a sales, political, entertainment ,or other type of highly extraverted culture, it can be helpful for the leader to have a high score on E in order to be more like the other people in the department.</td></tr>
</table>

Table 22.1 (continued)

To the Left of the Optimum Score Range	*Optimum Leader Score Range (Note: Score ranges change.)*	*To the Right of the Optimum Score Range*
O: Originality Note: The following are general statements and need to be examined along with the leader's subtrait scores on the WorkPlace 4.0 Profile.		
Score Range: 0-54	**Score Range:** 55-60	**Score Range:** 61-100
Benefits: Preserver and moderate; may be primarily concerned with the here-and-now, tactics, and implementation; likely focuses on the details (especially when scores are E- and C+); typically good as a project manager; typically better as a manager in a maintenance/ status quo situation where little change is needed or required. Moderates can alternate between thinking tactically like most preservers and strategically like most explorers and will be a little more open to change than preservers.	**Benefits:** Borderline moderate and explorer; appropriately imaginative; anticipates future needs; focuses on strategy; handles theory, complexity, and uncertainty well; embraces change when the situation calls for it.	**Benefits:** Many. Explorer; naturally creative and imaginative; comfortable focusing on theory, complex problems, and the future; sees opportunities for change and problem-solving as enjoyable and challenging.
Concerns: Tends to focus more on the here and now, rather than the big picture and future needs; may minimize the need for change. Might be surprised by seemingly sudden new technological developments or a competitor's new products/ services that were not anticipated.	**Concerns:** None	**Concerns:** May enjoy change for change's sake, even initiating it at times when it may not be necessary or helpful; likely to resist spending sufficient time on the details; if C-, will have difficulty being on time and within budget on projects; will probably become bored with routine, repetitive responsibilities that don't challenge the imagination; may generate lots of new ideas that are delegated to others to research or implement but later discarded in favor of a different approach.
Options: Invite an associate, vendor, consultant, or customer who is O+ to come in from time to time and challenge your assumptions about your short- and long-term thinking and planning.	**Options:** None needed.	**Options:** Have a colleague or team member who has permission to keep you in line with respect to being practical, meeting stated project objectives, and creating future plans.
Notes: In more established or conservative organizations where there is little technology change or few upgrades from year to year, an appropriate leader may function quite adequately with a midrange or slightly lower score.	**Notes:** The "typical" leader on O, while more strategic and oriented toward the future, may not be as effective in dealing with day-to-day administrative details and implementing policies and procedures. Make sure there is someone else on the management team who can handle these tasks.	**Notes:** In a highly technical industry where change occurs very rapidly, a leader needs to score well into the high range in order to grasp the possibilities and global implications of change while creating an innovative, cutting-edge plan for the future of the department or the organization.

Table 22.1 (continued)

To the Left of the Optimum Score Range	*Optimum Leader Score Range (Note: Score ranges change.)*	*To the Right of the Optimum Score Range*
A: Accommodation Note: The following are general statements and need to be examined along with the leader's subtrait scores on the WorkPlace 4.0 Profile.		
Score Range: 0-39	**Score Range:** 40-50	**Score Range:** 51-100
Benefits: Depends. Challenger; tough-minded, has to win, independent, thick-skinned (if also N-), enjoys center stage (especially if also N- and C+), enjoys a strong, lively debate. In tougher, more competitive situations, you as a leader will rarely back down from a challenge.	**Benefits:** High challenger and low negotiator. Typically effective at negotiating; goes for the win-win approach; sufficiently tough, but also able to understand others' needs and interests; can wheel and deal without either caving in to others or crushing them. Appropriately humble.	**Benefits:** Depends. Adapter; can excel in a friendly, trusting, nurturing environment that emphasizes teamwork, cooperation, building consensus, and openly sharing information.
Concerns: Can come across as arrogant, untrusting, and superior; can alienate team members and others; may even withhold key information from others. Playing to win may result in frequent conflicts that can damage internal or external relationships over time. You not only want to win, but you often want to crush the competition.	**Concerns:** None.	**Concerns:** Is subject to being duped, tricked, and outmaneuvered by associates, vendors, or customers who are more competitive and manipulative; doesn't like to fight and avoids conflict, especially with strong challengers who insist on debating every matter.
Options: Reconsider any decision made in the heat of the moment; do aerobic exercise before meetings in which you need to be softer; give a colleague permission to give you feedback when your ego has exceeded accepted norms, has come across too strongly, or offended others.	**Options:** None needed.	**Options:** Identify an associate or consultant who can assist you in negotiations or other situations in which you know that you must stand up to persons who play hardball, such as giving feedback to strong challengers.
Notes: Don't assume that all accept your ideas. You may be such a tough leader that people won't confront you. Try holding your opinion until the end of a discussion to allow colleagues to discuss options instead of caving in to you. Don't miss out on some valuable information by discounting those who won't stand up to you.	**Notes:** This score range spans 10 points rather than 5 points that the other four supertraits show for the Optimum Leader Score Range. That is due to a tendency in the early 2000s for some leaders to become kinder and emphasize servant leadership with associates. We could see the range revert to the earlier 40-45 span after the economy reemerges from recession.	**Notes:** Your tendency may be to reach consensus by discussion with others. Don't be surprised if strong challengers say they agree in a meeting (just to get out of it), then leave the meeting, and do a project exactly the way they want to rather than doing what was decided in the meeting by consensus, knowing that you probably won't object. If this happens frequently, you may wish to involve some A- colleagues in helping you confront the challenger.

Table 22.1 (continued)

To the Left of the Optimum Score Range	*Optimum Leader Score Range (Note: Score ranges change.)*	*To the Right of the Optimum Score Range*
C: Consolidation Note: The following are general statements and need to be examined along with the leader's subtrait scores on the WorkPlace 4.0 Profile.		
Score Range: 0-54	**Score Range:** 55-60	**Score Range:** 61-100
Benefits: Few. Flexible and balanced; spontaneous and enjoys wearing different hats, can serve well typically in a staff-type position which must respond to a variety of ever-changing needs and demands from line management or which requires much multitasking, can flex fairly easily when goals change or when the organization goes through reorganization.	Benefits: Borderline balanced and focused; tends to stay organized with minimal effort; disciplined, ambitious, naturally stays focused on immediate and long-term priorities and goals; appropriately cautious in decision making; has high standards for self and others; likely to have well-balanced work and personal lives.	**Benefits:** Many. Focused; very ambitious; highly disciplined and difficult, if not impossible, to distract from the task or goal at hand; strong preference for finishing one project before beginning another; a perfectionist who maintains very high standards; one who can always be trusted to deliver what is promised and stick to the plan.
Concerns: May lack discipline, organization, and ambition; can work hard and long but is often distracted from immediate or long term goals; may not begin a project in a timely fashion or may be pulled away from it by a sudden interruption, often makes decisions quickly without studying the hard data or facts.	**Concerns:** None.	**Concerns:** Often is a workaholic who can cause C- associates to resent having to match your long hours, untiring drive, and strong will to achieve; has difficulty flexing when in reorganization, goals change, or projects are put on hold.
Options: Can excel when a job is highly structured with minimal allowance for discretion and autonomy; otherwise, may need an associate to remind you of deadlines, to attend to details, to avoid distractions, or to stick to the budget, as these tasks do not come as easily to this type of leader.	**Options:** None Needed.	**Options:** Understand that your associates are not like you with your high comfort level for long hours and dedication to goals; occasionally, take yourself less seriously to show associates that you are aware of your excesses; make a point of being playful or spontaneous on occasions when it won't jeopardize your goal attainment and will make you appear more human to others.
Notes: You can succeed as a leader if the job demands constant multitasking, as long as you have help from your team in organizing, collecting/publishing meeting notes, polishing documents before they are sent, and reviewing data before a decision is made.	**Notes:** Most "typical" leaders score in this range, but there are circumstances in which scores below and above this range can succeed.	**Notes:** The lower your N score, the more you will understand that your coworkers are working hard even if they can't match you. The higher your N score, the more their coming in late, leaving early, or even working just their scheduled hours will bother you if you are putting in more time on a project than others.

Meanwhile, in the next chapter, we will explore the world of relationships and how traits influence one's satisfaction in a relationship, both of the romantic and nonromantic variety.

A Case Study in Leadership: Ben Encounters the World of Politics

Contributed by Emily Crowder, UNC-Chapel Hill student and CentACS Research Intern

Ben: N- E= O+ A- - C+

Ben was always a shining student. He made top grades, was involved in clubs and sports, and the teachers doted on him. So when he ran for class president for his junior year of high school, he won. No one was surprised. He was, after all, a natural leader for his fellow students. In class, he was always one to take charge. In math, he would show people their mistakes when they were writing answers to problems. He took charge of the lab experiments in biology and delegated jobs to lab partners. In English, he initiated the discussion about the assigned book. He said what he thought about the reading and argued his point strongly. When others disagreed or gave additional ideas, he asked questions of them and responded with his opinion about what they said. Overall, he was quite effective in getting the rest of the class involved. Even outside of the classroom, these behaviors carried over. He would jump into a conversation and question people's statements, then express his own strong opinion.

Towards the end of the year, it was time for class elections. Again, he ran for class president. However, this time, he lost. He was upset and confused. He couldn't understand why he lost. He was always the one to take charge and lead a group. But even with his natural leadership abilities, people found some faults. They were tired of him always correcting their errors and annoyed that he always questioned what they said. Some people complained that he always had opinions about everything and that he was too competitive.

Given Ben's traits listed above, he was very close to the ideal profile of a leader. With his low need for stability, he didn't worry much or get mad often, which helped keep his classmates calm. He was patient and steady. In classes, his midrange extraversion level prompted him to speak up and take charge, while his high originality led to his curiosity, questioning the status quo, and an ongoing desire for further discussion. He wanted to hear more ideas and opinions and wasn't satisfied with simple answers. His low accommodation level also contributed to his questioning, but from a more competitive stance. He wanted to question people in order to strengthen his ideas, and he was not afraid to argue, to speak up, or debate with others. When someone's answer or argument was flawed, he readily addressed the problem. Ben's high consolidation score drove him to be number one and led him to set the goal of being class president. After he achieved the position once, he was even more interested in retaining that achievement a second time. However, these same traits that initially helped Ben also caused him some trouble.

At first, his peers didn't mind his behavior, but as time went on, they grew tired of it. His high originality (O+), which contributed to his exploration of new ideas, eventually annoyed others. Sometimes they wanted to just answer a question and leave it alone without further discussion. Likewise, he invariably made problems or ideas too complex when a simple solution would do. Even more harmful to his reputation, was his low accommodation (A-) level. Other students didn't appreciate his constantly questioning them and disagreeing. They were also annoyed that he seemed to dominate the conversation and would interrupt or argue with others when he disagreed. As a result, people began to think he was too confident in his own ideas and too self-centered to listen to others. Any time he pointed out a problem with their answer, it made his peers even more annoyed because they saw it as arrogance. Thus, when the time came to choose a class president, most people voted against him. In fact, the girl who won the election was similar to Ben in all of the traits except the two that caused him the most problems among his classmates—originality and accommodation. Her low O was completely opposite from his. While he wanted complexity, she craved simplicity. And unlike his questioning, competitive nature, her high A made her more likely to listen to her peers and promote their ideas over hers. People saw her as a team player, and they were ready to embrace this change in leadership after a full year of Ben's too strong leadership.

Ben got carried away with his leadership role. He also overlooked his negative behavioral tendencies. In another situation, Ben could lead, but he would need to be aware of his natural drawbacks. For example, he should try to limit himself to a specific amount of time in a discussion in order to let others get a chance to speak. He should also wait until someone is clearly finished talking before he chimes in. When he notices others' errors, he should avoid bluntly saying they're wrong and instead find a way to tactfully help them realize their mistake. With respect to his high originality, he needs to learn a way to distinguish between what deserves a lengthy discussion and what is better left alone. If he had tried these strategies as class president, his classmates wouldn't have resented his leadership role as much, and he most likely would have been re-elected the following year.

23

The Big Five in Love and Like

How Traits Affect Short-Term Romance and Long-Term Relationships

> "Birds of a feather, flock together."
> "Opposites attract."
>
> --Two opposing folk sayings dating from at least the 16th century

Guide to This Chapter:

- Kinds of Relationships
- Effects of Similarity/Dissimilarity in Relationships
- Achieving Rapport and Intimacy
- Developmental Phases in Relationships
- Predicting Long-Term Satisfaction in Relationships
- Summary of What We Know About Relationships

Would-be sages have opined for centuries on the desirability of mating with similar or dissimilar persons. Athletes should marry athletes, extraverts marry extraverts, creatives marry creatives, neatniks marry neatniks, math genii marry math genii, and so forth. Technically, this subject is typically referred to as "assortative mating (or pairing)." In this chapter we will explore what the research has to say about bonding with those of similar/dissimilar feathers (i.e., traits, abilities, values, experiences, physical characteristics). In fact, both "Birds of a feather…" and "Opposites attract" statements are true, but for different reasons. For example, opposites tend to attract for the short term, like a solitary person being drawn to the outgoing energy of a socialite, while the research shows that, in many ways, long-term satisfaction in relationships is grounded in similarity, as in the couples who grow old together enjoying ballroom dancing or reading together in silence through their evenings.

The Big Five and Major Life Choices

N	E	O	A	C
Need for Stability	**Extraversion**	**Originality**	**Accommodation**	**Consolidation**
N+ Reactive	E+ Extraverted	O+ Explorer	A+ Adapter	C+ Focused
N= Responsive	E= Ambiverted	O= Moderate	A= Negotiator	C= Balanced
N- Resilient	E- Introverted	O- Preserver	A- Challenger	C- Flexible
N1: Worry	**E1: Approach Level**	**O1: Imagination**	**A1: Service**	**C1:Thoroughness**
N2: Temper	**E2: Group Orientation**	**O2: Range of Interests**	**A2: Compliance**	**C2: Structure**
N3: Outlook	**E3: Pace**	**O3: Innovation**	**A3: Humility**	**C3: Ambition**
N4: Coping Level	**E4: Leadership**	**O4: Zoom Scale**	**A4: Speak Out Level**	**C4: Concentration**
	E5: Trust			**C5: Methodicalness**
	E6: Tact			

The Kinds of Relationships

Many kinds of relationships fill our lives, and much of what we have to say about relationships applies to all these different kinds or pairings:

- romantic partners (short term)
- romantic partners (long term)
- parent/child
- siblings
- employer/employee
- teacher/student
- peers
- colleagues
- best friends
- roommates
- buyer/supplier
- leader/follower
- coach/coachee
- counselor/counselee
- mentor/mentee
- ...the list goes on

Each of these kinds of relationships shares a common core: the desire to maintain the relationship indefinitely with minimum maintenance and maximum satisfaction. A friend of mine (Pierce's), Dale Higbee, who also plays the recorder well and has done so for a lifetime, once compared it to other instruments. The difference between the recorder and the violin or trumpet, he asserted, is that it requires minimal practice in order to achieve pleasing results. You don't have to worry about keeping up the calluses on your fingers or keeping your embouchure in condition. You can pick up the recorder off the shelf after a six months' absence and play for hours as though you'd never stopped practicing. "Minimal effort for maximal reward," he quipped. Well, that is the dream of every relationship. The fact, however, is that some relationships require more maintenance than others, and some entail more reward than others.

Various researchers (e.g., Bradford Brown, in Lerner and Steinberg, 2004; Cobb, 2007) have identified three levels of relationships: dyads, cliques, and crowds. A "dyad" is two people in a relationship—the kind of pair this chapter is about. A "clique" is a group of three to ten; most regard each other as a friend. Among youth, cliques are typically comprised of a single sex, while as we age, our cliques typically become more diverse—some single sex, some mixed. About three-fourths of teens belong to at least one clique (Lerner and Steinberg, 2004, p. 363). The one-fourth who do not identify with a clique likely corresponds to the more introverted end of the E supertrait. A "crowd" is typically 20 or more individuals comprising multiple cliques that have a reason for associating with each other—a football team "crowd" with cliques such as offensive line, defensive line, defensive backs, offensive backs, special teams, coaching staff, trainers, cheerleaders, and so on. Or a chorus "crowd" comprised of cliques such as sopranos, altos, tenors, basses, and scholarship students. Normally, all crowd members are members of a clique, but there are individuals who hang with the crowd without clear membership in one of its cliques (e.g., an accompanist who considers it just a job, or a solitary person who comes for the music/sport and makes no effort to bond with a clique—Kobe Bryant has often been described in this way).

Young people typically are engaged in all three: dyads, cliques, and crowds. Those who prefer to experience dyads only, with no membership in cliques or crowds have been described as "isolates." (Cobb, 2007, p. 260) Roughly 15% of teens exhibit this pattern, again, most likely E- and A-, solitary and self-absorbed, like a computer devotee, philosopher, or craftsperson. They have few friends, and their interactions with them tend to be mostly one-on-one, not all together. They typically have either no interest or no ability in joining a clique or crowd. Some youth are described as "liaisons," in that they are a part of two or more cliques but central in none. "Clique members" differ from liaisons in that they are central within a particular clique—they have clear dyadic relationships within the clique. About half of teens identify with one crowd (musicians, jocks, geeks, etc), one-third with two or more crowds, and the remaining one-sixth with no crowds (again, very likely low in both E and A).

Teens normally stick with one crowd or move from one crowd to a similar crowd, rarely changing identity by claiming a crowd significantly different (Cobb, 2007, p. 373). Singers may associate with instrumentalists, footballers with baseballers, mathematics students with programmers, debutantes with sororities, but you rarely see youth associating with two or more crowds that represent different norms or values, such as math whizzes and debutantes, party animals and pre-ministerials, poets and scientists (although there are clearly the rare cases of such). Sometimes a youth happens to acquire—unintentionally—the reputation of being a part of a crowd deemed undesirable, such as being a do-gooder, community-service type. In order to dissociate oneself from an undesirable crowd label, one can publicly violate the assumptions, stereotypes, practices, habits, haunts, fashions, and so forth that are publicly associated with the unwanted crowd label. For example, if the environmental activist crowd sports baggy clothes with little need for upkeep, someone who wants to distance themselves might sport expensive, designer clothes, wear a fur or leather coat, or spend lots of time on makeup and hair, in a silent statement of "I'm not one of them—don't call me that."

Moving in and out of these kinds of groups and relationships invites the question of the relative importance of popularity as opposed to friendships. Recall the conversation of Charlie Bartlett (from the eponymous movie) and his mom, where she suggests that there are more important things in high school than popularity, to which he retorts, "Like what?" The core of their dialog is the difference in quality between popularity and friendship. Charlie is skimming the surface of multiple dyads and enjoying it, but it is doing him no particular good developmentally. Rather, his myriad of surface relationships only gives him a false sense of security and acceptance.

> "What is a friend? A single soul dwelling in two bodies."
>
> --Aristotle

A friendship is a dyad characterized by intimacy. This is the basic unit. The quality of one's dyads is extremely important for developing self-esteem. A dyad without intimacy (more on that word later) is merely an acquaintance. Membership in multiple cliques and crowds may or may not entail an individual's experiencing high-quality dyads. At worst, one could feel that one is a member of many cliques and crowds yet has no friends—merely acquaintances, while at its best, one could feel that one is a member of many cliques and crowds and has many friends. Nancy Cobb (2007, p. 249) asserts that popularity (defined as having many dyadic relationships across many cliques/crowds) results in one's feeling socially competent but not necessarily in having high self-esteem. However, strong, intimate, dyadic friendships (even just a few) have a significant influence on improving self-esteem through intense clarification of one's sense of self. There is simply not enough time for a multiplicity of casual friendships to provide the depth and satisfaction that comes with fewer, more intimate relationships.

Of course, as we shall see, just having a relationship doesn't mean that it is any good! There are two key ingredients for satisfaction in relationships: intimacy and compatibility of temperament. We will now explore these two features in turn.

The Effects of Similarity/Dissimilarity in Relationships

More than two millennia in our past, Aristotle said what contemporary research has confirmed. Over the long haul, the more similar two individuals are, the more satisfying the relationship (we will deal with the exceptions in a moment). In a 1989 "B.C." comic strip, a bold ant sings from the top of her anthill, "I gotta be meee!" No sooner is the lyric sung than the ant is zapped off the top of her hill by the anteater, who laments unapologetically, "Unfortunately, so do I." Clearly, according to Aristotle, these two could never be friends, because they don't share the same soul, the same values, the same trait infrastructure.

Two relatively recent studies of interpersonal relationships have clarified the importance of trait similarity to satisfaction in relationships. Burgoon, Stern, and Dillman (1995, pp. 117 ff.) emphasize the beneficial effects of similarity between two partners. They find that partners who begin on a positive footing actually become more like each other. The traits converge, as it were. They call this process "reciprocity." Partners who start off more shakily, and who, in fact, are relatively more different than similar, undergo a process they label "compensation," in which the partners change away from each other. Their traits diverge, moving even farther apart. Other research confirms that although opposites seem more appealing in the short term, both in business and in romance, being with people with similar profiles is more satisfying over the long haul.

Neil Diamond sang to Barbra Streisand, "You don't bring me flowers anymore." The subtext of that lyric is: "My behavior doesn't elicit from you the validating behaviors it used to." Whether people are in a marriage, a business partnership, a boss-subordinate relationship, a relationship between two work associates, a corporate or team culture, or a school friendship with a classmate, they prefer a context in which they can behave naturally. Introverts want to introvert, challengers want to challenge, and Trusters want to be able to trust. Anything different is unsatisfying. And, the easiest way to be yourself is to be with someone similar to you.

Dag Hammarskjöld is credited with once suggesting that world peace might result if each of us could establish just one healthy relationship with another person. Sometimes the going is difficult, in spite of our similarities and often because of our differences. Nothing is as powerful in sustaining relationships as accepting others for who they are. This is easier when we are similar, but nobler when we are different. As Katherine quips in *The African Queen,* "Nature, Mr. Allnut, is what we are put in this world to rise above." Well, as Kate surely knew, it is not quite that easy. For every combination of traits, there is a positive as well as a negative effect possible. Table 23.1 summarizes the high points. And this is just for the supertraits. A table listing the positive and negative effects of combinations of all 23 subtraits would be quite lengthy, and we have not presumed to spell out this amount of detail for our readers. If you peruse Table 23.1, you will get the idea of how each of the six possible combinations of a trait (i.e., partner A is high in the trait and partner B is low, A is high and B is mid, and so on) within a relationship might be analyzed. Clearly, the most dramatic effects are those associated with large differences. For trust (E5), for example, if one partner is a 65 and the other is a 35, then the danger is that the lower trust partner will see the other as naïve, while the more trusting partner will see the other as self-absorbed and unable to give others the benefit of the doubt. Over time, these attitudes can do real damage in a relationship, unless both partners understand their innate difference and are able to regard it with a sense of humor. Otherwise, the high-trust person will take the partner's doubts personally and begin to think that the distrust is directed personally and only at them. To regard such major differences in traits as impersonal—"my partner is not only skeptical of me, they're skeptical of everyone!"—is the beginning of acceptance and sanity. At some point, the trusting partner can even grow to see their partner's doubts as a strength in certain situations, and be thankful for it.

The Big Five and Major Life Choices

I (Jane) am less trusting than Pierce, and I have caught many an error in restaurant tabs that Pierce was too trusting to detect! I've also negotiated major legal partnerships with other companies where one needs to plan in advance how the partnership will deal with unexpected or unanticipated issues that probably won't happen. Likewise, I have backed off of many an accusation of a friend or family member before actually expressing it to them, as a result of Pierce's insistence on finding real evidence before accusing, and considering different possible ways of interpreting that evidence.

Table 23.1 The Effects of Congruence in Relationships

The effects of similarity/dissimilarity of **NEED FOR STABILITY** scores

CONDITION:	POSITIVE EFFECTS:	NEGATIVE EFFECTS:
Both Reactive	Nothing escapes your attention Strong sense of needing each other Respect for each other's emotionality	High stress Mutual dependencies Argument-proneness
Both Responsive	Even-tempered	Could take stability for granted
Both Resilient	Essentially stress-free Problem-solve well together	Could miss important cues Occasional outbursts Could be misread as noncaring
React. + Respons.	Reac. will admire Resp.'s control	Resp. can tire of Reac.'s reactions
Resil. + Respons.	Resp. will envy Resil's steadiness	Resil.'s needs may not get expressed
Reactive + Resil.	Reac. can convey interest in others for Res. Resil. can provide stability for Reac.	Reac. will think Resil. has no feelings Resil. will see Reac. as out of control Resil. will not take Reac.'s stress seriously Reac. may resent Resil.'s tranquillity

The effects of similarity/dissimilarity of **EXTRAVERSION** scores

CONDITION:	POSITIVE EFFECTS:	NEGATIVE EFFECTS:
Both Extraverts	Many friends	Little time for reflection
Both Ambiverts	Plenty of time for friends and solitude	Regrets over not being committed to either extreme--could have more friends or more solitude
Both Introverts	Close, intimate relationship	Inadequate communication
Extravert + Ambivert	Ext. will be attracted to Amb.'s balance	Amb. may wish Ext. would be more private about personal life
Introvert + Ambivert	Amb. will draw Int. out socially Amb. will admire Int.'s stillness	Amb. will grow impatient having to read Int.'s mind
Extravert + Introvert	Ext. can handle external relationships while the Int. churns out the work Recognition of each one's unique strengths	Int. may see Ext. as shallow and afraid of being alone Ext. may resent Int.'s reluctance to socialize and communicate Ext may tire of having to read Int's mind Int may tire of Ext's talking

Table 23.1 (continued)

The effects of similarity/dissimilarity of **ORIGINALITY** scores

CONDITION:	POSITIVE EFFECTS:	NEGATIVE EFFECTS:
Both Explorers	Enjoy dreaming together Mutually enjoy trying new things	Never become truly expert in anything Fail to achieve efficiencies
Both Moderates	A relationship full of common sense	Fail to develop a competitive edge
Both Preservers	Respect for each other's expertise	Can be rigid in outlook and miss opportunities
Explorer + Moderate	Mod. can help keep Exp.'s feet on the ground	Mod. can resent Exp.'s risk-proneness
Preserver + Moderate	Mod. will respect Pre.'s constancy	Mod. may resent Pre.'s unwillingness to take off on flights of fancy
Explorer + Preserver	Pre. will balance Exp.'s dreams with the capability to implement them	Pre. resent Exp.'s unrealistic theorizing Exp. may see Pre. as boring, too few risks May spat over traditional vs. progressive

The effects of similarity/dissimilarity of **ACCOMMODATION** scores

CONDITION:	POSITIVE EFFECTS:	NEGATIVE EFFECTS:
Both Adapters	Strong bonds; many mutual friends	Become overly dependent on one another
Both Negotiators	Strong at making good decisions	Can get caught up in politics
Both Challengers	Will respect each other's fighting spirit	May fight constantly May become too independent of one another
Adapter + Negotiator	Neg. will help draw out the Adap's needs	Neg. may grow impatient with Adap's martyrdom
Challenger + Negotiator	Neg. will help Chal. take others' needs into consideration	Neg. may grow impatient with Chal.'s rigidity or need to be right
Adapter + Challenger	Will (can) fight to synthesize a decision out of both group and individual needs	A may get taken to the cleaners C may get thrown out into the cold C may see A as a conflict avoider A may see C as rigid, inflexible, cold

The effects of similarity/dissimilarity of **CONSOLIDATION** scores

CONDITION:	POSITIVE EFFECTS:	NEGATIVE EFFECTS:
Both Focused	High achievement Accepting of each others' ambition	All work and no play Little time for pure relationship building
Both Balanced	Well-organized with time for work and play	Neither individual goes for the gold May look outside the relationship for models
Both Flexible	A life of spontaneity and discovery	Constantly out of time and money Will feed each others' bad habits
Focused + Balanced	Bal. can coax the Foc. into relaxing	Foc. may feel held back by the Bal.
Flexible + Balanced	Bal. can help the Flex. stay within budget	The Bal. may resent the Flex.'s poor time and financial management
Flexible + Focused	Flex. can handle crises while the Foc. wins the campaign Can develop a healthy tension between spontaneity and achievement, between play and work	Constantly at each other--slob and the drill sergeant (Beetle Bailey syndrome) Foc. will be both envious and resentful of Flex.'s spontaneity/capacity for fun Flex. will be both envious of and threatened by Foc.'s self-control, need for order, and will to achieve

The Big Five and Major Life Choices

In an extensive study of the literature on relationships, McCrae and Costa (2003, p. 213) concluded that "...the adage that opposites attract has rarely been supported by research." Satisfaction increases the closer together partners are on traits. The number of marriage therapy sessions required to maintain a relationship increases as differences in trait scores increase (Hamer and Copeland, 1998, p. 50). The most problematic combination is a female who is high in "sensation-seeking" (a quality comprised of E+ and O+) with a male who is low in sensation seeking. High-sensation-seeking males paired with low sensation-seeking females are less problematic, probably because it fits more with the male stereotype, and women tend to be more accepting of it (than men are accepting of the reverse situation). Hamer and Copeland (1998) report evidence of assortative mating on sensation seeking, regardless of the level (p. 50). This means that a person tends to marry or partner with someone who has a similar level of this behavior: Strong appetites like to be with others with strong appetites, while the bland like being with the bland. One of the strongest bases of assortative mating is the O (originality) dimension, whereby creative people like to partner with creatives, practicals with practicals, complex with complex, status quo with status quo, and so on.

So, in the event that two partners/friends are opposite on a trait, how do they manage the gap so as to build on it rather than to resent it? They take a personality assessment early in their relationship (we recommend the SchoolPlace Big Five Profile™ and the WorkPlace Big Five Profile™!). They discuss the results, they get real clear on the fact that these scores are unlikely to change very much, and they decide if they can live with each other and not resent the other's differences, not take it personally. I (Pierce) did not do this before my first marriage back in my 20s—I wish I had. Later, I learned that my first wife had an angry temperament. I had been taking it personally during those years we were together—perhaps having gone through an assessment would have prevented that—I would have learned that she was angry at many things, not just at me, and that could be easier to take, perhaps. However, I do not personally react well around anger—I sort of crawl into a shell and wait for it to go away. Then I'm happy to talk about it later. Having this kind of information early in a relationship should result in one of two things: You can either terminate the relationship because you know the behaviors are unlikely to change, and you can't live with them, or you can understand the differences and accept them with a sense of humor and swear never to take them personally.

On the other hand, is having the same level of all traits necessarily a good thing? The research says it is good for everything but N (need for stability). Two high Ns tend to fight all the time. For the N trait, a high N is best paired with a low N, who can take the reactivity of the high N like water off a duck's back—feathers unruffled, rock of Gibraltar, staying cool, and all that. On the other traits, similarity of level appears to be fine. But what about two partners who are both high in E4, take charge. Shouldn't they be constantly vying for who is in charge? Not necessarily. Research suggests that such couple tend to divide the areas of responsibility such that one partner is in charge of one set of responsibilities (e.g., bill paying, cleaning, gardening) and the other is in charge of another set (e.g., maintenance, grocery shopping, decorating). As McCrae and Costa (2003, p. 213) observe:

> Couples seem to develop a pattern of complementary behavior. Two assertive individuals may make a couple in which one is clearly dominant, or they may carve out separate domains in which to exercise their dominance (traditionally, the wife ran the house and the husband made decisions about the car).

This is clearly the case with us. We are both high in O (originality) and low in C (consolidation), such that we both prefer the creative, complex, spontaneous, multitasking way of life. So who pays the bills, washes the clothes? How do basic low O, high C chores get done? We divide them up: Jane shops for groceries, bakes, buys gifts, and pays the bills, and Pierce does the laundry, cooks stews, reads technical manuals, and maintains the media center.

There is one major area where romantic couples *must*, or perhaps I ought to say *should*, be different. That has to do with what is called "histocompatibility." Evolution has ensured that we not marry our relatives by making our close kin smell less alluring to us than others. Close kin have a scent that comes from the histamines that they secrete. We tend to be attracted to persons whose histamines are different than ours. This reduces the risk of genetic abnormalities. Now, in a twist of fate, it so happens that taking the birth control pill masks the partner's scent for the woman taking the pill. So, after a long period of intimacy, a female who, for whatever reason, goes off the pill, could be in for a rude surprise, as in "Who's this stinker I thought I was in love with?"

Achieving Rapport and Intimacy

If intimacy is the difference between friends and mere acquaintances, then how does one recognize when intimacy is present in a relationship? In Chapter 19, we based our definition on that of Nancy Cobb (2007, p. 159): "sharing of one's feelings and thoughts in an atmosphere of caring, trust, and acceptance." Intimacy between two people means that each feels free to share whatever is on one's mind without fear of judgment, without fear of breaking the relationship somehow, of losing the other's acceptance, trust, and care. It is knowing that one does not have to risk going crazy by keeping the lid on thoughts and feelings. It is having a shoulder to cry on, an ear to listen, a mind to bounce things off of, an audience to appreciate one's joys and prides, and a kind of confessor to hear of one's regrets and trespasses without fear that one will be judged as weird, unworthy, unlovable. Clearly, not every "friend" can hear 100% of what is on one's mind, but among one's friends hopefully there is always at least one whom we know we can go to for a particular topic. "Best friends" come close to being able to hear 100% of what is on our minds, including concerns about the best friend. It is friends who believe there is no such thing as a dumb question, but only the unasked question. Friends may not always approve, but they always accept. If they are told something in confidence, they are expected to maintain the confidentiality of what their friend has told them.

With friends, there are rarely surprises in our development. Because we share so much, our friends have a sense of who we are and the path we are carving out for ourselves. The accepting stance of the intimate friend is a requirement for growth and change, for they make risk-taking seem less risky. Nancy Cobb (2007, p. 163) writes: "If they hope to build a lasting relationship, young couples need to be willing to accept changes in their partner's self-definition." When friends are continually sharing what is going on inside, such changes in one's self-definition are easier to take. If one holds back, if one goes through a lengthy process of self-analysis and redefinition without consulting with one's friend, it is likely that the effect could break the friendship. Incremental change is easier to accept than makeovers. Baby steps are easier to keep up with than giant steps. Intimate friends stay in touch; they let each other know of the small steps. Like the frog in cold water on the stove, I am more likely to stay in the pot if the temperature increases incrementally. If the change in temperature is abrupt, I am likely to jump out, to jump ship. I (Pierce) recall friends in high school who went to different colleges than I did. They changed during their first year, and upon renewing our friendship the next summer, after a nine-month absence full of change, we found ourselves unable to talk with one another. We hadn't changed incrementally with one another. Not all relationships are doomed as the result of such major change with incremental sharing, but typically a change in identity will crush a relationship when intimacy, continual sharing, is missing. Additionally, I (Pierce) recall a summer during college in which I experienced a major identity change—switching my major, switching my career choice, and acquiring new habits and tastes. Several of my friends at the time were not with me that summer, and I did not communicate by letter or phone. They found my changes too strident, too abrupt, and the friendships ruptured, never to return to their former closeness. A good example of the failure to share on a continuing, day-to-day basis, is the couple Frank and April Wheeler (played by Leonardo DiCaprio and Kate Winslet in the 2009 film *Revolutionary Road.* Rather than frequently sharing their feelings of emptiness, they periodically explode in rage and/or hopelessness. Perhaps in a touch of irony, the "Wheelers" have no wheels—no ongoing intimacy to help avoid such major potholes.

Kiesler (1996, p. 6) describes another important aspect of intimacy. Not only can we share most anything, but a good friend reacts to our behavior in a way that makes us feel validated, o.k. He calls this phenomenon "behavior concordance":

> Any interpersonal act is designed to elicit from a respondent reactions that confirm, reinforce, or validate the actor's self-presentation and that make it more likely that the actor will continue to emit similar interpersonal acts.

I think that Kiesler is trying to say that when we behave a certain way in the presence of our partner, we expect that partner to react in a way that is accepting of us as an individual. If we see a news story about our friend's family member and mail it to them, we certainly don't expect them to say, "Don't you have something better to do with your time?" or "I've already got two dozen emails about it." Kiesler goes on to conclude that when behavior is concordant, when my behavior gets a response from you that is accepting and validating, then the chances of satisfaction in the relationship are high. He further points out that the likelihood of such concordant behavior is highest when two partners are similar with respect to their trait infrastructure (as well as having similar intelligence and physical characteristics). In addition to such concordant behavior, similarity of traits also encourages reciprocal behavior, which involves responding in kind. I ask you over today, and tomorrow you ask me. Such reciprocity is another way of validating or accepting another's value as an individual.

We are going to be most satisfied when we can be ourselves and don't have to put on an act. Kiesler observes that midrange people, whose traits are more moderate, act like universal donors, able to be satisfied with the widest possible range of partners. They have a wider range of potential intimate friends because they find it natural to be accepting of persons on either side of the midrange. In Chapter 19, we mentioned that "facilitative" people make intimacy possible, and that midrange scores make it easier to be facilitative. It is not natural, but also not impossible, for a sociable, gregarious person to be intimate with a solitary, private one. These two would need to value other areas of their relationship and essentially overlook their big difference(s). That doesn't mean they can't talk about them. They can, pensively, but not judgmentally:

> "Sometimes I wish you would be content to stay home with me and just read a book in the same room for an evening, but I know that we are built differently in that regard. I wish we weren't, but I really don't take it personally. I know you go out because that is just you, and not because you don't want to be around me. But I have to really make an effort to be accepting and rational about it. Maybe over time it'll get easier."

One of the enemies of intimacy is a phenomenon called the "fundamental attribution error." This refers to the tendency most people have to generalize from limited samples of others' behavior, whether for good or for ill. You may have the opportunity, for example, to see someone at their best, and to assume from the one episode the person is that way all the time. For example, you may see us helping an elderly person cross the street and so assume that we're always courteous, thoughtful, generous, helpful. You may be right, or you may be wrong. You are attributing to us a characteristic that is based on observing it only once. Or you may see us at our worst and assume we're that way all the time. For example, you may see us lose our temper and then assume that we can't control our temper most of the time. You may be right, or you may be wrong. The "fundamental attribution error" is based on the universal expectation that people will be consistent. Once a jerk, "always" a jerk. Once a chauvinist, "always"... Friendships can be won or lost based on this kind of assumption. It is through the act of intimacy—sharing our concerns—that we are able to get beyond the fundamental attribution error and pave the way for possible friendships maybe by saying, "Are you always like that?"

If the fundamental attribution error (actually, it is closely related to stereotyping and prejudice) is the enemy of intimacy, then establishing rapport is intimacy's best friend. Rapport puts people at ease, allows them to let their guard down, makes them feel accepted. The trick to establishing rapport is "mirroring" another's behavior. By mirroring, we mean trying to be like them. If you are walking briskly, and I am walking with you, then if I lag behind you, it will be difficult to establish rapport. I need to keep up with you, or you need to slow down for me, in order for both of us to feel rapport between us. This goes for many other aspects of behavior, e.g., the kind of language we use (jargon versus technical), the volume and tempo at which we talk (loud versus soft, fast versus slow). Figure 23.1 portrays the many ways in which people can mirror each other as a way of establishing rapport. Of the many contexts indicated in Figure 23.1, the more contexts we can match our partner on, the better our chances are of establishing rapport. The more elements on which we differ, the more distance we cre-

Figure 23.1 The Many Contexts for Establishing Rapport through Mirroring (from Howard, 2000)

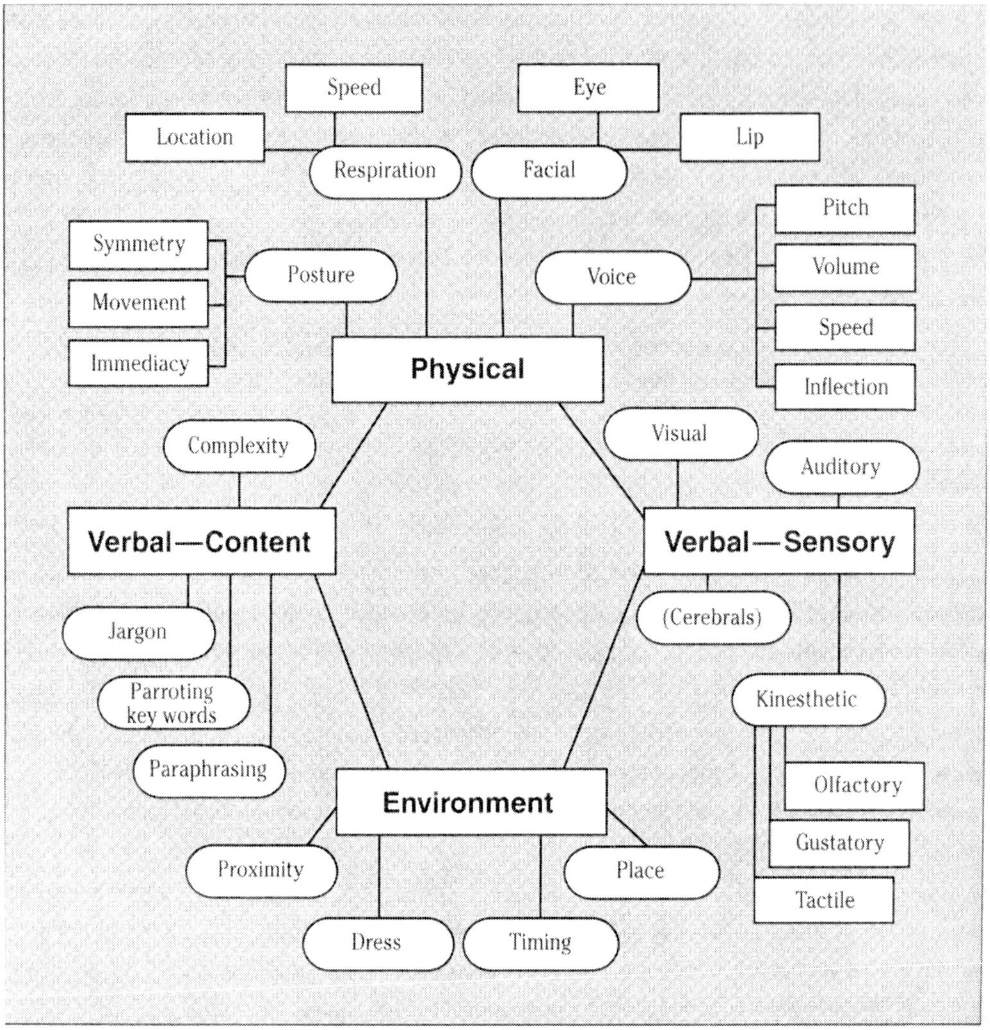

ate between ourselves. We cannot change everything about ourselves in order to establish rapport, but we can certainly be aware of some distancing differences that we could soften and still be true to ourselves. I (Pierce) love to walk fast, but I don't *always* have to walk fast! I can slow down on occasion in order to feel closer to Jane! I don't like to wear a coat and tie when I go out to dinner, but I have one particular friend who always does. Occasionally, I don't mind dressing up a little just to make him (and actually me!) feel more comfortable, to make us feel more in rapport with each other.

Earlier, we discussed four models that contribute towards greater intimacy in relationships: the Johari Window (Chapter 13), Values Clarification (Chapter 3), Coping Strategies (Chapter 17), and Conflict Management Strategies (also Chapter 17). Refresh your understanding of these four models with a view towards how they can promote intimacy among your important friendships. The Johari Window increases what others know about you through self-disclosure, asking for feedback, and appropriate risk-taking. The Values Clarification approach does it through a seven-step interview that explores the maturity of one's strongly held values. It provides hundreds of exercises that friends could use to get to know each other more deeply. An example of these exercises is "Three Things That Would Improve My Quality of Life." We were walking down a North Carolina beach one spring day, and we asked each other the question. One of my (Jane's) three things was how important it was for me to do my share (with respect to my two sisters) in caring for my aging parents. We discussed ways I could act on this value and came up with the idea of inviting my parents to move from Alabama to Charlotte to be closer to us so we could care for them. This simple exercise resulted in a clear action which brought us closer together as partners, as well as closer in the relationships with the rest of my family. The coping and conflict management strategies provide definite options for dealing openly with stress and conflict without trying to submerge them or me, ignore them, or just wishing them to just go away.

Given that we understand now the value of practicing rapport and intimacy, we are now ready to move through the phases of a relationship that has minimal "storm and stress."

Developmental Phases in Relationships

Steven R. Covey (1989) and his son Sean (1998) have made famous a three-phase model of relationship development that moves from dependence to independence and ultimately to interdependence. In the first phase, dependence, the euphoria of mutual discovery is associated with feeling inseparable—doing things together as often as possible. As two friends become more comfortable in their relationship through continuing intimacy, the natural evolution of the relationship is to move towards greater independence. In this more mature level of a relationship, each person feels greater freedom to do things that do not necessarily involve the other person. The continuing intimacy serves as a home basis; frequent sharing of feelings, thoughts, and experiences serve to maintain a feeling of trust, acceptance, and caring. Ultimately, assuming the continuation of authentic intimacy, the two friends will arrive at a state of interdependence, whereby both members feel that, while they can be independent of each other, they prefer to be together as much as possible.

Most people have understood the first two phases—dependence and independence—and have found corroboration of these two phases in a multiplicity of relationships, both romantic and nonromantic. Friendships tend to originate with a sense of inseparability. But such togetherness can be stifling and must of necessity be followed by allowing each other some "rope," some freedom to be on one's own. To deny such freedom prevents a child from forming their identity, a lover from appropriate growth opportunities, a "best friend" from having enriching experiences with others, and an employee from achieving greater challenges and promotion opportunities.

However, we never fully understood Covey's meaning of "interdependence." Not until we came upon the writing of Harold Kelley (1978, 1979). Kelley describes interdependence in a relationship as a state characterized by a roughly equal sharing of drudgery and delights. Interdependence, according to Kelley, is a kind of scale or balance in which both members of a relationship feel that the inevitable chores that are intrinsically boring, monotonous, onerous, and mindless are equally shared by both. Or at least neither member of the relationship feels like the other expects them to do all or most of the grunt work—cleaning up, washing up, picking up, putting up, documenting, paying bills, organizing, and so on. Every relationship entails both pleasing and nonpleasing tasks. We could call them enrichment and maintenance tasks. With parents, it is playing games with a child versus washing dishes. With peers it might be making music versus proofreading papers. In a truly interdependent relationship, both have reached the state whereby, through the revelations of intimacy and the magic of acceptance, trust, and caring, the two sense what is drudgery and delight to the other and ensure that neither senses that the relationship has become one-sided, with one member having proportionately more drudgery and less delight, with the other having proportionately more delight and less drudgery. Kelley says the person with more drudgery is in a dependent position relative to the other, while the "more delight" person holds a more independent position. Over time, someone in the dependent position tends to develop resentments toward the more independent person, while someone in the independent position tends to develop contempt for the other, more dependent person. Those most likely to allow themselves to become dependent in this sense are those higher in A, with those lower in A more likely to become independent. Both extremes in A should take special pains to swear fealty to the process of intimacy, of sharing one's thoughts, feelings, and concerns. Frequently! Don't put it off.

Predicting Long-Term Satisfaction in Relationships

Let us now focus specifically on choosing a mate for life—marriage. The single most important prerequisite for a satisfying, long-lasting marriage is having a firm sense of one's identity before committing to a life-long relationship. That goes for both parties! This does not mean that one cannot, or will not, be able to change in meaningful ways after marrying. What it does mean is that we need to know our traits, our abilities, our values, our skills, and which of these qualities form the core of our passions in life. We know our traits and abilities, but not all of them are core for us. For example, we are moderately low on C2 (organization) but that does not necessarily mean that we *need* low order, chaos, or disarray in order to be happy. Some with low C2 have a passion for disarray: They simply do not feel at home, do not feel comfortable, unless there is a certain casual, unpicked-up appearance in their home and work life. In other words, they feel passionately about being in disarray. Order and disarray are not important for us: We don't feel passionate about either. We tend to be casual but are perfectly comfortable around order and neatness. On the other hand, we score very high on all four subtraits of O (originality), and we feel passionately about them. Being creative, working with complexity, being innovative, and dwelling on the big picture are part of our bliss—we are unhappy if confined to their opposites. So, in considering a mate, it is not important that we marry a neatnik or a slob, but it is crucial that we marry someone who respects, accepts, and positively regards our high O behavior and values. A partner who is low in O could be that person, but it is more likely that another high O would fit the bill more naturally. Fortunately, we found each other.

In a sense, what we are saying is that, in negotiating the marriage "contract," we need to know what our non-negotiables are, and those are our core personal qualities that we must express, live, and breathe daily in order to flourish. The clearer we are as to our passions, our limits, and the sources of our bliss, then the easier it is for us and our prospective mate to recognize and affirm the possibility for acceptance and even high regard for the other. One of our former pastors, Dr. Guy D. Griffith, once told us his favorite definition of love. He remembered it from a class with the noted theologian James Loder at Princeton Theological Seminary: "Love is the non-possessive delight in the particularity of the other." It is much easier to have such generous esteem for another when both you and the other have a clear sense of self, like showing one's deck to the other before playing cards. It is very much like "truth in lending," whereby all the relevant information is shared before signing a contract. No surprises. McCrae and Costa (2003, p. 218) underscore the importance of having this personal sense of clarity of who we are before making long-term commitments:

> Choosing a major in college, deciding whom to marry, accepting a job transfer, planning for retirement—all depend on the knowledge that our basic motives and styles will endure....*We choose and create environments that will reinforce our dispositions*; regardless of the reasons, stability is a fact we must and do count on. [italics ours]

In other words, we must understand that our traits, abilities, and values are unlikely to change; so we must select a mate (or career) that is supportive of whom we are. In effect, we need to draft up a kind of personal mission statement that says something like this:

> "These are my core traits, abilities, and values. Can you accept and feel good about living with them for a lifetime? Now, let me see your core traits, abilities, and values, so I can see if I can live with them. What we see is what we're going to get!"

In spite of our best preparation, our best negotiation, our fullest disclosure before committing to marriage, there are certain risk factors that, while not dooming a marriage, certainly increase the risk of stormy weather ahead. Two stand out—early tantrums and impulsiveness. First, research has found that someone who exhibited a pattern of strong temper tantrums in their early years tends to have more than their share of stormy weather in their career and in their marriage. Such individuals, who are likely to be very low in A and very high in N, are highly likely to experience divorce and/or limited career options (McCrae and Costa, 2003, p. 219). This does not mean that N++A- - individuals are doomed to divorce and job stagnation. But it does mean that such individuals should be forewarned now that they are at risk, and that they should strategize with someone how they might reduce the risk. For example, knowing their tendency to make decisions in the heat of the moment, they should commit, now, to revisiting *every* decision they make during such intense moments, revisiting them when calm and more rational, and involving those affected by the decision. Early on, they also need to develop a regular habit of aerobic exercise (easier if they are also C+).

The second risk factor is impulsiveness, or the tendency to make decisions on a spontaneous basis without thinking through alternatives and consequences. This behavioral pattern is associated with a blend of high N and low C (and intensified when accompanied by E+). Specifically, where both members of a couple are high in N, and the male is also low in C, research points towards the increased likelihood of divorce. This pattern entails two features: Both partners are highly emotionally reactive, having quick fuses for anger, fear, and sadness, and the male has a greater likelihood of sexual wandering, substance abuse, and physically abusive responses to the wife's reactions to such behavior (McCrae and Costa, 2003). Again, forewarned is forearmed. N+C- men (and, to a lesser degree, the same for women) should strategize, now, how they can manage their impulsivity and its consequences. Impulsivity in and of itself is neutral—it can be good for an artist, who needs spontaneity of expression; good for a service worker, who needs to be highly reactive and attuned to customers' needs; good for many roles that benefit from a spontaneous, nervous edge (a defensive specialist in basketball comes to mind, such as Dennis Rodman). However, these individuals are especially at risk for negative expressions of spontaneity, such as taking dares, experimenting with drugs, and succumbing to sexual opportunities. They must learn strategies to use in permitting the positive impulses and avoiding the negative ones. And should the negative ones win out, learn strategies to use in remedying, compensating, atoning for their effects. The "WWJD" mantra is one way of self-monitoring: "What would Jesus (or Mohammed, Moses, Gandhi, Mother Teresa, my daddy, my mother, my big brother) do in this situation?" In other words, have a sense of those you wish to emulate, and invoke them in situations that tempt you to otherwise violate what they stand for. And should you yield, find ways to show genuine contrition and offer/negotiate meaningful methods of reparation. One of the best ways to avoid temptation is to stay busy. To submit oneself to a job and a home life that keeps one on a full-time straight and narrow path is a way of acknowledging one's weakness.

To embark on marriage is serious business. Joseph Campbell, in dialog with Bill Moyers (Campbell and Moyers, 1991, pp. 6-7), establishes the standard in this way:

> Campbell: I would say that if the marriage isn't a first priority in your life, you're not married. The marriage means the two that are one, the two become one flesh. If the marriage lasts long enough, and if you are acquiescing constantly to it instead of to individual personal whim, you come to realize that that is true—the two really are one.
>
> Moyers: So marriage is utterly incompatible with the idea of doing one's own thing.
>
> Campbell: It's not simply one's own thing, you see. It is, in a sense, doing one's own thing, but the one isn't just you, it's the two together as one.

Their dialog is an echo of our earlier reference to Aristotle: "What is a friend? A single soul dwelling in two bodies." How is this accomplished? By full disclosure of whom we are to each other, followed by full acceptance and positive regard for each other. And this is far easier when both partners share the same traits. The primary exception is need for stability, where higher Ns benefit from being with lower Ns, as a storm-tossed boat needs a harbor.

A Note About Abusive Relationships

Estimates of the prevalence of both physical and emotionally abusive relationships among teens are sobering, if not alarming. When young people, especially girls, first sense that their partner is being more than aggressive (N+E+A-), that they have moved from insistence to abuse, they should immediately notify parents, friends, or school authorities, wherever they feel secure in getting help. Every school should have policies and educational programs on how to detect and report abuse. As victims tend often to be girls with an underdeveloped sense of identity, they need their community to provide abundant lifelines. Many states have passed laws that aim to protect against dating violence. Here are some resources:

- www.jenniferann.org
- www.aneesamichelle.org
- www.hazelden.org/safedates
- www.chooserespect.org
- www.breakthecycle.org/resources-state-law-report-cards-2009.html
- www.cdc.gov/mmwr/PDF/wk/mm5519.pdf
- www.loveisnotabuse.com/surveyresults_teens2006.htm

Summary of What We Know About Relationships

- Fewer, closer friendships are more satisfying than more, surface acquaintances (i.e., intimacy is more satisfying than popularity).
- Intimacy is achieved through frequent, incremental sharing of what's going on inside.
- Similar trait profiles in a relationship are more satisfying over the long term, with similarity on O (originality) being the most important, and N being the exception (with N+ benefiting from pairing with N-).
- Intimacy is difficult when one individual does not have a clear sense of who they are with respect to traits, abilities, and values.
- Marriage needs to be based on full disclosure of each person's core traits, abilities, and values, with unqualified acceptance and positive regard for each other's core.

Now, let us turn to the other major lifetime commitment: one's career.

Relationship Case Study #1: The Roommates

Contributed by Emily Crowder, UNC-Chapel Hill student and CentACS Research Intern

Gaby and Katie are roommates in college who were selected randomly to live together. Before meeting Katie, Gaby didn't know what to expect, but she figured it would work out fine because Gaby could normally adapt pretty well to others' needs or habits. On the other hand, Katie was very nervous. She worried that Gaby would be too much of a partier for her and that she would always be bringing friends over to the room. Fortunately, there are no such problems. The two of them get along great and have become not only roommates, but also friends who eat together, study together, and go out together. Even with all the time they spend together, they have never fought, or even had a serious disagreement. They both adjust their activities to accommodate the other. If Gaby wants to do homework while Katie is listening to music, Gaby will either go to a study lounge or just do less demanding homework first, while Katie will often put in earphones if she notices; however, Gaby has begun to notice that Katie often has difficulty sleeping. Katie will be exhausted and get in bed, but a few times a week she gets up after being unable to fall asleep. Gaby notices that this happens even more frequently when Katie has a test or has been having trouble with her boyfriend. Gaby can tell she's worried and asks her the next morning if she's okay. Normally Katie responds with, "Yeah fine. I just couldn't sleep well last night." But later in the day, after dinner, Katie normally confesses what she's been thinking about. Although it's hard for Gaby not to push Katie's original response that she's fine, she knows that if Katie is really worried about something, she will eventually express it.

Traits provide an explanation for their relationship:
Katie is N+E-O=A++C+ Gaby is N-E=O=A+C=

Unlike some living situations, the one for this pair has, fortunately, worked out. As is seen by their tendency to adjust to each other's needs, whether with music or otherwise, they are both high in accommodation (A). This similarity enables the two to form a strong bond, without either taking advantage of the other. While they are very similar on the accommodation scale, their scores on need for stability (N) are quite different. Gaby, who wasn't even worried about getting a new roommate, is on the lower end of the scale, whereas Katie, who was very nervous at first and who has difficulty sleeping because she's racked with worry, is much higher in N. With her higher N, Katie is more likely to get upset; however, Gaby's lower level of Need for Stability can calm Katie down. Plus, both of their higher Accommodation levels make it unlikely that either will knowingly press the other's buttons or confront the other when she does. Though not as drastic as the differences in N, they also have variations in Extraversion (E). Katie, as an Introvert, was worried about a roommate who would be too active, outgoing, or sociable. But Gaby, an Ambivert, figured she could handle someone who was either introverted or extraverted as a roommate and wasn't concerned. This difference in Extraversion levels also helps to explain why Gaby wants to talk over a problem with the more private Katie who is more likely to hold things in. Fortunately, they are able to overcome such differences. When Katie is worried, it is obvious to Gaby that something is wrong; so she asks Katie what is going on to invite her to open up. Though Katie wouldn't respond at first, her worry is so great that she really needs to talk it through, and later, after thinking on the issue, she is able to express her thoughts. Without knowing their personalities, the two still manage to handle the situation well. Gaby, being more extraverted and high in A, wants to hear what Katie is thinking but doesn't press the issue. Katie, an Introvert, doesn't want to talk about it immediately, especially when she hasn't had time to think it over. Her introversion plus her high A make her hold back her thoughts; however, her worry eventually causes her to share her feelings. The approach of asking Katie if she is all right and then waiting for an answer works well because it gives Katie time alone to think and invites her to discuss the issue at her will. When dealing with similar issues involving Extraversion and Introversion, it's helpful to remember a popular quote from Isabel Briggs Myers, "If you don't know what an Extravert is thinking, you haven't been listening. If you don't know what an Introvert is thinking, you haven't asked."

Relationship Case Study #2: Opposites Attract

Contributed by Emily Crowder, UNC-Chapel Hill student and CentACS Research Intern

Robert is N++E+O- -A+C- Allison is N- -E-O- -A- -C+

While more similar temperaments are more likely to foster a healthy, long-lasting relationship, there are plenty of exceptions. Allison and Robert are one such exception where their understanding of their differences enables them to have a positive relationship.

Allison and Robert are seniors at the same university and have been dating since high school. Having dated for so long, they are renting an apartment together. Robert's sister, her husband, and their two daughters recently moved to the city where Allison and Robert are living. His sister is going to graduate school at their university. However, her husband just got a promotion and has little time to stay home with the kids while Robert's sister juggles class and work. In need of help, she just asked Robert to watch the kids when she's in class and he's free. Though he knows it will be difficult to babysit and complete his schoolwork, he agrees because, as an Adapter (A+), he wants to help others above his own needs. Allison, who loves children, decides to help out and watch the girls when possible. When Robert and Allison are both watching the kids, their caregiving styles are observably different. Allison, who is lower in N (Need for Stability), tends to remain calmer with the kids even when they're whining, but Robert (N+) gets frustrated with their crying and tells them that he'll put them in time-out if they don't calm down. With her high activity level (E3++), Allison likes to take the kids out to parks or playgrounds when she's with them, but Robert (E3=) would rather play a relaxing game with them at home.

Away from the kids, Robert and Allison are just as different. When he's repairing something in their apartment, she (C+, high in Consolidation) makes sure it's perfect even though he would accept it as long as it works (C-); however, he doesn't complain (A+). If she tells him that she wants something hung differently or that a picture doesn't look good, he accepts her opinion and asks her what she wants to do about it. Though Robert tends to keep things generally neat, Allison organizes further and makes sure everything is in its place (C+). When they go out, their behaviors once again differ. As an Extravert, he talks to everyone and takes a short time to get to know people as he tells jokes. Allison, an Introvert, is friendly, but she takes longer to open up and normally is not the one to walk around and initiate greetings with those she doesn't know. Instead, she lets Robert introduce her to his friends. Yet among these many differences, they do have similar interests which they first discovered in high school when they ended up taking many of the same classes. Not only do they appreciate the other's interests, but his goofy humor makes her laugh, while her steadiness under stress tends to calm him down.

While some relationships would struggle with such drastic differences, Allison and Robert's similar interests (both low in Originality) and acceptance of each other's different traits helps them stay together. They not only accept each other's differences, but they enjoy them as well, such as the more introverted Allison watching Robert make jokes or the more reactive Robert being calmed by Allison's stability under stress. In fact, when they first took the SchoolPlace Big Five Profile™, they acknowledged that they would be opposites. When told that their traits were quite interesting to compare, Allison replied, "Oh I'm sure we're opposites on everything. We're probably both on the extremes." And she, in fact, was right on four out of five supertraits.

Relationship Case Study #3: A Souring Relationship

Contributed by Emily Crowder, UNC-Chapel Hill student and CentACS Research Intern

Greg and Emma have been dating on and off for four years. They met in high school and started dating their freshman year. As their relationship progressed, they became each other's best friend, confiding everything in the other. Yet, even with their high dependence on each other, they started having problems. She was always hanging around Greg and his friends, and rarely with her own friends. In addition, he would take advantage of her by getting her to do parts of his schoolwork for him, having her pay for all their dates, and refusing to talk about things that interested her. Unfortunately, she wouldn't speak up for herself and continued to do whatever Greg asked. She would put up with his continuous chatter about sports and video games, while getting no word in about herself. Eventually Emma had enough and broke it off; however, Greg didn't take it seriously—he knew if he pestered her enough, she would give in and get back together with him. She did. The cycle of good times followed by break-ups continued for four years. Sometimes he broke up with her to date other people or because he wanted independence. Sometimes she broke up with him, frustrated with his inconsideration towards her and doubtful of his intentions with other girls. Though they would get back together, nothing was ever resolved, and resentment and doubts of loyalty remained on both sides. Finally, after many breakups and reunions, Emma decided to part ways permanently. Both struggled to let go of the other, which resulted in heated arguments followed by crying on both sides. Emma was worried that if she continued to talk to him, they would get back together even though it wasn't what she wanted. But with support from friends, both Greg and Emma eventually cut off contact. What went wrong in the relationship which, at first, was so close?

To get a better understanding, it would help to know the traits of each:
Greg's traits are N+E=O-A- C- Emma's traits are N+E-O-A++C=

The results of this combination of traits are easy to see in this relationship. The initial strong mutual dependency which caused both enjoyment and difficulties in the relationship was due to the high emotionality from the two N+s. The high Need for Stability within the relationship also led to arguments characterized by hot tempers and strong emotions whenever conflict arrived. With respect to O, both of them appreciated the same low level of Originality; however, their difficulty accepting change probably led them to stay in an unsatisfactory relationship for so long because it was comfortable. One of the reasons Emma (O-) worried about getting back together with Greg after their final break-up was that she knew how difficult it would be for her to follow through with such a drastic change in her life. Perhaps the most notable combination in their relationship was the contrast of scores on the Accommodation scale, which resulted in several problems. While Greg (A-) welcomed conflict, Emma (A++) shied away from it, giving into Greg's wants and needs and letting hers get overlooked. As a result, she neglected her friends to be with his, and she didn't speak up for herself when she was unhappy with Greg and his actions. This lack of communication caused Greg to believe that Emma was happy with the existing relationship while, in truth, she was angry and resented him but held it in to prevent more fights. Thus, when she would break up with him, he thought it was a spontaneous, emotional decision and used his assertiveness to talk her back into continuing the relationship.

Fortunately, both have started to move on and are less stressed without the strain of the relationship; however, if both had understood the inherent traits of the other, they might have been able to employ strategies such as counting to 10 before speaking when angry or by trying to allot specific amounts of time in a conversation for each to talk about a topic of one's choice. It proved futile to stay in the relationship and hoping that things would get better without implementing such strategies. As much as you may try, you cannot truly change your natural traits. For any relationship—friend, family, romantic, or otherwise, it is important to accept this limitation.

Relationship Case Study #4: Chris and Katherine

Contributed by Emily Crowder, UNC-Chapel Hill student and CentACS Research Intern

Chris and Katherine have been dating for over two years. They have very few arguments, and even when they are upset with one another, neither has ever yelled at the other. In fact, Chris has never even seen Katherine get really mad. Her parents find this funny because whenever they play tennis, cards, putt-putt golf, or other games, she gets angry if she's not doing well. She never gets as worked up around Chris because he always calms her down when she starts to get frustrated. When Chris gets upset, he tends to hold it in and has a hard time expressing what's on his mind even though he knows he should talk about it to Katherine. Fortunately, Katherine understands when this happens and tries to find out what's wrong without being too pushy.

When they first started dating, their biggest problem was making decisions. Neither of them would voice what they wanted to do because they are typically fine doing whatever the other wants. While this is still a small problem, they have both agreed that they will speak up when they have a strong preference for something. They tend to do the same activities on dates, but lately they've been trying to find new options. In their relationship, Chris is typically the planner. He likes to know what they are doing ahead of time and when to be there, but she is more flexible and willing to change plans. He often plans group outings like dinner or ice cream with friends, but lately he has been frustrated that Katherine tends to always be beside him at these gatherings. Though he enjoys being around her, he wants the chance to just talk to his friends for a little bit. He doesn't want to tell her about his annoyance because he doesn't want her to take it the wrong way and doesn't think it's worth risking the conflict to discuss it.

Here are their traits: Chris: N-E=O-A+C+ Katherine: N=E=O=A+C-
How their traits affect the relationship:

Their lack of arguments is attributed to two personality traits: Need for Stability (N) and Accommodation (A). As one is a resilient and one is a responsive, neither of them tends to get angry quickly. This pairing of lower tempers leads to few fights and no yelling, as neither tends to be overly emotional. When Katherine would normally be upset around others, she remains calm around Chris whose lower N steadies her and helps relax her. Chris, on the other hand, has a hard time expressing his anger because of his higher A, which makes it hard for him to speak up. Knowing this, Katherine, who is also high in A, tries not to push him into an explanation, but she still wants to know what's wrong. The high Accommodation of the two also contributes to fewer fights because both dislike arguing and tend to submit to the other's needs. When they do get upset, they don't stay mad because their desire for harmony encourages them to apologize.

In addition to their management of disagreements, their high Accommodation levels make it hard for them to make decisions. Neither wants to voice a preference that would conflict with the other's, so both try to defer to the other's desire, which results in slow decision making. Fortunately, their new agreement on speaking up should help both to feel more comfortable stating opinions. Their repetition of dates is due to Chris's lower score on Originality, which makes it unnatural for him to think of and embrace new ideas. Chris's higher Consolidation score and his slightly higher Sociability score (E2) tend to make him the planner, as he is comfortable with more people at times and is uncomfortable being spontaneous. While interacting with these groups, a new problem has arrived. Katherine's lower Sociability and higher Need for Stability scores make her more dependent on Chris in social situations. In order to overcome this new obstacle, Chris needs to find a way to carefully express his feelings to Katherine. Another possibility could be for them to do something for just the two of them together before the gathering, so that Katherine might be a bit more willing to venture away from Chris's side later.

Relationship Case Study #5: Anna and the Queen of Math—a Teacher/Student Case

Contributed by Emily Crowder, UNC-Chapel Hill student and CentACS Research Intern

Anna was very nervous when she entered her junior-year high school math class for the first time. Not only was her class rumored to be the hardest math class at the school, but she feared her new teacher. Mrs. Cannon had been teaching at the school for over 10 years and was one of the best math teachers; however, she was best known to students as someone who would get mad and yell when she saw them doing inappropriate, sometimes stupid things. Likewise, she was not reputed to be very warm and enthusiastic, which was another uncertainty to the usually smiling Anna. For the first half of the year, Anna dreaded math. She feared Mrs. Cannon's getting angry with her, and she also had difficulty with the math material. As hard as she tried, she could not understand the complex problems that seemed so easy to Mrs. Cannon and other classmates. Although she was struggling, she wouldn't ask questions out of embarrassment. If someone asked a basic question, Mrs. Cannon would respond with, "My five year-old granddaughter can do that in her head." While Mrs. Cannon didn't find this harsh, others would be embarrassed or would avoid asking another question out of fear that they would receive the same response. In addition to these habits, Mrs. Cannon's intolerance for chit-chat, preference to get the lesson started on time, and low display of warm emotions made her hard to read and to get to know.

Eventually, Anna realized that the only way for her to keep up with the complex material was to get individual tutoring from Mrs. Cannon. Anna was worried at first that Mrs. Cannon would be upset with Anna's widespread confusion, but Mrs. Cannon encouraged her to try the problems she found difficult in order to address her issues. With Mrs. Cannon's willing help, Anna's math grade greatly improved, and she became more comfortable with her teacher. Outside of class, Mrs. Cannon welcomed more questions and was willing to take more time to work through difficulties. And as Anna and the rest of the students got to know her, she didn't seem as harsh. They began to understand that when she wrote "SHAME" over one of their incorrect answers she was trying to both point out an error and make it somewhat comical. Once the class had made it through the majority of the syllabus, she began to joke around with them more. As the students began to both like and respect her, they still made sure that they didn't act out of line because they knew she would be upset and would not hesitate to confront the students. The following year, she taught many of the same students, including Anna. By then, Anna understood that Mrs. Cannon was not as uncaring as she had once seemed. She knew that, in class, her teacher was intimidating, even scary, and it was not a good idea to joke around or waste time with lots of questions. But outside of the class, Mrs. Cannon was very welcoming to any questions that students had and took time to get to know her students.

This grizzly/teddy routine (being tough in one situation and nice and nourishing in another) can be difficult for others to follow; however, if we look at the traits of both student and teacher, we can find some explanation.

Mrs. Cannon's traits are: N=E=O=A=C=
Subtraits: N2+E1- -E2-O2++A2-

Anna's traits are: N-E=O-A+C+
Subtraits: N2-E1+E2=O2-A2++

(Case Study #5, continued)

Though Anna generally tends to be calmer and more of a Resilient, the reputation of her math teacher, plus Anna's past difficulties with math, were enough to make her worry about the coming school year. Mrs. Cannon was known for her temper, which is shown in her high N2 (Intensity) level. Also contributing to her intimidating reputation was her very low E1 (Warmth) level, which explains her general coolness
and aloofness. These two of Mrs. Cannon's traits helped contribute to Anna's worry. With Anna's high Accommodation level (A+), she was extremely uncomfortable with Mrs. Cannon's raising her voice in class, which Anna perceived as conflict. The contrast of Anna and Mrs. Cannon's O2 (Complexity) scores caused some issues as well. Anna, who is O2-, had a hard time understanding the complexity of the mathematics equations as easily as Mrs. Cannon (O2++) could. This, plus Anna's hesitation to speak up and ask questions (A+), made it difficult for her to keep up with the material. Mrs. Cannon's low Sociability (E2-) also made it difficult for Anna to get to know her teacher the first of the year and grow more comfortable because there was little time for chit-chat.

However, outside of class, Mrs. Cannon didn't seem as driven. Because there was no lesson plan for tutoring, she was willing to take time and answer specific questions. Yet in class, she wanted to make it through the lesson and was less patient with time-consuming questions. This contrast of focus levels helps demonstrate her mid Consolidation (C) score. After class, Anna got to know Mrs. Cannon better, which made her more comfortable in the classroom. Before, Anna had misunderstood Mrs. Cannon's behavior and traits. For instance, when Mrs. Cannon replied, "My five-year-old granddaughter can do that in her head," she didn't think that others would take it offensively because she tended not to worry or be as sensitive as others. Similarly, Anna had thought that Mrs. Cannon was too confrontational, but she began to understand that Mrs. Cannon only confronted people when she was enforcing discipline. With this new understanding, Mrs. Cannon and her students were able to form a bond, and she became one of their favorite teachers. They enjoyed watching her scorn and scare the younger students who were causing trouble outside the room, only to return to the classroom laughing. And though it took a while to understand her, it is this grizzly/teddy routine that perhaps makes Mrs. Cannon such a successful teacher. With her "grizzly" side, she demands discipline and that her students listen and do their best to avoid silly mistakes. But with her "teddy" side, she gives them the help and support they need to push through their difficulties and insecurities to comprehend the mathematics challenges.

Also note that with her midrange score on every supertrait, Mrs. Cannon could readily display behaviors on both ends of the spectrum; so it was hard to know what to expect from her. In one situation, she might display the "grizzly" behavior on one end of the spectrum, while in another setting she might behave in an opposite manner, such as returning to the classroom laughing after scolding students in the hallway.

24

The Big Five Paying Your Way

How Traits Affect Career Choice and Job Performance

> We are in the midst of an epidemic of work-life unreadiness because an alarming number of emerging adults are unable to find a good fit between their minds and their career directions. Like seabirds mired in an oil spill, these fledgling men and women are stuck, unable to take flight toward a suitable career. Some are crippled before they have a chance to beat their wings; others have tumbled downward in the early stages of their trajectories. Because they are not finding their way, they may feel as if they are going nowhere and have nowhere to go.
>
> --Mel Levine, *Ready or Not, Here Life Comes* (2005, p.4)

Guide to This Chapter:

- Defining the Landscape of Career
- The Typical Process for Selecting a Career
- The Importance of Keeping Your Options Open
- Formulating a Personal Career Mission Statement, or Shaping One's Niche, or Finding the Statue Within
- The Ingredients of Bliss: Work Objects, Traits, Abilities, Roles, Content, Work Attributes, and Values
- Two Important Career Resources: The 12 Career Competencies and the O*NET
- The 19 Most Common Causes of Career Derailment and How to Avoid Them

Like Michelangelo, who believed that every stone had a hidden figure, or statue, within, and that the artist's task was to chip away irrelevant material in order to reveal the statue, our task in this chapter is to lay the groundwork for every individual to find their optimal career by removing the irrel-

The Big Five and Major Life Choices

N	E	O	A	C
Need for Stability	**Extraversion**	**Originality**	**Accommodation**	**Consolidation**
N+ Reactive	E+ Extraverted	O+ Explorer	A+ Adapter	C+ Focused
N= Responsive	E= Ambiverted	O= Moderate	A= Negotiator	C= Balanced
N- Resilient	E- Introverted	O- Preserver	A- Challenger	C- Flexible
N1: Worry	E1: Approach Level	O1: Imagination	A1: Service	C1:Thoroughness
N2: Temper	E2: Group Orientation	O2: Range of Interests	A2: Compliance	C2: Structure
N3: Outlook	E3: Pace	O3: Innovation	A3: Humility	C3: Ambition
N4: Coping Level	E4: Leadership	O4: Zoom Scale	A4: Speak Out Level	C4: Concentration
	E5: Trust			C5: Methodicalness
	E6: Tact			

evant behaviors and focusing on the core. Dr. Mel Levine (1994, 2005, 2006), noted Professor of Pediatrics at the University of North Carolina at Chapel Hill, makes a plea in the above quote for society to take the time to facilitate young people in finding their career within. A suitable metaphor for this internal statue is the popular Renaissance word "niche," which referred to a recess, usually in a wall, door, or tower, that was shaped to contain a statue of a specific shape. Not just any statue would fit within a niche, only one that conformed to the dimensions of the recess intended for it. Similarly, each of us must find our own career "niche," the career that conforms to the shape of our traits, abilities, values, and experiences. Throughout this book, we have expanded on a variety of ways to define oneself. In this chapter, we will hone in specifically on how to define oneself with respect to the kind of lifework that accepts, recognizes, and values the unique constellation of qualities that we bring to the world of work. As we wrote in the previous chapter on selecting a mate, selecting a career must take into account our qualities. These qualities will not change—they will not bend to adapt to the constraints of an ill-chosen niche. As we quoted McCrae and Costa (2003) earlier—and it bears repeating—choosing a career

> depend[s] on the knowledge that our basic motives and styles will endure....*We choose and create environments that will reinforce our dispositions*; regardless of the reasons, stability is a fact we must and do count on (p. 218). [italics ours]

Defining the Landscape of Career

So, we begin at the beginning, with definitions. What is a career? The word comes from the Latin *carrus* for "car" and also from the medieval Latin *carraria* for a "road for vehicles." Hence the common phrase "career path" has evolved. It is the road we travel in the world of work. We are the car. We must know our car's limitations and potentials and strengths, and select the road that best suits us. All the metaphors! Niche, statue within, road for vehicles....The abundance of images for describing one's career is testimony to its importance.

Career needs to be understood on different levels, from the more general to the more specific. Accordingly, we can create a taxonomy, an organizational chart, by identifying four levels of career:

- **Work Objects**. At its most general level, career deals with four kinds of work objects: people, things, ideas, and data. We all have to work with each of these four work objects—for example, a police officer must deal with people, must operate equipment and other things, must develop strategies and ideas for effective neighborhood policing, and must analyze reports and data to identify significant patterns. Every career entails some degree of involvement with all four of these work objects. But some careers emphasize one or two over the others. As we will see later in this chapter, our traits guide our preference for these four work objects. Our preference is for working with ideas, yet we cannot ignore the other three. Later in this chapter, we will identify a resource for identifying the fields that are associated with specific work objects (the O*NET).

- **Field**. Now we get a little more specific: One's field is the technical specialty, the body of knowledge, that one commits to studying, mastering, and keeping up with for a lifetime, or at least for the duration of one's career. Each work object is associated with hundreds of different fields. Knowing one's work object preference helps to narrow one's selection of field. For example, if one's preference is for working with things, then one doesn't consider the field of philosophy. Or if one's preference is for working with ideas, then one doesn't consider the field of auto mechanics. Surely, auto mechanics entails some degree of working with ideas (e.g., wrestling with aerodynamic principles and issues of efficiency), and philosophy entails some degree of working with things (e.g., using machinery to illustrate philosophical principles), but ideas are not the primary focus of auto mechanics, just as things are not the primary focus of philosophy.
- **Specialty**. Choosing one's field is typically not specific enough. One needs to study one's field, and then home in on a specialty within that field. For example, one might choose medicine as a field, and then pediatrics as a specialty within medicine. Persons who are higher in O normally select multidisciplinary specialties such as pediatric cardiology or pediatric neurology, while those lower in O will be more prone to take a single specialty and refine it even more, as in a pediatric orthopedic specialist who treats the wrist.
- **Role**. This is where the pedal hits the metal, where the rubber meets the road. Oh no, more metaphors! This is the most specific way of defining a career: the role in which one practices a specialty. Edgar Schein (1993) has identified eight such roles, which he calls "career anchors," the sort of style that provides you stability, hence an anchor, in your specialty. In the definitions below, we provide an example of how each of his eight roles might express itself in the specialty of pediatric medicine.

    1. **Technical:** being an expert in one's chosen skill area, success associated with being perceived as highly knowledgeable/skilled (examples: medical school pediatrics professor, pediatric medicine researcher, medical writer/illustrator for a pediatrics journal)
    2. **Managerial:** being responsible for leading others towards successful goal attainment, sense of success tied to the organization (example: chief medical officer in a pediatric hospital or clinic)
    3. **Autonomy:** able to do things one's own way, on one's own terms; success comes from achieving independence (example: pediatrician in private practice, pediatrics medical research with an organization that permits self-direction)
    4. **Security:** achieving predictability and stability in employment and income in exchange for loyalty to the employer, success associated with feeling needed by the organization (example: pediatric physician attached to a clinic for military dependents)
    5. **Entrepreneurial:** building one's own business/organization from zero to a point of financial success, success associated with using one's ability to build an organization (example:

starting a pediatric treatment and/or research hospital with a unique mission and an aim towards franchising nationally or globally)

6. **Service:** making a contribution to a cause, a community, or some other entity; success associated with sensing that one's work makes a difference for someone (examples: pediatric medical missionary, pediatrician in a public health clinic, spending one week a year volunteering in third world nations on health problems)
7. **Challenge:** overcoming complex circumstances in order to beat out the competition, success associated with the challenge—if it's easy and repetitious, it is boring and not challenging (example: pediatrician on a research team trying to be first to bring a new treatment, drug, or other child-oriented therapy to market)
8. **Lifestyle:** flexibility to balance work and personal life, success associated with perceiving self as a whole person, not one-sided (examples: pediatricians practicing medicine but also teaching and writing about pediatrics, coaching kids' soccer, enjoying hobbies, etc.)

Each of these roles is associated with its own pattern of trait scores, as we shall see later in this chapter when we present a process for zeroing in on one's career choice. So, we have now defined what we mean by a career: performing a role in a specialty that is in a field that focuses on one's preferred work objects. While this logical approach to defining one's career is relatively easy to describe and also relatively easy to identify for each individual, we shall see later in this chapter that it leaves out an important aspect of career—the feeling in your gut that you are passionate about what you are doing, that you could go on doing it forever with little chance of tiring, much less burnout. Research suggests that one begins to feel these passions—and most of us have many more than just one passion—before we reach age 10 and certainly by the time we enter college. These passions are such that their expression can change but their nature doesn't.

For example, I (Jane) wanted to sing and act on Broadway in New York City from a very young age. Since I am naturally calm and rational under stress (N-), comfortable taking charge (E4+), curious and imaginative about others' lives/emotions/work/feelings (O+), naturally comfortable being in front of or presenting to others (A4-), and somewhat ambitious (C3=), I thought my career choice was clear. Yet my practical (O-) parents, who had gotten married in 1932 during the Great Depression, urged caution and pushed me toward becoming a teacher. My undergraduate degree in education and my teaching in a classroom for three years showed me that I could do it. Yet, I wasn't passionate about it (probably not high enough in E and A). Having worked in an office to help put myself through college and in my dad's office in high school, it slowly came to me that I enjoyed the business world. Before shifting to the training and consulting field in 1982, I worked as a manager of the education department at an arts center. By the time I had my MBA and Pierce and I launched our company in 1986, it was clear to me that combining business and education has become my passion. I relish helping a client work through a problem rationally. I am energized by explaining personality traits during a training program by acting them out in front of the class. I become most engaged when I need to come up with an example on the spot in response to a client's question. My motivation to write (e.g., this book) is to help others learn to figure out themselves in relation to others so that they can be as satisfied in their careers as I have become. I was sidetracked at times between 1996 and 2008 when I handled the day-to-day management of our company. Now that we have another partner who does that well, I am free to be more of my natural self in my career.

For another example, when I (Pierce) was in junior high school (we didn't have middle schools back then), I knew in my gut that I wanted to be a preacher when I grew up. What that meant was that I had a passion for being helpful, for providing insights to others, for promoting health and happiness in the world. To a 16-year-old, that meant training to become a preacher in a church. Now, at age 69, it means conducting research on personality and the brain and finding ways to disseminate information and insight—by writing books, making speeches, blogging, conducting online and face-to-face training sessions. From preacher to researcher/teacher, but both of them based on the same passion, a kind of evangelical zeal for some way of helping others learn. My kind of helping. In the last section of Chapter 20, we summarized the approach of the Attwoods in identifying one's passions.

The Typical Process for Selecting a Career

Eli Ginzburg describes three stages of career exploration that each of us tends to go through, beginning in elementary school and culminating in high school or during the undergraduate or graduate school years. First comes *fantasy*, followed by a *tentative* stage, and finally landing in the *realistic* stage. Doesn't every child at some point want to be a fire chief (or at least a firefighter!), or to be an Olympic star, or to be president of the United States (hmmm, U.S. President Bill Clinton had this fantasy as a child, especially after shaking hands with President John F. Kennedy—turned out that his fantasy made it all the way to reality). These fantasies of our youth are subject to the tests of two significant criteria: interest and ability. As we get to know the ins and outs of a particular career—whether through internships, reading, exposure in the community, or by bumping up against the reality of a career's everyday demands while actually employed—we come face to face with whether we 1) are really interested in living that kind of life and 2) whether we sense that we have the ability to master the demands of the career. Just to be interested, or passionate, about a career is not enough, we must also have the ability to perform to the satisfaction, not only of others' standards, but of our own standards. Growing up in my (Pierce's) hometown of Kinston in eastern North Carolina, I heard the story of a bright young man whose lawyer-father wanted him to become a doctor. Ely Perry, Jr., completed his medical degree, only to turn it over to his father with the comment, "Well here's my diploma, and I hope that satisfies you." Ely Junior went on to be a successful farmer, then later joined his two lawyer brothers in their real estate development business. Ely Junior's brother, Dan Perry (2008, pp. 175 ff.), has documented this story in his book, *More Than I Deserve* (Chapel Hill Press). Here was a clear case of a man who had the ability (he got his degree and his license), but who lacked the interest—no fire in the belly, no passion for medicine and all that it entailed. It all has to match up: ability and interest, skill and passion, competence and traits/values.

Progressing from the fantasy stage to the reality stage requires testing one's fantasy against the real world. Four out of five high school students embrace the goal of some day being a "professional"—doctor, lawyer, architect, professor, scientist... The traditional definition of a professional involves a career that requires an advanced degree. I (Pierce) recall my first day as a freshman at Davidson College. The Dean of Students told 300 of us: "Two out of three of you freshmen have indicated that you want to be doctors, that you plan to major in pre-med. By the time you graduate, that will be one out of three." That is testament to either a deficit in ability or interest: lack of ability and you fail the tests in spite of your interest, and lack of interest where you simply don't put in the hours required to make sufficiently high grades to get accepted into medical school. Passion and ability. Some of these freshmen had moved from the fantasy of wanting to be a doctor to the tentative phase of committing to a pre-med major. Reality in the form of demanding coursework was to clarify that this path was not for them.

Progress through the three stages is governed by the tension between the things we enjoy and the things we're good/natural at, such that we should ideally, either abandon interests not supported by ability or try gaining ability to support our interest and see if it is forthcoming. The ways to test one's interest and/or to discover/test one's ability are actually the same. Parents and teachers/counselors can help youth clarify their interests and abilities by suggesting, offering, and supporting activities that develop knowledge, attitude, and skills associated with a particular career. For example, a child wishing to be an architect could visit worksites, collect postcards of famous buildings, draw sketches of buildings or cityscapes, keep a drawings notebook, read biographies of architects (e.g., for book reports), play with architecture-oriented toys/games from the more simple (Legos) to the more complex (a model railroad landscaping kit), take relevant courses in school or online (math, drawing, computer applications), subscribe to an architecture-oriented magazine, start a library of book and other resources, be encouraged to design and execute home improvement projects, design a science project that demonstrates the geometry behind the Roman and Greek arches, collect and digest all the work of David Macaulay, develop a collection of tools for making scale models and drawings, intern with architecture and engineering firms, plan family vacations around visiting outstanding architectural examples (read about them in advance, and make drawings of them while viewing), watch DVDs as a family on the work of famous architects, and so forth.

One career blinder some people must deal with is a parent's desire for a child to follow in the footsteps of a parent. In fact, fewer children wish to do this than might be apparent. Studies show (McCrae and Costa, 2000, p. 44) that not even one in five teens wishes or expects to pursue the same career as either of their parents. Sometimes the parents urge the child to follow in a career or become an employee in the family business in order to inherit it in the future, and sometimes a child accepts the mantle willingly, eagerly. With so many of us wishing to find new paths unlike our parents' and the ongoing evolution of technology that gives rise to new career options, it underlines the importance of internships and other opportunities for observing role models for our careers of interest. Joseph Campbell, the originator of the "follow your bliss" mantra for career exploration, writes (1991, p. 193): "I did go into business with Dad for a couple of months, and then I thought, 'Geez, I can't do this.' And he let me go. There is that testing time in your life when you have got to test yourself out to your own flight." In further explaining the importance of knowing one's traits, abilities, values, and interests , plus the importance of finding a good fit between them and one's life work, Campbell urges against blindly, rationally following parents' or others' expectations for one:

> Consciousness thinks it's running the shop. But it's a secondary organ of a total human being, and it must not put itself in control. It must submit and serve the humanity of the body. When it does put itself in control, you get a man like Darth Vader in *Star Wars,* the man who goes over to the consciously intentional dark side....If the person insists on a certain program, and doesn't listen to the demands of his own heart, he's going to risk a schizophrenic crackup. Such a person has put himself off center. He has aligned himself with a program for life, and it's not the one the body's interested in at all. The world is full of people who have stopped listening to themselves or have listened only to their neighbors to learn what they ought to do, how they ought to behave, and what the values are that they should be living for. (p. 181)

The Importance of Keeping Your Options Open

In a stark conclusion from examining the factors associated with readiness for college work, a report released in 2008 by ACT, Inc., called *The Forgotten Middle* stated that "Students who leave eighth grade without the essential skills they need to be on target for college and career readiness too often leave high school not ready for any kind of meaningful future." The report goes on to detail the "essential skills," but suffice it to say that the middle school years must produce ninth graders who are proficient writers, who have mastered the mathematics required that will lead them to taking calculus later, who are well on their way to proficiency in at least one foreign language, who have mastered the basic principles of scientific investigation, and who know the basics of world history and geography. This means that middle school is not the time to coast, putting off rigorous learning until high school. Middle school should be as serious and effortful as the practice before a concert. Otherwise, a casual approach to learning in middle school may well lead to an unsatisfying performance in senior high.

> "I've never done a single thing I've wanted to in my whole life! I don't knows I've accomplished anything except just get along....But I do get a kind of sneaking pleasure out of the fact that you knew what you wanted to do and did it. Well, those folks in there will try to bully you, and tame you down. Tell 'em to go to the devil! I'll back you. Take your factory job, if you want to. Don't be scared of the family. No, nor all of Zenith. Nor of yourself, the way I've been. Go ahead, old man! The world is yours!"
>
> --Father to son in Sinclair Lewis's novel, *Babbitt*

To take middle school seriously is to keep one's options open. One doesn't need to know one's career of choice in the seventh grade (unless one lives in Mexico and must select a career interest at a young age in order to attend the appropriate school), but one does need to know one's abc's. It is the academic equivalent of being in good shape physically: running, lifting weights, eating well, sleeping properly—all these keep the body honed, so that one is ready once a preference becomes apparent for what to do with one's body, be it basketball, skiing, or track and field. The same is true for the mind: Learn reading, writing, arithmetic, science, and history, regardless of whether one will at a future point choose medicine, architecture, police work, or social work. All too often, when we make a choice of career, we find that we have omitted critical preparation. When that is the case, we either must abandon our choice or backtrack and make up the work we opted out of earlier. My (Pierce's) major regret along this line of reasoning is that I never took calculus. I have since read a textbook on the subject, but it is not the same that it would have been if I had taken calculus as a teen and been able to integrate it into my last 40 years of professional life.

Formulating a Personal Career Mission Statement, or Shaping One's Niche, or Finding the Statue Within

Moving from *fantasy* to the *tentative* phase of career exploration involves two steps:

1. **Identify the elements**, or raw materials, that comprise your core personality, and
2. Organize these elements/raw materials into the final product: **Write your personal career mission statement**.

The first step involves making a long list, while the second leads to writing a brief paragraph/essay that pulls together in one place all of the traits, abilities, values, and experiences that you want a career to build on, and even those that you want to make sure to avoid! In the following section, we provide a framework for identifying the elements, and then in the next section, we will present a step-by-step process for writing your mission statement. These two steps are similar to the writer's process of making an outline and then writing the story, essay, or book.

The Ingredients of Bliss: Work Objects, Traits, Abilities, Roles, Content, Work Attributes, and Values

Joseph Campbell (1991) writes passionately about the need for each individual to define their own uniqueness and to build a career around that uniqueness. He contrasts this process with the traditional career paths of Asia (and much of the West):

> This, I believe, is the great Western truth: that each of us is a completely unique creature and that, if we are ever to give any gift to the world, it will have to come out of our own experience and fulfillment of our own potentialities, not someone else's. In the traditional Orient, on the other hand, and generally in all traditionally grounded societies, the individual is cookie-molded. His duties are put upon him in exact and precise terms, and there's no way of breaking out from them. When you go to a guru to be guided on the spiritual way, he knows just where you are..., just where you have to go next.... That wouldn't be a proper Western pedagogical way of guidance. We have to give our students guidance in developing their own pictures of themselves. What each must seek in his life never was, on land or sea. It is to be something out of his own unique potentiality for experience, something that never has been and never could have been experienced by anyone else.... Hamlet's problem was that he wasn't [up to his imposed destiny]. He was given a destiny too big for him to handle, and it blew him to pieces (pp. 186-7).

In order to avoid the cookie cutter approach, we must, in fact, search for the cookie cutter that fits us! Cookie cutters are not intrinsically bad for career planning—they are only bad when we select a cookie cutter that doesn't match our niche, our design within the stone. Another metaphor that Campbell uses in talking about our core inner qualities is the concept of the "force" in the film *Star Wars*. Here, Campbell is in dialog with Bill Moyers (from the Public Broadcasting System series the book is based one):

> Moyers: The voice of Ben Kenobi says to Skywalker in the climactic moment of the last fight, "Turn off your computer, turn off your machine and do it yourself, follow your feelings, trust your feelings." And when he did, he achieved success, and the audience broke out into applause.
>
> Campbell: When Ben Kenobi says, "May the Force be with you," he's speaking of the power and energy of life, not of programmed political intentions.
>
> Moyers: I was intrigued by the definition of the Force. Ben Kenobi says, "The Force is an energy field created by all living things. It surrounds us, it penetrates us, it binds the galaxy together (pp. 178-179).

So our personal, unique constellation of traits, abilities, physical characteristics, values, and experiences is our force, and we must know it and build on it. In this section we will guide you through the process of estimating each of these elements so that you might build your career mission statement. Actually, our Center for Applied Cognitive Studies has an assessment that you can take—the SchoolPlace Big Five Profile™—and therefrom receive a 30+ page report with all of this information spelled out. If you would like to receive this report you can contact a Certified CentACS Big Five Consultant in your area. Go to our website, www.centacs.com, to find a consultant to assist you.

Here, we simply invite you to estimate what these results would be. We call this report the Career Guider Report, and it serves the purpose much like what Campbell and Moyer refer to as "Ariadne's thread":

> Moyers: "Theseus says to Ariadne, 'I'll love you forever if you can show me a way to come out of the labyrinth.' So she gives him a ball of string, which he unwinds as he goes into the labyrinth, and then follows to find the way out. You say, "All he had was the string. That's all you need.... Sometimes we look for great wealth to save us, a great power to save us, or great ideas to save us, when all we need is that piece of string...."
>
> Campbell: "That's not always easy to find. But it's nice to have someone who can give you a clue. That's the teacher's job, to help you find your Ariadne thread.... All a teacher can do is suggest. He is like a lighthouse that says, '"There are rocks over here, steer clear. There is a channel, however, out there.'" (p. 185)

Accordingly, one by one, let us build the thread of Ariadne for you or someone close to you, as a way to find your path and avoid dead ends. For each of the elements that follow in the Personal Career Table of Elements, Table 24.1, we will provide for you the Big Five traits that tend to be associated with them. Some of the elements are not associated with traits, so they will have only definitions. In the far right column, simply indicate whether you want to *build* on that element or to *avoid* it (or to maximize or minimize it). A sample that has been completed by Emily Crowder (in preparation for her Personal Career Mission Statement that you will read in the next section) is included as Appendix B. Now, begin your analysis of your own Personal Career Table of Elements.

The Big Five and Major Life Choices

Table 24.1 Personal Career Table of Elements

Work Objects

Object:	**Definition ("A preference for working with..."):**	**Associated Traits:**	**Value for You:**
People	groups, meetings, interviews, audiences, conversations	E+ A+	
Things	machinery, animals, equipment, supplies, material	E- O-	
Ideas	theories, stories, experiments, problems, planning, decisions	O+	
Data	numbers, spreadsheets, databases, formulas	O-	

Traits

Subtrait:	**Work Characteristics Associated with the Three Levels:** (Leftmost phrase refers to lower levels of the trait, middle phrase to mid level, and rightmost phrase to higher levels of the trait.)	**Pre-ferred Level:**
N1: Worry	Can handle high stress levels, Balance of calm/stress, Low stress levels	
N2: Temper	Can handle high conflict, Balance of conflict/at ease, Low conflict	
N3: Outlook	Need to be optimistic, Balance of opt./pess., Need to be pessimistic	
N4: Coping Level	Can handle crises as way of life, Moderate number of crises, Few crises	
E1: Approach Level	Seldom needs to show enthusiasm, Moderate enth., Constant enth.	
E2: Group Orientation	Usually alone, Balance of others/alone, Always around other people	
E3: Pace	Usually sitting, Balanced sitting/up and about, Usually up and about	
E4: Leadership	Independent, Half/half indep./responsible, Responsible for others	
E5: Trust	Needs to be skeptical, Moderate skepticism, Needs to be trusting	
E6: Tact	Little need to be tactful, Sometimes tactful, Always tactful	
O1: Imagination	No need to be creative, Sometimes creative, Always creative	
O2: Range of Interests	Complexity is uncommon, Moderate complexity, Complexity is con-stant	
O3: Innovation	Change is seldom, Change is occasional, Change is frequent	
O4: Zoom Scale	Work with the details, Half/half, Work with the big picture	
A1: Service	Do your own thing, Half/half, Serve/help others	
A2: Compliance	Stand up to others' demands, Negotiate, Follow others' wishes	
A3: Humility	Needs to show pride, Moderate pride, Needs to show humility	
A4: Speaking Out	Needs to speak mind, Moderate assertiveness, Stays in background	
C1: Thoroughness	Casual about quality, Moderate quality focus, Constant quality focus	
C2: Structure	Organization unimportant, Moderate org., Organization is imperative	
C3: Ambition	Comfortable with status quo, Moderate ambition, Driven to achieve	
C4: Concentration	Multi-tasking, Moderate focus, Focus on a single task at a time	
C5: Methodicalness	Spontaneous, Moderate use of plans, Constantly follow the plan	

Note: Due to space limitations, the middle level (a score between 45 and 55) is often referred to as a "balance" or "half/half" of the two extremes, meaning that the work would require one extreme about half the time, and the other the other half. If you have your SchoolPlace or WorkPlace Big Five Profile 4.0 results, then a score below 45 would be associated with the leftmost level, and a score over 55 with the rightmost level.

Table 24.1 **Personal Career Table of Elements** (cont.)

Abilities

Ability:	Definition:	Want to Build on It?
Auditory	Remembering and discriminating between a variety of sounds	
Visual/Spatial	Reading diagrams, understanding and remembering complex images	
Verbal	Good vocabulary, grammar, composition w one/more languages	
Logical/Math	Working with number systems, symbols, codes, puzzles	
Natural Observer	Working with nomenclatures, biology, taxonomies	
Kinesthetic	Peak physical condition, coordination, and muscle control	
Interpersonal	Managing personal relationships/influencing others (N-E+A=)	
Intrapersonal	Being introspective, perceiving feelings and nonverbal (N+E-O+)	

Roles

Role:	Definition:	Traits:	Important?
Technical	Need to be an expert with reputation of being knowledgeable	N+E-O-A-	
Managerial	Responsible for leading other people and directing the organization	N-E+A-C+	
Autonomy	Being independent of others/bosses and doing things one's own way	N+O+	
Security	Enjoying the promise of lifetime employment; loyalty to employer	O-C+	
Entrepreneurial	Starting and building one's own business to a financial success	N+E-A-C-	
Service	Making a contribution for some cause or entity	E+A+	
Challenge	Overcoming difficult, challenging situations to beat the competition	N-E+A-C+	
Lifestyle	Having flexibility to balance demands of work &personal life	N+A+	

Content, or Occupational Theme (Based on the Holland Hexagon)

Holland Area:	Definition:	Traits:	Important?
Realistic	Physical work, esp. outdoors, with animals, machines, construction, transportation, agriculture, equipment	E-O-	
Investigative	Research, gathering information, reading, study	N-O+	
Artistic	The arts, writing	E+O+	
Social	The helping professions: teaching, counseling, social work	E+O+A+	
Enterprising	Selling, managing	N-E+O-A-C+	
Conventional	Office work: planning, organizing, working with office equipment	O-C+	

Work Attributes (Based on the American College Testing [ACT] Program model)

Attribute:	Definition:	Traits:	Important?
Authority	Similar to management, but towards non-employees, as in a traffic cop job—telling others what to do/not do	E+O+A-C+	

The Big Five and Major Life Choices

Table 24.1 Personal Career Table of Elements (cont.)

(*Work Attributes*, continued)

Certification	Careers certifying competence by a degree, license, etc. (doctor, actuary, realtor)	O-C+	
Creating Order	Using rules to arrange things (quality inspector, administrator)	N-E+C+	
Easy Re-entry	Easy to move, or quit and come back, as after maternity leave (sales, mechanic)	E+O+A-	
Financial Challenge	Advising others so that much could be gained or lost (investment/financial planner)	N-E+O+A-C+	
40-Hour Week	Work that entails no overtime, taking work home, on-call status, etc. (postal clerk, governmental analyst)	O-A+C+	
High Income	To be in the top 25% of money earners (NFL quarterback, executive)	N-E+O+A-C+	
Immediate Response	Working around others where immediate feedback is the norm—applause, laughs, boos, cheers, attaboys, attagirls, handshakes, etc. (comedian, flight attendant)	N+E+O+A-	
Influencing Others	Convincing without authority (sales, counseling, health care, social work)	N-E+O+A-C+	
Making or Fixing Things	Working with your hands or tools on electro-mechanical objects (mechanic, manufacturing work)	N-C+	
Management	Planning, directing, and evaluating the work of others (manager, supervisor, etc.)	N-E+O+A-C+	
New Ideas	Creating new ways to do things—trying new combinations of ideas (advertising, consultant, research and development)	N-E+O+A-	
Non-Standard Hours	Preferring work that is seasonal, temporary, part-time, shifts, etc. (consultant, waiter, tennis/golf pro)	E+O+A-C-	
Occasional Travel	Out-of-town travel about once a quarter (small business owner)	E-O-A+C-	
Physical Activity	Work resulting in significant amount of exercise—walking, lifting, sports (stevedore, chef, park ranger, material handler)	N-E+O+A-C+	
Precision	Work that is done according to exact standards or procedures (assembler, fabricator, lab technician, nurse)	N-E+O-C+	
Problem Solving	Spending time figuring out how to do things, to get things done, to repair things (consultant, R & D, team leader)	N-E+O+A-C+	
Project Work	Tasks lasting one week or longer (project manager, engineer, architect)	N-E+O+C+	
Public Contact	Work in which you can talk and be seen by non-coworkers (customer service, sales, trainer)	N-E+O+A-C+	
Routine Travel	Getting out of the office/town once a week or more (many sales positions, consultant, pilot, flight attendant)	E+O+A-C+	
Short Training Time	Less than 6 months required training after high school (construction work, receptionist, cook)	N+E-O-C-	
Working in an Office	Work most of the time inside, in an office (accountant, writer, banker, lawyer, dentist, telephone sales, administrator)	N+E-O-A+C-	

Table 24.1 **Personal Career Table of Elements** (cont.)

(*Work Attributes*, continued)

Working In/Out	Partially inside and partially outside (material handler, elementary school teacher, coach, baggage handler, external sales)	E+	
Working Outside	Working outdoors in the weather, good or bad (cowpoke, mail delivery, door-to-door sales, park ranger, road construction)	N-E+O+A-C+	
Working Separately	Solitary work that requires little talking or other contact with co-workers (bookkeeper, writer, Internet entrepreneur)	N+E-O-A+C-	

Values

Value:	Definition:	Traits:	Important:
Achievement	Setting goals and attaining them, from writing a book to building a house	C+	
Aesthetics	The pursuit of interests in the visual and/or performing arts	O+	
Affiliation	Having high-quality relationships	E+A+	
Charity	Giving one's material wealth to those in need	A+	
Compassion	Serving those in pain or general need of help	A+	
Creativity	Originating novel ideas or things with utilitarian or entertainment value	O+	
Entertainment	Providing diversion to others for relief from work, stress, or boredom	E+	
Escape	Providing diversion for oneself for relief from work, stress, or boredom	N+	
Family	Furthering the interests and needs of one's family members	A+	
Health	Minimizing disease or death risk through attention to diet, exercise, etc.	C+	
Hedonism	Experiencing pleasure through the five senses	N+E+A-C-	
Learning	Increasing one's own knowledge in one or more domains	O+	
Maintenance	Keeping all of one's possessions/responsibilities in peak condition	O-C+	
Materialism	Maximizing the accumulation of physical possessions; consumerism	N+A-	
Politics	Being involved in pursuit of or execution of an elected office	E+A-	
Position	Having the goal of rising to highest position in one or more hierarchies	A-C+	
Power	Being in control of others' ability to satisfy their needs	E+A-C+	
Professionalism	Being regarded as a role model within one's chosen career	A-C+	
Romance	Creating a mood that promotes or maintains a love relationship	E+A+	
Safety	Minimizing the risk of accidents for self or others	N-E-O-A+C+	
Security	Ensuring a steady, unending supply of resources necessary for survival	N+O-	
Spirituality	Pursuit of non-material goals such as truth, beauty, goodness, or the "Divine"	N-E-O+	

Table 24.1 Personal Career Table of Elements (cont.)

(Values, continued)

Sport	The love of competition and winning, whether athletic or otherwise	E+A-	
Tolerance	Pursuing the social goal of universal mutual acceptance and equality	O+A+	
Wealth	The accumulation of maximum items of financial value	E+A-C+	

Miscellaneous Career Requirements

Category:	**Specifics from These Categories that Your Career Should (or Shouldn't) Involve:**
Physical Characteristics (myopia, allergies, etc.)	
Experiences (features of one's personal history)	
Specific Roles (parent, researcher, teacher, guide)	
Bodies of Knowledge (physics, history, horticulture)	
Other:	
Other:	

Going From Your "Personal Career Table of Elements" to Your "Personal Career Mission Statement"

After having made your entries in the rightmost column of each table above, you can now compose your Personal Career Mission Statement, using the outline suggested in Table 24.2. You can use this outline, or template, for pulling the previous information—your "Table of Elements"—together in a summary sheet. Table 24.2 presents this template in two versions: a blank one (for you to use in beginning to think through your own Personal Career Mission Statement) and a completed one (using the career interests of our research intern, Emily Crowder) for you to review as a sample.

> If you follow your bliss, you put yourself on a kind of track that has been there all the while, waiting for you, and the life that you ought to be living is the one you are living. Wherever you are—if you are following your bliss, you are enjoying that refreshment, that life within you, all the time.
>
> --Joseph Campbell, *The Power of Myth* (1991, p. 113)

Note that the template begins with identifying the work objects and continues with traits, abilities, roles, occupational themes, work attribute preferences, and values. Also note that the mission statement not only identifies the qualities that you want to build on—it also identifies the qualities that you want to avoid! It is important in thinking through a career that you consider what you don't want to do as well as what you want to. To get into a career and find, for example, that it involves extensive proofreading could be discouraging for someone high in O4 (zoom scale, preference for the big picture). It is not that this person wouldn't want to do *any* proofreading, just that they wouldn't want to make it a regular feature of their work.

Once you have a draft of your Personal Career Mission Statement, start sharing it with persons who are in a position to help you a) refine the statement, b) suggest specific jobs or careers that would satisfy all or most of your requirements, and c) help identify the path between here and there (i.e., education, skill, and experience prerequisites). In Appendix B, we have provided you with an example of all three steps of this process as completed by Emily Crowder. First, she completed the detailed checklist that you have just reviewed. This checklist is a way of conducting a thorough self-study for the purpose of identifying the elements of one's passion. Second, she pulled the salient entries from her checklist into a "summary sheet," so that all of the elements of her passion might be captured in one place (this is the same summary sheet you will encounter in Table 24.2). Then Emily composed her Personal Career Mission Statement using the words and phrases in her summary sheet. That's the complete process: self-study, summary, statement, sharing, and landing the position you want.

Table 24.2 Personal Career Mission Statement: a. Blank Template for Summary Sheet, b. Sample Summary Sheet Based on Template, c. Sample Personal Career Mission Statement

a. Blank Template:

I want a career that focuses primarily on the work object(s) ______________________.

I also want to find a career that will build on the following personality traits: ____________

____.

I want a career that will not expect me to exhibit these traits:______________________

____.

I want a career that will build on these abilities that I consider my strengths: ____________

____.

And I want to make sure that the career does not expect me to build on these weaknesses:

____.

The primary role(s) that I want to perform in this career is (are): __________________.

The content(s), or occupational theme(s), I want to build on are __________________, and I would like to avoid ____.

Table 24.2 **Personal Career Mission Statement: a) Blank Template for Summary Sheet, b) Sample Summary Sheet Based on Template, c) Sample Personal Career Mission Statement** (cont.)

I would also like to incorporate these work attribute preferences: ______________________

I want to build on, and accommodate these values: ________________________________.

Finally, I want these miscellaneous characteristics to be taken into consideration: ________

____.

b. Sample Completed Summary Sheet for Personal Career Mission Statement for Emily Crowder

I want a career that focuses primarily on the work object(s) ____People_________________________.

I also want to find a career that will build on the following personality traits: ____Balance of Low/High Stress, Balance of Sociability and Solitude, Helping Others, Moderate Ambition_____________________________.

I want a career that will *not* expect me to exhibit these traits: ____Need to be Skeptical, Solitude, Creativity, Assertiveness, Comfort with Conflict, Spontaneity__________________________.

I want a career that will build on these abilities that I consider my strengths: ____Verbal, Kinesthetic, Interpersonal, and Natural Observer____.

And I want to make sure that the career does *not* expect me to build on these weaknesses: ____ Visual/Spatial, Logical/Mathematical____.

The primary role(s) that I want to perform in this career is (are): ____Security, Lifestyle, and Service.

The content(s), or occupational theme(s), I want to build on are ____Social, Conventional_________ and I would like to avoid ____Realistic, Enterprising_______________________.

I would also like to incorporate these work attribute preferences: ____Easy Re-entry, Problem Solving, Creating Order, Project Work, Working In/Outside______________________________.

I want to build on, and accommodate, these values: ____Affiliation, Compassion, Family, Achievement, Security____.

Finally, I want these miscellaneous characteristics to be taken into consideration: ______Serve as a Guide to Others, Motion Sickness____.

c. Sample Personal Career Mission Statement Based on the Information in the Preceding Summary Sheet

"My ideal career would focus on people in a way that expresses my interests in social and conventional work. My career should allow me to have a balanced lifestyle along with security and a sense of service to others. I prefer a work style that involves problem solving, organizing, easy re-entry, and hopefully working both in and outside. I would like to build on my interpersonal, kinesthetic, and natural observer abilities in a job that recognizes my values of compassion, family, achievement, and security."

The purpose of composing the Personal Career Mission Statement is not to hang it on your wall. The purpose is to begin showing it to people in your social network—teachers, family members, religious leaders, counselors, employers, and friends—and to invite them to suggest careers that would be most likely to build on your preferences while avoiding your aversions. Then, as you begin to hear suggestions that make sense to you, you can try to move them from the *tentative* to the *realistic* phase by learning more about them through internships, employment, reading, touring, and so forth. Your goal is to identify at least one career that will allow you to build on your strengths and not expect you to be accountable for your weaknesses or aversions. Once you have settled on a career that meets your criteria, you can then begin asking appropriate persons how best to get started preparing for that career: what education is necessary, what experiences, what credentials, what career path they have followed, and so forth.

Two Important Career Resources: The 12 Career Competencies and the O*NET

The National Occupational Information Coordinating Committee (NOICC), a federal government interagency committee charged with monitoring, consolidating, and making accessible career planning resources, has published a series of handbooks for student career planning. These handbooks come in four versions: one each for elementary school students, middle/junior high school, high school, and post high school. Simply doing a online search for "NOICC" or "National Career Development Guidelines" will lead you a variety of websites that provide information on the handbooks. The core of their work is a set of career competencies for each student level, elementary through post secondary. These competencies have been endorsed by many professional associations and educational agencies, and they are extremely helpful in planning career guidance programs.

Another major resource for career exploration is a project of the U. S. Department of Labor called the O*NET (for occupational network). Based on the inputs of thousands of occupational specialists, this Internet resource enables the career planner to explore thousands of specific jobs with respect to their requirements and characteristics—what traits are important, what abilities are important, what specific daily activities are associated with the job, and so forth. It is beyond the scope of this book to go into detail about the contents of this enormous, and helpful, database, but we urge you to go to the website at http://online.onetcenter.org and to begin gaining proficiency in using it.

The 19 Most Common Causes of Career Derailment, and How to Avoid Them

The Center for Creative Leadership, headquartered in Greensboro, North Carolina, has identified 19 behavioral tendencies that can derail a person in mid-career. These derailers are listed and defined in Table 24.3. Each of the 19 derailers is associated with a Big Five infrastructure that predisposes a person towards a specific derailer. For example, too much partying could "derail" a student in his/her school career and lead to grades too poor to get into the higher schooling or employment of his/her choice. The trait "infrastructure" associated with "too much partying" would be E+C-, or an outgoing, energetic person who is spontaneous. That is not to say that every E+C- student will party too much and not accomplish his/her goals. It is just to say that an E+C- student needs to be aware of such natural leanings and resist them as appropriate. Each of the 19 derailers listed below has its own set of traits. In the far right column, there is a space for you to indicate whether or not any one of the 19 should be of a concern to you, either because your trait profile matches the profile for that derailer or simply because of your knowledge of your tendencies. For each derailer that you consider to be a potential threat in your future career, it would behoove you to do some thinking and planning around how you might offset the threat, so that it does not occur and prevent you from attaining your goals. For each threat, determine which traits are the primary source of the threat, and plan accordingly. While this research was done with managers/leaders in mind, certainly most of these derailers apply to non-managerial careers as well.

Table 24.3 **The 19 Derailers**

Derailer:	Definition for This Derailment Risk:	Associated Traits:	Concern?
Arrogant	Excessive pride in one's work, failure to recognize others	E-A-C+	
Betrayal of Trust	Indiscriminate release of what should be private information	A-C-	
Blocked Personal Learner	Resistance to keeping up with new developments and technology	O-A-	
Defensiveness	Failure to take responsibility, preference for blaming others	N+O-A-	
Failure to Build a Team	Allowing a team to develop as individuals with little emphasis on subordinating individual needs to those of the team	E-A-C-	
Failure to Staff Effectively	Staffing with clones of oneself rather than keeping an eye on the unique needs of specific positions	Extremes*	
Insensitive to Others	Failure to acknowledge, accept, and constructively deal with the needs of others	N+A-	
Key Skill Deficiencies	Failure to hone skills to increasing levels of quality, comfort with the status quo with respect to skill level	C-	
Lack of Composure	Losing one's cool in crisis, conflict, emergency, and other situations	N++A-C-	
Lack of Ethics and Values	Nonadherence to an accepted code of conduct	N+A-C-	
Nonstrategic	Planning and performing for the short term only, failure to take the long term view, quick profits versus long term investment	O-	
Overdependence on an Advocate	The classic case of letting a relative, mentor, friend, or other ally explain and cover your shortcomings	N+E-A+C-	
Overdependence on Single Skill	Wearing blinders and declining to familiarize oneself with allied skills that are related to one's core skill set	O-C-	
Overly Ambitious	Placing personal advancement over the goals of the team or organization	N+E+A--C+	

Table 24.3 The 19 Derailers (continued)

Overmanaging	Failure to delegate properly, keeping a close eye on the work of others when they are capable of more independence	N+E+A--C+	
Performance Problems	Failure to acknowledge and conform to accepted standards of performance	C-	
Political Missteps	Offending, denigrating, puzzling, or otherwise alienating key potential allies for the advancement of oneself or one's team	Extremes*	
Poor Administrator	Failure to place adequate attention and standards to planning, organizing, and coordinating the details of one's overall operation	O+A+C-	
Unable to Adapt to Differences	Failure to acknowledge, accept, and value the contributions of person's different in background, values, ethnicity, personality, etc., compared to oneself	N+E+O-A-C+	

*For this derailer, any extreme scores—either high or low, are at risk, as midrange scores are optimally preventive.

For some people, career is everything. For the rest of us, our career is one part of who we are. This chapter has focused on planning for a satisfying career, one that gives expression to our "bliss," our passions. In the next, and final, chapter, we will take a look at planning our lives from a larger perspective—how to set goals based on a realistic understanding of who we are, and how to achieve those goals.

Career Case Study: David and his Goliath (aka Grandpa's Manufacturing Plant)

Contributed by Emily Crowder, UNC-Chapel Hill student and CentACS Research Intern

David (17 yrs): N=E+O=A+C=

Hoping to make some money during the summer, David decided to work at his grandfather's farming company. He was thrilled to have a paying job, even if it was not the most desirable. He was working in the manufacturing area of the company. From seven in the morning to five in the afternoon, he would stand in an assembly line, putting together feeders for the animals. He worked hard and would often get ahead of others working; so he would have to wait idly until they caught up to resume working. Each day, he had a 30-minute break for lunch, along with two other 10-minute breaks. Finally, after his 10-hour day, he would return home. By the time he got home, he was so worn out that he just stayed home instead of going out to see friends. He was extremely frustrated with his situation, but he continued to work in order to please his grandfather, who had happily given him the job. Two weeks into work, he made a mistake, and someone yelled at him. Though he was very upset with being yelled at, he didn't fight back. And when he got home that day, all he wanted to do was quit. However, he didn't. Even as miserable as he was, he couldn't face his grandpa and explain how he despised the job.

There are several reasons that David was so unhappy in his job. His first complaints arose based on his high extraversion (E+) level. As an extravert, David would be more satisfied in a job that has more contact with others. On the assembly line, no one talked much, so his desire to socialize was unmet. While his breaks could have provided an opportunity to chat, they were so short that he had little time to do anything other than take a quick bathroom break or get lunch. When he got home, he was so tired from his day that he didn't socialize with his friends. Sadly, this made him even more miserable because he felt isolated from others, both when he was working and when he got home. Like his extraversion, his mid-range originality (O=) level was not a good fit for the highly repetitive job. For 10 hours each day, he did the exact same thing over and over. The repetition drove him crazy, and he couldn't handle the boredom. Again, staying home in the evenings made the problem even worse because he didn't get to change up the routine. Though he was obviously frustrated, he continued to work because of his high accommodation (A+). He put his grandfather's desire for him to work in the company above his own hatred of the job, and he didn't want to seem ungrateful by quitting. Had he been lower in accommodation, he might have been more willing to confront his grandfather about his frustrations, even if it would lead to conflict. Luckily, David's job ended when he went back to school. But as David looks for other jobs in the future, he needs to be aware of the compatibility of a job with his natural traits.

Unfortunately, many people have difficulties picking a job suitable for their traits. Some people go into a profession to appease a parent, only to realize that they absolutely despise the job. For example, someone high in accommodation would be miserable in a position where it is a necessity to constantly argue a point, as in a trial lawyer. One way to avoid landing in an unsuitable career is to have an understanding of one's traits and how they affect job preferences. To explore careers that fit one's personality, try using the Personal Career Table of Elements, Table 24.1, and the Personal Career Mission Statement, Table 24.2 Also see my (Emily's) completed Personal Career Mission Statement in Appendix B.

Concluding the Book . . .

. . . While Laying the Stage for a Lifetime

25

The Challenge of Living with Traits

Setting and Attaining Goals

> People say that what we're all seeking is a meaning for life. I don't think that's what we're really seeking. I think that what we're seeking is an experience of being alive . . . so that we actually feel the rapture of being alive. That's what it's all finally about, and that's what these clues help us to find within ourselves.
>
> --Joseph Campbell (1991, p. 5)
>
> "I want to be used up when I die."
>
> --Julia Bergman, in *Three Cups of Tea* (Mortenson and Relin, 2006)

Guide to This Chapter:

- Self-Esteem is Attainable and Powerful.
- Savvy Goal-Setting (and Attainment!) is the Key to Self-Esteem.
- Plan Well for Goal Attainment.
- Happiness is Not the Goal for All.

Joseph Campbell states the theory, and Julia Bergman applies it. The world's philosophies and religions have all strived with the question of the meaning of life. Campbell throws it all out of the window by saying that it is not meaning we search for, but rather the feeling that our bodies and minds are engaged in a satisfying way. Or, as Quaker philosopher Bernard Phillips once sermonized, "The Search Will Make You Free." It is not the answers, but the search for answers, that enlivens us. As we will see in the next section on self-esteem, we can define this satisfying way of life in a way that is both simple and attainable. In this chapter we introduce nothing new, but rather we pull everything together in a framework that invites us to catch our own personal form of satisfaction with life.

N	E	O	A	C
Need for Stability	**Extraversion**	**Originality**	**Accommodation**	**Consolidation**
N+ Reactive	E+ Extraverted	O+ Explorer	A+ Adapter	C+ Focused
N= Responsive	E= Ambiverted	O= Moderate	A= Negotiator	C= Balanced
N- Resilient	E- Introverted	O- Preserver	A- Challenger	C- Flexible
N1: Worry	**E1: Approach Level**	**O1: Imagination**	**A1: Service**	**C1:Thoroughness**
N2: Temper	**E2: Group Orientation**	**O2: Range of Interests**	**A2: Compliance**	**C2: Structure**
N3: Outlook	**E3: Pace**	**O3: Innovation**	**A3: Humility**	**C3: Ambition**
N4: Coping Level	**E4: Leadership**	**O4: Zoom Scale**	**A4: Speak Out Level**	**C4: Concentration**
	E5: Trust			**C5: Methodicalness**
	E6: Tact			

Self-Esteem is Attainable and Powerful.

Self-esteem is the fuel that drives us. A two-headed Janus, self-esteem looks back at our past achievements and forward in anticipation of new successes (Csikszentmihalyi and Schneider, 2000, p.221). One's memory of recent and remote successes gives birth to our desire to pursue more success, more achievement. The memory can be mundane (winning a round of cards, writing a letter to the editor) or momentous (winning a gold medal at the Olympics, writing a book). Goal attainment is addictive. The pleasure we feel while in pursuit of a goal increases to a maximum point just before the moment of attainment, with actual attainment being something of a letdown, and with the pleasure only to be renewed with taking on a new goal and making progress towards it. The memory of past success makes us want more, just like the memory of the last Godiva chocolate....

However, there are two major threats to self-esteem: resting on one's laurels and inability to let go of failed goals. In the first case, we reach an agreeable level of achievement and, from that point forward, take on only those goals that are similar in terms of challenge, competition, difficulty. To run a four-minute mile, to be satisfied with that, and not to try to shave off hundredths of a second in additional races, is to risk one's self-esteem. One begins to question oneself: Could I have done better, why haven't I tried to run a faster mile, am I lazy, am I a spoiled brat, am I afraid of failure? As we discussed in earlier chapters, Carol Dweck (2006) calls this the difference between a fixed mindset and a growth mindset. The former plays it safe, while the latter takes on "stretch" goals. It might be doing something one has done before, but doing it faster, better, different. Or it could be taking on a goal in a different domain, like a runner taking on the challenge of learning a new language. The key to the growth mindset is the willingness to embrace goals that one has never taken on before. It is the difference between undertaking something that one is assured of completing successfully, versus undertaking something for which success is not guaranteed. For these growth goals, we have to explore the unknown, to take risks, to take a chance on failure. But, as Mihalhi Czikszentmihalyi explains in his book *Flow* (1990), as our chance of success in any given endeavor rises above 50%, we run the risk of boredom. On the other hand, as our chance of failure rises above 50 %, we run the risk of frustration. It is that zone around 50% chance of success that totally engages us, that keeps us alert and bent on maximum effort.

Laura King and Joshua Hicks (of the University of Missouri-Columbia) write (2007) about the same phenomenon, but with a twist. They define maturity as the ability to remain engaged in progressively more challenging goals, and immaturity as the tendency to remain stuck in the past, whereby one focuses on all of one's lost goals, failures, and missed opportunities. This focus on past failure tends to disengage one from the pursuit of new goals in the present. As they write, "The failure to disengage from lost goals is associated with lowered well-being" (p. 629). Maturity is predicated on acknowledging one's losses or limitations (missing out on a promotion, death of loved one, health issues of self or family, etc.) but nonetheless totally engaging in present goals. The temperament for developing in this manner requires acknowledging that one has erred, or has experienced trouble or loss, yet is still capable of being surprised by new and unexpected successes. To be mature, to maintain one's self-esteem, is to show humility at not being totally in control. It is having the courage to explore new goals and risk new losses and failures. Cutting one's losses, learning from them, and moving on are the path of well-being. It is a matter of using our memory of the past—both successes and failure—to shape ever more challenging goals for the future.

Savvy Goal-Setting (and Attainment!) is the Key to Self-Esteem

Jari-Erik Nurmi summarizes (in Lerner and Steinberg, 2004, p. 85) the task of adolescence this way:

> Adolescents face two broad challenges during the transition from childhood to adult life: the entrance into production and reproduction fields of the culture and society.

In other words, for society to progress, teens must learn to make an income and to build relationships, whether through a family, friends, organizations, or other networks. As we wrote earlier, failure to achieve either of these two superordinate goals tends to result in mental illness. The failure to hold a job or to keep a relationship is death to self-esteem. The secret to health and happiness is to continually take on goals that will result in a satisfying career and a satisfying relationship. That is not to say that we can't have multiple careers or multiple relationships, but one satisfying career and relationship must be at the center of our target for setting goals.

Here is something of what we know about setting goals (Latham and Yukl, 1975; Gollwitzer, 1999; Locke and Latham, 2002):

1. **Goal-setters achieve more**. First, and foremost, people who set goals achieve more than people who do not set goals. The very act of committing oneself to a goal—writing it down (in a journal, in a To-Do List, on a piece of paper), sharing it (with a friend, parents, teachers, the world), and posting it in some visible place (bedroom/study wall, bathroom mirror, car dashboard, class notebook) makes it more likely that we will attain it. Goal-setting is not a guarantee of attainment, but it helps minimize the risk of nonattainment. Any goal is better than no goal at all.
2. **Prefer specific goals**. It is not enough to set a general goal—specific goals are more likely to be achieved. "I'm going to try harder this year" is less likely to result in improved performance than something like "I'm going to study one hour more per day this year in comparison to last year."

3. **Goals with plans are surer bets**. A goal is more likely to be achieved if one plans out the what, who, when, and where of working towards the goal. It is not enough to say that one is going to apply for and get into Harvard—one is more likely to be accepted at Harvard if, in addition to just having the goal, one forms a plan with specific steps and target dates as to what one will do that will result in acceptance by Harvard. Again, having a plan is not a guarantee, but it increases the chance of success.

4. **Aim higher**. Goals that are not guaranteed to succeed result in more effort and higher performance than goals that are too easy and unchallenging. This is all about maintenance goals versus improvement goals: Do I maintain my batting average, or do I try to increase it? Do I maintain my B average, or go for a B+? These relate to the distinction between "task mastery" and "performance ability" motivations discussed in Chapter 13. Both Nancy Cobb (2007) and Carol Dweck (2006) refer to task mastery as a focus on aiming higher. Performance ability focuses on playing it safe for the purpose of only engaging in sure bets, slam dunks, gimmes, and the like. Do you simply want to perform well? In that case, do what you're comfortable with. Or do you want to conquer a new challenge? If so, you must venture outside of your comfort zone, or aim higher or differently. "Aiming higher" implies that we are talking about doing better at the same thing. That is not what we intend. Aiming higher could also mean aiming at a new and different target, as in moving from still targets to skeet shooting. Or from shooting at targets to learning a new language.

5. **Salami approach**. The previous paragraph leads to this one: A salami (or watermelon...) cannot be eaten all in one bite; so we cut it into more manageable slices. Accordingly, major goals—goals that take much time and resources, like earning Phi Beta Kappa, a Rhodes Scholarship, or a seat in the U.S. Senate—must be broken up into incremental goals, with each goal being slightly more challenging than the previous one. The point here is not to run for president of the U.S.A. your first year out of college. That is not only aiming *too* high—it fails to acknowledge the fact that, as for many of life's larger goals, there are many incremental goals that must be attained before the ultimate prize. Of course, one can always have an eye on the big goal while pursuing the next step on the way. However, remember what the great athletes say: "I'm not thinking about the season championship—I'm thinking about tonight's game."

6. **Positive phrasing**. Goals that are worded positively ("respond with humor when insulted") tend to be more achievable than goals that are worded negatively ("avoid getting angry when insulted").

7. **Create synergy.** Find ways to conjoin two goals such that doing one entails doing the other. For example, for the goals of "spend more time with my father" and "reorganize my computer directory," invite your father to help you plan and execute your computer directory reorganization.

These seven characteristics of goals help us to understand the qualities that are common to all goals, but they do not say anything about the content of the goals themselves. What does it mean to lead one's life by setting one goal after another? In fact, we are setting goals during all of our waking hours, as a goal is really nothing other than what we decide to do. It can be as mundane and instantaneous as going to check our mailbox, or as momentous and drawn out as running for political office. We set a goal when we consciously decide to focus on something, anything.

We have talked elsewhere about following our bliss, about spending our energy on things that we feel passionately about. I (Pierce) look every day at my four passions—learning, writing, developing relationships, and experiencing sensory pleasure. If any o f these passions is underattended, I set new goals for them. I have the most trouble with developing relationships, as I tend to work long hours. So, by working in the same company with my wife, Jane, and in fact locating my office next to hers, I create synergy by working on my relationship with her while working on my other passions.

These goals need to build on my natural energy—my traits, abilities, values, physical characteristics. To ignore my natural energies is to risk 1) not attaining my goals and 2) stress bordering on burnout. Case in point: Two friends of mine married in graduate school. He was gay. Nonetheless, she committed her life to him in marriage, thinking to herself that she could change him, remake him into heterosexual. They had a baby. The marriage fell apart after about three years. Her prolonged stress emanating from the futile efforts to reorient his sexuality was likely related to the cancer that ultimately ravaged her body soon after their separation, leaving her parents to care for the baby. The father, guilt-ridden, plunged into the temporary escape of alcohol abuse and one-night stands.

We must respect our natural energies, our genetic inheritance. In 1986, we both were faced with career decisions. I (Jane) was asked to continue as the Director of Sales and Marketing for the consulting and training company where Pierce and I worked. A client had asked me to lead a training program for his company, and I was tired of sales. I had done a great job in the position for four years even though my E is midrange (not E+ as is really needed in sales over time). Another problem was my very high O++. I was bored with the same work after four years. And my low C was getting in my way of constantly following up with clients. (It really helps if sales people are higher in C.) I clearly had the very low N score sales people need to recover from rejection, and it had allowed me to tolerate a job that was not completely natural for me for over four years. The only trait I really had on target for sales was very low A.

Meanwhile, I (Pierce) was asked to be manager of the research division of our growing consulting firm. My responsibilities would focus on quality control—ensuring that all reports had reliable numbers. Essentially, this promotion was a proofreading job. It called for someone relatively low in O and A, while being relatively high in C. I was the opposite: very high in O, moderate in A, moderately low in C. I have the natural energy to proofread for limited amounts of time, but that energy runs out rather quickly, and my body yearns to be free of it and engaged in exploration, discovery, invention, imagination, and complexity. Rather than accept this promotion with its higher salary, Jane and I chose to leave the firm and become our own "boss." We started our own company on July 1, 1986, Independence Day (almost). Ever since, we have been free to be high O. While the nature of my (Pierce's) work does require substantial poofreading (☺), fortunately I do not have to do it all.

Perhaps you will quote Katherine Hepburn (see sidebar) to say that we are wrong—that we should regard our genetic inheritance, our nature, as something like modeling clay that can be shaped at our command. But Hepburn's character, the missionary Rose Sayer, is simply admonishing Mr. Allnut, who has just suggested that occasionally having one too many for the road is just "human nature." Allnut (played by Humphrey

> "Nature, Mr. Allnut, is what we are put in this world to rise above."
> --Katharine Hepburn, in *The African Queen*

Bogart) is referring to the basic instincts here—the appetites, whether sexual, alcoholic, or sweets. Certainly, it is human nature to want one more cookie, one more drink, one more dalliance. And certainly missionary Rose is right that the growth and progress of civilization is predicated on resisting the urge for just one more metaphorical cookie. But resisting an appetite's urge is not the same as acknowledging the bent of our temperament. We all have different gifts and are meant to use them. We are not put in this world to resist our extraverted (or introverted, or ambiverted) natures—we are here to harness them in a way that is satisfying to us and productive to society. So extraverts sell, ambiverts teach, and introverts do lab work. Challengers debate, adapters serve others, and negotiators make peace.

In the process outlined in the previous chapter, we use our natural sources of energy to shape our personal mission in life. In considering the many goals that populate our days, we constantly assess for the goals that build on our strengths and don't overtax our limited sources of energy. Remembering the Human Resource Optimization "trees," we attempt to make of our lives fully developed trees based on strong root systems.

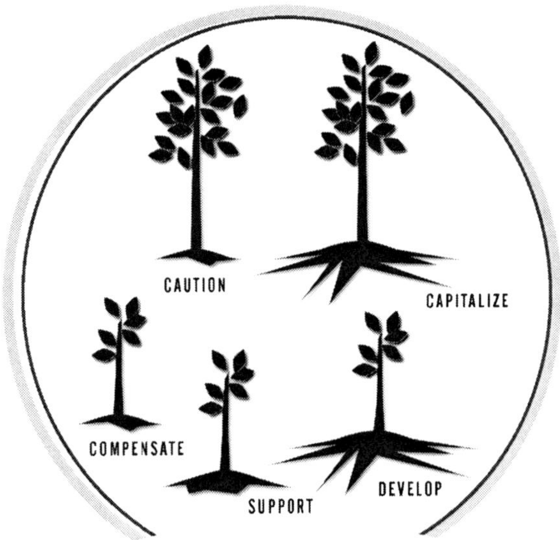

HUMAN RESOURCE OPTIMIZATION

Planning Well for Goal Attainment

As goals move from simpler (make a cup of noodles in the microwave) to more complex (earn a superior rating at the state music contest), the risk of failure increases. In order to insure attainment or more complex goals, we need a plan. At a minimum, a plan involves a series of steps, with each step specifying three aspects: what (i.e., the sub-goal), when (i.e., the target date for completion), and resources required (permissions, budget, subcontracting, delegation). Here is our plan for writing this book:

Step:	What:	When:	Resources Required:
1.	Write a book proposal.	11/1/07	Get team approval.
2.	Conduct relevant research.	11/1/08	Consult experts for books and authors to read.
3.	Revise book outline.	12/1/08	Get team approval.
4.	For each chapter, review relevant research, draw up a mind map, and write the chapter.	One week per chapter	For early chapters, get team's input and support on design; get agreement to leave office daily at 4 for home writing sessions.
5.	Schedule four off-site writing retreats.	Jan., Feb., April, and May	Coordinate with team; find appropriate locations for writing retreats that are quiet, cheap (or free), and reasonably inspiring.

6.	Find intern to serve as editorial research. assistant.	June-August 2009	Secure office space; have manuscript ready for review; complete first revision.
7.	Secure 20 readers and send manuscripts.	7/1/09	Solicit recommendations, feedback, and make corrections.
8.	Complete first draft.	7/1/09	As deadline nears, set aside time required to finish on schedule.
9.	Secure publishing arrangements.	9/09	Discuss options with current publisher.
10.	Complete revisions.	12/1/09	Identify editor.
11.	Prepare for printing.	6/1/10	Secure agreements on cover and overall design; conduct market research.
12.	Receive completed books.	1/11	Prepare promotion campaign and list for sending comp copies.

Clearly, there are more subgoals than this brief plan specifies, but you get the idea. The core of the process is allocating one week for each chapter. At 25 chapters, that means completing the first draft in six months. Some weeks will be disasters, with no time available for writing. We make up that time by going away for "writing retreats"—long weekends at the beach or mountains with no interruptions. Without the commitment to averaging a chapter a week, the likelihood is that the project would drag out interminably. In fact, as I (Pierce) write this sentence, today is Sunday, June 21, 2009. I am close to finishing this, the final chapter. In fact, having started writing just before Christmas last winter, we have come close to averaging the set goal of one chapter a week.

One way to increase the chances of sticking to your plan is to share the plan with those around you. This does two things: By their knowing your plan, they are in a better position to help you in a variety of ways. And by publicly committing to the plan, it lights a fire under you to get cooking! You certainly don't want to lose face by not doing what you say.

Sometimes a goal is overwhelming. It is something you really want to do—you really have a passion for it. However, you are not clear on how to proceed, and you are not guaranteed success just because you want to do it. Some examples of overwhelming, large, complex goals might be: applying for a major scholarship, running for an elective office, applying for an important job or role, creating a new organization, inventing a product and taking it to market, or writing a book. These overwhelming goals deserve special consideration with respect for how we plan them out. John Kotter (1985) has written the book *Power and Influence* to suggest how this might be done. His plan is simple, and it works:

1. Write a brief statement about what it is you want to accomplish.
2. Make a list of your key stakeholders—persons who could help or hinder you in accomplishing your goal, whether through ideas, support, resources, recommendations, or some other way.
3. Share your goal statement with each of them, and ask them what suggestions they have about how you might proceed, what you might do to increase your chances of attaining your goal.
4. Listen to what they say, and write it all down.

Concluding the Book

5. Evaluate all of the suggestions and incorporate them into a plan.
6. If necessary, revise your goal statement, and repeat steps 1 through 5 as appropriate.

Happiness is Not the Goal for All

A closing comment: Happiness is a false god (or goal). We expanded on this early in this book (and you'll see a book by Pierce on this subject in the near future). Only one person in nine is happy by nature—those few individuals who are high in E (maximum positive emotions) and low in N (minimal negative emotions). Maria in *Sound of Music*, Guido in *Life is Beautiful*, and Evelyn Ryan in *The Prize Winner of Defiance, Ohio*. These are people who simply can't be kept down and out—they are born happy, and pepper their days with laughter, smiles, curiosity, joy, and delight. They seldom experience fear, sadness, or anger.

So what is there for the rest of us? Put simply, it is goal attainment. As self-esteem is the remembrance of past achievement and the anticipation of future success, our satisfaction with life hinges on setting goals that build on our strengths and attaining them. The sense of making progress towards goals is the ultimate satisfaction. Slow but sure. We may have to revise some of the major goals. We may have setbacks. But we do not dwell on lost opportunities—we refocus and continue our steady progress. When we are totally engaged in pursuit of a goal, we are in flow, and happiness is not even an issue. To be absorbed in making progress is better than happiness. Happiness is fun, it is nice, but it does not suffice alone. We make our own version of happiness by forming challenging goals and staying in pursuit of them.

What's that? A distraction? Does it relate to one of our goals, our passions? Then, sorry, can't deal with it today!

> "The Constitution only gives you the right to pursue happiness. You have to catch it yourself."
> --Benjamin Franklin

Appendices

Appendices

Appendix A

Table for Estimating Scores on the SchoolPlace Big Five Profile

Instructions: To the right of each subtrait (N1, N2, etc.), highlight or circle the one out of the five statements that best describes you (or someone else you wish to describe) under normal, relatively carefree circumstances. The bottom row in each section is the overall supertrait for the preceding subtraits. On that row, estimate your likely overall level of the supertrait by averaging the preceding subtrait levels you circled. You might find this an interesting exercise to do in discussion with family and/or friends. In order to obtain the most accurate estimate of your trait levels, we suggest that you contact a school counselor or other professional to assist you in taking and interpreting the full SchoolPlace Big Five Profile 4.0™ questionnaire offered by the Center for Applied Cognitive Studies, Charlotte NC, USA, www.centacs.com. A version for adults—the WorkPlace Big Five Profile™—is also available, as is a version for the mentally disabled—the DisAbilities Big Five Profile™.

	0 – 35	35 – 45	45 – 55	55 – 65	65 – 100
	N1- -	N1-	N1=	N1+	N1++
N1: Worry	Most people worry more than I do—I am extremely calm even in stressful situations.	A few people are calmer than I am, but I am usually calm and seldom worry.	About half of my acquaintances seem to worry more than I do, while the other half seem to be calmer.	I seem to worry more than most people, but a few people appear to worry more than I do.	I seem to worry more than most people.
	N2- -	N2-	N2=	N2+	N2++
N2: Temper	Most people seem to have more of a temper than I do—I am extremely cool, even during arguments and conflict.	A few people are cooler than I am during arguments and conflict, but I seldom have a burst of temper.	About half of my acquaintances appear to have more of a temper than I do, while the other half are cooler in conflict.	I appear to have more of a temper than most people, but a few people seem to have even more of a temper than I.	I appear to have more of a temper than most people.
	N3- -	N3-	N3=	N3+	N3++
N3: Outlook	I seem to be more optimistic than most of the people that I know.	Although a few of my acquaintances are more optimistic than I am, I tend to be more optimistic than most.	I tend to be rather realistic, neither particularly optimistic nor pessimistic.	Although a few of my acquaintances are less optimistic than I am, I tend to be less optimistic than most.	I seem to be less optimistic than most of the people that I know.
	N4- -	N4-	N4=	N4+	N4++
N4: Coping Level	I seem to bounce back from crises and intense stress more quickly than my acquaintances.	A few people bounce back from crises and stress more quickly than I do, but I recover more quickly than most.	I bounce back from crises and stress more quickly than half the people I know, and less quickly than the other half.	I seem to take longer to bounce back from crises and stress than most people do, but some take even longer than I do.	I seem to take longer to bounce back from crises and stressful situations than most people do.
	N- -	N-	N=	N+	N++
N: Need for Stability	**Very Resilient**	**Resilient**	**Responsive**	**Reactive**	**Very Reactive**
	0 – 35	35 – 45	45 – 55	55 – 65	65 – 100

Appendices

	0	35	45	55	65 100
E1: Approach Level	E1- -	E1-	E1=	E1+	E1++
	I keep my positive feelings to myself—others show more enthusiasm than I do.	Some people seem to keep their positive feelings to themselves more than I do, but I show less enthusiasm than most people do.	I show more positive feelings to others than about half of my acquaintances, and I show fewer positive feelings than the other half.	Although a few of my acquaintances show more positive feelings than I do, I show more enthusiasm than most people I know.	I seem to share more of my positive feelings and enthusiasm than most people do.
E2: Group Orientation	E2- -	E2-	E2=	E2+	E2++
	I see myself as more solitary than most of the people I know. I am very comfortable being alone.	I am more solitary than most of my associates, but some are more solitary than I am.	I am comfortable being alone for about half the time, while for the other half I enjoy being around others.	I enjoy others' company more than most of my associates, but some of them are even more sociable than me.	I enjoy the company of others more than most of my associates do; I am seldom alone.
E3: Pace	E3- -	E3-	E3=	E3+	E3++
	I appear to prefer sitting and staying in one place more than most of the people I know—they are much more active than I am.	I appear to prefer sitting and staying in one place more than most of the people I know, but some of them are even less active than I am.	I appear to be more active than about half the people I know and less active than the other half.	I appear to be more active than most of the people I know, yet a few of them are even more active than I am.	I appear to be more active than most of the people I know—I seldom like to sit still or stay in one place.
E4: Leadership	E4- -	E4-	E4=	E4+	E4++
	I do not like to take the leadership role—I prefer to be either independent or to follow others' leadership.	I avoid taking leadership roles, but a few of my associates avoid leadership responsibility even more than I do.	I am comfortable being the leader about half the time, while for the other half I prefer to be independent or to follow.	I typically enjoy being the leader, but some of my associates enjoy it even more than I do.	I typically enjoy being the leader and being in charge of other people.
E5: Trust	E5- -	E5-	E5=	E5+	E5++
	I do not typically take other people at their word—I am very skeptical and questioning.	While I do not typically take other people at their word, a few of my associates are even more skeptical than I am.	I am trusting of others about half of the time, and the other half I tend to be skeptical and not take others at their word.	While I typically trust others and take them at their word, some of my associates are even more trusting than I am.	I typically trust other people and take them at their word.
E6: Tact	E6- -	E6-	E6=	E6+	E6++
	I tend to be blunt and direct most of the time, seldom trying to chose tactful ways of saying things.	While I tend to be blunt and direct most of the time, a few of my associates are even more so than I am.	I tend to be blunt and direct for about half of the time, while the other half I tend to be more tactful in what I say.	I tend to be tactful in most situations, but a few of my associates are even more tactful than I am.	I tend to be tactful in most situations, rarely speaking in a blunt or direct manner.
E: Extraversion	E- -	E-	E=	E+	E++
	Very Introverted	**Introverted**	**Ambiverted**	**Extraverted**	**Very Extraverted**
	0	35	45	55	65 100

Appendix A

	0	35	45	55	65 100
O1: Imagination	O1- -	O1-	O1=	O1+	O1++
	I tend to be less interested in coming up with new ideas and more interested in implementing the good ones that already exist.	Compared to other people, I am less interested in coming up with new ideas—I prefer being an implementer; some people are less inventive than I am.	I am more imaginative than about half of the people I know, while the other half appear to be more imaginative than I am.	I have an active imagination that is frequently coming up with new ideas, but some of my associates are even more imaginative than I am.	I have an extremely active imagination and am constantly coming up with new ideas, some of which are not really doable.
O2: Range of Interests	O2- -	O2-	O2=	O2+	O2++
	My interests are limited to no more than a few special subjects or areas—I like to keep it simple.	My interests are limited to a few subjects, as I like to keep it simple, but some of my associates like it even simpler.	I like to keep much of my life as simple as possible, while in other areas I am comfortable with greater complexity.	I am interested in many subjects and enjoy complexity, but some people like even more complexity than I do.	I am interested in many different subjects and areas and enjoy their complex interrelationships.
O3: Innovation	O3- -	O3-	O3=	O3+	O3++
	I prefer a way of life that that exists now and that involves relatively little change.	I prefer a stable life with little change, but some prefer even less change than I do.	I'm comfortable with change in some areas of my life, but prefer less change in other areas.	I welcome change in most areas of my life, but some people like even more change than I do.	I welcome change in most areas of my life.
O4: Zoom Scale	O4- -	O4-	O4=	O4+	O4++
	I thoroughly enjoy focusing on the details of any situation and seldom tire of them.	I enjoy focusing on the details of most situations, but some people like the details even more than I do.	About half the time I enjoy working with the details of a situation, while during the other half I like dealing with the big picture.	I am a big picture person who doesn't particularly enjoy handling details, but some other people like details even less than I do.	I am a big picture person who really doesn't enjoy handling the details.
O: Originality	O- -	O-	O=	O+	O++
	Strong Preserver	**Preserver**	**Moderate**	**Explorer**	**Strong Explorer**
	0	35	45	55	65 100

Appendices

	0 35	45	55	65	100
	A1- -	A1-	A1=	A1+	A1++
A1: Service	I typically do not inconvenience myself for others—I address my own needs before attending to others'.	I tend to address my own needs before attending to those of others, but some of my associates are even more that way than I am.	About half the time, I focus on attending to my personal needs, while the other half, I attend to the needs of others.	I tend to focus more on the needs of others than on my own personal needs, yet some of my associates are even more that way than I am.	I typically focus on the needs of others, with my own needs only getting attended to when those of others have been satisfied.
	A2- -	A2-	A2=	A2+	A2++
A2: Compliance	In most any conflict situation, my primary goal is winning.	Normally in conflict situations, my goal is winning, but some of my associates have an even stronger need to win than I do.	When in a conflict situation, I normally try to find a way that both the other person and I can win; if a win-win isn't possible, then the outcome is in my favor about half the time and in the other person's favor the other half of the time.	I value harmony, so in conflict situations I normally let the other person get their way; Some of my associates are even more deferential in that regard than I am.	I place a high value on harmony; so in most conflict situations, I tend to let the other person get their way.
	A3- -	A3-	A3=	A3+	A3++
A3: Humility	When I do a good job, I expect praise and recognition from others.	Most of the time after doing a good job, I expect praise and recognition from others; some of my associates want even more recognition than I do.	Sometimes I like to get praise and recognition for a job well done, but it is not that important to me.	After doing something well, I get uncomfortable when I am singled out for praise and recognition; some of my associates like praise even less than I do.	After doing something well, I get uncomfortable when I am singled out for praise and recognition.
	A4- -	A4-	A4=	A4+	A4++
A4: Speak Out Level	I rarely keep my opinions to myself—I tend to speak my mind wherever I am, whenever I can, whomever I'm with.	I tend to express my opinions in most every situation; however, some of my associates are even more outspoken than I am.	About half the time I have an opinion, I tend to let others know it by speaking up; while the other half of the time, I tend to keep my opinions to myself.	I tend to keep my opinions to myself in most situations; however, some of my associates are even more reserved than I am.	I am very reserved and typically keep my opinions to myself.
A: Accommodation	A- -	A-	A=	A+	A++
	Strong Challenger	**Challenger**	**Negotiator**	**Adapter**	**Strong Adapter**
	0 35	45	55	65	100

	0	35	45	55	65 — 100
C1: Thoroughness	C1- -	C1-	C1=	C1+	C1++
	I am rarely, if ever, a stickler for making things as perfect as they can be—I'm more casual about getting things right.	I am not much of a perfectionist in the things I do, but I know some people who are even less perfectionistic than I am.	I am somewhat perfectionistic about some areas of my life and more casual about other areas.	I tend to be a perfectionist in most of the things I undertake, but I know some people who are even more perfectionistic than I am.	I have a strong need to be perfect in everything that I undertake.
C2: Structure	C2- -	C2-	C2=	C2+	C2++
	I am not naturally oriented towards getting and staying organized, and I tend to be rather comfortable with not being organized.	While I am comfortable not being particularly well organized, I know some people who are even less organized than I am.	I am moderately well organized in the various aspects of my life, with perhaps some areas better organized than other areas.	I tend to be well organized in most areas of my life, but I know some people who place an even higher value on organization than I do.	I place a very high value on getting and staying organized in just about every area of my life.
C3: Ambition	C3- -	C3-	C3=	C3+	C3++
	I basically have no interest in being the number one person in an organization—other people are welcome to be "numero uno."	I am relatively uninterested in being the number one person in an organization, yet I know some people who are even less interested in being "numero uno" than I am.	I aspire to be the number one person in some organizations that I'm involved with, but in other organizations being "numero uno" is not important to me.	As a general rule, if I'm a part of an organization, I want to be "numero uno" in that organization; however, I know some people who feel that urge even stronger than I do.	If I'm a part of an organization, then I want to be the number one person in that organization.
C4: Concentration	C4- -	C4-	C4=	C4+	C4++
	I tend to be very easily distracted from whatever I am doing at the time.	While I am easily distracted from the task at hand, I know some other people who are even more easily distracted than I am.	I find it relatively easy to concentrate in some situations, but find myself easily distracted in other situations.	As a rule, I find it easy to concentrate on the task at hand and am relatively difficult to distract; yet, I know some people who can concentrate and are even more difficult to distract than I am.	As a general rule, I find it easy to concentrate on the task at hand and am difficult to distract.
C5: Methodicalness	C5- -	C5-	C5=	C5+	C5++
	I dislike making and following plans, preferring instead to be spontaneous and to "wing it."	While I dislike plans and planning in most areas of my life, I know some people who are even more spontaneous than I am.	I find it natural to be a planner in some areas of my life, but in other areas I prefer to be spontaneous and "wing it."	I prefer having plans for most things I do and am seldom spontaneous, yet I know some people whose lives are more "planful" than mine is.	I prefer having plans for just about everything that I undertake—I am seldom spontaneous and rarely, if ever, find myself "winging it."
C: Consolidation	C- -	C-	C=	C+	C++
	Very Flexible	**Flexible**	**Balanced**	**Focused**	**Very Focused**
	0	35	45	55	65 — 100

Summary of SchoolPlace Big Five Profile Estimated Scores for: _________________________(name)

Directions: Transfer your estimated levels for each trait from the previous five pages to this summary sheet, then copy this sheet or tear it out to use as a reference while reading this book.

	0	35	45	55	65 100
Trait:	**Very Low**	**Low**	**Medium**	**High**	**Very High**
N: Need for Stability	**N- -**	**N-**	**N=**	**N+**	**N++**
N1: Worry	N1- -	N1-	N1=	N1+	N1++
N2: Temper	N2- -	N2-	N2=	N2+	N2++
N3: Outlook	N3- -	N3-	N3=	N3+	N3++
N4: Coping Level	N4- -	N4-	N4=	N4+	N4++
E: Extraversion	**E- -**	**E-**	**E=**	**E+**	**E++**
E1: Approach Level	E1- -	E1-	E1=	E1+	E1++
E2: Group Orientation	E2- -	E2-	E2=	E2+	E2++
E3: Pace	E3- -	E3-	E3=	E3+	E3++
E4: Leadership	E4- -	E4-	E4=	E4+	E4++
E5: Trust	E5- -	E5-	E5=	E5+	E5++
E6: Tact	E6- -	E6-	E6=	E6+	E6++
O: Originality	**O- -**	**O-**	**O=**	**O+**	**O++**
O1: Imagination	O1- -	O1-	O1=	O1+	O1++
O2: Range of Interests	O2- -	O2-	O2=	O2+	O2++
O3: Innovation	O3- -	O3-	O3=	O3+	O3++
O4: Zoom Scale	O4- -	O4-	O4=	O4+	O4++
A: Accommodation	**A- -**	**A-**	**A=**	**A+**	**A++**
A1: Service	A1- -	A1-	A1=	A1+	A1++
A2: Compliance	A2- -	A2-	A2=	A2+	A2++
A3: Humility	A3- -	A3-	A3=	A3+	A3++
A4: Speak Out Level	A4- -	A4-	A4=	A4+	A4++
C: Consolidation	**C- -**	**C-**	**C=**	**C+**	**C++**
C1: Thoroughness	C1- -	C1-	C1=	C1+	C1++
C2: Structure	C2- -	C2-	C2=	C2+	C2++
C3: Ambition	C3- -	C3-	C3=	C3+	C3++
C4: Concentration	C4- -	C4-	C4=	C4+	C4++
C5: Methodicalness	C5- -	C5-	C5=	C5+	C5++
	0	35	45	55	65 100

Appendix B

Sample Personal Career Mission Statement

In Chapter 24, we presented a series of tables and self-checklists intended to prepare one for composing a Personal Career Mission Statement. An individual can take this statement and share it with persons in their network who are in a position to advise them on career options that best fit with their personal characteristics.

In this appendix, we show how these checklists were completed by a 19-year-old rising college sophomore (our research intern, Emily Crowder) who was thinking through her career options. She underwent this process both to aid in selecting a major as well as to identify some internship experiences that would help clarify her career preferences. To aid in gaining some overall perspective on Emily's outlook, her supertrait profile is: N-E=O-/=A+C+.

The process of composing the Personal Career Mission Statement comprises three steps (blank versions of the Personal Career Table of Elements and Summary Sheet are provided in Chapter 24):

1. **The Personal Career Table of Elements**: Identifying personal characteristics that are important considerations for selecting a career. This checklist is a relatively thorough self-study.

2. **The Summary Sheet**: On the Summary Sheet, put the most important information, e.g., traits with the strongest emotional charge, as in, "I really don't like being alone—I have to be around people all or most of the time" (high E2: group orientation), from the Personal Career Table of Elements, so as to facilitate writing a Personal Career Mission Statement.

3. **The Personal Career Mission Statement**: Composing a brief, easy-to-read essay that presents one's personal career needs (passionate attractions/aversions) to individuals in one's network.

Part One: The Personal Career Table of Elements

Work Objects

Object:	**Definition ("A preference for working with…"):**	**Associated Traits:**	**Value for You:**
People	groups, meetings, interviews, audiences, conversations	E+ A+	Yes
Things	machinery, animals, equipment, supplies, material	E- O-	No
Ideas	theories, stories, experiments, problems, planning, decisions	O+	No
Data	numbers, spreadsheets, databases, formulas	O-	Yes

Traits

Subtrait:	**Work Characteristics Associated with the Three Levels:** (Leftmost phrase refers to lower levels of the trait, middle phrase to mid level, and rightmost phrase to higher levels of the trait.)	**Preferred Level:**
N1: Worry	Can handle high stress levels, Balance of calm/stress, Low stress levels	=
N2: Temper	Can handle high conflict, Balance of conflict/at ease, Low conflict	-

Appendices

N3: Outlook	Need to be optimistic, Balance of opt./pess., Need to be pessimistic	-
N4: Coping Level	Can handle crises as a way of life, Moderate number of crises, Few crises	-/=
E1: Approach Level	Seldom needs to show enthusiasm, Moderate enth., Constant enth.	=
E2: Group Orientation.	Usually alone, Balance of others/alone, Always around other people	=
E3: Pace	Usually sitting, Balance of sitting/up and about, Usually up and about	=
E4: Leadership	Independent, Responsibility is half/half, Responsible for others' work	-
E5: Trust	Needs to be skeptical, Moderate skepticism, Needs to be trusting	+
E6: Tact	Little need to be tactful, Sometimes tactful, Always tactful	+
O1: Imagination	No need to be creative, Sometimes creative, Always creative	-
O2: Range of Interests	Complexity is uncommon, Moderate complexity, Complexity is constant	-
O3: Innovation	Change is seldom, Change is occasional, Change is frequent	=
O4: Zoom Scale	Work with the details, Half/half, Work with the big picture	=
A1: Service	Do your own thing, Half/half, Serve/help others	=
A2: Compliance	Stand up to others' demands, Negotiate, Follow others' wishes	+
A3: Humility	Needs to show pride, Moderate pride, Needs to show humility	+
A4: Speaking Out	Needs to speak mind, Moderate assertiveness, Stays in background	+
C1: Thoroughness	Casual about quality, Moderate quality focus, Constant quality focus	+
C2: Structure	Organization unimportant, Moderate org., Organization is imperative	=
C3: Ambition	Comfortable with status quo, Moderate ambition, Driven to achieve	=
C4: Concentration	Multi-tasking, Moderate focus, Focus on a single task at a time	+
C5: Methodicalness	Spontaneous, Moderate use of plans, Constantly follows the plan	+

Note: Due to space limitations, the middle level (scores between 45 and 55) is often referred to as "moderate" (i.e., not preferring either extreme, as in E2= preferring small groups over either solitude or crowds), or a "balance"/"half/half" of the two extremes (i.e., preferring work that requires one extreme about half the time, and the other extreme the other half, as in practicing the piano half the day and teaching classes the other half). If you have your SchoolPlace or WorkPlace Big Five Profile 4.0 results, then a score below 45 would be associated with the leftmost level, and a score over 55 with the rightmost level.

Abilities

Ability:	**Definition:**	**Want to Build on It?**
Auditory	Remembering and discriminating between a variety of sounds	Yes
Visual/Spatial	Reading diagrams, understanding and remembering complex images	No
Verbal	Good vocabulary, grammar, composition w one/more languages	Yes
Logical/Math	Working with number systems, symbols, codes, puzzles	No
Natural Observer	Working with nomenclatures, biology, taxonomies	Yes
Kinesthetic	Peak physical condition, coordination, and muscle control	Yes
Interpersonal	Managing personal relationships/influencing others (N-E+A=)	Yes
Intrapersonal	Being introspective, perceiving feelings and nonverbal (N+E-O+)	No

Roles

Role:	**Definition:**	**Traits:**	**Important?**
Technical	Need to be an expert with reputation of being knowledgeable	N+E-O-A-	No
Managerial	Responsible for leading other people and directing the organization	N-E+A-C+	Somewhat
Autonomy	Being independent of others/bosses and doing things one's own way	N+O+	No
Security	Enjoying the promise of lifetime employment; loyalty to employer	O-C+	Yes
Entrepreneurial	Starting and building one's own business to a financial success	N+E-A-C-	No
Service	Making a contribution/difference for some cause or entity	E+A+	Yes
Challenge	Overcoming difficult, challenging situations to beat the competition	N-E+A-C+	Somewhat
Lifestyle	Having the flexibility to balance demands of work and personal life	N+A+	Yes

Content, or Occupational Theme (Based on the Holland Hexagon)

Holland Area:	**Definition:**	**Traits:**	**Important?**
Realistic	Physical work, especially outdoors, with animals, machines, construction, transportation, agriculture, equipment	E-O-	No
Investigative	Research, gathering information, reading, study	N-O+	No
Artistic	The arts, writing	E+O+	No
Social	The helping professions: teaching, counseling, social work	E+O+A+	Yes

Appendices

Enterprising	Selling, managing	N-E+O+ A-C+	No
Conventional	Office work: planning, organizing, working with office equipment	O-C+	Yes

Work Attributes (Based on the American College Testing (ACT) Program model)

Attribute:	Definition:	Traits:	Important?
Authority	Similar to management, but towards non-employees, as in a traffic cop job—telling others what to do/not do	E+O+A-C+	No
Certification	Careers certifying competence by a degree, license, etc. (doctor, actuary, realtor)	O-C+	Somewhat
Creating Order	Using rules to arrange things (quality inspector, administrator)	N-E+C+	Yes
Easy Re-entry	Easy to move, or quit and come back, as after maternity leave (sales, mechanic)	E+O+A-	Yes
Financial Challenge	Advising others so that much could be gained or lost (investment/financial planner)	N-E+O+A-C+	No
40-Hour Week	Work that entails no overtime, taking work home, on-call status, etc. (postal clerk, government analyst)	O-A+C+	Somewhat
High Income	To be in the top 25% of money earners (NFL quarterback, executive)	N-E+O+A-C+	Yes
Immediate Response	Working/performing around others where immediate feedback is the norm-- applause, laughs, boos, cheers, attaboys, attagirls, handshakes, etc. (comedian, flight attendant)	N+E+O+A-	No
Influencing Others	Convincing without authority (sales, counseling, health care, social work)	N-E+O+A-C+	No
Making or Fixing Things	Working with your hands or tools on electro-mechanical objects (mechanic, manufacturing work)	N-C+	No
Management	Planning, directing, and evaluating the work of others (manager, supervisor, etc.)	N-E+O+A-C+	Somewhat
New Ideas	Creating new ways to do things--trying new combinations of ideas (advertising, consultant, research and development)	N-E+O+A-	No
Non-Standard Hours	Preferring work that is seasonal, temporary, part-time, shifts, etc. (consultant, waiter, tennis/golf pro)	E+O+A-C-	No
Occasional Travel	Out of town travel about once a quarter (small business owner)	E-O-A+C-	Somewhat

Physical Activity	Work that results in a significant amount of exercise--walking, lifting, sporting (stevedore, chef, material handler, park ranger)	N-E+O+A-C+	Somewhat
Precision	Work that is done according to exact standards or procedures (assembler, fabricator, lab technician, nurse)	N-E+O-C+	Somewhat
Problem Solving	Spending time figuring out how to do things, to get things done, to repair things (consultant, research and development, customer service rep, team leader)	N-E+O+A-C+	Yes
Project Work	Tasks lasting one week or longer (project manager, engineer, architect)	N-E+O+C+	Yes
Public Contact	Work in which you can talk and be seen by non co-workers (customer service, sales, trainer)	N-E+O+A-C+	Yes
Routine Travel	Getting out of the office/town once a week or more (many sales positions, consultant, pilot, flight attendant)	E+O+A-C+	No
Short Training Time	Less than 6 months required training after high school (construction work, receptionist, cook)	N+E-O-C-	No
Working Inside	Work mostly inside, in an office (accountant, writer, banker, administrator, lawyer, dentist, telephone sales)	N+E-O-A+C-	Somewhat
Working In/Out	Partially inside and partially outside (material handler, elementary school teacher, coach, external sales, baggage handler)	E+	Yes
Working Outside	Working outdoors in the weather, good or bad (cowpoke, mail delivery, door-to-door sales, park ranger, road construction engineer)	N-E+O+A-C+	No
Working Separately	Solitary work that requires little talking or other contact with co-workers (bookkeeper, Internet entrepreneur, writer)	N+E-O-A+C-	No

Values

Value:	**Definition:**	**Traits:**	**Important:**
Achievement	Setting goals and attaining them, from writing a book to building a house	C+	Yes
Aesthetics	The pursuit of interests in the visual and/or performing arts	O+	No
Affiliation	Having high-quality relationships	E+A+	Yes
Charity	Giving one's material wealth to those in need	A+	No
Compassion	Serving those in pain or general need of help	A+	Yes
Creativity	Originating novel ideas or things with utilitarian or entertainment value	O+	No
Entertainment	Providing diversion to others for relief from work, stress, or boredom	E+	No
Escape	Providing diversion for oneself for relief from work, stress, or boredom	N+	Yes

Appendices

Family	Furthering the interests and needs of one's family members	A+	Yes
Health	Minimizing disease or death risk through attention to diet, exercise, etc.	C+	Yes
Hedonism	Experiencing pleasure through the five senses	N+E+A-C-	No
Learning	Increasing one's own knowledge in one or more domains	O+	Some-what
Mainte-nance	Keeping all of one's possessions/responsibilities in peak condi-tion	O-C+	No
Materialism	Maximizing the accumulation of physical possessions; consum-erism	N+A-	No
Politics	Being involved in pursuit of or execution of an elected office	E+A-	No
Position	Having the goal of rising to highest position in one or more hierarchies	A-C+	Some-what
Power	Being in control of others' ability to satisfy their needs	E+A-C+	No
Profession-alism	Being regarded as a role model within one's chosen career	A-C+	Yes
Romance	Creating a mood that promotes or maintains a love relation-ship	E+A+	Yes
Safety	Minimizing the risk of accidents for self or others	N-E-O-A+C+	Yes
Security	Ensuring a steady, unending supply of resources necessary for survival	N+O-	Yes
Spirituality	Pursuit of non-material goals such as truth, beauty, goodness, or the "Divine"	N-E-O+	Yes
Sport	The love of competition and winning, whether athletic or oth-erwise	E+A-	No
Tolerance	Pursuing the social goal of universal mutual acceptance and equality	O+A+	Yes
Wealth	The accumulation of maximum items of financial value	E+A-C+	Yes

Miscellaneous Career Requirements

Category:	**Specifics from These Categories that Your Career Should (or Shouldn't) Involve:**
Physical Characteristics (myopia, allergies, etc.)	Motion sickness, neck soreness
Experiences (features of one's personal history)	
Specific Roles (parent, researcher, teacher, guide)	Parent (eventually), Guide
Bodies of Knowledge (Physics, History, Horticulture)	French, Biology, Psychology, History
Other:	
Other:	

Part Two: The Summary Sheet *(After Emily completed the Checklist in Part One, she went back through it and highlighted the entries that she felt strongest about—career elements to ensure or to avoid, i.e., her strongest work attractions/aversions. Here, they have been highlighted in light gray.)*

I want a career that focuses primarily on the work object(s) ___People___________________.

I also want to find a career that will build on the following personality traits: ___Balance of Low/High Stress, Balance of Sociability and Solitude, Helping Others, Moderate Ambition_______.

I want a career that will *not* expect me to exhibit these traits: ___Need to be Skeptical, Solitude, Creativity, Assertiveness, Comfort with Conflict, Spontaneity_________________________.

I want a career that will build on these abilities that I consider my strengths: ___Verbal, Kinesthetic, Interpersonal, and Natural Observer_______________________________________.

And I want to make sure that the career does *not* expect me to build on these weaknesses: ___ Visual/Spatial, Logical/Mathematical____.

The primary role(s) that I want to perform in this career is (are): ___Security, Lifestyle, and Service____.

The content(s), or occupational theme(s), I want to build on are ___Social, Conventional_______ and I would like to avoid ___Realistic, Enterprising_________________________________.

I would also like to incorporate these work attribute preferences: ___Easy Re-entry, Problem Solving, Creating Order, Project Work, Working In/Outside_________________________________.

I want to build on, and accommodate, these values: ___Affiliation, Compassion, Family, Achievement, Security____.

Finally, I want these miscellaneous characteristics to be taken into consideration: _____Serve as a Guide to Others, Motion Sickness____.

Part Three: Sample Personal Career Mission Statement Based on the Previous Information

"My ideal career would focus on people in a way that expresses my interests in social and conventional work. My career should allow me to have a balanced lifestyle along with security and a sense of service to others. I prefer a work style that involves problem solving, organizing, easy re-entry, and hopefully working both in and outside. I would like to build on my interpersonal, kinesthetic, and natural observer abilities in a job that recognizes my values of compassion, family, achievement, and security."

Appendix C

Training and Other Resources that Apply the SchoolPlace Big Five Profile™ to the Needs of Teens

Program:	**Invisionit—Becoming You**
Audience:	One all-day program for high school students; one for college students
Description:	Uses three personality assessments—the SchoolPlace Big Five Profile™, Signature Themes®, and The Passion Test™—in an 8-hour classroom setting, plus a follow-up, one-on-one-coaching session (via telephone with an executive coach) to assist students in college, career, and life planning by identifying their optimal path for success based on strengths and passions. Special programs and services for educators and parents are also available.
Contact:	Judi Spear, Buffalo NY, USA — +1.716.845.5588 http://www.invisionitllc.com
Program:	**Go 2 the Peak Consulting**
Audience:	Middle school, high school and college—before entering the workforce
Description:	By using our Personal Preference Worksheet and participants' SchoolPlace results, we are able to work with participants to create a Personal Development Plan. This plan defines a person's unique learning strategy, a communication strategy, strengths, and potential career options. We then coach them on implementation of the plan. Our program is offered two ways—as a one-on-one coaching program that includes three sessions or as a one-day seminar. Both options are very interactive and engaging.
Contact:	Amy Ramsey, Charlotte NC, USA — +1.704.649.4810, amy.ramsey@go2thepeak.com Lou Minges, Wilmington NC, USA — +1.910.795.7711, lou.minges@go2thepeak.com http://www.go2thepeak.com
Program:	**Concept Communications**
Audience:	High school students, parents, and educators
Description:	Coaching, consulting, and workshops for a variety of organizations and nonprofits. Based on SchoolPlace Big Five Profile and Levine's Mental Abilities model.
Contact:	Jennifer Parker, MA, MSW, Charlotte NC, USA — +1.704.366.8028, jenniferwparker@gmail.com
Program:	**Piedmont Performance Evaluations, PLLC**
Audience:	Kindergarten through adult
Description:	We use the SchoolPlace Big Five Profile (along with other relevant assessments, such as Personality Assessment for Youth and the MMPI-A) with high school students who present with learning problems, diagnoses of ADHD, minor behavior issues, and conflict with parents. In addition to assessments, we offer tutoring services, especially for students in kindergarten through the middle school grades. We also work with schools that are interested in using the SchoolPlace as part of their assessment process (along with their own cognitive, academic and social measures), with results shared with teachers in a format that explains how the child learns best, their personality characteristics, and how the teacher may best relate with the child.
Contact:	Roslyn Walker, MA, LPA, Charlotte NC, USA — +1.704.763.7386, roslynwalker@piedmontevals.com www.piedmontevals.com

Appendix D

What's Happening to Boys?

In his March 28, 2010 column for *The New York Times*, Nicholas D. Kristof summarized recent research that points starkly towards a global downturn in scholastic, and personal, success for boys. Here are some of his stats:

- High school GPA for boys is 2.86 compared to girls' 3.09.
- Girls now score equal to boys in math (but boys more often score extremely high or extremely low).
- Girls outscore boys in verbal.
- Girls appear to make more effort.
- 64% of National Honor Society members are girls.
- In many colleges, boys are now given "special consideration" so ratios won't become out of balance (i.e., affirmative action for boys).
- Girls outread boys at all levels/grades and in all states of the U.S. , with the number of girls reading at a proficiency level in the high 70%, boys in the low 70%.
- Boys are two times more likely than girls to repeat a grade, two times more likely to be suspended, and three times more likely to be expelled.
- 25% more boys are dropouts in comparison to girls.
- 57% of master's degrees awarded to whites go to females, and 62% of doctorates go to females.
- Among Afro Americans, 66% of master's degrees go to females, and 72% of doctorates go to females.
- In the national writing exam, 32% of girls are proficient, but only 16% of boys.

` Why? Physician and psychologist Leonard Sax proposes in his 2007 book *Boys Adrift* (Basic Books) five underlying and interactive causes:

1. The current way schools do business does not typically permit boys to be boys.
2. When they do try to be boys, they tend to get (falsely) diagnosed with ADHD and (over) medicated, leading to an unmotivated, alienated anomie.
3. Meanwhile, years of consuming foods and beverages poisoned by estrogen-mimicking phthalates from plastic containers have led to endocrine imbalances and anomalies.
4. This triple whammy has nudged many boys into the "safe" virtual reality of video games and pornography, where they can have thrills without responsibilities.
5. The family and society have allowed negative cultural role models (epitomized by Homer Simpson) to reinforce an image of boys and men as lazy, unambitious, and lacking in courage, with too few positive role models demanding that young boys exhibit courage and service in approaching manhood (epitomized by the Scouting movement)—what is known as "rites of passage."

So, that's the situation. The solution is straightforward, if not easy:

1. Schools and parents need to delay boys' reading instruction and permit more play and exploration; Sax encourages: single-sex schools and classrooms (see http://www.singlesexschols.org); adjustable height tables so boys can stand or kneel, even lie down, while doing schoolwork; following the German model of Waldkindergarten (http://www.waldkindergarteninc.com/).
2. Resist diagnosing active boys with ADHD; insist that all five DSM-IV criteria are met; if meds are required, start with weaker ones.

3. Eliminate plastic beverage and food containers, especially when they are heated (in a microwave, sitting in the sun, etc.); look for new PLA containers made by Cargill from corn.
4. Severely limit videogaming and provide "thrilling" alternatives, such as RaceLegal (http://www.sandiego.gov/qualcomm/event/tenants/racelegal.shtml) and Wii competitions with parents and kids.
5. Subject young boys to positive, demanding role models, whether through Scouting, sports, or other community programs and organizations.

That's it. Want more? For a little more, keep reading, and I'll share some of my notes from reading Dr. Sax's book. If you want more than this, visit his website http://www.boysadrift.com and read his book.

Here is some more detail about each of the five areas. These notes should give you a good feeling for Sax's reasoning.

1. Schools

Sax writes about the difference in two modes of learning: rote (*Wissenschaft*) or experience (*Kenntnis)*, or knowledge and understanding, like the difference between being able to recite the steps involved in building a radio and actually being able to build a radio from raw materials. The current emphasis in schools, where the emphasis is on raising test scores, is on "book learning" (Wissenshaft) and not on experiential learning (Kenntnis), learning by doing. It is like the difference between memory and mastery—the memory of the steps involved in winning friends and influencing people, versus the mastery of actually winning friends and influencing people.

A consequence of the emphasis on testing is that kids at earlier and earlier ages are expected to be able to read and do math. Girls are ready for these activities earlier than boys, who require one or more extra years to acquire the developmental maturity to focus on letters and numbers. The solution is to hold boys back from entering kindergarten and/or select a kindergarten/early grade that permits more play and hands-on activity until signs emerge that a boy is ready and interested in mastering reading. Don't worry about not starting school until later: Finland, where children do not begin school until seven years of age, comes in first on international tests of school performance (p. 20). Why? Fewer kids alienated by school will result in a higher average. Turned-off kids sink your average performance scores. Readiness is everything.

Many schools have deemphasized competitive activities, with the result of fewer outlets at school for competitive kids to become engaged. Cooperation has been promoted too often at the expensive of healthy competition.

Boys used to outscore girls on tests of science understanding, but now the gap has vanished. Sax attributes this to less time being spent in play, experimentation, trial-and-error, and more spent on listening and reciting. Girls do not necessarily like such rote learning, but the typical girl appears to be more willing to put up with it than the typical boy. But this doesn't exist in isolation. The other four factors interact with and exaggerate the boy-unfriendly classroom.

Sax mentions illegal car racing in city streets as an example of boys not engaged by school and seeking thrills. San Diego began "RaceLegal," in which teens pay to race cars against, e.g., police officers in their cruisers. The program has spread to Atlanta and other cities, with the result that street racing has virtually disappeared. Who says legal thrills can't still be thrilling?! (pp. 190-191)

2. ADHD

The excessive use of ADHD medications leads to decreased testosterone (pp.88 ff.). However, stimulants improve school performance, both of ADHD students and non-ADHD students. As a consequence, many students who do not have ADHD, but who are diagnosed with it, are mistakenly diagnosed *post hoc* as having ADHD, since the med led to improved performance. The problem is that "...even relatively short-term use of these drugs [Ritalin, Concerta, Metadate, Dexedrine, Adderall], for just a year or perhaps less, can lead to changes in personality. The boy who used to be agreeable, outgoing, and adventurous becomes lazy and irritable."

Why? These drugs damage the nucleus accumbens, the area of the brain that "translates motivation into action. If a boy's nucleus accumbens is damaged, he may still feel hungry or sexually aroused. He just won't feel motivated to do anything about it." (p. 90) Studies show an inverse relationship between the size of the nucleus accumbens and the degree of apathy in an individual. Rat studies show this relationship conclusively—studies are afoot to determine the degree to which humans show the same relationship between nucleus accumbens size and strength of drive. This apathy resulting from nucleus accumbens damage is not the same thing as depression (p. 91).

Always question ADHD diagnoses, keeping this in mind: "Very often, when a boy isn't paying attention, the problem is not with the boy but with the way he is being taught." For diagnosis of ADHD, see my book, *The Owner's Manual for the Brain,* 3rd Ed. Sax (pp. 195-6, adapted from DSM-IV) says ADHD must meet 5 criteria:

1. Hyperactivity/impulsivity/inattention
2. Begins before age 7
3. Not just one setting, e.g., school, home, church, friend's home
4. Impaired school and social skills
5. No other disorder or cause apparent

If ADD diagnosis is unavoidable, start with the mildest meds (e.g., Wellbutrin, Strattera), keeping the stronger ones as a last resort (Adderall, Ritalin, Concerta, Metadate, Focalin, Daytrana, all amphetamines and methylphenidates), and accompany meds with talk therapy/training/behavior mod.

3. Plastics

Plastic containers bleed toxins into contents, with the effect of disrupting the endocrine system. Transparent plastics (polyvinyl chloride/PVC, polycarbonates) used for bottles, food storage, etc., contain polyethylene terephthalate (PET), bisphenol A (BPA), and other building blocks for the purpose of keeping the plastic from being rigid, as well as having other properties. The problem is that the toxins leach into its contents, especially in the presence of heat. That's why a plastic bottle of water, juice, or soda tastes plasticky after sitting in the car on a warm day. The problem is that these so-called phthalates (and others) disrupt the endocrine system, effectively feminizing humans or animals that consume them. Thus, girls and female animals achieve puberty early if they consume phthalates regularly, and boys and male animals are emasculated. In essence, phthalates act as estrogen. Other chemicals are thought to have a similar effect. For examples, endosulfan is used to keep insects off of crops, but it disrupts the endocrine system in humans/animals who eat the crops endosulfan has permeated.(p. 105)

Also, the various endocrine disruptors appears to foul up a neural process based on PACAP (pituitary adenylate cyclase-activating polypeptide), with the result that the PACAP system's normal dampening effect is prevented, with the consequence of nonstop activity, or ADD. Sax mentions (p. 107) that 1) India and China have little ADHD, and 2) India and China also have the lowest use of plastic beverage containers, except for tourists. Apparently, these two immense populations are using more and more plastic beverage containers, and it will be of interest to see if ADHD rates increase accordingly—a natural, if unintended, experiment.

Estrogen disruption is also related to the overweight epidemic, as estrogen governs the size of fat cells (p. 109). Increases in estrogen levels enlarge fat cells. And phthalates et al increase estrogen. As children don't make estrogen, their unnatural acquisition of estrogen through phthalates et al appear to be a prepotent explanation of the weight epidemic among children.

The evidence is that phthalates et al cause three disorders (p. 110), all because of endocrine disruption: ADHD, overweight, and delayed (for boys) or early (for girls) puberty. And Sax thinks that the incidence of bone fractures among boys, having doubled since 1960, is largely attributable to these endocrine disruptors—increases in estrogen make girls bones dense, but not so with boys (p. 111).

"There's growing evidence that the end result of our increasingly toxic environment is girls who are both masculine and feminine, and boys who are neither masculine nor feminine." (p. 112) In another study, women across the country who drank water from plastic bottles during pregnancy had boys who were 10 times more likely to have genital defects (p. 113). Meanwhile, their girl babies were OK. And, in a similar vein, rural men (e.g., farmers and others exposed to more pesticides than city dwellers) have been found to carry lower quantity and quality sperm than city-dwelling men.

Sax recommends (p. 114-115):

1. Prefer glass/paper to plastic food and beverage containers.
2. Insure that food and beverages being heated do not come into contact with plastic of any kind.
3. When you must have plastics, look for PVC-free labels
4. Insure that your dentist does not place phthalate-containing compounds in your family's mouths.
5. If you must take food or beverage in plastic containers, keep them out of the heat as much as possible.
6. Be on the lookout for a new container made of corn: PLA (polylactic acid), by Cargill. Looks just like other plastic bottles (PET, made from petroleum), but is compostable, is not a plastic, and does not contain toxins.

4. Videogaming

Sax writes (p. 58) that the "average teenage boy today spends more than thirteen hours a week playing video games, compared with five hours per week for the average teenage girl." The bad video games (Grand Theft Auto, SpyHunter, Halo, Doom, Madden NFL, etc.) emphasize power, violence, and thrills achieved in a safe environment in which the worst thing that can happen to you is to have to restart. You don't have to deal with the 24-7 of ongoing relationships. You can do whatever you want to without real world consequences, and you can watch as virtual people kill etc. without consequences. Games like SimCity and The Sims do not entail violence, but they can permit an individual to opt for a virtual existence rather than a flesh-and-blood one. There are "good ones" that permit person-to-person interaction, as in parent and child playing with Wii systems, MTX Motocross, NASCAR: Dirt to Daytona.

The amount of time spent playing video games is inversely related to school performance, regardless of grade level (p. 63). Sax calls it a "clear and unambiguous" relationship. Studies show that time spent on video games "engorges" (91) the nucleus accumbens with blood, in the same fashion that cocaine does. This shuts down blood to the area of the brain—the dorsolateral prefrontal cortex—associated with providing a balanced view of the world. The kid on video games is like the rat with an electrode in the nucleus accumbens, who is so ecstatic from the electrode that it neglects to eat. Both the rat and the kid lose perspective because the engorgement of the nucleus accumbens robs the dorsolateral prefrontal cortex of blood flow necessary to provide some perspective, i.e., addiction is setting in—video gaming morphs into something akin to crack cocaining.

Sax recommends:

1. No games allowed in which you can kill good people.
2. Play no more than an hour on weekends or 40 minutes Monday through Thursday and only AFTER other responsibilities are completed.
3. Establish priorities: Family is first, school second, friends third, then and only then come things like video games.
4. Initiate alternative ways to get thrills: polar bear club, legal racetracks, sports, music, service clubs, etc. My teammate takes her sons mountain biking.

5. Cultural Role Models

Current cultural norms (e.g. Bart Simpson, Seinfeld) provide unambitious, weak, uncaring role models, rather than the more traditionally rigorous rites of passage that emphasize achievement, courage, and altruism. The percentage of men who are either not working nor not looking for work has quadrupled since the middle of the twentieth century.(p. 128) Sax attributes this to two principle factors: first, the collective influence of the previous four factors, and, second, the decreasing profile of the traditional male ideal. The latter is typified in the popularity of Homer Simpson on television and Matthew McConaughey's character Tripp in the film *Failure to Launch*. The malaise results in 1 of 3 college-age males with erectile dysfunction, which Sax sees as the result of a preference for virtual reality (video games, pornography) and its guarantee of hassle-free, easy-success relationships and ventures, such that real world encounters simply aren't arousing (p. 132). When youth have Homers and Tripps as their model, taking refuge in virtual reality ensues. The antidote is exposure—and exposure from which you can't retreat—to male role models that exude courage and kindness, a kind of global, cross-cultural male ideal that pours mental, emotional, physical, and financial energy into the service of the planet. Whether it is parents, coaches, bosses, teachers,

Scout leaders, community organizers, church workers, etc., it must be a grown man, not a peer, who engages the youth and mentors them into prosocial goals and behaviors. As Sax writes: "A boy does not naturally become a gentleman—by which I mean a man who is courteous and kind and unselfish. That behavior is not hardwired. It has to be taught." (p. 163) He gives the example of several single-sex schools that emphasize positive male role models. Whether it is killing an animal to feed the family or completing an Eagle Scout service project, youth must pass through a series of tests under the leadership of men. "There is no enduring culture in which cowardly men are esteemed, or in which brave men are held in contempt. There is no enduring culture in which lazy men are celebrated while hardworking men are despised." (p. 168) "The explicit motivation behind the founding of the Boy Scouts was to 'make men of little boys' and foster 'an independent manhood.' There was no assumption that an independent manhood would just happen naturally. As in other cultures, there was an urgent awareness that boys must be led to manhood." (p. 172)

Bibliography

Allen, N. B., et al. (2006). *The neuroanatomical basis of temperament in early adolescents.* Paper presented at the Society for Neuroscience, Atlanta, GA.

Allik, J., Laidra, K., Realo, A., & Pullmann, H. (2004). Personality development from 12 to 18 years of age: Changes in mean levels and structure of traits. *European Journal of Personality, 18*, 445-462.

American Psychological Association Zero Tolerance Task Force. (2008). Are zero tolerance policies effective in the Schools? An evidentiary review and recommendations. *American Psychologist, 63*(9), 852-862.

Arnett, J. J. (1999). Adolescent storm and stress, reconsidered. *American Psychologist, 54*, 317-326.

Attwood, J. B., & Attwood, C. (2007). *The passion test.* New York: Hudson Street Press.

Belenky, M. F., Clinchy, B. M., Goldberger, N. R., & Tarule, J. M. (1997). *Women's ways of knowing: The development of self, voice, and mind* (10th anniversary ed.). New York: Basic Books.

Bransford, J. D., et al. (2000). *How people learn: Brain, mind, experience, and school.* Washington, DC: National Academy Press.

Braun, S. (1996). *Buzz: The science and lore of alcohol and caffeine.* New York: Oxford University Press.

Burgoon, J. K., Stern, L. A., & Dillman, L. (1995). *Interpersonal adaptation: Dyadic interaction patterns.* New York: Cambridge University Press.

Busato, V. V., Prins, F. J., Elshout, J. J., & Hamaker, C. (1999). The relation between learning styles, the Big Five personality traits and achievement motivation in higher education. *Personality and Individual Differences, 26*, 129-140.

Bush, B. J. (1986, June). *A study of innovative training techniques at the Defense Language Institute Foreign Language Center.* (Research Report 1426). Alexandria, VA: U.S. Army Research Institute for the Behavioral and Social Sciences.

Campbell, J., & Moyers, B. (1991). *The power of myth.* New York: Anchor Books/Doubleday.

Caron, A. F. (1991). *"Don't stop loving me": A reassuring guide for mothers of adolescent daughters.* New York: Henry Holt.

Carroll, J. B. (1993). *Human cognitive abilities: A survey of factor analytic studies.* Cambridge, England: Cambridge University Press.

Ceci, S. J. (1990). *On intelligence—more or less: A bio-ecological treatise on intellectual development.* Englewood Cliffs, NJ: Prentice Hall.

Cervone, D., & Mischel, W. (Eds.). (2002). *Advances in personality science*. New York: The Guilford Press.

Cervone, D., & Shoda, Y. (Eds.). (1999). *The coherence of personality: Social-cognitive bases of consistency, variability, and organization.* New York: The Guildford Press.

Cloninger, C. R. (2004). *Feeling good: The science of well-being*. New York: Oxford University Press.

Cobb, N. J. (2007). *Adolescence: Continuity, change, and diversity.* (6th Ed.). New York: McGraw-Hill.

Coleman, J. C., et al. (1974). *Relationships in adolescents.* London: Routledge and Kegan Paul.

Costa, P. T., Jr., & McCrae, R. R. (1992). *NEO PI-R: Professional manual.* Odessa, FL: Psychological Assessment Resources.

Costa, P. T., Jr., & Widiger, T. A. (Eds.). (1994). *Personality disorders and the Five-Factor Model of Personality.* Washington, DC: American Psychological Association.

Costa, P. T., Jr., Parker, W. J., & McCrae, R. R. (2000). *Adult development, Episode I: Personality change from 12 to 16.* Paper presented at the 1st annual Conference of the Society for Personality and Social Psychology, Nashville, TN.

Courneya, K. S., & Hellsten, L. M. (1998, May). Personality correlates of exercise behavior, motives, barriers and preferences: An application of the Five-Factor Model. *Personality and Individual Differences*, *24*(5), 625-633.

Covey, S. (1998). *The 7 habits of highly effective teens*. New York: Fireside/Simon & Schuster.

Covey, S. (2006). *The 6 most important decisions you'll ever make: A guide for teens.* New York: Fireside/Simon & Schuster.

Covey, S. R. (1989). *The 7 habits of highly effective people.* New York: Fireside/Simon & Schuster.

Csikszentmihalyhi, M. (1990). *Flow: The psychology of optimal experience.* New York: HarperCollins.

Csikszentmihalyhi, M., & Schneider, B. (2000). *Becoming adult: How teenagers prepare for the world of work.* New York: Basic Books.

Dennissen, J. J. A., Asendorpf, J. B., & van Aken, M. A. G. (2008). Childhood personality predicts long-term trajectories of shyness and aggressiveness in the context of demographic transitions in emerging adulthood. *Journal of Personality, 76*(1), 67-99.

Detterman, D. K., & Sternberg, R. J. (1993). *Transfer on trial: Intelligence, cognition, and instruction.* Norwood, NJ: Ablex.

DeYoung, C. G., Hirsh, J. B., Shane, M. S., Papademetris, X., Rajeevan, N., & Gray, J. R. (2010). Testing predictions from personality neuroscience: Brain structure and the Big Five. *Psychological Science, 21*(6), 820-828.

DeYoung, C. G., Shamosh, N. A., Green, A. E., Braver, T. S., & Gray, J. R. (2009). Intellect as distinct from Openness: Differences revealed by fMRI of working memory. *Journal of Personality and Social Psychology, (97)*5, 883-892.

Druckman, D., & Swets, J. A. (Eds.). (1988). *Enhancing human performance: Issues, theories, and techniques.* Washington, D.C.: National Academy Press.

Druckman, D., & Bjork, R. A. (Eds.). (1991). *In the mind's eye: Enhancing human performance.* Washington, DC: National Academy Press.

Dweck, C. S. (2006). *Mindset: The new psychology of success.* New York: Random House.

Eccles, J. S., & Barber, B. L. (1999). Student council, volunteering, basketball, or marching band: What kind of extracurricular involvement matters? *Journal of Adolescent Research, 14*(1), 10-43.

Epstein, R. (2007). *The case against adolescence: Rediscovering the adult in every teen.* Sanger, CA: Quill Driver Books

Erikson, E. H. (1950). *Childhood and society*. New York: Norton.

Flanders, N. A. (1970). *Analyzing teaching behavior*. Menlo Park, CA: Addison-Wesley.

Freeman, D. (1999). *The fateful hoaxing of Margaret Mead: A historical analysis of her Samoan research.* Boulder, CO: Westview Press.

Gardner, H. (1983). *Frames of mind: The theory of multiple intelligences*. New York: Basic Books.

Gilligan, C. (1982). *In a different voice: Psychological theory and women's development.* Cambridge, MA: Harvard University Press.

Gladwell, M. (2008). *Outliers: The story of success*. New York: Little, Brown.

Goleman, D. (2006). *Social intelligence: The new science of human relationships.* New York: Bantam Books.

Gollwitzer, P. M. (1999). Implementation intentions: Strong effects of simple plans. *American Psychologist, 54*(7), 493-503.

Graham, P. (2004). *The end of adolescence.* Oxford, England: Oxford University Press.

Haan, N., Millsap, R., & Hartka, E. (1986). As time goes by: Change and stability in personality over fifty years. *Psychology and Aging, 1,* 220-232.

Hall, G. S. (1904). *Adolescence: Its psychology and its relation to physiology, anthropology, sociology, sex, crime, religion, and education* (Vols. I & II). Englewood Cliffs, NJ: Prentice-Hall.

Hamer, D., & Copeland, P. (1998). *Living with our genes: Why they matter more than you think.* New York: Doubleday.

Harris, J. R. (1998). *The nurture assumption: Why children turn out the way they do.* New York: Free Press.

Harris, J. R. (2006). *No two alike: Human nature and human individuality.* New York: W.W. Norton.

Hofstede, G. (2001). *Culture's consequences.* (2nd Ed.). Thousand Oaks, CA: Sage Publications.

Hogan, R. (2007). *Personality and the fate of organizations.* New York: Psychology Press.

Hoge, R. D. (1999). *Assessing adolescents in educational, counseling, and other settings.* Mahwah, NJ: Lawrence Erlbaum.

Hosseini, K. (2003). *The kite runner.* New York: Riverhead Books/Penguin.

Howard, P. J. (2000, February). *Preliminary report on results of CentACS research questionnaire #2.* (Research bulletin #2). Charlotte, NC: Center for Applied Cognitive Studies.

Howard, P. J. (2000). *The owner's manual for the brain: Everyday applications from mind/brain research.* (2nd ed.). Austin, TX: Bard Press.

Howard, P. J. (2006). *The Owner's manual for the brain: Everyday applications from mind/brain research.* (3rd ed.). Austin, TX: Bard Press.

Howard, P. J., & Howard, J. M. (2001). *The owner's manual for personality at work.* Austin, TX: Bard Press.

Howard, P. J., & Howard, J. M. (2007). *Professional manual for the SchoolPlace Big Five Profile 2.0.* Charlotte, NC: Center for Applied Cognitive Studies.

Howard, P. J., & Howard, J. M. (2009). *Professional manual for the WorkPlace Big Five Profile 4.0.* Charlotte, NC: Center for Applied Cognitive Studies.

Howard, P. J., & Howard, J. M. (2010). *The owner's manual for personality at work.* (2nd ed.). Charlotte, NC: Center for Applied Cognitive Studies.

Howard, P. J., Howard, J. M., & Medina, P.L. (1996). The Big Five locator: A quick assessment tool for consultants and trainers. *The 1996 Annual.* San Diego: Pfeiffer.

Jacques, E. (1994). *Human capability.* Falls Church, VA: Cason Hall.

James, L., & Bissinger, B. (2009). *Shooting Stars.* New York: The Penguin Press.

Johnson, C. D., Howard, P. J., Roebuck, D. B., Lesesne, T., & Brock, S. J. (2010). *Schein's career anchors and its relationship with the Five-Factor Model of Personality.* Unpublished manuscript.

Johnson, D. W., Johnson, R. T., & Holubec, E. J. (1993). *Cooperation in the classroom* (6th ed.). Edina, MN: Interaction Book Company.

Kandel, E. (2006). *In search of memory.* New York: W.W. Norton.

Kane, T. J., Staiger, D., & Gordon, R. (2006). *Identifying effective teachers using performance on the job.* Washington, DC: The Brookings Institution.

Kelley, H. H. (1979). *Personal relationships.* Hillsdale, NJ: Erlbaum.

Kelley, H. H., & Thibaut, J. W. (1978). *Interpersonal relations: A Theory of Interdependence.* New York: John Wiley & Sons.

Kernberg, P. F., Weiner, A. S., & Bardenstein, K. K. (2000). *Personality disorders in children and adolescents.* New York: Basic Books.

Kiesler, D. J. (1996). *Contemporary interpersonal theory and research: Personality, psychopathology, and psychotherapy.* New York: John Wiley & Sons.

King, L. A., & Hicks, J. A. (2007). Whatever happened to "What might have been"? Regrets, happiness, and maturity. *American Psychologist, 62*(7), 625-36.

Kleiner, B., Porch, R., & Farris, E. (2002). *Public alternative schools and programs for students at risk of education failure: 2000-01*. Washington, DC: National Center for Education Statistics, U.S. Department of Education, Office of Educational Research and Improvement.

Kolb, D. (1985). *Learning Style Inventory*. Boston: McBer.

Kounin, J. S. (1970). *Discipline and group management in classrooms*. New York: Holt, Reinhardt and Winston.

Laney, M. O. (2002). *The introvert advantage: How to thrive in an extravert world.* New York: Workman.

Laney, M. O. (2005). *The hidden gifts of the introverted child: Helping your child thrive in an extraverted world.* New York: Workman.

Lareau, A. (2003). *Unequal childhoods: Class, race, and family life.* Berkeley: University of California Press.

Latham, G. P., & Yukl, G. A. (1975). A review of research on the application of goal setting in organizations. *Academy of Management Journal, 18*, 824-845.

Lerner, R. M., & Steinberg, L. (Eds.) (2004). *Handbook of adolescent psychology.* (2nd Ed.). New York: John Wiley & Sons.

Levine, M. D. (1994). *Educational care: A system for understanding and helping children with learning problems at home and in school.* Cambridge, MA: Educators Publishing Service.

Levine, M. D. (2005). *Ready or not, here life comes.* Cambridge, MA: Educators Publishing Service.

Levine, M. D., with Reed, M. (1999). *Developmental variation and learning disorders*. (2nd Ed.). Cambridge, MA: Educators Publishing Service.

Levitin, D. J. (2006). *This Is your brain on music: The science of a human obsession.* New York: Dutton.

Levitin, D. J. (2008). *The world in six songs: How the musical brain created human nature.* New York: Dutton.

Liedloff, J. (1977). *The continuum concept: In search of happiness lost.* Cambridge, MA: Da Capo Press/Perseus Books Group.

Locke, E. A., & Latham, G. P. (2002). Building a practically useful theory of goal setting and task motivation: A 35-year odyssey. *American Psychologist, 57*(9), 705-717.

Luft, J. (1969). *Of human interaction.* Palo Alto, CA: National Press Books.

Marcia, J. E., Waterman, A. S., Matteson, D. R., Archer, S. L., & Orlofsky, J. L. (1993). *Ego identity: A handbook for psychosocial research.* New York: Springer-Verlag.

McAdams, D. P. (1993). *The stories we live by: Personal myths and the making of the self.* New York: The Guilford Press.

McCown, W., Keiser, R., Mulhearn, S., & Williamson, D. (1997, October). The role of personality and gender in preference for exaggerated bass in music. *Personality and Individual Differences, 23*(4), 543-547.

McCrae, R. R. (2001). Trait psychology and culture: Exploring intercultural comparisons. *Journal of Personality, 69*(6), 819-846.

McCrae, R. R., & Allik, J. (Eds.). (2002). *The Five-Factor Model of personality across cultures.* New York: Kluwer Academic/Plenum Publishers.

McCrae, R.R., & Costa, P.T., Jr. (2003). *Personality in adulthood: A Five-Factor Theory perspective.* (2nd Ed.). New York: The Guildford Press.

McGowan, J., & Gormly, J. (1976). Validation of personality traits: A multicriteria approach. *Journal of Personality and Social Psychology, 34,* 791-795.

Mischel, W., & Shoda, Y. (1995). A cognitive-affective system theory of personality: Reconceptualizing situations, dispositions, dynamics, and invariance in personality structure. *Psychological Review, 102,* 246-268.

Morrison, T., & Conaway, W. A. (2006). *Kiss, bow, or shake hands: The bestselling guide to doing business in more than 60 countries.* Avon, MA: Adams Media Corporation.

Mortenson, G., & Relin, D. O. (2006). *Three cups of tea: One man's mission to fight terrorism and build nations . . . one school at a time.* New York: Penguin.

National Center on Education and the Economy (2007). *Tough choices or tough times: The report of the new commission on the skills of the American workforce.* San Francisco: John Wiley & Sons.

Nettle, D. (2007). *Personality: What makes you the way you are*. New York: Oxford University Press.

Nisbett, R. E. (2009). *Intelligence and how to get it: Why school and culture count*. New York: W.W. Norton.

Pashler, H., McDaniel, M., Rohrer, D., & Bjork, R. (2010). Learning styles: Concepts and evidence. *Psychological Science in the Public Interest, 9*(3), 105-119.

Paton, A. (1948/1987). *Cry, the beloved country*. New York: Scribner.

Patterson, G. R. (1982). *Coercive family process*, Eugene, OR: Castalia.

Paunonen, S. V., & Ashton, M. C. (2001, September) Big Five factors and facets and the prediction of behavior. *Journal of Personality and Social Psychology, 81*(3), 524-539.

Perry, D. E. (2008). *More than I deserve*. Chapel Hill, NC: Chapel Hill Press.

Peter, L. & Benson, P. L. (2008). *Sparks: How parents can help ignite the hidden strengths of teenagers*. San Francisco: Jossey-Bass.

Pianta, R. C. (1999). *Enhancing relationships between children and teachers*. Washington, DC: American Psychological Association.

Piedmont, R. L., Hill, D. C., & Blanco, S. (1999, October) Predicting athletic performance using the Five-Factor Model of Personality. *Personality and Individual Differences, 27*(4), 769-777.

Pinker, S. (2003). *Blank slate: The modern denial of human* nature. New York: Penguin.

Potok, C. (1975). *In the beginning.* New York: Fawcett Crest.

Putnam, R. D. (2000). *Bowling alone: The collapse and revival of American community.* New York: Simon & Schuster.

Ravitch, D. (2010). *The death and life of the great American school system: How testing and choice are undermining education.* New York: Basic Books.

Rentfrow, P. J., Gosling, S. D., & Potter, J. (2008). The geography of personality: A theory of the emergence, persistence, and expression of regional variation in basic traits. *Perspectives on Psychological Science, 3*(5), 339-369.

Ridley, M. (2003). *Nature via nurture: Genes, experience, and what makes us human.* New York: HarperCollins.

Roberts, B. W., Wood, D., & Smith, J. L. (2005). Evaluating Five Factor Theory and social investment perspectives on personality trait development. *Journal of Research in Personality, 39*, 166-184.

Rosen, J. (2006). *The supreme court: The personalities and rivalries that defined America.* New York: Times Books/Henry Holt and Company.

Rowe, D. C. (1994). *The limits of family influence: Genes, experience, and behavior.* New York: The Guilford Press.

Sax, L. (2007). *Boys adrift: The five factors driving the growing epidemic of unmotivated boys and underachieving young men*. New York: Basic Books.

Scarr, S. (1992). Developmental theories for the 1990s: Development and individual differences. *Developmental Psychology, 63,* 1-19.

Schargel, F. P., Thacker, T., & Bell, J. S. (2007*). From at risk to academic excellence: What successful leaders do*. Larchmont NY: Eye on Education.

Schein, E. (1993). *Career anchors: Discovering your real values.* San Francisco: Jossey-Bass Pfeiffer.

Schlegel, A., & Barry, H., III. (1991). *Adolescence: An anthropological inquiry*. New York: The Free Press.

Seligman, M. E. P. (1991). *Learned optimism*. New York: Knopf.

Silverthorne, C. (2001). Leadership effectiveness and personality: A cross-cultural evaluation. *Personality and Individual Differences, 30*(2), 303-309.

Steinberg, L. (1996). *Beyond the classroom: Why school reform has failed and what parents need to do*. New York: Simon & Schuster.

Steinberg, L. (2004). *The ten basic principles of good parenting.* New York: Simon & Schuster.

Steinberg, L., & Levine, A. (1997). *You and your adolescent: A parent's guide for ages 10 to 20.* New York: Harper Perennial.

Sternberg, R. J. (1988). *The triarchic mind: A new theory of human intelligence.* New York: Viking Penguin.

Stoner, S., & Bandy, M. A. (1977, August). Personality traits of females who participate in intercollegiate competition and nonparticipants. *Perceptual and Motor Skills, 45*(1), 332-334.

Tuckman, B. W. (1965). Development sequence in small groups, *Psychological Bulletin, 63,* 384-389.

Valenstein, E. S. (1998). *Blaming the brain: The truth about drugs and mental health.* New York: Free Press.

Vermunt, J. D. H. M. (1994). *Inventory of learning styles in higher education: Scoring key for the Inventory of Learning Styles in higher education,* Tilburg, Netherlands: Tilburg University, Department of Educational Psychology.

Wagner, M. J., and Tilney, G. (1983, March 17). The effect of 'superlearning' techniques on the vocabulary acquisition and alpha brainwave production of language learners." *TESOL Quarterly,* 7(1), 5–17.

Wang, M. (1997). *Personality traits and athletic behaviors: An examination of personality in college aged athletes and their sport behaviors.* (Senior Thesis). Davidson College, Davidson, NC. Retrieved from Center for Applied Cognitive Studies.

Whittle, S., Allen, N. B., Lubman, D. I., & Yücel, M. (2005). The neurobiological basis of temperament: Towards a better understanding of psychopathology. *Neuroscience and Biobehavioral Reviews, 30,* 511-525.

Wilson, G. D. (1994). *Psychology for performing artists: Butterflies and bouquets.* London: Jessica Kingsley.

Wolf, A. E. (2002). *Get out of my life, but first could you drive me and Cheryl to the mall?* New York: Farrar, Straus, Giroux.

Wright, W. (1998). *Born that way: Genes, behavior, personality.* New York: Alfred A. Knopf.

Yoshino, K. (2006). *Covering: The hidden assault on our civil rights.* New York: Random House.

Index

How to Order Additional Copies of this Book

To order additional copies of:

The Owner's Manual for Personality from 12 to 22

Paperback: $24.95

VISA / MASTERCARD / DISCOVER / AMERICAN EXPRESS Accepted

Quantity Discounts Are Available

To order, visit www.amazon.com, or contact us as listed below:

Contact:	Customer Relationship Representative
Publisher:	The Center for Applied Cognitive Studies 4701 Hedgemore Drive, Suite 210 Charlotte, NC 28209-2200 / USA
Telephone:	+1.704.331.0926
US Toll Free:	+1.800.244.5555 (800-BIG-5555)
Fax:	+1.704.331.9408
E-mail:	info@centacs.com
Website:	www.centacs.com

CENTER FOR

APPLIED COGNITIVE STUDIES

CPSIA information can be obtained at www.ICGtesting.com
Printed in the USA
269581BV00004B/2/P

9 780578 053370